The Orators and Their Treatment of the Recent Past

Trends in Classics – Supplementary Volumes

Edited by
Franco Montanari and Antonios Rengakos

Associate Editors
Stavros Frangoulidis · Fausto Montana · Lara Pagani
Serena Perrone · Evina Sistakou · Christos Tsagalis

Scientific Committee
Alberto Bernabé · Margarethe Billerbeck
Claude Calame · Kathleen Coleman · Jonas Grethlein
Philip R. Hardie · Stephen J. Harrison · Stephen Hinds
Richard Hunter · Giuseppe Mastromarco
Gregory Nagy · Theodore D. Papanghelis
Giusto Picone · Alessandro Schiesaro
Tim Whitmarsh · Bernhard Zimmermann

Volume 133

The Orators and Their Treatment of the Recent Past

Edited by
Aggelos Kapellos

DE GRUYTER

ISBN 978-3-11-153668-2
e-ISBN (PDF) 978-3-11-079187-7
e-ISBN (EPUB) 978-3-11-079196-9
ISSN 1868-4785

Library of Congress Control Number: 2022946559

Bibliographic information published by the Deutsche Nationalbibliothek
The Deutsche Nationalbibliothek lists this publication in the Deutsche Nationalbibliografie; detailed bibliographic data are available on the Internet at http://dnb.dnb.de.

© 2024 Walter de Gruyter GmbH, Berlin/Boston
This volume is text- and page-identical with the hardback published in 2023.
Editorial Office: Alessia Ferreccio and Katerina Zianna
Logo: Christopher Schneider, Laufen

www.degruyter.com

In memory of Peter Rhodes

Contents

Aggelos Kapellos
The Orators and their Treatment of the Recent Past: Introduction —— 1

Thomas G.M. Blank
Methodical Remarks on the 'Truthfulness' of Oratorical Narrative —— 23

Michael Gagarin
Antiphon and the Recent Past —— 47

Peter Rhodes
[Lysias], 20 *for Polystratus*. Polystratus and the Coup of 411 B.C. —— 53

Frances Pownall
Andocides, the Spartans, and the Thirty —— 65

Edward M. Harris
Recent Events in Assembly Speeches and [Andocides] *On the Peace* —— 81

Cinzia Bearzot
Lysias' *Against the Subversion of the Ancestral Constitution of Athens*: A Past not to be Forgotten —— 101

Dino Piovan
The Athenian Civil War according to Lysias' Funeral Oration —— 119

Markus Zimmermann
Lysias' Speech 14 and the Use of the Recent Past for Political Purposes —— 135

Aggelos Kapellos
Plato's *Menexenus* on the Sea Battle-trial of Arginousai and the Battle of Aegospotami —— 151

David Whitehead
Isocrates and the Peloponnesian War —— 171

Yun Lee Too
Back to the Future: Temporal Adjustments in Isocrates —— 189

Stefano Ferrucci
The Recent Past in Isaeus' Forensic Speeches —— 205

Nicolas Siron
The Forensic Time Machine: Play on Times in Apollodorus' *Against Timotheus* —— 225

Brad L. Cook
Family Portraits in Demosthenes' Inheritance Speeches: Between Rhetoric & History —— 241

Gunther Martin
Reusing Invective: Demosthenes on Androtion's Past —— 257

Jeremy Trevett
A Tale of Two Sea-battles: Demosthenes' Praise of Chabrias in the Speech *Against Leptines* —— 275

Nathan Crick
The Rhetoric of Deflection: Demosthenes's *Funeral Oration* as Propaganda —— 291

Patrice Brun
Demosthenes, between Fake News and Alternative Facts —— 307

Peter A. O'Connell
Facts, Time, and Imagination in Demosthenes and Aeschines —— 323

Dániel Bajnok
Peace and War with Philip: Aeschines' *Against Ctesiphon* on the Recent Past —— 343

Joseph Roisman
Lycurgus and the Past —— 363

Craig Cooper
Remembering Chaeronea in Hyperides —— 377

Janek Kucharski
Hyperides, Diondas, and the First Ascendancy of Demades —— 397

Zhichao Wang
Hegesippus and his Treatment of the Recent Past —— 413

Ian Worthington
Dinarchus, the 'Recent' and the 'Very Recent' Past: Lessons from Aeschines, Demosthenes and Lycurgus? —— 431

Joshua P. Nudell
Remembering Injustice as the Perpetrator? Athenian Orators, Cultural Memory, and the Athenian Conquest of Samos —— 447

James Sickinger
State Inscriptions from the Recent Past in the Attic Orators —— 465

Pierre Chiron
The *Rhetoric to Alexander* and its Political and Historical Context: The Mystery of a (Quasi-) Occultation —— 481

List of Contributors —— 493
General Index —— 499
Index of Passages —— 507

Fig. 1: Peter Rhodes

Aggelos Kapellos
The Orators and their Treatment of the Recent Past: Introduction

The Athenian orators emphasized the importance of time (χρόνος) in their speeches.[1] However, it was not possible for all men to make an objective assessment of it appropriately. Gorgias explains this in his *Encomium of Helen* by saying that if all men in all matters had both memory of the past and awareness of the present, speech would not be equally deceptive; but now neither remembering a past event nor investigating a present one nor prophesying a future one is easy (εἰ μὲν γὰρ πάντες περὶ πάντων εἶχον τῶν <τε> παροιχομένων μνήμην τῶν τε παρόντων <ἔννοιαν> ... οὐκ ἂν ὁμοίως ὅμοιος ὢν ὁ λόγος ἦ<πά>τα· νῦν δὲ οὔτε μνησθῆναι τὸ παροιχόμενον οὔτε σκέψασθαι τὸ παρὸν οὔτε μαντεύσασθαι τὸ μέλλον εὐπόρως ἔχει) (11.3 (ed. Schollmeyer).[2] This means that perfect knowledge of every subject is not easy, for one has to possess knowledge of the past, understanding of the present and foreknowledge of the future. If this happened, then speech would not be as powerful.[3] Thus, human incapacities make the capacities of *logos* even stronger, since it becomes a way of fabricating things out of the flux of past and present appearances, capable of regulating collective practices in the name of a desired good. Therefore, *logos* became a powerful means in political life through which men acquired opinions which granted them solace from the past, security for the present, and hope for the future.[4] About the past in particular, men gave in to *logos* because they do not remember it.[5]

Enquiry into the past and how this fitted to the present was not easy too. Reading the rhetorical corpus, we realize that there seems to be a trichotomy in the way the orators treated the past. There is:

The late Peter Rhodes had read a previous draft of my introduction. I heartily thank G. Martin, B. Cook, N. Crick, N. Siron, J. Roisman and the anonymous readers for their comments. For possible omissions or mistakes I am solely responsible.

1 See Antiph. 5.14,94, 6.2,45, Andoc. 3.37, Lys. 2.1,54, Isocr. 5.47, Dem. 2.25, [Dem.] 7.11, Dem. 18.310, 22.13, 25.97, 60.11, Aesch. 3.106, Hyp. 6.2.
2 I base my translation of the passage on MacDowell 1982, 25, which is slightly modified on the basis of the new edition of the text made by Schollmeyer; see 2021, 256–260.
3 See Constantinidou 2008, 59.
4 See Crick 2015, 84.
5 See Hunter 1986, 422.

(a) The distant past. In this 'category' the speakers say that none of the listeners can remember old events but they know them through hearing. The Athenian envoys at Sparta say just before the outbreak of the Peloponnesian War that the best source of information for the very distant past is the stories that men hear (τὰ μὲν πάνυ παλαιὰ ... ἀκοαί) and not the listeners' autopsy (Thuc. 1.73).[6] In 415 B.C., when Alcibiades' opponents claimed that both the affair of the Mysteries and the mutilation of the Herms had been done in order to subvert the people, and that neither of these things had been done without his connivance, alleging as evidence all of his other undemocratic habits (Thuc. 6.28.2), the people took everything suspiciously because they knew from what they heard (ἀκοῇ) how oppressive the tyranny of Peisistratus and his sons had been in its later stages, and, further, that it was not because of themselves and Harmodius that it had come to an end, but because of the Spartans (Thuc. 6.53.3). The people's opinion derived from oral tradition.[7] In 325/24 B.C. the speaker of Dem. 26 refers to Miltiades and Pericles and how the Athenians had punished them, calling these stories as περὶ τῶν παλαιῶν and mentioning as his sources 'some men' who φασιν (26.6–7), obviously what they have heard.[8]

(b) The middling past, about which an orator can say 'the older ones will remember and they can tell the younger'. In 355/54 B.C. Demosthenes remembers in his speech *Against Leptines* how some brave Corinthians helped the Athenians, following their defeat against the Spartans near the Nemea river in 394, forty years earlier, and says that he is describing these events, relying on what he has heard from the older men among them (παρ' ὑμῶν τῶν πρεσβυτέρων αὐτὸς ἀκήκοα) (20.52).[9] In 343 B.C. Demosthenes said about the Phocians, whose towns had been demolished at the end of the Third Sacred War (356–346 B.C.), that they had once voted against the Thebans when they made a proposal for our enslavement, I hear from you all [ὑμῶν ἔγωγ' ἀκούω πάντων] (19.65). Demosthenes is alluding to an event that took place in 404, sixty-one years earlier.[10] In 330 B.C. Lycurgus says that there is none among the elders or the younger who does not remember or has not heard respectively that Callistra-

---

[6] See Schepens 1975, 262.

[7] Munn 2000, 114–116 argues that the Athenians interpreted the scandal through their knowledge of Herodotus and not through oral tradition, but this is an extreme view (see Schenker 2001, 315).

[8] For this date of the speech and its author, who is not Demosthenes, see MacDowell 2009, 139–141, 312–313. Harris 2018, 195–197 argues that the speech was composed during the Hellenistic period. Even if he is right, this does not affect my argument.

[9] For this and other relevant passages see Canevaro 2019, 139–141.

[10] See Steinbock 2012, 41–42.

tus was condemned to death by the city (μέμνηται τῶν πρεσβυτέρων ... τῶν νεωτέρων οὐκ ἀκήκοε) (1.93). This man was executed in 361 B.C., thirty one years earlier than Lycurgus' speech, at a time when the youngest of the jurors would have been infants or too young to remember this event themselves.[11]

And **(c) the recent past**, about which a speaker say that 'we/you all know'. In 386 B.C. Plato's Socrates says in his funeral speech in the *Menexenus*, supposedly delivered for those who had died in the Corinthian War, that he should not prolong the story of this war, because it is not a tale of ancient history about men of long ago (οὐ γὰρ πάλαι οὐδὲ παλαιῶν ἀνθρώπων γεγονότα λέγοιμ' ἂν τὰ μετὰ ταῦτα· αὐτοὶ γὰρ ἴσμεν) (244d1–3).[12] In 330 B.C., in his speech *On the Crown*, Demosthenes referred to his involvement in the war against Philip before Chaeronea and called these events νέα καὶ γνώριμα πᾶσι (Dem. 18.85), since they took place eleven years earlier.[13]

This temporal distinction is artificial. Even though the orators usually acknowledge the division of the past into a mythical and historical period and distinguish between examples from the distant and the recent past, this distinction is never clear-cut, and the border between myth and history is rather fluid.[14] This happens because arguments related to the past constitute a part of the arsenal of each orator. In fact, a speaker could lump the distant, middling and recent past together. We can see this by reading the funeral speeches of Lysias, Demosthenes and Plato, Isocrates' pamphlets, who used the mythological past in order to enlighten his students about the recent past,[15] and Lycurgus' speech *Against Leocrates*.[16]

Nevertheless, the treatment of the three rhetorical periods of the past is not of equal weight in the orators. The distant past and myths loom large in the funeral speeches and in Isocrates' oeuvre, but they are rarely referred to in symbouleutic and forensic speeches. In the latter the orators show a marked predilection for recent events, because they were considered more familiar, more

---

11 Taddei 2012, 168 n. 70 argues that Lycurgus is referring to the recent past of Athens, but this cannot be right. See further below.
12 See more about this text in Kapellos' chapter in this volume.
13 Usher 1993, 199.
14 See Steinbock 2012, 26–28.
15 See Too in this volume.
16 For Lysias see 2.3–66 with Todd 2007, 212–268. For Plato's *Menexenus* see 242b5–c5, where he uses μετὰ δὲ ταῦτα, jumping from the aftermath of the Persian wars to the Peloponnesian war (see Henderson 1975, 40). For Demosthenes' funeral speech see Crick in this volume. For Lycurgus see Roisman in this volume. Nouhaud, 1982, 10 rightly says that the temporal distinction is artificial, but he does not cite any proof.

relevant to the present and provided stronger proofs about the importance of an argument.[17] For instance, Aeschines explicitly privileges recent historical time above mythical time by providing evidence not from ancient myths but from events of their own time (οὐκ ἐν τοῖς ἀρχαίοις μύθοις, ἀλλ' ἐφ' ἡμῶν γεγενημένα) (2.31).[18]

Taking into consideration the Greeks' difficulty of conceiving the past, the orators' trichotomy of time and their predilection for the recent past, this volume focuses on it and investigates the following issues: *a)* the time span of the recent past; *b)* the ability of the orators to interpret the recent past according to their interests; *c)* the inability of the Athenians to make an objective assessment of persons and events of the recent past; *d)* the unwillingness of the citizens to hear the truth, make self-criticism and take responsibility for bad results; and *e)* the superiority of the historical sources over the orators regarding the reliability of their historical precision. On the basis of these issues, in what follows: *a)* I try to explain the methodology that the contributors follow in approaching the recent past in the orators; *b)* I pinpoint the historical events and persons the orators are referring to in the speeches under investigation and *c)* I make a short presentation of the arguments of each chapter.

First, what needs further clarification is the time span that we could define as recent. Nouhaud distinguishes current events from historical ones[19] and believes that it took twenty years for an event to pass from current politics to the realm of history; a time limit of thirty one years is excessive, because it would give a false impression of reality.[20] He does this after a short discussion of the appeal to "what the older ones will remember" in the speech *Against Leptines*; so this twenty-year distinction is perhaps prompted by Demosthenes' remarks. I agree with him. We saw above that Lycurgus mentioned the execution of Callistratus, not a recent event for the younger jurors, because it took place three decades before his speech, so we can say that this constitutes evidence of time that people could not hear as contemporary.

We saw earlier Gorgias' positions about the past. What must be said now is that his positions were familiar to the Greeks of his day.[21] This is important because it helps us understand the role of the orators. The speakers in the Assembly or the courts knew that their audiences could not have true knowledge of all

---

17 See Gotteland 2001, 94–103 and Grethlein 2014, 328–334.
18 For this point see Westwood 2020, 263.
19 Nouhaud 1982, 248, 254, 302, 307.
20 See Nouhaud 1982, 10, 369.
21 See Adkins 1977, 11.

past things, so they used their speech and covered their listeners' gap of knowledge with their opinion about the past. In some cases a speaker could be accurate.[22] However, the opposite was the rule. An orator could allude to the recent past,[23] recall it,[24] shape and/or distort it,[25] interpret it from his own perspective or even lie, believing that it would help him win his case.[26] Moreover, an orator could create an official memory — interpretation of specific incidents, which would suppress unpleasant events of the city, such as inner conflicts and military defeats, play down its failures and give a more optimistic view of the future. This kind of rhetoric finds a unique proof in Athens when we read the funeral orations in honour of those who died for Athens every year.[27]

This does not mean that listeners passively accepted what speakers said about the recent past. On the contrary, they participated in the rhetorical reinterpretation of the past. Xenophon gives a clear example of this by reporting the reaction of Alcibiades' supporters when he returned to the Peiraeus in 407 B.C. These men acted as if they were defending him in court, judging him in the light of recent victories. They claimed that his conduct of military affairs was excellent; they remembered his generosity towards the city through *choregiai*, trierarchies and taxes; argued that he had not wanted to profane the Mysteries; claimed that he went to Sparta against his will, foresaw the Athenian mistakes regarding the Sicilian expedition and believed that if he had remained in command of the fleet there it would have succeeded. However, they conveniently forgot that Alcibiades wanted to conquer Sicily and Carthage and that he considered himself socially superior to his fellow citizens; they deliberately forgot that they had helped unconsciously the sycophantic action of his enemies by not putting him on trial immediately, and thus they exculpated themselves from the responsibility for his unjust condemnation from the city. Moreover, they knew that no necessity had forced Alcibiades to flee to the Spartans and instruct them how to support Syracusan forces in Sicily and harm his city by fortifying Deceleia. Finally, nobody could know whether Alcibiades would have succeeded as a general in Sicily.[28]

When things could or did turn bad for the Athenians, they did not want to take responsibility for the bad outcome, but they wanted to put the blame on

---

22 See Harris on Demosthenes' Assembly speeches in this volume.
23 See Gagarin in this volume.
24 See Worthington in this volume.
25 See Trevett in this volume.
26 See Brun, O'Connel, Bajnok, Roisman in this volume.
27 See Piovan, Kapellos and Crick in this volume.
28 See Kapellos 2019, 63–64.

others. When news was brought to Athens that their men as well as their ships had been destroyed at Syracuse, they became furious with the orators who had joined in promoting the expedition, the soothsayers, and prophets, and all who by the influence of religion had at the time inspired them with the belief that they would conquer Sicily. Thucydides criticizes this reaction of his fellow citizens, saying that it was not justified, because they had voted the expedition themselves (8.1).[29] Xenophon says in his *Hellenica* that those who disapproved of Alcibiades' second return to Athens said that he alone had been responsible for their past evils; and there was a danger that he alone would be the author of future evils that they feared would befall the city (1.4.17). This fierceness against Alcibiades is striking, because these Athenians forgot that they had consented to the opinion of those politicians who argued that Alcibiades should participate in the Sicilian expedition but should be put on trial sometime after that. Moreover, there is no doubt that Alcibiades' betrayal was astonishing, but the disaster of the force in Sicily lay with Nicias, who had the central role in it.[30] After the Arginousai trial the Athenians put the blame on Callixenus and those who had accused the generals but not on themselves (*Hell.* 1.7.35).[31] After the defeat of the Athenian fleet at Aegospotami by Lysander, the Athenians realized the evils that would affect them and got angry even with the trierarchs, forgetting that it was they who had approved of the campaign in the Hellespont and had ratified the demagogic policy of the generals.[32] Afterwards, they surrendered their city to the Spartans, and some of them accused Adeimantus of betraying the fleet at Aegospotami to the Spartans (Xen. *Hell.* 2.1.32). However, these men had forgotten that Adeimantus was the only one who had spoken against a decree proposed by his colleague, the general Philocles, according to which in case of victory the Athenians would cut off the right hands of all prisoners. These men remembered only that Adeimantus had not been killed by Lysander.[33]

These events justify Demosthenes' comment in his speech *On the Crown* that if recent events are favourable, they are gratefully received, and if otherwise, they incur punishment (18.85).

If an event or a person's actions were open to different interpretations by the orators after a few years they took place, a possible trace of the facts and

---

[29] For the responsibility of the Athenians see the remarks of Osborne 2003, 257.
[30] See Kapellos 2019, 65–66.
[31] See Kapellos 2019, 209–215.
[32] See Lys. 21.9 with Kapellos 2014, 96.
[33] See Kapellos 2009, 257.

their rhetorical treatment become more difficult for modern readers of the past. On the other hand, we are not at a loss. A useful way to assess the factual content of oratory and its distortion of reality because of the need for persuasion is to use other more trustworthy sources.

First, one of these sources, are the Greek historians.[34] Thucydides' claim to authority on the Peloponnesian War should not be accepted so easily. It would have been very difficult for a man who came from a leading family, served in the war as a general and was finally exiled for failing to keep Amphipolis to Sparta to write an impartial history and get the facts right all the time, and he did not get the facts right all the time. Nevertheless, Thucydides tried to get the events right, and he was successful in most cases. Xenophon cared about the truth and he did not write things he knew were false or invented others, except at a trivial level. Some of the Atthidographers, such as Androtion and Philochorus, wanted to write serious histories of their own time (Phanodemus was more interested in the legendary past). Regarding Diodorus, we can recognize good material where he was following Ephorus, who was using the *Hellenica Oxyrhynchia*, but also his own direct knowledge. But his limitations are due to his carelessness and a tendency to invent things: his attitude to truth was not the same as Thucydides', but not even he can be said to have written without any regard for the truth.[35]

Second, [Aristotle] and his *Athenaion Politeia*. This author used Thucydides, Xenophon, Ephorus, the *Atthides* (especially Androtion), political writings, Solon, comedy, anecdotes, oral tradition, documents and laws, and observed current practice.[36]

Third, Plutarch, who, although a biographer, is useful because he had a splendid library of works, many of them lost to us, capable of illuminating the course of events.[37]

Finally, inscriptions can play a leading role in such investigation, especially when the historians do not preserve information about events that we should like to know.[38]

Such an approach is not new in modern scholarship. Nouhaud has treated the theme of the recent past in his valuable monograph *L'utilization de l'histoire par les orateurs attiques*, by comparing the orators with the historical sources.

---

34 Worthington 1991, 55 points out that we must check whether there are serious clashes between the orators and the historical authors and therefore be skeptical with their arguments.
35 See Rhodes 1994, 161–168.
36 See Rhodes 1981, 15–37.
37 See Kagan 1987, ix, and now in detail Schettino 2014, 417–421, 425–426.
38 See Rhodes and Osborne 2003.

However, he has not analyzed the orators' treatment of the recent past in detail and in chronological order.[39] The aspiration of the present editor is to treat the subject more thoroughly. In this volume we study [Lysias] 20, the ten orators of the Canon, Plato's *Menexenus*, Apollodorus and Hegesippus. Recent important studies on the orators have given more attention to orators outside the canon, but not to the analysis of the recent past, at least in depth because of their different focus.[40]

Twenty-eight scholars have written chapters for this volume to this end, aiming at advanced students and professional scholars. The contributors have approached the orators' treatment of the recent past, aspiring to give a new or different interpretation of the texts under investigation. The volume deals with a wide range of themes, in terms both of contents and of chronology, from the fifth to the fourth century B.C. Each contributor has written a chapter which analyzes one or more historical events mentioned or alluded in the corpus of the Attic orators and cover the three species of Attic oratory, dicanic, symbouleutic and epideictic (funeral speeches). Chapters that treat other issues collectively are also included. At the end of each chapter the authors provide bibliography related to their topic. All chapters have approximately the same length, except for that on Antiphon, because he offers a very limited use of the recent past. The common feature of each contribution is an outline of the recent events that took place and influenced the citizens and/or the city of Athens and its juxtaposition with their rhetorical treatment by the orators either by comparing the rhetorical texts with the historical sources and/or by examining the rhetorical means through which the speakers model the recent past. In this way the present author has tried to produce a volume written in a uniform manner.

The historical events and persons mentioned in the orators under examination in this volume are: the revolution of Mytilene, the regime of the Four Hun-

---

39 In Nouhaud 1982, 79–80 he mentions Din. 1.72–32 and the destruction of Thebes. In p. 81 Nouhaud characterizes Lysias' attack on Alcibiades in 14.30–38 as unjust, refers to Isocr. 16 as a biographical defence of Alcibiades' father and points out that Lys. 18.2 refers to the general Nicias, who died in Sicily. In p. 93 he refers to Dem. 18.169 and the dramatic hours of the Athenians after the occupation of Elateia. In p. 111 n. 23 he remarks that Dem. 19 and Aesch. 3 disagree on the real events during their embassy to Philip. In pp. 248, 279–280 he analyzes the Arginousai trial and the battle of Aegospotami in Plato's *Menexenus*. In p. 252 n. 14 he mentions [Lys.] 20.24 and Polystratus' order to his son to serve in Sicily for Athens. In p. 254 he refers to Isocr. 18.59 and the destruction of the Athenian fleet in the Hellespont and Athens' blockade by Lysander. In p. 295 he makes a concise analysis of Alcibiades' involvement in the scandals of 415 B.C. and their treatment of Isocrates and Lysias.
40 See Edwards 1994, 68–69, Αποστολάκης 2003, Alexiou 2020, 79–309.

dred, the Arginousai trial, the defeat of the Athenian fleet by Lysander at Aegospotami, the regime of the Thirty, the amnesty, Phormisius' proposal of limiting citizenship rights in Athens, the role of Alcibiades in Athenian politics, Demosthenes' inheritance problems, the military deeds of the generals Chabrias and Timotheus, the peace of Philocrates, the role of Demosthenes and Aeschines in Athenian politics, the defeat of the Athenian army at Chaeronea by Philip, the political power of Demades, the destruction of Thebes by Alexander, the war of Agis III, and the Harpalus Affair. Finally, we consider Anaximenes' treatment of the recent past in his treatise *Rhetorica ad* Alexandrum.

Although this collective enterprise is not (it could not be) an exhaustive treatment of the recent past in the orators, I hope it will prove to offer a deeper understanding of Attic oratory.

The volume proceeds presenting these historical events across the course of the fifth and fourth century B.C. and traces their treatment in the orators.

It is time to describe what the contributors argue.

Thomas G.M. Blank ('Methodical Remarks on the 'Truthfulness' of Oratorical Narrative') shows that earlier scholarship studied uses of history in the corpus against the backdrop of 'historical fact' and used to emphasize that oratory regularly instrumentalized historical data, often supposedly distorting such information, that was considered true from modern perspectives. Recent scholarship, by contrast, has highlighted the differences between ancient Greek and modern concepts of historical truth. Unquestionably, deceit plays a significant role in oratory, but not all distortion of historical fact is deceitful or unhistorical. Considering the centrality of oratorical stages to the formation of public culture in Athens, the notion of historical truth itself proves to be situative and based on spontaneous assent rather than only on factual data. Without a necessary intent of deceit or of presenting counter-factual narratives, the instrumental use of relevant *lieux de mémoire* in public speeches played its own authentical part in the shaping of historical memory in Athens. This renders oratory a valuable source for contemporary public history and culture, regardless of the factual 'reliability' of the historical narratives it contains.

Michael Gagarin ('Antiphon and the recent past') argues that the only mentions of historical events in the preserved speeches of Antiphon come in his speech *On the Murder of Herodes* (Ant. 5). These mentions are of two sorts. First, in the speech for the prosecution, the speaker's father and his role in the fairly recent Mytilenean revolt were apparently criticized in order to cast the speaker, named Euxitheus, in a bad light; Euxitheus therefore needs to defend his father, as well as himself, against these charges (Ant. 5.74–80). Second, after Euxitheus finishes his main arguments in his defense, he adds several relatively minor additional arguments, during the course of which he includes three historical incidents from the more distant past (5.67–73) that are meant to warn the jurors against convicting him too hastily. In relating these events, and also in discussing the Mytilenean revolt, Euxitheus appears to be, at the very least, slanting the facts.

Peter Rhodes ('[Lysias] 20 for Polystratus. Polystratus and the coup of 411 B.C.') argues that there are various ways in which the speaker seeks to make the best of what was probably a weak case: e.g. that Polystratus had (democratically) good intentions, that he was a "good" oligarch rather than a "bad" oligarch, that he served as a *katalogeus* only under compulsion and registered as many men as possible, that he paid a fine under the intermediate régime of the Five Thousand when men who were guiltier escaped. There are arguments of the kind which we should expect of a man in his position, that he had held democratic offices, that he had not concealed his property but had paid *eisphorai* and had performed liturgies. The narrative is in general consistent with that which we can construct from Thucydides and *Ath. Pol.* — (whether, as the author believes, Thucydides' Assembly at Colonus and *Ath. Pol.*'s Assembly are the same, or *Ath. Pol.*'s Assembly was earlier than Thucydides'); it confirms *Ath. Pol.*'s statement that the 100 *katalogeis* were appointed and at least started work, but it does not match Thucydides' account of how the Four Hundred were appointed. Most likely to be misleading is the claim that Polystratus and Phrynichus, members of the same small deme, and both resident in the city when the Spartans were occupying Decelea, had nothing to do with each other.

Frances Pownall ('The Thirty in Andocides' *On the Peace*') points out that there is a very unusual passage in *On the Peace* in which Andocides elides the Spartans' responsibility in 404/3 for the imposition upon the Athenians of the Thirty (3.10–11), the oligarchical junta that was later so despised that it became known as the Thirty Tyrants. Furthermore, Andocides' apparent rehabilitation of the Spartans' collusion in tyranny is very much at odds with his attempt to bolster his democratic credentials in his first two speeches, where he emphasizes the assistance of his family in the expulsion of the Peisistratid tyranny (1.106; 2.26), an episode in which the role of the Spartans was very much contested in later tradition. Pownall examines the significance of Andocides' apparent willingness to act as an apologist for the Spartans in 403 in terms of what it can tell us about both his own political ideology and the memory of the regime of the Thirty.

Edward M. Harris ('Major Events in the Recent Past in Assembly Speeches and the Authenticity of [Andocides] *On the Peace*') examines the accuracy of statements about the recent past and contemporary institutions in Demosthenes' speeches to the Assembly. He shows that the orator does not misrepresent recent events or existing relations between states; allusions to the past are also short and to the point; and there are no long narratives. Then he shows that the statements about the recent past in *On the Peace* attributed to Andocides are not reliable and could not have been delivered to the Assembly in 391 B.C. The speaker says that the Athenians did not have a fleet or walls at the time, that the Boeotians had made peace with Sparta, that the Athenians held only two-thirds of Euboea up to 411 B.C. and that the Athenians violated a peace treaty with the Persian King by supporting the rebel Amorges. All these statements and others are contradicted by Thucydides, Xenophon, Diodorus and other sources. The speaker also does not understand the institution of *presbeis autokratores*. These mistakes confirm the judgment of Dionysius of Halicarnassus that the speech is a forgery and point to composition during the Hellenistic period.

Cinzia Bearzot ('The recent past in Lysias 34') shows how this speech, written for a democratic politician against Phormisius' proposal to restrict the rights of citizenship to landowners, deals with various issues referring to the most recent past of Athens, recently emerging from the civil war: the continuity between the oligarchical experiences of 411 and 404, which is likely to recur for the third time (§ 1); the controversy against the amnesty and "forgetting" the evil suffered, exposing democracy to serious risks (§ 2); the presence of unreliable people, from the democratic point of view, in the so-called Peiraeus Party; the theme of *soteria* (§§ 6 and 8) and the tendency of the assembly to be deceived and to vote against its own interest (§ 3); the different behavior of oligarchs and democrats towards the civic body (§§ 3, 4–5); the greed for money of antidemocratic people (§ 5); allusions to the strategy of Pericles (§ 9), to a past, remote and recent, in which the Athenians fought for freedom and justice (§ 11), and to the case of the Argives and Mantinaeans, constantly anti-Spartan (§§ 7–8). All in all, Lysias tries to offer a reconstruction of the recent past in a democratic key, foreshadowing the risks that the democracy is still running.

Dino Piovan ('The Athenian civil war according to Lysias' funeral speech') reviews some passages in Lysias' *Funeral Oration* that allude to events that took place between 405 and 403 B.C, in particular § 58 on Aegospotami. The author presents an interpretation consistent with the thesis that the defeat was due to treason, previously found in Lys. 12, although here it is less explicit; and §§ 61–64 on the democratic resistance as a heroic struggle for justice and freedom, in which there are some distortions and glaring omissions. Afterwards he compares this Lysianic account of the Athenian civil war with those present in other funeral orations, and in particular in Plato's *Menexenus*. Finally, contrary to the interpretation offered by N. Loraux according to which the exaltation of harmony by Lysias watered down the more democratic traits of the anti-oligarchic resistance, Piovan argues that Lysias' rhetoric develops values and symbols without creating them from scratch and helps to instil them further into the city's culture, thus influencing civic behaviour.

Markus Zimmermann ('Alcibiades in Lys. 14') deals with Lysias' speech against Alcibiades, the son of the famous Athenian politician Alcibiades, and analyses how the historical events during the Peloponnesian War in which Alcibiades took part are presented in the speech, and also how the Lysianic version of Alcibiades' participation in this events is used by the orator to discredit his son. Zimmerman compares the narrative of Lysias with Thucydides, Xenophon and the *Hellenica Oxyrhynchia* and analyses the differences between them. The completely negative and one-sided version of Lysias is interesting because: *a*) most Athenians must still have known what happened during the Peloponnesian War and how Alcibiades was related to those events and *b*) Alcibiades was not hated by all of the Athenians, since he returned to Athens in 408, was elected *stragetos autokrator*, while even after his second flight he was not convicted *in absentia* and there was no trial. This leads to the question to what extent (if at all) historical accuracy was necessary to convince the audience.

Aggelos Kapellos ('Plato's *Menexenus* on the sea battle-trial of Arginousai and the battle of Aegospotami') examines Plato's selective treatment of the battle of Arginousai, his silence about the trial that ensued (a subject which he also briefly treated in the *Apology*) as well as his omission of the Athenians' defeat at Aegospotami, which reflects contemporary rhetoric. This becomes clear through a comparison of the relevant sections of the *Menexenus* with other funeral orations which treated similar subjects but mainly through the historians Thucydides, Xenophon and Diodorus. In the end, Plato's readers come to the same conclusion as the historians, i.e. that the Athenians were defeated because of their own mistakes, so they were unwilling to trace them. Plato's contemporaries could forget the real events, but his readers should not forget the truth, which could be achieved through their knowledge of the events but mainly through Xenophon's account.

David Whitehead ('Isocrates and the Peloponnesian War') examines Isocrates and his rhetorical treatment of the Peloponnesian War. Whitehead points out that of those Athenians who were born before the Peloponnesian War's outbreak in 431 and survived beyond its end in 404, Isocrates belongs to a select, literate, few whose surviving writings we can examine for traces of its impact. Both in (i) his early speeches for the courts and (ii) throughout his later, more numerous, epideictic compositions Isocrates does make mention of the War — which destroyed his family's fortunes; when forensic circumstances called for this (*re* i) and when he himself felt inclined to do so (*re* ii). This material falls into three main categories: the terminology that he employs to refer to the War and its several phases; specific events and people mentioned or ignored (some of them surprising); and, of particular note, passages like *On The Peace* 92, where personal feelings seems to persist.

Yun Lee Too ('Back to the Future: Temporal Adjustments in Isocrates') points out that Isocrates is an extremely conservative author, who prefers the past to what he sees as the currently chaotic present of Athens. For him, any hope for the future lies in lessons on behaviour and statesmanship provided by Athens' ancestors such that the past becomes the now and the future. The actual duration of history becomes inconsequential because the past is simply the past which is not now and which is intended as a template for now. The past is a pedagogical template for Athens to imitate. Too considers the *Areopagiticus*, *Antidosis*, *Panathenaicus* and *Evagoras*, texts where Isocrates resorts to a prior time in order to present the lessons that Athens needs to learn. Through these texts, Isocratean rhetoric treats history as a fluid substance while claiming that it is fixed and immutable.

Stefano Ferrucci ('The Recent Past in Isaeus' Forensic Speeches') shows that references to past events are limited in number and concise in Isaeus' speeches. The recent past is recalled to back up narratives on the causes' protagonists: family and individual memories that, at times, intertwine with the wider history of the *polis*. Such references may have an argumentative function, to display the reasons or explain the origin of a specific circumstance useful to the case, or an encomisastic/denigratory one, while constructing a character in the speech. In both cases events of the recent past come as pure facts, without any paradigmatic intent or judgment. The purpose in using the past is to illuminate the *ethos* of the characters, as good or bad citizens, by displaying individual attitude towards military or fiscal obligations. Identifying past facts was not Isaeus' concern; he used them as a given element within the narrative. Finally, Ferrucci analyzes Isaeus V as a relevant case-study.

Nicolas Siron ('The forensic time machine. Play on time in Apollodoros' *Against Timotheus*') deals with Apollodorus' *Against Timotheus* and the *eisangelia* this general faced, because although he was sent to rescue the Corcyreans, he sailed towards the Cyclades to gather money and men. Siron analyzes Apollodorus' ability to play with time in the construction of his narrative: the endless back and forth movement through time gives the opportunity to recall the *eisangelia* on several occasion and to cover up the good reputation of his opponent. Through a style said to be poor he manages to manipulate reality.

Furthermore, Apollodorus' calling for the jurors' testimony is a brilliant strategy using their various levels of knowledge in order to win his case.

Brad L. Cook ("Permit me to speak of myself': Demosthenes' Account of his Early Years') shows how Demosthenes in his inheritance speeches, then in his early twenties, speaks of his family at the time of his father's illness and death, over a decade earlier, and the repercussions of that loss. Because of the nature of the estate and Demosthenes' later fame, historians have much mined these speeches. Demosthenes does not, however, tell all that we would like but offers only glimpses within the house, carefully framed to serve his immediate rhetorical goals. This essay articulates the design and purpose of these glimpses to showcase the orator's nascent rhetorical skill in fashioning character portraits, and to qualify, and nuance, the uses that some studies have made of these glimpses into Demosthenes' household.

Gunther Martin ('Demosthenes' attacks on Androtion's record and their importance for *Against Timocrates*') deals with the attack that Diodorus (or his logographos Demosthenes) launches against Androtion with regard to two past activities: the collection of outstanding war tax and the melting of old gold crowns into processional vessels. This attack forms the end of *Against Androtion* and is repeated largely *verbatim* in *Against Timocrates*. Martin first deals briefly with what we know about Androtion's actions and then looks at Demosthenes' narrative technique in their presentation and the changes he made for the later version. His main point is the close correspondence between this section and the arguments in the rest of *Against Timocrates*. Martin shows that the shared motifs raise questions about how much the pre-existing section on recent political events influenced the production process and the rhetorical strategy of *Against Timocrates*.

Jeremy Trevett ('Demosthenes' Praise of Chabrias in the speech *Against Leptines*') explores Demosthenes' presentation in his early public speech *Against Leptines* (Dem. 20) of the career of the Athenian general Chabrias. Trevett shows that Demosthenes' arrangement is loosely chronological, from Chabrias' early successes to the battle of Naxos to his death at Chios, but the coverage is uneven. The early years are dealt with briskly and without appeal to any supporting evidence: Demosthenes assumes knowledge of Chabrias' manoeuvring at Thebes, his defeat of Gorgopas, and his service in Cyprus and Egypt. Unsurprisingly he devotes more space to the battle of Naxos in 375 B.C., where he both appeals to the memories of older members of his audience and provides documentation in the form of the decree honouring Chabrias and his own list of his achievements. However, when Demosthenes the recent Athenian defeat at Chios, in which Chabrias lost his life, he makes a vague and eulogistic account of the latter's death serves in order to minimize his responsibility for a humiliating military reverse.

Nathan Crick ('The Rhetoric of Deflection: Demosthenes's *Funeral Oration* as Propaganda') argues that when Demosthenes was chosen by the Athenians to deliver the funeral oration for those who had died fighting Philip II of Macedonia at the battle of Chaeronea in 338, he was given an unenviable task. Not only had the Athenians been decisively defeated, but Demosthenes had been an outspoken advocate for the disastrous campaign. His solution was to craft what Max Goldman has called a "rhetoric of defeat" whereby the Athenians could claim that "true victory is in the excellence of the city itself that produced the citizens who fought nobly." This chapter explores the rhetorical nuances of this type of rhetoric in more detail. Using Kenneth Burke's *War of Words*, Crick argues that Demosthenes combines strategies of *reversal* and *spiritualization* in order to reverse victory into defeat by changing the register of a valuation from a materialistic to an idealistic standard that produces emotional satisfaction at the expense of realistic evaluation.

Patrice Brun ('Demosthenes and the fake news') analyzes: (*a*) the decision of the Athenians to accept the so-called Peace of Philocrates in the situation of 346 (*On the False Embassy*) and (*b*) the formation of a military alliance with Thebes in 339 (*On the Crown*). These events help us learn from the way Demosthenes had re-invented recent history in his favour. In 346 B.C., Athens had no other choice but sue for peace with Philip II of Macedon and Demosthenes agreed with this position. Three years later, he tried to make the Athenians believe that they could have continued the war, showing that the Peace of Philocrates was faulty from the very start and trying to make Philocrates and Aeschines responsible for the situation. This assertion is utterly untrue, because the Athenians themselves were forced to accept peace, while Philip was not. In 18.168–216, repeating the events that led to the alliance with Thebes in 339 B.C., Demosthenes recalls that the speech he delivered on that occasion in front of the Assembly as ambassador prompted the Thebans to become allies to Athens. However, if Demosthenes only talks about himself and never about the others, Hyperides' *Against Diondas* puts him back in his right place and get things into perspective, since Hypereides' version is rather different from the one given by Demosthenes.

Peter A. O'Connell ('Facts, Time, and Imagination in Demosthenes and Aeschines') considers two ways that Demosthenes tries to make the version of the recent past he presents in his speech *On the False Embassy*, seem factual. First, he treats the second embassy, when he maintains Aeschines was working on Philip's behalf, as though it belongs to the distant past. This lets him present his argument as a search for facts about Aeschines's behavior that time has made hard for other people to obtain or recall. Second, through a strategy of enactive narration, he encourages the judges to imagine experiencing one of the events he describes, a symposium in Pella where he claims Aeschines got violently drunk. O'Connell also briefly considers similar rhetorical strategies in Demosthenes 18 and Aeschines 2 and 3.

Daniel Bajnok ('Peace and War with Philip: Aeschines' *Against Ctesiphon* on the recent past') examines how Aeschines presented the peace of Philocrates in 346 and the battle of Chaeronea in 338) in the trial *One the Crown*, trying to convince the judges to prefer his interpretation of events over that of Demosthenes. In general, Aeschines seems to have tried to turn Demosthenes into a scapegoat responsible for all the mishaps of Athens. As for the peace, Aeschines decided to omit his own service as envoy and to turn back a number of charges (used by Demosthenes against him in 343) against his opponent, while managing not to blame the disadvantageous peace on Philip II of Macedon. Concerning the antecedents and the aftermath of Chaeronea, Philip played again a markedly positive role as opposed to Demosthenes. Aeschines expected that the general Athenian attitude towards the Macedonians had been adapted to the political realities, therefore using the sorrowful memories of a historical disaster and turning his opponent a scapegoat might prove to be a successful strategy again.

Joseph Roisman ('Lycurgus and the Past') deals with Lycurgus' attempt to shape the memory and historical record of the recent past in his sole surviving speech *Against Leocrates*. Beginning with events roughly twenty years prior to Leocrates' trial (371–331 B.C.), the paper discusses how Lycurgus uses the recent past for examples and precedents that he hopes will sway the court to convict the defendant and sentence him to death. He makes purposeful and creative use of the past for his other mission: to inspire citizens with uncompromising patriotism and strong adherence to traditional values and practices. These goals affected Lycurgus' treatment of the battle of Chaeronea, the Athenians' frame of mind aftermath, the measures they took to defend themselves and the Macedonian perceived threat to the city. The result is a "history", which, though credible in its substance, is highly imbalanced, at times even bordering on invention.

Craig Cooper ('Remembering Chaeronea in Hyperides') treats the issue of Hyperides' proposal of a series of emergency measures in the Assembly in the aftermath of Chaeronea in 338 B.C. that involved evacuating women and children to the Peiraeus, arming the Boule, restoring all exiles and disenfranchised citizens, granting citizenship to metics, and freeing and arming slaves for a possible attack on Athens by Philip. Although the proposal was approved, it was never implemented given Philip's conciliatory attitude towards Athens. Still

Hyperides was indicted for introducing an illegal decree, but successfully defended himself, arguing that Macedonian arms obstructed the words of the laws prohibiting his proposal. In the many trials that followed Athens' defeat, Hyperides justified the city's involvement in the battle by recasting the memory of Chaeronea into a critical moment in Athens' history, like epic struggles of the past. This chapter, then, examines how he recalls and uses the memory of Chaeronea rhetorically in his forensic speeches to attack his political opponents and assist his clients in court.

Zinchao Wang ('Hegesippus and his treatment of the recent past') writes about Hegesippus, who is a neglected orator due to the lack of relevant historical sources. However, according to scholars, he is the author of *On Halonnesus*, namely, the seventh oration of the corpus of Demosthenes. As an orator with an anti-Macedonian stance, Hegesippus has some commonalities and some peculiarity with other Attic orators, especially Demosthenes, when he used the recent past in his speeches. First of all, like other orators, his speeches tended to use the recent past as an argument or object of discussion, but when he used it, he showed a tendency to distort, invent, and interpret facts in a way that favored Athens. Secondly, compared with Demosthenes, Hegesippus also shows some differences: his interpretation of the recent past tends to be factual, and rarely rises to the general principle; his attack on Philip was intended only to prove that Philip was dishonest, not to portray him as a tyrant, which was repugnant to the Greeks; although he displays a fierce style, his use of the recent past and his attacks on Philip seem to be confined to words rather than the strong direction of action of Demosthenes' public speech.

Ian Worthington ('Dinarchus. How to Succeed with No Evidence: Dinarchus vs. Demosthenes') shows that in his speech against Demosthenes of 323, Dinarchus alludes to several episodes from Athens' recent past, including the pivotal battle of Chaeronea, the war of Agis III, and the Harpalus affair, the last folding into Demosthenes' trial. All the jurors had lived through and so remembered these momentous events, especially the scandal surrounding Harpalus. Yet without a shred of evidence against Demosthenes, Dinarchus (and nine other prosecutors including Hyperides) was able to secure his conviction for taking a bribe from Harpalus. In dealing with an event so recent, still so fresh in everyone's minds, Dinarchus' success raises the question of how he was able to persuade the jury. Worthington examines how Dinarchus (and to a lesser extent Hyperides, given that his speech is fragmentary) manipulated events to create maximum rhetorical prejudice against Demosthenes, and the extent to which his audience was really ignorant of them or was beguiled by his presentation.

Janek Kucharski ('Hyperides, Diondas, and the First Ascendancy of Demades') writes about the recently deciphered Hyperidean speech *Against Diondas* (22–23 Horvath), which provides a glimpse into the early period of Demades' ascendancy in the 330s. In the relevant passage the orator deplores the fact that Demades and his clique monopolized Athens' policy, and seems to impute to him a tyrannical attempt to enslave the city paired with embarrassing flattery towards his Macedonian sponsors. Although the latter accusations may be a case of misunderstanding, taken together they provide a clear illustration of the rhetorical distortions to which events from recent history are subjected in ancient Athens: treachery may be a label given to prudence, while rational appeasement of a much stronger enemy could be misconstrued as a case of debased fawning. Traitor and flatterer were indeed the two principal shades with which the image of Demades was painted in later authors. The preserved fragment of *Against Diondas* is one of the earliest known testimonies in which these unflattering traits are outlined, and that in rather crisp detail.

Joshua P. Nudell ('Remembering injustice as the perpetrator?: Athenian orators, cultural memory, and the Athenian conquest of Samos') Timotheus' conquest of Samos in 366 and the alleged expulsions of the Samian demos that followed came to be remembered as one of the worst excesses of Athenian imperialism. Despite the hostile memory of Athenian overreach in the wider Greek world, however, the Attic orators universally characterize Timotheus' conquest as the "liberation" of Samos. Rhetorical manipulation of facts is well established; the question is whether the orators could shape the collective memory about a gross violation of Greek interstate norms to create a collective amnesia about an event from the recent past. An analysis of four speeches from three Attic orators (Isoc. 15; Dem. 15; Din. 1 and 3) suggests that they could not, which, in turn, casts doubt on the orthodox interpretation of this period in the history of Samos.

James Sickinger ('Inscriptions from the Recent Past in the Attic Orators') examines how the Attic orators integrated recent inscriptions — ones set up within a few decades of the date of the speeches in which they are mentioned — into their speeches in order to support and enhance their arguments. He notes that scholars have often discussed the fourth-century practice of citing older, fifth-century documents, especially inscribed documents, for the moral exempla and models of behavior that they provide for their audiences. Nevertheless, less often explored are how and why the Attic orators turned to more recently inscribed texts to support their cases and reinforce specific arguments. Several speeches include references to recent inscriptions and requests to have their texts read out, but unlike the fifth-century *stelae* cited by the orators, these citations are not meant to illustrate behavior of a distant era or provide models that an audience should emulate. Instead, their texts provide specific evidence in support of some aspect of a speaker's case. Sickinger shows that the orators and their audiences recognized that inscriptions of different dates could serve different functions, and that ones close to their own time were a potentially valuable source for information more immediately relevant to the issue at hand.

Finally, looking not at speeches but at a work at speeches, Pierre Chiron ('The *Rhetoric to Alexander* and its political and historical context: the mystery of a (quasi-) occultation') argues that technical treatises as *tekhnai rhetorikai* have suffered what philologists call "fluid transmission". It means that their content may have been adapted to their various contexts of use or fraudulent attributions. In the case of *Rhetoric to Alexander*, if we admit the testimony of Quintilian (3., 4., 9) describing under the name of Anaximenes a doctrine very close of that of the treatise in its current state but not identical to it, we have the proof of such adaptations and a quite clear motive for them: accrediting the attribution of the text to Aristotle. This is why, examining the scarce echoes left on the *Rhetoric to Alexander* by contemporary events, Chiron begins with textual hypotheses. But he examines other possibilities too: political reasons (the links of Anaximenes to Macedonian power, the bad image of logography), communicational reasons (addressing a larger audience than democratic Athens), or "philosophical" reasons, linked to the influence of Isocrates on the treatise and the preeminence of personal imitation on the transmission of models or experiences.

I wish to thank the contributors not only for their keenness to participate but also for bearing the present editor, who made various comments during the writing of their chapters, even at at the last stages of the volume. In return, I may excuse myself by saying that I have tried to be worthy of their scholarship. I am grateful to Professor Gunther Martin and Professor Joseph Roisman to help me and other contributors to improve this volume. I must also add that I am most grateful to the man whom I considered my second father, Professor Peter Rhodes. Peter supported my idea to edit this volume from the moment he heard about it, when we met in Athens, and he proved that during its creation. However, now, and with great sadness, I have to say that I dedicate this book to his memory. I thank the anonymous readers who examined the volume. Last, but not least, it is my honour, obligation and pleasure to express my gratitude to the editors-in-chief of De Gruyter, *Trends in Classics*, Professors Franco Montanari and Antonios Rengakos, for accepting and hosting this volume. For the latter specifically, I ought to say that he embraced my enthusiasm for this project through an instant e-mail of approval.

Bibliography

Adkins, A. (1977), "Form and Content in Gorgias' Helen and Palamedes: Rhetoric, Philosophy, Inconsistency and Invalid Argument in some Greek Thinkers", *The Society for Ancient Greek Philosophy Newsletter* 73, 1–14.

Alexiou, E. (2020), *Greek Rhetoric of the 4th Century BC: The Elixir of Democracy and Individuality*, Berlin/Boston.

Αποστολάκης, Κ. (2003), [Λυσίου] *Υπέρ Πολυστράτου*, Αθήνα.

Canevaro, M. (2019), "Memory, the Orators and the Public in Fourth Century BC Athens", in: L. Castagnoli/P. Ceccarelli (eds.), *Greek Memories. Theories and Practices*, Cambridge, 136–157.

Constantinidou, S. (2008), *Logos into Mythos: The Case of Gorgias' Encomium of Helen*, Athens.

Crick, N. (2015), *Rhetoric and Power: The Drama of Classical Greece*, Columbia.

Edwards, M. (1994), *The Attic Orators*, Bristol.

Gotteland, S. (2001), *Mythe et Rhétorique : Les exemples mythiques dans les discours politique de l'Athènes classique*, Paris.

Grethlein, J. (2014), "The Value of the Past Challenged: Myth and Ancient History in the Orators", in: J. Ker/C. Pieper (eds.), *Valuing the Past in the Greco-Roman World*, Leiden/Boston, 326–354.

Harris, E.M. (2018), *Demosthenes: Speeches 23–26*, Austin.

Henderson, M.M. (1975), "Plato's Menexenus and the Distortion of History", *Acta Classica* 18, 25–46.

Hunter, V. (1986), "Thucydides, Gorgias and Mass Psychology", *Hermes* 114, 412–429.

Kagan, D. (1987), *The Fall of the Athenian Empire*, Ithaca/London.

Kapellos, A. (2009), "Adeimantos at Aegospotami: Innocent or guilty?", *Historia* 58, 257–275.

Kapellos, A. (2014), *Lysias 21: A Commentary*, Berlin.

Kapellos, A. (2019a), *Xenophon's Peloponnesian War*, Berlin.

MacDowell, D.M. (2009), *Demosthenes the Orator*, Oxford.

Munn, M. (2000), *The School of History: Athens in the Age of Socrates*, Berkeley/Los Angeles.

Nouhaud, M. (1982), *L'utilisation de l'histoire par les orateurs attiques*, Paris.

Osborne, R. (2003), "Changing the Discourse", in: K. Morgan (ed.), *Political Tyranny*, Austin, 251–272.

Rhodes, P.J. (1981), *A Commentary on the Aristotelian Athenaion Politeia*, Oxford.

Rhodes, P.J. (1994), "In defence of the Greek Historians", *G&R* 41, 156–171.

Rhodes, P.J./Osborne, R. (2003), *Greek Historical Inscriptions 478–404 BC*, Oxford.

Rosenbloom, D. (1993), "Shouting 'Fire' in a crowded Theater: Phrynichos' *Capture of Miletos* and the politics of fear in early Attic tragedy", *Philologus* 137, 159–196.

Rowe, G. (1997), "Review of M. Edwards, *The Attic Orators*", *CW* 90, 372.

Sato, N. (2019), "Inciting thorybos and narrative strategies in attic forensic speeches", in: M. Edwards/D. Spatharas (eds.), *Forensic Narratives in Athenian Courts*, London/New York, 102–118.

Schenker, D.J. (2001), "Review of M. Munn, *The School of History*", *CR* 51, 314–316.

Schepens, G. (1975), "Some Aspects of Source Theory in Greek Historiography", *AncSoc* 6, 257–274.

Schettino, M.T. (2014), "The use of historical sources", in: M. Beck (ed.), *A Companion to Plutarch*, Oxford, 417–436.

Schollmeyer, J. (2021), *Gorgias' Lobrede auf Helena*, Berlin/Boston.

Steinbock, B. (2012), *Social Memory in Athenian Public Discourse: Uses and Meanings of the Past*, Ann Arbor.

Steinbock, B. (2017), "The Multipolarity of Athenian Social Memory: Polis, Tribes and Demes as Interdependent Memory Communities", in: R. Bernbeck/K.P. Hofmann/U. Sommer (eds.), *Between Memory Sites and Memory Networks. New Archaeological and Historical Perspectives*, Berlin, 97–125.

Usher, S. (1993), *Demosthenes On the Crown*, Warminster.

Taddei, A. (2012), *Licurgo Contro Leocrate*, Milano.

Todd, S.C. (2007), *A Commentary on Lysias: Speeches 1–11*, Oxford.

Westwood, G. (2020), *The Rhetoric of the Past in Demosthenes and Aeschines*, Oxford.

Worthington, I. (1991), "Greek Oratory, Revision of Speeches and the Problem of Historical Reliability", *C&M* 42, 55–74.

Thomas G.M. Blank
Methodical Remarks on the 'Truthfulness' of Oratorical Narrative

Abstract: In older scholarship the use of historical arguments in the Attic Orators was primarily interpreted against the backdrop of an insistence on 'historical fact'. There used to be an emphasis on how public speech quite commonly instrumentalised historical data, often distorting information that was considered 'true' from the perspective of modern research. Recent scholarship, by contrast, has highlighted the differences between ancient Greek and modern concepts of historical truth. Unquestionably, deceit plays a significant role in oratory, but not all distortion of historical fact is deceitful or un-historical. Considering the centrality of oratorical stages to the formation of public culture in Athens, the notion of historical truth itself proves to be situative and based on spontaneous assent rather than only on factual data. Without a necessary intent of deceit or of presenting counter-factual narratives, the instrumental use of relevant *lieux de mémoire* in public speeches played its own authentical part in the shaping of historical memory in Athens. This renders oratory a valuable source for contemporary public history and culture, regardless of the factual 'reliability' of the historical narratives it contains.

1 Introduction

Notwithstanding the crucial role that the power of *logos* played in the stabilisation of political identities and decision-making processes in Hellenic democracies,[1] modern scholarship for a long time tended to interpret the uses of the past in Greek oratory along the lines of an alleged opposition of truthfulness and trickery. Historians who tried to assess the worth of Classical oratory as a historical source, often regarded the information that these texts contained a slippery and treacherous matter — a speaker could be seen as either sticking to the facts or lying for selfish (or other oratorical) motives; historians simply needed to understand which was the case in order to judge 'true' from 'false' accounts of

---
I need to thank Aggelos Kapellos for inviting me to contribute, for helpful suggestions and, most of all, for his admirable patience.

1 Cf. Fontana 2004; Yunis 2013; Pernot 2014.

the past. On the other hand, philological and rhetorical studies were primarily focused on the persuasive goal of a given speech: Oratorical manipulation of facts and instrumental uses of narrative were, less pessimistically, regarded as purely functional, their mastery as proof of the art itself.[2] Such readings usually assumed that it needed to be on purpose if a speaker's account of the past did not match modern scholarly opinion about a particular event. In this sense it was — and sometimes still is[3] — common to view modern reconstructions of history as the sole canon by which to judge the truthfulness or honesty of ancient narratives of past events. In recent scholarship, however, there has been a considerable shift and diversification of interest in studying such narratives in Greek oratory. In this essay I will survey some theoretical and methodological implications that these recent developments have for assessing the representation of the recent past in the Attic orators. I will do so by outlining the complexities of public communication and the various circumstances that may have been influential for a given orator's retelling of events.

2 Facts = Truth(s)? Persuasion and the roots of history

That a narration of the past, indeed history itself, proved its 'truthfulness' solely by the standard of the facts it contained is a both modern and a historical point of view. It is modern, on the one hand, in its premise that truthfulness resulted from factual accuracy alone: the equation of fact and truth emerged as an epistemological principle as late as in the 18th and 19th centuries, in the wake of the rise of science as a paradigm for method and epistemic rigour in the academic world and beyond. By contrast, history as an academic discipline was defined both in opposition and in imitation to those scientific methods. While 'historist'[4] historians acknowledged that their object of study did not allow for the induction of universally applicable theories, they developed a historical method (still fundamental today) inspired by theological exegesis that aimed to meet the

---

[2] E.g Jost 1936; Schmitz-Kahlmann 1939; Pearson 1941; Perlman 1961; Allroggen 1972; Nouhaud 1982; Todd 1990; cf. on these tendencies Piepenbrink 2012, 101; Wojciech 2022, 20–22; Canevaro 2017, 174–175.
[3] See Wojciech (*forthcoming*), 23–24.
[4] On the term see Berger 2001.

standards of scientific empiricism in identifying the facts behind historical traditions.⁵

On the other hand, an equation of history with factual information on past events would be ahistorical from even the most traditional historist perspective. Even in Ranke's view historical sources do not plainly mirror but narrate and reflect facts, wherefore they implicitly transmit authorial bias and persuasive strategies.⁶ Historist source criticism was never meant to establish history by simply reconstructing or retelling facts, but it intended to reconstruct the facts to be able to understand how past cultures faced and perceived the world they encountered and how this shaped their actions (and narrations).⁷ That all memory of past events consists in narratives (which may or may not conform to facts about the events) was thus never neglected theoretically by modern historical research, though many scholars during the 19th and 20th centuries were more interested in reconstructing the facts than in studying how facts were translated into memory.⁸ Also, influenced by nationalist perspectives older historical scholarship overstated the homogeneity, if not uniformity, of historical memory and identity.⁹ Consequently, it was easy to overestimate certain interpretations of the past that were particularly widespread in a society as stable and authoritative. Deviations from these tended to appear as deliberate counter-narratives, whether with provocative or deceptive intent.

Narratives of the past in oratory are, of course, functionalised as to serve the rhetorical goal of the argument, and some oratorical narratives may be consciously driven by the intent to deceive the audience about the facts of the matter.¹⁰ But to be aware of the rhetoricity of all history complicates the issue. Recent scholarship has, therefore, abandoned the idea that deviations from (supposedly) more impartial historical accounts were sufficient to qualify a particular speech as reliable or untrue to 'history'.¹¹ In order to understand the

---

5 On predecessors in 18th century philosophy see Pflug 1971=1954.
6 See Kapellos' Introduction in this volume on the Greek historians.
7 Beiser 2011; cf. on Ranke Berding 2005.
8 For the study of Greek oratory and rhetoric see above n. 2.
9 Hesk 2012, 208–209; Barbato 2017, 215–216 and Wojciech 2022, 9 11, 21 22 deplore traces of this tendency in works as influential to current scholarship (and far from historist positivism) as Ober 1989; 2007 or Pownall 2004; but cf. the suggestion in Ober 2003 that democratic ideology (and its narratives) in Athens was merely based on a *thin coherence*.
10 See e.g. Worthington 1994 and 2020; Hesk 2012, 207–208.
11 Wojciech 2022, 174–175. Recently, Kremmydas 2019a introduced psychological criteria that allow to analyse the methods of rhetorical manipulation without necessarily measuring orator-

intentions, qualities and effects of a particular narration of the past we not only must take into account how Athenian orators and their audiences would have conceived of 'truthfulness' (e.g. based on *doxa*) as a criterion to judge an oration (a criterion which speechwriters needed to consider if they wanted to be persuasive),¹² but also how historical memory as a collective phenomenon usually evolves from an amorphous polyphony and multipolarity of very different personal accounts of a given event. In fact, cultural memory never achieves a status of perfect homogeneity, but remains in a constant state of change. This social quality of history as 'communicative memory' seems particularly relevant for the narration of very recent events.¹³

Different occasions for oratory require different degrees of factual plausibility or historical truthfulness for a speech to be persuasive¹⁴ — in some cases emotional arguments, scandalous or frivolous narratives may have been opportune,¹⁵ in others historical detail (or even cultural memory in general) may simply not have been of interest.¹⁶ What is more, particularly as regards recent events, historical narratives evolve over time, and to a certain degree they need the prevalence of an authoritative tradition to achieve a status as a 'cultural memory' stable enough to be used as rhetorical proof or moral exemplum.¹⁷ Such a tradition almost never exists right after the event, and it seldom did in

---

ical narrative against the idea of a homogenous democratic master narrative; cf. Edwards 2019 with Kremmydas 2013.

12 Allen 2014, 57–59; Farenga 2014, esp. 97–100. Cf. Canevaro 2017, 171–172 who observes the discrepancies between the self-perception of an audience and the complex realities of the formation of mnemonic communities. On *doxa* see also Kapellos (Introduction to this volume).

13 See Assmann 2008; 2011 on the distinction of 'communicative memory' (=polyphonic, functionalised negotiation of different interpretations of the past) and 'cultural memory' (=fixed, retold in hegemonic discourse); cf. Feitscher 2020. On social memory in Athens and the role of oratory within that context see Steinbock 2013a; 2017a; 2017b, 135–143; Canevaro 2017, 171–175; Wojciech 2018; 2020; Westwood 2020, 9–64.

14 Wojciech 2022, 35–48.

15 E.g. Spatharas 2011 on Apollodorus' rationale for including so many erotic anecdotes in *Against Neaira*; cf. Mossé 1993.

16 Arist. *Rhet.* 1414a30–b3 defines διήγησις as requirement only of dicanic oratory (on this see generally Volonaki 2020; cf. Calboli Montefusco 1988; Kirby 1991; Wojciech 2022, 6–8), not neglecting that some rhetoricians did not categorically exclude it from other genres of speech.

17 See e.g. Chaniotis 2009a; cf. 2009b; Osmers 2013; Wojciech (*forthcoming*), 53–67. The formation of authoritative historical traditions involved public 'forgetting', even of whole events; on this see Loraux 1980; 1997; Flaig 1991; 2004a; 2004b; Piepenbrink 2012; Canevaro 2017; Wojciech 2022, 70–140; cf. also Chaniotis 2010, 151–153; on the intentionality of history as a cultural practice see Foxhall and Gehrke (eds.) 2010; Gehrke 2010; 2014; Grethlein 2014a; Thomas 2014.

Athens.¹⁸ To the contrary, we should expect a variety of different, even contradictory, narrations: this was the case, for example, with the battle of Aegospotami and its catastrophic effects for Athens' warfare, safety and politics. Different narratives of the events surrounding this battle could be and were used in postwar Athens to either whitewash or denigrate the image of politicians like Alcibiades and their affiliates. Speakers who participated in such oratorical struggles were confronted with audiences whose members would each hold their very individual personal memories of the events, depending on the role they had played as soldiers in the Athenian fleet or part of the urban population at Athens.¹⁹

How, then, should we imagine the communicative processes by which social memories of persons or events of the recent past took shape in Classical Athens? It seems reasonable to believe that soon after an event there was more room for, but also more at stake in, controversy and alternate versions of a given 'story' than years or decades later.²⁰ For years, for example, Demosthenes and Aeschines were involved in a public and legal struggle to gain control over public interpretations of their respective roles in bringing about the "Peace of Philocrates" in 346 B.C.²¹ This dispute was not only influenced by the rhetorical skills of the opponents, but also by the commotions that arose on a daily basis as a result of the precipitating events leading up to the aftermath of the defeat of the anti-Macedonian coalition at Chaeronea.²² In some cases drama may have been influential in stabilising "official narratives" of single events, but it seems hard to tell how successful a particular play actually was in such an effort, not to speak of the fact that we do not even know how many alternate readings of the recent past may have been presented at the very same or different festivals by competing playwrights.²³ Remembrance of the war dead, in fact, was homog-

---

18 Grethlein 2013; 2014a and 2014b; Wojciech 2022; cf. Maltagliati 2020a and 2020b.
19 Whitehead (this volume), pp. 180–181; Zimmermann (this volume), pp. 139–143; cf. Wojciech 2022, 142–144; Worthington 2020, 22. Eckstein 2018 highlights the critical remarks of Thucydides on the reliability of eyewitness accounts. On the preference for eyewitness testimony over other types of sources in Greek (and other premodern) historiography see Luraghi 2014 and the further entries in Rösigner and Signori (eds.) 2014; cf. Schepens 2007.
20 See Kucharski (this volume) on Demades; in general Grethlein 2014a. Cf. Proietti 2017 on the multipolarity of memory of war events.
21 On these events and their depiction in Demosthenes and Aeschines see Brun (this volume).
22 See O'Connell (this volume) and Bajnok (this volume); cf. Westwood 2020, 223–327; Wojciech 2022, 174–183, 244–274; Worthington 2020, 20–22. See Steinbock 2013b on the potential role of distinct mnemonic traditions in the use of historical exempla in these speeches.
23 See e.g. Darbo-Peschanski 2017; Proietti 2017, 89–92; Ruffell 2017. That drama had an impact on public sentiment about the past is concisely illustrated by the story of Phrynichus'

enised to a certain degree in the public funerals at the Kerameikon cemetery, but, as far as we can tell, detailed narratives of recent events were no regular part of the funeral monuments or orations (though the heroization of the fallen soldiers helped to establish or uphold interpretations of those events as meaningful). Instead, in their presentation of moral paradigms the extant (mostly literary) *epitaphioi* (with the exception of Hypereides) focus on much earlier *exempla* such as the Persian Wars, events whose narrative transmission had long before taken a more or less definite form and which are referred to in order to suggest analogies or discrepancies between past, present (or most recent past), and future.[24] In a similar way, public processions were part of Athens' mnemonic culture, but not as much part of negotiating the recent past.[25] Other monuments would mark the existence of a narrative acceptable to the majority at the time of the popular decree (often soon after an event) by which their erection was enacted, but that does not mean that such narratives would necessarily remain stable over time.[26] Historiography, on the other hand, would take years to be published and, more importantly, almost certainly circulated among rather small audiences.[27]

On a daily basis markets, shops, taverns, and other places of public leisure — places not very prominent in the literary record[28] — were influential in shaping public opinion about recent events; most important, of course, were the stages of public oratory: Assembly, Council, courtrooms, and (sometimes) plac-

---

Miletou Halosis which met with shock and awe among the audience and led to the dramatist being fined by the *polis* (Hdt. 6.21.2).
24 Westwood 2020, 62–63; Wojciech 2022, 244–250 (on Demosthenes' use of epitaphic exempla in the aftermath of Chaeronea; cf. Hesk 2013, 52–55 and Cooper, this volume, on Hypereides). On the Funeral Oration in general see Loraux 1981; Pritchard (ed. *forthcoming*) and the articles of Kapellos and Crick (this volume). On 'intentional history' in the Funeral Oration see Proietti 2015; Barbato 2017, 215–222. Athens' decline in the recent past was sometimes mentioned as contrasting to the achievements of the fathers, cf. Lys. 2.58–59; see Piovan (this volume); cf. Bearzot 2002, 177–198. Cf. Bremner 2020 for a similar pattern in symbuleutic oratory. On the cultural relevance of monuments in the Ceramicus see Low 2012.
25 Hölkeskamp 2010.
26 On references to monuments in Greek oratory see Kostopoulos 2019; cf. Shear 2007; Hölscher 2010; Proietti 2017, 78–89; Westwood 2020, 1–23; Kapellos 2022, 11. Low 2012 argues that not even memorials for the war dead represented a homogenous public discourse. On inscribed narratives see also Chaniotis 2010; Osborne 2011 and Harris 2016 (decrees and chronicles).
27 Wojciech 2022, 5–6; cf. Canevaro 2017, 178–179 on the little use Athenian orators made of historiography. On the relation of historical culture and historiography cf. Nicolaï 2007.
28 See Matuszewski 2019.

es of informal meetings. When it came to narrating the recent past, Athenian orators were, in fact, less using or manipulating established narratives than they were at the forefront of shaping such narratives from the background noise of many-voiced rumour and publicly tangible moods.

3 Reasoning with the past: Between memorial culture, composition, reception and editorial process

What, then, are the complexities that orators needed to take account of when mentioning events of the recent past? The following section of this essay will delineate some of the more important contexts of communication that one should consider relevant for the analysis of 'historical' arguments. The elements discussed below will not be altogether new to many readers. Still, they are not always thoroughly recognised, and they have seldom been expressed as a hermeneutical program.

3.1 Event and memory

First, there (unsurprisingly) still is a fundamental need to assess what we factually know of the events under discussion on a source basis as broad as possible. However, it will not be sufficient to simply fact-check the narration of event X as given by orator Y in speech Z by comparing it to all types of parallel sources, be they literary, epigraphic, iconographic or whichever (each of which may pose their own problems of interpretation). To the contrary, it will be necessary to establish as precisely as possible, which narrative versions of X were current, or prevalent, among the immediate audience of Z, whether or not there were any predominant views on X, if they were contested or not and whether or not there was any known oratorical tradition of narrating X.

Speechwriters (and orators) needed to take into account how the audience would potentially react to a specific narrative version of an event: they would have speculated about this on the basis of their assumptions about what facts of the event may effectively have been known to the audience, which and how many different narrations of it the audience may have been presented in earlier orations, in literary and dramatic pieces, by polis-wide and local epigraphic, iconographic and performative commemorations and the like. All of these were sources of public memories of the past that could be and were easily used as points of reference in speeches.[29] It should be clear that once a certain version of interpreting or narrating the event came near to being an *opinio communis* it would have required different and more elaborate rhetorical strategies if an orator were to present a contrasting view. This also means that in the depiction of very recent events, a speechwriter could usually refer to a greater variety of opinions than if he wanted to treat important events of earlier history, on which the audience was more likely to share the culturally dominant view of a 'democratic master narrative'.[30] On the other hand, he may have encountered more emotional and controversial reactions and a much stronger conviction among the audience that they individually knew the events very well, since a considerable number of citizens or judges would hold opinions on the event that rooted in personal experience. And, finally, it could even be unavoidable for a speaker to mention a particular event if it was still a controversial talk of the day,[31] whereas the more distant past was more freely available for speakers to make use of or disregard as a paradigm.

Examples in case are references to the events in between the Sicilian disaster, the oligarchic coups of 411 and 404 B.C. and the restoration of democracy in 403 B.C. In the decade after 403 public memory of these events, especially those directly linked to the regime of the Thirty, was not only in an early stage of formation but also highly contested — the tensions are obvious in regulations of public and legal discourse surrounding the amnesty of 403 with its famous formula "no malicious memory/no memory of malice" (μὴ μνησικακεῖν).[32] For Lysias and his clients the memory of catastrophic events like Aegospotami, regardless of the amnesty (which in practice only referred to the civil war of 404/3), was heuristically useful for character assassination, but they needed to carefully heap all reproach on single individuals so that the jurors who might

---

29 See Kostopoulos 2019; cf. e.g. Hobden 2007, 495–498 (on Aeschin. or. 3); above n. 26.
30 See above n. 2.
31 See Zimmermann (this volume), pp. 139–146; cf. Canevaro 2017, 181.
32 E.g. Andoc. 1.81; Lys. 18.19; Isocr. 14.14. The speaker of Isocr. 18.3 and 42–44 explicitly claims that the amnesty helped to prevent that partisan interpretations of the past deepen the division between "democrats" and "moderates". He also appeals to the audience to be aware of his opponent's lies by making use of their personal experience of the events (18.9–10; 38; 52–54); cf. Lys. 21.9 and 2.58 (see Piovan, this volume); cf. Flaig 1991 and Wolpert 2002, esp. 75–118 on the importance of the amnesty for cultural memory in Athens. For the differing voice of Andocides see Pownall (this volume). Decades later, by contrast, Dem. 23.193 could refer to the amnesty in a qualifying sense, clarifying that not all remembrance of past crimes would fall under the category of 'malicious memory'.

have been part of the fleet would not themselves feel subject to those attacks.[33] It may be for similar reasons that the battle and (implicitly) trial of Arginusae was mentioned reproachfully (and explicitly) only more than twenty years after the event, in Plato's parody of funeral orations in the *Menexenus* which as a fictitious speech was not even addressed at the Athenian public, but at a private elite audience.[34] Half a century after the restoration of democracy, authors like Isocrates[35] and politicians like Demosthenes or Aeschines were already addressing audiences who shared more common interpretations of Athens' failures at the end of the 5th century B.C.,[36] but also had not personally been involved in the events.[37]

The sort of discourse analysis required to take these contexts into account is confronted with a considerable number of further variables such as the establishment of a fixed chronology of events (particularly in synchronising events in several distant places)[38] and, most generally, measuring the public relevance of the narrated event. If we consider the different kinds of events narrated in the *Corpus Oratorum*, especially in dicanic oratory, we should expect that in private cases, many of the narrated facts were completely new to the majority of the

---

33 See Kapellos 2009; 2013, 465–468; 2017, 314–319; 2019a on scapegoating and personal motives of litigants; see also Whitehead (this volume on Isocrates). On the need for historiographers to consider both public knowledge and opinion see Kapellos 2012; 2013, 468–470; 2014, 43–45, 91–100; 2018, 394–398, 404–406; 2019b. On the impact of local and tribe-traditions see Steinbock 2017a. On circumnavigation of the amnesty in the *Corpus Lysiacuum* see also Bearzot 2002, 37–86, 141–176; Piovan 2011 and Volonaki 2019.
34 Plat. *Men.* 243d2–6; Trivigno 2009, 39 and Balot (*forthcoming*); cf. Kapellos (this volume). Compare the approving statements in earlier oratory, e.g. Lys. 12.36; see Kapellos 2019c and 2022.
35 E.g. Isoc. 7.62–70; 8.84–88; Whitehead (this volume), esp. 182–186 reads Isocratean discourse as evidence for the diachronical formation of a coherent cultural memory of the later Peloponnesian War, a 'master narrative' that Isocrates decided to subvert.
36 See Hesk 2012; Steinbock 2013b and Barbato 2017, 229–243 on Demosthenes' and Aeschines' diverging take on the final years of the Peloponnesian War in 2.74–78 Steinbock in particular argues that Aeschines picked up existing (but not dominant) readings of Athenian history in order to confront his 'warmongering' opponents with the very type of historical evidence they were used to cite. Traditions were subject to changes as well; see Steinbock 2017b on the memory of Nicias role in the Sicilian Expedition.
37 Westwood 2020, 26–31 notes that in such cases orators could use the "'identical audience' topos" to reduce the critical distance of audiences who had, in fact, not been involved in the past narrated in a speech. When it came to narrating contemporary events, of course, Demosthenes as well was speaking to an audience who would have been personally involved; see Worthington 2020, 20–21.
38 See Clarke 2008.

audience. For many such private or semi-private events, we furthermore do not dispose of parallel sources that could allow us to reconstruct possible alternative views in contemporary audiences. Nevertheless, many such events were narrated as if they were widely known to all listeners, putting the individual listener under pressure to either agree or feel (implicitly) accused of being ignorant of the obvious.[39] Such is the case with a lot of the information Demosthenes gives about his family and opponents in the inheritance suits against Aphobus and Onetor. Obviously, the Athenian system of taxes and liturgies afforded publicity of some information about a citizen's wealth. Demosthenes makes use of this publicity in claiming that the wealth of his father was widely known. But that surely does not mean that he was unable to fashion to his own use the details of his narration of the events that over the span of more than a decade allegedly led him to be deprived of his father's property and assets and money.[40]

3.2 *Kairos*: situation and performative context

Audiences, naturally, varied from one rhetorical stage or event to another. It may be possible to describe something like an 'Athenian public discourse' in general terms – particularly concerning moments of grave political crisis, which may have facilitated the emergence of a unified public opinion on the immediate/recent past[41] –, but in most cases it is unlikely that the Athenian public was unanimous on topics of the recent past. Furthermore, different views on an event may not have been spread arbitrarily among citizens, but were in-

---

39 Arist. *Rhet.* 1408a33–6; Wojciech 2018, 165–167, 171; Westwood 2020, 24–26. Cf. the speculations about Andocides' activities abroad in [Lys.] 6.6–7, Apollodorus' allegations against Timotheus (see Siron, this volume, pp. 227–231) or Demosthenes' claims about the publicity of his humiliation by Meidias (see Cook, this volume, pp. 12–13). Canevaro 2017, 195–199 argues that references to the audience's "common knowledge" should be read as a means of concealing the potential ignorance or dissent of parts of the audience or even to cover the orator's creative modifications in his narration of the past.
40 Dem. 27.4–48 *passim*; 28.3–16; see Cook (this volume), pp. 244–247; cf. Siron (this volume), pp. 227–229 on [Dem.] 49. In similar ways, public expenditures are regularly listed as proof for calculations of any person's wealth (and civic commitment), e.g. Lys. 12.20; 19.55–59; 21.1–5 (on the latter see Kapellos 2104, 11–14, 41–42, 61–79). On the use of numbers as rhetorical proof in Greek oratory see van Berkel 2017. The publicity of decrees and honorific decrees could even be used as an argument when the respective decisions were no longer valid, see Bearzot 1981; cf. Wojciech 2022, 163–166.
41 See Worthington 2010 on how the destruction of Thebes could be instrumentalised as a 'commonplace' argument; cf. Banjok and Worthington (this volume).

fluenced by social class, deme affiliation, age group, kinship and the like: in this respect, Athens formed not but one but consisted of several 'mnemonic communities' which shared many, but not all views on the past.[42] Finally, there was the influence of eyewitness testimony, rumour and hearsay, which was so important in the formation of public opinion in Athens (and Graeco-Roman cultures in general) that it shaped the methodological discussion not only of rhetoric but of historiography.[43]

How different an impression an argument could have made under changing circumstances (concerning the composition of the audience and other cultural factors as mentioned above) was already seen by contemporary observers of Athenian oratory. For Alcidamas, the decisive factor for the success of a speech was *kairos*, and (unlike Isocrates) he deemed it impossible to do justice to the daily different conditions on Athenian stages in a pre-written speech.[44] In the *Menexenus*, Plato's Socrates addresses a very general issue of cultural determination when he argues that the litmus test for a technically brilliant argument from history was to be plausible to those who would otherwise oppose its narrative thrust: an *epainos* of fallen Athenian soldiers should convince Athens' enemies, not just the Athenians themselves.[45] What underlies this Platonic claim is an awareness of the fact that the persuasive power of any argument depends on the preconceptions of the audience, and that one and the same argument may therefore have quite different effects in front of different audiences.[46] In this sense, too, the composition of the audience had to be calculated by the speechwriter with a view to the specific (institutional, political, seasonal etc.) occasion at which the speech was to be performed.

3.3 Circumstances of composition

A further factor that could take influence on narrations of the recent past was institutional circumstance. While we can assume that for epideictic speeches the almost ritual recurrence of certain topics and modes of argumentation al-

---

[42] Steinbock 2013a and 2017a.
[43] On positive evaluations of φήμη as an indication of truth in Greek oratory (particularly with regard to the recent past) see Gotteland 1997; Bajnok 2013; Bultrighini 2014. On eyewitness-testimony and its importance for rhetoric and historiography see above n. 18.
[44] Vallozza 1985.
[45] Plat. *Men.* 234c1–235d7.
[46] See also Barbato 2017 on the different uses to made of elements of the epitaphic "Tatenkatalog".

lowed for a rather autonomous, if thematically static, creative approach — the very kind of textbook-rhetoric that Socrates ridicules in the *Menexenus* —, the heuristic situation of a typical Assembly speech was altogether different: here, a speaker should need to address both common ethical values (as represented in cultural memory by historical paradigms) and issues of contemporary politics which might often be part of public controversy.[47] In dicanic oratory, to the contrary, the narration of events was often required to establish the (judicial and/or public) relevance of the case in question.[48] By definition the facts of the matter and many of the events to be narrated were contested among the parties at court, but there was not normally a public discourse (nor personal experience) by which the audience's views of those narrations should have been preconceived. If parts of the audience were prejudiced, this would rather have been an effect of the public image of that person, not of the event *per se*. In consequence, judicial speeches beyond narrating the facts of the case itself often also narrated recent events in the course of *ad personam ethos*-arguments. While in the first type of narrative, by which the speaker's version of the case was introduced to the audience, the speaker could shape those narrations almost unrestricted by any established *doxa*, in the latter he should try to form his arguments in accordance with such public opinion.

While genre thus had an impact on the way events could be told or retold, judicial procedure had as well: both parties had to present all evidence and witnesses, and even their main line of argument, to the *archōn* in the course of the (pre-trial) *anakrisis*; all testimony (witnesses, contracts, laws etc.) had to be acknowledged by the chair, was recorded in writing and laid down in a sealed box (*echinos*) from which it would be taken during the trial and read to the jurors by the clerks whenever cited by one of the speakers.[49] This, to be sure, included evidence for the events immediately related to the indictment only, but would not (necessarily) involve material for ethical arguments apart from it. If the narration of a particular event was, therefore, to be used as proof for the immediate case under discussion, the speechwriter needed to be aware of the fact that the opponent knew the facts he was going to refer to and could use the

---

[47] A particular problem, for example, arose after the defeat at Chaeronea from Athens' collaboration with Thebes in the war against Philip. Thebes had long been an ally that stirred controversy in Athens. But getting to terms with the legacy of Chaeronea (that Macedon did not want to be forgotten) now meant to recall the dire fate of Athens' ally; see Banjok and Worthington (this volume).

[48] Gagarin 2019.

[49] On the need to argue on the basis of the material documented in the *anakrisis* see Todd 2002, 159–165; Kremmydas 2019b; on the procedure see Thür 2008.

same material for his own argument.⁵⁰ On the other hand, neither the moral exaltation of those who supported one's own case nor the denigration of an opponent was subject to such objectivity. It, therefore, needs to be taken into account, whether a speaker made use of a particular event's narration with regard to the facts of the matter or with regard to *ad personam* arguments.

Finally, there is the problem of authorship. Litigants in Athenian courts generally had to present their case in person, regardless of their rhetorical education or experience as speakers. Some litigants surely did write their own speeches, and quite a number of such speeches are extant.⁵¹ Also, litigants could present one support speaker (*synēgoros*) by arguing that the case in question touched the interest of that person. This *synēgoros* could be a professionally trained orator, and *synēgoros*-speeches often exceeded the length of the actual litigants' speech: the trained orator would then present the arguments that were crucial for the litigant's case.⁵² The perspective in which an event of the recent past was presented thus partly depended on the speaker and his or her relationship to the events. Yet the majority of dicanic speeches, were written by professional speechwriters (*logographoi*) like Lysias or Isaeus, or influential politicians like Demosthenes.⁵³ In narrating events these logographers had to take on the role of the litigant in their writing, and for this they had to externally empathise with the speaker's *persona*. The information that a speechwriter could process for this purpose probably came from the litigant himself, from the *anakrisis* and — in the case of events of public relevance — from public discourse. Eventually, however, it was the speechwriter who had to evaluate and processes

---

50 Remarkably, Aeschines (3.99, see Wojciech 2018, 168–169) reproaches Demosthenes with presenting false testimony, by which he tried to dissimulate his lies. The thrust of this attack lies in its contrast to the trustworthiness usually ascribed to the documents presented by the clerks. On the relation of written testimony and oral performance see Taddei 2016. On witness testimony see e.g. Todd 1990; 2002; Rubinstein 2000; 2005; Thür 2005; Siron 2019a. On the (imputed and actual) credibility of witnesses see Mirhady 2002; cf. Siron 2019b.

51 Among these are some rather famous cases like Lysias' speech *Against Eratosthenes* (12), Andocides' apology (1), Demosthenes' guardian trials (27–31), or some of the speeches of the *parapresbeia*-affair (Dem. or. 19; Aesch. or. 2). The earliest extant case of a speech delivered by its author, the speech for Polystratus delivered by his son (=[Lys.] 20; see Apostolakis 2003, 83–90, cf. 289–290; cf. Rhodes, this volume), probably qualifies as a *synēgoros*-speech, although the speaker does not mention any speech of the actual defendant.

52 Rubinstein 2000; cf. Blank 2019, 65–66. Some of the most famous speeches of Greek oratory were held by *synēgoroi*, e.g. Demosthenes' *On the Crown* (18); for [Lys.] 20 see n. 52.

53 On professional speechwriting see Edwards 2000; Usher 2010. On Din. 1 see Worthington (this volume).

the information available to him so to transform it into a coherent narrative.⁵⁴ In this respect, such speeches present narratives that have emerged in a more complex way, and it may usually be difficult to determine in detail how much a logographer may have altered the narratives that a client had told him.

3.4 Circumstances of performance and reception

A last aspect to be considered is the diverging circumstances of performance and reception of speeches on different political stages. At court, each party was allowed a clearly defined amount of time to present their case (multiple plaintiffs needed to share their amount of time);⁵⁵ and they were allowed to include one *synēgoros* in support. Importantly, there normally was no cross-examination of any if the evidence or arguments presented, nor was there any room for discussion in general.⁵⁶ Each side presented its argument coherently, first plaintiff, then defendant. This reduced the speakers' control over the effect of their words on the audience: what was once spoken could not be corrected or extended later. Plaintiffs in particular had to ensure that their version of events anticipated and invalidated as many of the other side's arguments as possible (*prokatalēpsis*). As a result, while we mostly dispose of one side of the speeches held in a given trial, important arguments of the opposing side (including diverging narrations of events) can still sometimes be more or less clearly inferred from that speech.

The situation was mostly similar when speeches were held in front of the Assembly. Yet there were some important differences. As far as we can tell, the length of speeches could vary, but they were usually much shorter than speeches at court. This probably had to do with the fact that most sessions of the Assembly treated more than just one issue, and also that the Assembly allowed citizens to come forward to speak spontaneously.⁵⁷ Even if we assume that only a minority of Assemblymen would actually dare to speak up in front of an audience of often several thousand,⁵⁸ the greater number of potential speakers limited the time available for single speeches. We also know that audiences in the Assembly could be very engaged and would, at times, react very strongly. De-

---

54 Winter 1973; Usher 1976; Worthington 1993; cf. Todd 2002, 159–165.
55 Worthington 1989 and 2003 may be right to argue that some exceptional political trials exceeded one day (especially if there were several plaintiffs).
56 Todd 2002.
57 Blank 2019, 59–62.
58 Wojciech 2022, 6–8.

mosthenes seems to have been all but booed off stage in some instances, and speakers could be ridiculed for this by their opponents.⁵⁹ Speakers in the Assembly probably had an increased interest in seeking to unite ideologically with the majority of the audience, and this may have led to a certain preference for better established takes on past events. On the other hand, we also find an almost topical form of self-representation by speakers who presented themselves as 'teachers' or 'critical friends' of the citizens, teachers who corrected their audiences' misconceptions and who in the interest of the common good would even risk to fall out of favour with them.⁶⁰

Not all speeches were even delivered at the occasion from which they purport to spring. While only Isocrates is known to have primarily written speeches for written circulation only, some single speeches included in the corpora of Lysias, Demosthenes and others might have been as well.⁶¹ If such oratory was composed for reading audiences, we should at least consider it possible that they took into account the very different ways of reception of such a reading audience when writing those texts. Isocrates even reflected this in some of his works, as S. Usener and Y.L. Too were first to demonstrate.⁶² Importantly, unlike live audiences, readers would be able to re-read arguments that made use of contemporary events and incidents of the recent past and assess them critically against the backdrop of other versions. Isocrates clearly realised this and repeatedly comments on the danger of inconsistencies that might emerge even within his own body of discourses.⁶³ On the other hand, the author of a fictional speech would have faced little immediate consequences if he presented controversial or provocative views that failed to convince a majority of readers — the stakes thus being rather low he potentially could be more outspoken than if he was to speak in front of a genuine political or judicial Assembly. It is, therefore,

---

59 Dem. 19.45–46; cf. Aesch. 1.80. On audience reactions: Lanni 1997; Worthington 2017; Blank 2019, 66–69; Sato 2019.
60 Schenkeveld 2007.
61 See e.g. Bearzot 2002, 158–175 on [Lys.] 6; Pownall (this volume) on Andoc. 3.
62 Usener 1994 (on addresses to reading audiences); Too 1995 (on Isocrates' awareness of the particularities of written speeches and the need for a coherently stylized authorial *persona*); cf. Blank 2014, 57–63; Westwood 2020, 63; 76; Wojciech 2022, 14–16.
63 Isocr. 5.9–11; 12.172–174, 199–263; see Blank 2014, 457–459, 557 n. 245, 563–579. It seems appealing (though methodically impossible to prove) to argue that at least some of the manipulation of facts and their interpretation in, for example, the speeches of Demosthenes and Aeschines should have been obvious to a reading audience; cf. Brun (this volume).

unsurprising that Isocrates appears as a most severe critic of contemporary politics, the Second Athenian League in particular.[64]

To identify the precise relation of author/orator and audience is relevant not only for speeches that were originally composed for reading audiences, but also for original oratory that was later revised for publication. To what degree published speeches were revised or even thoroughly reworked in the process of their publication is a highly controversial question.[65] It should be safe to say, though, that published speeches normally were revised but that the degree to which the published versions differed from the spoken word strongly depended on the reasons for a speech's publication. If an orator (e.g. Demosthenes) intended to publish a speech (e.g. *On the False Embassy*) in order to disseminate his points of view beyond the original occasion, then revisions are likely to have been made according to different criteria than, for example, in the case of the publication of a court speech as a model piece for rhetorical education. Regardless of this interest, however, there certainly were limits to the degree to which speeches might be reworked. The published speech still had to conform to the essential argumentation of the original version, since the number of those who would have witnessed the original delivery of the speech in person was very large (especially immediately after publication).[66]

4 Conclusion

The outline given above is neither comprehensive nor are there too many individual speeches for which its elements are relevant in their entirety. What I want to highlight is the variety and diversity of circumstances that potentially had an influence on oratorical narrations of the recent past. Beyond personal memory and conviction, there were numerous factors to consider that helped determine what could be said or should be omitted in public discourse. Procedural rules in public institutions influenced the level of knowledge of speakers and audiences, contemporary politics could potentially have an impact on pub-

---

[64] Cf. Isoc. 7.1–13; 8 (*passim*); in both discourses 5th century *exempla* are introduced as standards by which the recent past can be measured; see Blank 2014, 392–393, 413–436.

[65] See e.g. Worthington 1991; 1996; 2020; Vatri 2019, 195–257 (on linguistic differences); Westwood 2020, 74–78; Wojciech 2022, 15–19. Worthington argues that inaccuracies in narratives of the past/history were not only due to rhetorical manipulation of facts but potentially also to later revisions; cf. Pownall (this volume).

[66] Gagarin in Gagarin and MacDowell 1998, xv.

lic sentiment about the events under discussion; different institutional occasions afforded different kinds of speeches; personal training in rhetoric (or the lack of it) would decide whether a speaker presented his own arguments or rather those construed by professional speechwriters etc. Circumstances like these should be taken into account in any study of the narratives of the recent past in oratory, since they could have an impact on the form and content of these narratives. An orator would normally form his narratives according to the implications such circumstances might have. This, to be sure, has nothing to do with the question whether an orator wanted to honestly convince his audience of what he considered true himself, or if he, instead, did not care too much about the facts behind his arguments as long as he managed to persuade.

Bibliography

Allen, J.V. (2014), "Aristotle on the Value of 'Probability', Persuasiveness, and Verisimilitude in Rhetorical Argument", in: V. Wohl (ed.), *Probabilities, Hypotheticals, and Counterfactuals in Ancient Greek Thought*, Cambridge, 47–64.

Allroggen, D. (1972), *Griechische Geschichte im Urteil der attischen Redner des vierten Jahrhunderts v. Chr.*, Univ. Diss. Freiburg i.Br.

Apostolakis, K. (2003), *[Λυσίου] Ὑπὲρ Πολυστράτου. Εἰσαγωγή, Μετάφραση, Σχόλια*, Athens.

Assmann, J. (2008), "Communicative and Cultural Memory", in: A. Erll/A. Nünning (eds.), *Cultural Memory Studies. An International and Interdisciplinary Handbook*, Berlin, 109–118.

Assmann, J. (2011), *Cultural Memory and Early Civilization. Writing, Remembrance, and Political Imagination*, Cambridge (orig: Das kulturelle Gedächtnis, Munich 1992).

Bajnok, D. (2013), "The Goddess of Report in the Courtroom", *Acta Classica Universitatis Scientiarum Debreceniensis* 49, 181–189.

Balot, R. (forthcoming), "Plato's Menexenus", in: D.M. Pritchard (ed.), *The Athenian Funeral Oration: 40 Years After Nicole Loraux*, Cambridge.

Barbato, M. (2017), "Using the Past to Shape the Future: Ancestors, Institutions and Ideology in Aeschin. 2.74–8", in: E. Franchi/G. Proietti (eds.), *Conflict in Communities. Forward-looking Memories in Classical Athens*, Trento, 213–253.

Bearzot, C. (1981), "A proposito del decreto ML 85 per Trasibulo uccisore di Frinico e i suoi complici", *RIL* 115, 289–303.

Bearzot, C. (2002), *Vivere da democratici: studi su Lisia e la democrazia ateniese*, Roma.

Beiser, F.C. (2011), *The German Historicist Tradition*, Oxford.

Berding, H. (2005), "Leopold von Ranke", in: P. Koslowski (ed.), *The Discovery of Historicity in German Idealism and Historism*, Berlin, 41–58.

Berger, S. (2001), "Stefan Berger Responds to Ulrich Muhlack", *Bulletin of the GHI London* 23, 21–33.

Blank, T.G.M. (2014), *Logos und Praxis. Sparta als politisches Exemplum in den Schriften des Isokrates*, Berlin.

Blank, T.G.M. (2019), "Politisch-rhetorische Praxis in der Polis", in: A. Burkhardt (ed.), *Handbuch Politische Rhetorik*, Berlin, 53–76.
Bremner, S. (2020), "The Rhetoric of Athenian Identity in Demosthenes' Early Assembly Speeches", *GRBS* 60, 544–573.
Bultrighini, U. (2014), "Eschine e la 'phéme' in giudizio", *Rivista di Cultura Classica e Medioevale* 56, 317–330.
Calboli Montefusco, L. (1988), *Exordium, narration, epilogus. Studi sulla teoria retorica greca e Latina delle parti di discorso*, Bologna.
Canevaro, M. (2017), "La memoria, gli oratori e il pubblico nell'Atene del IV secolo a.C.", in: E. Franchi/G. Proietti (eds.), *Conflict in Communities. Forward-looking Memories in Classical Athens*, Trento, 171–212.
Chaniotis, A. (2009a), "Überzeugungsstrategien in der griechischen Diplomatie. Geschichte als Argument", in: A. Chaniotis/A. Kropp/C. Steinhoff (eds.), *Überzeugungsstrategien*, Berlin, 147–165.
Chaniotis, A. (2009b), "Travelling Memories in the Hellenistic World", in: R.L. Hunter/ I.C. Rutherford (eds.), *Wandering Poets in Ancient Greek Culture. Travel, Locality and Pan-Hellenism*, Cambridge, 249–269.
Chaniotis, A. (2010), "Mnemopoetik: Die epigraphische Konstruktion von Erinnerung in den griechischen Poleis", in: O. Dally (ed.), *Medien der Geschichte – Antikes Griechenland und Rom*, Berlin, 132–169.
Clarke, K. (2008), *Making Time for the Past. Local History and the Polis*, Oxford.
Darbo-Peschanski, C. (2017), "Multiple Ways to Access the Past: The Myth of Oedipus, Sophocles' *Oedipus Rex* and Herodotus' *Histories*", in: L.I. Hau/I. Ruffel (eds.), *Truth and History in the Ancient World: Pluralising the Past*, Oxford, 81–103.
Eckstein, A.M. (2018), "Learning from Thucydides: An Ancient Historian Writes Contemporary History", *Histos* 12, 97–115.
Edwards, M.J. (2019), "Deceptive Narratives in the Speeches of Isaeus", in: M.J. Edwards/ D. Spatharas (eds.), *Forensic Narratives in Athenian Courts*, London, 71–80.
Farenga, V. (2014), "Open and Speak your mind: Citizen Agency, the Likelihood of Truth, and Democratic Knowledge in Archaic and Classical Greece", in: V. Wohl (ed.), *Probabilities, Hypotheticals, and Counterfactuals in Ancient Greek Thought*, Cambridge, 84–100.
Feitscher, G. (2020), *Erinnerung und Gedächtnis*, in: Compedium heroicum 2020/02/12 (SFB 948 Helden – Heroisierungen – Heroismen), URL http://dx.doi.org/10.6094/heroicum/egd1.1.20200212 [last visited: 2021/02/23].
Flaig, E. (1991), "Amnestie und Amnesie in der griechischen Kultur. Das vergessene Selbstopfer für den Sieg im athenischen Bürgerkrieg 403 v. Chr.", *Saeculum* 42, 129–149.
Flaig, E. (2004a), "Der verlorene Gründungsmythos der athenischen Demokratie. Wie der Volksaufstand von 507 v. Chr. vergessen wurde", *Historische Zeitschrift* 279, 35–61.
Flaig, E. (2004b), "Politisches Vergessen. Die Tyrannentöter – eine Deckerinnerung der athenischen Demokratie", in: G. Butzer/M. Günter (eds.), *Kulturelles Vergessen: Medien – Rituale – Orte*, Göttingen, 101–114.
Fontana, B. (2004), "Rhetoric and the Roots of Democratic Politics", in: B. Fontana/C.J. Nederman/G. Remer (eds.), *Talking Democracy. Historical Perspectives on Rhetoric and Democracy*, Pennsylvania, 27–56.
Foxhall, L./Gehrke, H.-J./Luraghi, N. (eds.) (2010), *Intentional History: Spinning Time in Ancient Greece*, Stuttgart.
Gagarin, M./MacDowell, D.M. (1998), *Antiphon and Andocides*, Austin (TX).

Gagarin, M. (2019), "Storytelling in Athenian Law", in: M.J. Edwards/D. Spatharas (eds.), *Forensic Narratives in Athenian Courts*, London, 11–21.
Gehrke, H.-J. (2010), "Historiographie: Die Gegenwart in der Geschichte", in: O. Dally (ed.), *Medien der Geschichte – Antikes Griechenland und Rom*, Berlin, 37–53.
Gehrke, H.-J. (2014), *Geschichte als Element antiker Kultur: Die Griechen und ihre Geschichten*, Berlin.
Gotteland, S. (1997), "La rumeur chez les orateurs attiques : vérité ou vraisemblance?", *AC* 66, 89–119.
Grethlein, J. (2013), "Democracy, Oratory, and the Rise of Historiography in Fifth-Century Greece", in: J.P. Arnason/K.A. Raaflaub/P. Wagner (eds.), *The Greek Polis and the Invention of Democracy. A Politico-Cultural Transformation and its Interpretations*, Chichester, 126–143.
Grethlein, J. (2014a), "The Many Faces of the Past in Archaic and Classical Greece", in: K.A. Raaflaub (ed.), *Thinking, Recording, and Writing History in the Ancient World*, Malden (MA), 234–255.
Grethlein, J. (2014b), "The value of the past challenged. Myth and Ancient History in the Attic Orators", in: C. Pieper/J. Kerr (eds.), *Valuing the Past in the Greco-Roman World*, 326–354.
Harris, E.M. (2016), "Alcibiades, the Ancestors, Liturgies, and the Etiquette of Addressing the Athenian Assembly", in: S.T. Farrington/V. Liotsakis (eds.), *The Art of History: Literary Perspectives on Greek and Roman Historiography*, Berlin, 145–155.
Hesk, J.P. (2012), "Common Knowledge and the Contestation of History in Some Fourth-Century Athenian Trials", in: J. Marincola/L. Llewellyn-Jones/C. MacIver (eds.), *Greek Notions of the Past in the Archaic and Classical Eras. History Without Historians*, Edinburgh, 207–226.
Hesk, J.P. (2013), "Leadership and Individuality in the Athenian Funeral Orations", *BICS* 56, 49–65.
Hobden, F. (2007), "Imagining Past and Present. A Rhetorical Strategy in Aeschines 3, *Against Ctesiphon*", *CQ* 57, 490–501.
Hölkeskamp, K.-J. (2010), "Raum – Präsenz – Performanz. Prozessionen in politischen Kulturen der Vormoderne – Forschungen und Fortschritte", in: O. Dally (ed.), *Medien der Geschichte – Antikes Griechenland und Rom*, Berlin, 359–395.
Hölscher, T. (2010), "Monumente der Geschichte – Geschichte als Monument? ", in: O. Dally (ed.), *Medien der Geschichte – Antikes Griechenland und Rom*, Berlin, 254–284.
Jost, K. (1936), *Das Beispiel und Vorbild der Vorfahren bei den attischen Rednern und Geschichtsschreibern bis Demosthenes*, Paderborn.
Kapellos, A. (2009), "Adeimantos at Aegospotami: Innocent or Guilty?", *Historia* 58, 257–275.
Kapellos, A. (2012), "Philocles and the Sea-battle at Aegospotami (Xenophon *Hell.* 2.1.22–32)", *CW* 106, 97–101.
Kapellos, A. (2013), "Xenophon and the Execution of the Athenian Captives at Aegospotami", *Mnemosyne* 66, 464–472.
Kapellos, A. (2014), *Lysias 21. A Commentary*, Berlin.
Kapellos, A. (2017), "Alcibiades at Aegospotami and the Defeat of the Athenian Fleet: History and Rhetoric", *PP* 72, 303–323.
Kapellos, A. (2018), "Lysander and the Execution of the Athenian Prisoners at Aegospotami (Xenophon, *Hell.* 2.1.31.–32)", *Mnemosyne* 4 71, 394–407.
Kapellos, A. (2019a), "Lysias, Isocrates and the Trierarchs of Aegospotami", *Erga-Logoi* 7, 85–101.

Kapellos, A. (2019b), "The Greek Reaction to the Slaughter of the Athenian Captives at Aegospotami and Xenophon's *Hellenica*", in: A. Kapellos (ed.), *Xenophon on Violence*, Berlin, 161–168.

Kapellos, A. (2019c), "Xenophon and Lysias on the Arginusae Trial", *Erga-Logoi* 7, 19–44.

Kapellos, A. (2022), "Xenophon and the orators on the Topography of Arginusae and Aegospotami", *Mnemosyne* (online), 1–27.

Kirby, J.T. (1991), "Mimesis and Diegesis: Foundations of Aesthetic Theory in Plato and Aristotle", *Helios* 18, 113–128.

Kostopoulos, K. (2019), *Die Vergangenheit vor Augen. Erinnerungsräume bei den attischen Rednern*, (Hermes Einzelschriften 116), Stuttgart.

Kremmydas, C. (2013), "The Discourse of Deception and Characterization in Attic Oratory", *GRBS* 53, 51–89.

Kremmydas, C. (2019a), "Truth and Deception in Athenian Forensic Narratives: An Assessment of Demosthenes 54 and Lysias 3", in: M.J. Edwards/D. Spatharas (eds.), *Forensic Narratives in Athenian Courts*, London, 211–229.

Kremmydas, C. (2019b), "Anakrisis and the Framing of Strategies of Argumentation in Athenian Public Trials", in: C. Carey/I. Giannadaki/B. Griffith-Williams (eds.), *Use and Abuse of Law in the Athenian Courts*, Leiden, 110–131.

Lanni, A.M. (1997), "Spectator Sport or Serious Politics? *Oi peristēkontes* and the Athenian Lawcourts", *JHS* 117, 189–189.

Loraux, N. (1980), "L'oubli dans la cité", *Le temps de la réflexion* 1, 213–242.

Loraux, N. (1981), *L'invention d'Athènes. Histoire de l'oraison funèbre dans la cité classique*, Paris.

Loraux, N. (1997), *La cité divisée. L'oubli dans la mémoire d'Athènes*, Paris.

Low, P. (2012), "The Monuments of the War Dead in Classical Athens. Form, Contexts, Meanings", *Proceedings of the British Academy* 160, 13–39.

Luraghi, N. (2014), "The Eyewitness and the Writing of History. Ancient and Modern", in: A. Rösinger/G. Signori (eds.), *Die Figur des Augenzeugen: Geschichte und Wahrheit im fächer- und epochenübergreifenden Vergleich*, Konstanz, 13–26.

MacDowell, D. (1982), *Gorgias, Encomium of Helen*, Bristol.

Maltagliati, G. (2020a), "Persuasion Through Proximity (and Distance) in the Attic Orators' Historical Examples", *GRBS* 60, 68–97.

Maltagliati, G. (2020b), "Manipolare il passato, prefigurare il futuro: esempi storici, emozioni e deliberazione nell'oratoria attica", *Rhesis* 11, 290–298.

Matuszewski, R. (2019), *Räume der Reputation. Zur bürgerlichen Kommunikation im Athen des 4. Jahrhunderts v. Chr.*, Stuttgart.

McCoy, M.B. (2008), *Plato on the Rhetoric on Philosophers and Sophists*, Cambridge.

McCoy, M.B. (2009), "Alcidamas, Isocrates, and Plato on Speech, Writing, and Philosophical Rhetoric", *Ancient Philosophy* 29, 45–66.

Mirhady, D.C. (2002), "Athens' Democratic Witnesses", *Phoenix* 56, 255–274.

Mossé, C. (1993), "Neera, la cortigiana", in: N. Loraux (ed.), *Grecia al femminile*, Rome, 197–227.

Nicolaï, R. (2007), "The Place of History in the Ancient World", in: J. Marincola (ed.), *A Companion to Greek and Roman Historiography*, Malden (MA), I/13–26.

Nouhaud, M. (1982), *L'utilisation de l'histoire par les orateurs attiques*, Paris.

Ober, J. (1989), *Mass and Elite in Democratic Athens. Rhetoric, Ideology, and the Power of the People*, Princeton (NJ).

Ober, J. (2003), "Culture, Thin Coherence, and the Persistence of Politics", in: C. Dougherty/ L. Kurke (eds.), *The Cultures Within Ancient Greek Culture. Contact, Conflict, Collaboration*, Cambridge, 237–255.

Ober, J. (2007), "Ability and Education. The Power of Persuasion", in: E. Carawan (ed.), *Oxford Readings in the Attic Orators*, Oxford, 271–311.

Osborne, R. (2011), "Greek Inscriptions as Historical Writing", in: A. Feldherr/G. Hardy (eds.), *The Oxford History of Historical Writing 1: Beginnings to AD 600*, Oxford, 97–121.

Osmers, M. (2013), *"Wir aber sind damals und jetzt immer die gleichen." Vergangenheitsbezüge in der polisübergreifenden Kommunikation der klassischen Zeit*, Stuttgart.

Pearson, L. (1941), "Historical Allusions in the Attic Orators", *CP* 36, 209–229.

Perlman, S. (1961), "The Historical Example. Its Use and Importance as Political Propaganda in the Attic Orators", *Scripta Hierosolymitana* 7, 150–166.

Pernot, L. (2014), "L'invention de la rhétorique démocratique en Grèce ancienne", in: J. Jouanna/L. Pernot/ M. Zink (eds.), *Colloque "Charmer, convaincre: la rhétorique dans l'histoire*, Paris, 19–38.

Pflug, G. (1971=1954), "The Development of Historical Method in the Eighteenth Century", *History and Theory* 11, 1–23.

Piepenbrink, K. (2012), "Vergangenheitsbezug in interkultureller Perspektive. Die Rhetorik der attischen Demokratie und der späten römischen Republik im Vergleich", *Klio* 94, 100–121.

Piovan, D. (2011), *Memoria e oblio della Guerra civile: strategie giudiziarie e racconto del passato in Lisia*, Pisa.

Pownall, F.A. (2004), *Lessons from the Past. The Moral Use of History in Fourth-Century Prose*, Ann Arbor (MI).

Pritchard, D.M. (ed. forthcoming), *The Athenian Funeral Oration: 40 Years After Nicole Loraux*, Cambridge.

Proietti, G. (2015), "Beyond the 'invention of Athens': the 5th Century Athenian 'Tatenkatalog' as Example of 'intentional history'", *Klio* 97, 516–538.

Proietti, G. (2017), "Fare i conti con la Guerra. Forme del discorso civico ad Atene nel V secolo (con uno sguardo all'età contemporanea)", in: E. Franchi/Ead. (eds.), *Conflict in Communities. Forward-looking memories in Classical Athens*, Trento, 69–108.

Rösinger, A./Signori, G. (eds.) (2014), *Die Figur des Augenzeugen: Geschichte und Wahrheit im fächer- und epochenübergreifenden Vergleich*, Konstanz.

Rubinstein, L. (2000), *Litigation and Cooperation. Supporting Speakers in the Courts of Classical Athens*, Stuttgart.

Rubinstein, L. (2005), "Main Litigants and Witnesses in the Athenian Courts", in: M. Gagarin/ R.W. Wallace (eds.), *Symposion 2001. Vorträge zur griechischen und hellenistischen Rechtsgeschichte*, Wien, 99–120.

Ruffell, I. (2017), "Tragedy and Fictionality", in: L.I. Hau/I. Ruffell (eds.), *Truth and History in the Ancient World: Pluralising the Past*, Oxford, 32–54.

Sato, N. (2019), "Inciting *thorubos* and Narrative Strategies in Attic Forensic Speeches", in: M.J. Edwards/D. Spatharas (eds.), *Forensic Narratives in Athenian Courts*, London, 102–118.

Schenkeveld, D.M. (2007), "Theory and Practice in Fourth-Century Eloquence. The Case of the Speaker as a Teacher of the Demos", in: D. Mirhady (ed.), *Influences on Peripatetic Rhetoric. Essays in Honor of William W. Fortenbaugh*, Leiden, 25–36.

Schepens, G. (2007), "History and *historia*: Inquiry in the Greek Historians", in: J. Marincola (ed.), *A Companion to Greek and Roman Historiography*, Malden (MA), 39–55.

Schmitz-Kahlmann, G. (1939), *Das Beispiel der Geschichte im politischen Denken des Isokrates*, Univ. Diss. Berlin.

Shear, J. (2007), "Cultural Change, Space, and the Politics of Commemoration in Athens", in: R. Osborne (ed.), *Debating the Athenian Cultural Revolution: Art, Literature, Philosophy, and Politics 430–380 BC*, 91–115.

Siron, N. (2019a), *Témoigner et convaincre. Le dispositif de vérité dans les discours judiciaires de l'Athènes classique*, Paris.

Siron, N. (2019b), "Identifier les témoins dans les procès athéniens du Ve–IVe siècle av. J.-C., in: R. Gouicharrousse et al. (eds.), *L'identification des personnes dans les mondes grecs*, Paris, 219–241.

Spatharas, D. (2011), "Kinky Stories from the Rostrum. Storytelling in Apollodorus' *Against Neaira*", Ancient Narrative 9, 99–120.

Steinbock, B. (2013a), *Social Memory in Athenian Public Discourse: Uses and Meanings of the Past*, Ann Arbor (MI).

Steinbock, B. (2013b), "Contesting Lessons From the Past: Aeschines' Use of Social Memory", TAPA 143, 65–103.

Steinbock, B. (2017a), "The Multipolarity of Athenian Social Memory: Polis, Tribes, Demes as Interdependent Memory Communities", in: K.P. Hofmann/R. Bernbeck/U. Sommer (eds.), *Between Memory Sites and Memory Networks*, Berlin, 97–125.

Steinbock, B. (2017b), "The Contested Memory of Nicias After the Sicilian Expedition", in: E. Franchi/G. Proietti (eds.), *Conflict in Communities. Forward-looking Memories in Classical Athens*, Trento, 109–170.

Taddei, A. (2016), "Literacy and Orality in the Attic Orators", in: A. Ercolani/M. Giordano (eds.), *Submerged Literature in Ancient Greek Culture. The Comparative Perspective*, Berlin, 95–111.

Thomas, R. (2014), "The Greek Polis and the Tradition of Polis History. Local History, Chronicles, and the Patterning of the Past", in: A. Moreno/R. Thomas (eds.), *Patterns of the Past: Epitēdeumata in the Greek Tradition*, Oxford, 145–172.

Thür, G. (2005), "The Role of Witnesses in Athenian Law", in: M. Gagarin/D.J. Cohen (eds.), *The Cambridge Companion to Ancient Greek Law*, Cambridge, 146–169.

Thür, G. (2008), "The Principle of Fairness in Athenian Legal Procedure: Thoughts on the 'echinos' and 'enklema'", Dike 11, 51–73.

Todd, S.R. (1990a), "The Use and Abuse of the Attic Orators", G&R 37, 159–178.

Todd, S.R. (1990b), "The Purpose of Evidence in Athenian Courts", in: P. Cartledge/P. Millett/S.R. Todd (ed.), *Nomos: Essays in Athenian Law, Politics and Society*, Cambridge, 19–40.

Todd, S.C. (2002), "Advocacy, Logography and Erōtēsis in Athenian Lawcourts", in: P. McKechnie (ed.), *Thinking Like a Lawyer: Essays on Legal History and General History for John Crook*, Leiden, 151–165.

Too, Y.L. (1995), *The Rhetoric of Identity in Isocrates. Text, Power, Pedagogy*, Oxford.

Trivigno, F. (2009), "The Rhetoric of Parody in Plato's *Menexenus*", Philosophy & Rhetoric 42, 29–58.

Usener, S. (1994), *Isokrates, Platon und ihr Publikum. Hörer und Leser von Literatur im 4. Jahrhundert v. Chr.*, Tübingen.

Usher, S. (1976), "Lysias and His Clients", GRBS 17, 31–40.

Usher, S. (2010), "Apostrophe in Greek Oratory", Rhetorica 28, 351–362.

Vallozza, M. (1985), "Καιρός nella teoria retorica di Alcidamante e di Isocrate, ovvero nell'oratoria orale e scritta," QUCC 21, 119–123.

van Berkel, T. (2017), "Voiced Mathematics. Orality and Numeracy", in: N.W. Slater (ed.), *Voice and Voices in Antiquity*, Leiden, 321–350.
Vatri, A. (2017), *Orality and Performance in Classical Attic Prose. A Linguistic Approach*, Oxford.
Volonaki, E. (2019), "Reconstructing the Past: Forensic Storytelling About the Athenian Constitution in Lysias 12 and 13", in: M.J. Edwards/D. Spatharas (eds.), *Forensic Narratives in Athenian Courts*, London, 135–156.
Volonaki, E. (2020), "Narrative in Forensic Oratory: Persuasion and Performance", in: P. Papaioannou/A. Serafim/K. Demetriou (eds.), *The Ancient Art of Persuasion Across Genres and Topics*, Leiden, 56–72.
Westwood, G. (2020), *The Rhetoric of the Past in Demosthenes and Aeschines. Oratory, History, and Politics in Classical Athens*, Oxford.
Winter, T.N. (1973), "On the Corpus of Lysias", *CJ* 69, 34–40.
Wojciech, K. (2018), "Geschichte vor Gericht. Wahrheit und Wahrscheinlichkeit als Kriterien in der Vergangenheitsdarstellung attischer Redner", in: Thomas G.M. Blank/Felix K. Maier (eds.), *Die symphonischen Schwestern. Narrative Konstruktion von 'Wahrheiten' in der nachklassischen Geschichtsschreibung*, Stuttgart, 163–184.
Wojciech, K. (2022), *Wie die Athener ihre Vergangenheit verhandelt haben. Rede und Erinnerung im 5. und 4. Jahrhundert v. Chr.*, Berlin.
Wolpert, A. (2002), *Remembering Defeat. Civil War and Civic Memory in Ancient Athens*, Baltimore.
Worthington, I. (1989), "The Duration of an Athenian Public Trial", *JHS* 109, 204–207.
Worthington, I. (1991), "Greek Oratory, Revision of Speeches and the Problem of Historical Reliability", *C & M* 42, 55–74.
Worthington, I. (1993), "Once More, the Client/Logographos Relationship", *CQ* 43, 67–72.
Worthington, I. (1994), "History and Oratorical Exploitation", in: I. Worthington (ed.), *Persuasion. Greek Rhetoric in Action*, London, 109–129.
Worthington, I. (1996), "Greek Oratory and the Oral/Literate Division", in: I. Worthington (ed.), *Voice into Text. Orality and Literacy in Ancient Greece*, Leiden (Mnemosyne Supplementum 157), 165–177.
Worthington, I. (2003), "The Length of an Athenian Public Trial. A Reply to Professor MacDowell", *Hermes* 131, 364–371.
Worthington, I. (2010), "Intentional History: Alexander, Demosthenes and Thebes", in: L. Foxhall/H.-J. Gehrke (eds.), *Intentional History: Spinning Time in Ancient Greece*, Stuttgart, 239–246.
Worthington, I. (2017), "Audience Reaction, Performance and the Exploitation of Delivery in the Courts and Assembly", in: S. Papaioannou/A. Serafim/B. da Vela (eds.), *The Theatre of Justice. Aspects of Performance in Greco-Roman Oratory and Rhetoric*, Leiden, 13–25.
Worthington, I. (2020), "Fake News. The Greek Orators' Rhetorical Presentation of the Past", *Roda de Fortuna* 9, 15–31.
Yunis, H. (2013), "Political Uses of Rhetoric in Democratic Athens", in: J.P. Arnason/K.A. Raaflaub/P. Wagner (eds.), *The Greek Polis and the Invention of Democracy. A Politico-Cultural Transformation and its Interpretations*, Chichester, 144–162.

Michael Gagarin
Antiphon and the Recent Past

Abstract: The only mentions of historical events in the preserved speeches of Antiphon come in his speech *On the Murder of Herodes* (Ant. 5). These mentions are of two sorts. First, in the speech for the prosecution, the speaker's father and his role in the fairly recent Mytilenean revolt were apparently criticized in order to cast the speaker, named Euxitheus, in a bad light; Euxitheus therefore needs to defend his father, as well as himself, against these charges (Ant. 5.74–80). Second, after Euxitheus finishes his main arguments in his defense, he adds several relatively minor additional arguments, during the course of which he includes three historical incidents from the more distant past (5.67–73) that are meant to warn the jurors against convicting him too hastily. In relating these events, and also in discussing the Mytilenean revolt, Euxitheus appears to be, at the very least, slanting the facts.

The only speech of Antiphon that discusses historical events is *On the Murder of Herodes* (Ant. 5). This speech was delivered before a regular Athenian court about a decade after the revolt of Mytilene on the island of Lesbos in 428–427 B.C. As Thucydides presents it (3.2–18, 25–50), the revolt was a major event in the early years of the Peloponnesian war. The Mytileneans, nominally allies of Athens but in reality under Athenian dominance, wished to unify the various communities on the island, a move opposed by Athens. So the Mytileneans revolted. They expected help from Sparta, but when this was not forthcoming, Athens rather brutally suppressed the revolt, put to death more than a thousand men who had taken part in it, and imposed stiff penalties on the island.

Memories of this episode must have been fresh in the minds of the jurors and other members of the audience in court when Antiphon 5 was delivered. The defendant, a young Mytilenean probably named Euxitheus, had been arrested in Mytilene and brought to Athens for trial on a charge of killing Herodes, an Athenian citizen living on Lesbos. Understandably, he does not wish to remind his audience of the recent revolt, but he does mention it briefly toward the end of his speech (5.74–79) in order to defend his father against the accusation that he had participated in the revolt. It is likely that the prosecution had raised the issue of his father's role in the revolt in order to prejudice the jury against Euxitheus, even though he was just a child at the time of the revolt. His father's loyalty to Athens ought to have no bearing on Euxitheus' guilt or innocence in this case, but he understands that in a complex and circumstantial case, it

https://doi.org/10.1515/9783110791877-003

could have a decisive effect on the jury, and thus he feels obliged to defend his father as part of his own defense.

Euxitheus had earlier mentioned his father when he explained why he was traveling on the same boat as Herodes: "We were sailing to Aenus, I to visit my father — for he happened to be there at the time" (5.20). He is aware, however, that this small fact could be, and probably was, exploited by the prosecution to show that his father was disloyal to Athens, since Aenus, a town in Thrace, was outside of Athenian control.

In defending his father (74–79) Euxitheus maintains that he knows nothing about the revolt except for what he has heard; thus he must rely on hearsay to defend his father (74–75). This is not strictly true; although Euxitheus was young at the time, he must have remembered something about the revolt. Regardless, he affirms that his father was always loyal to Athens before the revolt (76):[1]

> But when the whole city wrongly decided to revolt and failed to meet your expectations, he was compelled to join with the whole city in that failure. Even during these events his feelings toward you remained the same, but he could no longer demonstrate the same loyalty, since he couldn't easily leave the city.

Euxitheus adds that his father was not a leader of the revolt, as shown by the fact that he was not executed afterwards, and he continues now to be loyal to Athens: "He has done everything required of him and has not neglected any of the special needs of either city, yours or Mytilene, but he has sponsored choral productions and paid his taxes" (77).

Then Euxitheus addresses the potentially damaging part of their criticism of his father, his residency in Thrace (78–79):

> If he likes to live in Aenus, his intent is not to avoid any of his obligations to the city. He has not become a citizen of any other state as I see others doing, some going to the mainland to live among your enemies while others bring suits against you under treaties, and he's not trying to avoid your courts. His only reason is that, like you, he hates sykophants. [79] It is not right for my father to be punished as an individual for things he did together with the whole city under compulsion, not by choice.

Clearly his father is rich and thus could be the victim of sycophants (i.e. nuisance lawsuits) and he is avoiding this problem by living out of the reach of Athenian courts. But this hardly acquits his father of the charge of disloyalty to Athens.

---

1 All translations come from Gagarin and MacDowell 1998.

Nonetheless, on the theory that the best defense is a strong offense, Antiphon turns the prosecution's criticism of Euxitheus' father back into an attack on their corrupt motives in bringing the case, alleging, as he has throughout his defense, that they are sycophants, who are only prosecuting him for their own enrichment (79):[2]

> Do not believe the slanderous charges these men have leveled against my father personally; for they have contrived this whole case against us for the sake of money. Many factors help those who want to get hold of other people's property; he is too old to assist me and I am much too young to be able to protect myself as I should.

This is the final point in Euxitheus' defense of his father. In all that I have cited so far he has said nothing about the Mytilenean revolt except to acknowledge that it happened and deny his father's role in it. Just before the last-cited remark, however, he does touch briefly on the revolt itself: "All Mytileneans will remember forever the mistake they made then. They exchanged great happiness for great misery and saw their own homeland devastated" (79).

It is obvious, and would have been obvious to the jury, that this statement is an exaggeration. Many Mytileneans, perhaps most, may have considered the revolt a mistake — after all, it failed — but surely not all did. And yet I would not call the statement a lie, since it clearly is not intended to be an expression of historical fact, but rather a rhetorical supplement to Euxitheus' defense of his father, whose opposition to the revolt was (he suggests) later shared by all Mytileneans.

In sum, the Mytilenean revolt forms the unstated context for this case as well as the background to Euxitheus' defense of his father, but he tells us nothing about the revolt except that it happened, that his father opposed it, and that the Mytileneans now consider it a mistake. For historians this is all the more regrettable in that Euxitheus himself was in Mytilene during the revolt, and even though he was young at the time, he must have been aware of what was happening around him. But Euxitheus understandably says as little as possible. Indeed, it would have been more advantageous for him to keep silent about the revolt if he were not forced to mention it by the prosecution's attack on his father.

We should note that since Antiphon had to compose this speech before the trial, he (and Euxitheus) could anticipate, but could not be certain, that the prosecution would attack Euxitheus' father. Antiphon thus composed the pas-

---

[2] It is not clear exactly how the prosecution might profit from bringing this case, but the charge of sycophancy comes up throughout the speech. See Gagarin 1997, 24, 75–76.

sage (74–79), together with a section on sycophants (80), as a self-contained unit, which could be omitted if the prosecution did not attack his father.

The Mytilenean revolt is the only historical event mentioned at length in Antiphon 5, but Euxitheus briefly mentions three other past events when he urges the jury not to jump to conclusions in this case because hasty decisions in the past have had, or might have had, unfortunate consequences (67–71). As he says, "many men have received the blame for other people's crimes and have been put to death before the facts became clearly known" (67). The three events mentioned probably all took place prior to the Mytilenean revolt, and thus Euxitheus knows about them only from hearsay (*akoēi epistamai*, 67).[3] The jurors would all be older than Euxitheus, ranging from 30 to 60 or older, and many of them would thus remember the events. As Euxitheus says, "I think you older jurors remember these events and the younger ones have heard about them, as I have" (71).[4] In only one of the three examples was someone actually executed wrongly, but the other two add different examples of uncertainty.

The most relevant example concerns the Hellenotamiai or State Treasurers (69–70):

> And then there were your Treasurers, who were blamed for financial wrongdoing, although, like me now, they were not guilty. They were all put to death in anger without any deliberation, except for one. Later the facts became clear. [70] This one man — they say his name was Sosias — had been sentenced to death but not yet executed, and when it was revealed in the meanwhile how the money had been lost, this man was rescued by you, the people, though he had already been delivered to the Eleven. The others had already been put to death, although they were innocent.

The message is clear: the jury must not rush to convict Euxitheus because they may make a mistake which would only be discovered after it was too late. No other source mentions this incident, but such an event is unlikely to be a complete fabrication, though we cannot know for certain whether Euxitheus is accurately describing an actual event.

A second example is even less certain (69):

> Then, not long ago a young slave, not twelve years old, tried to kill his master, and if he hadn't become frightened at the victim's cries and run off leaving his dagger in the wound but had had the courage to remain, all the servants in the house would have been put to

---

[3] For the middling past see Kapellos' Introduction in this volume.
[4] Of the three events, the murder of Ephialtes is securely dated (to 461). Tracy 2016, 207–215 makes a strong argument that the execution of the Treasurers occurred in 449/8. The incident involving the boy and his master could have occurred any time.

death. No one would suspect the boy would dare commit such a crime. As it was, however, he was arrested and later confessed.

Despite the absence of detail, it is possible that something like this had happened recently. In fact, I suspect that the incident did occur, because it is only hypothetically relevant to Euxitheus situation. Surely if Antiphon were inventing the facts, he would have created a story that was actually, not just hypothetically, relevant to his case.

The third example, the assassination of Ephialtes in 461, is the only one for which we have other sources, though they are all later than this speech (68):

> For example, the murderers of your fellow-citizen Ephialtes have never yet been found. Now, if someone thought that those who were with him should speculate about the identity of his killers, and if they didn't, they should be held responsible for the murder, that wouldn't be right for those who were with him. Moreover, those who killed Ephialtes did not try to get rid of the body and by so doing run the risk of exposing the crime, as the prosecution say I did, alleging that I let no one help me with plotting the crime, but enlisted help in lifting the body.

Like the second example, this event is only hypothetically relevant to Euxitheus' argument that the jury should be careful to avoid making a mistake — no one was even punished, let alone executed — but there is a kind of negative relevance related to disposing of the body of a homicide victim.

As for historical accuracy, although [Aristotle] *Ath. Pol.* 25.4 (written in the late fourth century) reports that Aristodicus of Tanagra was the assassin, other ancient sources suggest other names (see e.g. Plutarch, *Pericles* 10), and it seems likely that despite much speculation the killer was never known for certain.[5] Other details in Antiphon's account, such as that the corpse was not removed, are likely to be accurate, since those in his audience who remembered this famous incident would notice any inaccuracies. Euxitheus concludes by urging the jury not to decide this case in haste: "[These events] show how good it is to put things to the test of time. Perhaps this question too, how Herodes died, might become clear later" (71).

To conclude, Antiphon shows little interest in historical events even when, like the Mytilenean revolt, these are of direct relevance to the case. Besides the revolt Euxitheus briefly mentions three other events, only one of which was significant for Athenian history. He gives almost no details about any of the three, nor does his discussion of the Mytilenean revolt tell us anything about it

---

5 See Rhodes' discussion (1981, 322).

except that it happened. Antiphon, it seems, has no interest in historical events as history but only alludes to them for their broad relevance to the case at hand.

Bibliography

Gagarin, M. (1997), *Antiphon. The Speeches*, Cambridge.
Gagarin, M./MacDowell, M. (1998), *Antiphon and Andocides*, Austin.
Rhodes, P.J. (1981), *A Commentary on the Athenian Athenaion Politeia*, Oxford.
Tracy, S. (2016), *Athenian Lettering of the Fifth Century B.C.*, Berlin.

Peter Rhodes
[Lysias], 20 *for Polystratus*: Polystratus and the Coup of 411 B.C.

Abstract: The speech makes the best of what was a weak case: Polystratus had (democratically) good intentions; he was a "good" oligarch rather than a "bad" oligarch; he served as a *katalogeus* only under compulsion and registered as many men as possible; he paid a fine under the Five Thousand when men who were guiltier escaped; he had held democratic offices; he had not concealed his property but had paid *eisphorai* and had performed liturgies. The narrative is in general consistent with that which we can construct from Thucydides and *Ath. Pol.*; it confirms *Ath. Pol.* that the 100 *katalogeis* were appointed and at least started work, but it does not match Thucydides' account of how the Four Hundred were appointed. The claim that Polystratus and Phrynichus, fellow demesmen and resident in the city when the Spartans were occupying Decelea, had nothing to do with each other, is misleading.

This speech — or rather parts of two speeches: from § 11 onwards Polystratus is referred to as the speaker's father, and it appears that the speaker is the second of three sons, but there is no instance of that in §§ 1–10[1] — was written for a trial

---

My thanks to Dr. Kapellos for inviting me to contribute a chapter on this speech to this volume, and for sending me electronic versions of various studies. My thanks also to Dr. K.E. Apostolakis for Apostolakis 2003 (English summary on pp. 285–292) and 2017; and to Dr. D. Piovan for Piovan 2011.
  Apart from this speech, Lysias is not attested as the author of any speech before 403/2, and Todd writes of this speech as "universally agreed to be misattributed" (2007, 12; cf. 29–30 and 2000, 217). However, Dover 1968, 56, was not prepared to deny Lysias' authorship on political or ideological grounds, and at 115–147 noted features in which this speech but others too differ from 12. *Eratosthenes*.

---

1 Suggested by Wilamowitz-Moellendorff 1893, ii. 356–367 at 363–364, and widely accepted; but rejected by Gernet in Gernet/Bizos 1926, 60–61; Apostolakis 2003, 67–71 (English summary, 290). However, that "the defendant evidently delivered 20.1–10" (Todd 2007, 2 n. 7) is a slip: Polystratus is referred to throughout in the third person, and in § 3 "you can see his age"; § 4, in the first part of the speech, refers to the three sons in the third person and suggests that this speaker is not any of them. Apostolakis 2003, 39–42 (English summary, 288), followed the suggestion of A. Kirchhoff (*ap.* Thalheim 1876, 40) that the second son who was the speaker was Lycius, and that the similarity of the name led to the speech's being attributed to Lysias; but more probably the speaker of §§ 11–36 was the younger Polystratus. Cf. below n. 120.

shortly after the democratic restoration of 410 (cf. § 17), following the régimes of the Four Hundred and the Five Thousand. By this time Polystratus was apparently, unless his defender exaggerates, over seventy years old (§ 10 cf. § 3). The specific charge is not made clear, but it is alleged that Polystratus had held various offices, apparently before the overthrow of the democracy (§§ 5–7); that he was a kinsman and friend of Phrynichus, a member of the same deme, Deiradiotae[2] (§§ 11–12) (Phrynichus had opposed the oligarchic movement at first but joined it when it decided to go ahead without Alcibiades[3]); and that he had been a member of the Four Hundred and one of the *katalogeis* charged with drawing up a register of the Five Thousand (§§ 13–14).[4] His son in defending him mentions in the course of an argument that he was *demotikos* his repeated performance of military service, presumably before 411 (§ 23).

He had already before the current trial been sentenced to a large fine (§§ 14, 18); a slightly later passage probably refers to that and states that "immediately after the events", so under the régime of the Five Thousand, he had faced his trial and paid the penalty (§ 22).[5] If Polystratus were to be condemned in the current trial, (he would be unable to pay another large fine, and therefore (he and) his sons would lose their citizenship (§ 35), and so the speech also defends the three sons as good citizens: the speaker, who took part as a cavalryman in Athens' campaign of 415–413 in Sicily (§§ 24–27 cf. 4), the youngest son, who had served in Boeotia and served in the cavalry against the Peloponnesian occupying forces based in Decelea and Athenian exiles who were supporting them (§§ 4, 28), and the eldest son, who served in the Hellespont in 412/1 and in Boeo-

---

[2] Deiradiotae, Plut. *Alc.* 25.6. This was a small coastal deme, with two *bouleutai* in the fourth century: Traill 1975, Table IV.
[3] Thuc. 8.48.4 –51.3, 54.3–4, 68.3, 90.1–2.
[4] For these *katalogeis* see *Ath. Pol.* 29.5. Other groups of a hundred men at that time were the nucleus of the Four Hundred in Thucydides' appointment process (8.67.3) and the *anagrapheis* appointed to work out the details of the constitution (*Ath. Pol.* 30.1, 32.1): the groups were not necessarily identical in membership, but they may well have overlapped substantially. That they were identical was suggested e.g. by Busolt 1904, 1481–1482 n. 1, 1486, cf. Cavaignac 1925/6; Wilamowitz-Moellendorff 1893, ii. 356–367 at 356–358, argued that the men first appointed as *katalogeis* were afterwards used as the core of the Four Hundred; and a version of that is defended by Heftner 1999a (see further below).
[5] Todd 2000, 223 with n. 15, notes that this passage is ambiguous and could refer either to the earlier trial or to the current one, and in his translation he prefers the current trial, whereas I think the earlier trial is more likely. Gernet/Bizos 1926, 67, Lamb 1930, 465, and Apostolakis 2003, 109, all saw a reference to the earlier trial but translated δίκην δέδωκεν as "has submitted himself to justice"; but Lamb 1930, 453, thought that the fine was paid.

tia (§§ 4, 29).⁶ "The main value of the speech is as a historical source";⁷ but, as has regularly been acknowledged, we need to enquire carefully how far it fits what we know of these events from other sources, and how far and how reliably it adds to what we know from the other sources.⁸

Simple exaggeration is not a problem, and we can accept that Polystratus had performed military service reasonably often, and had held some offices; given the state of our fifth-century evidence, it need not worry us that there is no confirmation of the office-holding. § 6 mentions his having been an official (ἄρξας) in Oropus, without betraying it and setting up a different constitution, as "all" the others who held office did. This was presumably before the installation of the Four Hundred, since after their installation he sailed to Eretria (§ 14). If the speaker is not seriously distorting what happened, we should expect this to be in the spring of 411, very shortly before the installation, when Athens' oligarchs tried to set up oligarchies in other cities,⁹ and this can just be reconciled with Thucydides' narrative, in which the capture of Oropus from Athens by the Boeotians is the last episode in winter 412/1.¹⁰ If we make a greater allowance for distortion, Polystratus may have been in Oropus somewhat earlier, when the question of a change of constitution will not have arisen.

As for the alleged connection with Phrynichus, §§ 11–12 deny that Polystratus and Phrynichus were either kinsmen or friends; and claim that Phrynichus was brought up as a rural shepherd but as an adult migrated to the city, whereas Polystratus was brought up in the city but as an adult (presumably when he

---

6 For the three sons, Philopolis, Polystratus and Lycius, see Davies 1971, 467–468 no. 12076, following Kirchner's *IG* ii² in placing them in that order, whereas earlier Kirchner 1901–1903, ii. 220–221, had made the younger Polystratus who went to Sicily the eldest. Cf. above, n. 15. Philopolis' Hellespont campaign should be datable from Leon, who was general there in 412/1 and afterwards a pro-democratic general at Samos (Thuc. 8.23.1, etc., 73.4) – but Gernet in Gernet/Bizos 1926, 58, dated it 411/0, cf. Apostolakis 2003, 228, who thinks particularly of the battle of Cynossema in 8.104–106; and Davies dates it 410/09. While strictly we do not know the outcome of the trial for which the speech was written, it is clear that the sons neither lost their citizenship nor became paupers. However, on account of their father's record "these men apparently had no chance of a career in Attika" (Humphreys 2018, ii. 763, cf. 959–960).
7 Todd 2000, 217.
8 For the need to compare the orators with other more reliable sources see Kapellos' Introduction in this volume.
9 Thuc. 8.64.5, cf. Phrynichus in 48.5.
10 Thuc. 8.60. There is therefore no need for the emendation of Oropus to Oreus (in the north of Euboea) by Blass, entertained as a possibility by Todd 2000, 220 n. 3: see Gernet in Gernet/Bizos 1926, 56 n. 3. Apostolakis 2003, 38, 141, accepts Oropus and makes him garrison commander there before the Boeotian capture. But Develin 1989, 161, dates this under the Four Hundred in 411.

inherited his father's property) became a farmer — but owing to the Peloponnesians' presence at Decelea from 413 onwards the landed property in the country was worthless (§ 33).[11] That he could have converted his landed property to "invisible" property and thus have avoided paying *eisphorai* and performing liturgies, but was happy to accept those burdens (§ 23), is the kind of remark we should expect in defence of a man who did have "visible" property and did pay *eisphorai* and perform liturgies. It is claimed also in § 12 that when Phrynichus was paying a fine Polystratus did not contribute to the cost. Phrynichus by now was dead,[12] and could not have spoken about himself or his fine; we have no other evidence for the family circumstances of the two men, but there is the negative fact that Phrynichus has not qualified for an entry in Davies' *Athenian Properted Families*. But both men were politically active and at least not strongly opposed to oligarchy, both are likely to have been living in the city after Sparta's occupation of Decelea in 413, and Todd notes that members of this small deme are likely to have known one another.[13] It may be that the accusers had simply invented a connection on the basis of deme membership, but there may well have been more to it than that.

That brings us to Polystratus and the Four Hundred. Polystratus had been one of the hundred *katalogeis* after the Athenians had voted to entrust affairs to Five Thousand: this must refer to the Assembly at Colonus, of which probably Thucydides and *Ath. Pol.* each give incomplete accounts:[14] the Athenians did

---

[11] The speaker says, "We were deprived of all this". Legally, no doubt, Polystratus still owned the land, but at the time of the trial he could not exercise his ownership and there was no immediate prospect of his being able to do so again. Apostolakis 2003, 161, regards the contrast between Polystratus and Phrynichus as a rhetorical *topos* and compares Demosthenes' contrast between himself and Aeschines in Dem. 18.257–258.

[12] Thuc. 8.92.2.

[13] Todd 2000, 221 n. 9 (and the deme's fourth-century quota was not three members, as stated by Todd, but two); cf. Apostolakis 2003, 158–159. Humphreys 2018, ii. 959–960, goes so far as to suggest that Polystratus was 'probably recruited — despite later disclaimers' to the Four Hundred by Phrynichus.

[14] This is generally believed, and is accepted by Rhodes 1981, 363–365, and 2017, 282. However, Wilamowitz-Moellendorff 1893, ii. 356–358, supposed that first the decision for a citizen body of Five Thousand was made, as in *Ath. Pol.*, and the *katalogeis* were appointed, and subsequently the decision for a council of Four Hundred was made, as in Thucydides, and the *katalogeis* were used as the core of the Four Hundred. *Ath. Pol.*'s Assembly and Thucydides' Colonus Assembly were distinguished also by Lang 1948 and 1967; Hackl, 1960, 13–50, discussing this speech at 36–41; and more recently by Heftner 1999a. Heftner's version of this view is accepted by Apostolakis 2003 (Appendix 1: pp. 255–264 with English summary p. 291). Heftner writes further on these matters, again following Wilamowitz' view of a constitutional change in two stages, in 1999b; 2001, esp. 93–108; 2003.

then decide both on a powerful council of Four Hundred and on a restricted citizen body of Five Thousand, and elected a hundred *katalogeis* to enrol the Five Thousand.[15] Polystratus also served as a member of the council, i.e. of the Four Hundred, but both speakers stress that he served only for eight days before sailing to Eretria, and that he made no proposals about "your *plethos*" (§§ 7–10, 14–16). Objectors would say that, even if it is true that he himself made no antidemocratic proposals, which will not have been necessary when the basic decision to overthrow the constitution had already been taken and there was a body of *anagrapheis* working out the details, it is more important that he was sufficiently compliant with the régime to serve as a member of the Four Hundred and a *katalogeus*, and then to depart to Eretria in an official capacity.[16]

If Thucydides' account of how the Four Hundred were appointed is correct, five *proedroi* chose a hundred men (presumably including themselves) and the hundred chose a further three hundred; the forty from each tribe, from a larger body of tribal *prokritoi*; in *Ath. Pol.*'s "immediate" constitution, was perhaps envisaged for 411/0 but never implemented.[17] The speech's claim that Polystratus was chosen for the Council, i.e. the Four Hundred, by members of his tribe, who would know his character (§§ 1–2), is closer to *Ath. Pol.*'s "immediate" constitution than to Thucydides, though we can reduce the difficulty if we assume (what is not inherently unlikely) that there was some tribal element in the composition of the Four Hundred which Thucydides has not mentioned.

In *Ath. Pol.*'s narrative the *katalogeis* were ten men from each tribe (without a statement of how they were appointed), aged over forty, who swore an oath. In the speech, Polystratus did not want to be *katalogeus* or to swear the oath, but "they" compelled him, imposing *epibolai* and fines (*sc.* on those who refused), and so he did swear and serve;[18] and, whereas the decision had been to enrol five thousand men, he registered nine thousand, "so that none of the demesmen should quarrel with him, but so that he should register anybody who wanted it, as a favour if it was not possible for anybody" (§§ 13–14). It is encouraging that both the speech and *Ath. Pol.* refer to an oath in connection with the

---

15 Thuc. 8.67.2–3 (mentioning the Four Hundred, but not the Five Thousand, who had been mentioned in 65.3), *Ath. Pol.* 29. 4–5 (mentioning the Five Thousand and the *katalogeis*, but not the Four Hundred, who were to be mentioned in the "immediate constitution" in 31).
16 Apostolakis 2003, 174, rightly rejects the alternative interpretation of Lang 1948, 287, that Polystratus was sent away from Athens because he was not a sufficiently enthusiastic supporter of the oligarchs.
17 See *Ath. Pol.* 31.1 with Rhodes 1981 and 2018, *ad loc.*
18 But Wilamowitz-Moellendorff 1893, ii. 356–357, followed by Heftner 1999a, 77–79, argued from §14 that Polystratus' oath was his oath as a member of the Council, i.e. the Four Hundred.

katalogeis; tribal membership is credible, while it was impossible that each of the demes should have been represented in a body of a hundred, but the registers of citizens were deme registers, and it is likely enough that the list of the Five Thousand was to be organised by demes.[19] Beyond that, for a trial under the restored democracy it is natural that Polystratus should have claimed to have served only under compulsion, whatever the truth; and to have been generous rather than mean in accepting men for registration — but, in whatever way and with however much zeal the *katalogeis* set about their task, as has been remarked, it is hard to imagine that Polystratus did much registering before he left Athens after only eight days.[20]

According to *Ath. Pol.*, the council of 412/1 was paid off on 14 Thargelion and the Four Hundred were inaugurated on 22 Thargelion: probably 14 Thargelion was soon after the Assembly at Colonus, 22 Thargelion marked the formal beginning of the new régime,[21] and probably 22 Thargelion was the first of Polystratus' eight days before he departed for Eretria.[22] With Spartan forces permanently in Attica, Euboea was of great importance to Athens;[23] after the installation of the Four Hundred Thucydides does not mention it again until the episode which led to their overthrow, in Boedromion 411/0,[24] but his account of that episode indicates that before it there were already some Athenian ships there, and so it is credible that Polystratus did go on the occasion which the speech claims.[25] His opponents claim that he left Athens to make money (§ 17): modern readers are reminded of Demosthenes' later allegations that Midias used his service as a trierarch sent to Euboea to enrich himself;[26] but we can probably infer from the speaker's response that in his earlier trial Polystratus was not found guilty on that count. "He was not weak-spirited in the naval bat-

---

19 Cf. Hurni 1991, 223–224.
20 Andrewes, in Gomme/Andrewes/Dover 1981, 202; Todd 2000, 218. Hurni 1991, 223–224, suggests that a list could have been compiled in a few days if each *katalogeus* was instructed to coopt fifty men from his deme or group of demes, and Polystratus coopted not fifty but ninety. In the two-stage scenario of Wilamowitz and others, Polystratus would have had somewhat more time to work as a *katalogeus*. Apostolakis 2003, 264–267 (English summary, 292), suggests that there were about 9,000 citizens of hoplite status or above, who could "serve with their possessions and their bodies", and that they were all registered by the *katalogeis*.
21 *Ath. Pol.* 32. 1 with Rhodes 1981 and 2017 *ad loc.*
22 But Heftner 2001, 172, makes the eight days 14–22 Thargelion.
23 Thuc. 8.1.3,96; also 2.14, 7.28.1.
24 The Four Hundred lasted about four months, *Ath. Pol.* 33.1.
25 Cf. Andrewes, in Gomme/Andrewes/Dover 1981, 318 (citing also Thuc. 8.74.2); Todd 2000, 222 n. 11.
26 Dem. 21. *Meidias* 160–167.

tles", which must refer particularly to the autumn battle reported by Thucydides, which led to the overthrow of the Four Hundred;[27] he claims to have been wounded, and after that battle it will indeed be true that the Four Hundred had been overthrown by the time he returned to Athens (§ 14).

His first trial followed, under the intermediate régime of the Five Thousand, and presumably in some connection with his involvement in the régime of the Four Hundred: perhaps a form of *euthynai* (§§ 14, 18–22).[28] That he was sentenced to a large fine is presumably true; as indicated above, my understanding of § 22 is that he paid the fine, and would therefore be in a weaker financial position if he were convicted again in the current trial, but as Todd notes if he had failed to pay by the time the democracy was restored the democratic régime would probably have considered his condemnation under the previous régime invalid.[29] That he was convicted when others more guilty than he was acquitted is the kind of thing a man in his position would be expected to say, and we do not have the evidence to investigate.

As for the three sons, for two of them we are given nothing substantial: the eldest, Philopolis, had served in the Hellespont in 412/1, and in Boeotia, and the youngest, Lycius, had served in Boeotia, and in the cavalry against the Peloponnesian occupying forces and Athenian exiles, when he had killed one of them. Thucydides does not mention Athenian forces in Boeotia in 411, but it is not unlikely that there should have been an attempt to prevent the Boeotian capture of Oropus or a retaliatory expedition after it.[30] He does not mention Athenian exiles supporting the occupying forces at Decelea, but it is likely enough that there were some, and they are mentioned elsewhere in Lysias' speeches;[31] he does mention Athenian cavalry demonstrations against Decelea,[32] and the claim that Lycius killed a member of "the enemy" is more probably true than untrue.

Not surprisingly, the younger Polystratus, the speaker of the second part, says more about himself (§§ 24–27). His father sent him on the Sicilian campaign of 415–413 as a cavalryman. After the failure of that campaign, he escaped to Catana, and then engaged in successful raiding (this seems to have been the

---

27 Thuc. 8.94–97.
28 *Euthynai*, e.g. Andrewes, in Gomme/Andrewes/Dover 1981, 203; Bearzot 2000. Bearzot notes that the restoration of 410 seems to have been a much less difficult matter than the restoration of 403.
29 Todd 2000, 217 n. 1.
30 Apostolakis 2003, 40, suggests the first.
31 They are mentioned again in Lys. 18. *Nicias' Brother* 9, fr. 170. 184–189 (Carey).
32 Thuc. 7.27.5; 8.71.2.

period during which he was a hoplite), the proceeds of which were spent on ransoming men who had been captured. Thucydides mentions Catana as the destination of those who managed to get away; he does not say what became of the Athenian captives after their eight months in the quarries, but it is not unlikely that some were ransomed, and it is not unlikely that the younger Polystratus did spend at any rate some of his booty in this way.[33] He continues by stating that the people of Catana compelled him to serve in the cavalry (of their own army: war in Sicily continued after the defeat of the Athenians), and the service is probably authentic though the compulsion may not be. More mysterious is the claim that a man from Syracuse was making men swear an oath, perhaps to desert the Catanaeans and join the Syracusans,[34] but Polystratus opposed him and explained the situation to an unidentified Tydeus. The elder Polystratus sent a letter to his son, advising him to return to Athens when things were going well in Sicily, but there is no indication of when and under what régime the letter was sent, or of when and under what régime the son did return to Athens, so we cannot draw conclusions from this about attitudes to democracy.

What do we find overall? There are certainly many passages where the speech makes the best of what was probably a weak case: that Polystratus was chosen for the Four Hundred because he had good intentions (§ 2), that he had held offices (previously, under the democracy) without doing wrong (§§ 5–6), that as one of the Four Hundred he had not made any anti-democratic proposals (§§ 7–10), that he served as a *katalogeus* reluctantly and was generous in accepting men for registration (§§ 13–14), that he fought bravely and was wounded in the naval battle in the Euripus (§ 14), that he nevertheless paid a fine under the régime of the Five Thousand when men who were guiltier escaped (§§ 14–22), that (earlier) he performed military service and did not hide his property but paid *eisphorai* and performed liturgies (§ 23), that he brought up his sons to be good citizens (§§ 4, 23–30). More doubtful is the suggestion that he had no connection with his fellow-demesman Phrynichus (§§ 11–12); and the circumstances in which he invited his son, the younger Polystratus, to return to Athens from Sicily and the son did return are not made clear. There are further *motifs* with which we are familiar from other lawcourt speeches: that there was nothing in his past to make him want to oppose the democracy (§ 4),[35] that the family had

---

33 Thuc. 7.85.4; 87.2–3, cf. Grote 1869/1884, vii. 186, Kelly 1970, 127–131, citing this passage and others, Hornblower 2008, 743 *ad loc.* and 641, citing *IG* i³ 125 and Dem. 20. *Leptines* 41–42; but Diod. Sic. 13.33.1 and Plut. *Nic.* 29.1 suggest that the Athenians were left to die.
34 Thus Apostolakis 2003, 219.
35 Cf. Lys. 25. *Overthrowing Democracy* 7–11, with Piovan 2011, 198–200.

done well by Athens so that if it fell into trouble this would be remembered to its credit (§§ 30–31); here (as an inversion of a common *motif*) we have not a father pleading for his children but the children pleading for their father (§§ 34–36);[36] and there are parallels in other speeches to the attempt to distinguish between comparatively good oligarchs and truly bad oligarchs (§§ 1–3, 5–10, 13–15, 18–21), for instance in the attempt of Eratosthenes, one of the Thirty of 404/3, to associate himself with Theramenes.[37]

As regards the relation of statements made here to what we know from other sources, it is problematic that the speech's account of the appointment of the Four Hundred (§§ 1–2) does not clearly match Thucydides' account; on the other hand, that the Assembly at Colonus did decide on a restricted citizen body of the Five Thousand, and that, although the definitive list of the Five Thousand was never published, *katalogeis* were appointed at the beginning of the oligarchic régime and were made to swear an oath (§§ 13–14), confirms something that we are told by *Ath. Pol.* which has no counterpart in Thucydides.[38] That a force was sent to Eretria earlier than the autumn (§§ 10, 14), that there were some Athenian exiles supporting the occupying forces at Decelea (§ 28), and the activities of the younger Polystratus at Catana (§§ 24–26), are consistent with what we know from other sources and there is no reason why they should not have a factual basis.

Bibliography

Apostolakis, K.E. (2003), *[Λυσίου] Υπερ Πολυστράτου· Εισαγωγή, κείμενο, μετάφραση, σχόλια*, Athens.

Apostolakis, K.E. (2017), "Pitiable Dramas on the Podium of the Athenian Law Courts", in: S. Papaioannou/A. Serafim/B. da Vela (eds.), *The Theatre of Justice: Aspects of Performance in Greco-Roman Oratory and Rhetoric* (Mnemosyne Supp. 403), Leiden, 133–156.

Bearzot, C. (2000), "La XX orazione pseudolisiana e la 'prima restaurazione' della democrazia nel 410", in: M. Capasso/S. Pernigotti (eds.), *Studium atque urbanitas: miscellanea in onore di Sergio Daris* (Papyrologica Lupiensia 9), 83–99.

Busolt, G. (1904), *Griechische Geschichte*, iii. 1, Gotha.

Cavaignac, E. (1925/6), "Les Quatre cents, Thucydide, Aristote et les Discours pour Polystratos", *RUB* 31, 317–322.

---

36 See Apostolakis 2017, 141–144.
37 Lys. 12. *Eratosthenes* 50, 62–79: see on that Piovan 2011, 66–90, Kapellos 2018, 56, 62; also Shear 2011, 63–65, who cites that and other examples.
38 Cf. Andrewes, in Gomme/Andrewes/Dover 1981, 201–206. On the Assemblies of Thucydides and of *Ath. Pol.* cf. above, p. 41 with nn. 127–128.

Davies, J.K. (1971), *Athenian Propertied Families, 600–300 B.C.*, Oxford.
Develin, R. (1989), *Athenian Officials, 684–321 B.C.*, Cambridge.
Dover, K.J. (1968), *Lysias and the Corpus Lysiacum*, Berkeley/Los Angeles.
Gernet, L./Bizos, M. (1926), *Lysias, Discours*, ii (Budé edition), Paris.
Gomme, A.W./Andrewes, A./Dover, K.J. (1981), *A Historical Commentary on Thucydides*, v, Oxford.
Grote, G. (1869/1884), *History of Greece* ("new edition" in 12 volumes), London.
Hackl, U. (1960), Die *oligarchische Bewegung* in Athen am Ausgang des 5. Jahrhunderts v. Chr., München.
Heftner, H. (1999a), "Die Rede für Polystratos ([Lysias] XX) als Zeugnis für den oligarchischen Umsturz von 411 v. Chr. in Athen", *Klio* 81, 68–94.
Heftner, H. (1999b), "Die Rede für Polystratos ([Lys.] 20) und die Katalogisierung der Fünftausend während des athenischen Verfassungsumsturzes von 411 v. Chr.", in: P. Scherrer/H. Taueber/H. Thür (eds.), *Steine und Wege: Festschrift für D. Knibbe*, Wien, 221–226.
Heftner, H. (2001), *Der oligarchische Umsturz des Jahres 411 v. Chr. und die Herrschaft der Vierhundert in Athen: quellenkritische und historische Untersuchungen*, Bern/Frankfurt am Main.
Heftner, H. (2003), "Bemerkungen zur Rolle der Probuloi während des oligarchischen Umsturzes in Athen 411 v. Chr.", *Prometheus* 29, 213–227.
Hornblower, S. (2008), *A Commentary on Thucydides*, iii, Oxford.
Hurni, F. (1991), "Comment les Cinq-Mille furent-ils sélectionnés en 411?", *MH* 48, 220–227.
Humphreys, S.C. (2018), *Kinship in Ancient Athens*, Oxford.
Kapellos, A. (1918), "Lysias Interrogating Eratosthenes on the Murder of Polemarchus" *Erga-Logoi* 6.2, 51–64.
Kelly, D.H. (1970), "What Happened to the Athenians Captured in Sicily?", *CR* n.s. 20, 127–131.
Kirchner, J. (1901–1903), *Prosopographia Attica*, Berlin.
Lamb, W.R.M. (1930), *Lysias*, London.
Lang, M.L. (1948), "The Revolution of the 400", *AJP* 69, 272–279.
Lang, M.L. (1967), "Revolution of the 400: Chronology and Constitutions", *AJP* 88, 176–187.
Piovan, D. (2011), *Memoria e oblio della guerra civile: Strategie giudiziarie e racconto del passato in Lisia*, Pisa.
Rhodes, P.J. (1981), *A Commentary on the Aristotelian Athenaion Politeia*, Oxford.
Rhodes, P.J. (2018), *The Athenian Constitution Written in the School of Aristotle*, Liverpool.
Shear, J.L. (2011), *Polis and Revolution: Responding to Oligarchy in Classical Athens*, Cambridge.
Thalheim, T. (1876), *Des Lysias Rede für Polystratos*, Breslau.
Todd, S.C. (2000), *Lysias*, Austin.
Todd, S.C. (2007), *A Commentary on Lysias, Speeches 1–11*, Oxford.
Traill, J.S. (1975), *The Political Organization of Attica* (*Hesperia* Supp. 14), Princeton.
Wilamowitz-Moellendorff, U. von (1893), *Aristoteles und Athen*, Berlin.

Frances Pownall
Andocides, the Spartans, and the Thirty

Abstract: There is a very unusual passage in *On the Peace* in which Andocides elides the Spartans' responsibility in 404/3 for the imposition upon the Athenians of the Thirty (3.10–11), the oligarchical junta that was later so despised that it became known as the Thirty Tyrants. Furthermore, Andocides' apparent rehabilitation of the Spartans' collusion in tyranny is very much at odds with his attempt to bolster his democratic credentials in his first two speeches, where he emphasizes the assistance of his family in the expulsion of the Peisistratid tyranny (1.106; 2.26), an episode in which the role of the Spartans was very much contested in later tradition. Pownall examines the significance of Andocides' apparent willingness to act as an apologist for the Spartans in 403 in terms of what it can tell us about both his own political ideology and the memory of the regime of the Thirty.

There is a startling passage in Andocides' *De Pace* (the third speech in his corpus) in which he elides over the Spartans' responsibility at the conclusion of the Peloponnesian War for the imposition upon the Athenians of the Thirty, a short-lived oligarchical regime that was later so despised that its members became collectively known as the Thirty Tyrants. The Thirty technically were not tyrants, as they did not usurp power but were elected constitutionally by the Athenians to form a government, as even Xenophon (whose influential narrative of their reign of terror in the *Hellenica* has done much to enshrine the impression that their rule was tyrannical) concedes,[1] and the silence of the orators on the institution of their rule confirms. Nevertheless, the brutality of their regime,[2] along with the recasting of the restoration of democracy in Athens (again, with Spartan collusion) as a liberation from tyranny, almost immediately solidified the popular perception that the Thirty were tyrants, and no orator could risk alienating his audience by portraying them as constitutional rulers. The role that the Spartans played in the regime of the Thirty, however, offered more scope for rhetorical manipulation. Even so, Andocides' apparent willingness to act as an apologist for the Spartans' recent collusion in "tyranny" seems jarring

---

I thank Aggelos Kapellos for his help with the bibliography.

1 Xen. *Hell.* 2.3.11; cf. Diod. 14.3. See also Krentz 1982, 50; Krentz 1995, 123; Pownall 2012, 2–3.
2 On the violence of the regime of the Thirty, see Wolpert 2006 and 2019.

https://doi.org/10.1515/9783110791877-005

in light of his efforts in his first two speeches to bolster his democratic credentials by distancing himself from the oligarchical governments of both the Four Hundred and the Thirty. In this contribution, I examine Andocides' attempt to rehabilitate the involvement of the Spartans just over a decade after the events of 404/3 in terms of what it can tell us about both his own political ideology and the Athenian collective memory of the regime of the Thirty.

Andocides' *De Pace* reflects a set of unsuccessful peace negotiations that took place at Sparta during the Corinthian War in 392/1, resulting in the condemnation and exile of the ambassadors when they failed to persuade the Athenians to accept the terms.[3] Although the speech has generally been considered authentic by modern scholars,[4] Dionysius of Halicarnassus is alleged to have dismissed it as spurious, and Harpocration expresses scepticism that it is genuine.[5] E. Harris has offered a vigorous challenge to the *De Pace*'s authenticity, arguing that it (like the fourth speech attributed to Andocides) is a later forgery composed as a rhetorical exercise.[6] Harris' arguments have not won universal acceptance,[7] however, and I wonder if it might be more productive to

---

[3] These peace negotiations are also mentioned by Didymus, *Commentary on Demosthenes' Fourth Philip*, col. 7, 11–27 and the anonymous author of the *Hypothesis* to Andocides' *De Pace* (both on the authority of Philochorus BNJ 328 F 149a and b, who provides the archon year); cf. [Plut.] *Mor.* 835a; Phot. *Bibl.* 261b. Demosthenes (19.276–277) makes it clear that the ambassadors did not await trial, but voluntarily went into exile to avoid a sentence of capital punishment. On the historical circumstances, see Edwards 1995, 106–107; Pownall 1995; Keen 1995 and 1998; Harding 2006, 165–177. Tordoff 2017, demonstrates that these failed peace negotiations are reflected in the atmosphere of political crisis in Aristophanes' *Ecclesiazusae*, produced later in the same archon year of 392/1.

[4] E.g. Kennedy 1958, 40–41; Albini 1964, 17–24; Missiou 1992, 56 n. 1; Edwards 1995, 107–108; Grethlein 2020, 128–145.

[5] Hypothesis to the *De Pace* (= Philochorus BNJ 328 F 149b): ὁ δὲ Διονύσιος νόθον εἶναι λέγει τὸν λόγον. Cf. Harpocration's εἰ γνήσιος (*ter*) s.v. Ἑλληνοταμίαι, Νεώρια, Πηγαί.

[6] Harris 2000 and in this volume. For the view that *Against Alcibiades* is a rhetorical exercise, see Rhodes 1994, 88–91; Edwards 1995, 131–136; Gazzano 1999, xviii–xxii; Gribble 1999, 154–158; Carey 2005, 97. We should not, however, discount the possibility that it could be a contemporary pamphlet designed to influence political opinion in 416; Furley 1996, 7–8 and Todd 2020, 465.

[7] Although Harris' thesis is strongly endorsed by Couvenhes 2012, 109–114 (see also Canevaro and Gray 2018, 90 and n. 69), his arguments against authenticity are convincingly refuted by Ueno 2008; Magnetto 2013; Rhodes 2016, 182–186 (who observes *inter alia* that the style of Andocides 1, 2, and 3, is the same, unlike Andocides 4); cf. Grethlein 2010, 128 n. 9. The further arguments that Harris adduces in his contribution to this volume and Harris 2021 (which has the same title) are not conclusive against the speech's authenticity, based as they are on the premise that historical inaccuracies necessarily imply inauthenticity rather than tendentious

consider the *De Pace* as an example of an authentic speech that was originally composed for oral delivery and subsequently revised by Andocides himself for circulation as a written pamphlet.[8] It is worth noting that another symbouleutic speech belonging to the fraught aftermath of the rule of the Thirty, and one that is often discussed in connection with the *De Pace*, is attributed to Lysias (34 in his corpus) by Dionysius (*Lysias* 32).[9] He introduces his long citation with the comment that he is unsure if Lysias' speech was actually given on that occasion; it is generally viewed as a political pamphlet.[10] Similarly, the *De Pace* in its current form likely does not represent the original speech delivered to the Athenian Assembly during the attempted ratification of the peace terms in 392/1, where Andocides attempted to persuade his fellow citizens that it was to their advantage to change their minds about Sparta. Although Aristotle (*Rhet.* 1358b20) identifies "advantage" (τὸ συμφέρον) as a goal of symbouleutic rhetoric, Andocides was unsuccessful in making his case to the Athenian Assembly in the original speech.[11] Thanks to his lengthy absence from Athens during his exile and aristocratic background, he was out of touch with the outlook of the masses and his speech was spectacularly unpersuasive to the Athenian Assembly, as is indicated by the severe penalty incurred by the hapless ambassadors. Instead,

---

rhetoric required by the narrative context. Nor is it clear that the term *presbeis autokratores* is necessarily misused in the *De Pace*; as Harris demonstrates in his fuller discussion of the issue (Harris 2021), the term was used to designate special (but limited) powers to enable negotiation in specific circumstances. Thus, it is difficult to argue to that there was a recognized set of requirements for the use of this designation that do not fit the peace negotiations of the *De Pace*.

8 Cf. Edwards 1995, 106. For evidence that speeches were revised for circulation after oral delivery, see Worthington 1991, 1995, and 2020/1; Hubbard 2008, Clarke 2021, 179–185 (addressing the circulation of Demosthenes 8 to a reading audience); as Worthington 2020/1 observes, the revision of speeches explains how the orators were able to include historical inaccuracies or even outright falsehoods; cf. Todd 2020, 385 and 478. It is unclear whether Andocides' (no longer extant) *To his Comrades* (πρὸς τοὺς ἑταίρους), written in an oratorical format, began life as a speech as well; the work is generally considered "a piece of oligarchic propaganda" (so MacDowell 1962, 2 and 190–192; cf. Missiou 1992, 22–23; Edwards 1995, 3). Although Harris 1998, 19 suggests that it is not genuine, it is more likely an authentic speech composed by Andocides for written circulation to a like-minded audience; Ober 1985, 53–54, Roisman and Worthington 2015, 115–116; cf. the still valuable remarks of Calhoun 1913, 113–115.
9 On Lysias 34, see Bearzot in this volume.
10 E.g. Hansen 1984, 60; Edwards 1995, 105–106; Todd 2000, 335–338; Carey 2005, 92–93; Usher 2007, 220–222.
11 As noted by Grethlein 2010, 136, it is difficult to believe that Andocides did not attempt to persuade his audience; *pace* Missiou 1992, who contends that his true intent was to subvert the democracy and the success of his speech was of less consequence.

the text of the *De Pace* as we have it is more likely a version reworked as a political pamphlet directed to those who were able to read written documents (i.e. the educated elite) and were in a position to be able to shape future policy.[12] It is no accident that Aristotle does not include political rhetoric in his analysis of rhetorical types, although he does comment that one of the most important topics of symbouleutic rhetoric is to advise an audience on the question of war or peace.[13] Thus, I follow recent scholarship in reading the *De Pace* as an oligarchic document,[14] but I hope to offer further refinement of how and why Andocides chooses to subvert democratic ideology.

In the *De Pace*, Andocides carefully and deliberately treads a fine line between arguments that conform to the "master narrative" of the Athenian democracy (i.e., elements remaining from the original speech) and those that are designed to subvert it (i.e., elements added and/or highlighted in the published version).[15] In other words, Andocides' intent in this revised version was not so much to persuade the Athenian democracy to vote for peace with Sparta on a particular occasion in 392/1,[16] but to furnish his fellow intellectual critics of popular rule with further ammunition to soften contemporary attitudes in Athens to Sparta as part of their ultimate goal of rehabilitating some form of moderate oligarchy.[17] My approach differs from previous scholarship on the essentially subversive nature of the *De Pace* in that I contend that Andocides is explicitly directing the version that we have to his fellow elites as a "working paper," rather than trying to influence the mindset of the Athenian democracy in

---

[12] On the circulation of revised speeches as "a contribution to a continuing struggle" waged by the educated elite, see Carey 2005, 92–97 (quotation on p. 93); cf. Worthington 1996.
[13] Arist. (*Rhet*. 1359b23–24). I owe this point to Aggelos Kapellos; cf. Yunis 1996, 16.
[14] Missiou 1992; Edwards 1995, esp. 105–113; Grethein 2010, 129–139. On Andocides' oligarchic stance and on the consistency of his political views throughout his career, see Furley 1996, 49–69 (although he does not believe that the *De Pace* is a subversive oligarchic document). For doubts that Andocides was an oligarch, see Harris 1998, 19.
[15] The useful term "master narrative" has been coined by S. Forsdyke 2005, 242 to represent the democratic version of the past; cf. R. Thomas' "official polis tradition" (1989, 196–237).
[16] As Edwards 1995, 113 observes, Epicrates, who was one of Andocides' fellow ambassadors, as an avowed populist politician who was personally involved in the restoration of the Athenian democracy in 403 (Dem. 19.277), was unlikely to endorse Andocides' version of events in the *De Pace* as we have it.
[17] On political dissent to the Athenian democracy, see Ober 1998 (although he does not discuss Andocides). On the hypersensitivity of the restored democracy to political dissent (real or perceived), particularly in the wake of the disastrous oligarchical experiments of the late fifth century, see Shear 2011; cf. Pownall 2018, esp. 137–139.

392/1.[18] This political agenda, as I shall argue, is what lies behind his attempt to skate around Spartan complicity in the establishment of the Thirty at Athens.

The overall thrust of the *De Pace* is that peace with Sparta does not represent a threat to the Athenian democracy,[19] a difficult point indeed to sell to an Athenian audience in the late 390s,[20] a scant decade after the eight-month siege of the city and surrender to the Spartans, which resulted in the rule of the hated Thirty, the memory of which was still fresh.[21] Andocides begins with a notoriously inaccurate survey of fifth-century Athenian history (later adapted by Aeschines 2.172–176) to illustrate his point that a negotiated peace with Sparta has never resulted in the overthrowing of democracy in Athens (3.3–9),[22] laying heavy emphasis on the substantial benefits (particularly financial and military) accruing to the Athenian democracy from these previous treaties. R. Thomas is undoubtedly correct in her observation that his utterly idiosyncratic rendition of fifth-century events stems ultimately from the oral transmission of family memories.[23] Despite the obligatory (if glancing) reference to the growth of Athenian sea power that permitted the naval defeat of the Persian king and the "barbarians" and the concomitant freeing of the Greeks (3.5), themes that are stereotypical of patriotic Athenian oratory, Thomas' further statement, "there is little in Andocides' description that can be identified as oligarchic,"[24] invites further scrutiny.

First of all, it is only Andocides (and after him, Aeschines) who employ the intra-Greek peace treaties struck during the Pentekontaetia as a historical example;[25] the other Attic orators avoid them altogether, which suggests that these

---

18 On Andocides' oligarchic mission in the *De Pace*, see esp. Missiou 1992, 182; cf. Edwards 1995, 113 and Grethlein 2010, 128–129. Edwards 1995, 113 and Harris 1998, 19 rightly doubt the ideological cohesion among Athenian oligarchs that Missiou postulates. On the inherently brittle nature of oligarchies in classical Greece, not least due to their difficulty in achieving unity, see Simonton 2017b.
19 On the rhetorical strategy employed by Andocides, whereby he employed examples from the past in order to mitigate fear for the future, see Maltagliati 2020, 293–295.
20 On the generally negative image of Sparta in Athenian oratory, see Bearzot 2007.
21 For a perceptive analysis of prosecutions for political murders committed during the rule of the Thirty in the years following the amnesty, see Loening 1987, 69–84.
22 On the rampant historical errors in this passage, see Nouhaud 1982, 230–234 and 267–270; Thomas 1989, 119–123; Edwards 1995, 194–196. Harris 2000, 481–487 (arguments elaborated in Harris 2020 and in his contribution to this volume) contends that a Hellenistic forger manipulated the very similar passage in Aeschines.
23 Thomas 1989, 118–123; cf. Edwards 1995, 194; Steinbock 2013b, 74–75.
24 Thomas 1989, 119 n. 77.
25 Cf. Nouhaud 1982, 229–234.

negotiations do not in fact form part of the mainstream democratic master narrative. Second, while the other orators make no mention of any of Athens' efforts to establish a land empire in central Greece in the 450s and early 440s, Andocides (3.3) refers blatantly to Athens' possession of Megara, Pegae, and Troezen (again probably through the influence of family memories).[26] Notably, the only other explicit reference in Attic oratory to the extension of Athenian imperial power from sea to land occurs in the funeral speech recited by Socrates in Plato's *Menexenus* (242a–b), in which the blatant historical errors serve to satirize the transparent falseness of the idealized portrait of the past in the master narrative of the Athenian democracy.[27] Third, in another set of historical examples (3.28–32), again buttressing his arguments with a direct family connection,[28] and containing (at the very least) further tendentious claims and chronological uncertainties,[29] Andocides criticizes the Athenian (democratic) penchant for intervening on behalf of the weak instead of siding with the strong. With this overt appeal to self-interest, he undermines the altruistic motive of helping the wronged and oppressed that is conventionally adduced by the orators as a justification for Athenian intervention in the internal affairs of other poleis (and was even retrojected to the legendary history of Athens in funeral orations).[30] Finally, in a third set of historical examples, Andocides (3.37) bluntly attributes the foundation of the Athenian empire to a somewhat shocking combination of persuasion, stealth, bribery, and force, rather than as a natural and fully deserved consequence of their moral superiority, as the saviours of Greece in the Persian Wars and the protectors of their fellow Hellenes in the ensuing struggle against the barbarians.[31] Instead of either omitting the openly imperialistic aspects of fifth-century Athenian history or endowing them

---

26 Andocides' homonymous grandfather commanded three tribes of Athenian hoplites in a successful campaign to the Megarid in 446; Osborne and Rhodes 2017, no. 130.
27 On the parodic function of the *Menexenus*, see Pownall 2004, 38–64 (with earlier bibliography). For recent scholarship on this perplexing and ambiguous dialogue, see Pappas and Zelcer 2015 and the essays contained in Parker and Robitzsch 2018 (the volume usefully opens with a reprint of Charles H. Kahn's seminal 1963 article); see also Kapellos in this volume.
28 Andocides' claim that his maternal uncle Epilycus negotiated a peace with the Persian king is possibly confirmed by an Athenian decree (Osborne and Rhodes 2017, no. 157).
29 Missiou 1992, 109–111; Edwards 1995, 198–199; Grethlein 2010, 132; cf. Tuci 2020, 172–175.
30 On Andocides' criticism of the Athenian democratic claim to the moral high ground in foreign policy, see also Missiou 1992, 1091–1039 and Edwards 1995, 111–112.
31 As noted by Missiou 1992, 78–79: "he makes use of concepts and terms which describe the empire, but immediately sets out to tarnish the memories they might evoke." Cf. Edwards 1995, 199.

with a moral justification,[32] Andocides deliberately undercuts the idealized version of the past generally found in the Attic orators.[33]

With this sustained subversion of the democratic master narrative, the overall subtext of the *De Pace* is highly oligarchic. It is in this ideological context that we must examine Andocides' presentation of the role of the Spartans in the establishment of the Thirty. Andocides concludes his first set of historical examples, illustrating his overall point that peace with Sparta has never harmed the democracy, with the following statement (3.10):

> ἤδη δέ τινων ἤκουσα λεγόντων ὡς ἐκ τῆς τελευταίας εἰρήνης τῆς πρὸς Λακεδαιμονίους οἵ τε τριάκοντα κατέστησαν, πολλοί τε Ἀθηναίων κώνειον πιόντες ἀπέθανον, οἱ δὲ φεύγοντες ᾤχοντο.

> I have previously heard some people saying that as a result of the last peace with the Spartans the Thirty were established, many Athenians died by drinking hemlock, and others were exiled.

Andocides proceeds to address what he portrays as a misconception connecting the Spartans to the violent regime of the Thirty with some rhetorical sleight of hand on the difference between a peace and a truce.[34] As he argues, the Athenian capitulation at the end of the Peloponnesian War was the result of a truce (not a negotiated peace) and the Athenians were forced to accept the Spartan terms unconditionally (3.11):

> ἡμῶν κρατήσαντες Λακεδαιμόνιοι τῷ πολέμῳ ἐπέταξαν ἡμῖν καὶ <τὰ> τείχη καθαιρεῖν καὶ τὰς ναῦς παραδιδόναι καὶ τοὺς φεύγοντας καταδέχεσθαι.

> After defeating us in the war, the Spartans ordered us to destroy our walls, hand over our ships, and restore our exiles.[35]

According to Andocides, one of the crucial differences between the compulsory truce of 404 and the negotiated peace proposed in the negotiations of 392/1 is the restoration of exiles (3.12):

---

32 Chambers 1975, esp. 182–187; cf. Pownall 2004, 41–42.
33 As Dillery 2017, 217 observes, Xenophon employs a very similar technique in the *Poroi* to subvert the standard justifications of Athenian imperialism.
34 Cf. Nouhaud 1982, 304: "son analyse de vocabulaire ne repose sur rien".
35 On Xenophon's equally tendentious narrative of the razing of the walls and the restoration of exiles, see Kapellos 2011.

> καὶ φεύγοντας νῦν μὲν οὐκ ἐπάναγκες οὐδένα καταδέχεσθαι, τότε δ' ἐπάναγκες, ἐξ ὧν ὁ δῆμος κατελύθη.
>
> Now there is no compulsion to recall exiles, whereas at that time there was compulsion, which resulted in the democracy being overthrown.

Thus, Andocides not only glosses over the role of the Lysander and the Spartans in the election of the Thirty, but unequivocally transfers responsibility for the dissolution of the democracy (and, by implication, the atrocities of the regime that ensued) from the Spartans to the Thirty themselves, a number of whom were political exiles who returned to Athens at the end of the war (cf. [Arist.] *Ath. Pol.* 34.3).[36]

The Spartans' responsibility for imposing upon the Athenians an oligarchical government, billed as a return to the ancestral constitution (*patrios politeia*),[37] as part of the peace terms of 404 has been doubted by some scholars because Xenophon (*Hell.* 2.2.11) fails to mention it in his own narrative (deliberately, as I shall argue, for exactly the same reasons as Andocides),[38] although significantly he plants a reference to Spartan involvement in the mouth of Critias (*Hell.* 2.3.25).[39] The Spartan demand for the dissolution of the Athenian democracy does appear, however, in [Arist.] *Ath. Pol.* 34.3, who introduces it with the comment: "Lysander established the Thirty in the following way" (Λύσανδρον καταστῆσαι τοὺς τριάκοντα τρόπῳ τοιῷδε), and is confirmed by Lysias (12.71–76), Diodorus (14.3.1–7), Plutarch (*Lys.* 15.1–2), and Justin (5.8.5–6).[40] Thus, the active role of the Spartans in the overthrowing of the Athenian democracy is hardly a common misconception, as Andocides somewhat disingenuously claims, and the question remains of why he chose to edit them out of the picture altogether.

How does Andocides' removal of responsibility from the Spartans for the fall of the democracy and the establishment of the Thirty jibe with his sweeping self-defense in the first speech of his corpus (delivered in 400) against the

---

[36] On the members of the Thirty, see Krentz 1982, 51–56 and Németh 2006, 16–25.

[37] This phrase, conferring political legitimacy, became a loaded slogan appropriated by both supporters of the Four Hundred and their opponents; see David 2014 (with previous bibliography); cf. Shear 2012, 19–69.

[38] On the historicity of this Spartan demand, see Ostwald 1986, 458 n. 165 and Stern 2003, 22–23 (who suggests that Theramenes may have been behind Lysander's dissolution of the democracy in favour of a constitution acceptable to Sparta).

[39] Cf. Pownall 2012, where I argue that Xenophon's rhetorical strategy in the *Hellenica* is to scapegoat Critias for the crimes of the Thirty.

[40] On Lysander's role in the subversion of democracy in Athens, see Kapellos 2018.

charge that he was involved in the profanation of the Mysteries and the mutilation of the Hermae in 415 (widely thought to have been an oligarchical conspiracy aimed at the overthrow of the democracy),[41] as well as the care he takes to dissociate himself from the Four Hundred in his (unsuccessful) attempt to return to Athens from exile in the second speech of his corpus (delivered probably in 409 or 408)?[42] The oligarchic revolution of the Four Hundred in 411/10 originated with the Athenian fleet at Samos where some of the commanders (with the collusion of the mercurial Alcibiades, who promised Persian aid in the war effort against Sparta), including Peisander (Andocides' nemesis), took advantage of the disastrous conclusion to the Sicilian expedition to conspire to overthrow the Athenian democracy. Ironically, however, once the oligarchs in Athens successfully intimidated the Assembly into supplanting the democracy with the Four Hundred, a counter-revolution occurred among the Athenian fleet at Samos upon rumours of atrocities taking place in Athens, and democracy was restored among the troops based on the island.[43] In Athens, a violent rift occurred among the moderate oligarchs (led by Theramenes) and the extremists (who appealed to the Spartans), a scenario prefiguring the events of the equally short-lived regime of the Thirty. After a naval defeat to the Peloponnesians near Eretria, the Four Hundred were deposed and replaced by a more moderate oligarchical government, the Five Thousand (Thuc. 8.97.1–2; [Arist.] *Ath. Pol.* 33.1).[44] Democracy was restored not long afterwards, following the victory over the Spartans at Cyzicus by the Athenian fleet now commanded by Alcibiades (Xen. *Hell.* 1.1.11–26),[45] and the ensuing (unsuccessful) Spartan attempt to negotiate a peace treaty (Philochorus BNJ 328 F 139a and b; Diod. 13.52.2).

To take the earlier speech first, the rhetorical context of *On his Return* dictates an emphasis on both Andocides' own and his family's services to the democracy. As concrete evidence of his democratic credentials, Andocides adduces his provision of the Athenian fleet at Samos (which was by then effectively functioning as the democratic government in exile) with grain (possibly from Cyprus, where he had connections),[46] bronze, and most importantly oar-spars from Macedonian timber (thanks to his guest-friendship with Archelaus). Ac-

---

41 Cf. Thuc. 6.27.3.
42 On the date, see Missiou 1992, 26 n. 35 and Edwards 1995, 89.
43 Cf. Simonton 2017a, 240: "The military Assembly has become a democratic hothouse".
44 On the oligarchical regime of the Four Hundred, see Shear 2012, 19–69 (who provides a useful comparison of the accounts of Thucydides and the Aristotelian *Athenaion Politeia*); cf. David 2014.
45 On Xenophon's narrative of the battle at Cyzicus, see Kapellos 2019, 16–21.
46 Andoc. 1.4; cf. 2.20–21.

cording to Andocides, it was with the resources that he provided to the fleet at Samos that the Athenians were able to inflict a major naval defeat upon the Peloponnesians (2.11–12), which implies the crucial victory at Cyzicus, although it should be noted that he does not say so explicitly. Andocides claims that it was thanks to these benefactions to the (democratic) fleet at Samos that he incurred the hostility of the Four Hundred, particularly Peisander, who had been one of the investigators into the mutilation of the Herms (Andoc. 1.27 and 36), resulting in his arrest and imprisonment (Andoc. 2.13–16). Andocides refers to the battle only in vague terms because the Four Hundred had already been deposed and replaced by the Five Thousand by then. But the juxtaposition of his generosity to the fleet at Samos with the defeat of the Peloponnesians by the newly-equipped ships allows Andocides to claim a direct association with one of the greatest victories of the Athenian democracy in the Peloponnesian War.

It is often thought that Andocides' references to his personal wealth and royal connections reflect oligarchic rather than democratic ideology and explain the Athenian rejection of his appeal to return to Athens.[47] But personal international connections served the elite in the Athenian democracy effectively as political capital and such arguments would conform to audience expectations.[48] Nevertheless, Andocides (2.19–21) does undercut his attempt to establish his support of the Athenian democracy in this speech by referring in vague terms to a second (unspecified) occasion when he supplied grain to Athens from Cyprus along with a secret proposal to the Council that more would be forthcoming, revealing a desire to thwart the vaunted openness of decision-making of the Athenian democracy, as well as a desire to bypass the Assembly (the chief democratic organ of the state).[49]

Andocides manipulates the Athenian memory of the recent past in a similar way by representing himself in *On the Mysteries* as a victim of the Thirty, although he had actually been in exile during their regime. As he claims (1.101–102), in a rhetorical sequence of contrafactual history, if he had been in Athens, the Thirty would have put him to death because he had not joined the Spartan base at Decelea, where the leaders of the Four Hundred fled after the fall of their government,[50] nor did he take any military action against Athens by land or by sea, help in demolishing its walls or overthrowing the democracy, or return to

---

[47] See e.g. Missiou 1992, 28–49; cf. Kennedy's 1958, 33 characterization of Andocides as a "haughty aristocrat" and Gray 2015, 328 on his "entitlement."
[48] Sato 2015; cf. Grethlein 2010, 131.
[49] Cf. Edwards 1995, 192.
[50] Thuc. 8.98.1.

the city by force. This claim that he had not actively joined the Thirty allows Andocides to distance himself from their regime (a particularly crucial aspect of his defense in view of the allegations that he had been complicit in previous oligarchical plots against the democracy), but more importantly offers him proof of his *bona fide* democratic credentials in light of the prevailing (if overly simplistic) conception that anyone who was not a supporter of the Thirty necessarily opposed their rule.[51]

Andocides further reinforces his loyalty to the democracy in emphasizing the remarkable nature of the amnesty that restored civic harmony to Athens in the aftermath of the defeat of the Thirty (1.80–91), an integral part of the democratic master narrative,[52] although it should be noted that his own self-interest required this approach, for he relied upon the amnesty for the success of his acquittal.[53] Notably, he opens this section by dissociating himself from the Thirty through studiously avoiding verbs in the first person (1.80):

> ἐπεὶ δ' αἱ σπονδαὶ πρὸς Λακεδαιμονίους ἐγένοντο, καὶ τὰ τείχη καθείλετε, καὶ τοὺς φεύγοντας κατεδέξασθε, καὶ κατέστησαν οἱ τριάκοντα, καὶ μετὰ ταῦτα Φυλῆτε κατελήφθη Μουνυχίαν τε κατέλαβον, ἐγένετό ὑμῖν ὧν ἐγὼ οὐδὲν δέομαι μεμνῆσθαι οὐδ' ἀναμιμνῄσκειν ὑμᾶς τῶν γεγενημένων κακῶν.

> When the truce was struck with the Spartans, and you demolished your walls and restored your exiles, and the Thirty were established, and subsequently Phyle was seized and they took Munychia, terrible things happened to you, none of which is it necessary for me to call to mind or remind you.

In this usefully polyvalent passage,[54] Andocides subtly switches from the third person to the second person plural to absolve the Spartans from responsibility for the events that occurred after the truce. Although Andocides employs the standard oratorical device of professing unwillingness to remind his auditors of unpleasant events of the past,[55] he does not entirely skate over the disastrous end of the Peloponnesian War. By attributing to the Athenians themselves the demolition of the city's walls and the recall of political exiles (eliding over the fact that these had been terms imposed by the Spartan peace),[56] he subtly im-

---

51 Wolpert 2002, 106.
52 On the politics of social memory articulated in the amnesty, see e.g., Loraux 2002; Wolpert 2002; Carawan 2013.
53 Wolpert 2002, 50.
54 On the deliberate ambiguity of this passage, see Wolpert 2002, 122.
55 On this rhetorical *topos*, see Kapellos 2014b, 95.
56 Andocides employs a similar tactic at 1.109.

plies that the establishment of the brutal regime of the Thirty, and the atrocities that followed, including the civil war (with the requisite allusions to Phyle, the base used by the democratic resistance,[57] and Munychia, where the decisive battle against the Thirty took place),[58] were consequences of their own actions. This passage, therefore, corresponds with Andocides' absolution of the Spartans from responsibility for the establishment of the Thirty in the *De Pace*, although in the context of pleading the case for his acquittal to the restored democracy he is much more careful not to do so explicitly. Notably, in both speeches he portrays the Spartans as the saviours of Athens for preventing their allies from the complete destruction of the city (1.142 and 3.21). The only other reference to Sparta's benefaction to Athens in the wake of the city's surrender occurs in Xenophon (*Hell.* 2.2.19–20; cf. 2.3.41),[59] who had a similar agenda (as I shall argue below).

Another connection between the *De Pace* and Andocides' earlier speeches is his emphasis on his family's previous service to the democracy. Significantly, the event on which he chooses to focus in the two earlier speeches is his ancestor's alleged role in the expulsion of the Peisistratids (2.26 and 1.106), an event enshrined in the democratic master narrative as the foundation of Athenian democracy, in which the pivotal military assistance of the Spartans was conveniently excised from popular memory.[60] Although the inaccuracies and confusion contained in this historical allusion,[61] like those in the *De Pace*, are generally attributed to the process of oral transmission of family memories,[62] I would suggest that another (not necessarily mutually exclusive) explanation is possible. In the fraught political circumstances after the reconciliation of 403, there was renewed public interest in Athens in the city's previous liberation from tyranny (juxtaposed in public memory with the foundation of the democracy), the pre-

---

[57] On the importance of the "heroes of Phyle" in the civic memory of the Athenian democracy, see Wolpert 2002, 88.
[58] On the use of Phyle and Munychia as democratic shorthand for the events of the civil war, see Dillery 1995, 141.
[59] See Bearzot 2004–2005 and Kapellos 2010; cf. Bearzot 2017, 50.
[60] On the role of the Spartans in the expulsion of the Peisistratids, see Hdt. 5.62–65 and 6.123; Thuc. 6.59.4; [Arist.] *Ath. Pol.* 19; cf. Ar. *Lys.* 1155–1156. On the juxtaposition of the liberation of Athens from tyranny and the foundation of Athenian democracy in the master narrative, see, e.g., Pownall 2012a, esp. 329–334 and 2018, esp. 137–146 (both with previous bibliography).
[61] The anachronism of democracy in pre-Cleisthenic Athens, the confusion of the precise generation to which Andocides' ancestor belonged, and the conflation of the Battle of Pallene with the expulsion of the Peisistratids.
[62] So Thomas 1989, 139–144.

cise details of which lay far enough in the past to be manipulated to provide a more exact parallel.⁶³ But the recent liberation from the "tyranny" of the Thirty offered the opportunity to rewrite the past not only to Athenian democrats, but also to oligarchs,⁶⁴ who could not voice their true political allegiance openly in an atmosphere of hyper-sensitivity to real or perceived dissent, where elite opponents to democracy ran the risk of being labelled as aspiring tyrants.⁶⁵ Thus, the historical errors in Andocides' narrative of his ancestor's efforts on behalf of a proto (that is, pre-Cleisthenic) *demos* hint that his true intention is to undermine the master narrative,⁶⁶ and perhaps, just like the particularly egregious ones in the *De Pace*, are a subtle nod to those "in the know" that the Spartans were the ones actually responsible for liberating the city from tyranny, thereby laying the groundwork for the (re)foundation of democracy.

Because philo-laconism was a marker of the political sensibilities of those opposed to the radical democracy of the late fifth-century,⁶⁷ the association of the Spartans with the liberation of the city from tyranny serves as a clarion call to this particular readership to withdraw from quietism and return to active participation in political life. In the *Hellenica*, a work directed to the educated elite, Xenophon goes to very great lengths to obscure the fact that the Thirty modelled their conception of the *patrios politeia* upon the Spartan constitution, thereby denying them any ideological basis to their rule, choosing instead to follow the democratic master narrative in painting them as an utterly bloodthirsty set of tyrants.⁶⁸ Furthermore, like Andocides, Xenophon removes responsibility from the Spartans for colluding in the overthrow of the democracy and the institution of the regime, claiming that the Thirty were elected (i.e., by the *demos*) after the destruction of the walls,⁶⁹ and it was the Thirty who summoned the Spartan garrison and *harmost* to enforce their government (Xen. *Hell.* 2.3.13–

---

63 See, e.g., Shear 2012; Teegarden 2014, 43–47; Azoulay 2014, 97–120; Pownall 2018.
64 Cf. Larran 2014, who convincingly argues that the chronological manipulation in conflating the Battle of Pallene with the expulsion of the Peisistratids allows Andocides to reconcile oligarchic and democratic readings of the distant past.
65 On the witch-hunting atmosphere in Athens in the years immediately following the restoration of democracy in 403, see e.g. Pownall 2018, 137–139.
66 Cf. the much more blatant errors in Plato's *Menexenus* in comparison with the other (i.e., non-parodic) *epitaphioi*; Pownall 2004, 49–58.
67 See, e.g., Carter 1986, esp. 56–75 and Jordović 2014.
68 Pownall 2012b; cf. Pownall 2018.
69 Xen. *Hell.* 2.3.11: οἱ δὲ τριάκοντα ᾑρέθησαν; cf. 2.3.2: ἔδοξε τῷ δήμῳ τριάκοντα ἄνδρας ἑλέσθαι (although this passage is usually thought to be interpolated).

14). In his description of the violence of the regime of the Thirty,[70] Xenophon is willing to adhere to the democratic master narrative to some extent, for it suited his own political ends to distance support of moderate oligarchy on the Spartan model from what he portrays as the extremist views of a lunatic fringe (as is particularly evident in his narrative of the showdown between the "radical" Critias and the "moderate" Theramenes). But when it came to the restoration of democracy in 403, Xenophon deliberately deviated from the master narrative, which carefully omitted the role of the Spartans, the memory of which was already contested.[71] Instead of focusing on the amnesty that is so prominent in the democratic tradition (for it reflected well upon the self-image of the Athenians as magnanimous), Xenophon attributes the end of the civil war and the ensuing reconciliation between the two sides at least as much to the behind-the-scenes negotiations of the Spartan king Pausanias as to the military victories of the democratic resistance (Xen. *Hell.* 2.4.28–39).[72] Xenophon's narrative is carefully designed to rehabilitate the Spartans as an integral part of the recuperation of oligarchy as a viable political system in fourth-century Athens.

Like Xenophon, Andocides adheres to the democratic master narrative in some respects, but deviates from it in others. It therefore seems likely that his goal was a similar one of advocating a moderate form of oligarchic ideology (based on an idealized version of the Spartan constitution), which would strike a balance between the radical democracy of the late fifth-century, where unscrupulous demagogues misled the *demos* into making disastrous decisions ultimately resulting in the fall of Athens in 404,[73] and the violent and bloodthirsty "tyranny" of the Thirty. In order to advocate this type of political program, Andocides not only had to dissociate moderate oligarchy from the Thirty (a goal easily achieved by alluding to the brutality of their regime), but more crucially had to address the role of the Spartans, who were considered synonymous with oligarchic ideology in late fifth- and early fourth-century Athens. Unlike the recent memory of the abuses of the Thirty, which was unassailable and not open to rehabilitation,[74] the participation of the Spartans in the events

---

70 Cf. Wolpert 2019.
71 Cf. Dillery 1995, 141, who observes that the most profound differences in the extant accounts of the Thirty centre around the exact time and extent of the Spartan interventions. On Lysias' suppression of the role of the Spartans, see Piovan 2011, esp. 63–65.
72 Pownall 2018, 146–150.
73 Cf. Thuc. 2.65.10–12.
74 As Steinbock 2013a, esp. 91–95 observes, the convenient fiction that the whole *demos* was in exile during the regime of the Thirty allowed speakers in Athens to demonstrate their democratic credentials and gain political capital by claiming that their family members joined the

of 404/3 remained contested, and therefore could be manipulated to fit his immediate rhetorical purposes.

In conclusion, Andocides' whitewashing of the role of the Spartans in the regime of the Thirty in the *De Pace* in no way diminishes his rhetorical stance as a supporter of the democracy, and more importantly reinforces his latent agenda of legitimizing a moderate oligarchy on the Spartan model as a way of restoring economic prosperity through peace instead of through war and imperial power. Thus, there is no contradiction between Andocides' elision of the Spartans from the overthrow of democracy and the imposition of the Thirty in the *De Pace* and his attempt to garner democratic credentials in his earlier two speeches; his political ideology remains consistent across his corpus. Andocides' subtle balancing act between upholding and undermining the stereotypical tenets of the democratic master narrative in his narrative of the recent past permits the *De Pace* to be read on multiple levels and to appeal to audiences with varying political perspectives. Nevertheless, when reworking the speech as a written version to be circulated among like-minded elites, Andocides highlights the subversive subtext of his arguments by resorting to more blatant than usual historical inaccuracies, endorsing an open appeal to *Machtpolitik* instead of cloaking Athenian imperialism in the usual moral platitudes, and deliberately failing to conform to (democratic) audience expectations. The use of the recent past as political capital in Athenian oratory was not limited to those who bought into the democratic master narrative.

Bibliography

Albini, U. (1964), *Andocide: De Pace*, Florence.
Azoulay, V. (2014), *Les tyrannicides d'Athènes: Vie et mort de deux statues*, Paris.
Bearzot, C. (2004–2005), "Ateniesi e Spartani reciproci salvatori: un topos tra retorica e storiografia", *Acta Classica Universitas Scientiarum Debreceniensis* 40–41, 17–32.
Bearzot, C. (2007), "Uomini ed eventi del passato spartano nell' oratoria attica", in: P. Desideri et al. (eds.), *Costruzione e uso del passato storico nella cultura antica*, Alessandria, 63–97.
Bearzot, C. (2017), "La συμφορά de la cité. La défaite d'Athènes (405-404 av. J.-C.) chez les orateurs attiques", *Ktèma* 42, 41–52.
Calhoun, G.M. (1913), *Athenian Clubs in Politics and Litigation*, Austin.

---

resistance in 404/3. Similarly, it allowed supporters of the Thirty, like Mantitheus in Lysias 16, to claim that they were absent from Athens during the rule of the Thirty; cf. Kapellos 2014a.

Canevaro, M./Gray, B. (2018), *The Hellenistic Reception of Classical Athenian Democracy and Political Thought*, Oxford.

Carawan, E. (2013), *The Athenian Amnesty and Reconstructing the Law*, Oxford.

Carey, C. (2005), "Propaganda and Competition in Athenian Oratory", in: K.A.E. Enenkel/I.L. Pfeijffer (eds.), *The Manipulative Mode: Political Propaganda in Antiquity*, Leiden/Boston, 65–99.

Carter, L.B. (1986), *The Quiet Athenian*, Oxford.

Chambers, J.T. (1975), "The Fourth-Century Athenians' View of their Fifth-Century Empire", *PP* 30, 177–191.

Clarke, S. (2021), *Demosthenes 8: On the Chersonese*, Liverpool.

Couvenhes, J.-C. (2012), "L'introduction des archers scythes, esclaves publics, à Athènes: la date et l'agent d'un transfert culturel", in: B. Legras (ed.), *Transferts culturels et droits dans le monde grec et hellénistique*, Paris, 99–118.

David, E. (2014), "An Oligarchic Democracy: Manipulation of Democratic Ideals by Athenian Oligarchs in 411 BC", *Eirene* 50, 11–38.

Dillery, J. (1995), *Xenophon and the History of His Times*, London/New York.

Dillery, J. (2017), "Xenophon: The Small Works", in: M.A. Flower (ed.), *The Cambridge Companion to Xenophon*, Cambridge, 195–220.

Edwards, M. (1995), *Greek Orators IV: Andocides*, Warminster.

Forsdyke, S. (2005), *Exile, Ostracism, and Democracy: The Politics of Expulsion in Ancient Greece*, Princeton.

Furley, W.D. (1996), *Andokides and the Herms: A Study of Crisis in Fifth-Century Athenian Religion*, London.

Gazzano, F. (1999), *Pseudo-Andocide: Contro Alcibiade*, Genoa.

Gray, B. (2015), *Stasis and Stability: Exile, the Polis, and Political Thought, c. 404–146 BC*, Oxford.

Grethlein, J. (2010), *The Greeks and Their Past: Poetry, Oratory, and History in the Fifth Century BCE*, Cambridge.

Gribble, D. (1999), *Alcibiades and Athens: A Study in Literary Presentation*, Oxford.

Hansen, M.H. (1984), "Two Notes on Demosthenes' Symbouleutic Speeches", *C & M* 35, 57–70.

Harding, P. (2006), *Didymos: On Demosthenes*, Oxford.

Harris, E.M. (1998), Review of *Greek Orators IV: Andocides* by M.J. Edwards, *CR* 48, 18–20.

Harris, E.M. (2000), "The Authenticity of Andokides' *De Pace*. A Subversive Essay", in: P. Flensted-Jensen et al. (eds.), *Polis & Politics: Studies in Ancient Greek History*, Copenhagen, 479–505.

Harris, E. (2021), "Major Events in the Recent Past in Assembly Speeches and the Authenticity of [Andocides] *On the Peace*", *Tekmeria* 16, 19–68.

Hubbard, T. (2008), "Getting the Last Word: Publication of Political Oratory as an Instrument of Historical Revisionism", in: E.A. Mackay (ed.), *Orality, Literacy, Memory in the Ancient Greek and Roman World*, Leiden, 185–202.

Jordović, I. (2014), "The Origins of Philolaconism", *C & M* 65, 127–154.

Kagan, D. (1987), *The Fall of the Athenian Empire*, Ithaca/London.

Kapellos, A. (2010), "Xenophon and Sparta's Reaction to the Execution of the Athenian Captives at Aegospotami", *PP* 65, 385–391.

Kapellos, A. (2011), "Xenophon, *Hell.* II 2, 23 – A Note", *PP* 66, 132–138.

Kapellos, A. (2014a), "*In Defense of Mantitheus*: Structure, Strategy and Argument in Lysias 16", *BICS* 57, 23–47.

Kapellos, A. (2014b), *Lysias 21: A Commentary*, Berlin.
Kapellos, A. (2018), "Lysander and the Execution of the Athenian Prisoners at Aegospotami (Xenophon, *Hell*. 2.1.31–32)", *Mnemosyne* 71, 394–407.
Kapellos, A. (2019), *Xenophon's Peloponnesian War*, Berlin.
Keen, A.G. (1995), "A 'Confused' Passage of Philochoros (F 149a) and the Peace of 392/1 B.C.", *Historia* 44, 1–10.
Keen, A.G. (1998), "Philochoros F 149 A & B: A Further Note", *Historia* 47, 375–378.
Kennedy, G.A. (1958), "The Oratory of Andocides", *AJP* 79, 32–43.
Krentz, P. (1982), *The Thirty in Athens*, Ithaca/London.
Krentz, P. (1995), *Xenophon: Hellenika II.3.11–IV.2.28*, Warminster.
Larran, F. (2014), "La bataille de Pallènè aura encore lieu ou Pisistrate dans les rets de l'analogisme historique d'Andocide", *DHA* 40, 53–73.
Loening, T.C. (1987), *The Reconciliation Agreement of 403/402 B.C. in Athens: Its Content and Application*, Stuttgart.
Loraux, N. (2002), *The Divided City: On Memory and Forgetting in Ancient Athens*, trans. Corinne Pache with Jeff Fort, New York.
MacDowell, D. (1962), *Andokides: On the Mysteries*, Oxford.
Magnetto, A. (2013), "Ambasciatori plenipotenziari delle città greche in età classica ed ellenistica: terminologia e prerogative", in: M. Mari/J. Thornton (eds.), *Parole in Movimento: Linguaggio Politico e Lessico Storiografico nel Mondo Ellenistico*, Pisa/Rome, 223–241.
Maltagliati, G. (2020), "Manipolare il passato, prefigurare il futuro: esempi storici, emozioni e deliberazione nell'oratoria attica", *Rhesis* 11, 290–298.
Missiou, A. (1992), *The Subversive Oratory of Andokides*, Cambridge.
Németh, G. (2006), *Kritias und die Dreissig Tyrannen*, Stuttgart.
Nouhaud, M. (1982), *L'Utilisation de l'histoire par les orateurs attiques*, Paris.
Ober, J. (1985), *Fortress Attica: Defense of the Athenian Land Frontier 404–322 BC*, Leiden.
Ober, J. (1998), *Political Dissent in Democratic Athens: Intellectual Critics of Popular Rule*, Princeton/Oxford.
Osborne, R./Rhodes, P.J. (eds.) (2017), *Greek Historical Inscriptions 478–404 BC*, Oxford.
Ostwald, M. (1986), *From Popular Sovereignty to the Sovereignty of Law*, Berkeley.
Piovan, D. (2011), *Memoria e oblio della guerra civile*, Pisa.
Pownall, F. (1995), "*Presbeis Autokratores*: Andocides' *De Pace*", *Phoenix* 49, 140–149.
Pownall, F. (2004), *Lessons from the Past: The Moral Use of History in Fourth-century Prose*, Ann Arbor.
Pownall, F. (2012a), "A Case Study in Isocrates: The Expulsion of the Peisistratids", *DHA*, Suppl. 8, Besançon, 329–344.
Pownall, F. (2012b), "Critias in Xenophon's *Hellenica*", *SCI* 31, 1–17.
Pownall, F. (2018), "Tyranny and Democracy in Isocrates and Xenophon", *Trends in Classics* 10, 137–153.
Rhodes, P.J. (1994), "The Ostracism of Hyperbolus", in: R. Osborne/S. Hornblower (eds.), *Ritual, Finance, Politics*, Oxford, 85–98.
Rhodes, P.J. (2016), "Heraclides of Clazomenae and an Athenian Treaty with Persia", *ZPE* 200, 177–186.
Roisman, J./Worthington, I. (2015), *Lives of the Attic Orators*, Oxford.
Sato, N. (2015), "'Aristocracy' in Athenian Democracy", in: N. Fisher/H. van Wees (eds.), *Aristocracy in Antiquity: Redefining Greek and Roman Elites*, Swansea, 203–226.

Shear, J.L. (2011), *Polis and Revolution: Responding to Oligarchy in Classical Athens*, Cambridge.
Shear, J.L. (2012), "The Tyrannicides, Their Cult, and the Panathenaea: A Note", *JHS* 132, 107–119.
Simonton, M. (2017a), *Classical Greek Oligarchy: A Political History*, Princeton/Oxford.
Simonton, M. (2017b), "Stability and Violence in Classical Greek Democracies and Oligarchies", *CA* 36, 52–103.
Steinbock, B. (2013a), "Contesting the Lessons from the Past: Aeschines' Use of Social Memory", *TAPA* 143, 65–103.
Steinbock, B. (2013b), *Social Memory in Athenian Public Discourse: Uses and Meaning of the Past*, Ann Arbor.
Stern, R. (2003), "The Thirty at Athens in the Summer of 404", *Phoenix* 57, 18–34.
Teegarden, D.A. (2014), *Death to Tyrants! Ancient Greek Democracy and the Struggle Against Tyrants*, Princeton.
Thomas, R. (1989), *Oral Tradition and Written Record in Classical Athens*, Cambridge.
Todd, S.C. (2000), *Lysias*, Austin.
Todd, S.C. (2020), *A Commentary on Lysias, Speeches 12–16*, Oxford.
Tordoff, R. (2017), "Memory and the Rhetoric of σωτηρία in Aristophanes' *Assembly Women*", in: E. Baragwanath/E. Foster (eds.), *Clio and Thalia. Attic Comedy and Historiography* (*Histos* Supplement 6), 153–210.
Tuci, P.A. (2020), "Persian Refugees in Ancient Greece", *Pallas* 112, 167–190.
Ueno, S. (2008), "Some Remarks on πρέσβεις αὐτοκράτορες", *Journal of Classical Studies* 56, 51–64 (in Japanese, but with a summary in English).
Usher, S. (2007), "Symbouleutic Oratory", in: I. Worthington (ed.), *A Companion to Greek Rhetoric*, Malden, MA/Oxford, 220–235.
Wolpert, A. (2002), *Remembering Defeat: Civil War and Civic Memory in Ancient Athens*, Baltimore.
Wolpert, A. (2006), "The Violence of the Thirty Tyrants", in: S. Lewis (ed.), *Ancient Tyranny*, Edinburgh, 213–223.
Wolpert, A. (2019), "Xenophon on the Violence of the Thirty", in: A. Kapellos (ed.), *Xenophon on Violence*, Berlin, 169–185.
Worthington, I. (1991), "Greek Oratory, Revision of Speeches and the Problem of Historical Reliability", *C & M* 42, 55–74.
Worthington, I. (1994), "History and Oratorical Exploitation", in: I. Worthington (ed.), *Persuasion: Greek Rhetoric in Action*, London/New York, 109–118.
Worthington, I. (1996), "Greek oratory and the Oral/Literate Division", in: I. Worthington (ed.), *Voice into Text: Orality and Literacy in Ancient Greece*, Leiden/New York, 165–178.
Yunis, H. (1996), *Taming Democracy: Models of Political Rhetoric in Classical Athens*, Ithaca/London.

Edward M. Harris
Recent Events in Assembly Speeches and [Andocides] *On the Peace*

Abstract: This chapter examines the accuracy of statements about the recent past in Demosthenes' speeches to the Assembly. In general, Demosthenes does not misrepresent recent events or existing relations between states; allusions to the past are also short; and there are no long narratives. Then he shows that the statements about the recent past in *On the Peace* attributed to Andocides are not reliable and could not have been delivered to the Assembly in 391 B.C. Statements about a treaty between Athens and the Great King, about Athenian control of Euboea, about the fleet of Athens and the walls of the city in 391 B.C. and about other matters are contradicted by Thucydides, Xenophon, Diodorus and other sources. The speaker also does not understand the institution of *presbeis autokratores*. These mistakes confirm the judgment of Dionysius of Halicarnassus that the speech is a forgery.

When a speaker addressed the Athenian Assembly, he had to be very careful not to misrepresent major events in the recent past if he were to maintain his credibility. Speakers often used examples from the past to support their arguments about what the Athenians should do in the future. For their arguments to convince, these examples had to be familiar to the voters in the Assembly and to be accurate. A speaker could not lie about major political events everyone had witnessed. If a politician wanted the Assembly to enact his proposals, he could not state that the Athenians won the battles of Aegospotami[1] and Chaeronea[2] or that the Spartans won the battle of Leuctra or refer to treaties that never existed. A speaker could not misrepresent the causes of a recent war nor make errors about contemporary institutions.

This essay will start by reviewing the statements made by Demosthenes about major recent events in his speeches to the Assembly and show that they

---

I would like to thank Alberto Esu and David Lewis for reading over drafts of this essay. This is a short version of an essay published in *Tekmeria* 16 (2021), 19–68.

1 Cf. Piovan in this volume.
2 Cf. Crick in this volume.

are accurate and confirmed by other sources. These statements about familiar events also tend to be brief and to the point.³ The rest of the essay will show that the speech *On the Peace* attributed to Andocides makes major mistakes about contemporary and recent events and uses the term *presbeis autokratores* in a way that reveals the author of this work was not familiar with the institution. All this evidence confirms the judgement of Dionysius of Halicarnassus that the speech is not a genuine work of Andocides and the doubts of Harpocration about its authenticity.⁴

1 Major events in Demosthenes' public speeches

The historical allusions will be examined in the order the speeches were delivered.

The speech *On the Symmories* (14), delivered in 354/3, contains few allusions to contemporary events, but they are all confirmed by other sources. Demosthenes (14.13) says that the Athenians have about three hundred triremes available, which is close the figure found in the naval records the year 353/2 (*IG* II² 1613, lines 284–292).⁵ Demosthenes (10.19, 27) states that the taxable property available for the *eisphora* is 6,000 talents, which is close to the figure given for the year 378/7 by Polybius (2.62.6–7). Demosthenes also alludes to revolts by Orontes and the Egyptians, which are attested in other sources.⁶ And

---

3 On the expression "you all know" see Pearson 1941 and Canevaro 2019.
4 Earlier scholars have accepted the authenticity of *On the Peace* as a genuine work of Andocides. See for example, Hamilton 1979, 234–237, Missiou 1992, Edwards 1995, 107–108, MacDowell in Gagarin and MacDowell 1998, 148–158. My arguments against authenticity in Harris 2000 have been accepted by Martin 2009, 220 n. 4, Couvenhes 2012, 109–114, Conwell 2008, 220, Zaccarini 2017, 34 n. 46 ("probably a gross forgery") and Canevaro 2019, 140. Rhodes 2016 replies to my points but his arguments are not convincing. Magnetto 2013 only discusses my analysis of the term *presbeis autokratores*. See my reply below. This essay adds more evidence to the evidence presented in Harris 2000 and modifies some of the analyses in that essay. In this volume F. Pownall speculates that Andocides revised his speech to make it more appropriate for aristocratic readers. In my opinion, there is no reason to believe that orators ever revised speeches in this way and for this reason (Pownall does not cite any parallels). Besides, the mistakes such as the misuse of the term *presbeis autokratores* cannot be explained in this way. In this chapter I present evidence against authenticity, which Pownall does not consider.
5 See Gabrielsen 1994, 126–129.
6 For these revolts see Briant 2002, 662–666, 682–685.

the information Demosthenes gives about naval equipment is consistent with the epigraphic evidence.[7]

The speech *On the Freedom of the Rhodians* (15), delivered in 351/0, contains several allusions to recent events. Desmosthenes (15.3–4) alludes to the recent revolt from the Second Athenian Confederacy by Chios, Byzantium and Rhodes, which is confirmed by Diodorus (15.7.3). Demosthenes (5.9–10) also mentions the orders given to Timotheus about aid to the satrap Ariobarzanes and the conquest of Samos, which is confirmed by other sources (Ariobarzanes: Diod. 15.90–92; Samos: Isocr. 15.11).[8] The information Demosthenes (15.19) gives about oligarchs at Mytilene is confirmed in part by the eighth letter of Isocrates to the leaders there. Demosthenes (15.22, 24) also alludes to two events much earlier in the fourth century. First, he mentions that during the Thirty several Athenian exiles went to Argos (Diod. 14.6.2). Second, he mentions the unsuccessful attempt of Cyrus and Clearchus to overthrow the Persian king in 401 which is recounted at length in Xenophon's *Anabasis* (1.1–10.19). Finally, Demosthenes (15.27, 29) alludes to the King's Peace, which was concluded in 387/6 (Diod. 14.110.2–4; Xen. *Hell.* 5.1. 31 — see below for detailed discussion. In what follows all references to Xenophon are to the *Hellenica*) and was still in effect.

The speech *On the Megalopolitans* was delivered in 353/2 (D. H. *Amm.* 4) and concerns mainly events in the Peloponnese. The statements of Demosthenes accurately portray the situation there and elsewhere. Demosthenes (16.4, 25, 28) says that the Thebans have not allowed the cities of Orchomenus, Thespiae, and Plataea to be resettled, which is consistent with other information about their status at the time (Diod. 15.46.6; 79.3–6; Pausanias 9.1.4–8). Demosthenes (16.6) is also correct in recalling that the Athenians fought with the Spartans against the Thebans at the battle of Mantinea (Xen. 7; Diod. 15.84.4–87.6). The alliance between Athens and Messene mentioned by Demosthenes (16.6) is confirmed by Pausanias (4.28.2). Demosthenes (16.16) implies that Elis had lost Triphylia and alludes to a dispute over Tricaranum, which are also recounted by Xenophon (7.1.26; 4.4). Demosthenes (11–13, 18) also mentions Theban control over Oropus, which is confirmed by several other sources (Xen. 7.4.1; Aesch. 3.85; Diod. 15.76.1; Plut. *Dem*.5).

The *First Philippic* is dated by Dionysius of Halicarnassus (*Amm.* 4) to 352/1 and discusses the situation in Northern and Central Greece. Demosthenes (4.4–6) gives accurate information about the loss of Pydna, Potidaea, and Methone (see below) and about Athenian expeditions to Euboea, Haliartus and Thermopylae

---

[7] See Gabrielsen 1994, 146–169 with *IG* II^2 1604–1632.
[8] For discussion of Demosthenes' account of Timotheus' actions see Canevaro 2019, 154–155.

(Dem. 4.17 with Aesch. 3.85; Diod. 16.7.2; *IG* II² 124 [Euboea]; Xen. 3.5.18–19 [Haliartus]; Diod. 16.38.1 [Thermopylae]). He is also correct about the Athenian defeat of the Spartans at Corinth in 393 (Diod. 14.91.2–3). Demosthenes (4.27) gives accurate information about the hipparch at Lemnos ([Arist.] *Ath. Pol.* 61.6) and about Thasos and Skiathos as Athenian allies (*IG* II² 43, lines A86, B3).[9] His criticism of the Athenians for trying generals two or three times on capital charges is slightly exaggerated but has a large element of truth (Dem. 4.47).[10]

The three speeches about Olynthus were delivered in 349/8 (D.H. *Amm.* 4; Philochorus BNJ 328F 49–51) and also concern the situation in Northern Greece.[11] Demosthenes repeatedly mentions the cities captured in this area, defeats that are confirmed by other sources: Amphipolis (Dem. 1.5; 12; 2.6 with Diod. 16.6.2), Potidaea (Dem. 1.9; 2.7 with Diod. 16.8.5), Pydna (Dem. 1.5, 12 with Diod. 16.82.2–3), and Methone (Dem. 1.9 with Diod. 16.31.6; 34.4–5). There is not as much evidence in the sources about Thessaly in this period (Diod. 16.38.1), but Demosthenes' statements are not inconsistent with what is known about Philip's influence there (Dem. 1.13, 21–22; 2.11).[12] Demosthenes states that the Phocians desperately need help, which is in line with information supplied by Diodorus (16.37.3–38.2). The allusions of Demosthenes (1.13) to campaigns against Illyrians, Paeonians and Arybbas are confirmed by inscriptions (*IG* II² 127; *IG* II³ 1, 411).[13] The statement of Demosthenes (2.14) about Timotheus's campaigns against Olynthus is also confirmed (Nepos *Timotheus* 1.2; Polyaenus *Strat.* 3.10.7, 14; *IG* II² 110 [363/2]).

On the Peace was delivered in late 346 after the conclusion of the Peace of Philocrates (D. H. *Amm.* 4). At the beginning of his speech Demosthenes (5.5) alludes to the recent defeat of the Athenians on Euboea, which is recounted by Plutarch (*Phocion* 12–14) and mentioned in *Against Meidias* (Dem. 21.110). His statement that Argos, Messene and Megalopolis are hostile to Sparta (Dem. 5.18)

---

9 On Thasos see also Dem. 20.59 with Canevaro 2016, 291–292 with references to earlier discussions.
10 For trials of generals see Hansen 1975, 63–64.
11 On these speeches see Herrman 2019. On Demosthenes' portrayal of Philip in these speeches and elsewhere see Harris 2018. The distortions in this case relate to the internal affairs of the Macedonians, about which the average person in the Assembly had no knowledge.
12 Rhodes and Osborne 2003, 225 and Worthington 2008, 64–66 mistakenly believe that Philip was archon of Thessaly at this time. See Harris 1995, 175–176; Dmitriev 2011, 411–420; and Helly 2018, 139–150.
13 Errington 1975 and Heskel 1988 plausibly place the campaign against Arybbas around 350, but Griffith 1979, 504–509, followed by Rhodes and Osborne 2003, 353–355, place the campaign in 342, which is less likely.

is accurate as we saw in the speech *On the Megalopolitans*. His statements that the Phocians had seized Orchomenos and Coronea during the Third Sacred War and that the Thebans recovered them in 346 are certainly true (Dem. 5.20; Diod. 16.56.2), and the statement that the Thebans controlled Oropus at the time is also true as we saw above (Dem. 5.10, 16). Aeschines (2.119–120) corroborates the predictions made about Philip's intentions earlier that year (Dem. 5.10).

The *Second Philippic* was delivered in 344/3 (D. H. *Amm.* 4) and mentions several of the incidents discussed in earlier speeches regarding Amphipolis, Potidaea, and Olynthus (Dem. 6.17) and Philip's control of Thermopylae and the Phocians (Dem. 6.29, 35, 36). What is curious is that Demosthenes (6.11) also recalls the invitation from the Persian King brought by King Alexander of Macedon to the Athenians inviting them to rule Greece in return for obedience and the Athenian refusal, which is recounted by Herodotus (8.136, 140–143). Demosthenes (6.14) also alludes to Theban collaboration with the Persians during the Persian Wars (Hdt. 7.132). Both these events took place over one hundred and thirty years earlier.

The *Third Philippic* was delivered in 342/1 and contains many allusions to recent events. Demosthenes repeats many of his accusations about the events of 346 such as Philip's seizure of towns in Thrace during the peace (15) and the "destruction of the Phocians" (19, 26, 68). The first is misleading because Philip did capture these towns but not during the peace,[14] and the second an exaggeration because Philip only imposed a settlement that weakened the Phocians, but they are not false. Demosthenes (9.12) again alludes to Philip's control of Thessaly as he did in earlier speeches and mentions Philip's attempt on Megara (Dem. 9.17–18), which may be confirmed by a passage in Plutarch (*Phocion* 15). His statement that Philip administered the Pythian games in 346 is accurate (Dem. 9.32 with Diod. 16.60.2), and the information about the Athenians chasing out Plutarchus is also accurate (Dem. 9.57 with Plut. *Phocion* 12–14). Another section (59–62. Cf. 12, 17, 18) contains a discussion of the situation in Euboea and states that at Oreus Philistides, Menippus, Socrates, Thoas and Agapaeus controlled the city in Philip's interest. All these names are not mentioned in other sources, but the role of Philistides is confirmed by a fragment of Philochorus (BNJ 328 F 157. Cf. Stephanus of Byzantium *Ethnika* s.v. Oreus). His statement about the Theban victory at Leuctra is accurate (Dem. 9.23).[15] The figure of thirteen years for Philip's attacks on the Greeks would place the start of his

---

14 See Harris 1995, 79–80.
15 For discussion see Herrman 2019, 223.

aggression around 354, which is debatable but not unreasonable (Dem. 9.25).¹⁶ Yet one needs to take the rhetorical context into account here because Demosthenes wishes to contrast Philip's many crimes done in a short space of time with the crimes committed by the Athenians and the Spartans over a longer period of time.¹⁷

On the Chersonnese was delivered in 342/1 (D. H. *Amm.* 4), but large parts of it (Dem. 8.38–51, 52–67) are repeated in the *Fourth Philippic* (11–27, 55–70). Demosthenes once more mentions the tyrants in Euboea (36), and the capture of Olynthus by treachery (40), and the Athenian "liberation" of Euboea in 357 (73–75). Much of the speech is devoted to a discussion of Diopeithes' activities in the Chersonnese, which appears to be confirmed by evidence from the hypothesis to the speech, which may draw on independent sources.

In the *Fourth* Philippic, which was delivered in 342/1 or 341/0 (see Didymus col. 1.30), Demosthenes repeats much of the information found in earlier speeches about Serrion and Doriscus (8), Euboea (8, 9), Megara (9), Amphipolis (12), Potidaea (12), Thebes and Phocis (47), Olynthus (64) and Thrace (65), which we have found to be reliable. In one section he discusses Athenian relations with the Persian king, information which is confirmed by other sources. Demosthenes (10.31–32) mentions the Benefactors of the King, whose existence is well attested,¹⁸ and alludes to the arrest of Hermias, which is discussed at length by Didymus (cols. 4.59–6.62), and to cooperation between Perinthus and the satraps of Asia Minor (Dem. 10.31–33), which is also confirmed by Didymus (cols. 4.1–15). In the same section Demosthenes (10.34) refers to the help the Persian king gave the Athenians during the Corinthian War and his recent offer to help them again, which is confirmed by a fragment of Philochorus (BNJ 328 F 157).

A study of the use of recent events in Demosthenes' speeches to the Assembly reveals that the orator is generally reliable and accurate. What is also striking is that almost every mention of recent events is very brief, often only a few words, and never more than a few sentences. There are no lengthy narratives of past history in the speeches to the Assembly.

---

16 See Herrman 2019, 225.
17 For a similar case of Demosthenes' manipulation of dates see Dem. 21.154 with Harris 1989, 121–125. Daix and Fernandez 2017, 403 believe that the text may have been corrupted, but the evidence of Plutarch *Demosthenes* 12 and *POxy* 11: 1378, col. ii, 19–21 show that the reading of the manuscripts was the reading in antiquity.
18 Briant 2002, 303–304.

2 Events in the fifth century B.C. in *On the Peace*, Aeschines and other sources

We can now turn to the speech *On the Peace* attributed to Andocides. The speech purports to have been delivered in 391 when the Greeks had been fighting the Corinthian War, which began in 395, for four years (20). This paper will concentrate on events in the recent past mentioned in *On the Peace* and not discuss the events in the more distant past mentioned in the narrative given at the beginning of the speech (3–9) and their relationship to a similar but not identical account given by Aeschines (2.172–177).[19] Yet one needs to bear in mind what we observed in the previous section: speakers in the Assembly do not give long accounts of past events but refer to them briefly and succinctly. By contrast, lengthy accounts of past events occur in forensic speeches like Theramenes' career (Lys. 12.62–78), the siege of Plataea ([Dem.] 59.94–107), Philip's victory at Chaeronea (Lyc. 1.37–54), Charidemus' career (Dem. 23.144–211), and Philip's arrival at Elateia and Demosthenes' reaction in 339 (Dem. 18.169–180). This makes sense: speakers in the Assembly could not make long speeches, but litigants in court had up to three hours in a public case ([Arist.] *Ath. Pol.* 67.2–4). If therefore we take into account the way speakers in the Assembly used historical material, we would expect the account of Aeschines in *On the False Embassy* (2.172–177) to be much longer than the account of the same events in *On the Peace* ([Andoc.] 3.3–9), but we find the opposite: the account in the *On the Peace* is slightly longer in several places.[20] The person who composed *On the Peace* was clearly not familiar with the different discursive protocols of the Assembly and law courts. He took what he found in Aeschines' speech and added to this material but committed more errors.[21]

---

19 I discussed these events in Harris 2000, 480–487 and show how *On the Peace* makes more errors than Aeschines. Rhodes 2016, 183 admits that *On the Peace* makes more errors, but claims that 'Aeschines perpetuates fewer errors because of the way in which he is reusing the text.' Rhodes does not notice that Aeschines explicitly states that he is recalling these events to show the advantages of peace and the disadvantages of peace, which would lead us to expect that he would alter evidence to make it more compelling for his argument. But Aeschines (2.175) states that the Athenians had three hundred triremes during peace while *On the Peace* (9) puts the number at over four hundred, which is the opposite of what we would expect.
20 This point escapes Rhodes 2016, 183.
21 For a similar case with a forged document (Andoc. 1.96–98) see Harris 2013/2014 with a detailed refutation of Sommerstein 2014. Recently scholars have recognized that the evidence

In the lawcourts, it was not unusual for litigants to mention their ancestors by name. In orations delivered in the Assembly, however, speakers do not as a rule mention their ancestors by name.[22] In *On the Peace* (6, 29) we find the names of Andocides, the grandfather of Andocides, and of Epilycus, the uncle of Andocides. This is without parallel in all the preserved speeches given in the Assembly and provides additional evidence against authenticity.

Additional evidence against authenticity is provided by the mistakes about recent events in *On the Peace*. In Aeschines (2.175) one reads that the Athenians held Euboea during the Peace of Nicias. This is confirmed by other evidence. Thucydides (1.114.3) reports that Pericles recovered all of Euboea after its revolt in 447/6. Carystus sent a contingent for the expedition of Nicias against Corinth in 425, and Eretria, Chalcis and Carystus sent troops for the Sicilian expedition (4.24; 43.4; 7.57.4). Thucydides (8.95.7) later states that all of Euboea except Oreos revolted in 411. The Assessment list of 425 corroborates this information (*IG* I³ 71): the list includes the cities of Carystus (line 70), Styra (line 74), Chalcis (line 71), Eretria (line 67), the Diakrians (lines 79, 83–84, 92–93), Dion (line 78) and Athenai Diades.[23] But *On the Peace* (9) erroneously states that the Athenians held only two thirds of Euboea during this period, which was only a little over twenty years before 391. As we observed in the previous section, speakers in the Assembly do not make this kind of mistake about recent events.

One can add more examples of serious mistakes about recent major events. After their defeat in war, *On the Peace* (39) states that the Spartans took their walls and their ships as security (ἐνέχυρα). The use of ἐνέχυρα in an account of interstate relations is without parallel. A participial phrase then explains what this expression means: the Spartans took the ships of the Athenians and destroyed their walls. The speech continues by asserting that the Spartan ambassadors are now in Athens 'returning the securities' (ἀποδιδόντες) and allowing them to acquire walls and ships.[24] In an earlier section, *On the Peace* (36) states that if the Athenians accept the treaty, ships and the walls will return to the city, which implies that the Athenians did not have them at the time. This contains several serious errors. First, Xenophon (2.2.20) states that the Athenians surren-

---

against the authenticity of this document is overwhelming and rejected Sommerstein's flawed analysis. See Liddel 2020, 79 and Dilts and Murphy 2018, vi.

22 See Harris 2016. Alcibiades mentions his ancestors in his speech to the Assembly in 415 (Thuc. 6.16.1–3), but he does not name any of them.

23 The Athenians also had a cleruchy at Hestiaea. See Thuc. 1.114.3; Plut. *Per.* 23.4; *IG* I³ 41. For Athenian control of all of Euboea see Meiggs 1972, 565–570.

24 Edwards 1995, 199 and MacDowell in Gagarin and MacDowell 1998, 157 do not discuss this statement.

dered all their ships except for twelve. The Athenians were able to rebuild their navy earlier than 391 and contributed ships to the fleet commanded by Conon and Pharnabazus in the victory at Cnidus in 394 (Xen. 4.3.10–12. Cf. Diod. 14.83.4–7). Shortly after this, Conon had an Athenian fleet at his disposal (Xen. 4.8.9, 12). Second, according to Xenophon, the Athenians were also required to tear down their walls after their defeat though Lysias (13.14) says that the Athenians destroyed only the Long Walls and the fortifications of the Peiraeus. The Athenians rebuilt their walls not because the Spartans permitted them to do so in 391 but because they were in a position to do so as early as 395/4. (Cf. Philochorus (BNJ 328 F 40 with *SEG* 19: 145; *IG* II² 1660). Xenophon (4.8.9–10. Cf. Diod. 14.85.3; Dem. 20.68, 72–74) also places the reconstruction of the walls at this time.[25]

The expression ἐνέχυρα may be an odd way of referring to the act of destroying the wall, but what *On the Peace* states about the ships is very clear: the Spartans took them in 404 and are now returning them. One cannot transform the participle ἀποδιδόντες into a 'figurative' way of stating that the proposed terms 'would allow Athens to keep (...) its (new) ships.' If the author wanted to express the idea of 'allowing to keep,' he would not have used the participle ἀποδιδόντες ('giving back'). One should not place words in the text ('its [rebuilt] walls and its [new] ships' — there is nothing corresponding to 'rebuilt' and 'new' in the Greek of the passage) that are not in our manuscripts.[26] The text plainly states that the Spartans took the ships and are now returning them; the wording of the passage is clear as it stands and cannot be explained away as 'figurative.' Elsewhere in *On the Peace* (36), the speaker says that the Athenians will have walls and ships in the future as a result of the treaty (36: τείχη καὶ νῆες εἰ γενήσονται τῇ πόλει), which clearly implies that they do not have them at the present moment. In the following section (37) the speaker also implies that the Athenians do not have walls and ships right now by telling them 'if you wish now too (i.e. to acquire them), get them for yourselves.' Earlier the speaker says that the Spartans now are 'are giving (διδόασιν) to us the walls and the ships and the islands to be ours' (23). One does not give to someone else objects he

---

25 Cf. Theocharaki 2020, 27–28, who does not see how this information clashes with the information in *On the Peace*.
26 This is done by Rhodes 2016, 185.

already possesses.²⁷ These passages must have been written long after 391 by someone who knew very little about the historical circumstances of the period.

Let us turn to the statement in *On the Peace* (28. Cf. 32) that in 391 the Athenians faced a choice between joining with the Argives in a war against Sparta and making peace with Sparta as the Boeotians have done. Now if *On the Peace* is a genuine speech and dated to 391, the negotiations to which the speaker refers must have taken place after the failed negotiations of 392 reported in Xenophon (4.8.12–16). But according to *On the Peace* (20. Cf. 13) the Boeotians made peace with the Spartans and allowed the city of Orchomenos to be free and independent. Later the speaker claims that the choice facing the Athenians is between making war on Sparta with the Argives or making peace alongside the Boeotians (28. Cf. 32). This is contradicted by Xenophon (5.1.28–36) and Diodorus (14.110.2–4), who state that Thebes was still at war with Sparta in 387/6 and had not yet recognized the independence of the Boeotian cities. In the earlier negotiations, no promise was made to the Athenians about control of the islands of Lemnos, Skyros and Imbros, but according to *On the Peace* (14) the Spartans were making this promise in 391. This guarantee was not offered until 387/6. *On the Peace* (27) also states that the Argives had concluded a separate peace, but forbade the Athenians to make peace with the Spartans yet want to make war against them at the same time, which makes little sense. This also clashes with the evidence of Xenophon and Diodorus.

The speaker warns the Athenians not to repeat the error of supporting weak allies and abandoning strong allies, an error that they have made in the past. To support his point, the speaker adduces three examples in chronological order (29–31). First (πρῶτον), the Athenians made a treaty with the Great King negotiated by his uncle Epilycus but were persuaded by Amorges, the runaway slave of the Great King, to choose his friendship, which caused the Great King to side with the Spartans and give them five thousand talents until Athens was defeated. Second, when the Syracusans came to offer the Athenians their friendship, the Athenians chose to support the people of Egesta, which led to the defeat in Sicily. Third and later (ὕστερον), the Argives persuaded the Athenians to sail against Laconia while they were at peace with the Spartans, which led to their defeat in the Peloponnesian War.

Before examining the statements about these incidents, it is important to note the temporal sequence. According to *On the Peace*, the support for Amor-

---

27 The translation of Edwards 1995, 123 is very misleading and inaccurate: "offering to us to keep our walls, ships and islands." One cannot translate διδόασιν as "offering," and there is nothing in the Greek corresponding to "to keep" in Edwards' English translation.

ges came first, followed by the campaign in Sicily and finally the decision to side with Argos. Thucydides reports that the support for Amorges came in the late summer of 412 (8.28.2–4), the decision to support Egesta in 415 (6.6–8), and the decision to support Argos in the summer of 414 (6.105). Even though these events took place less than twenty five years before 391, the author has made a serious mistake about the date of the support for Amorges.[28]

Let us examine the second and third events. The story of the Syracusan invitation to conclude a treaty of friendship is contradicted by the narrative of Thucydides (6.6–8).[29] Once again, *On the Peace* makes a serious mistake about recent history. On the other hand, the Athenian support for Argos and its diplomatic consequences, which led to a resumption of hostilities, is confirmed by Thucydides (6.105; 7.18).

To return to the first example. Thucydides mentions Amorges in four passages. In the winter of 413/2 Tissaphernes sends an envoy to Sparta to offer financial assistance against the Athenians in Asia, one of his motives being to capture alive or kill Amorges, the bastard son of Pissuthnes, who had revolted (8.5.4–5). This passage does not indicate whether the Athenians were supporting Amorges at this time or not. Later after the revolts in Asia, when some ships from Chios sail to Anaia, the Spartan commander Chalcideus orders them to return home and that Amorges is about to arrive by land with troops (8.19.1–2), but nothing is said about Athenian support for Amorges. In the later summer of 412 Tissaphernes persuades the Peloponnesians to make an assault by sea against Iasos, which is the headquarters of Amorges and his mercenaries. This attack succeeds because the ships are thought to be Athenian. The Peloponnesians capture Amorges alive and turn him over to Tissaphernes. The fact that Amorges appears to have been expecting Athenian help is the first indication of any relationship between Amorges and the Athenians (8.28.2–4). During the following winter Peisander had Phrynichus dismissed by accusing him of betraying Amorges and Iasos. Thucydides (8.54.3) considers the charge false, a slander designed to remove an enemy of Alcibiades. There are two issues here: first, the relative chronology of Athenian support for Amorges and the offer of Persian support to Sparta (which occurred first?), and, second, the causal rela-

---

28 Cf. Westlake 1989, 108 sees the mistake but still assumes that *On the Peace* is a genuine speech of Andocides.
29 Rhodes 2016, 185, Edwards 1995, 199, and Harris 2000, 496–497.

tionship between the two events (did Athenian support for Amorges cause the Persians to support Sparta?).[30]

It is clear that Thucydides does not indicate that the revolt of Amorges occurred before the embassy sent by Tissaphernes and the start of Persian aid to Sparta. It has been suggested that an inscription dated to the eighth prytany of 415/4, that is, March of 415, and recording a payment to an Athenian general ἐν Ἐφ[–] (*IG* I² 302, line 69 = *IG* I³ 370, line 79) was made to a general at Ephesus and that 'Athenian support for Amorges would be a reason for a general being there.'[31] As Westlake rightly noted, other explanations for the general's presence at Ephesus are more likely and an Athenian expedition to support Amorges would have been sent to Miletus or Iasos.[32] The passage about the embassy requires further scrutiny. Thucydides (8.5.4) states that Tissaphernes had recently been appointed 'general' either of 'the people of the lower part (i.e. western part of the Persian Empire)' or 'of the lower (i.e. western) areas' (τῶν κάτω).[33] Whatever his precise remit, the instructions he had received from the Great King were clear: he was in the process of collecting payments of tribute (φόρους) from those in the area of his command, which he owed (ἐπωφείλησεν) because he was unable to collect from the Greek cities because of the Athenians. This tribute was assessed in the time of Artaphernes, and the assessment continued until the lifetime of Herodotus even when the king could not collect the taxes.[34] The passage clearly indicates that the reason why Tissaphernes wanted the alliance with the Spartans was because he thought that he stood a better chance of collecting the tribute if he could damage the Athenians. The main reason for the alliance has nothing to do with Athenian support for Amorges. Tissaphernes wants to attack the Athenians because they are preventing him from accomplishing his task of collecting tribute, something *On the Peace* does

---

30 Rhodes 2016, 185 admits that Thucydides "does not make it clear when Athens began to support Amorges' and "does not give Athens' support for Amorges as Persia's reason for supporting Sparta." Rhodes does not list the incidents found in *On the Peace* in the order they are given in the speech and therefore fails to note the error in chronology. Rhodes admits that the statement about the Syracusan embassy "probably is a mistake," the statement about Amorges "may well not be" without giving a reason and without taking into account the evidence of Thucydides.
31 Wade–Gery 1958, 222–223; Andrewes 1961, 5 and Lewis 1977, 86.
32 Westlake 1989, 105–106. Westlake suggests that suspicions about the loyalty of Ephesus or a mission to collect tribute are more likely explanations. Thonemann 2009, 174 with 187 note 59 arbitrarily dismisses Westlake's analysis without giving any reasons.
33 For the debate about his position see Andrewes 1981, 13–16 (military commander of western Asia Minor) and Hornblower 2008, 776–777 (military commander and satrap).
34 See Hdt. 6.42.2 with Murray 1966.

not mention. The attack on the Athenians therefore has nothing to do with any support for Amorges but with their interference with Tissaphernes' financial obligations. This is a completely different explanation for the alliance with the Spartans than the one given in *On the Peace*. One should also note that Thucydides separates the aim of harming the Athenians from the aim of capturing Amorges, which suggests that the two objectives were strictly separate. If the Athenians were helping Amorges at this time, the attack on the Athenians would have been linked to this aim. Thucydides (2.65) elsewhere in his history does not give Athenian support for Amorges as one of the reasons by the Athenians lost the war.[35] One cannot reconcile the information given by Thucydides and that given by *On the Peace*.

Yet we can go further. *On the Peace* (29) claims that when the Athenians sent help to Amorges, there was a treaty between the Athenians and the Great King concluded by Epilycus. On the other hand, the passage in Thucydides about Tissaphernes clearly implies that there was no treaty between the Athenians and the Persians at this time. First, the Great King could not expect his officer to collect tribute from territories subject to Athens if he had a treaty with him. Several sources indicate that there a treaty earlier in the fifth century, known today as the Peace of Callias. This treaty granted the Athenians control the cities in Western Asia Minor, which were members of the Delian League. Some scholars have questioned the reliability of the sources for this treaty, but recent studies have shown that the objections are groundless.[36] This treaty imposed limits on Persian movements. The sources differ on the precise boundaries of these limits: Diodorus (12.4.5) states that no large ship (i.e. military vessel) was to sail beyond Phaselis and Kyaneai and that Persian satraps were not to approach the sea (i.e. the Aegean) within a three days' journey while Isocrates (12.59) places the limit for ships at Phaselis and the limit an army at the River Halys. If these terms were still in effect, Tissaphernes would not have been able to collect any tribute from the Greek cities in Western Asia Minor.

The Peace of Callias was concluded with king Artaxerxes I (Diod. 12.4.4), who died in 424. According to Thucydides (4.50), Aristides, son of Archippus, captured at Eion a Persian Artaphernes, who was on his way to Sparta from the King of Persia. Artaphernes was carrying letters in Assyrian characters from the King, who stated that despite several Spartan embassies, he could not under-

---

35 Westlake 1989, 109.
36 Rhodes 2016, 178 n. 6 believes that the treaty was forged in the fourth century but see especially Meiggs 1972, 487–495 and Badian 1993b, 1–72 with the modifications of Samons 1998 for full discussion of the evidence.

stand what the Spartans wanted because the ambassadors never said the same thing and asked them to send men back with Artaphernes. The Athenians then sent Artaphernes in a trireme to Ephesus with their own embassy. There they learned that Artaxerxes had recently died and returned home, that is, without continuing their journey to the Persian King. This is one of the most frustrating passages in Thucydides, but the diplomatic implications of the king's death are clear: the Peace of Callias was no longer in effect because the Athenians had made the treaty not with the Persian state, a political entity that did not exist, but with Artaxerxes, the Persian King (for the Persian King himself swearing the oaths see *IG* II^2 34, lines 6–7: τὰς οὔσας συνθῆκας]|[ἃ]ς ὤμοσεν βασιλ[εὺς). After the death of Artaxerxes, the treaty lapsed and to take effect anew would have to be sworn by his successor Darius. Now if the treaty of Epilycus was a renewal of the Peace of Callias with the same terms, then Tissaphernes would not have been able to collect tribute from the Greek cities on the coast. The fact that the Persian King expected Tissaphernes to collect tribute from these cities indicates that as far as he was concerned, there was no treaty with the Athenians at this point.[37] And if Tissaphernes thought that he was free to harm the Athenians and make an alliance with their enemies the Spartans, Tissaphernes also obviously thought that he was not bound by the terms of any treaty with the Athenians. Now if the Athenians or Tissaphernes violated a treaty concluded by Epilycus, why does Thucydides not say so? Thucydides is very attentive to such violations of interstate agreements. The entire debate in Athens about the treaty with Corcyra reflects a keen awareness of this potential implication of this agreement for the Thirty Years Peace between Athens and Sparta (Thuc. 1.31–44). Thucydides is also careful to record the alleged Spartan violations of the truce with Sparta in 425 (4.16; 23) and lays much emphasis on the Athenian violation of the Peace of Nicias in 414 (6.105). The information provided by Thucydides therefore contradicts *On the Peace* not only about the reason for the Persian decision to support Sparta but also about the existence of a treaty between Athens and the Persian

---

[37] Cf. Stockton 1959, 66–67 ("Either the Great King had a legal title to these revenues, or he had not. If he had, the Athenians were breaking their bond by preventing the King's representative from collecting them. If, however, by the Peace of Callias he had surrendered his title to such revenues, then we have here an open avowal by the King that he is not longer ready to abide by the terms of the Peace. Whichever alternative we choose, the Peace of Callias must be highly relevant, if it existed. Yet it seems that Thucydides is not of this mind; nor do we find Tissaphernes taking the obvious step of remonstrating with Athens over her obstructive attitude – he just turns to Sparta."). Stockton was arguing against the existence of the Peace of Callias, but the argument is directed against the alleged Peace of Epilycus as an extension of the Peace of Callias.

king in 412.³⁸ It should come as no surprise that *On the Peace* has invented a treaty that never existed. If the author of this work could invent an embassy and an offer of friendship from Syracuse that never occurred and could claim that the Athenians had no walls or fleet in 391, this author was quite capable of fabricating a treaty to score a rhetorical point. The speech *On the Peace* was clearly not written for delivery in the Athenian Assembly but for a performance in a rhetorical school sometime after the Classical period.

This finding advances our understanding of relations between Athens and the Persian king in the fifth century. The Persians made no attempt to renew the peace treaty after the death of Artaxerxes on 424 because the situation had changed. Instead of the unchallenged power in Greece, the Athenians were now at war with Sparta. Even after the Peace of Nicias, the Persian king could bide his time and wait for an opportunity to claim his ancestral lands in Western Asia Minor. When he did renew these claims in 412, he was no longer bound by the terms of any treaty and was free to support the enemies of Athens. We also do not have to explain why Thucydides neglected to mention the alleged Peace of Epilycus or to state that either the Persians or the Athenians violated this treaty in 412.³⁹ And there is no reason to believe that an inscription granting *proxenia* to Heracleides of Clazomenae has anything to do with a treaty between Athens and the king of Persia negotiated by Epilycus because such a treaty never existed.⁴⁰

---

38 The existence of this treaty has been accepted by many scholars including Meiggs 1972, 134, 135, 330; Lewis 1977, 76–77; Briant 2002, 591–592; Badian 1993, 40.

39 *Pace* Andrewes 1961, 5 ("The most striking omission is of course that Thucydides, so soon after his description of the uncompleted embassy of winter 425/4, should leave out entirely the successful embassy and treaty of 423.")

40 This finding shows that the attempt of Rhodes 2016 to identify the treaty mentioned in *IG* I³ 227 as the treaty negotiated by Epilycus is untenable. For other more convincing proposals see Culasso Gastaldi 2004, 35–55, who identifies the treaty with the alliance between the Athenians and the King of Persia in the 390s. Rhodes 2016, 178–182 claims that even though there was cooperation between the Athenians and the Persians there was no formal treaty, but this is inaccurate. Xenophon (4.8.24) states that the Athenians had the king as their friend in the late 390s, and this is the same language Xenophon (4.1.32; cf. Thuc. 6.34) uses to describe the relationship between the Spartans and the king.

3 The use of the term *presbeis autokratores* in classical sources and in *On the Peace*

Greek communities sent *presbeis autokratores* (ambassadors with full powers) in two situations.[41] First, they sent this kind of embassy to start negotiations with another community by giving them an open mandate to negotiate about peace an alliance. This was in effect an invitation for another community or foreign leader to make specific proposals, which the *presbeis autokratores* would bring back to their own community for ratification. There are several examples of this use of *presbeis autokratores*: 1) they are sent by the Spartans to the Athenians in 420 B.C. (Thuc. 5.44.3), 2) by the Athenians to the Spartans in 405 (Xen. 2.2.16–17. Cf. Lysias 13.9–11), 3) by the Spartans and their allies to the Athenians in 370/69 B.C. (Xen. 7.1.1), 4) allegedly by Philip II to the Athenians in 346 B.C. (Aeschin. 3.63), and 5) by the Athenians to Antipater in 322 B.C. (Plut. *Phoc.* 26.1–2. Cf. Diod. 18.183–184). This type of embassy is in contrast to a regular embassy, which has specific orders and not an open mandate. In most cases, the weaker party sends *presbeis autokratores* to the stronger party (cf. Aristoph. *Lys.* 1009–1012; *Birds* 1591–1595). Second, if a community decided to surrender or accept a treaty, they would send *presbeis autokratores* to swear the oaths to this treaty. The Olynthians sent this kind of embassy to the Spartans in 379 B.C. (Xen. 5.3.26. Cf. Diod. 15.23.3), the people of Aspendus to Alexander in 334/3 B.C. (Arr. *An.* 26.2–3) and the Oxydracae to Alexander in 326/5 B.C. (Arr. *An.* 6.14.1–3) (cf. *OGIS* 265, lines 9–10; *Milet* I 3, 149 [early second century B.C.]). In all attested cases *presbeis autokratores* are sent either to start negotiations or to finalize them by swearing oaths. This is the reason why there is never a set of negotiaions where different communities each send *presbeis autokratores* to the other. They are also never found in multilateral negotiations. One does not find *presbeis autokratores* in the discussions of the Peloponnesian League that led to the declaration of war against Athens and its allies in 431 B.C. (Thuc. 1.67, 119–125), the negotiations about the Peace of Antalcidas (Xen. 5.1.30–34), the discussions about the Common Peace in 367/6 (Xen. 7.1.33–40), or the formation of the League of Corinth (Diod. 16.89.2–3).

---

[41] This section corrects Magnetto 2013, on which Rhodes 2016, 184 with note 47 relies uncritically. Magnetto believes that "ambassadors having power" mentioned in an inscription (*IG* I³ 61) and by Thucydides (4.118.10) are similar to *presbeis autokratores*, but they are a separate and much different institution and not relevant to the discussion.

The term *presbeis autokratores* is used three times in *On the Peace*. In the first passage *On the Peace* (6) states that ten ambassadors were sent with full powers to negotiate with the Spartans about peace. The passage does not say enough about this embassy to compare this information with the other sources for the institution. Further on, the speaker of *On the Peace* (33) states that he and his fellow ambassadors were sent to Sparta with full powers 'so that we would not have to refer back (πάλιν ἐπαναφέρωμεν).' Despite their powers, they have decided to grant the Assembly the right to discuss the terms they have brought back (πεμφθέντες αὐτοκράτορες ἔτι ἀποδώσομεν ὑμῖν περὶ αὐτῶν σκέψασθαι). This is completely at odds with the information about *presbeis autokratores* in contemporary sources, which show that any proposals received by such ambassadors had to be brought back home to be ratified in the Assembly. This was not left up to the discretion of the ambassadors. Finally, *On the Peace* (39) states that the Spartans have sent *presbeis autokratores* restoring the securities and allowing the Athenians to acquire walls and ships and the islands. The use of the term *presbeis autokratores* is inconsistent with the practice attested in contemporary sources in five ways. First, *presbeis autokratores* are sent to start negotiations, not once they are already underway. Second, *presbeis autokratores* are sent by one party with an open mandate and receive proposals from the other party; here they are making proposals, not receiving them. Third, in *On the Peace* (33, 39) both sides send *presbeis autokratores*, but this never happens in the sources for the Classical period and is inconsistent with the rationale behind the institution. Fourth, the negotiations in *On the Peace* (24–26, 32, 34, 41) are multilateral, not bilateral; as noted above, *presbeis autokratores* are never used in multilateral negotiations where they would be out of place.[42] Fifth, the speaker of *On the Peace* claims that the ambassadors had the option to ask for approval for any proposals made by the Spartans, implying that it was not compulsory as we know it was.

4 Conclusion

Once we recognize that the evidence against the authenticity of *On the Peace* is overwhelming and the information in it unreliable, we can improve our understanding of Athenian history in the late fifth and early fourth centuries B.C.

---

[42] Pownall 1995 does not see how the use of the term in *On the Peace* is not consistent with its use in Classical sources.

First, there is no longer any reason to believe that there was a Peace of Epilycus between the Great King and the Athenians between 424 and 412 or that the Persian King decided to conclude an alliance with the Spartans because of Athenian support for Amorges. Second, we no longer have to explain why Thucydides omits the alleged Peace of Epilycus because this treaty never existed. Third, there is no evidence for a conference at Sparta in 391 convened to discuss peace after the failure of the proposals of Tiribazus. Speeches delivered to the Athenian Assembly had to contain reliable information about the recent past and the contemporary situation. Any speech that did not contain reliable information about major events could not have been a genuine speech composed in the fourth century B.C.

Bibliography

Albini, L. (1964), *Andocide: De Pace*, Florence.
Badian, E. (1991), "The King's Peace", in: M.A. Flower/M. Toher (eds.), *Georgica. Greek Studies in Honour of George Cawkwell, BICS* Suppl. 58, London, 25–48.
Badian, E. (1993), *From Plataea to Potidaea: Studies in the History and Historiography of the Pentecontaetia*, Baltimore/London.
Briant, P. (2002), *From Cyrus to Alexander: A History of the Persian Empire*, Winona Lake.
Canevaro, M. (2019), "Memory, The Orators and the Public in Fourth-Century Athens", in: L. Castagnoli/P. Ceccarelli (eds.), *Greek Memories: Theories and Practices*, Oxford, 136–157.
Conwell, D.H. (2008), *Connecting a City to the Sea: The History of the Athenian Long Walls* (*Mnemosyne* Supplement 293), Leiden/Boston.
Couvenhes, J.P. (2012), "L'introduction des archers scythes, esclaves publics, à Athènes: la date et l'agent d'un transfert culturel", in: B. Legras (ed.), *Transferts culturels et droits dans le monde grec et hellénistique*, Paris, 99–118.
Culasso Gastaldi, E. (2004), *Le prossenie ateniesi del IV secolo: Gli onorati asiatici*, Alessandria.
Daix, D.A/Fernandez, M. (2017), *Démosthène : Contre Aphobos I & II suivi de Contre Midias*, Paris.
Dilts, M.R./Murphy, D.J. (2018), *Antiphontis et Andocides Orationes*, Oxford.
Dmitriev, S. (2011), *The Greek Slogan of Freedom and Early Roman Politics in Greece*, New York/Oxford.
Edwards, M.J. (1995), *Greek Orators IV: Andocides*, Warminster.
Errington, M. (1975), "Arrybas the Molossian", *GRBS* 16, 41–50.
Gagarin, M./MacDowell, D.M. (1998), *The Oratory of Classical Greece I: Antiphon and Andocides*, Austin.
Gomme, A.W./Andrewes, A./Dover, K.J. (1981), *A Historical Commentary on Thucydides. Volume V: Book VIII*, Oxford.

Hamilton, C.D. (1979), *Sparta's Bitter Victories: Politics and Diplomacy in the Corinthian War*, Ithaca/London.
Harris, E.M. (1989), "Demosthenes' Speech *Against Meidias*", *HSCP* 92, 117–136.
Harris, E.M. (1995), *Aeschines and Athenian Politics*, Oxford/New York.
Harris, E.M. (2000), "The Authenticity of Andokides' *De Pace*: A Subversive Essay", in: P. Flensted-Jensen/T. Nielsen/L. Rubinstein (eds.), *Polis and Politics: Studies in Ancient Greek History*, Copenhagen, 479–506.
Harris, E.M. (2016), "Alcibiades, the Ancestors, Liturgies, and the Etiquette of Addressing the Athenian Assembly", in: V. Liotakis/S. Farrington (eds.), *The Art of History: Literary Perspectives on Greek and Roman Historiography*, 145–155.
Harris, E.M. (2018), "The Stereotype of Tyranny and the Tyranny of Stereotypes: Demosthenes on Philip II of Macedon", in: M. Kalaitzi/P. Paschidis/C. Antonetti/A.-M. Guimer-Sorbets, (eds.), Βορειοελλαδικά: *Tales from the Lands of the Ethne: Essays in Honour of Miltiades B. Hatzopoulos* (= ΜΕΛΕΤΗΜΑΤΑ 78), 167–178.
Hatzfeld, J. (1951), *Alcibiade*. 2nd. ed. Paris.
Helly, B. (2018), "La Thesssalie au 4ᵉ s. av. J.-C.: entre autonomie et sujétion", in: M. Kalaitzi/ P. Paschidis/C. Antonetti/A.-M. Guimer-Sorbets (eds.), Βορειοελλαδικά: *Tales from the Lands of the Ethne: Essays in Honour of Miltiades B. Hatzopoulos* (= ΜΕΛΕΤΗΜΑΤΑ 78), 123–158.
Heskel, J. (1988), "The Political Background of the Arrybas Decree", *GRBS* 29, 185–96.
Hornblower, S. (2008), *A Commentary on Thucydides*. Vol. III. *Books 5.25–8.109*, Oxford.
Liddel, P. (2020), *Decrees of Fourth-Century Athens (403/2–322/1 BC)*, Volume 1: The Literary Evidence, Cambridge.
MacDowell, D.M. (2009), *Demosthenes the Orator*, Oxford.
Magnetto, A. (2013), "Ambasciatori plenipotenziari dell città greche in età classica ed ellenistica", *Studi Ellenistici* 27, 213–241.
Martin, G. (2009), *Divine Talk. Religious Argumentation in Demosthenes*, Oxford.
Missiou Ladi, A. (1987), "Coercive Diplomacy in Greek Interstate Relations", *CQ* 37, 336–345.
Missiou, A. (1992), *The Subversive Oratory of Andocides*, Cambridge.
Pearson, L. (1941), "Historical Allusions in the Attic Orators", *CP* 36.3, 209–229.
Pownall, F.S. (1995), "*Presbeis Autokratores*: Andocides' *De Pace*", *Phoenix* 49.2, 140–149.
Rhodes, P.J. (2016), "Heraclides of Clazomenai and a Treaty with Persia", *ZPE* 200, 177–186.
Rhodes, P.J./Osborne, R. (2003), *Greek Historical Inscriptions, 404–323 BC*, Oxford.
Ryder, T.T.B. (1965), *Koine Eirene. General Peace and Local Independence in Ancient Greece*, London.
Samons, L.J. (1998), "Kimon, Kallias, and Peace with Persia", *Historia* 47, 129–149.
Stockton, D. (1959), "The Peace of Callias", *Historia* 8, 61–79.
Theocharaki, M. (2020), *The Ancient Circuit Walls of Athens*, Berlin/Boston.
Thonemann, P. (2009), "Lycia, Athens and Amorges", in: J. Ma/R. Parker/N. Papazarkadas (eds.), *Interpreting the Athenian Empire*, London, 167–194.
Trevett, J.C. (1994), "Demosthenes' Speech *On Organization*", *GRBS* 35, 179–193.
Trevett, J.C. (2011), *Demosthenes, Speeches 1–17*, Austin.
Westlake, H.D. (1977), "Athens and Amorges", *Phoenix* 31, 319–329.
Westlake, H.D. (1989), *Studies in Thucydides and Greek History*, Bristol.
Worthington, I. (2008), *Philip II of Macedonia*, New Haven.
Zaccarini, M. (2017), *The Lame Hegemony: Cimon of Athens and the Failure of Panhellenism, ca. 478–450 BC.*, Bologna.

Cinzia Bearzot
Lysias' *Against the Subversion of the Ancestral Constitution of Athens*: A Past not to be Forgotten

Abstract: This chapter shows how this speech, written for a democratic politician against Phormisius' proposal to restrict the rights of citizenship to landowners, deals with various issues referring to the most recent past of Athens, recently emerging from the civil war: the continuity between the oligarchical experiences of 411 and 404, which is likely to recur for the third time (§ 1); the controversy against the amnesty and "forgetting" the evil suffered, exposing democracy to serious risks (§ 2); the presence of unreliable people, from the democratic point of view, in the so-called Peiraeus Party; the theme of *soteria* (§§ 6 and 8) and the tendency of the Assembly to be deceived and to vote against its own interest (§ 3); the different behavior of oligarchs and democrats towards the civic body (§§ 3, 4–5); the greed for money of antidemocratic people (§ 5); allusions to the strategy of Pericles (§ 9), to a past, remote and recent, in which the Athenians fought for freedom and justice (§ 11), and to the case of the Argives and Mantineans, constantly anti-Spartan (§§ 7–8). All in all, Lysias tries to offer a reconstruction of the recent past in a democratic key, foreshadowing the risks that the democracy is still running.

Oration 34 of Lysias' *corpus*, *Against the Subversion of the Ancestral Constitution of Athens*, is the orator's only deliberative speech which has been preserved (or rather a large fragment of it, consisting of 11 paragraphs). This is one of the earliest of Lysias's speeches, together with the *Against Eratosthenes*, dating back to the period shortly after the return of the democrats and to the application of the amnesty clause that imposed on the Thirty Tyrants and on their closest collaborators to render their accounts.[1] Medda even assumes that it was written before the *Against Eratosthenes*, but I do not share this opinion, since it is difficult to imagine that constitutional proposals could be made until the

---

I would like to thank Professor P.J. Rhodes for reading my chapter and for his suggestions.

1 For the date of *Against Eratosthenes* see Bearzot 1997, 42–44 and Kapellos 2014, 55–56, against Loening 1981. For the clause about the rendering of accounts see Andoc. 1.90–91; [Arist.] *Ath. Pol.* 39.6.

https://doi.org/10.1515/9783110791877-007

experience of the Thirty was definitely over.² Ostwald thinks that Phormisius' proposal precedes that of Thrasybulus, who would have citizenship to foreigners who had collaborated with the democratic resistance;³ but taking into account the fact that Thrasybulus' decree, not casually aprobouleumatic, was most probably one of the first proposals put forward in the Assembly after the return of the democrats in autumn 403, it is difficult to support the anteriority of a motion like Phormisius' one;⁴ in fact, Phormisius' project, proposing a reduction of citizenship rights after two anti-democratic *coups d'état*, demanded at least a partial normalization of the political climate.

Oration 34 did not receive particular attention from the scholars after Usener:⁵ the overall survey about orators and the recent past, which is the subject of this volume, provides the occasion for reconsideration.

1 Dionysius of Halicarnassus' testimony

The title indicated by Dionysius is already of great interest: περὶ τοῦ μὴ καταλῦσαι τὴν πάτριον πολιτείαν Ἀθήνησι. *Patrios politeia* is intended to be a system in line with the constitutional tradition of the country, which owing to its antiquity and to its intrinsic goodness it deserves to be preserved or restored. The slogan of the *patrios politeia* finds application in the political propaganda within the framework of the democratic crises of the end of fifth century: this phrase offers a model as authoritative (due to its location in a distant past) as vague in its contents and therefore very useful in the ideological clash between factions, which attributed different characteristics to it according to need.⁶

In the constitutional history of Athens, the *patrios politeia* could be identified in many ways. For the oligarchs the *patrios politeia* was a constitutional form which predates the development of the radical democracy and it is related to politicians like Draco, Solon and Cleisthenes or to the Areopagites of the age of Cimon (see the debate of 411 testified by [Arist.] *Ath. Pol.* 29.3; or once again the *patrios demokratia* of Isoc. *Areop.* 16–17 and 26–27 and Arist. *Pol.* 1273 b35–

---

2 Medda 1995, 439.
3 Ostwald 1986, 504.
4 Phormisius' decree: D4 Liddel; Thrasybulus' decree: D5 Liddel.
5 Usener 1887 = 1912.
6 This issue has been widely studied: see Fuks 1953; Cecchin 1969; Finley 1971; Lévy 1976, 191–197; Mossé 1978; Caire 2016, 262–286.

41);⁷ for the democrats, on the contrary, it was Pericles' classical form of democracy. A significant example is the use of the phrase *patrios politeia*) by the oligarchic circles that were active in 411 and in 404 in Athens and, on the other side, the reuse in a democratic perspective by Thrasybulus (Thuc. 8.76.6; Xen. *Hell*. 2.4.40–42).

The expression *patrios politeia* is attested for the first time in a fragment of Thrasymachus of Calchedon (Diels-Kranz 85 B1 = Dion. Hal. *Dem*.3), generally dated to 411; it has been proposed to place it in different contexts (407 and 404), but I believe that the framework of the events of the year 411 is the most convincing one, on the ground of the topics mentioned in the fragment.⁸

The title of oration 34 is an example of reappropriation by the democrats, as happened with other *slogans* used in the democratic crises of the late fifth century B.C., such as *soteria* and *homonoia*.⁹ The true *patrios politeia* of Athens is not the extremist oligarchy, but neither is it the "moderate" regime of [Arist.] *Ath. Pol.* 34.3: it is, simply, democracy.

This as for the title. Dionysius of Halicarnassus' summary is of extreme utility to frame the oration. First of all, the orator recalls the return of the democrats from Peiraeus, the reconciliation with "those of the city" and the promulgation of the amnesty, based on the principle "do not remember the evil suffered" (*me mnesikakein*).¹⁰ In this context, he continues, it was feared that the people, once their ancient power was recovered, would do violence to the rich (verb *hybrizo*). Wide discussions took place on this theme: at that time Phormisius, who was among those who had returned from Peiraeus together with the people, proposed a decree (*gnome*), asking on the one hand for the return of the exiles, on the other for the attribution of citizenship rights not to everyone, as it was foreseen in the Athenian democratic system, but to the landowners only. This proposal was appreciated by the Spartans: if approved, it would have deprived of their rights five thousand Athenians. The assumption is that, against this proposal, Lysias wrote the speech for a politician of notable importance (*episemos*).

---

7 On Aristotle's passage see Pezzoli 2012, 389.
8 White 1995; Yunis 1997.
9 Cecchin 1969, 85–92; Lévy 1976, 16–27, 209–222; Bearzot 2013b; Bearzot 2015.
10 Todd 2000, 336, questions Dionysius' reliability owing to the use of the verb *psephizo* referring to the reconciliation, which, technically speaking, was not a decree of the Assembly but an agreement between the parties with the mediation of the Spartan king Pausanias II. The verb, however, can have a non-technical sense (e.g., in oration 13 *psephizo* refers to the vote of the judges), nor it can be excluded that there had been some ratification of the provision in the Assembly. See Loening 1987, 28–30.

Dionysius expresses doubts as to whether the speech was actually delivered, however without explaining them.[11]

The pieces of information provided by Dionysius deserve careful reflection. Some of them are clearly taken from the text, but other might come from a different source: the fear of the *hybris* of the people, Phormisius' name, the issue of the return of the exiles, the number of those who were at risk of *atimia*.[12]

1. The fear of the people and of its possible manifestations of *hybris* against the *euporoi* (δέους δὲ ὄντος μὴ πάλιν τὸ πλῆθος ἐς τοὺς εὐπόρους ὑβρίζῃ τὴν ἀρχαίαν ἐξουσίαν κεκομισμένον) leaves us puzzled in the context of the application of the amnesty: violation attempts were immediately terminated ([Arist.] *Ath. Pol.* 40.2) and both Xenophon (*Hell.* 2.4.43) and [Aristotle] (*Ath. Pol.* 40.2-3) recognize that the amnesty was scrupulously observed.[13] In any case, the reference can be a chronological indication which brings us close enough to the return of the democrats, when the possibility to go to Eleusis for those who did not feel safe in Athens reveals similar concerns ([Arist.] *Ath. Pol.* 39.1-5).

2. The proposal, in the form of a decree, comes from Phormisius (Φορμίσιός τις τῶν συγκατελθόντων μετὰ τοῦ δήμου γνώμην εἰσηγήσατο):[14] a well known character, whom Ps-Aristotle (*Ath. Pol.* 34.3) considers, together with Archinus, Anytus and Cleitophon, an exponent of the Theramenian line, neither extremely oligarchic nor radically democratic.[15] The formulation of the proposal and its presentation to the Assembly reveal the influence of Theramenes' supporters under the democratic restoration:[16] the authority they had acquired thanks to Theramenes' death and to the collaboration with the democratic exiles gave them the opportunity to propose once again a timocratic reform, which recalled the "hoplites' *politeia*" in the center of the propaganda of 411 (Thuc. 8.65.3; [Arist.] *Ath. Pol.* 29.5) and was accomplished for a few months in the government of the Five Thousand.

---

11 Dover 1968, 172. The assumption of a pamphlet, proposed by Cloché 1915, 424 n. 1, is rejected by Bizos in Gernet/Bizos 1926, 206–207.
12 Naturally, these pieces of information could come from the part of the oration which is lost for us, but that Dionysius was able to read: see Lehmann 1972, 228; Todd 2000, 336.
13 Cf. also Plat. *Ep.* VII, 326b.
14 Traill nr. 962695
15 Rhodes 1981, 427–433. I do not understand why Todd 2000, 336–337 considers the *Athenaion Politeia* as a not reliable source about this: Theramenes' median position, real or pretended as it was, is declared by himself in Xen. *Hell.* 2.3.48 and Phormisius' position is clear from his project to exclude the thetes from the government.
16 Natalicchio 1996, 7–8, 38–41.

3. The proposal to recall the exiles has been differently interpreted. According to someone, these exiles would have to be identified with the "men of Peiraeus", therefore with the democratic exiles.[17] However, this interpretation seems to me quite improbable, because the "men of Peiraeus" had already returned thanks to their military success and to the subsequent agreements between the parties, and because their return is, in Dionysius' introduction too, the premise of the whole affair. The legitimacy of their position must have been sanctioned already in the Assembly summoned by Thrasybulus immediately after the return (Xen. *Hell.* 2.4.39). It is more probable that Phormisius was worried about the oligarchic exiles, when he proposed the official recall in a spirit of pacification; their return was indeed foreseen by the peace treaty with Sparta (Andoc. 3.11–12; Plut. *Lys.* 14.8), but probably there were particular situations still waiting to be regulated, first of all the presence of the oligarchic enclave of Eleusis.[18]

4. The figure of five thousand Athenians who were at risk of losing their political rights is interesting: doubts have been raised about the figure,[19] but if the proposal was intended to exclude the propertyless, this is a perfectly adequate number, indeed even low.[20] Correctly S. Todd underlines that Dionysius could be quoting here a part of the speech which is not preserved or us; however, the

---

17 Medda 1995, 441, of the basis of Bizos in Gernet/Bizos 1926, 206–207; this last suggests for the sentence γνώμην εἰσηγήσατο τοὺς μὲν φεύγοντας κατιέναι, τὴν δὲ πολιτείαν μὴ πᾶσιν, ἀλλὰ τοῖς [τὴν] γῆν ἔχουσι παραδοῦναι παραδοῦναι a simple-occasion sense ("une fois les exilés rentrés, il fallait n'accorder les droits politiques qu'aux propriétaires du sol"). The translation is accepted by Albini 1955, 309 and 451, and by Aujac 1978, 110.
18 On the clauses of the peace see Bearzot 1997, 215–220. For the identification of the exiles with exponents of the oligarchy see Cloché 1915, 280–281; Todd 2000, 339 n. 7. Lehmann 1972, 228, and Ostwald 1986, 504, identify them more precisely with the oligarchs who had taken refuge in Eleusis, an assumption perhaps too curtly excluded by Bizos in Gernet/Bizos 1926, 206–207.
19 Medda 1995, 440.
20 On the wish to exclude the thetes expressed by the proposal see Ruschenbusch 1979, 135–136. On the number of the thetes, Strauss 1986, states, in p. 81, that in 394 there were in Athens no more than five to seven thousand thetes ("it is difficult to imagine more than 5,000–7,000 thetes in 394"); in p. 99 and in p. 117, note 35, he says, however, that at the time of Phormisius' proposal the thetes were probably more than five thousand ("the thetes ... who may, however, have numbered more than 5,000"; "Ruschenbusch ... calculates 5,000 thetes; there may have been considerably more"). According to Lehmann 1972, 229, those excluded would have represented roughly the 20–25% of the population. Ostwald 1986, 505, observes that if the citizens deprived of their rights were only five thousands, the basis of the new regime was probably wider in comparison with the projects of 411: however, much depends on the demographic situation of contemporary Athens.

use that the orator is making of the figure, which could be either too large or too small, is not clearly reconstructed for us. The orator might want to underline the high level of it, to highlight the antidemocratic nature of the provision, or, on the contrary (if the figure was mentioned in the course of Phormisius' arguments), to state that the provision would have touched only a limited number of Athenians.[21]

Dionysius does not provide us the name of the politician for whom the speech was written: he only defines him as an *episemos*, that is as an important man, who has distinguished himself; after all, the speaker defines himself as superior to his opponents in *ousia* and for *genos*, in wealth and in ancestry, and he says he does not run the risk of losing his rights in case Phormisius' proposal is approved. He is therefore a democrat of high extraction: his ideological perspective could make us think of Thrasybulus, a staunch defender of democracy both in 411 and in 404. However, the clues are not fully congruent: undoubtedly some aspects of the speech evoke Thrasybulus' thought (§§ 3, the theme of citizenship; §§ 4–5, the theme of the generosity of the people and of his indifference to money, §§ 3, 6 and 9, the theme of *soteria*; § 10, the invitation to trust in the gods), but other elements of the argumentation, first of all the invitation to preserve the memory of the past and not to forget the evil suffered, seem to me to be in contrast with his political position, which put reconciliation in the foreground.

Dionysius therefore directs us, firstly, towards a proposal which comes from a man, Phormisius, of Theramenes' circle, and aimed to limit full citizenship rights to the middle class of the small landowners; secondly, a proposal that was put forward probably between the closing of Eratosthenes' trial and the end of the Eleusinian experiment (401/400: also the mention of Spartan interests is consistent with this dating, since it would be less and less justifiable the further we go from the autumn of 403);[22] finally, a proposal which was opposed, clearly successfully, by an authoritative democratic politician.

---

[21] Todd 1990, 164; Todd 2000, 336. Davies 1977, 118, n. 72, also assumes an attidographic origin of the news (*contra* Lehmann 1972, 228).

[22] Todd 2000, 337–338, connects Phormisius' proposal with Pausanias II's trial: a condemnation of King Pausanias would probably have increased Sparta's claims and some concession in an antidemocratic sense might have seemed prudent.

2 The text of the oration (§§ 1–11)

Let us now see what information can be drawn from the text of the oration.

§ 1. The orator addresses the *Athenaioi*. This directs towards a speech in the Assembly: one thing that was, after all, obvious, since the proposal would have deprived of their rights a considerable number of Athenians and that the popular Assembly was responsible for personal rights. Wilamowitz's proposal, resumed by Bizos and by Medda,[23] according to which the addressees of the oration would be, on the contrary, the *timemata parechomenoi* mentioned by [Arist.] *Ath. Pol.* 39.6,[24] does not seem sustainable to me: that of the *timemata parechomenoi* was a special tribunal tasked with auditing of the accounts of the oligarchs, and it is unlikely that their duties went further, nor that they were entitled to judge a proposal to reduce citizenship rights.[25]

The proposer of the decree is presented as someone who is trying to deceive (*exapatesai*), by the means of the same proposals already put forward twice, who has suffered "past misfortunes" and experienced both governments: the orator thus identifies a precise continuity line between the two oligarchic experiences of 411 and 404 and the new proposal by Phormisius. The speakers belong to the same political area; the proposals, presented in a "moderate" form, are similar. The continuity between the different oligarchic experiences of the end of the fifth century is a profound conviction of Lysias, who expresses himself in a similar way also in 12.65, where he outlines the ambiguous career of Theramenes starting from 411, and in 25.11: in both places he speaks of the "first oligarchy" for the regime of the Four Hundred.[26]

A second theme that emerges from the outset is that of memory. The disasters suffered, says the speaker, should be a sufficient lesson (*ikana mnemeia*) for the people. This also is among Lysias' favourite themes (see 12.87–100, in particular 96; 13, 95; in both places the verb *anaminnesko* recurs),[27] who rejects a

---

23 Wilamowitz-Moellendorff 1893 = 1966, II, 226; Bizos in Gernet/Bizos 1926, 207–208; Medda 1995, 404–441.
24 Rhodes 1981, 470–471.
25 On this court see Bearzot 1997, 21, with the discussion of the proposal of Loening 1987, 48–49, to understand *timemata parechomenoi* not in the sense of a census-based court, but of a court "enabled to fix the penalty".
26 Bearzot 1997, 174–176.
27 Bearzot 1997, 238–239; 339–340.

too generous amnesty:²⁸ the evil suffered must not be forgotten, not so much in order to take revenge (as suggested by the last paragraphs of the *Against Eratosthenes* and of the *Against Agoratus*, in opposition to the amnesty) but rather to take from the past a lesson that enables mistakes not to be repeated.

§ 2. Once again on the theme of memory, the speaker represents the Athenians as "the men most ready to forget" or, in case they have not forgotten, most willing to suffer offenses (πάντων ἐστὲ ἐπιλησμονέστατοι ἢ πάσχειν ἑτοιμότατοι κακῶς). In a political-cultural context that insisted a great deal on forgetting the evil suffered, Lysias, on the contrary, proposes memory, not so much as a precondition of vengeance but as a defence against recurring attacks against the democracy. This is an aspect of the opposition to the amnesty which characterizes Lysias' position: perhaps not by chance, in §§ 4–5 mention is made of the great generosity shown by the people after the democratic restoration.

A second noteworthy aspect is the opposition to those who, although they had returned with "those of Peiraeus", had only by chance been on their side, because indeed, in their opinions, they were "of the city" (οἳ τῇ μὲν τύχῃ τῶν <ἐν> Πειραιεῖ πραγμάτων μετέσχον, τῇ δὲ γνώμῃ τῶν ἐξ ἄστεως). The polemic concerns Theramenes' supporters such as Archinus, Anytus and indeed Phormisius, who, after Theramenes's death, left Athens, fearing the revenge of the Thirty, and joined the democrats of Thrasybulus, thus recovering an unexpected authority after the democratic restoration.²⁹ The attack on democracy now comes from them, not from the extremist oligarchy;³⁰ this attack was very dangerous because this proposal surely picked up the idea of the "different democracy" and the "moderate" regime of hoplites (Thuc. 8.53.1) of 411.³¹

§ 3. The risk envisaged by the orator is that the Athenians may vote against their own interest, becoming slaves through a vote by show of hands. A danger that the recent past envisaged as real, since both the coup of 411 and that of 404, which had led to the advent of Thirty, had been regularly voted in the Assembly, even if by unrepresentative and heavily conditioned Assemblies.³² It is a theme

---

28 On this theme I refer to the essays collected in Bearzot 2007.
29 For Anytus see Traill nr. 139460; Placido Suarez 1984/85; Strauss 1986, 94–96; Bertoli 2002; Lenfant 2016, 258–274; for Archinus, see Traill nr. 213880; Strauss 1986, 96–101; Bertoli 2003.
30 Evidently the democratic restoration was not accepted by all as an accomplished fact (see Wolpert 2002, 43): there were those who had not yet given up on the revolutionary projects that had upset Athens in recent years, despite their double failure.
31 David 2014.
32 See Bearzot 2013a, 62–70, 150–154.

that is deeply felt by Lysias (see 12.43–44; 12.71–72),[33] according to whom one of the objectives of the oligarchic conspirators was indeed to induce the people to vote against their own interests, so as to legitimize the provisions passed in the framework of the *coups d'état*.

The orator then identifies in the maintenance of the citizenship for all the Athenians the true *soteria* of the city:[34] Athens of the glorious imperial past did not study how to deprive of their citizenship some categories of citizens, but rather was generous in concessions, like the *epigamy* of the Euboeans.[35] Implicitly the idea that is expressed here is: if during the time of our hegemony we were generous, there is no reason to undo now behavior adopted in better times. Naturally the issue of the grant of the right of marriage to the Euboeans has nothing to do with the regulation of the right of citizenship in Athens; moreover, the presentation of Athens when holding the hegemony as generous towards foreigners matches the classic self-representation of Athens as a hospitable and available receptive city rather than the historical reality. The arguments in defence of the maintenance of citizenship for all the Athenians leads us to the figure of Thrasybulus and of his wish to reward with citizenship foreigners who had participated in the resistance, thus expanding the civic body.

The evocation of *soteria*, identified with maintaining the rights of citizenship for all the Athenians, and therefore with the protection of democracy, is still an example of the overthrow and the re-appropriation of oligarchic slogans (see also §§ 6–9): a further theme characteristic of Thrasybulus.[36]

§ 4. The military weakening that would be caused by a decrease in the number of citizens is highlighted here. As a matter of fact, the ouster of the thetes would not have affected either the number of hoplites (coming from the middle class) or of the cavalry (provided by the first two classes), nor the number of the archers, who in general were foreigners.[37] It is curious that no reference is made to the fleet, the traditional seat of the military service of the thetes: probably the

---

33 12.44: οὕτως οὐχ ὑπὸ τῶν πολεμίων μόνον ἀλλὰ καὶ ὑπὸ τούτων πολιτῶν ὄντων ἐπεβουλεύεσθε ὅπως μήτ' ἀγαθὸν μηδὲν ψηφίσησθε; 12.72: ἵνα μήτε ῥήτωρ αὐτοῖς μηδεὶς ἐναντιοῖτο μήτε διαπειλοῖτο, ὑμεῖς τε μὴ τὰ τῇ πόλει συμφέροντα ἕλοισθε, ἀλλὰ τἀκείνοις δοκοῦντα ψηφίσαισθε. See Bearzot 1997, 142 and 209–210.
34 On Lysias' interest in the theme of citizenship see Piovan 2011, 244–246.
35 Oranges 2013.
36 Bearzot 2013a, 171–196; Bearzot 2013b, 115 and 118–119.
37 Davies 1977, 120 (= 2004, 38), does not consider the problem. For information on the Athenian military organization see now Bettalli 2019, with bibliography; for the archers, Tuci 2004; Pritchard 2018.

reason should be identified in the fact that in Athens, forced in 404 to surrender all but twelve ships, the reconstruction of the fleet and the use of the penniless people in it could not yet be foreseen.[38] This element too would confirm, however, a rather high date for the oration.

§§ 4–5. A corruption of the text has been tentatively corrected through different proposals. Medda, following the Teubner edition of Thalheim, prints the following text:

> ἐπίστασθε γὰρ <τὰ ἐν> ταῖς ἐφ' ἡμῶν ὀλιγαρχίαις γεγενημένα [καὶ] οὐ τοὺς γῆν κεκτημένους ἔχοντας τὴν πόλιν, ἀλλὰ πολλοὺς μὲν αὐτῶν ἀποθανόντας, πολλοὺς δ' ἐκ τῆς πόλεως ἐκπεσόντας, [5] οὓς ὁ δῆμος καταγαγὼν ὑμῖν μὲν τὴν ὑμετέραν ἀπέδωκεν, αὐτὸς δὲ ταύτης οὐκ ἐτόλμησε μετασχεῖν.

And he translates:

> Sapete infatti cosa è accaduto durante le oligarchie dei nostri tempi, and sapete anche che non erano i possessori di terre ad avere in mano la città; anzi molti di loro sono stati messi a morte and molti sono stati espulsi dalla città; il popolo invece li ha fatti rientrare e vi ha restituito la vostra sovranità sullo stato, mentre non ha osato averne parte direttamente.

Different is the Oxford text of Hude, which is later adopted also by Gernet/Bizos in the Belles Lettres edition, by Lamb in the Loeb Classical Library, by Albini and by Carey; this is their version with translation by Lamb:

> ἐπίστασθε γὰρ <ἐν> ταῖς ἐφ' ἡμῶν ὀλιγαρχίαις γεγενημέναις [καὶ] οὐ τοὺς γῆν κεκτημένους ἔχοντας τὴν πόλιν, ἀλλὰ πολλοὺς μὲν αὐτῶν ἀποθανόντας, πολλοὺς δ' ἐκ τῆς πόλεως ἐκπεσόντας, [5] οὓς ὁ δῆμος καταγαγὼν ὑμῖν μὲν τὴν ὑμετέραν ἀπέδωκεν, αὐτὸς δὲ ταύτης οὐκ ἐτόλμησε μετασχεῖν.

> You are well aware that in the previous oligarchies of our time it was not the possessors of land who controlled the city: many of them were put to death, and many were expelled from the city; and the people, after recalling them, restored your city to you, but did not venture to participate in it themselves.

As a matter of fact, however you try to adjust the text of the first sentence, the meaning remains substantially unchanged. The problem is rather how τὴν ὑμετέραν is understood: "your sovereignty over the state" according to Albini and

---

[38] According to Lehmann 1972, 230–231, the absence of the fleet deprived the thetes of their role in the Athenian forces, and with this the basis for enjoying citizenship rights; hence the need to envisage their enlistment in other sectors. It was also suggested that, during the last phase of the Peloponnesian War, the thetes, owing to the reduction of military potential, were enrolled as hoplites (see Cloché 1915, 433 n. 1).

Medda, "your city" according to Lamb and Todd.³⁹ I believe that we should instead understand "your land": the orator has just spoken of land, and the expression evokes the territorial clauses of the peace agreements in which *ghe* is often implied (see Thuc. 5.79.1–2, treaty between Argos and Sparta in 418: τὰν αὑτῶν ἔχοντες; Isoc. *De pace* 16, peace of 375/4: τὴν αὑτῶν ἔχειν ἑκάστους; Xen. *Hell.* VII, 4, 10, peace of 366/5: ἔχειν τὴν ἑαυτῶν ἑκάστους).⁴⁰ I therefore propose to understand it as follows: you know that it was not the landowners who held the city in their hands during the oligarchies (much more extremist, in fact, than the moderate regime of the *hoplites* which they said they were pursuing), indeed many of them were killed and exiled; the people brought them back to Athens and returned their property to everyone. The speaker means that Athenian landowners have nothing to fear from the *demos*, including the propertyless thetes: indeed, the *demos* should be considered, as a whole, a benefactor (*euergetes*). The theme of the different behavior of oligarchs and democrats towards their fellow citizens and of the generosity of the people, uninterested in money, is also present in Thrasybulus' speech in Xen. *Hell.* 2.4.39–42.

§ 5. The orator addresses the audience with an invitation to look at the facts and not at the words (i.e. propaganda), at the past and not at the future: it is necessary that the Athenians "remember" (*memnemenoi*) what happened, that is, that the oligarchic faction in word supported an anti-democratic political line, but in fact it aimed, much more concretely, to take possession of the goods of its adversaries. The accusation of greed against the oligarchs, characterized as driven by personal interests, is constantly present in Lysias: a good example, about the Thirty Tyrants and their supporters, can be found in 12.5–24.⁴¹

§ 6. We find here a recurrence of the theme of *soteria*, which is used by Phormisius in the same sense in which Theramenes uses it in Xen. *Hell.* 2.2.22: to save oneself one must obey Spartan orders (verbs *keleuo*, *prostasso*: εἶτα τοιούτων ἡμῖν ὑπαρχόντων ἐρωτῶσι τίς ἔσται σωτηρία τῇ πόλει, εἰ μὴ ποιήσομεν <ἃ> Λακεδαιμόνιοι κελεύουσιν;). The speaker replies that obeying Spartan orders would deprive the people (*plethos*) of any chance of salvation (ἐγὼ δὲ τούτους εἰπεῖν ἀξιῶ, τίς τῷ πλήθει περιγενήσεται, εἰ ποιήσομεν ἃ ἐκεῖνοι προ-

---

39 Todd 2000, 340, note 10: the proposed alternatives are *polis* (city), *ousia* (property), *politeia* (constitution).
40 Above all see also § 8: κἂν πολλάκις εἰς τὴν τούτων ἐμβάλωσι. Thus Blass 1887, 451 n. 1, and Voegelin 152 n. 47: the hypothesis is rejected with excessive arrogance by Albini 1955, 451.
41 Bearzot 1997, 246–249.

στάττουσιν;). It is the defense of democracy that saves the city (see § 3): in fact, he urges people also to take up arms, because dying fighting would be in any case better than voting by decree your own death (πολὺ κάλλιον μαχομένοις ἀποθνῄσκειν ἢ φανερῶς ἡμῶν αὐτῶν θάνατον καταψηφίσασθαι).[42]

The reference to Spartan orders is interesting also as a chronological indication, because it leads us to a time before the beginning of the emancipation of Athens from enemy control: that started at the end of 397 or at the beginning of 396 by sending aid to the Persian ships led by Conon and through contacts with Persia (*Hell. Oxy.* 10.1 Chambers), and it was finally completed in 395, when a series of inscriptions reveals to us that the reconstruction of the walls had already been started (*IG* II², 1657–1664), and when in any case Athens welcomed, even if not without some reserve, the request an of alliance from the Thebans in an anti-Spartan perspective (Xen. *Hell.* 3.5.7–16);[43] we are therefore brought back to a moment not very far from autumn 403.

§ 7. Medda supposes a gap after κίνδυνον, on the basis of Usener[44] and against Thalheim; similarly Gernet/Bizos, Lamb and Todd; Carey registers the hypothesis of Usener in his apparatus but does not accept it. The topic that the speaker seems to be expressing is in any case the following, according to Gernet/Bizos and Albini: if we fight, we and our enemies will be on the same level and we will be at a similar risk.[45]

§§ 7–8. The example of the Argives and of the Mantineans is here introduced: while much lower in number than the Athenians, they systematically opposed Spartan interference; the objective is to support the need for the Athenians to defend themselves against the arrogance of the Spartans, discouraging their aggression with a will to resist similar to that of the two Peloponnesian cities. The Spartans as a matter of fact do not want to take any risk in the absence of certain advantages.

§ 9. The speaker states that the Athenians also reasoned in a similar way when they had the *arche* and they let their land be devastated, convinced as they were

---

[42] A similar contrast between fighting and voting (in such a case, fighting as the strong but voting as the weak) can be found in 12.79 (μηδὲ μαχομένους <μὲν> κρείττους εἶναι τῶν πολεμίων, ψηφιζομένους δὲ ἥττους τῶν ἐχθρῶν); see Bearzot 1997, 224.
[43] Strauss 1986, 106–110.
[44] Usener 1887, 157 and 170–171 = 1912, 275 and 291.
[45] Gernet/Bizos 1926, 211; Albini 1955, 451.

that it was not worth fighting for it. He evokes the Periclean strategy, consisting in abandoning Attica to devastation in order to base their survival on the empire and to obtain greater advantages (Thuc. 2.13). But today, when Athens has lost everything, only the will to resist Spartan impositions can ensure salvation for the city (and here the theme of the *soteria* returns again).

§ 10. Recalling (*anamnesthentas*) the deeds done in the past in favor of others who suffered injustice, the Athenians must now show themselves *andres agathoi* towards their homeland. In this paragraph too, the era of hegemony is idealized, with full adherence to democratic propaganda. The theme of memory assumes here a different meaning: the point is not to remember a negative past that is liable to occur once more, but to remember a glorious past of which they should be worthy.

Particularly interesting is the invitation to trust in the gods, even if the text is corrupted and it has been differently amended, leading therefore to different translations.

This is Thalheim's text, with the consequent translation:

ἀλλὰ γὰρ χρὴ ἀναμνησθέντας ὅτι ἤδη καὶ ἑτέροις ἀδικουμένοις βοηθήσαντες ἐν τῇ ἀλλοτρίᾳ πολλὰ τρόπαια τῶν πολεμίων ἐστήσαμεν, ἄνδρας ἀγαθοὺς περὶ τῆς πατρίδος καὶ ἡμῶν αὐτῶν γίγνεσθαι, πιστεύοντας μὲν τοῖς θεοῖς, καὶ ἐλπίζοντας κατὰ τὸ δίκαιον μετὰ τῶν ἀδικουμένων ἔσεσθαι.

In fact, remembering that we already raised many trophies over enemies in a foreign land, coming to the aid of those who were wronged, we need to be noble men towards our homeland and towards ourselves, trusting in the gods and hoping that, according to justice, they will be on the side of those who are offended (my translation).

Gernet/Bizos' text, with the related translation, is the following:

ἀλλὰ γὰρ χρὴ ἀναμνησθέντας ὅτι ἤδη καὶ ἑτέροις ἀδικουμένοις βοηθήσαντες ἐν τῇ ἀλλοτρίᾳ πολλὰ τρόπαια τῶν πολεμίων ἐστήσαμεν, ἄνδρας ἀγαθοὺς περὶ τῆς πατρίδος καὶ ἡμῶν αὐτῶν γίγνεσθαι, πιστεύοντας μὲν τοῖς θεοῖς, καὶ ἐλπίζοντας ἐπὶ τὸ δίκαιον μετὰ τῶν ἀδικουμένων ἔσεσθαι.

Rappelons nous que déjà, lorsque nous nous sommes portés au secours d'autres Grecs opprimés, nous avons dressés maints trophées victorieux, et montrons-nous des hommes de cœur pour la cause de la patrie et la nôtre ; ayions confiance dans les dieux, et espérons qu'ils seront avec les opprimés pour la justice.

Medda (like Albini) translates Hude's text, which accepts Scheibe's (ἐλπίζοντας δὲ) and Reiske's (ἔτι for ἐπί) emendations, and it is adopted also by Carey;

ἀλλὰ γὰρ χρὴ ἀναμνησθέντας ὅτι ἤδη καὶ ἑτέροις ἀδικουμένοις βοηθήσαντες ἐν τῇ ἀλλοτρίᾳ πολλὰ τρόπαια τῶν πολεμίων ἐστήσαμεν, ἄνδρας ἀγαθοὺς περὶ τῆς πατρίδος καὶ ἡμῶν αὐτῶν γίγνεσθαι, πιστεύοντας μὲν τοῖς θεοῖς, ἐλπίζοντας δὲ ἔτι τὸ δίκαιον μετὰ τῶν ἀδικουμένων ἔσεσθαι.

Ma bisogna anche, ricordando che già in altre occasioni, portando aiuto ad altri che subivano dei soprusi, abbiamo innalzato molti trofei sui nemici in terra straniera, che ci dimostriamo valorosi nei confronti della patria e di fronte a noi stessi, confidando negli dei e nutrendo la speranza che la giustizia sarà ancora una volta dalla parte degli offesi.[46]

The invitation to trust in the gods, as allies, is present in quite similar terms in Thrasybulus' speech before Mounichia (Xen. *Hell.* 2.4.13–17) and it could confirm that the speech was written for him. But, apart from the well-known deterioration of the relations between Lysias and Thrasybulus after the invalidation of the decree which involved citizenship for the foreigners who had been collaborators with the resistance (and therefore for Lysias too),[47] other elements conflict with this assumption; among them, in addition to the already mentioned exhortation to "remember", I would count also the unconditional praise of the Athenian hegemony (see §§ 9 and 11), which does not seem persuasive coming from Thrasybulus.[48]

§ 11. This fragment closes by comparing the situation of the democratic exiles who had fought the Thirty to that of the Athenians after their return, who were at risk of being sent into exile for not wanting to fight; and also by comparing that of the Athenians at the time of their hegemony, when they fought for the freedom of others, to that of the Athenians compelled nowadays to defend their own freedom. This look at the past proposes here examples to be imitated and of which they must be worthy.

---

[46] Lamb 1930 thus reads the text and translates: πιστεύοντας μὲν τοῖς θεοῖς καὶ ἐλπίζοντας ἐπὶ τὸ δίκαιον μετὰ τῶν ἀδικουμένων ἔσεσθαι, "let us trust in the gods, and hope that they will stand for justice on the side of the injured"; Todd 2000: "and that we have placed our trust in the gods and in the hope that once again justice will be on the side of those who are wronged".
[47] Bearzot 1997, 89–92, 150–152.
[48] For a definitely anti-imperialist Thrasybulus see Accame 1956; *contra* Seager 1967 and Cawkwell 1976; for a median position see Buck 1998, 91–92, who thinks of a moderate imperialism of the Periclean type.

3 The recent past in Lysias 34

The speech focuses on the invitation to remember the past: the recent past, with the *symphorai* suffered later by Athens owing to the defeat in war and the painful experiences of the first and second oligarchy, and even the most distant past, that of the empire.[49] It is necessary to learn from the past: in the first case not to repeat past mistakes and to avoid new *symphorai;* in the second, to be worthy heirs of a glorious tradition.

First of all, there emerge from the oration precise historical judgments: the continuity between the first and the second oligarchy;[50] the presence in the political framework of the city of "fake democrats", always willing to attack democracy with subversive proposals presented with great propaganda skills, and capable of deceiving the people once more; the re-enactment in a positive perspective of the *arche*, built by the *progonoi*, a period during which Athens intervened to correct wrongs and to defend the freedom of others, a period of which it is necessary to prove to be worthy heirs. Particularly for the first two points, other speeches by Lysias, in the first place 12 and 13, convey similar judgments: the re-enactment of the past is accompanied by clear political judgments.

Does this re-enactment show distortions? For the less recent past, it does: the period of the *arche* is idealized and presented in a perspective of the exaltation of Athens, champion of freedom and justice and capable of acceptance and availability to foreigners. The situation is different for the recent past: Lysias evokes a painful reality, which is well known to his audience; he may emphasise some aspects, but he never lies. After all, the plea to remember, and not to forget the misfortunes suffered, is addressed to protagonists and eyewitnesses of the events, which minimizes the possibility of manipulation. Perhaps an element of distortion can be found in the loss of "hoplites, archers and knights" that would follow a provision to restrict the citizenship (§ 4): certainly this would not have happened by depriving the thetes of their citizenship; the use of the argument of military weakening puzzles us (unless, in absence of a fleet, a different military use of the thetes was planned).

Nor it is possible to say that the orator counts on the ignorance of the audience[51]: on the contrary the opposite is true, as he counts on direct knowledge of

---

49 For the allusive reference to the battle of Aegospotami cf. Kapellos 2014, 91–100 and Bearzot 2017.
50 For this continuity of men and techniques see Bearzot 2013a.
51 On this point cf. Kapellos' Introduction.

the events, events that he invites them indeed "not to forget", and thus to act accordingly. The relation between orator and audience is similar to that which can be found in orations 12 and 13: the speaker addresses persons who have lived in their own lives what is to be revoked, and who are invited to keep a watchful awareness of that experience (and this is one of the reasons for defending Lysias' reliability about the political vicissitudes of the late fifth century).

The facts recalled have a significant role in the speaker's strategy: everything, in fact, is focused on the memory of what happened, which must prompt the Athenians to take the consequent decisions. The aim is to avoid repeating past mistakes, i.e. being deceived through the slogans of "salvation" and "emergency", according to which it would be obligatory to obey the Spartans. The opponent, Phormisius, is not expressly quoted in the fragment, but his political position is accurately described: he is one of the fake democrats who took advantage of the situation by joining the *demos*, but the fact that he sided with the "men of Peiraeus" is certainly not honest, because their *gnome*, their political orientation, was on the contrary in line with that of the "men of the city".

The past discussed by Lysias in oration 34 is too recent to be heavily manipulated and, perhaps, too painful to be a simple subject of propaganda: manipulation and propaganda are limited to the farthest past of Athens' hegemony. Phormisius' proposal was indeed "une prolongation des luttes civiles", to borrow an expression of Cloché.[52] Before the reappearance of the ghosts of a recent past, which was believed to be outdated for ever, our speaker, an exponent of the democratic party, tries rather to lead the Assembly to develop a clear awareness of the events and an objective judgement on them and on their protagonists; the speaker aims to assure them that, despite the tendency of the *demos* to forget the past and to be deceived, that past will not recur. History, also recent history, is here really a *ktema es aei*, to borrow the words of Thucydides: remembering the past is useful to avoid making the mistakes of the past once more and to prevent Athens, after getting rid of the Thirty Tyrants, from paradoxically falling again into the experience of a "third oligarchy".

---

52 Cloché 1915, 446.

Bibliography

Accame, S. (1956), "Il problema della nazionalità greca nella politica di Pericle e Trasibulo", *Paideia* 11, 241–253.
Aujac, G. (1978) (ed.), Denys d'Halicarnasse, *Opuscules rhétoriques*, I, Paris.
Bearzot, C. (1997), *Lisia e la tradizione su Teramene. Commento storico alle orazioni XII e XIII del corpus lysiacum*, Milano.
Bearzot, C. (2007), *Vivere da democratici. Studi su Lisia e la democrazia ateniese*, Roma.
Bearzot, C. (2013a), *Come si abbatte una democrazia*, Roma/Bari.
Bearzot, C. (2013b), "Soteria oligarchica e soteria democratica tra 411 e 404", in: N. Cusumano/ D. Motta (eds.), *Xenia. Studi in onore di Lia Marino*, Caltanissetta/Roma, 113–122.
Bearzot, C. (2015), "Il tema dell'*homonoia* nell'azione politica di Trasibulo", *RaRe* 5, 99–116.
Bearzot, C. (2017), "La συμφορά de la cité. La défaite d'Athènes (405–404 av. J.-C.) chez les orateurs attiques", *Ktema* 42, 41–52.
Bertoli, M. (2002), "Anito tra democrazia e teramenismo", in: D. Ambaglio (ed.), *Syngraphé. Materiali e appunti per lo studio della storia e della letteratura antica*, 3, Como, 87–102.
Bertoli, M. (2003), "Archino tra oratoria e politica: l'epitafio", *RIL* 137, 339–366.
Bettalli, M. (2019), *Un mondo di ferro*, Roma/Bari.
Blass, Fr. (1887), *Die attische Beredsamkeit*, I², Leipzig.
Buck, R.J. (1998), *Thrasybulus and the Athenian Democracy* (Historia Einzelschriften, 120), Stuttgart.
Caire, E. (2016), *Penser l'oligarchie à Athènes aux Ve et IVe siècles. Aspects d'une idéologie*, Paris.
Carey, C. (ed.) (2007), *Lysiae Orationes cum fragmentis*, Oxford.
Cawkwell, G.L. (1976), "The Imperialism of Thrasybulus", *CQ* 26, 270–277.
Cecchin, S.A. (1969), *Patrios politeia. Un tentativo propagandistico durante la guerra del Peloponneso*, Torino.
Cloché, P. (1915), *La restauration démocratique à Athènes en 403 avant J.-C.*, Paris.
David, E. (2014), "An Oligarchic Democracy: Manipulation of Democratic Ideals by Athenian Oligarchs in 411 BC", *Eirene* 50, 11–38.
Davies, J.K. (1977 = 2004), "Athenian Citizenship. The Descent Group and the Alternatives", *CJ* 73, 105–121 = in: P.J. Rhodes (ed.), *Athenian Democracy*, Edinburgh, 18–39.
Dover, K.J. (1968), *Lysias and the Corpus Lysiacum*, Berkeley/Los Angeles.
Finley, M.I. (1971), *The Ancestral Constitution*, Cambridge.
Fuks, A. (1953), *The Ancestral Constitution*, London.
Gernet, L./Bizos, M. (eds.) (1924–1926), Lysias, *Discours*, I–II, Paris.
Hude, C. (ed.) (1912), *Lysiae orationes*, Oxonii.
Kapellos, A. (2014), *Lysias 21. A Commentary*, Berlin/Boston.
Lamb, R.M. (ed.) (1930), *Lysias*, Cambridge (MA) – Harvard.
Lehmann, G.A. (1972), *Die revolutionäre Machtergreifung der „Dreissig" und die staatliche Teilung Attikas (404–401/0 v. Chr.)*, in: *Festschrift Stier*, Münster, 201–233.
Lenfant, D. (2016), "Anytos et la corruption massive de juges dans l'Athènes démocratique", *Historia* 65, 258–274.
Lévy, E. (1976), *Athènes devant la défaite de 404. Histoire d'une crise idéologique*, Paris.
Liddel, P. (2020), *Decrees of Fourth-Century Athens*, I, Cambridge.

Loening, Th.C. (1981), "The Autobiographical Speeches of Lysias and the Biographical Tradition", *Hermes* 109, 280–294.
Loening, T.C. (1987), *The Reconciliation Agreement of 403/2 in Athens. Its Content and Application* (Hermes Einzelschriften, 53), Stuttgart.
Medda, E. (ed.) (1991–1995), Lisia, *Orazioni*, I–II, Milano.
Mossé, C. (1978), "Le thème de la *patrios politeia* dans la pensée grecque du IVe siècle", *Eirene* 16, 81–89.
Natalicchio, A. (1996), *Atene e la crisi della democrazia. I Trenta e la querelle Teramene/ Cleofonte*, Bari.
Oranges, A. (2013), "La concessione dell'epigamia agli Eubei", in: C. Bearzot/F. Landucci (eds.), *Tra mare e continente: l'isola d'Eubea*, Milano, 173–189.
Ostwald, M. (1986), *From Popular Sovereignty to the Sovereignty of Law. Law, Society and Politics in Fifth-Century Athens*, Berkeley/Los Angeles.
Pezzoli, F. (2012), Aristotele, *La Politica, Libro II*, ed. by F. Pezzoli/M. Curnis, Roma.
Piovan, D. (2011), *Memoria e oblio della guerra civile. Strategie giudiziarie e racconto del passato in Lisia*, Pisa.
Placido Suarez, D. (1984/85), "Anito", *SHHD* 2-3, 7–13.
Pritchard, D.M. (2018), "The Archers of Classical Athens", *G & R* 65, 86–102.
Rhodes, P.J. (1981), *A Commentary on the Aristotelian* Athenaion Politeia, Oxford.
Ruschenbusch, E. (1979), *Athenische Innenpolitik im 5. Jahrhundert v. Chr. Ideologie oder Pragmatismus?*, Bamberg.
Seager, R. (1967), "Thrasybulus, Conon and Athenian Imperialism, 396–386 B.C.", *JHS* 87, 95–115.
Strauss, B.S. (1986), *Athens after the Peloponnesian War: Class, Faction and Policy 403–386 B.C.*, London/Sidney.
Thalheim, Th. (ed.) (1913²), *Lysiae orationes*, Lipsiae.
Todd, S.C. (1990), "The Use and Abuse of the Attic Orators", *G & R* 37, 159–178.
Todd, S.C. (2000), *Lysias*, Austin.
Traill, J.S. (1994–2016), *Persons of Ancient Athens*, I–XXII, Toronto.
Tuci, P.A. (2004), "Arcieri sciti, esercito e democrazia nell'Atene del V secolo", *Aevum* 78, 3–18.
Usener, H. (1873 = 1912), "Lysias' Rede über die Wiederherstellung der Demokratie", in: *Jahrbücher für klassische Philologie* 107, 145–174 = in: *Kleine Schriften*, I, Berlin/Leipzig, 262–295.
Voegelin, W. (1943), *Die Diabole bei Lysias*, Basel.
White, S.A. (1995), "Thrasymachus the Diplomat", *CP* 90, 307–327.
Wilamowitz-Moellendorff, U. von (1893 = 1966), *Aristoteles und Athen*, I–II, Berlin.
Wolpert, A. (2002), *Remembering Defeat. Civil War and Civic Memory in Ancient Athens*, Baltimore.
Yunis, H. (1997), "Thrasymachus B1: Discord, not Diplomacy", *CP* 92, 58–66.

Dino Piovan
The Athenian Civil War according to Lysias' Funeral Oration

Abstract: In this chapter the author reviews some passages in Lysias' *Funeral Oration* that allude to events that took place between 405 and 403 B.C, in particular § 58 on Aegospotami, about which the author presents an interpretation consistent with the thesis that the defeat was due to treason, previously found in Lys. 12, although here it is less explicit; and §§ 61–64 on the democratic resistance as a heroic struggle for justice and freedom, in which there are some distortions and glaring omissions. Afterwards he compares this Lysianic account of the Athenian civil war with those present in other funeral orations, and in particular in Plato's *Menexenus*. Finally, contrary to the interpretation offered by N. Loraux according to which the exaltation of harmony by Lysias watered down the more democratic traits of the anti-oligarchic resistance, Piovan argues that Lysias' rhetoric develops values and symbols without creating them from scratch and helps to instil them further into the city's culture, thus influencing civic behaviour.

In this essay I will analyze some passages from Lysias' Funeral Oration (Lys. 2), dealing with the period between the defeat at Aegospotami and the democratic restoration (405–403 B.C.), a two-year period that saw a series of tragic events in Athenian history, from defeat in the Peloponnesian War to the fall of the maritime empire and of democracy up to the civil war between democrats and oligarchs; a succession of catastrophes destined to have a long-lasting effect on the city and its public memory.

Certainly, some scholars have disputed Lysias' authorship of the speech and even have denied it. It is not possible here to deal with this question in depth; based on a previous study, I believe that there is no substantial reason to exclude Lysias' paternity whereas there are some good reasons to support it.[1]

I would like to thank Aggelos Kapellos for inviting me to contribute to this volume, sending me electronic versions of many useful studies and providing me with feedback of the first draft. I am also grateful to Giovanni Giorgini and Claudia Zatta for their readings of this essay and helpful suggestions to improve it; and the late Peter Rhodes for his careful attention and generous comments.

1 On the question of authorship and chronology of Lys. 2 cf. Todd 2007, 157–164, and Piovan 2011, 286–295, with much further bibliography.

The first passage includes an allusion to the battle of Aegospotami in the Hellespont, where the Spartan navy, commanded by Lysander, destroyed the Athenian fleet catching it unprepared on the beach (late summer 405 B.C.). It seems that the Spartan victory was gained without really fighting at sea; nevertheless, this victory was decisive because only nine Athenian ships, led by Conon, were able to escape; Athens lost control of the sea and its empire and was destined to suffer a terrible siege before the final surrender (spring 404 B.C.). Therefore the event of Aegospotami signalled the military end of the Peloponnesian war.[2]

Lysias writes:

Ἐπέδειξαν δὲ καὶ ἐν ταῖς δυστυχίαις τὴν ἑαυτῶν ἀρετήν. ἀπολομένων γὰρ τῶν νεῶν ἐν Ἑλλησπόντῳ εἴτε ἡγεμόνος κακίᾳ εἴτε θεῶν διανοίᾳ, καὶ συμφορᾶς ἐκείνης μεγίστης γενομένης καὶ ἡμῖν τοῖς δυστυχήσασι καὶ τοῖς ἄλλοις Ἕλλησιν, ἐδήλωσαν οὐ πολλῷ χρόνῳ ὕστερον ὅτι ἡ τῆς πόλεως δύναμις τῆς Ἑλλάδος ἦν σωτηρία. (Lys. 2.58)[3]

The defeat that put an end to the Peloponnesian war emerges as due either to the wickedness of a commander or to the will of the gods. The crucial word is κακία, which can be translated in different ways: badness, cowardice, vice, evil, etc.[4] Most translators prefer 'incompetence'.[5] Dover maintains that the meaning here is 'incompetence' without any reference to the charge of treason or coward-

---

[2] The main sources on the battle at Aegospotami are Xenophon (Hell. 2.1.22–29) and Diodorus (13.106.1–7), with partly conflicting accounts about the course of the events. Robinson 2014 reexamines them and proposes to harmonize them; instead Kapellos follows Xenophon against Diodorus: see Kapellos 2012; Kapellos 2014a, 9–10; Kapellos 2019b, chapter 4, where he argues that it was the Athenian generals that were responsible for the defeat and that the Athenian people reacted searching for "a scapegoat for their own mistakes at Aegospotami" (2019b, 251).
[3] "They displayed their merits even in times of misfortune: for when the fleet was destroyed in the Hellespont (either because of incompetence on the part of a commander, or else as a result of divine intervention), and there occurred what was a notorious disaster both for us who suffered it and for the rest of the Greeks, they made clear not long afterwards that the power of our city meant the security of Greece" (trans. by Todd 2007). The Greek text is quoted from Carey 2007.
[4] In particular, LSJ, s.v., suggests these translations under section I: 1) 'badness' as opposed to ἀρετή; 2) 'cowardice'; 3) 'moral badness', 'vice'; 4) 'evil'. Stephanus in TLG, s.v., suggests: 'improbitas, vitum, etiam vitiositas', even 'fraus'; only then 'ignavia', 'timiditas', finally 'probrum, dedecus'.
[5] Snell 1887 translates "incompetence", Gernet/Bizos 1924/26 "impéritie", Lamb 1930 "fault", Fernandez-Galiano 1953 "incapacidad", Albini 1955 "inettitudine", Medda 1991/95 "imperizia", Huber 2004/5 "Schuld", Todd 2007 "incompetence".

ice.⁶ This interpretation seems to find support in some of the words in the following paragraphs,⁷ i.e. συμφορά, 'misfortune', which is often used in referring to the battle at Aegospotami,⁸ and the verb δυστυχέω, 'to be affected by misfortune'. However, both words are euphemisms generally used for the events of 405–403 B.C. even when Athens' misfortunes are attributed to a precise group of people, be they oligarchs or sycophants.⁹ To really catch the meaning of κακία one has to look at § 65 below:

> ἔργοις δὲ μεγίστοις καὶ καλλίστοις ἀπελογήσαντο, ὅτι οὐ κακίᾳ τῇ αὐτῶν οὐδ' ἀρετῇ τῶν πολεμίων πρότερον ἐδυστύχησεν ἡ πόλις· εἰ γὰρ στασιάσαντες πρὸς ἀλλήλους βίᾳ παρόντων Πελοποννησίων καὶ τῶν ἄλλων ἐχθρῶν εἰς τὴν αὐτῶν οἷοί τε ἐγένοντο κατελθεῖν, δῆλον ὅτι ῥᾳδίως ἂν ὁμονοοῦντες πολεμεῖν αὐτοῖς ἐδύναντο.¹⁰

Here too the word κακία appears doubtlessly with the meaning of 'cowardice'; but the more interesting element is another. If the Athenians were able to return to their own land during a civil war, it is evident that they could have defeated

---

6 Dover 1968, 55 with n. 9; he quotes as parallels Aristoph. *Th.* 837, Thuc. 6.38.2, Plat. *Phaedr.* 248b. Instead Dover 1960, 72 had suggested a different explanation of ἡγεμόνος κακία: "the delinquency of a leader, i.e. of some person who was on that occasion in a position, morally or politically, to take an effective lead". Kapellos 2009, 260 thinks that "both interpretations hint at Philocles' deficient plan to confront Lysander, since he was in charge of the fleet on the fifth day and not Adeimantos". On Philocles' negative role at Aegospotami see also Kapellos 2012, 97–98.
7 Lys. 2.59: ἑτέρων γὰρ ἡγεμόνων γενομένων ἐνίκησαν μὲν ναυμαχοῦντες τοὺς Ἕλληνας οἱ πρότερον εἰς τὴν θάλατταν οὐκ ἐμβαίνοντες, ἔπλευσαν δ' εἰς τὴν Εὐρώπην, δουλεύουσι δὲ πόλεις τῶν Ἑλλήνων, τύραννοι δ' ἐγκαθεστᾶσιν, οἱ μὲν μετὰ τὴν ἡμετέραν συμφοράν, οἱδὲ μετὰ τὴν νίκην τῶν βαρβάρων ("For it was when others became leaders that those who had not previously manned a fleet defeated the Greeks in a sea-battle, sailed to Europe, and are enslaving the cities of the Greeks. Tyrants were established, some in the aftermath of our misfortune, and others following the victory of the barbarians", trans. by Todd 2007).
8 In Lysias' speeches συμφορά is used many times as an allusion either to Aegospotami or to all the events that begin with that battle and end with the reconciliation agreement (but in this case it is more frequent the plural συμφοραί); cf. Lys. 12.43; 16.4; 21.9; 31.8; fr. 170 Carey ll. 155–156, etc.
9 Cf. e.g. Lys. 12.92; 13.43, 48; 14.16; 25.25–26. In Lys. 12.43 συμφορά is used for Aegospotami while shortly before (§ 36) the responsibility for the defeat is attributed to an oligarchic plot; cf. Piovan 2011, 42–48. On συμφορά as the term used by the Attic orators for referring to Aegospotami see Kapellos 2014a, 98–99, and Bearzot 2017.
10 "They defended themselves by means of very great and very glorious deeds, showing that the city's previous misfortune was not the result of its own cowardice nor of the enemy's bravery. If they were able to return to their land while engaged in military conflict against fellow-citizens and in the face of the Peloponnesians and other hostile forces, it is clear that united they would easily have defeated them" (trans. by Todd 2007).

their enemies if they had been united. There is a clear allusion to the δυστυχία of Aegospotami, which is interpreted as a fruit of the lack of internal concord in Athens. In the κακία of § 58, therefore, it does not seem to me possible to see merely a reference to a commander's incompetence or to alleged cowardice, but rather to a greater fault such as the treason of an Athenian general. The reference could be to Adeimantus, one of the Athenian generals who led the fleet at Aegospotami, who according to Xenophon was "charged by some people with having betrayed the fleet" (ἠτιάθη μέντοι ὑπό τινων προδοῦναι τὰς ναῦς, Xen. *Hell.* 2.1.32).[11] It was Adeimantus that Conon, who also was a general on that occasion, blamed for the defeat after his own return to Athens, i.e. a little time before the likely date of the drafting of this speech.[12] Besides, some time earlier Lysias had written the speech against Alcibiades the Younger, in which both Alcibiades Senior and Adeimantus were considered responsible for the defeat because of treason (Lys. 14.38).[13] However, perhaps this reference is not so pre-

---

[11] On Adeimantus' role in the battle of Aegospotami and the suspicion against him cf. Kapellos 2009, 257–266; Piovan 2011, 44–47; Bearzot 2017, 47–48. Kapellos 2019b, 251, argues that Xenophon's wording at *Hell.* 2.1.32 expresses his disapproval of those men who blamed Adeimantus.

[12] Dem. 19.191 says that Conon accused Adeimantus συστρατηγήσας, 'after having been strategos with him', without specifying when or why. According to MacDowell 2000, 285, the date of the accusation should be after Conon came back to Athens in 393 B.C.; besides, the accusation could not have been of treason but a kind of character assassination during another legal action. Kirchner also thought of a date following Conon's return to Athens (cf. *PA* 586); so also Strauss 1983, 314 n. 24. Another hypothesis is that the accusation was launched by way of an intermediary (cf. Nouhaud 1982, 334); a possible parallel could be the letter sent by the generals of Arginusae before returning home, the letter which Theramenes used later to accuse them of failing to save the shipwrecked (Xen. *Hell.* 1.7.4). Demosthenes does not say explicitly that Conon's charge concerned Aegospotami but that is suggested by the verb συστρατηγέω, which recalls the most famous event in which they both were generals. Nouhaud assumes that Demosthenes could have invented this detail but I would reject that; in other passages Demosthenes shows he accurately knows things concerning Conon, like the honours granted to him (cf. Dem. 20.68–74). For a possible reconstruction of the trial against Adeimantus and Conon's role see Kapellos 2009, 266–276.

[13] Certainly, also the authorship of Lys. 14 is disputed, although it seems to me most likely: cf. Carey 1989, 147–148, Todd 2020, 479. See also Zimmerman in this volume. It is noteworthy that Lysias and Isocrates had an opposing position in the debate about Alcibiades Senior, the former against (cf. Lys. 14), the latter for, as it is shown by Isocr. 16, even if this latter speech, written in defence of Alcibiades the Younger, was for a different trial from that of Lys. 14. On the relationship between Lys. 14 and Isocr. 16 see Carey 1989, 148–150 and Todd 2020, 477–478; on the possible beginnings of the competition between Lysias and Isocrates see Kapellos 2019a; about Alcibiades as a scapegoat for the disaster of Aegospotami but actually not responsible for the defeat see Kapellos 2017.

cise and could be just a more generic allusion to the thesis of the defeat as due to treason, i.e. to a conspiracy against democracy. The conspiracy against democracy is the core around which the narration of the events of 405–403 B.C. is built in other speeches by Lysias, such as, especially, Lys. 12 (*Against Eratosthenes*) and Lys. 13 (*Against Agoratus*), and also Lys. 30 (*Against Nicomachus*) and Lys. 18 (*On the Property of Nicias' Brothers*).[14] Very briefly, the theory of conspiracy is a tool intended to both explain the formidable sequence of the tragic events ranging from Aegospotami to the Thirty in a simple yet effective and deeply reassuring way; this tale points to the search for scapegoats, usually represented by the adversary in the trial, but also by people such as Theramenes, who was long gone. Scapegoats were indispensable to relieve the citizens of responsibility for the evils that occurred, such as the momentous defeat of Aegospotami or the vote that established the government of the Thirty. As with the conspiracy interpretation, resorting to concrete scapegoats aimed to contribute to the restoration of civic harmony. On the other hand, the theory of an oligarchic conspiracy is missing from other speeches such as Lys. 25 (*On a Charge of Overthrowing the Democracy*), written for the defence of someone charged with supporting the Thirty's oligarchy, Lys. 31 (*Against Philon*), Lys. 16 (*For Mantitheus*) and Lys. 26 (*Against Evandrus*).[15]

It is true that this theme is here evoked only vaguely, but it could not be otherwise, given the context; the funeral oration had to be delivered on a solemn occasion in which it was the greatness of Athens that was celebrated and there was no place to remember the misfortune of the city, except in an evasive way; and the fall of the democracy was experienced and remembered just as a misfortune. Such vagueness can be compared to Thucydides' famous passage in which the historian attributes the Athenian defeat to the internal struggle among the political leaders eager to stand out at all costs.[16] The idea that Athens would have won if there would not have been internal treason or dissension is

---

14 I thoroughly examined all these speeches in Piovan 2011, 15–94 (Lys. 12), 95–179 (Lys. 13), 261–279 (Lys. 30), 279–286 (Lys. 18). About oligarchic plots in the *Lysiacum corpus* see also Roisman 2006, 72–85; Kapellos 2019c, esp. 38–39; about the selective memory of the above-mentioned events in Athens after the restoration of democracy see also Wolpert 2002.
15 On Lys. 25 see Piovan 2009 and Piovan 2011, 181–230; on Lys. 31 Piovan 2011, 233–246; on Lys. 16 Piovan 2011, 246–252 (cf. also Kapellos 2014b); on Lys. 26 Piovan 2011, 252–260.
16 Cf. Thuc. 2.65, 7, 10–12; on this crucial passage see Hornblower 1991, 340–349; Fantasia 2003, 483–507.

common in different ancient authors, even if they do not agree on the nature of such divisions.[17]

However, the context of the funeral oration is different from that of the law-courts, where the speaker has to win against the opposing party; here one cannot emphasize the oligarchic plots but rather the final victory of democracy. An ample section, §§ 61–64, is devoted to this point:

> [61] I have been led into uttering these lamentations on behalf of the whole of Greece. But it is right that we should commemorate both privately and in public those men, who fled from slavery, struggled for justice and fought for democracy (ὑπὲρ τῆς δημοκρατίας στασιάσαντες); they had all sorts of enemies (πάντας πολεμίους κεκτημένοι), but returned from exile to Peiraieus. They were not compelled by *nomos*, but persuaded by their own noble nature. In new situations of danger, they copied the ancient bravery of their ancestors, [62] in the hope that by means of their own bravery they would gain a *polis* that would be shared with other people as well. They preferred death accompanied by freedom, rather than life with slavery. Their motive was not so much shame at the disasters they had suffered (ταῖς συμφοραῖς αἰσχυνόμενοι), but anger directed at their enemies. They preferred to die in their own land rather than to live as inhabitants of other peoples'. They made the oaths and the agreements into their allies (συμμάχους μὲν ὅρκους καὶ συνθήκας ἔχοντες), whereas their enemies were not just those who had previously fulfilled this rôle, but also their own citizens (πολεμίους δὲ τοὺς πρότερον ὑπάρχοντας καὶ τοὺς πολίτας τοὺς ἑαυτῶν). [63] Nevertheless, they did not fear the number of those against them, but risked danger in their own bodies. They put up a trophy over their enemies (τρόπαιον μὲν τῶν πολεμίων ἔστησαν) and created witnesses of their own bravery, in the shape of the tombs of the Spartans which are near this monument (ἐγγὺς ὄντας τοῦδε τοῦ μνήματος τοὺς Λακεδαιμονίων τάφους). They proved that the *polis* was great instead of being weak, and showed that it was united instead of being crippled by civil strife (ὁμονοοῦσαν δὲ ἀντὶ στασιαζούσης); they put up walls in place of those which had been destroyed. [64] Those of them who returned from exile showed that their counsels were equal to the deeds of those who lie here—they turned their attention not to the punishment of their opponents but to the safety of the *polis*. They could not be defeated, and did not desire to possess more, but gave a share in their own freedom to those prepared to en-

---

[17] Cf. Plat. *Men.* 243d: "And in truth it was by our own dissensions that we were brought down and not by the hands of other men; for by them we are still to this day undefeated, and it is we ourselves who have both defeated and been defeated by ourselves" (trans. W.R.M. Lamb). Socrates' insistence here that Athens was never defeated by others but only by herself is interpreted by Trivigno 2009, 39, as part of an ironic strategy; cf. also the interesting suggestion by Henderson 1975, 30–31, according to which Lysias' Funeral Oration could have been a target of Plato just in this section of *Menexenus* (see now Kapellos in this volume). The idea that the city was defeated because of its internal divisions seems present also in Aeschin. 2.176, in which, however, the meaning of the key word ἀψιμαχία (τῶν ῥητόρων ἀψιμαχίας) is uncertain: 'altercation' for LSJ, 'obstinacy' for Natalicchio 1998, 443 n. 235.

dure slavery, whereas they themselves refused to share the slavery of those men" (trans. by Todd 2007).

The democrats' resistance here becomes a heroic struggle for justice and liberty against slavery; this struggle was fought against an overwhelming mass of enemies by brave men, who were able, first, to come back to Peiraeus (§ 61), then, to erect a trophy over the Spartans (§ 63); after the victory they restored the city's greatness, choosing concord instead of civil war, salvation instead of revenge, the sharing of freedom instead of prevarication (§§ 63–64).

This narrative includes important distortions of the facts, some of which we will now analyze. The most resounding distortion concerns the Spartan tombs in the cemetery of Ceramicus, which are shown as a sign of Athens' ability to defeat its enemies.[18] Xenophon's account in the *Hellenica* provides us with a different version: that fight was just a partial victory by the democrats and was not decisive; later there was again a siege of Peiraeus by the Spartans, until peace talks were opened among the parties involved in the conflict, and only after they were concluded could the men of Peiraeus come back to the city.[19] In Lysias' account no word is said about this phase nor about the important Spartan intermediation. It is impossible to undervalue this omission; from the Funeral Oration it would seem that the democratic exiles had come back to the city after defeating both their internal and their external enemies, without negotiating any agreement with the city's party. The silence on the fundamental Spartan mediation between the two Athenian parties is a part of the selective reenactment of the events in Lys. 12 too.[20] In this way the merit for having ended the civil war pertains solely to the Athenians themselves. This omission also helps them to forget the gravity of the division of a city torn between two parties.

Quite peculiar also is the way in which the city's party is alluded to; the men of Peiraeus, it is said, became a faction (στασιάσαντες) but for democracy (ὑπὲρ τῆς δημοκρατίας); against whom? The answer is very elusive, just a generic "having all enemies". Only later we understand the identity of the opposition; it consists in: "their open enemies of aforetime and their own fellow citizens". This is an unusual way to speak: on the one hand, the speaker wants to re-evoke the victory of the democracy in order to counterbalance the mention of the defeat of Aegospotami and all its consequences; on the other hand, remembering

---

18 About this spacial reference to Ceramicus in Lysias' speech cf. Bakker 2012, 383.
19 Cf. Xen. *Hell.* 2.4.10–39. On Xenophon and the Athenian civil war cf. Dillery 1995, 146–163; Piovan 2010; Piovan 2011, 60–64 and *passim*; Canfora 2013.
20 On the silence on the Spartan mediation in Lys. 12 see Piovan 2011, 63–65.

the στάσις which divided the city is too embarrassing to be stated clearly.[21] Why does not the speaker choose to be completely silent about it? Silence, for instance, hovered over the events of 404/403 in the other funeral orations, with the exception of Plato's *Menexenus*.[22] But Pericles' funeral oration in Thucydides is imagined as pronounced in the winter of 431/430, therefore much earlier than the civil war, whereas both Demosthenes and Hyperides delivered theirs much later, in, respectively, 338 and 322.[23] The reference in Plato's *Menexenus*[24] seems

---

[21] About the negative meaning of στάσις in ancient Greek see Finley 1960, 5–6; Bertelli 1989; Bertelli 1996; Gehrke 1997. About the use of στάσις and πόλεμος referred to the events of 404/3 cf. Bearzot 2001; according to her, πόλεμος would reflect the contemporaries' point of view while στάσις a subsequent one, after the democratic restoration, in a moment in which the split in the citizenry had not healed yet; the use of στάσις in this speech, combined with positive terms such as justice and democracy (§ 61), would aim to justify the democrats. I think that another explanation is possible. The fact that πόλεμος is used by Xenophon, who presumably wrote a long time after the events, and still more by non-contemporary authors such as Aristotle and Diodorus, could suggest that they are not using the fighters' definition but following the tendency to conceal the internal struggle, a trend that arose very early; see the analysis of the Lysian speeches already mentioned such as Lys. 12 and Lys. 13 in Piovan 2011. It was the Spartan troops fighting with the Athenian oligarchs that contributed to the representation of the war as against an external enemy when it had been, first of all, a war within the community. The recurrence of the term στάσις, both in Lysias and in other sources, shows that a total removal was impossible, or at least the perception that the definition of that conflict was imbued with ambiguity.

[22] On all the questions about Plato's *Menexenus* see Clavaud 1980 and Tsitsiridis 1998. I find convincing the parodic interpretation (see Trivigno 2009) and not plausible that of "a serious political pamphlet of an unknown Athenian author from the 4th century" (Engels 2012, 30). See also Kapellos's chapter in this volume.

[23] For Demosthenes' Funeral Oration see Crick's chapter in this volume; for Hyperides' see Hermann 2009, 3.

[24] Cf. Plat. *Men.* 243e–244b: "After these happenings, when we were at peace and amity with other States, our civil war at home (ὁ οἰκεῖος ἡμῖν πόλεμος) was waged in such a way that — if men are fated to engage in civil strife (στασιάσαι) — there is no man but would pray for his own State that its sickness might resemble ours. So kindly and so friendly was the way in which the citizens from the Peiraeus and from the city consorted with one another, and also — beyond men's hopes — with the other Greeks; and such moderation did they show in their settlement of the war (πόλεμος) against the men at Eleusis. [...] For it was not through wickedness (κακία) that they set upon one another, nor yet through hatred (ἔχθρα), but through misfortune (δυστυχία)" (trans. Lamb). It is worth noting a few things: a) that Plato, differently from Lysias, avoids the term στάσις for πόλεμος, which is used twice in the passage (first as 'civil war', then as 'war against the men at Eleusis'), whereas he uses the verb στασιάζω with a vague reference; b) that the conflict is attributed not to wickedness nor hatred but to misfortune; c) that this passage does not explain what was at stake, by not distinguishing Peiraeus and city, an element which makes more evident the democratic tone of Lysias' passage.

to show that it was not possible to be completely silent over events whose impact was too heavy and still present. The tangle of misfortunes that began at Aegospotami and continued for two years, such as the siege, the peace, the fall of the democracy, the end of the empire and the destruction of the walls,[25] constitutes a black hole about which the city continued to ponder for years, trying to find a reason for the loss of its former power and glory. Lysias chooses to allude with elusiveness to all this series of disasters, which he reconstructs much more accurately in other speeches such as Lys. 12 and Lys. 13. The mention of the misfortunes is balanced by the alleged victory of the democratic exiles as well as by the other successes attributed to the restored democracy, such as the recovery of internal harmony, the salvation of the city, the reconstruction of the walls.

In other words, Lysias' choice is to exalt the unity of the city without passing completely in silence over the dissension; according to Nicole Loraux, this strategy is not without costs. In particular, the value of the democratic fighters is celebrated, that's true, but what is distinctively democratic would be denied; in particular, she observes that the sentence οὐχ ὑπὸ νόμου ἀναγκασθέντες, ἀλλ' ὑπὸ τῆς φύσεως πεισθέντες, "not compelled by law, but induced by nature" (§ 61), which associates law and compulsion, persuasion and nature, represents a reversal of the opposition, traditional in ancient Greek political thought, between force and persuasion; instead, this association seems to her to recall the preference for nature at the expense of law in some antidemocratic intellectuals of the fifth century B.C.;[26] finally, the emphasis on harmony or the salvation of the city would mirror issues and the lexicon of the political thought of the period around the end of the fifth century and the beginning of the fourth century. As if it were possible to praise democracy only as far as to pervert it, to cover it with aristocratic traits.[27]

It is true that ὁμόνοια, 'harmony', is certainly a keyword in the years of the democratic restoration, while the salvation of the city had been a much-debated

---

[25] For the events after Aegospotami see Xen. *Hell.* 2.2.1–23; Diod. 13.107, 14.3.2–7; Plut. *Lys.* 13–15, *Alc.* 37.5; Just. 5.8.

[26] Also for Todd 2007, 261 it is "an unusually negative reading of *nomos* (law and/or custom)". I share Peter Rhodes' view that "Lysias' main point is that the returning democrats made their effort not under compulsion but from their own virtuous nature, and *nomos* has been used rather artificially for the sake of the contrast with *physis*" (private communication).

[27] Cf. Loraux 1981, 198–204; in this famous book, the French scholar analyses the theme of the aristocratic language used to praise democracy in all the surviving funeral orations, and in the conclusion she argues that the Athenian democracy was not able to mould its own language (*ibidem*, 339–340). For a criticism of Loraux's thesis see Ober 1989, 289–292.

theme in the final years of the Peloponnesian war, one which was used even by those who wanted to reform or subvert the democratic constitution.²⁸ The fact that these two expressions recur more times in the passage cannot be considered casual.²⁹ However, I would suggest that the explanation of Loraux is not the only possible one. Her analysis is acute but it overlooks the way in which the reconciliation agreement of 403 B.C. is here recalled. Indeed, it is evoked (§ 62) but in a paradoxical way: it appears as an event internal to the democratic resistance, as if the democrats had made among themselves those agreements and oaths for which they will later be praised even by Xenophon and Isocrates, authors who did not fight against the oligarchy. It seems almost as if the democrats were already disposed to reconciliation even before they came back.

We cannot know exactly what Lysias exactly thinks about this matter, if the question ever makes sense. We must not forget that every mental operation is opaque to itself.³⁰ In general, the question whether Lysias is personally convinced of what he writes or is just an unscrupulous manipulator often recurs in the studies of Lysias' accounts of the Athenian civil war; I believe it is not possible to give a definitive answer. Studies of how collective memory works have, however, shown how the memory of the individual is socially conditioned and influenced by the needs of the community in which one lives, communicates and interacts. In short, Lysias is certainly influenced by a collective memory that is formed during the years of the democratic restoration and, in his turn, helps to shape it.³¹ What I would suggest is that in this speech Lysias not only

---

28 Cf. e.g. for ὁμόνοια Isocr. 18.44, 68; Andoc. 1.73, 76, 106, 109, 140; for σωτηρία Thuc. 8.53, 72, 86; Lys. 12.68, 74; Lys. 34.6. For additional examples see Lévy 1976, 16–23 (about the theme "salvation of the city") and 209–222 (about "internal harmony"). In any way it is doubtful that "harmony" and "salvation" belonged to the aristocratic language as much as such words as *kosmiotes* or *sophrosyne*, as Peter Rhodes has pointed out to me (private communication).
29 It is may be worth observing that the noun ὁμόνοια and the verb ὁμονοεῖν are used ten times in Lysias' *corpus*: four times in Lys. 25, twice in Lys. 18 and even four times in Lys. 2 (§§ 18, 43, 63, 65). As to σωτηρία, there are forty-two occurrences in the same *corpus*, mostly concentrated in speeches posterior to the democratic restoration of 403, in which the events of 405/403 play an important role, such as Lys. 6 (four times), Lys. 12 (five), Lys. 25 (four), Lys. 34 (three) and precisely Lys. 2 with even eight occurrences. Of course, σωτηρία in Lys. 2 is often used with reference to Greece saved by Athens from the Persians, however it appears twice in this passage as "salvation of the city" (§§ 64 and 66).
30 So Loraux 1981, 342, about the ideological dimension of the genre "funeral oration".
31 For the notion of collective memory see the still seminal studies of M. Halbwachs, especially Halbwachs 2001 [1950]; Assman 1997 [1992] has suggested that there are more types of collective memory; for a very good discussion of general characteristics of social memory see Steinbock 2013, 7–19, and 19–47 for its application to ancient Greece and classical Athens.

speaks as an orator loyal and attached to the democracy, but he also tries to claim for the democratic party themes and key words of the language of those who had fought against democracy or at least had not openly defended it as Thrasybulus and his fellows had done. This strategy is similar to that adopted by other orators of the classical period. They, implicitly or explicitly, answer the objections of the critics of democracy by defining or redefining words seminal in the contemporary political debate. It is not only a verbal match but an ideological one too; it is a kind of speech which aims to produce truth and not simply propaganda, to use a concept elaborated by M. Foucault.[32] In sum, it is not only a question of words but also of values and symbols; the rhetoric elaborates them but does not create them from nothing, and it contributes to introducing them into the civic culture and to influencing the citizens' behaviour. Harmony indeed cannot be considered only a flag of the former Three Thousand, the only full citizens under the Thirty, who had, up to a point, actively or passively supported the oligarchy. Rather harmony should have been a need felt by the Athenian people beyond the split of 404/403;[33] it is for this reason that Lysias includes it in the constellation of values that define democracy beside freedom, justice, law and reason in an interesting passage of the Funeral Oration (Lys. 2.18–19).[34]

About the dynamics of memory in the Athenian funeral orations see now Shear 2013, 513, who rightly underscores that "the speeches [i.e. the *epitaphioi*] show in exemplary fashion how one individual's memory may become collective remembrance". I share the idea that "even if one assumes that Lysias' *Funeral Oration* was only intended as a written text for private circulation, the speech is nonetheless made to reflect an ideal *epitaphios logos*" (Barbato 2017, 219 n. 22).
32 For examples of democratic orators replying to critics on the basis of political-ideological language see Piovan 2008, §1; for the speech producing truth see Foucault 1977, 3–28. For propaganda cf. Crick's analysis in this volume.
33 Actually, it was a need felt immediately after Aegospotami, if we can believe And. 1.73 and 76; certainly, the noun 'harmony' is not used in Patrocleides' decree about the rights to be restituted to the disfranchised people (Andoc. 1.77–79), that is its stated aim; but the authenticity of this document is contested: cf. Canevaro and Harris 2012 and Canevaro and Harris 2016–2017; the opposite opinion is argued by Hansen 2015.
34 "[18] They were the first people, and at that time the only ones, to have driven out those who held autocratic power among them, and to have established democracy, in the belief that freedom for all is the greatest source of harmony. They allowed everybody to share in the hopes that arise out of danger, and governed themselves with freedom of spirit. [19] They honoured according to *nomos* those who were good, and punished those who were bad, in the belief that to be ruled forcibly by each other was an *ergon* for animals, but that it was fitting for humans to determine justice by means of *nomos*, to persuade by using *logos*, and to serve those purposes by their *ergon*, while being ruled by *nomoi* and taught by *logos*." (trans. by Todd 2007).

It is noteworthy that the interpretation of this last passage has an impact on the interpretation of Athenian democracy, especially that of the fourth century. That democracy has often been considered more moderate than the fifth century's one for various reasons, such as the demise of the empire, the part played by the moderates, etc.[35] However, J. Ober has radically challenged the traditional interpretation in many volumes and in a different way M. Hansen too has shown that the democratic institutions were not at all in decline in the fourth century.[36] This is not the right place for an in-depth discussion of this topic. But the fact that Lysias incorporates harmony within the constellation of democratic values can be considered not so much a sign of subordination to the values of the moderates as a clue to a complex process of redefinition of democracy itself, which tries to take into account the past evils and, in doing so, reveals an ongoing vitality.[37]

Bibliography

Albini, U. (ed.) (1955), *Lisia, I Discorsi*, Firenze.
Assman, I. (1997) [1992], *La memoria culturale*, Torino (=*Das Kulturelle Gedächtnis*, München 1992).
Bakker, M.P. de (2012), "Lysias", in: I. De Jong (ed.), *Space in Ancient Greek Literature*, Leiden/Boston, 377–392.

---

[35] Cf. e.g. Cloché 1915 and Cloché 1916; more recently, the thesis of a basic transformation of the Athenian democracy at the end of the fifth century has been argued by Ostwald 1986 and, many times, by M. Hansen, in part. Hansen 1999. For a critical evaluation of this thesis see Piovan 2017; against the use of the adjectives 'radical' and 'moderate' for the Athenian democracy of, respectively, fifth and fourth century B.C., see Strauss 1987 and Millett 2000.
[36] See Ober 1989; 1996; 2005; Hansen 1991. A different position from both Ober and Hansen is represented by Rhodes, who thinks that changes in the early fourth century were in the spirit of the fifth-century democracy, but later changes were not: see Rhodes 1980; Rhodes 1994, 565–571. Cf. also Cartledge 2018, 203–217, on the so-called 'Lycurgan' democracy.
[37] Cf. Ober and Strauss 1990, 241: "consensus (*homonoia*) was regarded by the Athenians as a central democratic virtue"; and Wolpert 2002, 130: "Using what was traditionally aristocratic language to praise those who had fought against the oligarchs, they rendered elite values serviceable to democratic ideals. This coopting of aristocratic language does not suggest that the Athenians accepted aristocratic pretensions at face value or that they were attempting to elevate the democratic resistance by portraying it as if all of its members were part of the political and social elite. Rather, the use of this language shows how memory of the civil war enabled the Athenians to democratize elite values".

Barbato, M. (2017), "Using the Past to Shape the Future: Ancestors, Institutions and Ideology in Aeschin. 2.74–78", in: E. Franchi/G. Proietti (eds.), *Conflict in Communities. Forward-looking Memories in Classical Athens*, Trento, 213–253.
Bearzot, C. (2001), "Stasis e polemos nel 404", in: M. Sordi (ed.), *Il pensiero sulla guerra nel mondo antico*, Milano, 19–36; reprint in: C. Bearzot, *Vivere da democratici. Studi su Lisia e la democrazia ateniese*, Roma 2007, 101–120.
Bearzot, C. (2017), "La συμφορά de la cité. La défaite d'Athènes (405–404 av. J.–C.) chez les orateurs attiques", *Ktèma* 42, 41–52.
Bertelli, L. (1989), "Stasis: La "rivoluzione" dei greci", *Teoria politica* 5, 53–96.
Bertelli, L. (1996), "La stasis dans la démocratie", in: M.-L. Desclos (ed.), *Réflexions contemporaines sur l'antiquité classique*, Grenoble, 11–38.
Canevaro, M./Harris, E.M. (2012), "The Documents in Andocides' *On the Mysteries*", *CQ* 62, 98–129.
Canevaro, M./Harris, E.M. (2016–2017), "The Authenticity of the Documents at Andocides' *On the Mysteries* 77–79 and 83–84", *Dike* 19/20, 9–49.
Canfora, L. (2013), *La guerra civile ateniese*, Milano.
Carey, C. (1989), *Lysias, Selected Speeches*, Cambridge.
Carey, C. (ed.) (2007), *Lysiae orationes cum fragmentis*, Oxford.
Cartledge, P. (2018), *Democracy. A Life*, 2nd edn., Oxford.
Clavaud, R. (1980), *Le Ménexène de Platon et la rhétorique de son temps*, Paris.
Cloché, P. (1915), *La restauration démocratique à Athènes en 403 avant J. C.*, Paris.
Cloché, P. (1916), "Les Trois-Mille et la restauration démocratique à Athènes en 403", *REG* 29, 14–28.
Dillery, J. (1995), *Xenophon and the History of His Times*, London/New York.
Dover, K.J. (1960), "ΔΕΚΑΤΟΣ ΑΥΤΟΣ", *JHS* 80, 61–77.
Dover, K.J. (1968), *Lysias and the Corpus Lysiacum*, Berkeley/Los Angeles.
Engels, D. (2012), "Irony and Plato's *Menexenus*", *AC* 81, 13–30.
Fantasia, U. (2003), *Tucidide, La guerra del Peloponneso, Libro II*, Pisa.
Fernandez-Galiano, M. (ed.) (1953), *Lysias, Discursos I–XII*, Barcelona.
Finley, M.I. (1974), "Athenian Demagogues", in: M.I. Finley (ed.), *Studies in Ancient Society*, London/Boston, 1–25 (or. ed.: *Past & Present*, 1960, 21, 3–24).
Foucault, M. (1977), *Microfisica del potere. Interventi politici*, ed. A. Fontana and P. Pasquino, Torino.
Gehrke, H.-J. (1997), "La stasis", in: S. Settis (ed.), *I Greci. Storia cultura arte società*, vol. 2, t. II, Torino, 453–480.
Gernet, L./Bizos, M. (eds.) (1924/26), *Lysias, Discours*, I–II, Paris.
Halbwachs, M. (2001) [1950], *La memoria collettiva*, ed. by P. Jedlowsky and T. Grande, Milan (= *La memoir collective*, Paris 1950).
Hansen, M.H. (1999), *The Athenian Democracy in the Age of Demosthenes*, 2nd ed., Oxford.
Hansen, M.H. (2015), "Is Patrokleides' Decree (Andoc. 1.77–79) a Genuine Document?", *GRBS* 55, 884–901.
Henderson, M.M. (1975), "Plato's *Menexenus* and the Funeral Oration", *Acta Classica* 18, 25–46.
Herrman, J. (2009), *Hyperides, Funeral Oration*, New York.
Hornblower, S. (1991), *A Commentary on Thucydides, Volume I: Books I–III*, Oxford.
Huber, I. (ed.) (2004/5), *Lysias Reden*, Darmstadt.

Kapellos, A. (2009), "Adeimantos at Aegospotami: Innocent or Guilty?", *Historia* 53 (3), 257–275.
Kapellos, A. (2012), "Philocles and the Sea-Battle at Aegospotami (Xen. *Hell*. 2.1.22–32)", *CW* 106 (1), 97–101.
Kapellos, A. (2014a), *Lysias 21. A Commentary*, Berlin/Boston.
Kapellos, A. (2014b), "In Defence of Mantitheus: Structure, Strategy and Argumentation in Lysias 16", *BICS* 57, 23–47.
Kapellos, A. (2017), "Alcibiades at Aegospotami and the Defeat of the Athenian Fleet: History and Rhetoric", *PP* 72 (2), 303–323.
Kapellos, A. (2019a), "Lysias, Isocrates and the Trierarchs of Aegospotami", *Erga-Logoi* 7 (1), 85–102.
Kapellos, A. (2019b), *Xenophon's Peloponnesian War*, Berlin/Boston.
Kapellos, A. (2019c), "Xenophon and Lysias on the Arginusai Trial", *Erga-Logoi* 7 (2), 19–44.
Lamb, W.R.M. (ed.) (1930), *Lysias*, London/Cambridge (MA).
Lévy, E. (1976), *Athènes devant la défaite de 404. Histoire d'une crise idéologique*, Paris.
Loraux, N. (1981), *L'invention d'Athènes. Histoire de l'oraison funèbre dans la «cité classique»*, Paris.
MacDowell, D.M. (ed.) (2000), *Demosthenes, On the False Embassy (Oration 19)*, Oxford.
Medda, E. (ed.) (1991/95), *Lisia, Orazioni*, I–II, Milano.
Millett, P. (2000), "Mogens Hansen and the Labelling of Athenian Democracy", in: P. Flensten-Jensen/T. Nielsen/L. Rubinstein (eds.), *Polis & Politics. Studies in Ancient Greek History Presented to M. H. Hansen*, Copenhagen, 337–362.
Natalicchio, A. (ed.) (1998), *Eschine, Orazioni*, Milano.
Nouhaud, M. (1982), *L'utilisation de l'histoire par les orateurs attiques*, Paris.
Ober, J. (1989), *Mass and Elite in Democratic Athens. Rhetoric, Ideology, and the Power of the People*, Princeton.
Ober, J. (1996), *The Athenian Revolution. Essays on Ancient Greek Democracy and Political Theory*, Princeton.
Ober, J. (2005), *Athenian Legacies. Essays on the Politics of Going Together*, Princeton/Oxford.
Ober, J./Strauss, B. (1990), "Drama, Political Rhetoric, and the Discourse of Athenian Democracy", in: J.J. Winkler/F.I. Zeitlin, *Nothing to Do with Dionysos? Athenian Drama in Its Social Context*, Princeton, 237–270.
Ostwald, M. (1986), *From Popular Sovereignty to the Sovereignty of Law*, Berkeley/Los Angeles.
Piovan, D. (2008), "Criticism Ancient and Modern. Observations on the Critical Tradition of Athenian Democracy", *Polis* 25 (2), 305–329.
Piovan, D. (ed.) (2009), *Lisia, Difesa dall'accusa di attentato alla democrazia*, Padova/Roma.
Piovan, D. (2010), *L'antidemocrazia al potere. La tirannia dei Trenta in Senofonte*, Milano.
Piovan, D. (2011), *Memoria e oblio della guerra civile. Strategie giudiziarie e racconto del passato in Lisia*, Pisa.
Piovan, D. (2017), "Nomos Basileus o demos basileus? Sulla democrazia ateniese di V e IV secolo a.C.", *Rivista di diritto ellenico* 7, 139–152.
Robinson, E. (2014), "What Happened at Aegospotami? Xenophon and Diodorus on the Last Battle of the Peloponnesian War", *Historia* 63 (1), 1–16.
Rhodes, P.J. (1980), "Athenian Democracy after 403 B.C.", *CJ* 75 (4), 305–323.
Rhodes, P.J. (1994), "The *Polis* and the Alternatives", in: *Cambridge Ancient History*, 2nd ed., vol. VI, *The Fourth Century B.C.*, ed. by D.M. Lewis, J. Boardman, S. Hornblower, M. Ostwald, Cambridge, 565–591.

Roisman, J. (2006), *The Rhetoric of Conspiracy in Ancient Athens*, Berkeley/Los Angeles/London.
Shear, J.L. (2013), "Their Memories Will Never Grow Old: The Politics of Remembrance in the Athenian Funeral Orations", *CQ* 63 (2), 511–536.
Snell, F.J. (ed.) (1887), *Lysias Epitaphios*, Oxford.
Steinbock, B. (2013), *Social Memory in Athenian Public Discourse: Uses and Meanings of the Past*, Ann Arbor.
Strauss, B.S. (1983), "Aegospotami Reexamined", *AJP* 104, 24–35.
Strauss, B.S. (1987), "Athenian Democracy: Neither Radical, Extreme, Nor Moderate", *AHB* 1, 127–129.
Todd, S.C. (2007), *A Commentary on Lysias, Speeches 1–11*, Oxford.
Todd, S.C. (2020), *A Commentary on Lysias, Speeches 12–17*, Oxford.
Trivigno, F. (2009), "The Rhetoric of Parody in Plato's *Menexenus*", *Philosophy and Rhetoric* 42 (1), 29–58.
Tsitsiridis, S. (1998), *Platons Menexenos*, Stuttgart/Leipzig.
Wolpert, A. (2002), *Remembering Defeat. Civil War and Civic Memory in Ancient Athens*, Baltimore/London.

Markus Zimmermann
Lysias' Speech 14 and the Use of the Recent Past for Political Purposes

Abstract: This chapter deals with Lysias' speech against Alcibiades, the son of the famous Athenian politician Alcibiades, and analyses how the historical events during the Peloponnesian War in which Alcibiades took part are presented in the speech, and also how the Lysianic version of Alcibiades' participation in this events is used by the orator to discredit his son. The completely negative and one-sided version of Lysias is interesting because: *a)* most Athenians must still have known what happened during the Peloponnesian War and how Alcibiades was related to those events and *b)* Alcibiades was not hated by all of the Athenians, since he returned to Athens in 408, was elected *stragetos autokrator*, while even after his second flight he was not convicted *in absentia* and there was no trial. This leads to the question to what extent (if at all) historical accuracy was necessary to convince the audience.

After the restoration of the Athenian democracy, Lysias made a living as a logographer. All the orations known to us today whose attribution to Lysias is relatively certain were written roughly between 403 to 380 B.C.[1] Thus, they are an important source for the social — and to some degree even political — history of Athens after the Peloponnesian War.

The domestic policy of Athens in the first years of the 4th century B.C. was dominated by efforts to maintain the amnesty and by conflicts regarding the city-state's proper relationship with Sparta. Another problem was the conflict between the men who had restored democracy and those who had supported the Thirty or were accused of having done so. This political climate lasted until Athens decided to support the Boeotians against Sparta.[2] It was in these eventful years that Lysias wrote his 14th speech. Lysias wrote the speech for a trial against Alcibiades the Younger, the son of the famous 5th-century politician Alcibiades. The plaintiff in this trial was a certain Archestratides (§ 3), who was supported by two *synegoroi* whose names are unknown. Lysias wrote his speech for one of the *synegoroi*, who may have been a member of the Athenian upper

---
[1] Paulsen 2011, 439–440; for the biography of Lysias and the chronology of his speeches see also Dover 1968, 28–46.
[2] Funke 1980, 7–11; see also Wolpert 2002, 48–71.

class,³ while we do not know Archestratides' speech. The trial took place after the battle of Haliartus, where Athens supported the Boeotians against Sparta. It was a successful campaign for Athens, even though they only arrived after the Boeotians' victory and the death of the Spartan commander Lysander.⁴ The *synegoros* accuses Alcibiades the Younger of having illegally served in the cavalry. He thus charges him with failure to perform his military duties (ἀστρατεία), desertion (λιποτάξιον) and cowardice (δειλία) (§ 7).⁵ As was common in these kinds of lawsuits, the jury consisted of soldiers who had participated in the battle, while the generals presided over the trial.⁶ The latter took place shortly after the military campaign and therefore most probably still in the year 395 B.C.⁷ This was not the first lawsuit which Alcibiades the Younger had to deal with. Probably in 397 B.C., a man named Teisias also took him to court because of something his father had allegedly done. Teisias accused the famous but already deceased Alcibiades of stealing a team of horses from him for his participation in the Olympic Games of 416 B.C.; he sought to get Alcibiades the Younger to reimburse the theft.⁸ We know about this trial form Isocrates' 16th speech, which he wrote for Alcibiades the Younger.⁹ According to Isocrates, this trial was not the first one which Alcibiades the Younger had to undergo. Alcibiades the Younger claims in this speech that in all those trials he had to face, it was not so much the actual indictment which was debated in court, as his father's alleged crimes, for which he himself was held responsible by the plaintiffs.¹⁰ Lysias' 14th speech must be viewed in the same context: for although the defendant is Alcibiades the Younger, much of the speech is devoted to the alleged crimes of his father.

---

3 Rubinstein 2000, 144 n. 59.
4 Xen. *Hell.* 3.5.16–25; Buck 1998, 98–99.
5 Dombrowski 1934, 19; for the legal aspects see also Todd 2020, 472–474.
6 Dombrowski 1934, 2 and 19; Carey 1989, 144; see also Todd 2020, 469–471.
7 Carey 1989, 141; F. Blass, D. Gribble and S. Todd think that 395 and 394 B.C. are both possible dates for the trial: Blass 1887, 489; Gribble 1999, 93; Todd 2020, 467.
8 Blass 1874, 204–205; Gribble 1999, 93 (397/396 B.C.).
9 Isoc. 16; Plutarch thinks that the speech was given at a real trial: Plut. *Alc.* 12. Ober 1989, 49 maintains that all the published forensic speeches must be very similar to those which were actually given in court. Worthington 1991 is convinced of the opposite and argues that all forensic speeches were revised before publication.
Many people think that Isoc. 16 may have been revised before publication because it presents many features which are more commonly found in encomia: Carey 1989, 149; Gribble 1999, 112–117; Alexiou 2011, 316–319. Häusle 1987/88, 96, by contrast, is convinced that the speech is only an encomium and was never delivered in court.
10 Isoc. 16.1–2.

When writing the speech for the trial, Lysias must have known about Isocrates' speech, since he refers to it;[11] but we do not know the outcome of either of the two trials.[12] An acquittal in the desertion case is considered likely by G. Hertzberg[13] and F. Blass[14] because of the influential supporters mentioned in Lysias' 14th speech (§ 21). The charges made in this speech seem far-fetched and therefore S. Feraboli is convinced that all of the accusations are legally untenable and that the prosecutors are bringing a very weak case to court.[15] In Lysias' 15th speech,[16] which was written for another *synegoros* participating in the same trial, it is also said that the generals are claiming that they allowed Alcibiades the Younger to join the cavalry.[17] Furthermore, he was not the only one joining the cavalry on this military campaign without having passed the proper military examination, as we are told in Lysias' 16th speech. In this speech, which was written in defence of a certain Mantitheus, the orator claims that several men joined the cavalry because it seemed less dangerous to them to serve in this unit.[18] Even if several men did so without permission, Athens seems to have benefited from this arbitrary act, since Xenophon mentions the strength of the cavalry as one of the reasons why the Spartans under Pausanias' command avoided a second battle and marched back home after the Boeotians won the first battle without the help of Athens.[19] In the end, Athens participated in a successful military campaign against Sparta without any losses; therefore, the predominant feelings in the army must have been of joy for the easy victory and not of anger towards some men who were serving in the cavalry without proper examination. So it is plausible that the jury found Alcibiades the Younger not guilty. In any case, it is highly interesting that the young man had to face several trials once he reached the legal age in 398/97 B.C.[20] and that in all those trials his famous deceased father would appear to have been in the dock as the co-defendant.

In the years following the end of the Peloponnesian War there was a vivid debate about the evaluation of the famous politician Alcibiades and his deeds.[21]

---

11 Gribble 1999, 108.
12 Hertzberg 1853, 358.
13 Hertzberg 1853, 358.
14 Blass 1887, 489.
15 Feraboli 1980, 83–86; see also Carey 1989, 145.
16 For Lysias' authorship see Carey 1989, 148; Todd 2020, 479.
17 Lys. 15, 6; see also Todd 2020, 588.
18 Lys. 16, 13; see also Kapellos 2014, 34–35; Todd 2020, 656–657.
19 Xen. *Hell.* 3.5.23.
20 Gribble 1999, 92; see also Todd 2020, 466–467.
21 Gribble 1999, 95–96.

This debate first broke out when Alcibiades was still alive, as Aristophanes tells us in his *Frogs*, which was performed in 405 B.C., at a time when Alcibiades was living in self-chosen exile in Thrace. Aristophanes wrote in this play that the Athenians loved yet at the same time also hated Alcibiades.[22] This must be understood as an allusion to the debate about the possibility of recalling Alcibiades to Athens and of assigning him once again command over the troops,[23] a prospect which not all Athenians were keen on. This discussion continued in Athens even after the end of the war and the murder of Alcibiades in 404 B.C.[24] One of the reasons for this may have been Athenian domestic politics, as the political opponents of former companions of Alcibiades strove to put them in a bad light by discrediting the man with whom they had been closely connected. This was probably the main reason why Alcibiades the Younger had to defend himself against the charges made by Archestratides: the trial was also meant to harm Thrasybulus — a former companion of Alcibiades — and his supporters.[25] Therefore, the plaintiffs' motivation was probably a political one.[26] D. Gribble seems right to assume that Thrasybulus is one of the important officials (§ 21), which is to say one of the *strategoi* at Haliartus,[27] who are mentioned in the speech as supporters of Alcibiades the Younger in court.[28] This support from the victorious *strategoi*– including Thrasybulus, the leader of the democratic party in the civil war[29] — makes it highly plausible that the charges were dismissed. This is why the speaker of Lysias' 15th speech tries very hard to weaken the commanders' intercession in favour of Alcibiades the Younger.[30]

Besides these insights into the domestic policy of Athens in the early years of the 4th century B.C., which will be discussed in more detail later, it is also of great interest to note how the orator tries to discredit Alcibiades the Younger and his father. One line of argumentation is the presentation of Alcibiades and Alcibiades the Younger as morally degenerate persons who do not care about the moral principles of the *polis*.[31] He tries to prove this by telling stories about

---

22 Aristoph. *Frogs* 1425.
23 Bleckmann 1998, 586–587; Heftner 2011, 177–178.
24 Concerning the various accounts about Alcibiades' murder in the ancient sources see for example Perrin 1906; Heftner 2011, 186–188.
25 Strauss 1987, 93.
26 Strauss 1987, 112; Gribble 1999, 97.
27 Carey 1989, 161; see also Todd 2020, 526–527.
28 Gribble 1999, 96.
29 Xen. *Hell*. 2.4.2–5; 2.4.10–43.
30 Lys. 15.
31 Gribble 1999, 118–119.

the debauchery of Alcibiades the Younger when he was still a kid (§ 25) and about how he betrayed his father (§ 26). He also tells us that the latter event led to a quarrel between father and son and that the father hated his son so much that he wantonly put his life at risk (§ 27). Another line of argumentation presents us Alcibiades as primarily responsible for the decline of Athens, since he is accused of being the initiator of all the bad things which have befallen the *polis* (§ 35).[32] This seems to have been a common accusation at the time and one not limited to Alcibiades' deeds, since the speaker of Lysias' 13th speech directs the same charge at Agoratus.[33] However, the orator does not limit himself to this kind of blanket charge, as he also uses specific events of the recent past to emphasize Alcibiades' guilt for the decline of Athens and therefore, at least partially, the guilt of his former companions too. To prove this point he also talks about historical events which had taken place over the previous two decades and which most people in the audience would therefore have recalled. This is of particular interest because the orator presents alternative views on important historical events which are contrary to the accounts in the historical sources. His aim in doing so is to present Alcibiades and his son in the worst possible light. However, since most people would presumably have remembered those events, the question arises as to whether this is a promising strategy.

A good example of the presentation of alternative interpretations of recent events in Lysias' 14th speech is the Athenian defeat at Aegospotami. This was one of the most important events in the recent history of Athens and it happened only ten years before the speech was given in court.[34] One can assume that every Athenian had at least some memory of this event, based either on personal experience or on others' accounts. Therefore, it is quite astonishing that the event is presented in a way which is not covered by any other source. Because of this, modern scholars may feel inclined to say that this is a misrepresentation of the past.[35] According to the oration, Alcibiades and Adeimantus committed treason before the Athenian defeat at Aegospotami by cooperating with Lysander (§ 38). This is a view which is neither congruent with the ancient accounts given by Xenophon,[36] Diodorus,[37] Plutarch[38] and Cornelius Nepos[39] nor

---

[32] See also Häusle 1987/88, 108.
[33] Lys. 13.33; see also Kapellos 2009, 263.
[34] Concerning the historical background of the battle, see for example Bleckmann 1998, 115–128 and 572–603; Kapellos 2014a, 1–11.
[35] Caimo 1935, 254; Seager 1967, 13; Carey 1989, 174–175; Kapellos 2009; Kapellos 2017.
[36] Xen. *Hell*. 2.1.25–32.
[37] Diod. 13.105–106.
[38] Plut. *Alc*. 36–37.

with the interpretation of this event favoured by the vast majority of modern scholars.⁴⁰ Thus, one wonders whether a correct account of recent historical events was actually necessary in forensic speeches or if the jury also tolerated other interpretations of the past, even if they seemed to be absurd ones. Maybe there was no generally accepted narrative about Athens' defeat in the Peloponnesian War and therefore the speech offers us some insight into the interpretive struggle about who was to blame for Athens' decline. This leads to the question whether an alternative account of the recent past, as given in Lysias' 14th speech, was a promising litigation strategy to persuade the jury of the defendant's guilt, or whether this was only of secondary importance because the main objective of the trial was not so much to have Alcibiades the Younger convicted, as to damage the reputation of his father and his former companions. If the latter is the case, one may also ask why it was necessary to attack the reputation of a dead man.

Regarding the last question, it is of great interest that public opinion about Alcibiades in Athens was divided not only at the time when Aristophanes wrote his *Frogs*,⁴¹ but even earlier. This ambiguous attitude towards him can be traced back to 415 B.C., when Alcibiades was accused of having profaned the mysteries of Eleusis,⁴² and it endured far beyond his death. Therefore, at the time of the trials against his son there was no unanimous opinion about the most famous Athenian politician of the last decades. This is why Isocrates tries to justify and glorify Alcibiades' deeds, which would have been a useless defence strategy if all Athenians had seen him as the public enemy, which is how he is presented to us in Lysias' 14th speech. The same applies to Alcibiades the Younger's imitation of his father's behaviour, as reported in a fragment of a comedy by Archippus,⁴³ performed in the years 397–395 B.C.⁴⁴ and thus at the time of the trials against him. Of course, Alcibiades the Younger may have imitated not only the bad habits of his father, as Archippus informs us, but his behaviour more generally. Since Alcibiades the Younger certainly hoped that at least some Athenians would appreciate this, we can draw the conclusion that some, if not

---

39 Nepos *Alc.* 8.
40 Strauss 1983; Bleckmann 1998, 594–603; Kapellos 2009, 261–263; Kapellos 2017; Todd 2020, 552–554.
41 Aristoph. *Frogs* 1425.
42 Bleckmann 1998, 467–468; on the divided public opinion before Alcibiades' recall to Athens in 408 B.C. see Kapellos 2017, 304–305.
43 Archippus (Frg. 48 Kassel–Austin): βαδίζει ⟨⟩/ διακεχλιδώς, θοἰμάτιον ἕλκων † ὅπως/ ἐμφερὴς μάλιστα τῷ πατρὶ δόξειεν εἶναι †/ κλασαυχενεύεταί τε καὶ τραυλίζεται.
44 Miccolis 2017, 280.

many, Athenians still admired his father.⁴⁵ This is supported by a statement in Lysias' 14th speech in which the plaintiff appeals to the jury not to spare the son in consideration of his father (§ 17). This appeal only makes sense if the plaintiff was afraid that at least some members of the jury still admired Alcibiades.

Let us now turn to the question of why the orator presents events of the recent past in a way which seems historically incorrect and therefore very implausible to the modern scholar. One wonders whether the ancient Athenians believed these kinds of stories. In this regard, K. Wojciech points out that an active citizen of Athens was expected to be able to distinguish between truth and falsehood in forensic speeches concerning recent events of importance for the city. This is why the orators often asked the jury to recall a certain event.⁴⁶ But this was also a rhetorical strategy, as Aristotle tells us. The philosopher points out that telling people to remember a specific event of the past could work in favour of the orator, because people not familiar with this event might be too embarrassed to admit their ignorance⁴⁷ and so the orator could hope that at least some individuals would believe his lies. In addition to this, it was very difficult for members of the jury who were insecure about the validity of the oration to verify its content,⁴⁸ because they had to decide whether to acquitt or convict the defendants right after the speeches. Hence, forensic speeches provided several opportunities for orators not to be too exact about the truth, as long as their argumentation was persuasive enough. One might object that while this was perhaps true for minor events, the defeat of Aegospotami decided the Peloponnesian War and there were also quite a number of survivors who had returned to Athens. A. Kapellos estimates the number of these survivors to be at least 2.200,⁴⁹ whereas B. Strauss posits an even higher figure: he thinks that the majority of the approximately 30.000 participants in the battle returned home.⁵⁰ Whatever the exact number may be, a significant number of people must have known about the event, which had occurred only ten years earlier,

---

45 According to Gribble 1999, 71, this was an attempt to stand out and a deliberate display of aristocratic behaviour. In itself, it was also an imitation of Alcibiades the Elder, who acted in the same way when he was an active politician. This behaviour differed completely form how other politicians conducted themselves and it was a violation of the common social norms of democratic Athens. Despite all this, Alcibiades' behaviour was appreciated by enough citizens to allow him to be elected several times. See Mann 2007, 226–229.
46 Wojciech 2018, 166.
47 Arist. *Rhet.* 1408a 33–36; see also Wojciech 2018, 171.
48 Wojciech 2018, 177.
49 Kapellos 2009, 272.
50 Strauss 1983, 33–34.

from first-hand accounts. The fact that the jury included people who had fought at Aegospotami is also mentioned in another speech by Lysias, delivered in 402 B.C.[51] At first glance, the alternative version of Alcibiades and Adeimantus' betrayal of the fleet does not seem to be a very promising reinterpretation of the event. However, it may have been possible to create doubt among the jurymen, since although most of the participants in the battle knew that Alcibiades had visited the Athenian camp and talked to the commanders,[52] the content of this conversation and what he did after the commanders denied his help offer may have been unknown to most of them and therefore left room for speculation.[53] In Lysias' own speeches, one can find different versions of this event. In his funeral speech for the soldiers who had died in the Corinthian War, he wrote that the defeat at Aegospotami was either the fault of the commanders or the will of the gods.[54] Therefore, Alcibiades, who was not one of the commanders, is not among those potentially responsible in this version of the event. Furthermore, a comparison with the perception of participants in battles in later epochs shows us that the common soldiers' perceptions differed significantly from those of their commanders.[55] Therefore, it is plausible that different stories about the same event were circulating in Athens and were or were not believed to be true depending on the witness.[56] Because of this, the orator may have had a good chance to influence the jury in his own terms if the jurors did not already have a very firm opinion about the event reinterpreted by him. Normally an orator would only say things that the jury was likely to believe;[57] thus, the alternative version of the defeat of Aegospotami gives us some insight into the internal battle waged within Athens over the representation of this event.[58] It also shows us that at the time of the trial this battle was not over, since a version which

---

[51] Lys. 21.10; see also Kapellos 2014a, 105–107.
[52] Xen. *Hell*. 2.1.25–26; Diod. 13.105; Plut. *Alc*. 36; Nepos *Alc*. 8.
[53] According to Plutarch, Alcibiades himself suspected that the generals' decision not to change their base was due to treason. Plutarch also tells us that when Alcibiades had to leave the camp, he talked to some Athenians about his plans and how the generals had dismissed them. We are also informed that some of the Athenians believed in Alcibiades' plans while others did not: Plut. *Alc*. 37. This shows that different stories about Alcibiades' visit to the camp were circulating in Athens and that different people believed different stories to be true.
[54] Lys. 2.58.
[55] See for example Münkler 1985.
[56] This problem was already recognized by Thucydides, who had to deal with it when he tried to reconstruct the battle actions of the Peloponnesian War (Thuc. 1.22.2–3).
[57] Dover 1974, 13.
[58] Gribble 1999, 94–95.

most of the Athenians would have rejected would not have been presented in court.

The betrayal of the fleet is not the only accusation levelled by the orator against Alcibiades. He also holds Alcibiades responsible for other negative events in the recent history of Athens. Some of these accusations may have been relatively convincing. He accuses Alcibiades of having persuaded the Spartans to take Decelea as a fortress in the Peloponnesian War, of having encouraged members of the Delian League to quit the alliance (§ 30) and of having told the Spartans about Athens' weaknesses (§ 37). Unlike the betrayal of the fleet, these accusations are more or less justified and the jury must have known about Alcibiades' temporary support of Sparta during the Peloponnesian War.[59] The orator adds to this list of true accusations the false one of the betrayal of the fleet at Aegospotami as the triumphant culmination of Alcibiades' misdoings,[60] which also led to Athens' defeat in the Peloponnesian War. The orator mentions Adeimantus, who was still active in Athenian politics, in the role of co-conspirator, in order to have not only a dead scapegoat but also a living one. This addition was also a means to strengthen the plausibility of the accusation, because Adeimantus had been one of the commanders at Aegospotami and other people had already accused him of being responsible for the defeat.[61] Immediately after finishing his enumeration of accusations against Alcibiades, the orator tries to stir and exploit the jury's emotions by appealing to their pity (ἐλεέω) for the soldiers who died in the battle, their shame (αἰσχύνω) at the prisoners of war sold into slavery, their indignation (ἀγανακτέω) at the destruction of the city walls and, finally, their anger (ὀργίζω) at the tyranny of the Thirty (§ 39). The orator wants the jurors to believe that all these things are the result of Alcibiades' misdoings. He hopes to trigger such strong emotions that the jurors will also convict Alcibiades the Younger, to whom he then turns in the speech, to demand his conviction (§ 40). By appealing to compassion and anger, the orator uses two powerful emotions which, according to Aristotle, are very useful to influence an audience.[62] Stirring emotions in this way was a common rhetorical

---

59 Regarding Decelea: Thuc. 6.91.6–7 and 7.18.1; regarding Chios: Thuc. 8.6.3; 8.12.1; see also Kapellos 2019a, 56–57.
60 Gribble 1999, 120–121 also thinks that the accusation of the betrayal of the fleet is not meant seriously, but must be seen as part of a rhetorical strategy designed to blame Alcibiades for the overall misfortune of Athens.
61 Xen. *Hell.* 2.1.32; see also Kapellos 2009, 257–258.
62 On the importance of the audience's emotions for a speech: Arist. *Rhet.* 1377b16–1378a6; on the importance of anger, compassion and fear as a means to influence an audience's opinion:

strategy in forensic speeches.⁶³ Therefore, listing Alcibiades' real misdoings to elicit certain emotions among the jurors before adding an invented crime, the worst one of all, might have achieved the intended effect on some of the jurors which was what really mattered at a trial.

That is why the orator also presented the jury some invented stories about the heavy drinking of Alcibiades the Younger and about how he betrayed his father (§§ 25–26). For the modern scholar these accusations might seem like fabrications, because back then Alcibiades the Younger should have been only eleven or twelve years old.⁶⁴ In court, however, these accusations might have worked because not all jurors were likely to know how old Alcibiades the Younger was. Therefore, even invented misdoings could have influenced the jury according to the orator's plans. Forensic speeches were not written to tell the truth but to convince the jury.⁶⁵ Even if the majority did not believe these accusations, the orator would at least have spread a rumour⁶⁶ which might have certain effects on the common people in the future. The Athenian court was certainly a suitable place to spread such rumours, since all trials were open to the public: especially when a prominent person was accused, many people would come to witness the trial.⁶⁷ Finally, we must bear in mind that forensic speeches like Lysias' 14th one were published after the trial and would be read within educated circles of Athens.⁶⁸ A forensic speech that proved unsuccessful in court could therefore have some impact after the trial. In the case of Lysias' 14th speech, the invective against Alcibiades may have driven some readers to think about his responsibility in the defeat at Aegospotami and some may have also concluded that Alcibiades and his companions were indeed responsible.

It seems that in 395 B.C. the responsibility for the defeat at Aegospotami and in the Peloponnesian War was still a matter of debate and that there was no scapegoat who was universally accepted as the person responsible for these military fiascos. Not only Alcibiades and Adeimantus but also some of the surviving trierarchs were held responsible and at least three of them were involved in trials after their return.⁶⁹ Furthermore, there was no unanimous opinion

---

Arist. *Rhet.* 1378a 20–23. For a general analysis of emotions according to the ancient Greeks see Konstan 2006.
63 Sanders 2012, 361–362.
64 Littman 1970, 263–264; Gribble 1999, 94.
65 Gagarin 2003, 202–203; Bearzot 2006, 143.
66 On the importance of rumours in Athenian politics see Ober 1989, 148–149.
67 On the public perception of trials see Lanni 2012, 120–127.
68 Kapellos 2019, 96.
69 Kapellos 2019, 89.

about Alcibiades' deeds in Athens.[70] This struggle over the interpretation of the greatest defeat in Athenian history was probably one of the reasons, if not the main reason why Alcibiades the Younger was brought to court, and why his father and Adeimantus were accused of betraying the fleet. B. Strauss points out that after the end of the Peloponnesian War Conon was especially keen to ensure that the Athenian public would consider him innocent in relation to the defeat at Aegospotami.[71] Conon's version of the story may have been less convincing than he had hoped, since as late as 346 B.C., long after his death, Isocrates had to emphasize that Conon was not responsible for the defeat at Aegospotami, but the other generals were.[72] The ineffectiveness of Conon's version of the defeat is related to Thrasybulus of Steiria, who was a political opponent of Conon,[73] and his supporters. Thrasybulus who was one of the leaders of the democratic party during the civil war became one of the leading politicians in Athens after the restoration of democracy in 403 B.C. He maintained this position until his defeats at Nemea and Coronea and Conon's return following his victory at Cnidus in 394 B.C.[74] Prior to his return in 394 B.C. Conon and his supporters may have tried to weaken Thrasybulus' position by all possible means; therefore, Thrasybulus' connection to Alcibiades and his son was an easy target. Furthermore, the cavalry was not very popular in the years following the restoration of democracy.[75] Consequently, Thrasybulus' enemies may also have hoped that his support for a member of the social elite who was part of a group of people whose loyalty to democracy was questioned by many Athenians would tarnish Thrasybulus' reputation. Especially after the victory at Haliartus, which Thrasybulus could claim as a success of his,[76] Conon and his supporters must have reached for any straw that might weaken Thrasybulus' position at least to some degree. In this respect, it was an advantage that the *demos* was also interested in identifying one or more individuals as responsible for the defeat at Aegospotami[77] and even more so for the defeat in the Peloponnesian

---

70 Heftner 2011, 192.
71 Strauss 1983, 27.
72 Strauss 1983, 31.
73 On the enmity between Conon and Thrasybulus: Beloch 1884, 119; Strauss 1984.
74 Strauss 1987, 14; on the popularity of Thrasybulus see also Strauss 1987, 92; on Thrasybulus' leading position see also Buck 1998, 87–88.
75 Xen. *Hell.* 3.1.4; Low 2002, 106–110.
76 The victory must have strengthened Thrasybulus' popularity: Buck 1998, 99.
77 "The greater the defeat, the greater the legends that grow up around it, the more eager the public is for scapegoats, the less fussy about evidence." (Strauss 1983, 27); on the debate about the alleged betrayal at Aegospotami see also Bearzot 2017, 47–48; Kapellos 2017, 314.

War. In the end, it was the *demos* itself which voted for the Sicilian expedition, sentenced the victorious commanders of the Arginusae battle to death and decided not to recall Alcibiades, but to appoint as commanders other men who were then defeated at Aegospotami. However, the *demos* was always right,[78] so other scapegoats were needed. Conon, who had been one of the commanders at Aegospotami, and who had managed to escape from the battlefield, had been too afraid to come back to Athens right after the defeat.[79] This behaviour must have made him a good target for his political opponents, making it necessary for him and his supporters to spread different narratives of the event. This might also be the reason why Conon brought Adeimantus to court after his return to Athens.[80]

Regarding the search for a scapegoat, it is also interesting to note that Archedemus'[81] participation in the Arginusae trial,[82] another important event of the recent past, is not mentioned by the orator in Lysias' 14th speech, even though he is mentioned in the speech as bad company kept by Alcibiades the Younger (§ 25). This trial was one of the least glorious chapters in Athenian legal history[83] and Xenophon describes it in a very negative way.[84] The *demos* cut a rather poor figure in this trial and regretted its decision shortly afterwards.[85] That is why the orator did not mention it: for it would have been a reference to an unpleasant event at least partially caused by the *demos*; therefore, such a story would not have been appreciated by the jury.[86] Pseudo-Aristotle also dis-

---

[78] According to Todd 1990, 174 the notion that the *demos* never acted wrongly was an important principle of Athenian democracy. Because of this attitude, in case of speeches where an orator described unpleasant events caused by the *demos* in an alternative way, so as to clear the *demos* of all blame, the jury may well have accepted these misrepresentations.
[79] Kapellos 2019a, 247.
[80] Concering the trial against Adeimantus see Kapellos 2009, 266–275.
[81] For the few things known about Archedemus see Hooper 2015, 500–505.
[82] Xen. *Hell.* 1.7.2; see also Kapellos 2019a, 142–144. According to Hooper 2015, 505–507, Archedemus' accusations against Erasinides were not a part of the Arginusae trial. However, Xenophon's narrative clearly points to Archedemus' accusations as the starting point of the Arginusae trial and therefore Lysias must have had other reasons for not mentioning it.
[83] On the trial, see for example Andrewes 1974; Bleckmann 1998, 509–571; Burckhardt 2000; Kapellos 2019a, 133–216; Kapellos 2019b.
[84] Xen. *Hell.* 1.7; see also Burckhardt 2000, 128.
[85] Xen. *Hell.* 1.7.35; see also Kapellos 2019a, 209–216.
[86] The same applies to Lys. 12.36, as Kapellos 2019b, 38 has shown. A similar phenomenon is the rhetoric of conspiracy used by Lysias with regard to the tyranny of the Thirty, which exculpates the *demos* for not having opposed the oligarchs when they seized power. See Roisman 2006, 78–79.

cussed this attitude of the *demos* in his *Athenaion Politeia*. According to him, the *demos* always got angry with men who had persuaded it to make a decision which in retrospect could be regarded a bad one.[87]

The identification of the supporters and opponents of Alcibiades the Younger and the inner-Athenian political conflicts related to the trial should not be seen as an attempt to dig up the old dichotomy between the rich pro-Spartan oligarchs and the poor and anti-Spartan democrats, which is not a convincing model since the political circumstances were far more complex.[88] Whether there were six major political groups in Athens in the early 4th century[89] — or maybe more or less — and what their political goals may have been, it is difficult to say. However, it is undeniable that various different groups existed[90] and that friendship was an important resource in Athenian politics.[91] Forensic speeches just give us an important snapshot of some political conflicts at the time of the trials. As regards Lysias' 14th speech, the accusations against Alcibiades the Younger must be seen as part of a political conflict between Thrasybulus and his supporters,[92] on the one hand, and Conon and his supporters, on the other.[93] Furthermore, the speech gives us some insight into the lively debate about Alcibiades' role during the Peloponnesian War and in the debate about the responsibility for Athens' defeat in this war. The speech also shows us that even decisive events of the recent past like the defeat at Aegospotami could be interpreted very differently depending on the context and audience. This is why forensic speeches are very often unsuitable to reconstruct historical events,[94] but in many cases they provide new insights into the prevailing political conflicts at the time of their delivery and show how certain accusations could be used to weaken a politician's position even after a trial. Despite all these interesting insights, the political importance of the trial against Alcibiades the Younger should not be overstated. In the end, the trial was only one of presum-

---

87 [Arist.] *Ath. Pol.* 28.3; see also Rhodes 1981, 357.
88 Funke 1980, 1–26. For a general discussion about the problem of identifying political groups in the study of the history of 5th century Athens see Gehrke 1984. For an overview of the scholarship discussing the possibility of identifying political groups in Classical Athens see Piovan 2015, 39–43.
89 Strauss 1987, 104.
90 Funke 1980, 23.
91 Rhodes 1986, 138–139; Mitchell and Rhodes 1996, 11–12.
92 For Thrasybulus' supporters see Strauss 1987, 96.
93 According to Strauss 1987, 112 Alcibiades the Younger was brought to court by Cephalus, Epicrates, Agyrrhius and Thrasybulus of Collytus, who supported Conon.
94 Todd 1990, 173; Worthington 1991, 55.

ably many conflicts and without the defeats of Thrasybulus at Nemea and Coronea and Conon's victory at Cnidus the return of the latter and his temporary political success might never have occurred.

Bibliography

Alexiou, E. (2011), "Isokrates 'de bigis' und die Entwicklung des Prosa-Enkomions", *Hermes* 139, 316–336.
Andrewes, A. (1974), "The Arginousai Trial", *Phoenix* 28, 112–122.
Bearzot, C. (2006), "Dritto e Retorica nella Polis Democratica Ateniese", *Dike* 9, 129–155.
Bearzot, C. (2017), "La συμφορά de la cite. La défaite d'Athènes (405–404 av. J.-C.) chez les orateurs attiques", *Ktèma* 42, 41–52.
Beloch, J. (1884), *Die attische Politik seit Perikles*, Leipzig.
Blass, F. (1874), *Die Attische Beredsamkeit. Zweite Abtheilung: Isokrates und Isaios*, Leipzig.
Blass, F. (1887), *Die Attische Beredsamkeit. Erste Abtheilung: Von Gorgias bis Lysias*, 2nd ed. Leipzig.
Bleckmann, B. (1998), *Athens Weg in die Niederlage. Die letzten Jahre des Peloponnesischen Kriegs*, Stuttgart/Leipzig.
Buck, R.J. (1998), *Thrasybulus and the Athenian Democracy. The Life of an Athenian Statesman*, Stuttgart.
Burckhardt, L. (2000), "Eine Demokratie wohl, aber kein Rechtsstaat? Der Arginusenprozeß des Jahres 406 v. Chr.", in: L. Burckhardt/J. von Ungern-Sternberg (eds.), *Große Prozesse im antiken Athen*, München, 128–143.
Caimo, I. (1935), "Alcibiade negli oratori attici", *A & R* 37, 244–260.
Carey, C. (1989), *Lysias. Selected Speeches*, Cambridge.
Dombrowski, H. (1934), *Die politischen Prozesse in Athen vom Archontat des Eukleides bis zum Ausgang des Bundesgenossenkrieges*, Diss. Greifswald.
Dover, K. (1968), *Lysias and the Corpus Lysiacum*, Berkeley/Los Angeles.
Dover, K. (1974), *Greek Popular Morality in the Time of Plato and Aristotle*, Oxford.
Feraboli, S. (1980), *Lisia avvocato*, Padova.
Funke, P. (1980), *Homonoia und Arche. Athen und die griechische Staatenwelt vom Ende des Peloponnesischen Krieges bis zum Königsfrieden*, Wiesbaden.
Gagarin, M. (2003), "Telling Stories in Athenian Law", *TAPA* 133, 197–207.
Gehrke, H.-J. (1984), "Zwischen Freundschaft und Programm. Politische Parteiungen im Athen des 5. Jahrhunderts v. Chr.", *HZ* 239, 529–564.
Gribble, D. (1999), *Alcibiades and Athens. A Study in Literary Presentation*, Oxford.
Häusle, H. (1987/88), "Alkibiades, der Tyrann. Ein Beitrag zur politischen Polemik in Reden des 5. und 4. Jahrhunderts v. Chr.", *Archaiognosia* 5, 85–129.
Heftner, H. (2011), *Alkibiades. Staatsmann und Feldherr*, Darmstadt.
Hertzberg, G. (1853), *Alkibiades der Staatsmann und Feldherr. Nach den Quellen dargestellt*, Halle.
Hooper, T. (2015), "Archedemus", *CQ* 65, 500–517.
Kapellos, A. (2009), "Adeimantos at Aegospotami. Innocent or Guilty?", *Historia* 58, 257–275.

Kapellos, A. (2014), "*In Defence of Mantitheus*. Structure, Strategy and Argumentation in Lysias 16", *BICS* 57 (2) 22–46.
Kapellos, A. (2014a), *Lysias 21. A Commentary*, Berlin.
Kapellos, A. (2017), "Alcibiades at Aegospotami and the Defeat of the Athenian Fleet. History and Rhetoric", *PP* 72, 303–324.
Kapellos, A. (2019), "Lysias, Isocrates and the Trierarchs at Aegospotami", *Erga-Logoi* 7, 1, 85–101.
Kapellos, A. (2019a), *Xenophon's Peloponnesian War*, Berlin.
Kapellos, A. (2019b), "Xenophon and Lysias on the Arginousai Trial", *Erga-Logoi* 7, 2, 19–44.
Konstan, D. (2006), *The Emotions of the Ancient Greeks. Studies in Aristotle and Classical Literature*, Toronto.
Lanni, A. (2012), "Publicity and the Courts of Classical Athens", *Yale Journal of Law & the Humanities* 24, 119–135.
Littman, R.J. (1970), "The Loves of Alcibiades", *TAPA* 101, 263–276.
Low, P. (2002), "Cavalry Identity and Democratic Ideology in early Fourth-Century Athens", *PCPS* 48, 102–122.
Mann, C. (2007), *Die Demagogen und das Volk. Zur politischen Kommunikation im Athen des 5. Jahrhunderts v. Chr.*, Berlin.
Miccolis, E. (2017), *Archippos. Einleitung, Übersetzung, Kommentar*, Heidelberg.
Mitchell, L.G./Rhodes, P.J. (1996), "Friends and Enemies in Athenian Politics", *G & R* 43, 11–30.
Münkler, H. (1985), "Schlachtbeschreibung. Der Zweite Weltkrieg in der Wahrnehmung und Erinnerung der Deutschen", *Leviathan* 13, 129–146.
Ober, J. (1989), *Mass and Elite in Democratic Athens. Rhetoric, Ideology, and the Power of the People*, Princeton.
Paulsen, T. (2011), "VIII. Rhetorik. 2.9 Lysias", in: B. Zimmermann (ed.), *Handbuch der Griechischen Literatur der Antike Bd. 1. Die Literatur der archaischen und klassischen Zeit*, München, 439–445.
Perrin, B. (1903), "The Death of Alcibiades", *TAPA* 37, 25–37.
Piovan, D. (2015), "Partiti e Democrazia in Atene Classica", *Filosofia Politica* 29, 39–52.
Rhodes, P.J. (1981), *A Commentary on the Aristotelian "Athenaion Politeia"*, Oxford.
Rhodes, P.J. (1986), "Political Activity in Classical Athens", *JHS* 106, 132–144.
Roisman, J. (2006), *The Rhetoric of Conspiracy in Ancient Athens*, Berkeley/Los Angeles.
Rubinstein, L. (2000), *Litigation and Cooperation. Supporting Speakers in the Courts of Classical Athens*, Stuttgart.
Sanders, E. (2012), "'He is a Liar, a Bounder, and a Cat'. The Arousal of Hostile Emotions in Attic Forensic Oratory", in: A. Chaniotis (ed.), *Unveiling Emotions. Sources and Methods for the Study of Emotions in the Greek World*, Stuttgart, 359–387.
Seager, R. (1967), "Alcibiades and the Charge of Aiming at Tyranny", *Historia* 16, 6–18.
Strauss, B. (1983), "Aegospotami Reexamined", *AJP* 104, 24–35.
Strauss, B. (1984), "Thrasybulus and Conon. A Rivalry in Athens in the 390s B.C.", *AJP* 105, 37–48.
Strauss, B. (1987), *Athens after the Peloponnesian War. Class, Faction and Policy 403–386 BC*, Ithaka.
Todd, S. (1990), "The Use and Abuse of the Attic Orators.", *G & R* 37, 159–178.
Todd, S. (2020), *A Commentary on Lysias, Speeches 12–16*, Oxford.

Wojciech, K. (2018), "Geschichte vor Gericht. Wahrheit und Wahrscheinlichkeit als Kriterien in der Vergangenheitsdarstellung attischer Redner", in: T. Blank/F.K. Maier (eds.), *Die symphonischen Schwestern. Narrative Konstruktion von ‚Wahrheiten' in der nachklassischen Geschichtsschreibung*, Stuttgart, 163–184.

Wolpert, A. (2002), *Remembering Defeat. Civil War and Civic Memory in Ancient Athens*, Baltimore.

Worthington, I. (1991), "Greek Oratory, Revision of Speeches and the Problem of Historical Reliability", *C & M* 42, 55–74.

Aggelos Kapellos
Plato's *Menexenus* on the Sea Battle-trial of Arginousai and the Battle of Aegospotami

Abstract: In this chapter I examine Plato's selective treatment of the battle of Arginousai, his silence about the trial that ensued (a subject which he also briefly treated in the *Apology*) as well as his omission of the Athenians' defeat at Aegospotami, which reflects contemporary rhetoric. This becomes clear through a comparison of the relevant sections of the *Menexenus* with other funeral orations which treated similar subjects but mainly through the historians Thucydides, Xenophon and Diodorus. In the end, Plato's readers come to the same conclusion as the historians, i.e. that the Athenians were defeated because of their own mistakes, so they were unwilling to trace them. Plato's contemporaries could forget the real events, but his readers should not forget the truth, which could be achieved through their knowledge of the events but mainly through Xenophon's account.

It is probable that Plato wrote the *Menexenus* in 386 B.C. or a little afterwards[1] and what he has mostly in mind is the genre of the funeral orations[2] and their argumentation, which he does not separate from the politics of Athens.[3] We are told that Socrates meets Menexenus, who comes from the agora (234a1–2). They probably meet in the Dromos, a wide road that cuts through the Cerameicus.[4] Menexenus tells him that Archinus and Dion are among the candidates to deliver the funeral speech (234b10). Both of them were active political figures, who participated in the recent political events of their city in 387 for the conclusion of the peace of Antalcidas, so the dramatic date is 386.[5]

Socrates expresses his disagreement with the funerary speeches, because far from reminding the citizenry of their roles and responsibilities, they distract

---

I am most grateful to Dr. G. Westwood for reading earlier drafts of this version. I also thank Professor W. Altman for reading my text. Professor Peter Rhodes had made useful comments.

---

1 See Tsitsiridis 1998, 41–52; Sansone 2020, 14–17.
2 See Coventry 1989, 3; Petre 2009, 152.
3 I do not share Shanske's opinion that Plato dichotomizes his attack on rhetoric and the Athenian *polis* (see Shanske 2007, 126).
4 See Corcoran 2016, 66.
5 See Pappas and Zelcer 2015, 40–41.

their listeners and dull their critical faculties.⁶ Socrates says that he can deliver the speech that Aspasia composed from Pericles' leftovers (236a8–c1). Those three were dead at that time, so Plato is making an anachronism,⁷ and one reason why he does this is to link his work with Thucydides, who was critical of the use of base rhetoric in Athens and its effect on the well-being of the polity.⁸ The importance of this sympathy between the two authors will appear later in my analysis. Menexenus urges Socrates to deliver this funeral speech, but the philosopher warns him that he might laugh at him, because, although he is old, he still wants to παίζειν (236c8–9). This word has Gorgianic connotations. Gorgias says in his *Encomium of Helen* 21 that his defence speech of Helen is a παίγνιον.⁹ Isocrates says in his *Encomium of Helen* that nobody can surpass sophists like Gorgias (10.2), who know how to contrive false statements on any subject that may be proposed but not the truth (10.4), and take most pleasure in those discourses which are of no practical service in any particular (10.6). In particular, they like to praise misfortunes (συμφοράς) (10.10). Such compositions follow one set road and this road is neither difficult to find, nor to learn, nor to imitate, while discourses that are trustworthy are difficult to learn and their composition is more difficult, as it is more arduous to practice seriousness than levity (παίζειν) (10.11). Gorgias and the sophists did not see persuasion as the primary goal of their works, but they wanted to display skill in intellectual argument, as well as to give pleasure. Among Gorgias' works which were intended to please his audience was his funeral speech.¹⁰ The infinitive παίζειν is one of the words which indicate playful, pleasurable laughter. This constituted a mechanism of release or psychological relaxation from something serious, which is accepted by those who participate in it.¹¹ Therefore Socrates implicitly equates himself with Gorgias; the speech that he will deliver follows the trends of the genre in the way he treats Athens' self-identity and self-praise (besides, his speech could be a part of Pericles' speech); he intends to show his intellectual ability in handling and offer pleasure and laughter to Menexenus, although the latter say that he will not laugh.¹²

---

6 See Stow 2007, 197.
7 See Engels 2012, 17, Pappas and Zelcer 2015, 25–26.
8 See Kerch 2008, 99–106.
9 See Gagarin 2001, 275–291.
10 See Gagarin 1999, 165 n. 12 for this opinion.
11 See Halliwell 1991, 280, 282–283.
12 Dodds 1959, 24 n. 2 says that Plato warns his readers that the funeral speech that follows is a παιδιά, but he did not analyze his remark.

When Menexenus urges him to continue, Socrates tells him that he would almost gratify him if he bade him strip and dance, now that they are alone (236c11–d2). Dancing is an expressive activity which aims to create pleasurable satisfaction for the participants. It is above all celebratory and joyful, and its principal setting is within some sort of festivity. All this is equally true of the conception of playful humour or laughter, so that it is not surprising to find laughter and dancing sometimes conjoined as prime features of festivity in Greek literature.[13] Socrates' warning about the speech is playful and the possibility to dance implies that he is distancing himself from what the genre performed.[14]

Menexenus agrees to hear the speech (236c5–7). The two men are moving and end up inside the cemetery.[15] The supposed occasion for such a speech must have been that for which Dion and Archinus could be elected to speak in 386 B.C. Menexenus seems to have no problem identifying the current event for which Socrates would deliver his speech, namely the Corinthian War; this becomes clear to Plato's audience by reading the speech to the end.[16] Given that this is the most recent event mentioned in the speech, it is plausible to believe that Plato represents popular opinion at Athens at the time of the King's Peace.[17]

The question that arises now is: could Menexenus examine the content of the speech and trace possible inaccuracies, omissions or falsifications? Following the norms of the genre, Menexenus would not stop Socrates or express his disapproval, but he would wait until the end of the speech,[18] and this is what really happens (see below). Concerning Plato's readers, as contemporaries of the recent events mentioned in the speech, they could have remembered them if they were personally involved or learned about them through those who had a personal experience. Thus the opinion of Pappas and Zelcer that Plato's readers would have known Athens' recent past and much more about the events recounted[19] seems right. On the other hand, even the protagonists' memories would fade away as time passed, or they would conform to the city's wish to

---

13 See Halliwell 1991, 283.
14 See also Haskins 2005, 31.
15 The phrase ἐνθάδε κειμένων (246a6) indicates that the two men are in the cemetery. See de Bakker 2013, 182.
16 See Engels 2012, 17.
17 See Bloedow 1975, 41–42.
18 For the relationship between funeral speakers and their audiences during the funeral speeches see Blanshard 2010, 206.
19 Pappas and Zelcer 2015, 84.

forget the bad moments of the past.[20] Thus Plato's readers should either read Socrates' speech and be led astray by it or compare it with some other literary sources. Pappas and Zelcer agree with this approach, saying that assessing the history in the narrative calls for consulting other historical writings of this time, because if Plato is distorting the facts, the rival sources will best reveal his distortions.[21] So they use Thucydides (and Diodorus Siculus), although they are not certain about Plato's sources,[22] because they believe that it is practically impossible to say what historical works were available in Plato's day and which of them he would have read himself.[23] However, this is wrong, because Thucydides was studied in the Academy.[24] Regarding Xenophon, the continuator of Thucydides, they say that because of the late date of the *Hellenica* it is possible that Plato never saw it or had not seen it by the time he wrote the *Menexenus*.[25] On the other hand, they find common pieces of information between the two authors, but they say nothing about a possible literary connection between them,[26] obviously regarding this as a coincidence.

I would be more optimistic that Plato had read Xenophon, although we do not have not proofs, for the following reasons: *a)* Xenophon's *Hellenica* I–II must have been written separately from the other Books, sometime between 404 and 401 B.C.,[27] while it seems that parts of the *Hellenica* were circulating in some form before the final form was completed, before 380;[28] *b)*, both Plato and Xenophon were associated with Socrates, so it is plausible that the former would have shown interest in reading the work of the latter, who was almost the same age as him;[29] *c)* the fact that both of them expressed, through their lexical convergence, the historical and political confusion of their era,[30] makes a literary connection between them probable; and *d)* the aim of Xenophon's history seems to have been close to Plato's critique of Athens, since he wrote his work

---

20 See Kapellos, Introduction in this volume.
21 Pappas and Zelcer 2015, 182.
22 See Pappas and Zelcer 2015, 186–190.
23 Pappas and Zelcer 2015, 195.
24 See Hornblower 1995, 55 and Morrison 2007, 230.
25 Pappas and Zelcer 2015, 195–196.
26 See Pappas and Zelcer 2015, 190.
27 See Anderson 1974, 61, 66.
28 See Luraghi 2016, 98.
29 Xenophon was born between 430 and 425 (see Lee 2017, 17), while Plato was born in 424/3 (see Nails 2002, 246).
30 Pontier 2006, 82.

for fellow aristocrats,[31] who knew the bare facts of the Peloponnesian War[32] and were keen to read his work, because it criticized the excesses and deficiencies of democracy and created an alternative aristocratic version of the past, opposed to the version of the orators.[33] Thus if Plato and his readers found information in Xenophon that was already known to them, they would just remember and verify what they already knew. But if they read things they did not know (for instance Theramenes' scheme against the generals – see below), then Socrates' account of the events would be under scrutiny and Plato's goal would become clearer.[34]

However, in this investigation I will also consider Diodorus who used Ephorus,[35] who used the *Hellenica Oxyrhynchia* as a source. This is necessary, because he narrates the same events as Xenophon, although their accounts are not always in agreement, and the information he provides could have been known to Plato's readers.

The surface discourse of the funeral orations was a hyperbolic self-praise.[36] Socrates claims that the strength and valour of the city was shown conspicuously in her fight against Sparta. When men thought that Athens had already been warred down (hence the prefix κατα in the infinitive καταπεπολεμῆσθαι) and the ships were cut off in Mytilene, the Athenians helped their fleet there with sixty ships, manned the ships themselves; and proved themselves by common agreement men of perfect valour by conquering their enemies and set free their friends; however, they met a undeserved fate, were not recovered from the sea and lie here. The Athenians must always remember and praise them; for it was owing to their valour that we were victors not only in the sea-fight at that time but in all the rest of the war. And it was due to them that men formed the conviction that the city of Athens could never be warred down, not even by all people. And in truth it was decided that it was by our own dissension that we were brought down and not by other men; for by them we are still to this day undefeated, and it is we ourselves who have both defeated and been defeated by ourselves.[37]

---

31 For Xenophon's writing for fellow aristocrats see Kelly 1996, 149–163; Pownall 2004, 65–112.
32 See Kapellos 2018, 397.
33 See Pownall 2004, 3–4.
34 Altman 2010, 33 argues that appreciating the *Menexenus* depends on having read the *Hellenica*.
35 See Hau 2016, 74.
36 See Walters 1980, 3.
37 *Men.* 243b7–d2: οὗ δὴ καὶ ἐκφανὴς ἐγένετο ἡ τῆς πόλεως ῥώμη τε καὶ ἀρετή. οἰομένων γὰρ ἤδη αὐτὴν καταπεπολεμῆσθαι καὶ ἀπειλημμένων ἐν Μυτιλήνῃ τῶν νεῶν, βοηθήσαντες ἐξήκο-

Socrates' reference to the blockaded Athenian fleet at Mytilene is a reference to Conon's being blockaded in the island (Xen. 1.6.16). Socrates avoids mentioning that Conon was the general of the ships there in order to put emphasis on the city's action. Moreover, he says that the Athenians sent sixty ships and that they embarked on the ships. Socrates is not accurate, because Xenophon reports that the Athenians voted to send one hundred and ten ships, and that they put on board (εἰσβιβάζοντες) all those who could be conscripted, slaves, free men and many of the hoplites (Xen. 1.6.24). The difference in the number of ships is striking. Given that Hyperides claims in his funeral speech that the Athenians were fewer than their enemies,[38] I suspect that Socrates asserts that his fellow citizens sent fewer ships than they actually did in order to maximize their achievement in defeating the Spartans.[39] For this reason he hides the fact that slaves served in the Athenian navy. In this way he presents the Athenians not as being in an urgent situation but as making a deliberate choice, and strengthens his claim that the warriors became ἄνδρες ἄριστοι in every man's mind. The noun ἀνήρ was used to emphasize the bravery in fighting,[40] the manly worth[41] and the death in battle[42] of the Athenian citizen-warriors. The adjective ἀγαθός denoted the risk of life and limb in military service.[43] From the surviving corpus of the funeral orations it is noteworthy that the orators tended to use the adjective ἀγαθοί in the normal and comparative degree, while the only occasion where we meet the adjective in the superlative degree is found in the *Menexenus*.[44] Thus Plato's Socrates places more emphasis on these dead than the other funeral orators do. This could be justified by the

---

ντα ναυσίν, αὐτοὶ ἐμβάντες εἰς τὰς ναῦς, καὶ ἄνδρες γενόμενοι ὁμολογουμένως ἄριστοι, νικήσαντες μὲν τοὺς πολεμίους, λυσάμενοι δὲ τοὺς φιλίους, ἀναξίου τύχης τυχόντες, οὐκ ἀναιρεθέντες ἐκ τῆς θαλάττης κεῖνται ἐνθάδε. ὧν χρὴ ἀεὶ μεμνῆσθαί τε καὶ ἐπαινεῖν· τῇ μὲν γὰρ ἐκείνων ἀρετῇ ἐνικήσαμεν οὐ μόνον τὴν τότε ναυμαχίαν, ἀλλὰ καὶ τὸν ἄλλον πόλεμον· δόξαν γὰρ δι' αὐτοὺς ἡ πόλις ἔσχεν μή ποτ' ἂν καταπολεμηθῆναι μηδ' ὑπὸ πάντων ἀνθρώπων—καὶ ἀληθῆ ἔδοξεν—τῇ δὲ ἡμετέρᾳ αὐτῶν διαφορᾷ ἐκρατήθημεν, οὐχ ὑπὸ τῶν ἄλλων· ἀήττητοι γὰρ ἔτι καὶ νῦν ὑπό γε ἐκείνων ἐσμέν, ἡμεῖς δὲ αὐτοὶ ἡμᾶς αὐτοὺς καὶ ἐνικήσαμεν καὶ ἡττήθημεν.
38 See Hyp. 6.19 with Herrman 2009, 84.
39 For another argument of this kind see Trevett in this volume.
40 See Adkins 1975, 156–157.
41 See Roisman 2005, 67–70.
42 See Loraux 1986, 99–100.
43 See Pritchard 2010, 35.
44 Cf. also Pl. *Men.* 243d1, where Aspasia characterizes the drowned men of Arginousai as ἄνδρες γενόμενοι ἄριστοι and Pl. *Men.* 246c2 the use of the adjective ἀρίστους. But note that Xen. *Mem.* 3.5.10 refers to the wars of the mythical ancestors of the Athenians and calls them ἀρίστους. I suspect that Xenophon has in mind the use of the adjective in funeral oratory.

fact that the present dead defeated their enemies (τοὺς πολεμίους), i.e. the Lacedaimonians, whom Socrates refuses to name in order to undermine them,[45] and set free their friends. Socrates does not name the place where the naval battle occurred, but given that he has already mentioned Mytilene, Menexenus and Plato's readers could assume that the Athenians defeated the Spartans there. However, Xenophon (1.6.28) and Diodorus (13.98.3) are more specific, saying that the battle took place near the Arginousai islands, but Socrates does not want to name them, following the general trend of the genre to avoid giving precise geographical information.[46]

Socrates proudly says that the dead warriors defeated (νικήσαντες) their enemies, because the Athenians displayed 'great deeds' by fighting collectively.[47] His claim finds proof in Xenophon and Diodorus. Although Xenophon (1.6.29–33) and Diodorus (13.98.4–99.6) give different accounts about the way the Spartans were defeated, both of them confirm that the Athenians achieved a great victory there. More specifically, Xenophon describes the alignment of the Athenians before battle (1.6.29–31) to show the preparation of the Athenians in order to win the battle. Then he narrates that they fought in order against the Spartans, who soon scattered and fled after Callicratidas' death (1.6.33).[48] Diodorus says that the Athenian crews sat in good order under the command of their generals; in the battle that ensued, both sides fought with intensity, but when Callicratidas was killed, the Peloponnesians fled (13.98.2–99.6).

Nevertheless, Socrates' allegation that the Athenians freed their allies from Sparta has nothing to do with reality. Socrates ascribes altruistic motives to the Athenians, something which was common in the funeral orations.[49] The truth was different of course. Diodorus reports that the Athenians and the Peloponnesians knew that the conquerors in this battle would put an end to the war (13.99.2). Concerning Athens, he says that the Boeotians, the Euboeans and other Greeks had revolted from her and now they were fighting with Sparta in this battle. When Callicratidas died, they continued to put up a stout fight as long as they could because they feared that if the Athenians regained their sovereignty, they would punish them for their revolt (13.99.6). Falsification of the recent past was something that Socrates did not hesitate to do.

---

[45] This is a tactic that Demosthenes also uses in his funeral oration. See Dem. 60.20: τοὺς πολεμίους with Frangeskou 1999, 333.
[46] See Kapellos 2022.
[47] See Pritchard 2010, 19.
[48] For an analysis of Xenophon's account see Kapellos 2019a, 131–132.
[49] For this issue see Christ 2012, 127–133.

All this comes in stark contrast with the end of the warriors, who met with an underserved fate (ἀναξίου τύχης), because they were not collected from the sea (οὐκ ἀναιρεθέντες ἐκ τῆς θαλάττης), and now they lie here (κεῖνται ἐνθάδε). Socrates focuses on the fate of the dead warriors and says that all of them were drowned. Socrates gives the impression that all the Athenians who fought at Arginousai were lost in this way, as if there were no losses during the actual battle.[50] This allows him to maximize the victory over the Lacedaimonians but also the number of the losses. Death in the sea does not deprive the warriors of glory, because, although they did not die during the naval battle, they should be treated as if they had because that was their intention.[51] The sentence 'they lie here', with which Socrates points with his finger to the tomb of the dead, if they are in the Ceramicus, as I argued above, is also used in Lysias and Demosthenes' funeral orations.[52] With it he is referring to the eleventh chest which was devoted to those whose body was not found, according to Thucydides' description of the burial custom,[53] and denotes that those who were drowned at Arginousai are now classified along with all the other warriors who are buried in the Ceramicus.[54]

However, this argument about the victorious dead, who, were unlucky and were not collected is not clear. Why did this happen? Were there any repercussions in Athenian society because of this? A close reading of Xenophon and Diodorus gives the necessary answers.

Xenophon focuses on the issue of the drowning men *and* the corpses and describes the trial that ensued in Athens. He reports that the Athenians had one hundred and fifty ships before the battle (1.6.25). After it they lost twenty-five ships together with their men, except for a few, who made their way to the shore. This happened because a strong wind and storm prevented the generals from saving their crews, who were drowned (1.6.34). This means that the losses were not so many, since they still numbered one hundred and twenty-five vessels.[55] According to his account, after the storm the whole area of Arginousai would be full of corpses, not only of those who lost their lives during the sea

---

50 See Yoshitake 2010, 374–375.
51 For the idea that the phrase ἄνδρες ἀγαθοί γενόμενοι denotes not death but the intention that motivates death see Loraux 1986, 101.
52 For the relevant passages see Frangeskou, 1999, 326 n. 52.
53 Thuc. 2.34.2: μία δὲ κλίνη κενὴ φέρεται ἐστρωμένη τῶν ἀφανῶν, οἳ ἂν μὴ εὑρεθῶσιν ἐς ἀναίρεσιν.
54 For this sentence meaning the war dead of all times see Todd 2007, 266; Grethlein 2010, 115; Yositake 2010, 361.
55 See Kapellos 2019a, 113–135.

battle but also of those who were drowned. The Athenian generals did not collect the bodies of their men, because they could not recover them because of a strong wind. This failure must have been shocking for the Athenians, because it was an old custom and ancestral law to bury the dead, but it was also acceptable that the recovery of corpses after a battle was not always possible. Although the generals sent a letter home, explaining why they had not collected the bodies, the Athenians deposed them and demanded that they return. Indeed, six out of eight commanders returned home. When this happened, the popular politician Archedemus accused Erasinides that he had embezzled public money, and he also attacked him for what had happened at Arginousai. Then the generals repeated in the Council what they had said in their letter, but Timocrates suggested that they should be put in jail, and the Councillors agreed. In the session of the Assembly that followed, Theramenes and others accused the generals of not having collected the shipwrecked men (οὐκ ἀνείλοντο τοὺς ναυαγούς – 1.7.4). The commanders replied that they had ordered Thrasybulus and Theramenes to assume this task (τὴν δὲ ἀναίρεσιν τῶν ναυαγῶν — 1.7.5). Nevertheless they did not blame them for the non-collection of the crews but only the weather (περὶ τῆς ἀναιρέσεως ... τὴν ἀναίρεσιν — 1.7.6). The adjournment of the Assembly gave the opportunity to Theramenes to organize a twofold scheme: first, fake mourners would appear in the Assembly as relatives of the lost men, and hence bring in the issue of their unburied bodies; second, the Councillor Callixenus convinced the *Boule* to pass a decree in which he used the participle τοὺς νικήσαντας, which was deliberately vague and could refer to the lost men as *both* shipwrecked and dead. An anonymous man spoke in the Assembly and claimed that the drowning men told him to bring the message to Athens that the generals had chosen not to rescue τοὺς ἀρίστους, those who had died for the fatherland (1.7.11). Thus he urged the Assemblymen to contemplate the fact that their bodies would remain unburied. Euryptolemus and some others were opposed to Callixenus and tried to block the process through a *graphe paranomon* (1.7.12). Nonetheless, the Assembly wanted to take revenge and do what it wished, thus violating the law according to which the generals had the right to be given the chance to defend themselves and not to be condemned without a proper trial.[56] One man called Lyciscus intimidated Euryptolemus and those who agreed with him by urging the Assemblymen to judge them with the same vote (1.7.13), so they withdrew their proposal. Some of the *prytaneis* tried to resist the mob's wish to violate the law, but when it shouted to serve a summons against those who refused to allow a vote (1.7.14), they were frightened and did

---

56 For the content of this law see Harris 2013, 342.

what the people wanted; only Socrates said that he would do nothing except in accordance with the law (1.7.15). Euryptolemus defended them and reminded his fellow citizens that the generals had defeated (νενικηκότας) the Lacedaimonians (1.7.25), but when Menecles made an objection on oath and demanded a repetition of the vote, the Athenians put the commanders to death (1.7.34). In the course of time the Athenians felt remorse, realizing that the harsh punishment of the commanders was wrong. Being unable to engage in self-criticism and assume responsibility for the condemnation of the generals, the Athenians took legal measures against those who had deceived them, i.e. Callixenus, Timocrates, Archedemus and Menecles, but these men escaped. Several events took place which Xenophon implicitly connects with the trial: Athens was defeated at Aegospotami (see below), democracy was subverted by the Thirty and a violent strife divided the citizens into democrats and oligarchs. When democracy was restored Callixenus took advantage of the amnesty and returned to Athens, but all the Athenians hated him and let him die out of hunger (1.7.35).[57]

Diodorus also reports that the Athenians had one hundred and fifty ships before the engagement at Arginousai and lost twenty-five ships with most of their crews because of the storm (13.100.2–3). He says that after the battle the Athenians filled the sea with corpses and the wreckage of ships. After this some of the generals thought that they should pick up the dead (ἀναιρεῖσθαι), since the Athenians were incensed at those who allowed the dead to go unburied; but others said they should sail to Mytilene and raise the siege with all speed. Nonetheless, a great storm arose, so that the ships were tossed about and the soldiers, because of the hardships they had suffered in the battle and the heavy waves, opposed picking up (πρὸς τὴν ἀναίρεσιν) the dead. In the end, they neither sailed to Mytilene nor picked up (ἀνείλαντο) the dead, but were forced by the winds to put in at Arginusai. As a result of the losses of ships and men the coastline of the territory of the Cymaeans and Phocaeans was strewn with corpses and wreckage (13.100.1–2).

When the Athenians learned of the generals' success at Arginousai, they commended the generals for the victory (τῇ νίκῃ – 13.101.1), but were incensed that they had allowed the men who had died to maintain their supremacy to go unburied. Since Theramenes and Thrasybulus had returned to Athens earlier, the generals, having assumed that it was they who had accused them before the people with respect to the dead, dispatched letters against them to the *demos*, stating that it was they whom the generals had ordered to pick up the dead

---

[57] For this analysis of Xenophon's text see Kapellos 2019a, 133–216. For the historicity of Theramenes' plan and Callixenus' punishment see Kapellos 2019b, 28–29, 34.

(ἀνελέσθαι — 13.101.2). Theramenes defended himself efficiently, so the Athenians grew angry and asked the generals to return. In the trial that took place in the Assembly the relatives of the dead appeared on their own and begged the people to punish the generals. In the end, the friends of these relatives and Theramenes' associates prevailed and the generals were condemned to death (13.102.1). Xenophon's account is in contrast with that of Diodorus in its estimate of Theramenes' role and the appearance of the mourners in the Assembly. Modern readers should prefer the historicity of the former, who is contemporary with the events, and consider the latter as not trustworthy, because the image of the 'democrat' Theramenes most probably comes from the Ephorian tradition, which is not credible.[58] However, Diodorus is clear-cut about the importance of the unburied corpses, so his information is also valuable. The rest of his account about what happened afterwards is similar to that of Xenophon. Soon the Athenians repented of executing the generals. Callixenus was brought to trial on the charge of having deceived the people, and was thrown into prison, but he escaped. Diodorus then makes a jump and explicitly connects the Arginousai trial with the end of the Peloponnesian War and the regime of the Thirty. He says that the Athenians paid the price for their choice by being ruled by the despotic Thirty (13.103.1, 14.3.7) and at a later point he describes the Athenians' defeat by Lysander at Aegospotami (13.106.1–6). Therefore, both historians confirm Socrates' mention of the non-collection of the crews and their drowning, the importance of the Athenian victory, the unjust execution of the generals, the defeat of Athens in the Peloponnesian War and the rule of the Thirty.

What is interesting is that Socrates was personally involved in the trial after Arginousai. Plato testifies to this in his *Apology of Socrates* and his veracity is quite certain.[59] He says that when all the Athenians decided (ἔδοξεν) to execute the Arginousai generals in violation of the law, he was the only one of the *prytaneis* who opposed doing anything contrary to the laws, because he thought he must run the risk to the end with law and justice on his side, rather than feel fear and join his fellow Athenians in their unjust wishes (32b1–c3). However, Socrates could not mention his role in the Arginousai trial, following the rule of the genre that no funeral orator referred to himself explicitly.[60]

---

58 See Bearzot 2012, 293–294, 297–300 and Bearzot 2015, 173–195.
59 For the historicity of the account of Plato's *Apology* see Kapellos 2019b, 32–34.
60 Hesk 2013, 62–63 argues that Pericles' speech would have been implicitly self-aggrandizing. Thucydides' Pericles praises his generation as being better than their ancestors (2.36.3), speaking in the first plural person, but he does not connect this praise with himself explicitly. Demosthenes refers to himself and his involvement in the battle of Chaeronea only allusively. See

Through Socrates' reference to the non-burial of the crews almost twenty years after the battle Plato reveals the uneasiness that the Athenians felt about this issue; but, most important, he indicates the unwillingness of his fellow citizens to remember Arginousai, the trial that ensued and its consequences. This becomes easier to understand by reading two of Lysias' speeches. First, in his speech *Against Eratosthenes*, which he wrote in 403/02 B.C. he claims that there was a strong conviction on the part of the Athenians that they should punish the generals, because they did not manage to collect the crews from the sea (τοὺς ἐκ τῆς θαλάττης ἀνελέσθαι) and he justifies this decision by saying that they considered the virtue of the dead (ἀρετῇ) (12.36). He knew that a brief reference to the Arginousai trial was enough for him to create a specific impression for the jurors about the need to punish the Thirty, but he was also aware that he could not insist on it any further, because the Athenians had changed their mind about the illegal condemnation of the generals.[61] Second, in his speech *Against Alcibiades*, written in the year 395 B.C, the speaker mentions Archedemus, the man who attacked Erasinides, as we saw earlier, and mentions him as bad company for Alcibiades the Younger (14.25).[62] However, since the trial was one of the least glorious chapters of Athenian legal history, Lysias did not mention it, because it would have been a reference to an unpleasant event at least partially caused by the *demos* and therefore such a story would not have been appreciated by the jury.[63]

Thus Socrates' urging that the Athenians must always remember and praise the dead (μεμνῆσθαί τε καὶ ἐπαινεῖν) follows the goal of the funeral orations to create memory (μεμνῆσθαι) for the relatives of the dead and thus unify them,[64] and the need to praise (ἐπαινεῖν) the missing men, but it must have seemed ironical to the readers who knew the historical facts.

Socrates' reason for this remembrance and praise is that owing to the virtue (ἀρετῇ) of the dead of Arginousai the Athenians were victorious not only in that battle which took place some time ago (hence the word τότε)[65] but also in the rest of the Peloponnesian War. Socrates exaggerates here, since he has already implied that all the men who fought at Arginousai were drowned, so is it is not possible that they defeated the Spartans in the war. Thus it is right to think that

---

Dem. 60.18, 19–22 with Worthington 2003, 154–156. Hesk 2013, 63 says that 'Hyperides does not explicitly praise himself, of course'.
61 See Kapellos 2019b, 36–38.
62 For Archedemus see Hooper 2015, 500–517.
63 See Zimmermann in this volume.
64 See Shear 2013, 515–528.
65 For the same use cf. e.g. Lys. 2.60, 12.46, 16.8, Dem. 18.20.

Socrates is making a grand statement for the fleet of Arginousai.⁶⁶ Possibly Plato is hinting at the Thucydidean (Periclean) insistence on Athens' invincibility in naval warfare.⁶⁷

Moreover, it is noteworthy that Socrates connects the battle of Arginousai with the end of the Peloponnesian war. This bridge was not Plato's invention. We have seen that Xenophon implicitly connected the Arginousai trial with the end of the war, while Diodorus connected it with the rule of the Thirty. Moreover, Lysias also makes a bridge between the Arginousai battle, the trial and the naval defeat at Aegospotami by connecting the generals with the Thirty, who supposedly participated in the military engagement in the Hellespont.⁶⁸ This allows us to think that Plato is making an argument based on contemporary politics by repeating a popular perception.

Then Socrates alleges that owing to these men Athens gave the impression (δόξαν) to the Greeks that she could never be defeated (καταπολεμηθῆναι) by all people. The word *doxa* appears often in the speech and puts an emphasis on appearances.⁶⁹ The Athenian fleet had achieved a great victory, because it had destroyed the biggest part of the Peloponnesian fleet. Xenophon reports that when a Spartan messenger boat carried news of the battle to Eteonicus at Mytilene, he ordered its crew to sail out and sail back to the camp, crying out that the division of their fleet at Arginousai had defeated the Athenians (Xen. 1.6.36).⁷⁰ Eteonicus was certain that if his men learned about the Athenian victory they would be shocked. Sparta's allies and Cyrus asked for Lysander as commander of the fleet again, because they believed that only he could break the stalemate (Xen. 2.1.6–7).⁷¹ The logical conclusion is that Athens must have seemed invincible to the Greeks at that time.

This impression of power is overturned with Socrates' next statement. It was a true decision (ἀληθῆ ἔδοξεν) that it was only by their own dissensions that the Athenians were brought down (τῇ δὲ ἡμετέρᾳ αὐτῶν διαφορᾷ ἐκρατήθημεν) and not by the hands of others (ὑπὸ τῶν ἄλλων). The verb ἔδοξε was used in the enactment clause of decrees: ἔδοξε τῇ βουλῇ καὶ τῷ δήμῳ. Socrates is using the language of inscriptions to provide solemnity and validity in his words to emphasize Athens' self-defeat.

---

66 See Yoshitake 2010, 370 n. 43.
67 See Kahn 1963, 233 n. 20.
68 See Kapellos 2019b, 37.
69 See Kahn 1963, 226; Coventry 1989, 12.
70 See Kapellos 2019a, 138.
71 See Kapellos 2019a, 218.

Plato's interpretation finds support in the historians. More specifically, he seems to follow closely Thucydides, who reports that the Athenians did not succumb to their enemies before they brought themselves down because of their own differences (αὐτοὶ ἐν σφίσι κατὰ τὰς ἰδίας διαφορὰς περιπεσόντες ἐσφάλησαν) (2.65.12),[72] probably having in mind the Arginousai trial,[73] and thus he lends support to Socrates' judgment.[74] Plato uses Thucydides to invert the image of Athens and keeps an ironic stance towards the funeral genre by intruding an analysis that could never be found in it. We have seen that Xenophon illustrates the *stasis* in Athens due to the determination of Theramenes and his associates to exterminate the Arginousai generals.[75] Diodorus also reports the aggressiveness of Theramenes and his group towards the commanders (13.101.3, 7, 102.5). It is noteworthy that Socrates does not use the word *stasis*, and this is not a coincidence. The people who fought each other in civil strife did not at that time call it that but as διαφορά. However, when the conflict was over and one side or both, had suffered total defeat, people used the word *stasis*.[76] This means that the proper word here would be *stasis*, but Plato used the word *diaphora* to show that his fellow citizens Athenians were still not willing to admit their mistake in civil strife.

In such a context, Socrates has to avoid naming who these ἄλλοι are, namely the Spartans,[77] and claims that it was the Athenians who defeated themselves and were defeated (ἐνικήσαμεν καὶ ἡττήθημεν). Plato is right. Xenophon reports that Alcibiades appeared in the Athenian camp at Aegospotami and warned them to move to Sestus in order to be safe, but the generals told him to leave, because they were afraid that the Athenians at home would execute them, as they had done with the Arginousai generals. In addition, they did not have a plan of action on how to force the Spartans to fight, but instead they showed negligence and arrogance towards Lysander, a fact which he exploited, so that he caught almost all of them by surprise on the beach.[78] Therefore, the Atheni-

---

[72] This is the remark of Usher 1999, 351–352.
[73] See Yunis 1990, 363; Rusten 1989, 215.
[74] Rosenstock 1994, 335.
[75] See Kapellos 2019a, 146–147, 151–163, 168, 172–173.
[76] See Price 2001, 35.
[77] For the use of the pronoun ἄλλος as a way of avoiding naming someone see Kapellos 2014, 27.
[78] The reasons that led to the Athenian defeat are different in Xenophon and Diodorus. I side with those scholars, who argue in favour of Xenophon: Strauss 1983, 24–35, especially 32–34, Gray 1987, 78–79; Bleckmann 1998, 572–580; Welwei 1999, 241. For Xenophon's account see Kapellos 2012, 97–98, Kapellos 2019a, 232–246.

ans suffered a heavy defeat. Henderson assumes that Socrates is making such an argument because Plato exposes, by taking it to an extreme, the chauvinist fiction which denied Athens' enemies credit for Athens' defeat.[79] I agree with this opinion. In his funeral speech Lysias refers to the defeat in the Hellespont, admits it[80] but puts the blame on the conspiracy of one of the Athenian generals who led the fleet there (2.58).[81] However, this reconstruction and concealment of the truth was necessary, because defeat threatened the representation of Athens as the prime-mover of history and as unrivalled in martial valour.[82] Socrates keeps for the Athenians what was considered to be the role of the Spartans in the Greek world after the defeat in the Hellespont. Lysias says in his *Olympiacus*, which was spoken in 388 B. C., i.e. the year before the Peace of Antalcidas, by which the Corinthian War was brought to a close,[83] and two years before the *Menexenus*, that the Spartans are justly champions of all the Greeks, because they are undefeated (ἀήττητοι) (33.7).

Moreover, this argument allowed Plato's Socrates not to mention the consequences of such defeat, i.e. that the Athenians surrendered their city to the Spartans under severe terms (Xen. 2.2.20, Diod. 13.107.4), saw the allies of the Spartans demolishing their walls and surrendering their ships (Xen. 2.2.23, Diod. 13.107.4, 14.3.2, 6),[84] the Thirty ruling their city (Xen. 2.3.2, 3.11–12, Diod. 14.2.1, 3.7, 4.2)[85] and a Spartan garrison occupying their citadel (Xen. 2.3.14, Diod. 14.4.4).

After the end of the speech, Socrates expects Menexenus to admire Aspasia and to be grateful to her for the speech (χάριν ἔχεις τοῦ λόγου). Menexenus says that he is exceedingly grateful to her or to him – whoever it was that repeated it to Socrates; and what is more, he owes many other debts of gratitude to the one who spoke it (χάριν ἔχω τούτου τοῦ λόγου ... ὁ εἰπών ... χάριν ἔχω τῷ εἰπόντι) (249d10–e2). The meaning of gratitude is flattery if we consider Platos' *Gorgias*. This text is significant for the present analysis, because it is approximately contemporary with the *Menexenus*[86] and Plato examines the theoretical basis of deceitful rhetoric.[87] When Callicles tells Socrates that he should speak to the

---

79 See Henderson 1975, 43.
80 See Henderson 1975, 42.
81 See Piovan in this volume.
82 Pritchard 1996, 147.
83 See Jebb 1893, 199.
84 For the demolition of the walls by Sparta's allies see Kapellos 2011, 132–138.
85 For the government of the Thirty see Krentz 1995, 122–123.
86 See Henderson 1975, 25.
87 Dodds 1959, 24.

Athenians in order to server their desires (πρὸς χάριν), the latter equates this with flattery (κολακεύσοντα) (521a3–b1). A little later on, Socrates talks about himself, saying that he is one of few, if not the only one, in Athens, who attempts the true art of statesmanship; the speeches he makes from time to time are not aiming at gratification (πρὸς χάριν) (521d6–9). Therefore, Socrates' speech was effective like all speeches of its genre[88] and its section on Arginousai and Aeogospotami was part of that success. Menexenus was bewitched by Socrates' speech, because he took it seriously in the end.[89] This implies that other contemporary Athenians, who would hear the speech would also be fascinated by it and would forget the real facts.

In conclusion, Plato alerts his audience to the dangers of funerary oratory. He condenses most of the events related to the battle of Arginousai and conceals the trial that ensued and the battle at Aegospotami. Seen in the context of Athenian society in the middle of the fourth-century, the content and rhetorical commonplaces of Socrates' speech seem to make sense as a possible and acceptable interpretation of the recent past of that time. This happens, because even these inglorious years of the Peloponnesian War provided an occasion for praise of the Athenians, something customary in the genre, since this was not the occasion for a discussion of the problems that had been made in the execution of the war.[90] At the end, he considers the Athenians themselves responsible for their defeat in the war, making a criticism that no funeral orator would do. The Athenians' difficulty in handling these problematic issues and their unwillingness for self-criticism becomes clear through the precise knowledge of these events, which Plato's readers could acquire in more detail through the use of Xenophon.

Bibliography

Adkins, A.W.H. (1960 – repr. Chicago 1975), *Merit and Responsibility: A Study of Greek Values*.
Altman, W.H.F. (2010), "The Reading Order of Plato's Dialogues", *Phoenix* 64, 18–51.
Anderson, J.K. (1974), *Xenophon*, Bristol.
Bearzot, C. (2012), "Eforo e Teramene", *Mediterraneo Antico* 15, 293–308.

---

[88] Thus I disagree with Wickkiser 1999, 65–74, who argues that the speech is not effective, because the greater ritual of the funeral ceremony is missing.
[89] Henderson 1975, 26 remarks that the fact that Socrates' speech bewitches is clear from Menexenus' enthusiastic response, since he accepts the speech at face value.
[90] See Stow 2007, 197.

Bearzot, C. (2015), "Diodoro sul processo delle Arginouse", in: U. Bultrighini/E. Dimauro (eds.), *Gli amici per Dino: Omaggio a Delfino Ambaglio*, Lanciano, 173–195.
Bosworth, A.B. (2000), "The Historical Context of Thucydides' Funeral Oration", *JHS* 120, 1–16.
Bleckmann, B. (1998), *Athens Weg in die Niederlage. Die Letzen Jahre des Peloponnesischen Kriegs*, Stuttgart/Leipzig.
Bloedow, E. (1975), "Aspasia and the 'Mystery' of the Menexenos", *WS* 9, 32–48.
Blanshard, A.J.L. (2010), "War in the law-court: some Athenian discussions", in: D. Pritchard (ed.), *War, Democracy and Culture in Classical Athens*, Cambridge, 203–224.
Corcoran, C. (2016), *Topography and Deep Structure in Plato: The construction of Place in the Dialogues*, Albany.
Coventry, L. (1989), "Philosophy and Rhetoric in the Menexenus", *JHS* 109, 1–15.
Christ, M. (2012), *The Limits of Altruism in Democratic Athens*, Cambridge.
de Bakker, M. (2013), "The *Epitaphios*, Civic Ideology and the cityscape of classical Athens", in: J. Heirman/J. Klooster (eds.), *The Ideologies of Lived Space in Literary Texts, Ancient and Modern*, Gent, 175–199.
Dodds, E.R. (1959), *Plato's Gorgias*, Oxford.
Engels, D. (2012), "Irony and Plato's Menexenus", *AC* 81, 13–30.
Frangeskou, V. (1999), "Tradition and Originality in Some Attic Funeral Orations", *CW* 92, 315–336.
Gagarin, M. (2001), "Did the Sophists Aim to Persuade?", *Rhetorica* 19, 275–291.
Gagarin, M. (1999), "The Orality of Greek Oratory", in: E.A. MacKay (ed.), *Signs of Orality: The Oral Tradition and its Influence in the Greek and Roman World*, Leiden/Boston, 165–180.
Gray, V.J. (1987), "The value of Diodorus Siculus for the years 411-386 B.C.", *Hermes* 115, 78–79.
Grethlein, J. (2010), *The Greeks and their Past: Poetry, Oratory and History in the Fifth Century BCE*, Cambridge.
Halliwell, S. (1991), "The Uses of Laughter in Greek Culture", *CQ* 41, 279–296.
Harris, E.M. (2013), *The Rule of Law in Action in Classical Athens*, Oxford.
Haskins, E.V. (2005), "Philosophy, rhetoric, and cultural memory: Rereading Plato's *Menexenus* and Isocrates' *Panegyricus*", *Rhetoric Society Quarterly* 35, 25–45.
Hau, I. (2016), *Moral History from Herodotus to Diodorus Siculus*, Edinburgh.
Henderson, M.M. (1975), "Plato's Menexenus and the Distortion of History", *Acta Classica* 18, 25–46.
Hesk, J. (2013), "Leadership and Individuality in the Athenian Funeral Orations", *BICS* 56, 49–65.
Herrman, J. (2009), *Hyperides: Funeral Oration*, Oxford.
Hooper, T. (2015), "Archedemus", *CQ* 65, 500–517.
Hornblower, S. (1995), "The Fourth-Century and Hellenistic Reception of Thucydides", *JHS* 115, 47–68.
Jebb, C. (1893), *The Attic Orators from Antiphon to Isaeus*, MacMillan/New York.
Kahn, C.H. (1963), "Plato's Funeral Oration: The Motive of the Menexenus", *CP* 58, 22–34.
Kapellos, A. (2009), "Adeimantos at Aegospotami: innocent or guilty?", *Historia* 58, 257–275.
Kapellos, A. (2011), "Xenophon Hellenica 2.2.23–A Note", *PP* 66, 132–138.
Kapellos, A. (2012), "Philocles and the Sea-Battle at Aegospotami (Xenophon *Hell*. 2.1.22–32)", *CW* 106, 97–101.
Kapellos, A. (2014), *Lysias 21: A Commentary*, Berlin.
Kapellos, A. (2018), "Lysander and the execution of the Athenian prisoners at Aegospotami (Xenophon *Hell*. 2.1.31–32)", *Mnemosyne* 71, 394–707.

Kapellos, A. (2019a), *Xenophon's Peloponnesian War: A Literary Presentation*, Berlin/Boston.
Kapellos, A. (2019b), "Xenophon and Lysias on the Arginousai trial", *Erga-Logoi* 7/2, 19–44.
Kapellos, A. (2022), "Xenophon and the Orators on the Topography of Arginousae and Aegospotami", *Mnemosyne* (on line), 1–27.
Kelly, D. (1996), "Oral Xenophon", in: I. Worthington (ed.), *Voice into Text: Orality and Literacy in Ancient Greece*, Leiden, 149–163.
Kerch, T.M. (2008), "Plato's Menexenus: A Paradigm of Rhetorical Flattery", *Polis* 25, 99–106.
Krentz, P. (1995), *Xenophon, Hellenica II.3.11–IV.2.8*, Warminster.
Lee, J.W.I. (2017), "Xenophon and his Times", in: M. Flower (ed.), *The Cambridge Companion to Xenophon*, Cambridge, 15–36.
Loraux, N. (1986), *The Invention of Athens: The Funeral Oration in the Classical City*, trans. A. Sheridan, Cambridge (MA).
Luraghi, N. (2016), "Xenophon's Place in Fourth-Century Greek Historiography", in: M. Flower (ed.), *The Cambridge Companion to Xenophon*, Cambridge, 84–99.
Morrison, J.V. (2007), "Thucydides' History Live: Reception and Politics", in: C. Cooper (ed.), *Politics of Orality*, Leiden, 218–233.
Pappas, N./Zelcer, M. (2015), *Politics and Philosophy in Plato's Menexenus: Education and Rhetoric, Myth and History*, London.
Petre, Z. (2009) "Revenants et sauveurs. Le *Ménexène* de Platon et le drame attique", in: M. Neambu/B. Tataru (eds.), *Memory, Humanity and Meaning*, Bucharest, 149–162.
Pontier, P. (2006), *Trouble et ordre chez Xénophon*, Paris.
Pownall, F. (2004), *Lessons from the Past: The Moral Use of History in Fourth-Century Prose*, Ann Arbor.
Price, J.J. (2001), *Thucydides and Internal War*, Cambridge.
Pritchard, D. (1996), "Thucydides and the Tradition of the Funeral Oration", *Ancient History* 26, 137–150.
Pritchard, D. (2010), "The symbiosis between democracy and war: the case of ancient Athens", in: D. Pritchard (ed.), *War, Democracy and Culture in Classical Athens*, Cambridge, 1–62.
Roisman, J. (2005), *The Rhetoric of Manhood: Masculinity in the Attic Orators*, Berkeley.
Rosenstock, B. (1994), "Socrates as Revenant: A Reading of the Menexenus", *Phoenix* 48, 331–347.
Rusten, J. (1989), *A Commentary on Thucydides II*, Cambridge.
Sansone, D. (2020), *Plato: Menexenus*, Cambridge.
Shanske, D. (2007), *Thucydides and the Philosophical Origins of History*, Cambridge.
Shear, J. (2013), "'Their Memories will never grow old': the politics of remembrance in the Athenian funeral orations", *CQ* 63, 511–536.
Stow, S. (2007), "Pericles at Gettysburg and Ground Zero: Tragedy, Patriotism, and Public Mourning", *The American Political Science Review* 101/2, 195–208.
Strauss, B.S. (1983), "Aegospotami Reexamined", *AJP* 104, 24–35.
Todd, S.C. (2007), *A Commentary on Lysias: Speeches 1–11*, Oxford.
Tsitsiridis, S. (1998), *Platons Menexenos: Einleitung, Text und Kommentar*, Stuttgart/Leipzig.
Usher, S. (1999), *Greek Oratory: Tradition and Originality*, Oxford.
Walters, K.R. (1980), "Rhetoric as Ritual: The Semiotics of the Attic Funeral Oration", *Florilegium* 2, 1–27.
Welwei, W.-K. (1999), *Das klassische Athen*, Darmstadt.
Wickkiser, B.L. (1999), "Speech in Context: Plato's *Menexenus* and the Ritual of Athenian Public Burial", *Rhetoric Society Quarterly* 29, 65–74.

Yoshitake, S. (2010), "Arete and the achievements of the war dead: the logic of praise in the Athenian funeral oration", in: D. Pritchard (ed.), *War, Democracy and Culture in Classical Athens*, 357–377.

Yunis, H. (1990), "Review of *The Fall of the Athenian Empire,* by D. Kagan", *CJ* 85, 360–364.

David Whitehead
Isocrates and the Peloponnesian War

Abstract: This chapter examines Isocrates and his rhetorical treatment of the Peloponnesian War. Whitehead points out that of those Athenians who were born before the Peloponnesian War's outbreak in 431 and survived beyond its end in 404, Isocrates belongs to a select, literate, few whose surviving writings we can examine for traces of its impact. Both in (i) his early speeches for the courts and (ii) throughout his later, more numerous, epideictic compositions Isocrates does make mention of the War — which destroyed his family's fortunes; when forensic circumstances called for this (*re* i) and when he himself felt inclined to do so (*re* ii). This material falls into three main categories: the terminology that he employs to refer to the War and its several phases; specific events and people mentioned or ignored (some of them surprising); and, of particular note, passages like *On The Peace* 92, where personal feelings seems to persist.

1 Preliminaries

'The Peloponnesian War' was the conceptual brainchild of its peerless contemporary historian, Thucydides. Despite the several questionable distortions of perspective entailed, his insistence that the twenty-seven years between 431 and 404 represented a single, unitary power-struggle in two phases (Thuc. 5.26), and that this was a conflict of unprecedented magnitude which drew in most of the inhabited world (Thuc. 1.1), is very hard to escape,[1] and nowhere more so than in its application to his own city.

Post-war Athens, besides being defeated and humiliated, was also a much smaller place than before. 'It has long been established that the number of Athenian citizens in 403 ... dropped dramatically since the beginning of the Peloponnesian War: there were less than half as many Athenians in 403 than in 431'.[2] Born five years before hostilities opened, Isocrates was one of the survivors. At the end of the twenty-seven years he was still alive; and he would live — and write — for a further two generations (until 338) thereafter. While Isocrates' avoidance of the

---

Aggelos Kapellos read earlier drafts of this paper and gave valuable advice for improving them.

---

1 See e.g. Strauss 1997; Hornblower 2002, 150–152.
2 Strauss 1986, 70.

wartime perils that proved fatal for so many of his fellow-citizens has to be attributed mainly to sheer good luck, the family's elevated socio-economic circumstances also played their part. His father Theodorus was probably a man of liturgical census; at any rate, of means.³ As such, Isocrates' (and by extension his family's) statistical chances of not succumbing to the Plague were high.⁴ The same applies, *mutatis mutandis*, to the likelihood of death in military service — something which in Isocrates' case can only have arisen, even theoretically, once the Peace of Nicias (421) had broken down into renewed, open hostilities. In any event, it was the enemy fortification and occupation of Deceleia (413) that lies behind the personal *metabolê* he mentions in 15.161: the loss, in 'the war against the Lacedaimonians', of the property he and his brothers had expected to inherit from their father. Besides land — retrievable, surely, after 404 — this patrimony had included slaves: the slave-labour-force, of unstated size, which Theodoros had acquired for manufacturing musicians' pipes (*auloi*). Such workmen were *cheirotechnai*, those skilled with their hands, whom Thucydides singles out for emphasis when reporting the mass defection of Athens' slaves to Deceleia (Thuc. 7.27.5).

Without expanding the point further: the Peloponnesian War transformed Isocrates' existence and what he could anticipate from it. For him it was (in his own word) a *metabolê*. During the remaining sixty-six years of his life he was to engineer, as Davies puts it, a 'return, via speech-writing and his school of rhetoric, to an economic position comparable to his father's',⁴ but that is not mycentral concern here. Rather, I maintain focus on the war itself: the extent to which, and the ways in which, it echoes through Isocrates' eight decades of writing.

This topic is hardly novel; it belongs in a field explored long ago by Lévy and latterly by Bearzot;⁵ but concentration on Isocrates, and on the war itself rather than the political and constitutional convulsions in Athens that it triggered, will shed some light on unnoticed areas.

An immediate complication arises. From the 380s onwards Isocrates devoted himself to genres which gave scope for expressing his personal opinions and for speaking in his own voice — a voice that, unsuited to public arenas (5.81, 12.9; [Plut.] *Vit.X Or.* 837a), resonated pleasurably inside his own head. Before that,

---

3 Davies 1971, 245–246 summarises the ancient evidence. The key item is Isocrates' own description of his father as 'serviceable to the polis' (15.161). On *chrêsimos* in that sort of context see generally Whitehead 1993, 63–64; Veligianni-Terzi 1997, 203–204.
4 Davies 1971, 246.
5 Lévy 1976; Bearzot 2017.

by contrast, his output consisted of true speeches, written for litigants (and others) appearing in court. Self-evidently, therefore, his first six compositions,[6] the very ones where we might otherwise have expected to find his responses to the War on open display, are the ones where the real-life requirements of the speech (and the character of the speaker) took priority.

Four of them — 21 *Prosecution Support-Speech Against Euthynous*, 20 *Against Lochites*, 17 *Trapeziticus*, 19 *Aigineticus* — contribute nothing to the present enquiry, but insights can be gained from the other two: 18 *Special Plea to block Callimachus*, and especially 16 *On the Horse-Team*. And what will be seen from Isocrates' oeuvre as a totality, though he was far from fixated on the War that had dominated his early years, is that it did leave various kinds of mark.[7]

2 Terminology and chronology

Extant appearances of the locution 'the Peloponnesian War' (ὁ Πελοποννησιακὸς Πόλεμος) do not occur until four centuries after it.[8] According to Strabo 13.1.39, 'Thucydides says that the Athenians took the Troad away from the Mytilenians in the Pachetian (*sc.* narrative/section) of the Peloponnesian War'.

Since we can read for ourselves Thuc. 3.18–50, on the 428 revolt of Mytilene and Athens' response to it, one must immediately comment that Thucydides' own words are very different from what Strabo implies — but no matter for my purposes here. Concerning Strabo's own vocabulary, the adjective 'Pachetian' (a *hapax legomenon* generated from the Athenian commanding general Paches) was perhaps his own; and, irrespective of that, it is obvious that 'Peloponnesian' subsumes it (ἐν τῷ Πελοποννησιακῷ πολέμῳ τῷ Παχητίῳ). Not obvious at all, though, is the chronological reach of 'Peloponnesian' here. Any assumption

---

[6] Nos. 16–21 in the traditional ordering that goes back to Hieronymus Wolf. Their chronological order, in my view, is: 21, 18, 20, 16, 17, 19. Details and argumentation in Whitehead 2022.

[7] Where more than one of Isocrates' works bears upon a topic they will be adduced in their chronological order — which, summarily, I take to be: (21, 18, 20, 16, 17, 19,) 13 *On the Sophists*, 11 *Bousiris*, 4 *Panegyricus*, 2 *To Nicocles*, 1 *To Demonicus*, 14 *Plataicus*, 3 *Nicocles*, 10 *Helen*, 6 *Archidamus*, 9 *Euagoras*, 7 *Areopagiticus*, 8 *On the Peace*, 15 *On the Antidosis*, 5 *To Philip*, 12 *Panathenaicus*.

[8] Thucydides himself never condenses his opening phrase 'the war of (the) Peloponnesians and Athenians' (1.1.1) into 'the Peloponnesian War', though in 5.28.2 the period 431–421 is (from an Argive standpoint) 'the Attic War'.

that it must embrace the entirety of 431–404 meets a cautionary obstacle in the other first-century instance of 'Peloponnesian War', in Diodorus Siculus 13.24.2: 'during the Peloponnesian War the Athenians confined many of the Lacedaimonians to the island of Sphacteria, and took them prisoner, but ransomed them to the Spartans'.

The passage is in fact noteworthy on two counts. One is the possibility, ever-present in that part of Diodorus' *Bibliothêkê*, that the phrase κατὰ τὸν Πελοποννησιακὸν πόλεμον has been taken over from Ephorus — a younger contemporary of Isocrates. The other is the strong likelihood that Nicolaus the Syracusan is made here to utter it (to his fellow-citizens after their rout of the Athenian invasion force in 413) in application to the conflict of 431–421, already in the past at the time of speaking. That decade is of course what many modern scholars conventionally label the 'Archidamian' War, following the lead of fourth-century writers cited by Harpocration, *Lexicon of the Ten Orators* (A247 Keaney): Lysias, Ephorus and Anaximenes.

Isocrates made a contribution to this piecemeal, un-Thucydidean approach to 431–404 in the shape of 'the Deceleian War' (ὁ Δεκελεικὸς πόλεμος), i.e. the fighting of 413–404. He deploys this phrase first in the *Plataicus* (14.31), at the end of the 370s: the Plataian speaker there rhetorically asks whether anyone did more harm to Athens ἐν τῷ Δεκελεικῷ πολέμῳ than the Thebans did. It then recurs — either once or twice — in the mid-350s, in *On the peace*: see 8.37 and, as a papyrus variant, 8.86.[9] Was it Isocrates' own coinage? Possibly so, but equally possibly not; and definitely not, if it is predated by either or both of the two instances in the Oxyrhyncus *Hellenica* (7.3, 19.2).

We might note that Isocrates had had an opportunity to use it as early as 402, in the *Special Plea to block Callimachus*, but what appears there (18.47) is the circumlocutory phrase 'during the ten years when the Lacedaimonians made war (*sc.* on Athens) continuously'.

When Isocrates wants or needs to encompass — implicitly — everything between 431 and 404, he can write (as in 15.161, quoted above) 'the war against the Lacedaimonians' or else simply 'the war' with an accompanying frame of refer-

---

[9] The passage lists three occasions when the Athenians suffered a catastrophic loss of warships or troops: Egypt and Cyprus in the mid-fifth century, and a third one. The primary manuscripts have the nonsensical ἐν Δάτῳ δέ; later ones proffer ἐν δὲ τῷ Πόντῳ, which is little better; so ἐν δὲ τῷ Δεκελεικῷ πολέμῳ in a London papyrus has been generally accepted. See Laistner 1921, 81–82; Norlin 1929, 60 with n.*d*; Raubitschek 1941; Papillon 2004, 154 n. 51.

ence. A case in point occurs in 4.122: the Spartans 'entered the war with the intention of liberating the Hellenes' (cf. Thuc. 4.85.1: speech of Brasidas).

What, though, where there is no such contextual material? In a language like English we can be confident that reference to 'the war' does mean one war in particular (and, with luck, an identifiable one) rather than 'war' as a generalised circumstance. But ancient Greek's use of the definite article can obscure this distinction.

Witness 18.31. There the speaker, Isocrates' client, invites the dikasts and other listeners in 402 to agree with him that nothing enhanced the Athenians' reputation more than the 404/3 reconciliation-agreements (between the competing factions of citizens), even though their forebears achieved many fine things ἐν τῷ πολέμῳ.

Translators of this phrase into languages which, like Greek, can preserve its ambiguity duly do so: 'à la guerre', 'im Krieg'.[10] Otherwise the choice is to make the phrase an explicit generalisation, as Van Hook did in the Loeb edition: 'many glorious deeds in war'.[11] In truth the matter is hard to determine with certainty. Does Isorates mean here (a) 'in war' or (b) 'in the (sc. Peloponnesian) War'? Arguments can be adduced in favour of either reading:

(i) *Isocrates' own (later) usage*. Inconclusive. The earliest relevant work, the *Panegyricus* (of c.380), furnishes an instance of a (ἐν τῷ πολέμῳ τῷ κατὰ γῆν is contrasted with ἐν τοῖς κινδύνοις τοῖς κατὰ θάλατταν: 4.21), but also two cases of b: in 4.98 the Persian 'War' of 480; in 4.142 Rhodian 'war' of the 390s, specified earlier in the sentence. Likewise the *Plataicus*, from the late 370s, appears to employ a specific sense of ἐν τῷ πολέμῳ in 14.14 but a generic one in 14.23; and the *Archidamus* (c. 366) has generic at 6.50 and 6.92 but specific at 6.44 and perhaps 6.104. See also: generic, 3.22; specific, perhaps 8.22. Sometimes Isocrates flags up a generic sense a by ἐν πολέμῳ, omitting the definite article; so in 4.35, 6.21, 12.77. But he does not do this consistently, as we have seen; and in 15.319 εἰς πόλεμον καταστάντες means the Peloponnesian War. Contrast with that 4.122 (mentioned above): the Spartans: εἰς τὸν πόλεμον κατέστησαν ὡς ἐλευθερώσοντες τοὺς Ἕλληνας.

(ii) *The usage of other orators*. Given that the first relevant comparanda within Isocrates' own oeuvre come two decades later than 18.31 (i, above), the

---

10 Mathieu and Brémond 1929, 26; Ley-Hutton in Brodersen and Ley-Hutton 1997, 210.
11 Van Hook 1945, 273. (Mirhady in Mirhady and Too 2000, 104 inadvertently omits the phrase from his translation of the present clause: 'while our ancestors accomplished many noble things'.) See also Carlotti 1966–1967, 365, 'in guerra'.

earlier these 'other orators' are, the better. Here again, however, the test is inconclusive. Lysias and Andocides exemplify both the generalising sense *a* (Lys 2.10 & 78, 14.13; Andoc. 3.11) and the particularising sense *b* (Lys. 17.3, 18.24, 25.12; Andoc. 3.39). Later orators too can be mustered on both sides of the argument, notably Demosthenes (*a*, the homicide law in Dem. 23.53 and 55 — cf. the Plataiai oath in Lyc. *Leocr.* 81; *b*, Dem. 8.57, 18.283, 20.42, 23.13) and Aeschines (*a*, Aesch. 3.7 & 154; *b*, Aesch. 2.70 & 100, 3.103).

(iii) *General and contextual considerations.* Again these pull indifferent directions. In context here in 18.31 it would have been good psychology for Isocrates to make his speaker remind listeners that during the course of the Peloponnesian War their parents and grandparents had indeed achieved 'many fine things' before Athens' ultimate failure in it. Yet a cogent reason for regarding the present passage as a generalisation about war(s) is that the very next sentence, linked by an explanatory γάρ, is one. It contrasts the many *poleis* which have a glorious military record with the single *polis* — Athens — supreme in wise resolution of civil strife, *stasis*. All the same, so soon after this particular war the dikasts' thoughts would inevitably turn to it; thus while giving due credit to their forebears the speaker goes immediately on to assert that wartime successes have been matched, even surpassed, by very recent achievements in peace-making.

In sum (and on balance): while πολλῶν καὶ καλῶν τοῖς προγόνοις ἐν τῷ πολέμῳ πεπραγμένων in 18.31 is probably a generalisation, we cannot exclude the Peloponnesian War's influence on it.

3 Events and people

Prominent personalities from great wars often remain in the memory more vividly than the abstract conflicts themselves. Involved in the Peloponnesian War were four individuals to whom Plutarch devoted full-dress biographies (Pericles, Nicias and Alcibiades from Athens, Lysander from Sparta); to them we might add, as resonant names, Archidamus, Phormion, Cleon, Brasidas, Gylippus, Thrasybulus, Cleophon, Cyrus. And the same goes for landmark events; here (e.g.) Pylos, Delion, Amphipolis, Sicily, Deceleia,[12] Arginousai,[13] Aegospotami. How does Isocrates measure up in this regard?[14]

---

[12] See Rhodes in this volume.

For reasons already acknowledged, only two of the six early forensic speeches bear upon this question. Only 18 and 16 bring the War into view at all; and even there, only those aspects of it relevant to the trial in progress.

The background to 18 *Special Plea to block Callimachus*, as recounted in 18.5–19 there, concerns events (and dealings between the litigants) in Athens immediately post-war; but even so the military conflict itself makes two appearances.

First and fleetingly — as we have registered here (under 2.2) — 18.47 uses the phrase 'the ten years when the Lacedaimonians made war (*sc.* on Athens) continuously', i.e. the Deceleian War (413–404) measured by inclusive Greek reckoning.[15] Isocrates' purpose there is a simple one, a negative one: the speaker is contrasting these 'ten years' with the 'not even a single day' when, allegedly, the opponent Callimachus had presented himself for military service.

Longer and more positive in intent is 18.59–61 (with 65); so positive, indeed, that the speaker introduces it, in 18.58, by claiming it as (ethically) decisive for his case a whole.

(59) When the *polis* had lost the ships in the Hellespont and was deprived of its military power, I stood out so far from the majority of the trierarchs in that I saved my ship — as did a few others; and from these few in that ... I alone did not bring my trierarchy to an end. (60) Instead, with the others gladly withdrawing from their liturgies and feeling demoralised in the face of the current situation ... I did not hold the same view as them. No, I persuaded my brother to be

---

13 See Kapellos in this volume.

14 The 'events' of the Peloponnesian War are unproblematically definable: they must occur within its 27-year span. As regards 'people' I leave aside three whose careers *as far as Isocrates is concerned* fell predominantly (*a*) before 431 or (*b*) after 404. Criterion *a* excludes PERICLES — for whom Isocrates' high regard is evident first in 16.28 ('by common consent the most self-controlled, most upright and most wise of the citizens', *sc.* in the 440s) and later in 15.111 (where 16.28's trio of virtues are repeated) with further elaboration at 15.234–235 and, tacitly, 15.307–308. Criterion *b* excludes, on the Athenian side, THRASYBULUS and ANYTUS (paired in 18.23) and CONON (not in the forensic speeches but see 4.142 & 154, 9.52 & 56–57, 7.12 & 65, 5.61 & 67, 12.105; also *Letters* 8.8) and LYSANDER among Spartans (21.2, 8.16 & 61, 16.41, 15.128).

15 In other circumstances this would have been an appropriate way to describe the Archidamian War, the first decade (431–421) of the Peloponnesian War: see esp. Thuc. 5.24.2 (ταῦτα δὲ τὰ δέκα ἔτη ὁ πρῶτος πόλεμος ξυνεχῶς γενόμενος γέγραπται), 5.25.1 & 3, 5.26.3 & 6. But as Isocrates' modern editors have realised (e.g. Mathieu and Brémond 1929, 30 n. 1; Van Hook 1945, 282 n. *a*), that cannot be so in the present context. For this see again 12.57 (the Athenians held out against massive opposition 'for ten years') and Cleocritus speaking in Xen. *Hell.* 2.4.21 (the Thirty have killed almost more Athenians in eight months than the Peloponnesians managed in ten years).

co-trierarch and, paying the sailors a wage out of our own pockets, we were giving the enemy a bad time. (61) Eventually, after Lysander had decreed that anyone importing grain to you would suffer the death-penalty, we exhibited such competitive ambition towards the *polis* that, with others not even bold enough to bring in their own, we were seizing the grain being shipped in to them and bringing it into the Peiraieus. In return for these things you yourselves voted to crown us, and to proclaim the award ... in front of the eponyms. ... (65) We are men whom you, taking deeds as your criterion, crowned by reason of 'manly worth', at a time when it was not so easy as it is now to win that honour.

The essential historicity of this account I take to be guaranteed by its appeal to the award of the honorific decree (for 'manly worth', *andragathia*). Isocrates would not have risked such a claim if enough of the listeners knew it to be false. In any event, while the passage is rich in commentary-worthy matters, here only one of them needs to be noted: its very opening words, 'When the *polis* had lost the ships in the Hellespont'. Present-day writers would have given this chronological fix as 'the battle of Aegospotami'.[16] And an Athenian court too, when a writer so chose, could be presented with the toponym Aigospotami, and be expected to recognise it; that is guaranteed by Dem. 23.212. Reference is made there to the steersman Hermon,[27] 'who with Lysander captured two hundred triremes on the occasion when we experienced our misfortunes at Aegospotami'. However, Dem. 23 (delivered in 352) is the exception which proves what is otherwise the rule in this genre.[17] For Isocrates' contemporaries see Andocides ('when we lost the ships in the Hellespont': 3.21) and particularly Lysias: e.g. Lys. 2.58 ('when the ships were lost in the Hellespont ... and that supreme disaster came upon not only us, who suffered the misfortune, but the other Hellenes too'), Lys. 12.43 ('when the sea-battle and the disaster for the polis occurred'), Lys. 13.5 ('when your ships had been destroyed'), Lys. 16.4 ('before the disaster in the Hellespont'), Lys. 19.17 ('when the sea-battle occurred in the Hellespont'), Lys. 21.9 ('when the ships were destroyed in the final sea-battle').[18]

As we see there, Lysias' habit is to call Aegospotami a 'disaster', a συμφορά. In Isocrates 18.59 (quoted above) the form of words he chose had required no all-encompassing noun, but such nouns do appear (and recur) in his long post-

---

16 Cf., likewise, Xen. *Hell.* 2.1.21 & 23, Diod. 13.105.3. On the battle see e.g. Wylie 1986; Strauss 1987; Kapellos 2009; Kapellos 2012; Kapellos 2013; Kapellos 2014, 13–22; Robinson 2014; Kapellos 2017.
17 See generally Bearzot 2017, 42.
18 In [Lys.] 6.46 the event is used as a chronological watershed: Andocides (it is claimed) has performed military service 'neither before the disaster nor after the disaster'. See Bearzot 2017, 44–45, proposing to add to this category Lys. 16.4 and Isoc. 12.99.

forensic output: ἀτυχία or δυστυχία, 'misfortune', and its cognates.[19] Witness 4.119 ('after the misfortune that occurred in the Hellespont'), 7.64 ('when we lost the ships in the Hellespont'), 8.86 (the fifth-century Athenians 'ultimately lost two hundred ships in the Hellespont'), 5.62 (Conon's 'misfortune in the sea-battle in the Hellespont') and 12.99 ('before the misfortune in the Hellespont occurred').[20] 14.31 also ('when we suffered our misfortune'), in Van Hook's opinion, is an allusion to Aegospotami; however, since the sentence goes directly on to mention the Thebans' wish that Athens be obliterated from the map (cf. Xen. *Hell.* 2.2.19), δυστυχησάντων ὑμῶν might more accurately be considered a broader encapsulation of the Athenians' loss of power, and scope for negotiation, in 405/4.[21]

The Peloponnesian War is brought much more copiously into play in 16 *On the Horse-Team*. Although the defendant in court in c. 397 (in a case stemming from events two decades earlier) is the son and namesake of a man by now dead, the speech as it stands focuses almost entirely on that celebrated figure: Alcibiades.

After his bitter-sweet start in life (orphaned young, but taken under Pericles' guardianship: 16.28) Alcibiades is presented in an unchronological series of episodes chosen to showcase his courage and patriotism: as serving soldier (16.29–30) and later as general and politician (16.5–21). His prowess in the former role (16.22) especially from 411 onwards, implicitly outweighs equivocal interludes such as his temporary defection to Sparta (16.10).

Isocrates' material on Alcibiades has long since been absorbed into biographies of the man, ancient and modern, which obviates any need to assess it at length here. The one overall point we might register is the omission of concrete detail, such as (other) names. The only (other) Athenian general mentioned by name is Phormion (16.29), who serves principally as a context/dating fix. The only other individuals who feature are the unnamed[22] king of Persia (16.18) and his satrap Tissaphernes (16.20); they play a narrative role without any colour or

---

[19] On Lysias' and Isocrates' different choice of vocabulary here see already Lévy 1976, 40–43; Bearzot 2017, 42.

[20] In 15.128 Isocrates needed a general — any general — to juxtapose with his protégé Timotheus. Timotheus' greatness as a general, according to Isocrates there, is his record of consistent success(es) over many years; this gives him the edge over anyone who had an unparalleled but single stroke of luck, 'like Lysander'. Plainly the allusion is to Aigospotami, with Lysander's good fortune the mirror-opposite of the Athenians' bad.

[21] Van Hook 1945, 152 n.*b*. Contrast Papillon 2004, 235 n. 24, who refers (rather obliquely), to 404.

[22] Dareius II.

emphasis.²³ And the same goes for the occasional geographical allusions: Argos, 16.9; Aspendos, 16.18; Deceleia, 16.10; Sicily, 16.6 & 15.

To say that the context here is biography, encomium even, is a statement of the obvious, but even so the speaker is made to gloss over much that could have reinforced his father's credit with the listeners. Note especially 16.21 (on the years after 411): 'To speak, item by item, of all the triremes he captured or battles he won or cities he took or talked into being your friends would be a considerable task'. Such summary treatment is justified in 16.22 by the argument that this is all common knowledge. Equally true is that Isocrates has little appetite for fine detail, especially in military matters.

In Lys. 14.38–39 the finger of blame for Aegospotami, and the events it led to, is pointed straight at Alcibiades (together with Adeimantus).²⁴ Given that that speech was written for a prosecution of the celebrity's son, this fact is no more surprising than the complete absence of any such suggestion from *On the Horse-Team* (Isocrates decided not even to draw attention to such a view by attacking it). Lys. 2.58, though, is noticeably more circumspect — in attributing the loss of Athens' war-fleet 'either to the *kakia* of a commander or the design of the gods'; and as Roisman has shown, both Lysias 2 and (on the Macedonian victory at Chaeronea) Demosthenes 60 exemplify the rhetorical role a Funeral Speech could play in focusing on the collective valour displayed by the armed forces, which has made their defeat no disgrace.²⁵

In his post-forensic output, where he has only himself to please, Isocrates is equally disposed to summon up memories of prominent Spartans from 431–404 as Athenians; and his choices are not always the ones we would have expected.

Athenians. Here 8.75 is the first passage of relevance: '... Aristeides and Themistocles and Miltiades were better men than Hyperbolus and Cleophon and present-day demagogues'.²⁶ Striking here is the wholesale omission of any figures from the Pentecontaetia, even Pericles. Aside from that, Hyperbolus, arguably, is an odd choice to pick out — why not Cleon?²⁷ In any event, whom from

---

23 Specifically, neither here nor elsewhere does Isocrates show the appreciation Thucydides had (2.65.12, 8.5.45) of the importance of Persian money in bankrolling the Spartans' fleet.
24 See generally Kapellos 2009, Kapellos 2017.
25 Roisman 2005, 67–70. For Chaeronea cf. Crick in this volume.
26 Papillon 2004, 151 mistakenly gives this name as Thrasybulus.
27 On Hyperbolus see Hornblower 2008, 968–972. This is his only appearance in Attic oratory (and he claims no place in the succession of popular leaders listed in [Arist]. *Ath. Pol.* 28, where there is no room for him between Cleon and Cleophon). In fact, Cleon too is mentioned only once in surviving oratory (in his case glowingly: the man who achieved the success at Pylos is

his youth does Isocrates find admirable (rather than the reverse)? *On the Horse-Team* has already foreshadowed the answer. Alcibiades is described in 11.5 as, by common consent, a man who stood far out from the crowd (πολὺ διήνεγκε τῶν ἄλλων),[28] and in 5.58–61 he is the first-named of four paradigms of success offered to Philip.[29] The passage is an encapsulation, in effect, of 16.5–21 — even down to the excuse for not itemising every detail (5.59).

Spartans. The *Archidamus* is voiced by an actual Spartan (the son of King Agesilaus II, himself later to rule as Archidamus III), so naturally[30] fellow-citizens furnish his trio of examples of men who successfully rescued allied cities under siege (6.52–53): Pedaritus at Chios,[31] Brasidas at Amphipolis,[32] Gylippus at Syracuse.[33]

For all three, this is their sole appearance in Attic oratory. Brasidas remained sufficiently celebrated in the fourth century as to merit a mention in Plato's *Symposium* (221C: Brasidas is a good parallel for Achilles, just as Pericles is for Nestor and Antenor) and in Aristotle's *Ethics* (*EN* 5.1134b23–24: his *post-mortem* heroization). The same cannot be said with confidence of Gylippus, though note the entry (Γ21 Keaney) in Harpocration: 'Gylippus, name of a Lacedaimonian'. Of course, Isocrates 6.53 might have generated the entry, as is explicitly the case with Π42: 'Pedaritus. Isocrates (*sc.* mentions him) in the *Archidamus*'.

---

the father of the speaker's mother's first husband: [Dem.] 40.25), though his persistence into fourth-century consciousness can be seen in Aristotle's *Rhetoric* (provided he is the unqualified 'Cleon' of 2.2.1, 3.5.2 and 3.8.1). As regards Cleophon, Aggelos Kapellos suggests to me that Isocrates had in mind the incident mentioned in [Arist.] *Ath. Pol.* 34.1 (C. wears body-armour in the Assembly, and is drunk, when he rejects Spartan peace-overtures). Be that as it may, Cleophon's persistence into even later oratorical memory can be seen in Aesch. 2.76 and 3.150.

28 In context this perhaps means that he was the best of Socrates' students.

29 The others are (post-Aegospotami) Conon, Dionysius I of Syracuse and, very briefly, Cyrus the Great of Persia.

30 Another relevant instance of Isokrates writing from a standpoint other than his own occurs in the *Plataicus* (14.26): 'we have twice been overthrown by siege' refers in the first instance to 427 (Thuc. 3.52–68).

31 In 412 (see principally Thuc. 8.28–55); Poralla and Bradford 1985, 104.

32 In 422 (see principally Thuc. 4.102–108, 5.6–11); Poralla and Bradford 1985, 36–37 with 177.

33 In 413 (see principally Thuc. 6.93–7.86 *passim*); Poralla and Bradford 1985, 38–39 with 178.

4 Impact and emotion

One thing shared in common by many of the passages quoted or cited so far is their relative matter-of-factness. Even when Isocrates uses one of his 'misfortune in the Hellespont' phrases, they convey little real emotion, and they anyway come and go too quickly for reflection on the part of the listener/reader. This contrasts sharply with Xenophon's pathos-driven narrative of the Athenians' immediate reaction to Aegospotami (Xen. *Hell.* 2.2.3–4 & 10–11). In that celebrated vignette the entire community is panic-stricken, facing immediate hunger and then the kind of punishment it had meted out to so many others. The genuine empathy for the mass of his fellow-citizens (and others) that Xenophon shows there is unparalleled anywhere in Isocrates' oeuvre – where reliance is usually on stock formulas. Occasionally, though, a longer passage gives a glimpse into stronger feelings that Isocrates has retained over the years (or, at least, can re-create to order).

A striking example comes in 8.84–88 (here abridged), on the Athenians' behaviour in the years from 413 onwards:

> (84) They reached such a peak of neglecting their own possessions and coveting those of others that when the Lacedaimonians had invaded our territory and the fortification at Deceleia had already been established they manned triremes for Sicily, and were not ashamed to watch the fatherland being hacked about and plundered while they were sending out an army against those who had never done us any harm... (86) ... In the Deceleian War they lost 10.000 hoplites of their own and of the allies, and in Sicily 40.000 men and 240 triremes, and finally 200 in the Hellespont. (87) And of the ships that were lost in fives and tens and more, and the men in thousands and two-thousands, who could make a count? ... (88) And finally, before they knew it, they had filled up the public burial-places with their fellow-citizens ...

That this flight of rhetoric bends facts to its purpose need not concern us.[34] What is important is the head of emotive steam Isocrates builds up, as he condemns the collective folly of his fellow-citizens during the culminating decade of the Peloponnesian War.

---

[34] I confine myself to noting the misleading impression given by 8.84 that no forces were sent against Sicily until 413 (rather than 415). As commentators have remarked (e.g. Laistner 1927, 103; Norlin 1929, 59 n.c; Papillon 2004, 154 n. 48), Isocrates' face can be saved by the assumption that he is referring to the *reinforcements* sent in 413 (Thuc. 7.20).

Contrast Isocrates there with the analysis that Thucydides incorporates into his celebrated "obituary" of Pericles (Thuc. 2.65). It begins with a contrast between Pericles and his unnamed political successors, who, in the historian's opinion, should have adhered to Periclean policies for Athens' survival, but did not: 2.65.7–11. In 2.65.12, however, the string of third-person plurals tacitly shifts from applying to political leaders to the Athenians as a whole. They suffer catastrophic losses in Sicily and revolution at home, hold out nevertheless for eight years against an enemy reinforced by Persian support and by their own revolting allies, but are ultimately obliged to surrender because of their own domestic disputes.[35] Isocrates, for his part, blames the collectivity of his fellow-citizens throughout. (Here, at any rate: 8.75 has already named Cleophon; see above, under 3.4.)

In any event, the high-political focus — and the power — that Isocrates displays in 8.84–88[36] continue in the ensuing paragraphs. But then 8.92 sees a shift, in part at least, into something more akin to *pathos*.

> Instead of garrisoning the *akropoleis* of other cities, [a] they saw the enemy become masters of their own; instead of taking children, dragged from their fathers and mothers, as hostages, [b] many citizens were compelled to raise and educate their own children, under (the) siege, less well than they deserved; and instead of farming the lands of others, [c] for many years they were not allowed even to see their own.

Here, it is plain, the trio of 'instead of (ἀντί) x' phrases allude (in broad brush terms) to the zenith of the Athenian Empire, and to three of the main tools of imperialism deployed then: imposition of garrisons, demand for hostages, dispatch of colonists/cleruchs.[50]

The three main clauses, though, take rather more fathoming. No problem is presented by *a*, because the only relevant occasion when Athens' own *akropolis* was in the hands of an enemy garrison is during the (post-war) rule of the Thirty.[37] However, neither *b* nor *c* belong in 404/3 with it,[38] and they are harder to

---

[35] 'The internal quarrels here are those of the last years of the war, the dismissal of Alcibiades after Notion and his retirement to the Chersonesus, the Arginousai trial, and the last struggles between Cleophon and his political enemies': Gomme 1956, 198. See also Kapellos 2019, 215–216.
[36] As indeed in most of the rest of *On the Peace*. See (e.g.) Moysey 1982, Davidson 1990, Michelini 1998.
[37] See Xen. *Hell*. 2.3.13 with Krentz 1995, 125–126. Within Isocrates, compare the outburst at 15.319: during the Peloponnesian War 'we saw some of our fellow-citizens going to their death, some taken by the enemy, some deprived of life's necessities; also the democracy twice over-

pin down precisely in time before it. Norlin flatly asserts that *c*, at any rate, relates to 413–404.[39] Contrast Papillon, on both *b* and *c*: '[t]he reference to children is more general [*sc.* than *a*] but describes the difficulties of the Athenians during the Peloponnesian War ... The people of Attica were called within the walls of Athens by Pericles and had to endure seeing the Attic countryside ravaged by Spartan forces each spring and summer'.[40] While Norlin might well be right, the broader interpretation is worth pursuing.

Though Thucydides memorably describes the 431 evacuation of Attica (2.14–17), he never records when — before 421 — it was altered or reversed. Modern opinions vary. On the one hand, fortified demes such as Eleusis, Oenoe, Phyle and Rhamnous (together with non-deme fortresses like Panactum) and cavalry sorties of the kind Thucydides does mention (2.19.2, 2.22.2, 3.1.2) will between them have safeguarded certain vital places and routes within Attica even during the first half of the 420s.[41] Also relevant is that the annual Spartan/Peloponnesian invasions ceased in 424, thanks to the Athenians' possession of the enemy troops captured on Sphacteria (Thuc. 4.41.1). On the other hand, at the Lenaia festival in early 425, the audience for Aristophanes' *Acharnians* had heard the protagonist Dicaeopolis lament that he was 'looking out [*sc.* from the Pnyx] into the countryside, passionate for peace, hating the town, yearning for his own deme' (lines 32–33). We learn later (line 406) that deme is Cholleidai. Assigned by Cleisthenes to tribe Leontis, Cholleidai was a small deme (furnishing two members of the *boulê* in the fourth century), and of indeterminable location.[42] Isocrates' deme, Aigeid Erchia, was much larger (six or seven *bouleutai*), and its site is known: beyond Mount Hymettos some twenty kilometres east of Athens, south of present-day Spata.[43] There, in the heart of Attica's

---

thrown, and the walls of the fatherland demolished; and worst of all, the entire *polis* in danger of being enslaved, and the enemy setting up house on the *akropolis*'.

38 The phrase ἐν τῇ πολιορκίᾳ — whether we translate it 'under siege' or 'under the siege' — might immediately suggest the actual Spartan/Peloponnesian blockade of 405–404 (cf. Andoc. 1.73, ἐπεὶ ... αἱ νῆες διεφθάρησαν καὶ ἡ πολιορκία ἐγένετο), but it did not last long enough to produce, even rhetorically, the results lamented here.

39 Norlin 1929, 65 n.*g*.

40 Papillon 2004, 156 n. 55. See also Ober 1985, 54, presenting 8.92 as an attack on Pericles' defensive strategy.

41 So e.g. Hanson 1983, 75–78, 105–106. See also Lewis 1992, 382.

42 See Traill 1986, 130 (more circumspect than Traill 1975, 46).

43 This is guaranteed by deme documents found there, notably the festival calendar *SEG* 21.541. On Erchia in general see Traill 1975, 41, 67; Whitehead 1986, deme-index s.v.

fertile Mesogeion, where the young Isocrates acquired the equestrian skills with which [Plutarch] credits him,[44] no fortresses lay close by.

Accordingly, there must be a real possibility that Isocrates, just like the fictional Athenian Everyman Dicaeopolis, spent seven years — between the ages of 5 and 12 in his case — confined to the *asty*.[45] In any event, that was indubitably true again, after the respite brought by the 421 Peace, during the Deceleia "decade" (his own 20s). For someone with such a well-developed sense of entitlement, this was hard to bear. The Peloponnesian War had robbed him, in his formative years, of what affluent and cultured young Athenians deserved (προσῆκεν αὐτοῖς: 8.92) from their parents. His own father, he acknowledges, had spared no expense to make the young Isocrates pre-eminent amongst his peers (15.161). Even so; half a century later the issue seems still to have rankled.

Bibliography

Bearzot, C. (2017), "La συμφορά de la cité: la défaite d'Athènes (405–404 av. J.-C.) chez les orateurs attiques", *Ktema* 42, 41–52.
Brodersen, K./Ley-Hutton, C. (1997), *Isokrates, Sämtliche Werke, Band 2: Reden IX–XXI*, Stuttgart.
Carlotti, E. (1966–1967), "L'orazione di Isocrate contro Callimacho", *Annali dei Liceo classico G. Garibaldi di Palermo* 3–4, 346–379.
Davidson, J. (1990), "Isocrates against imperialism: an analysis of *De Pace*", *Historia* 39, 20–36.
Davies, J.K. (1971), *Athenian Propertied Families 600–300 B.C.*, Oxford.
Dover, K.J. (1968), *Lysias and the Corpus Lysiacum*, Berkeley/Los Angeles.
Gomme, A.W. (1956), *A Historical Commentary on Thucydides, II*, Oxford.
Hanson, V.D. (1983), *Warfare and Agriculture in Classical Greece*, Pisa.
Hornblower, S. (2002), *The Greek World 479–323 BC* (third edition), London/New York.
Hornblower, S. (2008), *A Commentary on Thucydides, volume III*, Oxford.
Hyde, W.W. (1921), *Olympic Victor Monuments and Greek Athletic Art*, Washington DC.
Kapellos, A. (2009), "Adeimantos at Aegospotami: innocent or guilty?", *Historia* 58, 257–275.

---

44 Plut.] *Vit. X Or.* 839C; 'it is also said that he rode in a horse-race while still a boy, because a bronze statue of him, still a boy, is a dedication on the akropolis, ball-court of the Arrephoroi, as some say'. (For commentary on this see Roisman and Worthington 2015, 168.)
45 This is no more susceptible of proof than the belief of Lee 2017, 20–21 that Xenophon, Isocrates' younger fellow-Erchian, returned to the deme 'where there was space to ride and hunt' each winter once the invading forces had left. As regards the bronze statue (see preceding note) commemorating the horsemanship of the 'boy' (*pais*) Isocrates, Hyde 1921, 24 and 373 reasonably assigns it a date of c. 420; but a minimum of four-to-five years could have been enough to raise Isocrates' skills to the required standard.

Kapellos, A. (2012), "Philocles and the sea-battle at Aegospotami (Xenophon *Hell*. 2.1.22–32)", *CW* 106, 97–101.
Kapellos, A. (2013), "Xenophon and the execution of the Athenian captives at Aegospotami", *Mnemosyne* 66, 464–472.
Kapellos, A. (2014), *Lysias 21: A Commentary*, Berlin.
Kapellos, A. (2017), "Alcibiades at Aegospotami and the defeat of the Athenian fleet: history and rhetoric", *PP* 72, 303–323.
Kapellos, A. (2019), *Xenophon's Peloponnesian War: A Literary Presentation*, Berlin.
Krentz, P. (1995), *Xenophon, Hellenika II.3.11–IV.2.8*, Warminster.
Laistner, M.L.W. (1921), "Isocratea", *CQ* 15, 78–84.
Laistner, M.L.W. (1927), *De Pace et Philippus*, Ithaca (NY).
Lavency, M. (1964), *Aspects de la logographie judiciaire attique*, Louvain.
Lee, J.W.I. (2017), "Xenophon and his times", in: M.A. Flower (ed.), *The Cambridge Companion to Xenophon*, Cambridge, 15–36.
Lévy, E. (1976), *Athènes devant la défaite de 404: histoire d'une crise idéologique*, Paris.
Lewis, D.M. (1992), "The Archidamian War", in: D.M. Lewis *et al.* (eds.), *The Cambridge Ancient History* (second edition) Cambridge, vol. V, 370–432.
Mathieu, G./Brémond, É. (1929), *Isocrate, Discours: I*, Paris.
Michelini, A.M. (1998), "Isocrates' civic invective: Acharnians and On the Peace", *TAPA* 128, 115–133.
Mirhady, D.C./Too, Y.L. (2000), *Isocrates: I*, Austin.
Moysey, R.A. (1982), "Isocrates' *On the Peace*: rhetorical exercise or political advice", *AJAH* 7, 118–127.
Norlin, G. (1929), *Isocrates in three volumes: II*, London/Cambridge (MA).
Ober, J. (1985), *Fortress Attica: Defense of the Athenian Land Frontier 404–322 BC*, Leiden.
Osborne, R.G./Rhodes, P.J. (2017), *Greek Historical Inscriptions 478–404 BC*, Oxford.
Papillon, T. (2004), *Isocrates: II*, Austin.
Poralla, P./Bradford, A.S. (1985), *A Prosopography of Lacedaemonians from the Earliest Times to the Death of Alexander the Great*, Chicago.
Raubitschek, A.E. (1941), "Two notes on Isocrates", *TAPA* 72, 356–364.
Robinson, E.W. (2014), "What happened at Aegospotami? Xenophon and Diodorus on the last battle of the Peloponnesian War", *Historia* 63, 1–16.
Roisman, R. (2005), *The Rhetoric of Manhood: Masculinity in the Attic Orators*, Berkeley/Los Angeles.
Roisman, J./Worthington, I. (2015), *Lives of the Attic Orators: Texts from Pseudo-Plutarch, Photius, and the Suda* (trans. R. Waterfield), Oxford.
Strauss, B.S. (1986), *Athens after the Peloponnesian War*, Beckenham.
Strauss, B.S. (1987), "A note on the topography and tactics of the battle of Aegospotami", *AJP* 108, 741–745.
Strauss, B.S. (1997), "The problem of periodization: the case of the Peloponnesian War", in: M. Golden/P. Toohey (eds.), *Inventing Ancient Culture: Historicism, Periodization, and the Ancient World*, London/New York, 165–175.
Traill, J.S. (1975), *The Political Organization of Attica: A Study of the Demes, Trittyes, and Phylai, and their Representation in the Athenian Council*, Princeton.
Traill, J.S. (1986), *Demos and Trittys: Epigraphical and Topographical Studies in the Organization of Attica*, Toronto.
Van Hook, L.R. (1945), *Isocrates in three volumes: III*, London/Cambridge (MA).

Veligianni-Terzi, C. (1997), *Wertbegriffe in den attischen Ehrendekreten der klassischen Zeit*, Stuttgart.
Whitehead, D. (1986), *The Demes of Attica 508/7–c.250 B.C.: A Political and Social Study*, Princeton.
Whitehead, D. (1993), "Cardinal Virtues: the language of public approbation in democratic Athens", *C & M* 44, 37–75.
Whitehead, D. (2022), *Isokrates, The Forensic Speeches (nos.16–21); Introduction, Text, Translation and Commentary*, Cambridge.
Wylie, D. (1986), "What really happened at Aegospotami?", *AC* 55, 125–141.

Yun Lee Too
Back to the Future: Temporal Adjustments in Isocrates

Abstract: Isocrates is an extremely conservative author, who prefers the past to what he sees as the currently chaotic present of Athens. For him, any hope for the future lies in lessons on behaviour and statesmanship provided by Athens' ancestors such that the past becomes the now and the future. The actual duration of history becomes inconsequential because the past is simply the past which is not now and which is intended as a template for now. The past is a pedagogical template for Athens to imitate. Too considers the *Areopagiticus*, *Antidosis*, *Panathenaicus* and *Evagoras*, texts where Isocrates resorts to a prior time in order to present the lessons that Athens needs to learn. Through these texts, Isocratean rhetoric treats history as a fluid substance while claiming that it is fixed and immutable.

> Now I have come before you and spoken this discourse, believing that if we will only imitate our ancestors we shall both deliver ourselves from our present ills and become the saviours, not of Athens alone, but of all the Hellenes...
>
> Areopagiticus 84

So writes one of the most conservative thinkers in fourth century Athens, Isocrates. As far as this author is concerned, present day Athens is a state of chaos with orators running the state, litigants bringing the wealthy to trial for their money and warmongers leading the state into unnecessary conflicts with other states. The current democratic city is unpredictable and temperamental, with the interests of individuals taking precedence over those of the community as a whole. For him, hope for the future lies in the past, and M. Nouhaud has shown that Isocrates refers to the past more than any of other orators.[1] Furthermore, the past is somewhat malleable even though in the Isocratean fantasy, it is supposed to be fixed.

I thank Aggelos Kapellos for inviting me to join this project and for making me write a paper I otherwise would not have written!

---

1 See Nouhaud 1982, 8–9; cf. p. 360 on Isocrates as 'fantasiste'.

Yet the past is a construction. For K. Clarke,[2] it was a conceptual thing, far from fixed, as was evidenced by the fact that Athens had different systems of time-keeping simultaneously.[3] The past, even the distant past can be fast-forwarded, and as Clarke has observed some local historians of antiquity might blur the distinction between heroic and historical times when writing the history of a city.[4] The passage of time is compressed so that the distant past, even the mythical past, did not appear to be so remote, but was marked simply as a better bygone period.[5] G. Maltagliati similarly observes that Greek authors might draw temporally distant events together, engaging in a *praeteritio* so that there is an elision of temporal distance.[6] According to F. Pownall,[7] the past might be reinvented in accordance with the author's political agenda and Nouhaud sees Greek authors practising 'la deformation historique'.[8] Then, it is also the case that, as C. Carey observes,[9] orators, such as Demosthenes and Aeschines, and writers, such as Isocrates, might simply reinvent historical situations to suit their argument. And Pownall states that orators generally offered an idealized — and certainly, idealistic — version of the past in order to get their audience where they wanted them.[10] Events and people could be conveniently forgotten, misremembered and re-represented so that they appeared to be positive icons for the current period. This is how the orators manifest rhetorical καιρός, the sense of it being the right time to say something in their speeches.[11] Accordingly, the past, which might be remoulded to suit one's purposes, was far from fixed, and for Isocrates, looking backwards to distant ancestors, their institutions and their more moderate behaviours was a means of insulating oneself from, and a means of escaping, the political and social ills of the present. The past is, according to Isocrates, where Athenian society needs to find its salvation.

Let me further suggest that the past is so malleable because it is taken up and absorbed in the present: the past becomes the now and the future. This is because the Isocratean project is a pedagogical one. Nouhaud sees Isocrates

---

2 Clarke 2008, 2.
3 Clarke 2008, 8 and 14.
4 Clarke 2008, 197.
5 Hamilton 1979, 293, following Welles, sees no distinction between myth and history.
6 Maltagliati 2020, 78–81. See also Grethlein 2014, 326–336.
7 See Pownall 2013, 351.
8 See Verdin 1987, 329.
9 Carey 2017, 11.
10 Pownall 2013, 339.
11 Cf. Usher 2004, 52–61. Consequently, it is difficult, if not impossible, to regard oratory as a historical source; cf. Todd 1990, 173–174.

resorting to the past, and even to myth, because he is providing discourse as a model for current behaviour.¹² Athens is to imitate a prior and past model which generates the future so that the past is a state of affairs that influences and forms the present and future. The past is to be regarded as a worthy prototype for society and its politics. Isocrates presents the people from the past as being more honourable and inclined to watch out for the whole community rather than themselves. And thus the pastness of what went before is irrelevant and erased by the present.

Accordingly, in this paper I shall explore Isocrates' use of the past as a creative canvas for his idea(l) of a contemporary society, which is quite distinct from the present.¹³ I look at the *Areopagiticus* (post 355 B.C.), *On the Peace* (355 B.C.), *Antidosis* (c. 354–353 B.C.), *Panathenaicus* (c. 342 B.C.) and the *Evagoras* (cf. 370–365?) as a model for the present. But it is the case that even what has been the case and what has occurred in a previous time can become fluid as far as its representation in the present time is concerned, and the actual duration of history becomes inconsequential because the past is simply the past which is not now and which is intended as a template for now. A pedagogical context makes the past present again.

1 *Areopagiticus*

I begin this essay by examining the *Areopagiticus* as a lesson for a corrupted and troubled Athens. The *Areopagiticus* is a historical text only to the extent that it seeks to lead its audience into a certain viewpoint through historical example. As R. Wallace has observed, Isocrates' text indeed has an agenda to establish the prominence of the Areopagus as an institution for the fourth century, and this agenda is not actually representative of the institution's standing at this time.¹⁴ This text most emphatically proposes the past as a template for the present and future of Athens, but it will become apparent that this template is far from fixed, as the past should, or perhaps, might be — the past is brought into the latter times such that its pastness is overlooked and eventually disregarded because it is to be the future.¹⁵

---

12 Nouhaud 1982, 19 and 353.
13 See Natali 1982, 142–143.
14 Wallace 1989, x.
15 See Nouhaud 1982, 99.

The Areopagus in its foundation stood for a moral and upright Athens where privilege and status were based on birth and which Isocrates seeks to re-establish in, and restore to, the current day. The author creates this opposition between past and present, and between the static and unstable, in section 1 of his work where he enters into a hypothetical realm in speaking of the here and now. He asks the audience to imagine that Athens is in a condition which is quite different from that which she is actually in as a means of destabilising the present. The audience is asked to think of Athens *as if* (ὥσπερ) it had been in danger when in fact, she is not; she has more than two hundred ships of war, enjoys peace throughout her territory, has an empire on the sea and has many allies who will help her (1–2). She has every reason to feel secure and in fact, holds all of Hellas under her control (3).

Yet the security of the present is somewhat at risk because Athens, as is the wont of cities which are in the best circumstances, may assume the worst policies: the city's wealth and power lead to stupidity, which in turns leads to licence (4), while poverty and a humble station are accompanied by sobriety and moderation. Athens became the most powerful of the Hellenic states after it was laid waste by the barbarians, and after Spartan control of the Peloponnese (6–7). While enjoying a sense of security, it is actually the case that the city-state might be destabilised as it asserted its authority over the members of the Second Athenian League, namely Chios, Rhodes, Cos and Byzantium, perhaps as something of a second Athenian empire although initially standing to counter Persian influence and later opposing Spartan hegemony,[16] as the League's members rose up against Athens in the League War 357–355 B.C. I suggest that the hypothesis proposes that the present can be remade as the oration shows it can be: Isocrates aspires to raise up an Athens, which had lost a lot of her power and allies after the disastrous Social War, by the example of the formerly glorious institution of the Areopagus.

Destabilisation indeed happened before with Athens. When the city held all of Greece after the naval victory of Conon, which saw the destruction of the Spartan fleet, at the Battle of Cnidus[17] and after Timotheus' campaign, it then quickly lost its power in the Social War (357–355 B.C.), which Athens fought with Chios, Rhodes, Cos and Byzantium when they threw off Athenian democracy (12). And so, Isocrates suggests that it is an ancestral democracy, the one which was instituted by Solon and re-established by Cleisthenes, which would

---

[16] See Cargill 1981, who argues against tradition that the League was not a second Athenian empire; also Martin, 1984, 243–247.
[17] Cf. Xen. *Hell.* 4.3.11–12.; Diod. 14.83.5–7.

be of most benefit to the whole city (17). The past, which has already happened and is therefore supposedly unchangeable, is summoned back to fix the present and the future. Formerly democracy trained the citizens so that they did not regard democracy as insolence (ἀκολασία), lawlessness as freedom (ἐλευθερία), outspokenness as equality (ἰσονομία), and the freedom to do whatever they wish as happiness (εὐδαιμονία) (20).

Such was the obligation to fulfill one's public duty even to the point to putting their own private means into the service of the state that individuals did not rush to stand for public office (24–25). In former times democracy was such that the people remained the master and public servants were required to fulfill their tasks as servants of the state or else face the worst punishments (26–27). It was also the case that people treated one another in a better fashion. For instance, the rich did not despise the poor but helped them (32). Isocrates observes that in the ancestral democracy citizens were not supervised by preceptors in their youth only to be let free in adulthood. Rather they had the Council of the Areopagus, which kept the Athenian citizens hesitant to be themselves (37–38). From an idealistic perspective the Areopagus enforced moral discipline in the city-state, and furthermore, ensured that it was not so keenly populated with lawsuits, sycophantic law-suits, liturgy trials or poverty (caused by wars) as is the case in contemporary Athens where oratorical skill ensured one's prominence (51). As well according to this perspective, the Council provided the poor with work[18] and so with relief from their poverty, prevented corruption among those in office with the imposition of punishments and gave older men a sense of being active and useful in society by giving them public honours and allowing them to watch over the young (55).[19] Age, whether of individuals or of historical event, teaches.

For Isocrates to advocate the Areopagus council in this fashion and to call for its return to authority runs the risk of the author being thought an enemy of the people and being regarded as someone who seeks the transformation of the state into an oligarchy (57). Yet the author declares that he has recounted these details to demonstrate that he is not in favour of oligarchy or special privilege (70).

It appears from the *Areopagiticus* that the salvation of Athens' general present woes — the stereotypically endless litigation in the lawcourts, the continu-

---

[18] Isocrates may here mean pay for attendance in the lawcourt; see Humphreys 1970, 16–17. As Cecchet 2015, 230 observes, it is the fact that one works which defines the citizen as being poor.
[19] See Golden 2007, 277; also see Pl. *Laws* 657d and [Plut.] *Mor.*796a.

ous speechmaking in the Assembly often for personal gain, the lobbying for war abroad, and the poverty which these activities create[20] — can be found in a looking back to the past, where discipline and virtue supposedly held sway in the city-state such that it was in a state of order and peace. The past is held up as a model for imitation, in keeping with a pedagogical model where the young are to follow their elders and their ancestors. Indeed, he explicitly urges the city to imitate her ancestors to save both themselves and the Greeks as a whole (cf. ἢν μιμησώμεθα τοὺς προγόνους, 84). Elsewhere at *On the Peace* 41, a work which advocates quietism as far as foreign policy is concerned — A. Michelini suggests that the context is the peace proposal put forward in the Social War in the 350s —[21], the author goes so far as to observe that if someone were to visit Athens as a stranger he would find the Athenians mad because while they extol their ancestors, they do not actually follow their example.[22] Isocrates thus advises governance through this traditional system of education. De Bruyn observes that the Isocrates offers a vision of the Areopagus which is pre-Ephialtes, when the court was concerned with judicial matters.[23] As R.W. Wallace has observed,[24] it is the case that Isocrates' *Areopagus*, which is representative of a conservative ideology,[25] abolished the process of selection by lot, idealizing a return to a more exclusive role for the institution.[26] So the distant and recent past are brought together but in a manner that disregards historical accuracy; Isocrates remakes the past as he intends the future to be.

Writing can transform history and does in the case of the *Areopagiticus*. Yet it is necessary to realize that the stability of the past is only a proposition because the reality was that the Areopagus did not have an unchanging and immutable influence at Athens; rather it had an evolving role in accordance with the state of the Athenian democracy.[27] Yet with it, Isocrates seeks to create the impression of a strong and static institution in the past which stands in marked opposition to a present that is highly changeable.

---

[20] See Christ 1998; also see Carter 1986 for a study of the quietist, who resisted this culture.
[21] Michelini, 1998, 116.
[22] See Clarke 2008, 281; also Hamilton 1997, 297 and Michelini 1998, 116.
[23] O de Bruyn 1995, 109, 156.
[24] Wallace 1989, 150.
[25] Wallace 1989, 151.
[26] Hall 1990, 321–322.
[27] See Rhodes 1972 for a detailed and comprehensive study of the Council.

2 On the Peace

On the Peace is another work which, like the *Areopagiticus*, advocates the importance of learning from the ancestors but whereas the latter speech is grounded firmly in an ancient institution, the former speech deals with a contemporary situation. The speech appears to be written to seek an end to the Social War, which Athens fought with her former allies, Chios, Cos, Rhodes and Byzantium, advocating peace not just with these city-states but the whole world (cf. 16). Isocrates wishes that the Greeks states remain independent and that each state retains its own territory. And he advocates a quietistic stance in making his point: the present-day orators and demagogues are to be disregarded for inciting an imperialism that is not in the interests of the state, and the current arena of public speech is furthermore to be denigrated (1–11; cf. 36).

The current citizens of Athens no longer keep their ancestral laws but follow their passions so that they are plunged into confusion (103). Accordingly, the past is to instruct Athens, and Athens' education requires that the current orators and demagogues are replaced by examples from the past even though these individuals pay lip service to imitating precisely the ancestors (cf. λέγειν τολμῶσιν ὡς χρὴ τοὺς προγόνους μιμεῖσθαι, 36). He recalls that *previously* orators exhorted the people to cling to peace, something that has now been forgotten (12). The Athenians no longer act like their ancestors even if they take pride in their actions, producing such a contradiction between actual behavior and perceived behaviour that a stranger to the city-state would find matters depraved and crazy (41). Athens' ancestors were the happiest (cf. οἱ πρόγονοι ζῶντες εὐδαιμονέστατοι τῶν Ἑλλήνων, 64). Indeed, individuals such as Aristides, Themistocles and Miltiades were better men than the present-day demagogues Hyperbolus and Cleophon (75). These ancestors were responsible for making Athens great (122) and the example of Pericles shows that they were not interested in self-enrichment (126).

The past is thus presented as an escape from present evils, or, as Isocrates declares it near the end of this work: Τίς οὖν ἀπαλλαγὴ γένοιτ' ἂν τῶν κακῶν τῶν παρόντων (132).

3 Antidosis

The *Areopagiticus* demonstrates that the past as constructed in his writing is where Isocrates attempts to, and to some degree does, rewrite the present and the future that follows from the present. The *Antidosis* is a work that focuses on Isocrates as a teacher of the young, and indeed, highlights the pedagogical aspect of the author's work. Isocrates recalls past and more recent figures in order to eulogize them; however, encomium must be somewhat suspect in the writings of rhetoricians – after all, there are always two views of every subject – and it is perhaps the treatment of the general Timotheus (400 B.C.–354 B.C.) as completely laudatory in the *Antidosis* at sections 101–126 which demonstrates the rhetorician's ability to alter historical fact.[28] Just as Isocrates is physically impaired but still an excellent rhetorician, so too Timotheus lacks a strong bodily nature but has accomplished much in warfare (115–116). He had taken more cities than any other general, for instance, taking back the Chersonese[29] and liberating Cyzicus,[30] Samos,[31] Sesstus and Crithoe[32] (107) at no great expense to Athens (108–109, 111) and is presented as a good general (cf. τὸν στρατηγὸν τὸν ἀγαθόν, 117). (He was elected general in 366 or 365 B.C. (cf. Demosthenes 23.149) perhaps to succeed Iphicrates.[33] He knows against whom and with whom to wage war (118); he is able to gather a fit army (119) and he is able to withstand the hardships of military campaign (120). Timotheus appears in the portraiture provided by the *Antidosis* to be an ideal and most useful citizen above any reproach. He after all attempted to make Athens pre-eminent in the Second Athenian League and so, to reignite the city's imperialistic goals.

Yet, even though he helped Greece to attain ascendancy in the Hellenic World before the Social War, Timotheus is historically not a figure beyond reproach.[34] In any case, *On the Peace* offers an argument against Athens' imperialistic aspirations.[35] In 373 B.C. he delayed his fleet in its relief of Corcyra and was put on trial. He was acquitted after the intervention of Jason of Pherae and

---

[28] See Heskel 1997, 27, 'Since the orator wanted to glorify the deeds of Timotheus in this speech...'.
[29] Cf. Heskel 1997, 101.
[30] Cf. Heskel 1997, 116.
[31] Cf. Heskel 1997, 135 and 137.
[32] Cf. Heskel 1997, 147.
[33] Cf. Heskel 1997, 100.
[34] See Harding 1974, 139–140, notes Isocrates' embarrassment over Timotheus' behaviour.
[35] See e.g. Harding 1974, 145.

Alcetas, king of the Molossians. He then left Athens to undertake service with the king of Persia, who was an enemy of Athens. Then, Apollodorus, son of the banker Pasion, brought a case against Timotheus for the return of money loaned to him by his father (see Demosthenes oration 49). It seems that he had exhausted his own funds. Later in life the general Chares complained about Timotheus and Iphicrates so that they were put on trial and the former heavily fined the sum of one hundred talents due to his perceived arrogance. He had no means to pay the fine and withdrew to Calchis where he died. Athens later regretted Timotheus' punishment and reduced the fine by ninety per cent (see e.g. Nepos *Life of Timotheus* 4).[36]

And it is also in his praise of the city-state's ancestors that Isocrates is able to rewrite history somewhat. At *Antidosis* 313 the author states that in a previous era 'sophists' were admired, and they envied those who spent time with them as their students, blaming the sycophants instead for their troubles (313). The term 'sophist' has here been radically redefined in terms of its value; Isocrates has had to enact an archeology for the word to recall its original sense. He observes that the Athenians had made Solon the head of the state, an individual who had been given the title 'sophist', while punishing sycophants, individuals who brought lawcourt cases and suits for private gain, most severely (314). The noun 'sophist' is now clearly distinguished from the sycophants, who populate the *dikasteria* in contemporary Athens, although R. Osborne prefers to see 'sycophant' as a metaphor rather than an actual class of individual.[37] I suggest that the focus is not so much on Solon as on the rewriting of the more recent past with its corruption of language and of the present, where this corrupt language persists, through this reference to the past.

In the *Antidosis* Isocrates has erased the intervening period between the past and the present so that only the past exists as the new now. The period which follows the time of the ancestors is one where wrongdoers are currently appointed as the prosecutors and lawmakers for the people (315). As the city grew in power and influence, and gained the Hellenic empire, these men began to look with disfavour on the good men who had been responsible for the good situation of Athens, preferring instead those who had a lowly birth and were insolent (316–317). As a member of the privileged wealthy class, Isocrates seeks to maintain the privilege of those like himself against those who may have been

---

36 Cf. Siron and Nudell in this volume.
37 See Osborne 1990, 83–102. With Harvey, I accept the more traditional view of sycophant as an individual who made a living off court cases; see Harvey 1990, 103–122; also see Todd 1993, 93–94.

seeking to improve their situations. Security and success produced the change (μεταβολή), which for a conservative like Isocrates, who prefers a static condition in politics, is tantamount to disaster and revolution, for which the Greek word is a synonym. Indeed, according to the author, change has brought disasters and misfortunes upon the city-state as the best men were displaced by oligarchical and Spartan sympathies, war has come upon Athens with many dying and being reduced to extreme poverty (318–319). Placed in the mouth of the Spartan king Archidamus, the *Archidamus* may argue for war as is the wont of Sparta, but *On the Peace*, presented in a voice that is the author's or else one very close to his, advocates the abandonment of the city-state's pleonastic aspirations. Yet, furthermore, it is not a matter of determining whether Isocrates is accurate or not in his portrayal of matters at Athens. Rather he is engaging in a stereotypical portrait of his city-state: the past hated oligarchy and the present embraces it, and so the past is to be preferred over the here and now.

For Isocrates the past is superior and the old democracy surpasses the current one so that his writing always involved retrospection to the distant past as Athens' ideal template.[38] His writing and rhetoric have the power to restructure reality, and after all, we know from this text that the rhetorician can manufacture up a court case concerning an exchange with a fictional prosecutor, Lysimachus ('He who loses the battle').[39]

4 *Panathenaicus*

The *Panathenaicus* is a work in which Isocrates again and in a more extensive fashion lauds the past as responsible for the greatness of Athens. Athens has proven herself more adept than Sparta at keeping the barbarians in check beyond the Halys river and from sailing on their side of the Phaselis (59). If this is a reference to the Peace of Antalcidas (386 B.C.), an event that occurred some forty years before the writing of the *Panathenaicus*, it constitutes a remarkable rewriting of history, for the Peace left Sparta in a dominant position in Greece with the backing of Persia. Yet Isocrates insists that Athens deserves to be praised and honoured much more than Sparta, according to Isocrates (61).

But it is the case that currently Athens has shown herself contemptuous and slighting (cf. ὀλιγωρίας) so that one might praise the Spartans for their

---

38 Clarke 2008, 278.
39 Bearzot 2015, 167.

achievements and behavior (111). Being a sea-power has enabled Athens to fight off the Spartans and the Peloponnesians but it meant that the city had to forgo order (cf. εὐταξίας), moderation (cf. σωφροσύνης) and obedience (cf. πειθαρχίας) in order to be able to build and row ships, activities which require other qualities (116). Athens undertook this course of action in order to avoid being ruled by the Spartans (118). Power mars the city's formerly virtuous and just behavior.

Isocrates then goes on to say that while there are three types of polity — oligarchy, democracy and monarchy — it is the case that leaders who are most able and just govern well both at home and abroad, whereas when leaders are instead violent and greedy their government takes after them (132–133). The author offers a revisionary view of government here. It is the individuals who run government rather than the form of government which determines the nature of the polity. The fact that the ancestors of Athens have been men of character and courage has ensured that the city-state has enjoyed a fine government. They have been the best men, the wisest and those who have lived the best lives, and they were leaders of state, generals and ambassadors (143).

Traditional pedagogy is what Isocrates imagines to be the ideal governance of the state to be, so that the present and future are always bound to the past and the model it provides. And for this reason, the depiction of the author as the ideal teacher of Athens and the Greek world has more resonance than might initially appear to be the case: understanding that teaching concerns the following of ancestral models entails governing to the best ends.

5 *Evagoras*

The *Evagoras*, composed between 370–365 B.C.,[40] is a different genre of writing as an apparent encomium. It is an epideictic work that deals with a historical personage, the Cyprian king and father of Nicocles, who died in 374 B.C., and whom Isocrates could have actually known. It deals with a more recent past in a way which shows that history can be transformed for the purposes of changing the present.

As a eulogy, the *Evagoras* sets out an apparently reliable account of its subject. The Cyprian enjoyed beauty, strength and modesty, ensuring that his childhood was blessed (22) and upon adulthood also acquired courage, wisdom

---

40 Blass 1892, 285 and Jebb 1876, 104.

and justice (23). Due to a conspiracy, Evagoras had to flee to Soli in Cilicia (27) but planned his return to Cyprus with a band of not more than fifty men (29). This he achieved and his rule revealed him to be for the interests of the people, deft in the administration of the government and an able general (46). The Cypriot king had such a good government that he caused other Greeks to leave their own homelands to settle in Cyprus (51). Evagoras, however, was also a feared military leader with even the Persian king Cyrus in a state of terror where the Cypriot leader was concerned (59). And Evagoras turns out to be victorious against the Persian king, concluding a peace in 376 B.C. (64).[41]

Isocrates summarizes all of Evagoras' great achievements at sections 66–71 of the speech, from his return from exile to the Hellenizing of barbarians, to the civilizing of otherwise savage lands, to his military exploits which enabled him both to defend Cyprus against Persia and to side effectively with Persia, and to undertake the general administration of affairs (67–69). The author celebrates the Cypriot king overall in the concluding sections of the work, claiming that the verbal image of his subject's character and deeds are to be preferred to statues (74). He has accordingly become the subject of philosophical study for his son Nicocles (80–82). The image of Evagoras is an external one, and it may be the case that, as T. Hägg and S. Halliwell observe,[42] that Isocrates probably did not know his subject personally, since there is little attempt to present the subject inwardly and nothing was presented from Evagoras' own viewpoint.

Yet the contrast between the verbal image that rhetoric provides and statues in section 74 is noteworthy.[43] If a statue is a fixed and static plastic image, the verbal image, in contrast, has no place of fixed abode. It goes wherever it is spoken or read by whomsoever it is spoken or read. It is highly mobile, shifting and fluid.[44] The suggestion is that the portrait of Evagoras, which the oration presents, is open to some movement, some reinterpretation and change. And in fact, G. Heilbrunn reveals that the eulogy of the Cypriot leader is actually a celebration of tyranny, once something to be disapproved of and which now has become something strongly desirable, like Helen.[45] C. Atack notes that Evagoras is described as establishing himself as a τύραννος, or tyrant, of the city. She suggests that this is not because he was a tyrant but because he had seized the

---

[41] See Alexiou 2015, 47–61 for some of the historical and ethical issues raised by the speech.
[42] Hägg and Halliwell 2012, 40.
[43] See Noel 2009, 91–107.
[44] See Steiner 2001 for a discussion of these issues.
[45] Heilbrunn 1975, 171.

rule of Salamis from another tyrant (cf. 31).⁴⁶ Yet, the word 'tyrant' is a notably bad word in antiquity and an author would not name an individual such unless he exhibited the traits of a tyrant. Indeed, to mention that Evagoras had captured the palace, which is called a βασίλειον at 32 (cf. βασιλείαν, 25), highlights the contrast between tyrant and king, βασιλεύς. Earlier at section 25 Isocrates observes that deeds requiring impiety needed to acquire Evagoras' rule were accomplished by others while he seemed to behave with piety and justice (25–26), which Atack regards as a sign of the leader's good character.⁴⁷ The larger point is that the ruler had others do the dirty deeds so that he could appear to be blameless. After all, one notes that the speech omits to mention that Evagoras probably died by assassination (cf. Aristotle *Politics* 1311b),⁴⁸ and indeed tyranny was anathema to a fourth-century Athenian. Rhetoric has the capacity to depict a more changeable and changing history even while claiming history is fixed and stable.

The contrast between verbal and plastic image is also relevant because the *Evagoras* demonstrates that the past may be an area of contestation even though in the writing of Isocrates history is otherwise presented as a privileged era for being so distinct from the contentious and chaotic present. Different authors, whether they are prose writers, orators, or poets, offer vying views of individuals and events from history so that the fixity of what has gone before is in some doubt once it is open to re-representation. The figures Helen and Busiris (which I have not discussed in this paper because they are 'myth') may be open to censure and reproach according to some accounts, but Isocrates has shown that they are also to be the subjects of praise in his encomia of them as he offers an alternative historical perspective on these individuals. The rhetorician maintains the view that the past is a period from which the present may learn some valuable lessons about behaviour and statesmanship.

6 Conclusion

The past, no matter its distance from the present, appears to be a canvas on which Isocrates can paint the present and the future as he wishes them to be. The past, whether it is more recent or distant, seems to be populated with hon-

---

46 See Atack 2020.
47 Cf. Atack 2020; also see Alexiou 2015, 47–48, who wrongly assumes an overly idealizing view of Evagoras in Isocrates' work.
48 Hägg and Halliwell 2012, 39.

ourable and brave characters, e.g. Timotheus, Chabrias and Iphicrates, who may have modelled themselves on figures from an even earlier time. In the pedagogical context which Isocrates' writing assumes for itself, it is assumed that they are the 'teachers' of the recent politicians and generals who have acquitted themselves well. Their reputations cannot be altered, as it seems, because their deeds speak for themselves. It would appear that the past is claimed as a fixed and unmoving point, although Isocrates shows that it too can be a sphere of mutability as it is in the *Evagoras*, where he shows himself able to change what people think about the subjects of his work. But even the apparent fixity of the past is ultimately in question as the author demonstrates that the past can be telescoped or compressed so that it is more or less distant and so that the past virtually becomes the present and the hoped-for future. Time is indeed relative in Isocrates.

Statements about the past depend on present criteria and so, statements about it may change because they may be dependent on memory, on meaning, and on images, which may all be faulty or deficient.[49] And so, I maintain, it is the case with Isocrates. The past reality of the city-state of Athens may not seem to change but the present is transformed because the form of rhetorical discourse intervenes in knowledge of it. What is key to the mutability of the past is a changing historical perspective: one now views what has happened differently. Significant is the rhetorical intervention that the author makes in history. By refuting and rejecting the claims of other authors, which is claimed to be false or misleading, the rhetorician establishes a new prior 'reality'. In this way, rhetoric, a fluid discourse, demonstrates its power to alter the perception of events and people.

It is also the case with the *Areopagiticus*, the *Antidosis* and the *Panathenaicus* that Isocrates presents his reader with a past that offers a model for a present and future Athens. The past, which is supposedly fixed but actually transformed through rhetoric, becomes an ideal to replace a dysfunctional city-state as a location of moderation, modesty and courage. Rhetoric treats history as a fluid substance while claiming that it is fixed and immoveable.

---

[49] See Butler 1956, 305 and Blank in this volume.

Bibliography

Alexiou, A. (2015), "The Rhetoric of Isocrates' *Evagoras*: History, Ethics and Politics", in: C. Bouchet/P. Giavannelli-Jouanna (eds.), *Isocrate: Entre jeu rhétorique et en jeux politiques, Collection Études et Recherches de l'Occident Romain*, 47–61.
Atack, C. (2020), *The Discourse of Kingship in Classical Greece*, London.
Bearzot, C. (2015), "Isocrates et les dikastes athéniens", in: C. Bouchet/P. Giovannelli-Jouanna (eds.), *Isocrate. Entre jeu rhétorique et en jeux politiques*, Lyon, 163–174.
Blank, T. (2013), "Isocrates on Paradoxical Discourse: An Analysis of *Helen* and *Busiris*", *Rhetorica* 31, 1–33.
de Bruyn, O. (1995), *La Compétence de l'Aréopage en matière de process public: de origines de la polis athénienne à la conquête romaine de la Grèce (vers 700–146 avant J. C.)*, Historia supplement 90. Stuttgart.
Buck, R.J. (1965), "The Reforms of 487 B.C. in the Selection of Archons", *CP* 60, 96–101.
Butler, R.J. (1956), "A Wittgenteinian on 'The Reality of the Past'", *The Philosophical Quarterly* 6.25, 304–314.
Carey, C. (2017), *Democracy in Classical Athens*, London.
Cargill, J. (1981), *The Second Athenian League: Empire or Free Alliance?*, Berkeley.
Carter, L.B. (1986), *The Quiet Athenian*, Oxford.
Cartledge, P./Millet, P./Todd, S. (1990), *Nomos. Essays in Athenian Law, Politics and Society*, Cambridge.
Cecchet, L. (2015), *Poverty in Athenian Public Discourse from the Eve of the Peloponnesian War to the Rise of Macedonia*, Historia suppl. 239, Stuttgart.
Christ, M. (1998), *The Litigious Athenian*, Baltimore.
Clarke, K. (2008), *Making Time for the Past: Local History and the Polis*, Oxford.
Fornara, C./Samons, L.J. (1991), *Athens from Cleisthenes to Pericles*, Berkeley.
Gallego, J. (2017), "La Révolution Athénienne: Penser l'Événement Démocratique", *DHA* 43, 33–65.
Golden, M. (2007), "Gendering the Age Gap: Boys, Girls and Abduction in Ancient Greek Art", in: A. Cohen/J.B. Rutter (eds.), *Constructions of Childhood in Ancient Greece and Italy*, Hesperia supp. 41, 256–280.
Grethlein, J. (2014), "The Value of the Past Challenged: Myth and History in Attic Orators", in: C. Pieper *et al.* (eds.), *Valuing the Past in the Greco-Roman World*, Leiden, 326–336.
Hägg, T./Halliwell, S. (2012), *The Art of Biography in Antiquity*, Cambridge.
Hall, L. (1990), "Ephialtes, the Areopagus and the Thirty", *CQ* 40, 319–328.
Hamilton, C.D. (1979), "Greek Rhetoric and History: The Case of Isocrates", in: G.W. Bowersock/W. Burkert/M.C.J. Putnam (eds.), *Arktouros. Hellenic Studies Presented to Bernard M. W. Knox on the occasion of his 65th birthday*, Berlin/New York.
Hansen, M.H. (1986), "ΚΛΗΡΩΣΙΣ ΚΠΡΟΚΡΙΤΩΝ in Fourth-Century Athens", *CP* 81, 222–229.
Harding, P. (1974), "The Purpose of Isocrates' *Archidamos* and *On the Peace*", *CA* 6, 137–149.
Harvey, D. (1990), "The sycophant and sycophancy: Vexatious redefinition?", in: P. Cartledge/P. Millett/S. Todd (eds.), *NOMOS: Essays in Athenian Law, Politics and Society*, Cambridge, 103–122.
Heilbrunn, G. (1975), "Isocrates on Rhetoric and Power", *Hermes* 103, 154–178.
Heskel, J. (1997), *The North Aegean Wars, 371–60 B.C.*, Stuttgart.

Humphreys, S. (1970), "Economy and Society in Classical Athens", *Annali della Scuola Normale Superiore di Pisa. Lettere, Storia e Filosofia*, Serie II, Vol. 39, No. 1/2 1–26.
Jebb, R. (1876), *Attic Orators*, ii, London.
Maltagliati, G. (2020), "Persuasion through Proximity (and Distance) in the Attic Orators' Historical Examples", *GRBS* 60, 68–97.
Blass, F. (1892), *Die attische Beredsamkeit*, ii, Leipzig.
Michelini, A. (1998), "Isocrates' Civic Invective. Acharnians and On the Peace", *TAPA* 128, 115–133.
Natali, C. (1982), "Paradeigma: The Problems of Human Acting and the Use of Examples in Some Authors of the 4th Century B.C.", *RSJ* 19, 141–152.
Noel, M.P. (2009), "Painting or Writing Speeches? Plato, Alcidamas and Isocrates on Logography", in: L. Pernot (ed.), *New Chapters in the History of Rhetoric*, Leiden, 91–107.
Nouhaud, M. (1982), *L'utilisation de l'histoire par les orateurs attiques*, Paris.
Osborne, R. (1990), "Vexatious litigation in classical Athens: Sycophancy and the sycophant", in: Cartledge/Millett/Todd, 83–102.
Pownall, F. (2013), "A Case Study in Isocrates: the expulsion of the Peisistratids", *DHA* supplément 8, 339–354.
Rhodes, P.J. (1972), *The Athenian Boule*, Oxford.
Rhodes, P.J. (1993), *A Commentary on the Aristotelian* Athenaion Politeia, Oxford.
Steiner, D. (2001), *Images in Mind*, Princeton.
Todd, S. (1990), "The Use and Abuse of Attic Orators", *G& R* 37, 159–178.
Todd, S. (1993), *The Shape of Athenian Law*, Oxford.
Usher, S. (2004), "Kairos in Fourth-Century Greek Oratory", in: M. Edwards/C. Reid (eds.), *Oratory in Action*, Manchester, 52–61.
Verdin, H. (1987), Review of M. Nouhaud, *L'utilisation de l'histoire par les orateurs attiques* (Paris 1982), *AC* 56, 328–329.
Wallace, R.W. (1989), *The Areopagus Council, to 307 BC*, Baltimore.

Stefano Ferrucci
The Recent Past in Isaeus' Forensic Speeches

Abstract: References to past events are limited in number and concise in Isaeus' speeches. The recent past is recalled to back up narratives on the causes' protagonists: family and individual memories that, at times, intertwine with the wider history of the *polis*. Such references may have an argumentative function, to display the reasons or explain the origin of a specific circumstance useful to the case, or an encomisastic/denigratory one, while constructing a character in the speech. In both cases events of the recent past come as pure facts, without any paradigmatic intent or judgment. The purpose in using the past is to illuminate the *ethos* of the characters, as good or bad citizens, by displaying individual attitude towards military or fiscal obligations. Identifying past facts was not Isaeus' concern; he used them as a given element within the narrative. Finally, the author analyzes Isaeus V as a relevant case-study.

1 What kind of past do we find in Isaeus?

This paper aims at gathering some general information on the (quite rare) references to the recent past in Isaeus' works, and at analyzing in more detail Isaeus' fifth speech. According to Aristotle, forensic rhetoric was concerned about the past, περὶ τῶν γεγενημένων.[1] But what kind of past do we find in Isaeus' speeches? Inheritance cases deal with the 'private' past of a family, and the great events of a collective and shared memory has a very marginal role in Isaeus' argumentation.[2] He often focuses on genealogical demonstration, connected with a matter of fact, in order to offer a reconstruction of the events and the juridical titles, supported by suitable *pisteis*:[3] Family affairs' narrative was

---

I would like to express my deep gratitude to Agelos Kapellos and Mirko Canevaro for their precious remarks on the paper; I thank also Dr. Giacinto Falco for allowing me to cite his dissertation. I am the only responsible for all the contents of this paper.

1 Aristotle (*Rhet.* 1.3.1, 1358b4).
2 On the *corpus* of Isaeus' speeches cf. Ferrucci 1998, 57–63, Edwards 2007, 1–12, 199–201.
3 Matters of fact are largely prevalent on matters of law in attic forensic speeches cf. Harris 2013, 381–389; Canevaro 2019, 73–79, Falco 2020, 34 n. 197. On Isaeus' reconstruction of family past see Ferruci 2006.

addressed to the jurors' individual experiences, alluding, often explicitly, to their own family situations and recalling shared values and behaviors (considered or presented as such). Suggesting identification of the audience with the speaker was a relevant mean of persuasion.[4] References to historical facts and to the recent past in Isaeus therefore present an intent that goes beyond the event itself, and were used instrumentally for strategic and persuasive reasons. The motivation for their use, as we shall see, is always rhetorical, narrative or argumentative. This does not mean that such references are not historically reliable; however, accuracy or search for historical, political, military or ethical significance in the mentioned events is not among the orator's goals.

Reconstructing genealogies and introducing family events rarely involved recalling relevant facts from the recent Athenian past, except for brief references intertwined with the biographies of the people mentioned in the case, when their family and personal memories were part of a collective memory.[5]

I may suggest distinguishing three kind of references to the past in Isaeus' speeches:

1. as *enkomion* (praise), when Isaeus wishes to highlight civic values of a character, in particular if he died while serving the *polis* during a war or diplomatic activities. Such biographical notes imply a commendation and contribute to outline the *ethos* of people within the speech,[6] often the person whose death occasions the inheritance case: Dikaiogenes II,[7] Hagnias,[8] and Philoktemon[9] died for the homeland, Hagnias as ambassador, the other two as trierarchs. Reference to the past may also have a negative value (*psogos*): Dikaiogenes III, the opponent of Isaeus' client in the fifth speech, evaded all his obligations as taxpayer "except for the capture of Lechaion", nor does he actively take part in a war still in progress.[10]

2. as *pistis* (argument), when references provide support to a specific argument: the speaker's friendship with Chairestratus in the sixth speech is exem-

---

4 A clear example in [Dem.] 59.107–114; cf. now Serafim 2021.
5 On collective and social memory see Giangiulio 2010; shared memories in oratory: Steinbock 2013; Canevaro 2014; in Andocides: Pownall in this volume. Isaeus is rarely used as source while discussing the construction of public memories; on family memory see the seminal study of Thomas 1989, 95–153, who also includes but scanty references to Isaeus' speeches.
6 On *ethopoiia* (the construction of characters for persuasive purposes) as rhetorical tool cf. Carey 1994a; 1994b, 95–99; De Temmerman 2010, 34–37; Bruss 2013.
7 Isae. 5.6, 42 (*naumachia* at Cnidus).
8 Isae. 11.8.
9 Isae. 6.27, *naumachia* near Chios, short before the lawsuit was discussed.
10 Isae. 5.37, 46, cf. *infra*, § 4.

plified by joint participation in a mission to Sicily during the latter's trierarchy;[11] Astyphilus' military expeditions are listed to argue how implausible it would be if he had made a will after the last expedition while he never felt the need to make one before;[12] the will drawn up by Apollodorus before going to fight in Corinth would be a sign of his close relationship with Isaeus' client;[13] the role of *akolouthos* in the retinue of Harmodius for Chairestratus during the Corinthian war would demonstrate the contempt in which Dikaiogenes III held his relatives / opponents.[14]

3. as *diegesis* (narrative): some military or historical events prop the narrative, motivating its development towards a certain direction or explaining a specific stage. Participation in an expedition to Thrace following Iphicrates illustrates the timing of the speaker's adoption by Menecles, once he has returned, and also justifies the presence in his patrimony of assets unrelated to the *kleros* of the *oikos*;[15] the departure from Mounichia of an expedition set up by Timotheus describes the chaotic way in which Euctemon prepared the will for the presumed children;[16] the engagement in a *naumachia* as a trierarch and the false news of his death are recalled by the *synegoros* of Eumathes to illustrate the honesty and reliability of the banker and to explain why the speaker is acting in his defense.[17]

The three categories are to be understood merely as a general indication, illustrating how past events occur in Isaeus' speeches.

2 References to recent past in Isaeus: An overview

It is not surprising that all the episodes of Athens' recent past are briefly recalled by Isaeus without contextualization or description. The orator never enters the heart of the event, does not provide any information on its development: episodes are referred to simply as a matter of fact. As we shall see, some references represent a historiographical problem for us, due to the difficulty in

---

[11] Isae. 6.1.
[12] Isae. 9.14–15. On the argument's weakness cf. Wyse 1904, 635; Rubinstein 1993, 23; Griffith-Williams 2013, 170–171.
[13] Isae. 7.9.
[14] Isae. 5.11.
[15] Isae. 2.6.
[16] Isae. 6.27.
[17] Isae. fr. XVI, 66 B-S.

recognizing the episodes Isaeus mentions, which are not necessarily among those recorded by the available historical sources. An additional difficulty arises from the uncertainty in the dating of Isaeus' speeches, often dependent precisely on the historical events' identification.

Overall, Isaeus refers to 25 historical facts, 20 from recent past, as defined in this volume.[18] Almost all recent past events concern war: 12 military expeditions (*stateiai*), four individual battles (of which three are *naumachiai*), and two diplomatic missions related to war; only in one case is a peace mentioned (the peace of Antalcidas). One occurrence refers to a *stasis* that took place in the city, alluding to the years 404/4–401/400.[19]

In two cases, Isaeus mentions a military event as a whole: the *korinthikos polemos* and the *thebaikos polemos*. The definition of "Corinthian war" appears in Isaeus' tenth oration, generally dated between 378 and 371, and seems to refer to the years 395/4–386.[20] The designation Θηβαικὸς πόλεμος is generally intended to indicate the conflict between Sparta and Thebes of the years 378–371, but Rosivach has recently suggested that, from an Athenian perspective, a "Theban war" could only refer to the years 378–376, before the alliance with the Boeotian city, or 371–366, when Thebes returned to be an enemy; the scholar assumes that Isaeus is referring to these last years.[21] Corinthian and Theban war are two events of the recent past frequently recurring in Isaeus' speeches;[22] other references mention the Peloponnesian war;[23] war or diplomatic relations with

---

18 References to the recent past in Isaeus are gathered in the *Appendix*.
19 Military expeditions: Isae. 2.6; 4.7 (with Valkaener's emendation); 5.11 and 46; 6.27; 7.9; 9.4 (four *stateiai* mentioned); 10.20 and 22. Battles: 5.6 and 42 (battle of Cnidus); 5.37 (battle of the Lechaion); 6.27 (*naumachia* in Chius); fr. XVI 66 B–S (*naumachia*). Diplomatic missions: 6.1 (most likely a diplomatic mission than a military expedition); 11.8. Peace of Antalcidas: 10.20. *Stasis*: 5.7. The same prevalence of military events is to be found in the few references to the older past (5.42; 6.13–14).
20 Isae. 10.20: the mention in the same passage of a peace, the peace of Antalcidas, suggests that Isaeus considers the lower chronological limit of the *Korinthiakos polemos* the year 387/6. For the dating of the speech cf. Ferrucci 1998, 55 and n. 6; Cobetto Ghiggia 2012, 390; Griffith-Williams 2013, 196. Wevers 1969, 23–25, propose an alternative dating around 355, suggesting that the *polemos* mentioned at 10.22, in which Aristarchus died, should be identified not with the Theban war but with the social war, cf. Avramović 1997, 35. The definition of Κορινθιακὸς πόλεμος occurs also in Isocr. 14.27, composed around 373 and chronologically close to Isae. 10 (cf. Momigliano 1966, 447–450), and in Diod. 14.86.6, probably dependent on Ephorus. Isaeus uses more often the expression στρατεύεσθαι εἰς Κόρινθον (Isae. 5.11; 7.9; 9.14).
21 Isae. 9.14, cf. Rosivach 2005, 197.
22 Corinthian war: Isae. 5.11, 37, 46 (doubtful); 7.9; 9.14; 10.20; Theban war: 9.14, 10.22.
23 Isae. 5.6, 7.

Sicily,[24] military operations led by Iphicrates and Timotheus between the 70s and 60s of the 4th century,[25] the social war.[26]

Isaeus never enlightens chronology for recent historical events. An eponymous archon is named only twice and always for events from a more distant past: the Sicilian expedition of 415 (Arimnestus) and the confirmation of the law on citizenship in 403/2 (Eucleides).[27]

The speaker is not concerned that the audience could immediately identify the past events he mentions: battles, expeditions and embassies are alluded to almost *en passant*. This could mean that Isaeus took for granted the notoriety of the episodes, or that he had no particular interest in providing the audience with details about the event or with clues for identification. The alternative will have to be verified on a case-by-case basis, but the second explanation seems overall the most plausible.

3 Citizen stories and city history

War imposes itself among citizens' activities in Isaeus' speeches: citizens are portrayed mainly as soldiers. In at least 5 cases Isaeus reports military actions carried out as trierarchs; in one case as *lochagos*, most likely referring to a mercenary soldier.[28] Elective military charges (*stategos* and *phylarchos*) appear only for Dicaiogenes' II and Theophon's ancestors, not directly connected to the ongoing process and deceased from many years.[29] Statistics are meager, but the

---

24 Isae. 6.1.
25 Iphicrates: Isae. 2.6; 4.7 (conjectural); Timotheus: 6.27; 9.14.
26 Isae. 7.27; fr. XVI 66 B–S. As a whole, the events run from the last years of the 5th century to the middle of the 4th: Dionysius of Halicarnassus deduced though them a chronology for Isaeus' life "between the Peloponnesian war and the reign of Philipp II", Dion. Hal. *Isaeus*, 1, cf. Ferrucci 1998, 35–36, 57–64.
27 Isae. 6.13–14; the Sicilian expedition is recalled in order to refute the reconstruction of kinship relationships presented by the counterpart introducing a chronological argument: distant past helps unveiling distortions in the rhetorical presentation. The 403/2 law on citizenship occurs in two speeches, both pronounced almost 40 years after the law was promulgated: Isae. 6.47, 8.43; on the latter passage see Ferrucci 2005, 208–209.
28 Trierarchs: Isae. 5.6, 42 (Dicaiogenes I); 6.1 (Chairestratus), 27 (Philoctemon), 60 (Phanostratus, who is said to have served as trierarch seven times before 398); fr. XVI 66 B–S. *Locagos*: Isae. 9.14 (Astyphilus).
29 Isae. 5.42: Dicaiogenes I died as *strategos* in a battle in Eleusis (perhaps in 459/8, the identification of the battle is controversial, cf. Cobetto 2012, 214 n. 73); his son Menexenus died at

lack of references to institutional military positions seems quite remarkable within Isaeus' speeches, especially if compared to the greater frequency of trierarchies, or other liturgical services (*choregies, gymnasiarchies*).³⁰ Athenian citizen's good reputation and honour (*time*) would seem to pass mainly through the fulfilment of liturgies and in court the speaker chooses to enhance what felt more suitable to represent the citizen's bond with the *polis*, through the services rendered, better illustrated by liturgies than by institutional offices, which could arouse more controversial reactions.³¹ This may help explaining why military activity in Isaeus prevails in reconstructing the history and *ethos* of characters, while the political side, even if present, is essentially ignored.

An interesting case is represented by Hagnias, one of the few protagonists of Isaeus' speeches to have had a relevant political career, who died during an embassy; it is significant how Isaeus refers to the circumstance:³² [Ἁγνίας]… πρεσβεύσων ἐπὶ ταύτας τὰς πράξεις αἳ τῇ πόλει συμφερόντως εἶχον. The *praxeis* related to the mission are defined as important for the city (τῇ πόλει), not for Hagnias himself or for his *oikos*, as Wyse rightly noted.³³ The episode seems to have taken place about a decade before the inheritance lawsuit.³⁴ Isaeus does not go into Hagnias' conduct and avoids any possible shadow of the praise: the episode defines in itself Hagnias' civic virtue, and the speaker has no need to add many details. It is enough for him to pay homage to the deceased ancestor by emphasizing how he died in pursuit of the common interest.

Spartolus (429 a.C., cf. Thuc. 2.79), as *philarchon*. Isae. 11.41: Teophon *philarchon* (cf. Davies 1971, 84).
30 Wevers 1969, 72 provides a list of political, military and religious activities related, often through inscriptions, to the people in Isaeus' speeches: again trierarchs prevails, followed by decrees proposers and military officers.
31 The only *strategos* in Isaeus' speeches, as we have seen, is Dikaiogenes I (Isae. 5.42).
32 Isae. 11.8. The lawsuit was celebrated in 359 or 358, and resumed after a few years, as shown by [Dem.] 43.31; cf. Wyse 1904, 677; Wevers 1969, 25; Ferrucci 1998, 56.
33 Wyse 1904, 684.
34 Chronology of the embassy is disputed: Accame 1951, 48; Seager 1967, 95–96 and n. 6; Fornis 2008, 62–63 and n. 141, among others, propose to link it to an episode of 396, when the Spartan Pharax captured and killed some Athenian ambassadors (*Hell. Oxy.* 7.1 *FGrHist* 66 F1, c II, 1); for the identification of the Hagnias involved in this episode with the deceased *kyrios* of Isaeus XI, Harp s.v. Ἁγνίας (= Androt. BNJ 324 F18, and Philoc. BNJ 328 F 147) is decisive. Humphries 1983, 219–225 has raised several difficulties, suggesting that the embassy belongs instead to the 70s of the fourth century, as proposed by Blass 1892, 566–567 n. 6 and Wyse 1904, 684, who naturally could have no knowledge of the text of the *Hellenica*. Wyse believed the embassy was part of Athenian attempts to forge an alliance with Dionysius I, probably the most convincing chronology.

Among military stories narrated by Isaeus, in three cases soldiers who may have served as mercenaries are displayed: the adopted sons of Menecles (Isae. 2), Astyphilus (Isae. 9) and, with some more doubt, Nicostratus (Isae. 4).[35] In the first case, the speaker attests that he and his brother served in Thrace with Iphicrates, returning with many earnings. Participation in the campaign lasted at least two years, because on their return the older sister had given birth to two children, while the younger sister, married to Menecles, none.[36] This explains why the speaker has been adopted by his brother-in-law, some time later. Menecles survived 23 years after adoption; the cause for the inheritance took place at least 25 years after the Thracian expedition. Iphicrates was in Thrace probably from about 386 until 374, when Pharnabazus involved him in military operations against Egypt; he then went back to Thrace after the unsuccessful capture of Amphipolis (365/4).[37] Blass first suggested Isaeus' text should refer to Iphicrates' intervention to support to Cotys;[38] Cobetto recommends 357 as *termius post quem* for the speech and 383 as the expedition's date.[39]

Reference to an expedition "with Iphicrates in Thrace" provides a fragment of autobiographical memory shared with the jurors, but extremely generic and impossible to verify, especially after about three decades. Personal memory does not require the endorsement of any external authority or proof to be validated: the presence on site of the speaker is a sufficient guarantee. Wyse read in this memory a proud claim, connected to the fame of the Athenian general,

---

35 Isae. 4.7: τίς γὰρ οὐκ ἀπεκείρατο, ἐπειδὴ τὼ δύο ταλάντω ἐξ Ἄκῆς ἠλθέτην; The most accepted view sees Nicostratus as one of the mercenaries gathered at Akkos by Iphicrates in 374 for the Egyptian campaign; Nicostratus however is never explicitly said to be a mercenary and the reading ἐξ Ἄκῆς derives from Valkenaer's emendation instead of the ἐξάκις in the codes, accepted by many editors but not all (Wevers 1969, 21–23 and Edwards 2002, 87–88 and 2007, 68 prefer the manuscript reading). Cf. Ferrucci 1998, 85–88.
36 Isae. 2.6: ὄντες αὐτοὶ ἐν ἡλικίᾳ ἐπὶ τὸ στρατεύεσθαι ἐτραπόμεθα, καὶ ἀπεδημήσαμεν μετὰ Ἰφικράτους εἰς Θράκην.
37 Chronology is uncertain, cf. Davies 1971, 248–250; Pritchett 1974, 62–72; Sinclair 1978, 47; Archibald 1998, 219–234; Zahrnt 2015, 44; Falco 2020, 18–21, 312–314.
38 Blass 1892, 533 n. 2, followed by Roussel 1926, 35; Forster 1927, 39; Wevers 1969, 25.
39 Cobetto 2012, 57–58, 68 n. 15, based on Xen. *Hell.* 4.8.34; 5.1.25. Identification of the expedition also depends on Seneca the Elder's *Controversy* 6.5, and Nepos *Iphicr.* 2.1; 3.4: both mention the relationship between Cotys and Iphicrates and the latter marriage with the Thracian king's daughter, or more probably sister (cf. Dem. 23.129, 132), who gave birth to Menestheus; see Davies 1971, 249–250; Harris 1989, 267 and n. 15; Bianco 1997, 187 n. 29; Kremmydas 2012, 335. Wyse 1904, 236–237 was skeptical about identifying and dating the expedition alluded to by Isaeus. On Thracian campaign cf. Momigliano 1966, 451–455 and n. 36; recently Sears 2013, 118–127; Zahrnt 2015, 44–45; references to Thrace in Dem. 23 are analysed by Asmonti 2004.

introduced to balance the possible discredit of the mercenary activity, which the name of Iphicrates would have ennobled.⁴⁰ Iphicrates' connection with mercenaries goes back at least to the Corinthian war⁴¹ and the association made by Demosthenes of the honors bestowed on the general with the mercenary commanders Strabax and Polystratus corroborates the connection.⁴²

Isaeus does not make any comment on the brief reference to the expedition: he counted on the fact that the judges will not evaluate negatively the mention of the general and of his client's possible mercenary activity; frequency of occurrences of Iphicrates' Thracian campaigns in the orators (particularly Demosthenes and Aeschines) suggest that in the years following the commander's death the audience could be familiar with those events and look favorably on them. Mentioning Iphicrates between 365/4 and 354, when he stood trial with his son Menestheus and Timotheus after the battle of Embata, would probably have been unwise; in order to safely use the general's name, a better timing would have been after the trial or, maybe even better, after his death. This may suggest a post-354 date for the speech.⁴³

The case of Astyphilus in Isaeus 9 is more directly relevant to the purposes of this paper. Astyphilus was a man of arms: § 14 lists some of the expeditions he took part in, adding that he rushed "wherever else he heard that an army was being collected" to serve as *locagos* (καὶ ἄλλοσε ὅπου περ αἰσθάνοιτο στράτευμα συλλεγόμενον, ἁπανταχοῖ ἀπεδήμει λοχαγῶν).⁴⁴ "To Corinth" (εἰς Κόρινθον) is generally recognized to indicate the Corinthian war (395/4–386);⁴⁵ operations in Thessaly was connected by Wyse, with some caution, to the rise to

---

40 Wyse 1904, 244, cf. Aeschin. 2.149; Dem. 19.237. On Iphicrates' military career cf. Davies 1971, 249–250; Pritchett 1974, 62–72, 117–125; Bianco 1997; Sekunda 2017.
41 Xen. *Hell.* 4.5.11–18; Dem. 4.23; Just. *Epit.* 6.5.2; Aristoph. *Plut.* 173 and Harp. s.v. ξενικὸν ἐν Κορίνθῳ; cf. Develin 1989, 211; Burckhardt 1996, 91–92; Bianco 1997, 181–182; Fornis 2008, 245–250; Bettalli 2013, 374–376.
42 Dem. 20.84, cf. Kremmydas 2012, 337; Canevaro 2016, 330–331.
43 See for instance Aesch. 3.243; Dem. 23.130–132, 198; 21.62–63; cf. Canevaro 2016, 330–331. On Iphicrates' destitution of 365 cf. Bianco 1997, 199 and n. 66; 2007, 37–41; diverging positions about the accusation of treason in Harris 1989, 264–271 and Kallett 1983, 247–248 with Sealey 1993, 88; Dem. 23.149 provides strong support to Harris (1989, 270–271); cf. also Heskel 1997, 26–28. The date of the trial is also controversial: Sealey 1955 and Hansen 1975 propose 356/5; Cawkwell 1962, 45–49, following Schaefer 1885, 415, sets it in 354, quite convincingly; cf. Canevaro 2016, 331. The verdict was probably favorable to Iphicrates: Hansen 1975, 100; Hamel 1998, 155; Kremmydas 2012, 336.
44 On *locagoi in* mercenary armies cf. now Sekunda 2017; Griffith-Williams 2013, 151 and n. 9, 170 sees in this statement the strongest indication that Astyphilus was a mercenary.
45 Military operations εἰς Κόρινθον occur also in Isae. 5.11; 7.9.

power of Jason of Pherae in 379 or to the following years (not beyond 370, the year of the tyrant's assassination), a hypothesis recently maintained by Rosivach.[46] The Theban War, as we have seen, has been considered by Rosivach to refer to years 371–366, when Thebes was opposed to Athens: if we stick to the traditionally accepted chronology, it would instead be placed in 378–371.[47] The expedition to Mytilene, in which the soldier died, seems to be placed with some plausibility around 366, as part of Timotheus' Samian campaign.[48] If the lawsuit was discussed in 365, three of the four episodes would prove very recent and therefore easily recognizable by the audience.[49]

Rosivach and Bettalli recently discussed Astyphilus' military career as a mercenary.[50] Bettalli has highlighted how, in Isaeus' portrait, Astyphilus appears well integrated into the *polis*, without any trace of reproaches which, for example, Isocrates and Demosthenes reserve for mercenaries. It was certainly not in Isaeus' interest to introduce controversial topics and suggest comments on the role of mercenaries in the city community. While Isaeus' neutral summary can be considered a more realistic picture of the extent of mercenary activity in 4th-century Athens, and its substantial acceptance within the *polis*, it must be added that the speaker does his utmost to minimize the feature: since events are recent, the audience was able to make their own associations, and to draw conclusions on the nature of Astyphilus' activities, which, as Rosivach rightly notes, are not tinged with any patriotic color, and on the origin of its assets.[51]

---

46 Wyse 1904, 627, Rosivach 2005, 196; Griffith-Williams 2013, 170.
47 "Theban war" in the years 378–371: Roussel 1960, 161; Wevers 1969, 21; Cobetto 2012, 358; Griffith-Williams 2013, 151, 170; post-371: Rosivach 2005, 196–198.
48 Welsh 1991, 145–150, imagine a long permanence in Mytilene by Astyphilus, as part of garrison duties; he suggests a later date for the speech, between 360 and 355/4; see Rosivach 2005, 198–201.
49 Speech date on 365: Ferrucci 1998, 55; Cobetto Ghiggia 2012; Griffith-Williams 2013, 151–152 and n. 11. Wevers 1969, 11–13, 18, proposes 370 or 369, cf. Jebb 1893, II 329–331; Avramović 1997, 33–35 conjectures a later date, around 346/5, as Wyse 1904, 627 suggested, although very cautiously; it would be quite difficult, accepting this chronology, to explain the other military events of the speech. Proposal for early date: Schömann 1830; Burnett-Edmonson 1960.
50 Rosivach 2005; Bettalli 2013, 103–109, 416–418.
51 Bettalli 2006, 2 and 26 nn. 30–35; 2013, 103–109, 416–418. Cf. on mercenary citizens within the *polis* of classical era Hornblower 2002, 194; on their social *status* Van Wees 2004, 40; on Astyphilus' volontary and not compelled choice to serve as mercenary, cf. Davies 1971, 230. Isaeus restrains himself on referring to Astyphilus' patriotism, as noted first by Wyse 1904, 629; cf. Rosivach 2005, 198, who add as an argument for Astyphilus' mercenary *status* the fact that he was not buried in the *demosion sema*.

In the case of Astyphilus, it cannot be said that Isaeus is sparing in inserting references to past events within the narrative: individual and family memory crystallizes around the protagonist's military activity. The historical facts are recalled again without any specific detail, nor are they described in any way. Isaeus avoids explicit speculations on any possible 'public' meaning the events might assume in the collective memory. In the case of the second speech, the reference to Iphicrates could suggest a note of self-celebration by the speaker, although it was left to the audience to grasp that implication or not. For Astyphilus, Isaeus provides a pure sequence of military episodes, leaving the judges to place them in time and possibly to associate them with their own memories or personal knowledge.

No allusion is made by Isaeus to the sources of transmission for the memories of the events he listed, no expressions such as "you certainly remember" or "as the elderly tell us" recurs and this is remarkable, distinguishing Isaeus' attitude about common past and shared memory.[52] The concise list is merely introduced by ἐστρατεύσατο. The forensic context does not require discussing those memories or justifying their meaning or reliability.

The persuasive purpose does not have a collective dimension, but a private one: it aims at presenting the developments in the story of the family group and its members. The nature of inheritance lawsuits produces a sort of reversal of perspectives, in which the common past become subordinate to family or individual affairs.

Any celebratory intentions in the favor of clients or polemics against opponents, displayed by the attitudes held inside circumstances of public interest (as a more or less valiant participation in war, the fulfillment of a liturgical or fiscal service for the *polis*, the carrying out of a public office) are recalled in relation to the *ethos* of the individual involved and serve to illustrate his attitudes, maintaining a prudent distance from implications or judgments that the event could suggest.

The Corinthian War or the Theban War, the feats of the great Athenian generals, Iphicrates and Timotheus above all, are recorded but never discussed, accepted as the background against which the protagonists of the speeches move: the judgments, when suggested or expressed, concern always the way individuals interact with events, they never concern the event itself. A good example is offered by the Vth oration, *On the estate of Dikaiogenes*.

---

[52] See Canevaro 2014 and Kapellos' Introduction in the present volume.

4 Recent past and rhetorical strategies: Isaeus' V[th] speech

The Vth speech involves a prestigious Athenian family, bind, through the adoption of Dicaiogenes III, to the *genos* of the Gephyraioi, which could boast Harmodius the tyrannicide in his genealogy.[53] Isaeus' client accuses Dikaiogenes III of having violated a previous agreement on division of patrimonial assets with the daughters of Dikaiogenes II (the adoptive father), and illegitimately claimed the entire *oikos* for himself.

The mentions of historical events provide the only indications for a dating of the speech. The following events of the recent past are bespoken: 1. a battle at Cnidus, in which Dicaiogenes II died; 2. a *stasis* which took place in Athens, about 12 years after the death of Dicaiogenes II; 3. the war of Corinth, to which Cephisodotus is sent in the retinue of Harmodius as *akolouthos*; 4. the capture of the Lechaion; 5. a war still in progress in which the Olynthians and the islanders are said to be fighting alongside Athens;[54] Isaeus also adds a list of more ancient battles in which the *progonoi* of the family fought and died.[55]

The recent past is recalled mainly to mark the protagonists and their *oikos* affairs, starting from the death of Dicaiogenes II in Cnidus: καὶ ὁ μὲν Δικαιογένης, τριήραρχος ἐκπλεύσας τῆς Παράλου, ἐτελεύτησε μαχόμενος ἐν Κνίδῳ.[56] The mention is very short, information is meagre: placed in the first chapters of the speech and resumed at the end, it seems to have a narrative purpose, while recalling Dikaiogenes' noble death. The identification of the battle is not easy. Three possible candidates have been proposed: the Athenian attempt to besiege the city in 412; the naval battle of Syme of 411 and the well-known battle won by Pharnabazus and Conon against Sparta in 394.[57] The first option seems to fit

---

53 Cf. Wyse 1904, 402–405; Wevers 1969, 74–75; Davies 1971, 145–149; Cox 1998, 10–15; 2002, 59; Cobetto 2002, 59–78.
54 Isae. 5.6, 7, 11, 37, 46.
55 Isae. 5.47.
56 Isae. 5.6, cf. 5.42.
57 Thuc. 8.35.3–4 (battle at Cnidus, autumn 412) and 8.42 (battle of Syme, beginnings of 411). Battle of Cnidus of 394 cf. Xen. *Hell.* 4.3.10–14; Diod. 14.83.4–7; Paus. 6.3.16: Athenian fleet is never mentioned as part of the *naumachia* and Wyse 1904, 405, 412–413 argued that it could not be the battle Isaeus is referring to; cf. also Xen. *Hell.* 4.8.4 for the size of Athenian fleet's after the battle. On Athens' military and political condition in the years of the battle cf. Rhodes 2012, 113–115; on the Athenian attempt to gain merits on the victory, cf. Rhodes–Osborne, 2003, n. 11; Wilson–Hartwig 2009, with the observations in Rhodes 2011, 72. On the battle of Cnidus

better with what is stated immediately afterwards: the agreement between Dicaiogenes' four sisters and his adopted son, Dicaiogenes III, was violated twelve years later, when the latter successfully claimed for itself the whole *oikos*, taking advantage of a *stasis*.

Isaeus intertwines the family story with that of the *polis*: the agreement was maintained as long as the trials were held regularly (οὐσῶν δικῶν), before the city knew the misfortune of the stasis (πρὶν δυστυχησάσης τῆς πόλεως καὶ στάσεως γενομένης).[58] Calling into question the difficulties of the city is not a simple historical reminder: the speaker must criticize a previous sentence in favor of the opponent without offending the judges' sensibilities: he therefore evokes a context that absolves the jurors who at that time voted for Dicaiogenes III.

The city troubles after 404 are presented as an opportunity for Dicaiogenes to take possession of the whole estate. The intrigue, which presents some textual difficulties in paragraph 7,[59] is made clear in the next one: Isaeus attributes the reasons for the defeat in that lawsuit not to the *dikastai* but to the deception perpetrated by Dicaiogenes, during the internal troubles of the city, which provides the ideal context for machination.[60]

The combined reading of the two paragraphs clarifies the balance between collective and family events: when things worked regularly and "trials were held", the agreements within the family were respected; when the *stasis* arrives, an opportunity opens to violate pacts and rules: the city in the hands of enemies and tyrants, the *oikos* threatened by Dicaiogenes' plots; back to normal, the misfortunes suffered by the city have confused the right values, so that villains can deceive the judges in the process.[61]

---

see now Asmonti, 2015, 143–154. Hornblower 2008, 974, prefers the battle of 411; recently Bubelis 2010, 387–388, went back to the battle of 394, without discussing the reasons of his choice. Choosing 394 implies a speech date about 370, and would raise serious difficulties in identifying the other historical events mentioned throughout the speech; cf. Ferrucci 1998, 73–75 and n. 11; Cobetto Ghiggia 2002, 34–40.

58 Isae. 5.7. Cf. Cobetto Ghiggia 2002, 142–145 and nn. 93, 96, 98.
59 I follow the interpretation of the phase in Cobetto 2002, 137–139, 143–144; on the lawcourts' interruption cf. Dow 1990, 68–69; Hansen 1991, 243–246 Musti 2006, 449–451.
60 Isae. 5.8.
61 Wyse 1904, 414–415, underplays the significance of this passage: "Isaios' phrases contain no clear idea"; the 'historical' argument of the post-404 troubles occurs, however, also in Isoc. 21.7, with remarkable similarities; Isocrates too needs to criticize a previous verdict delivered as soon as the law-courts were active again, blaming not the jurors but the political context. A symmetrical case in Lys. 17.3: a verdict delivered in 401/400 was favorable, so the speaker chooses to briefly mention it without any further comments.

A decade later, the climate has changed: the city has regained its stability, judicial procedures are properly functioning. Dicaiogenes can now be represented in a dissonant light face to the community. Isaeus' strategy is clear, introducing the events of the recent past to capture the attention of the judges, soliciting personal memories related to the city's recent misfortunes in order to project them on the family affair and use them against the opponent.[62]

After recalling, among the misdeeds of Dicaiogenes III, now in possession of the whole of the inheritance, that he had sent the young Chairestratus to Corinth as *akolouthos*,[63] Isaeus prepares for the final attack. Compared to the illustrious *progonoi*, Dicaiogenes can boast only an inglorious *choregia* and an unfulfilled promise of payment of the *eisphora*, which would have placed him in a epigraphical "list of shame" (ἐπ' αἰσχίστῳ ἐπιγράμματι) posted in front of the statues of the eponymous heroes.[64] The occasion was the subscription that preceded the battle and capture of Lechaion by the Spartans in 392; a recent episode, certainly very much alive in the memory of the jurors, who could easily share the indignation of Isaeus' words, in a time when the tax burden on Athenian citizens was particularly high. The existence of such lists has no documentary confirmation, at least for the years at which the speech was pronounced; it cannot be excluded, however, that Isaeus overlaps the compulsory contributions of the *eisphorai* with the voluntary ones, the *epidoseis*. Migeotte seems right in considering the case a unique, and in being very cautious about his historical meaning.[65] Similar lists are documented not earlier than ca 330 a.C.[66] It is, however, hard to believe that Isaeus' statement could have been completely false. One can only speculate: is the speaker presenting a voluntary contribution as mandatory[67] and forcing the reference by suggesting that Dicaiogenes III

---

[62] Dikaiogenes III appears as the most accomplished rhetorical model for 'bad citizens' portraits in Isaeus' speeches: cf. Ferrucci 1998, 235–240.
[63] Wyse 2004, 419 rightly points out that *akolouthoi* were not necessarily slaves: cf. Thuc. 7.75, 5; Theophr. *Char.* 25.4; Dem. 54.4; but [Dem.] 49.22, 55, clearly refers to a free man. The correction proposed by Naber (ἄνευ ἀκολούθου for ἀντὶ ἀκολούθου), although brilliant, doesn't seems needed nor justified, cf. Wyse 1904, 416 and Cobetto 2002, 164 and n. 174. Chairestratus humiliation concerns not his enslavement but the denial of a citizens' hoplite *status*.
[64] Isae. 5.37.
[65] Migeotte 1983, 134–139; cf. also Cobetto 2002, 217–218 n. 386; 2012, 211 n. 66.
[66] Cf. *IG* II² 1627, 421–430; 1628, 563–570; 1629, 1039–1047.
[67] Wyse 1904, 455.

ended up in the ranks of public debtors, for what in fact was only a delay in payment, not implausible given the chronological proximity of the event?[68]

The portrait of the opponent as a bad citizen, developed in the last 10 paragraphs of the speeches, and focusing on public and private misconduct, never touches his political inclinations. His actions, however, are intertwined with key moments in recent Athenian history, so as to suggest in the audience that his behavior was incompatible with the values of the Athenian *politeia*: the machinations under the Thirty, the insolvency of the contribution for the war of Corinth, when he sent his nephew to fight as *akolouthos*, the absence of personal commitment, as contributor, as trierarch or even as soldier, when a war is still ongoing.[69] Isaeus uses the city's history as an effective argument for the construction of the obnoxious, annoying *ethos* of the adversary.[70] He never discusses historical facts nor narrates them: he mentions them to highlight the behavior of the various protagonists of the case, as a background against which to test and unfold the *ethos* emerging from those behaviors.

5 Conclusion

The recent past is recalled in Isaeus' speeches as known and unchallenged. The only concern is about the attitude of the citizen towards his obligations to the *polis*: wars must be fought, liturgies absolved, *eisphorai* paid; during a *stasis* the defense of democracy is expected. Isaeus puts in the foreground the representation of relationships between individuals and the community, in the assumption of unquestionable loyalty towards civic duties.

The assignment of ownership of an *oikos*, Isaeus' goal, requires the prerequisite of loyalty to be affirmed as a constant obligation, linking public interest to

---

[68] Also Dicaiogenes' *khoregia* presents some misrepresentation, cf. Wyse 1904, 454–457; for the rhetorical use of *leithourgiai* see Wilson 2000, 147 ("Bad performers make bad democrats"), 201–202.

[69] On the war involving Olinthians and islanders, cf. Wyse 1904, 480–481; Buckler 2003, 159–162.

[70] The rule of the Thirty belongs to the recent past, while other events involving the family ancestors, listed in paragraph 42, belongs to the middling past: the mention of the battle on Cnidus, in which Dikaiogenes' II died, is a sort of chronological boundary, overlapping the recent past with the history of the last generation of family members. The distinction between recent and middling past is here very fluid; cf. the remarks on middling past in Kapellos' Introduction to this volume (pp. 2–4).

private affairs. The past helps building the characters in the case, and that's it: there is no room for further considerations.

The audience may have identified past events, through a collective memory that retained notoriety for them, when they occur in public debate or civic commemorations, or through personal or family memories, or, finally, could simply fail to acknowledge them. What matters in Isaeus' perspective was the effectiveness that evoking the past could bring to the narrative: whether providing specific support to it (narrative-argumentative function) or revealing the *ethos* of those who had a part in it (narrative-celebratory function).

6 Appendix – References to the recent past in Isaeus' speeches

Or.	Greek Text	Historical Event	Date and Sources	Date of the Speech
II 6	ὄντες αὐτοὶ ἐν ἡλικίᾳ ἐπὶ τὸ στρατεύεσθαι ἐτραπόμεθα, καὶ ἀπεδημήσαμεν μετὰ Ἰφικράτους εἰς Θρᾴκην	Iphicrates' thracian military expedition	383 ? Sen. *Controv.* 6, 5; Xen. *Hell.* 4. 8, 24; 5. 1, 25	357–353 +25–30 years
IV 7	ἐπειδὴ τὼ δύο ταλάντω **ἐξ Ἄκης ἠλθέτην;** (Valckenaer's emendation, codd.: ἑξάκις)	Akkos (Egyptian campaign, 374)	374 Diod. 15. 41; Nep. *Datam.* 5; Polyen. 3. 9, 56	370 ca Few years before the speech
V 6; 42	(6) καὶ ὁ μὲν Δικαιογένης, τριήραρχος ἐκπλεύσας τῆς Παράλου, ἐτελεύτησε μαχόμενος ἐν Κνίδῳ (42) αὐτοὶ δ' ὑπὲρ τῆς πατρίδος πολεμοῦντες ἀπέθανον (…) Δικαιογένης δὲ ὁ Μενεξένου τριηραρχῶν τῆς Παράλου ἐν Κνίδῳ.	Battle of Cnidus with the sacred trireme Paralus	412 (or 411) Thuc. 8. 34, 3–4; 42	389 ca +22–23 years
V 7	ἐπειδὴ δὲ ἐνείμαντο τὸν κλῆρον (…) **ἐκέκτητο ἕκαστος δώδεκα ἔτη ἃ ἔλαχε·** καὶ ἐν τοσούτῳ χρόνῳ οὐσῶν δικῶν οὐδεὶς αὐτῶν ἠξίωσε τὰ	Stasis in Athens, already ended 12 years after the battle of Cnidus previously mentioned	404/3 – 400/399	389 ca +10–11 years

Or.	Greek Text	Historical Event	Date and Sources	Date of the Speech
	πεπραγμένα εἰπεῖν ἀδίκως πεπρᾶχθαι, **πρὶν δυστυχησάσης τῆς πόλεως καὶ στάσεως γενομένης** Δικαιογένης οὑτοσὶ (...) ἠμφισβήτει ἡμῖν ἅπαντος τοῦ κλήρου			
V 11	τὸν ἐκείνου ἀδελφιδοῦν Κηφισόδοτον τῷ ἑαυτοῦ ἀδελφῷ Ἁρμοδίῳ **συνέπεμψεν εἰς Κόρινθον ἀντ' ἀκολούθου**: εἰς τοῦτο ὕβρεως καὶ μιαρίας ἀφίκετο.	Corinthian war	394–390	389 A few years (<5 years)
V 37	Δικαιογένης οὐκ ἔστιν ἥντινα εἰσενήνοχε: πλὴν **ὅτε Λέχαιον ἑάλω**	Spartan occupation of the Lechaion	392 392: And. 3. 18; Xen. *Hell.* 4. 4, 7–18; Diod. 14. 86.	389 +3 years
V 46	ἀλλ' οὐκ ἐστράτευσαι τοσούτου καὶ τοιούτου γενομένου πολέμου, εἰς ὃν Ὀλύνθιοι μὲν καὶ νησιῶται ὑπὲρ τῆσδε τῆς γῆς ἀποθνήσκουσι μαχόμενοι τοῖς πολεμίοις	Ongoing war, Olynthians and *nesiotai* allied to Athens	390–389	389 +0
VI 1	ὅτε γὰρ εἰς Σικελίαν ἐξέπλει τριηραρχῶν Χαιρέστρατος, διὰ τὸ πρότερον αὐτὸς ἐκπεπλευκέναι (...) καὶ συνεξέπλευσα καὶ συνεδυστύχησα καὶ ἑάλωμεν εἰς τοὺς πολεμίους	Military raid or diplomatic mission to Sicily + previous mission, also to Sicily	370–367	365/4 or 364/3 + 6/7 years max.
VI 27	μετὰ ταῦτα τοίνυν ὁ Φιλοκτήμων τριηραρχῶν περὶ Χίον ἀποθνήσκει ὑπὸ τῶν πολεμίων	Battle near Chios	ante 366	365/4 – 364/3 + 5 years max.

The Recent Past in Isaeus' Forensic Speeches — 221

Or.	Greek Text	Historical Event	Date and Sources	Date of the Speech
VI 27	καὶ ὁ μὲν Φανόστρατος ἐκπλεῖν ἔμελλε τριηραρχῶν μετὰ Τιμοθέου, καὶ ἡ ναῦς αὐτῷ ἐξώρμει Μουνυχίασι	Military expedition from Mounichia, led by Timotheus	366 (?)	365/4 – 364/3 + 2 years ca.
VII 9	εἰς Κόρινθόν τε στρατεύεσθαι μέλλων, εἴ τι πάθοι, διέθετο τὴν οὐσίαν	Corinthian war	395/4–386	365/4 +21–30 years ca.
IX 14	πρῶτον μὲν γὰρ ἐστρατεύσατο εἰς Κόρινθον		394–390 (Corinthian war)	370 ca (Blass), 369 (Weissborn, Jebb, Wevers), 365 ca. (Wyse) + 25 years ca.
IX 14	ἔπειτα εἰς Θετταλίαν	Campaign in Thessaly	379–370	+ 5–14 years ca.
IX 14	ἔτι δὲ τὸν Θηβαικὸν πόλεμον ἅπαντα	Theban war	378–371 – 370–368 (Rosivach)	+ 3–13 years ca.
IX 14	ἡ δὲ εἰς τὴν Μυτιλήνην στρατεία τελευταία αὐτῷ ἐγένετο, ἐν ᾗ καὶ ἀπέθανε.	Expedition to Mytilene,	366 ?	+1 year ca.
X 20	μετὰ δὲ ταῦτα ὁ **Κορινθιακὸς πόλεμος ἐγένετο**, ἐν ᾧ ἐγὼ κἀκεῖνος στρατεύεσθαι ἠναγκαζόμεθα (...) εἰρήνης τ' αὖ γενομένης κτλ.	Corinthian war and peace (of Antalcidas)	394–386 (386: peace of Antalcidas)	ca. 370 + 16–24 years
X 22	ὡς ἀνὴρ ὢν ἀγαθὸς **ἐν τῷ πολέμῳ** τέθνηκε	Theban (?) war	378–371 ? Theban war?	370 + 1–8 years (recent fac, war still in action)
XI 8	Ἁγνίας οὖν, ὅτε ἐκπλεῖν παρεσκευάζετο πρεσβεύσων ἐπὶ ταύτας τὰς πράξεις αἳ τῇ πόλει συμφερόντως εἶχον, οὐκ ἐφ' ἡμῖν τοῖς ἐγγύτατα γένους, εἴ τι πάθοι, τὰ ὄντα κατέλιπεν,	Diplomatic mission	ca. 370? Possible expedition in 396; Harp.s.v. Ἁγνίας, Xen. *Hell.* 7, 1; Androt. BNJ 324 F 18; Philoc. BNJ 328 F 147	360–359 (cfr. [Dem.] 43, 31). + 10 years ca

Or.	Greek Text	Historical Event	Date and Sources	Date of the Speech
fr. 16. 66 B-S.	Τριηραρχοῦντος γάρ μου ἐπὶ Κηφισοδότου ἄρχοντος καὶ λόγου ἀπαγγελθέντος πρὸς τοὺς οἰκείους ὡς ἄρα τετελευτηκὼς εἴην ἐν τῇ ναυμαχίᾳ	Naumachia	358/7 (or 366/5, following the correction Cephisodorus for the name of the archon, proposed by Cawkwell)	?

Bibliography

Accame, S. (1951), *Ricerche intorno alla guerra corinzia*, Napoli.
Archibald, Z.H. (1998), *The Odrysian Kingdom of Thrace: Orpheus Unmasked*, Oxford.
Asmonti, L. (2004), "La (dis)organizzazione politica della Tracia, l'orazione contro Aristocrate e il lessico politico di Demostene", in: P. Schirripa (ed.), *I Traci tra l'Egeo e il Mar Nero*, Milano, 179–185.
Asmonti, L. (2015), *Conon the Athenian: Warfare and Politics in the Aegean, 411–386 BC*, Historia Einzelschriften 235, Stuttgart.
Avramović, S. (1997), *Iseo e il diritto attico*, Napoli.
Bettalli, M. (2006), "L'immagine del mercenario nella Grecia del IV sec. a.C.", in: M.A. Viaggiolo (ed.), *Guerra e pace in Sicilia e nel Mediterraneo antico. Arte, prassi e teoria della pace e della guerra*, I, Atti delle quinte giornate intern. di studi sull'area elima e la Sicilia occidentale nel contesto mediterraneo (Erice, 12–15 ottobre 2003), Pisa, 19–28.
Bettalli, M. (2013), *Mercenari. Il mestiere delle armi nel mondo greco antico*, Roma.
Bianco, E. (1997), "Ificrate, rhetor kai strategos", *MGR* 21, 179–207.
Bianco, E. (2007), *Lo stratego Timoteo, torre di Atene*, Alessandria.
Blass, F. (1892), *Die Attische Beredsamkeit. II: Isokrates und Isaios*, Leipzig 2.
Bruss, K.S. (2013), "Persuasive Ethopoeia in Dionysius's Lysias", *Rhetorica* 31, 34–57.
Bubelis, W. (2010), "The Sacred Triremes and their 'Tamiai' at Athens", *Historia* 59, 385–411.
Buckler, J. (2003), *Aegean Greece in the Fourth Century*, Leiden/Boston.
Burckhardt, L.A. (1996), *Bürger und Soldaten, Aspekte der politischen und militärischen Rolle athenischen Bürger im Kriegswegen des 4. Jahrhunderts v. Chr.*, Stuttgart.
Burnett, A.P./Edmonson, C.N. (1961), "The Chabrias monument in the Athenian agora", *Hesperia* 30, 80–91.
Canevaro, M. (2014), "Memory, the Orators and the Public in Athens", in: L. Castagnoli/P. Ceccarelli (eds.), *Greek Memories. Theory and Practises*, Cambridge, 136–157.
Canevaro, M. (2016), *Demostene, contro Leptine. Introduzione, traduzione e commento storico*, Berlin/Boston.
Canevaro, M. (2019), "Law and Justice", in: G. Martin (ed.), *The Oxford Handbook of Demosthenes*, Oxford, 73–86.
Carey, C. (1994a), "Rhetorical means of persuasion", in: I. Worthington (ed.), *Persuasion*, London, 26–45.
Carey, C. (1994b), "Artless proofs in Aristotle and the orators", *BICS* 39, 95–106

Cawkwell, G.L. (1962), "Notes on the Social War", *C & M* 23, 34–49.
Cobetto Ghiggia, P. (2002), *Iseo. Contro Leocare (Sulla successione di Diceogene)*, Pisa.
Cobetto Ghiggia, P. (2012), *Iseo. Orazioni*, Alessandria.
Cox, C.A. (1998), *Household Interests. Property, Marriage Strategies, and Family Dynamics in Ancient Athens*, Princeton.
Davies, J.K. (1971), *Athenian Propertied Families, 600–300 B.C.*, Oxford.
De Temmerman, K. (2010), "Ancient Rhetoric as a Hermeneutical Tool for the Analysis of Characterization in Narrative Literature", *Rhetorica* 28, 23–51.
Develin, R. (1989), *Athenian Officials 684–321 B.C.*, Cambridge.
Edwards, M. (2002), "A note on Isaeus 4.7", *Mnemosyne* 55, 87–88.
Edwards, M. (2007), *Isaeus*, Austin.
Falco, G. (2020), *Contro Timoteo ([Dem.] 49): introduzione, traduzione e commento*, PhD Thesis, SNS Pisa.
Ferrucci, S. (1998), *L'Atene di Iseo. L'organizzazione del privato nella prima metà del IV secolo a.C.*, Pisa.
Ferrucci, S. (2005), *Iseo, La successione di Kiron, introduzione, testo critico, traduzione e commento*, Pisa.
Ferrucci, S. (2006), "Iseo, Tucidide e l'indagine sul passato", *Incidenza dell'antico* 4, 99–109.
Fornis, C. (2008), *Grecia exhausta. Ensajo sobre la guerra de Corinto*, Göttingen.
Forster, E.S. (1927), *Isaeus*, Cambridge.
Giangiulio, M. (2010), "Le società ricordano? Paradigmi e problemi della memoria collettiva" (a partire da M. Halbwachs), in: M. Giangiulio (ed.), *Memorie coloniali*, Roma, 29–43.
Griffith-Williams, B. (2013), *A Commentary on Selected Speeches of Isaeus*, Leiden.
Hamel, D. (1998), *Military Authority in the Classical Period*, Leiden/Boston/Köln.
Hansen, M.I. (1975), *Eisangelia. The Sovereignty of the People's Court in Athens in the Fourth Century B.C. and the impeachment of Generals and Politicians*, Odense.
Hansen, M.I. (1991), *The Athenian Democracy in the Age of Demoshenes. Structure, Principles and Ideology*, London.
Harris, E.M. (1989), "Iphicrates at the Court of Cotys", *AJP* 110, 264–271.
Harris, E.M. (2013), *The Rule of Law in Action in Democratic Athens*, Oxford.
Heskel, J. (1997), *The North Aegean Wars, 371–360 B.C.*, Stuttgart.
Hornblower, S. (2002), *The Greek World*, London³.
Hornblower, S. (2008), *A Commentary on Thucydides. Volume III. Books 5.25–8.109*, Oxford.
Humphreys, S.C. (1983), *The Family, Women and Death. Comparative Studies*, London.
Jebb, R.C. (1893), *The Attic Orators from Antiphon to Isaeus*, London².
Kallett, L. (1983), "Iphicrates, Timotheos and Athens, 371–360 B.C.", *GRBS* 24, 239–252.
Kremmydas, C. (2012), *Demosthenes, Against Leptines, Commentary on Demosthenes Against Leptines. With Introduction, Text, and Translation*, Oxford.
Migeotte, L. (1983), "Souscriptions athéniennes de la période classique", *Historia* 32, 129–148.
Momigliano, A. (1966), *Terzo contributo alla storia degli studi classici*, Roma.
Musti, D. (2006), *Storia greca*, Roma/Bari².
Pritchett, W.K. (1974), *The Greek State at War*, Part II, Berkeley/Los Angeles/London.
Rhodes, P.J. (2011), "The Dionysia and Democracy again", *CQ* 61, 71–74.
Rhodes, P.J. (2012), "The Alleged Failure of Athens in the Fourth Century", *Electrum* 19, 111–129.
Rhodes, P.J./Osborne, R. (eds.) (2003), *Greek Historical Inscriptions, 404–323 B.C.*, Oxford.

Rosivach, V.J. (2005), "Astyphilus the Mercenary", *G&R* 52, 195–204.
Roussel, P. (1926), *Isée*, Discours, Paris.
Rubinstein, L. (1993), *Adoption in IVth Century Athens*, Copenhagen.
Schaefer, A. (1885), *Demosthenes und seine Zeit*, Leipzig 2.
Schömann, G.F. (1830), *Isäus der Redner*, Stuttgart.
Seager, R. (1967), "Thrasybulus, Conon and Athenian Imperialism, 396–386 B.C.", *JHS* 87, 95–115.
Sealey, R. (1955), "Athens after the Social War", *JHS* 75, 74–81.
Sealey, R. (1993), *Demosthenes and his Time: A Study in Defeat*, Oxford.
Sears, A.M. (2013), *Thrace and the Shaping of Athenian Leadership*, Cambridge.
Sekunda, N.V. (2017), "The locagoi of Iphicrates: Forming a Mercenary Army in the Fourth Century B.C.", in: T. Ñaco del Hoyo/F. López Sánchez (eds.), *War, Warlords, and Relations in the Ancient Mediterranean*, Leiden, 64–88.
Serafim, A. (2021), "I, He, We, You, They": Addresses to the Audience as a Means of Unity/ Division in Attic Forensic Oratory", in: A. Michalopoulos/A. Serafim/A. Vatri/F. Beneventano della Corte (eds.), *The Rhetoric of Unity and Division in Ancient Literature*, Berlin/ Boston, 71–98.
Sinclair, R.K. (1978), "The King's Peace and the Employment of military and naval forces 387–378", *Chiron* 8, 29–54.
Steinbock, B. (2013), *Social Memory in Athenian Public Discourse: Uses and Meaning of the Past*, Ann Arbor.
Thomas, R. (1989), *Oral Tradition and Written Record in Classical Athens*, Cambridge.
Van Wees, H. (2004), *Greek Warfare: Myth and Realities*, London.
Welsch, D. (1991), "Isaeus 9 and Astyphilos' Last Expedition", *G & R* 32, 133–150.
Wevers, R.F. (1969), *Iseus: Chronology, Prosopography, and Social History*, The Hague/Mouton.
Wilson, P. (2000), *The Athenian Institution of the Khoregia: The Chorus, the City, and the Stage*, Cambridge.
Wilson, P./Hartwig, A. (2009), "*IG* I^3 102 and the tradition of proclaiming honours at the tragic agon at the Athenian City Dionysia", *ZPE* 169, 17–27.
Wyse, W. (1904), *The Speeches of Isaeus, with critical and explanatory notes*, Cambridge.
Zahrnt, M. (2015), "Early History of Thrace to the Murder of Kotys I (360 BC)", in: J. Valeva/ E. Nankov/D. Graninger (eds.), *A Companion to Ancient Thrace*, Chichester, 35–47.

Nicolas Siron
The Forensic Time Machine: Play on Times in Apollodorus' *Against Timotheus*

Abstract: Timotheus is believed to have faced an *eisangelia* in November 373: sent to rescue the Corcyreans, he sailed towards the Cyclades to gather money and men. This *eisangelia* is mentioned in Apollodorus' speech *Against Timotheus*, probably delivered in 362. Apollodorus explains to the jurors that they remember the opinion that everyone had of Timotheus at that time. But the construction of his narrative tries to play with time in order to cover up the good reputation of his opponent. Through a style deemed poor, he manages to manipulate reality, which is now unknowable. By calling for judges' testimony, Apollodorus also alleges a common knowledge that appears to be a rhetorical loophole to gain the trust of his hearers.

If the fifth-century B.C. comes to mind most quickly when one thinks of the history of classical Athens, in particular the Delian League and the Peloponnesian War,[1] Athens' power does not permanently disappear after 403. The city reconstitutes an alliance in the 4th century, with the Second Athenian League from 378 to 371.[2] A character stands out in it: Timotheus of Anaphlystus, son of the famous general Conon, who already defeated Sparta's hegemony in the Aegean in 394, and a pupil of Isocrates.[3] As *stratēgos* from 376 to 373, he seizes Corcyra in 375, defeats the Spartans in Alyzeia and brings many cities into the league.[4] But the Lacedaemonians launch an expedition against Corcyra in 373

This chapter owes a lot to Aggelos Kapellos' repeated (but always kind) remarks and references. It would not have been the same without the proofreading of Paulin Ismard and Patrice Brun. I also thank Michel Massonnat and Aaron Kachuck for their help regarding English wording.

1 The handling of the 400's is thus treated in depth in this volume.
2 On the Second Athenian League, see Cargill 1981. The decree of Aristoteles shows the will to avoid all mistakes the Athenians had made during the Delian League: the allied cities are autonomous and can keep their constitution; without garrisons or governors, and without any tribute to pay; and the Athenian citizens cannot possess land in their territories.
3 On the origin and carrier of Timotheus, see Kirchner 1903, 314–318 and Davies 1971, 506–512 (no. 13 700). On Isocrates as Timotheus' teacher, see especially [Plut.] *Vit. X or.* 837c, Isoc. 15.101–139.
4 Xen. *Hell.* 5.4.63–66, Isoc. 15.108–109, Din. 1.14–16 (see also 3.17), Diod. 15.36.5–6, Nep. *Tim.* 2.1–2, Polyaenus, *Strat.* 3.10.

https://doi.org/10.1515/9783110791877-014

and Timotheus is sent by the Athenians to lead a fleet of sixty ships.[5] He nevertheless sails towards the Cyclades because he fails to gather enough money and men for the ships, and in November 373 (at the latest) he has to face an accusation led by Callistratus and Iphicrates, who takes his place and soon equips the fleet.[6]

This last event is mentioned in Apollodorus' speech *Against Timotheus* (§ 9–10), probably delivered in 362. E. Harris and J. Trevett had a debate about this dating: Harris wanted to show that the trial took place at some point between 370/69 and 367/6, but Trevett supported the traditional dating of Schaefer (midsummer 362).[7] Since then, the scholars seem to keep the earlier date. As A. Scafuro said, it is not surprising that Apollodorus waited for a dozen years to prosecute Timotheus, since he had to take into account his own schedule, his obligations and his opponents' presence in Athens.[8]

This passage will be useful in order to deal with several issues. First, is the account of events prepared by Apollodorus accurate? It will be interesting to deconstruct his strategy in order to reveal his way of organizing his story and manipulating the time. Then, how does the litigant attest to his narrative? The recent past combines facts that are both old enough to require usual evidentiary procedures in trials (for instance, testimonies), but also events which can be known to all. Finally, what does the speech tells us about the relation between the orator and his audience? Apollodorus' play on dicastic *thorubos* reveals and fights against the heterogeneity of the members of the jury.

---

[5] Xen. *Hell.* 6.2.2–11. For a chronological reconstruction of the events, see Roberts 1982, 41–42 (and especially 199–200 n. 50, with bibliography).
[6] Xen. *Hell.* 6.2.12–13, Diod. 15.47.2–3 (who speaks about a trip to Thrace). See Hamel 1998, 24 n. 63 on the difficulties of recruiting men: the responsibility could have lain on the trierarchs rather than Timotheus. Gray (1980, 315–317) tried to show that Iphicrates did not prosecuted Timotheus since he already left Athens to Corcyra, but Tuplin (1984, 538–539) demonstrated the opposite. Rice (1997) analyzes the trial within the context of the foreign policy of Athens.
[7] Harris 1988, Trevett 1991 (summarized in Trevett 1992, 35–36). See also Kapparis 2017, 288 n. 7.
[8] Scafuro 2011, 354 n. 1. For full discussion, see 359–361 (see also Trevett 1992, 128–129). She dates the speech of January 362. An argument can be added to those of Trevett and Scafuro: Harris states that Pasicles may have been a witness while he has not reached majority, but giving testimony implies the possibility of a trial for false testimony which can only concern free men, since they have to answer for it on their property (by a fine) or even their rights (by *atimia*).

1 Evoking the *eisangelia* of 373 in 362: Distortion of reality?

Apollodorus sues Timotheus for the repayment of several loans granted to the general by Pasio, the litigant's father. Pasio was a former slave of the bankers Archestratus and Antisthenes, otherwise unknown.[9] He began to work for them from the end of the fifth century, then was freed and became the owner of the bank, located in the Piraeus, before 394/3.[10] After numerous services to the city, he was granted Athenian citizenship and enrolled into the deme Acharnae.[11] Pasio had Apollodorus with his wife Archippe around 394.[12] But when he died in 370/69, he leased part of his property to Phormio, an ex-slave who managed the bank, and also gave him Archippe: the marriage happened in 368/7.[13] Apollodorus nonetheless had some money troubles with creditors, as his neighbour Nicostratus, and even had to go to court. He wrote speeches to defend himself: we know six speeches from him with certainty and two controversial ones, all included in the Demosthenic corpus.[14] They range from the beginning of the 360's to the end of the 340's, showing a long business and political career.

Apollodorus' indictment against Timotheus is probably an action for damages (*dikē blabēs*), even if the title of the speech may have suggested to some scholars that it was an action for debt (*dikē chreōs*), which is unknown elsewhere.[15] Even though the debts are a decade old, the question of prescription does not seem to be an issue.[16] Timotheus has contracted a total of four loans with Pasio: 1,351 drachmae 2 obols before his second expedition, in April 373; 1,000 drachmae to refund Antiphanes of Lamptrae (treasurer of the shipowner Philip) who paid the Boeotian trierarchs; a mine, blankets, coats and two silver cups to host Alcetas and Jason in his house in Peiraeus; finally the freight paid

---

9 Dem. 36.43. See Trevett 1992, 1–9 (with notes) for further details on Pasio's life.
10 See Dem. 36.48 and 52.8.
11 [Dem.] 59.2.
12 See Trevett 1992, 19 n. 5, from Dem. 36.22 and 46.13. On Apollodorus' life, see Trevett 1992, 8–17 and Kapparis 1999, 45.
13 See Gernet 1957, 156 n. 1 (with bibliography), from Dem. 45.3.
14 Dem. 45 (?), 46, 47 (?), 49, 50, 52, 53, 59. See Trevett 1992, 50–76. See MacDowell 2009, 115–121 and 136–141 for Dem. 45 and 47.
15 On the *dikē chreōs*, see Harrison 1971, 79 n. 3 and Todd 1993, 266–267 and 282–283. On the *dikē blabēs*, see Gernet 1959, 9–10 and Scafuro 2011, 354–355.
16 Gernet 1959, 10–11: Apollodorus should say a few words about it if the argument could be used against him by Timotheus.

to Philondas who returned with timber from Macedonia when Timotheus had fled to the Great King.[17] The sum thus reaches 4,438 drachmae 2 obols. Timotheus was a rich man. He seems to have received a patrimony of at least 17 talents from his father Conon at his death c. 390/89.[18] But all his properties are gradually mortgaged, as shown in Apollodorus' speech (§ 11–12). He then has to borrow money from Pasio several times. Trevett points out that these loans were peculiar, since they did not involve any guarantees or interest.[19] He solves this problem by explaining that Pasio "preferred to regard them as social rather than business transactions [in order] to have Timotheus under an obligation to him", which is confirmed by Apollodorus himself (§ 3).

Nevertheless, Timotheus' financial problems prevent him from sailing to Corcyra and he suffers a negative vote of confidence, *apocheirotonia* (§ 9): as the *Athenaion Politeia* says, in each *prytaneia*, i.e. ten times a year, a vote is taken at the main meeting of the Assembly to maintain or dismiss the magistrates (*epicheirotonia*) and the one who is rejected by the people is removed from his office (*apocheirotonia*).[20] Timotheus then has to face a trial, understood as an *eisangelia* (impeachment), launched by Iphicrates and Callistratus[21] because it is "under a very serious indictment" (αἰτίας τῆς μεγίστης, § 9), that is for treason (προδοσία), a word that includes treachery but also lack of will or circumstances beyond a *stratēgos*' control.[22] Iphicrates, son of Timotheus of Rhamnous, and Callistratus son of Callistrates of Aphidna, are two important statesmen of the

---

17 All the passages used for this list are shown in *Table 1*, which will be discussed later.
18 Dem. 46.13 for the date of the death and Lys. 19.39–40 for Conon's legacy, which amounts to 38 talents and 2,000 drachmae. See the detailed presentation in Davies 1971, 508–509.
19 Trevett 1992, 157–158. The following quote is on page 158.
20 [Arist.] *Ath. Pol.* 43.4 and 61.2.
21 The statement in the *Ath. Pol.* seems imprecise on the matter of the trial following the *apocheirotonia*. For MacDowell, it would not be compulsory, unlike *Ath. Pol.* asserts, even if it is logical that it should occur: the prosecutor can then choose whether he goes through a *graphē* or an *eisangelia*. *Ath. Pol.* also claims that the judgment after an *apocheirotonia* takes place in court, while Timotheus is charged with his *eisangelia* in the Assembly. This would be the result of the shift that happened at the beginning of the 350's, i.e. between the period of the trial and the Aristotle's time: see Hansen 1975, 52–54, Rhodes 1981, 683, Scafuro 2011, 366–367 n. 44 and Scafuro 2018, 201. On the *eisangelia* of Timotheus by Iphicrates and Callistratus, see Hansen 1975, 91 (no. 80), also listed in Hamel 1998, 150 (no. 42). Rubinstein 2000, 236 is not sure that Iphicrates and Callistratus initiated the *eisangelia*: it could be other supporting prosecutors.
22 See [Plut.] *Vit. X or.* 836D for the deduction. Scafuro 2018, 204 is reluctant to speak of *eisangelia*, since the word never occurs to refer to Timotheus' trial. On the multiple meanings of *prodosia* in Athenian political context, see Sinclair 1988, 147 and Queyrel Bottineau 2010 (for the 5th century only).

fourth-century, politically active from the end of the 390's and particularly in the 380–370's.²³ All three are, however, part of the "imperialist" side in favour of Athenian hegemony in the Aegean Sea: for some scholars, the opposition is based on ideology or factional struggle, because Timotheus is a member of the pro-Theban party whereas Callistratus supports the pro-Spartan peace; while for others, the trial comes from Timotheus' attentiveness which delays the achievement of the hegemonic goals.²⁴ Timotheus is supported by Alcetas, king of the Molossi in Epirus, and Jason, tyrant of Pherae in south-eastern Thessaly (§ 10).²⁵ They are at the same time allies of one another and members of the Second Athenian League after both were recruited by the Athenian general in 375 or around this date.²⁶ Cornelius Nepos even asserts that Jason comes to assist Timotheus without his escort although he was used to having guards to protect him at all times.²⁷

According to Apollodorus' speech, Timotheus would then be acquitted, but he would lose his command, and his treasurer Antimachus would be sentenced to death and confiscation of property. However, this source is the closest but also the most biased regarding this event and everything is problematic in this story. First, all the other sources speak only about the deposition (*apocheirotonia*):²⁸ the *eisangelia* against Timotheus appears in Apollodorus' speech alone, and the word itself is not even used. Then, there are major discrepancies regarding the outcome of the situation. Indeed, Diodorus of Sicily claims that Timotheus is reinstated in his command after his acquittal.²⁹ On the contrary, the *Lives of the ten orators* state that the speech delivered by Iphicrates during the *eisangelia* has been written by Lysias and was successful.³⁰ The authorship has been discussed, since Dionysius of Halicarnassus does not mention this speech

---

23 Iphicrates fights during the sea-battle of Cnidus in 394. Callistratus is one of the generals in 378/7 and 372/1. He is friend with Pasio (ἐπιτήδειος, Dem. 49.47). See Kirchner 1901, 511–515/ 541–542 and Davies 1971, 248–252, 277–282 (nos. 7737/8157). Iphicrates and Timotheus then become allies: Iphicrates' son marries Timotheus' daughter (Dem. 49.66).
24 For factional struggle see Sealey 1956 and Roberts 1982, 40–45. Against this view see Mossé 1974, 218–220.
25 The exact type of assistance is not clearly defined: see Harrison 1971, 164.
26 Xen. *Hell*. 6.1.7 and Cargill 1981, 43–44, even if Jason's name should not be restored in Aristoteles' decree.
27 Nep. *Tim*. 4.2–3.
28 Xen. *Hell*. 6.2.13 (the Athenians end up his charge of *stratēgos*: παύσαντες αὐτὸν τῆς στρατηγίας), Diod. 15.47.3 (he loses his charge, ἀπέβαλε τὴν στρατηγίαν).
29 Diod. Sic. 15.47.3. Stylianou 1998, 372 imagines that Diodorus only misunderstands Ephorus telling that Timotheus has been general again (but some years later).
30 [Plut.] *Vit. X Or*. 836d.

when he details Lysias' career.³¹ But the fact that Iphicrates won the trial may still be accurate, as M. Hansen considers it.³² It is nonetheless strange that Apollodorus talks about acquittal when the conviction would be a strong support to his indictment. On the other hand, it would be the only one acquittal of the three *apocheirotoniai* where a result is known for the secondary trial and one of three acquittals on twenty-one depositions (with the verb ἀποχειροτονέω or not) where the outcome is known.³³ Above all, it would be the only case of the twenty-seven known *eisangeliai* against generals found guilty between 432 and 355 where there is neither fine nor sentence to death.³⁴ The victory evoked by the Pseudo-Plutarch may therefore apply to Antimachus' trial and not to that of Timotheus.

But there is more. Indeed, the *Athenaion Politeia* claims that the acquitted *stratēgoi* were supposed to get their office back, a scenario that does not occur for Timotheus.³⁵ D. MacDowell is forced to work out a hypothesis that a decree of the Assembly is required to reinstall the deposed general.³⁶ Furthermore, Apollodorus contradicts himself regarding Timotheus' *euthynai tēs stratēgias*: first the general is twice depicted as rendering his accounts, then he fears the audit of his accounts and flees to Egypt to lead some of the Great King's troops (§ 12, 16 and 25).³⁷ A. Scafuro perceives Apollodorus as "disingenuous".³⁸ Therefore, the version of Apollodorus is not acceptable without the modification of his own narrative and other equally serious historical statements. Even if we may never be able to find out what exactly went down for Timotheus, it is clear that Apol-

---

31 Carey 2007, 464–465 sees the Κατὰ Τιμοθέου προδοσίας as fictitious and does not number it in the fragments of Lysias. Dover 1968, 45 explains how Dionysius wrongly rejected as unauthentic the speech for Iphicrates based on a miscalculation of the date of Lysias' death.
32 Hansen 1975, 91. Against this interpretation, see the arguments of Tuplin 1984, 567–568.
33 Hamel 1998, 140–157 (especially nos. 54 and 63 for the *apocheirotoniai*).
34 Hansen 1975, 63–64. Hansen is then obliged to invent a possible "symbolic fine" (Hansen 1975, 64 n. 47). Hamel 1998, 136–137 lists five trials against generals found guilty between 431 and 322 with unknown sentences (on 38).
35 Scafuro 2011, 368 n. 50 acknowledges this problem and recalls a situation where the generals get their office back (Dem. 58.27-28). Most recently, she proposes the idea that the reinstatement occurred in the next meeting of the Assembly and not because of a trial: see Scafuro 2018, 207–209.
36 MacDowell 1978, 169. See also Tuplin 1984, 566 n. 84 and Hamel 1998, 123 n. 2. Scafuro 2018, 206 n. 27 rather thinks that the Pseudo-Aristotle reports what is customary and not statutory: *stratēgoi* do not always get their office back after acquittal.
37 See Hansen 1975, 45 and Tuplin 1984, 567.
38 Scafuro 2011, 373 n. 70, resumed in Scafuro 2018, 213–214.

lodorus takes advantage of the remoteness of the *eisangelia* to elaborate a story suitable to his own interests.[39]

We may even wonder if the *eisangelia* against Timotheus actually existed. Never mentioned in the other sources, the accusation of the general is only a projection from the speech of Apollodorus that does not explicitly say the word. It would then be possible to think that Apollodorus uses the *eisangelia* against Antimachus, Timotheus' treasurer, to extrapolate a charge against Timotheus, thanks to the temporal distance of the trial.[40] This version would enable us to reconcile all the different statements related to this case: Timotheus has been subject to an *apocheirotonia*, that led some people to bring an *eisangelia* against Antimachus – because the financial problems were the main issue –, but Timotheus, even if he probably played a role in the defence of Antimachus, was not accused and, therefore, had no penalty but could not be reinstated in office. He may well have fled because of his *euthynai*, that has not been accounted for since there is no necessity brought by the inexistent *eisangelia*.

2 Playing with the timeline: An unstructured speech?

Apollodorus then talks about the Assembly's resentment towards Timotheus during the *eisangelia* (§ 13). It is interesting to note that this mention appears three sections after the account of the ending of the trial, but that is still the same sentence (§ 9–14). Scafuro describes it as a "monstrous sentence" and "one of the most poorly constructed and circular sentences in the corpus".[41] To analyze this development, scholars often highlighted Apollodorus' composition

---

39 See Scafuro 2018, 214: "Apollodoros' statement about Timotheus skipping town to avoid accountability is slanderous legal persiflage of the sort that Apollodoros was adept at producing – and who would notice, when he delivers the speech ca. ten years after the events to which he alludes?"
40 On the contrary, Roberts 1982, 42–43 offers an interesting explanation, with a strong list of arguments, about Timotheus' acquittal. But all of these are contradictory to Antimachus' death that is yet decided at the same time, as she acknowledges (Roberts 1982, 201 n. 54).
41 Scafuro 2011, 367 n. 48. Schaefer 1856, 190 ("ein wahres Ungetüm eines Satzes"). See also Trevett 1992, 107 ("the mammoth sentence") and Usher 1999, 340 ("one of the longest sentences in Greek literature").

difficulties, following criticisms of his style.⁴² But it is not necessarily a problem of oratorical skills: Apollodorus might have done it on purpose.⁴³ Indeed, Apollodorus' goal may be to conceal that the *eisangelia* does not concern Timotheus but Antimachus, and therefore needs to obliterate anything that may bring to mind Timotheus' great deeds. Thus, as Scafuro notes, the speaker refers to the "later" expedition (τὸν ὕστερον ἔκπλουν, § 6)⁴⁴ – the one that led him to be subjected to a trial according to Apollodorus –, but he forgets everything else. First, he never mentions Timotheus' successful "earlier expedition" in 375/4 against Corcyra and Alyzeia. The expression is even problematic later, when Apollodorus speaks of Timotheus as "sailing out on the later occasion while serving as general (στρατηγῶν τὸ ὕστερον)" (§ 8).⁴⁵ The construction of the sentence, close to the anacolouthon, gives the impression that Timotheus was *stratēgos* for the "second" time when he had already been general in 376/5: Apollodorus conceals his previous actions. Then, the statement "the later" avoids listing Timotheus' other acts of bravery, whereas he became very important in Athens in the 360s, being elected *stratēgos* on several occasions and taking Samos in 366, Sestos in 365/4 and Potidaea in 364/3.⁴⁶ He enjoys great prestige and has received many rewards.⁴⁷ Apollodorus thus takes care to speak of feelings that prevailed in the Assembly towards him "at that time" (τότε,

---

42 See Gernet 1959, 12: "Ils [Ses discours] sont tous mal composés, avec des interruptions et des reprises, des redites dans les choses et les mots, du bavardage." See also MacDowell, 2009, 105 ("such an ill written text"). This perceptive begins to change: see how Apollodorus used performance elements in his speeches to influence his audience in Kapparis 2019 (especially 288–290 and 296 on Dem. 49: Kapparis stresses the use of indirect and direct discourse). Kapparis points out the many different techniques that Apollodorus adopted from speech to speech and his ability to tell a lively and likely story which is entertaining for the members of the jury and capable of creating strong emotions in them.

43 My analysis is in line with the conclusions of Trevett 1992, 77, who wants to show "that the speeches [of Apollodorus] are not only competently written but also display a number of interesting features" and to pay attention "to the particular circumstances and demands of the individual cases for which they were written. Forensic speeches were practical works, written with the primary purpose of persuading the jurors to vote in favour of the speaker. They should therefore be judged in the first instance by their effectiveness in performing this function." See the whole chapter (77–110), even if, unfortunately, it devotes very little time to the narrative in speech 49 (88).

44 See Scafuro 2011, 365 n. 39.

45 See Scafuro 2011, 366 n. 43.

46 Isoc. 15.111–113, Din. 1.14, Diod. Sic. 15.81.6, Nep. *Tim.* 1.2–3, Polyaen. *Strat.* 3.10.7–10.

47 Dem. 20.84, 23.202, Aesch. 3.243. See also the praise for Timotheus in Isoc. 15.111–112, Dem. 15.9. On the statue erected for Timotheus in the Agora, see Tod 1962, 88–90 (no. 128) and Gauthier 1985, 102–103.

§ 13): he removes his actions after and before 373. This is a rhetorical way to stress the state of mind at the only time when Timotheus was not appreciated.

The construction of the extended sentence (§ 9–14) points to the same direction. After discussing the *eisangelia* (§ 9–10), Apollodorus goes backwards to tell the jurors about the debt of 7 minas that Timotheus owes to each of the sixty trierarchs (that is, 42,000 drachmae all in all) and about his fear that they give testimony against him during the *eisangelia* (§ 11–12).[48] Afterward, the orator does the same by returning to the Boeotian trierarchs to whom Timotheus distributes 1,000 drachmae, thanks to the loan of Philip via Antiphanes, to persuade them not to defect before the judgment (§ 14–15).[49] The general is also afraid that Philip may testify against him during the *eisangelia*, and that is why Pasio lent him 1,000 drachmae (§ 16–17): this is the second loan owed to Apollodorus' father. The whole sentence is therefore intended "to exhaust and confuse the hearer",[50] but these movements backwards and forwards in the timeline are also made to draw the jurors' attention to the *eisangelia* and especially to bring back the shadow cast by this moment on events that have nothing to do with it.

Apollodorus proceeds in the same way throughout the whole speech, based on constant reiterations, as Blass already noted.[51] *Eisangelia* itself is again mentioned, albeit implicitly, § 67. Above all, the detail of the four loans seems to follow a chronological progression but is actually separated into multiple parts, much more so than the division between narrative and evidence requires: for instance, the third loan is discussed five times (see Table 1: § 22–24, 31–32, 33, 55–58 and 62–64).[52] The same is true for the calling of evidence. Just after the end of the presentation of the second loan, which brought him back to the *eisangelia* four times, Apollodorus promises that he will provide testimonies, including that of Phormio and Antiphanes, "but, he told the jurors, only when I've told you about the other loan; this way, by hearing about the entire debt in the same deposition, you may know that I speak truly" (§ 18).[53] He thus post-

---

[48] On the potential threat of a general's colleagues and subordinates, see Hamel 1998, 119–121.
[49] On the place of Boeotian trierarchs in Athenian troops during the Second Athenian Confederacy, see Hamel 1998, 108–109.
[50] Trevett 1992, 107.
[51] Blass 1893, 525. Trevett 1992, 95–96 shows, on the contrary, that the organization is built in order to find the best way to convince the jurors.
[52] He indicates also without giving details that there have been an arbitration (§ 34, 44) and an exchange of oaths (§ 42, 65–67).
[53] All the extant translations come from the *Oratory in Classical Athens* series (transl. Scafuro for *Against Timotheus*).

pones these testimonies of 15 paragraphs, since they are produced at § 33, which is extremely unusual in forensic speeches. He therefore creates a new loop effect. Although he is careful to describe with precise details the moment of all the transactions,[54] Apollodorus plays on the temporal structure of his indictment to convince the jurors.

Tab. 1: Structure of the speech *Against Timotheus*.

§	Theme	Including
Proem (1–5)		
1–3	Overall presentation	The loan took place without pledge or witness
4	Cause of the trial	
5	Explanation of Apollodorus' knowledge	Bankers keep records of payments
Narrative (6–32)		
6–9	First loan	
9–21	Second loan	*Eisangelia* (9–10) Notification of the future calling of witnesses (18)
22–24	Third loan	
25–33	Fourth loan	Timotheus fled to the Great King to avoid his accounts (25)
31–32	Third loan	
Proof (33–67)		
33	Testimonies	Testimonies regarding the second, third and fourth loans
34–41	Fourth loan	Probability-arguments
42–44	Other proofs	Apollodorus' oath proposal at arbitration (42), testimony regarding Pasio's credits (42), bank records (43–44)
44–47	First loan	Probability-argument
48–54	Second loan	Probability-arguments
55–58	Third loan	Summons to torture (55–56) and probability-argument
59–61	Fourth loan	Probability-arguments and testimony (61)
62–64	Third loan	Probability-arguments
65–67	Oath summonses	Reference to the *eisangelia* (67)
Conclusion (68–69)		
68–69	Conclusion	Summary of the speech and call for the goodwill of jurors

---

54 Usher 1999, 340.

3 Appealing to the jurors' memory: A way to prove a statement?

The testimonies called in § 33 do not concern the *eisangelia* but the loans. So how does Apollodorus back up his precise statements about the indictment of Timotheus before the people? He addressed the jurors as follows: "you who heard these reports in the Assembly at that time recall how each of you felt about him, for you know the arguments that were made (ὧν ἀκούοντες ὑμεῖς ἐν τῷ δήμῳ τότε ἀναμνήσθητε πῶς ἕκαστος περὶ αὐτοῦ τὴν γνώμην εἶχεν· οὐ γὰρ ἀγνοεῖτε τὰ λεγόμενα)." (§ 13) Apollodorus refers to the knowledge of the jurors who listen to him. Asking the audience to remember the *eisangelia* without calling evidence about it turns the jurors into his own witnesses. This is not uncommon in forensic speeches, such as Demosthenes in *Against Meidias*: "For all these events that took place in the Assembly (ἐν τῷ δήμῳ) or in front of the judges in the theater, I have all you, men of the court, as witnesses (ὑμεῖς ἐστέ μοι μάρτυρες πάντες, ἄνδρες δικασταί). And one must certainly regard as most reliable any statements that those who are seated here testify to be true."[55] He mentions here the problems he had with his opponent during the preparation of his chorus, but this sentence could be pronounced by Apollodorus when he reminds the jurors of their place in the Assembly (ἐν τῷ δήμῳ). Members of the audience are therefore supposed to nod to the litigant's narrative, loudly signify their approbation or even talk to each other.[56] The noise that spreads among the jurors (*thorybos*) then acts as proof of the argument.[57]

In order to turn jurors into witnesses, Apollodorus assimilates the persons present in the courtroom to those who were in the Assembly ten years earlier, assuming that they were already citizens at that date and that they had no other business to deal with on that day.[58] This is a recurring strategy in the corpus of forensic orators, even if this topic has been a matter of debate. M. Hansen has demonstrated that only the Assembly is regarded as the *dēmos*: the jurors are only a fraction of the *dēmos* and can be referred to member of an ecclesiastic meeting because of the actual overlap in personnel.[59] J. Ober, on the other hand,

---

[55] Dem. 21.18, transl. Harris. See Siron 2019, 236–240 ("Le témoignage des juges").
[56] Bonner 1979, 85: "If only part of the jurors know, it was customary to ask them to inform those who sat near them." On the discussion between the jurors, see And. 1.37, 46, 69, Din. 1.42.
[57] On the *thorybos* in trials, see Bers 1985, especially 9–10, and more recently Sato 2020 (with bibliography).
[58] However, absenteeism was important during Assembly sessions.
[59] Hansen 1983, especially 140–148.

stated that the jurors stand for the whole citizen body as the Assembly, in a metaphorical perspective.[60] But the synthesis of A. Wolpert is quite convincing: the speakers build from the accurate overlap in personnel a larger metaphorical group of Athenian standing for the whole citizen body and transcending time and place, that is, including the citizens of the past.[61]

Litigants frequently appeal to the memory and, more generally, the knowledge of the jurors to testify to a point: there are more than two hundred occurrences identified for the memory and more than two hundred and fifty for the knowledge.[62] The scholars called it "the 'you all know' *topos*" to highlight the commonplace resulting from misleading expressions seeking to hide the lack of evidence.[63] S. Todd claims that, in the Demosthenic corpus, speakers adjust their speech to their audience by making a distinction between public and private trials: the sentence introduced by "many of you know" refers more to private matters while the phrase "you all know" applies to events in the public domain.[64] Apollodorus' assertion, which does not explicitly mention "all" jurors but involves the entire audience who came to listen to him, is consistent with this interpretation. Finally, some scholars have shown that litigants attempt, through these statements, to appear on a level with the jurors, in order to avoid appearing condescending.[65]

On the contrary, M. Canevaro has recently stated that speakers do not take such precautions: "references to the memory of the past [...] cannot be taken as evidence of the orators' restraint and reluctance to demonstrate an extensive knowledge of history, but are rather ways in which they claimed authority for their stories".[66] Furthermore, Canevaro has shown that the Athenians did not necessarily have the common knowledge that orators allege: litigants use such allusions to common knowledge as a rhetorical loophole to gain the trust of

---

60 Ober 1996, 118–119.
61 Wolpert 2003, especially 538–539.
62 Siron 2019, 225–233 ("L'expérience des juges") and 241–249 ("Formules pour se souvenir"). The first mention of the phenomenon comes from Bonner 1979, 84–85 ("The Personal Knowledge of the Jurors").
63 Leisi 1907, 110, Nouhaud 1982, 306, Ober 1989, 149, Hesk 2000, 227–231, from notably Arist. *Rhet.* 3.7 (1408a32–36) and Dem. 40.53–54. About this last occurrence, see Wolpert 2003, 541 n. 13: "Far from calling into question the "you all know" *topos*, Mantitheus reaffirmed it."
64 Todd 2007, 661.
65 Pearson 1941 (especially 218–219), Perlman 1961, 153, Ober 1989, 181, Wolpert 2003, 540, Steinbock 2013, 42–43.
66 Canevaro 2019, 147.

their hearers about questionable or false statements.⁶⁷ This is the exact goal of Apollodorus. The limit of Canevaro's explanation is the generalization of the members of the jury as a homogeneous group: why should they all have forgotten? The litigants themselves make the difference between older and younger jurors.⁶⁸ Moreover, Apollodorus' statement implies that he is aware of discrepancies among jurors: he asks "each" (ἕκαστος) member of the audience to remember. It thus divides the jurors in order to isolate them and prevent a potentially harmful communication between them. He then relies on the noise produced by general consensus to influence their decision before they take the time to recall the exact circumstances that occurred ten years earlier.⁶⁹ The voice of someone who finally disagrees is drowned out in the crowd's tumult.

4 Conclusion

The study of the speech *Against Timotheus* demonstrates Apollodorus' ability to play with the construction of his narrative in order to cover up the good reputation of his opponent by highlighting one particular moment of his career. The endless back and forth movement through time gives the opportunity to recall several times the *eisangelia* and to cast a shadow on all the events described. Through a style deemed poor, he manages to manipulate reality, which is now unknowable. The dispute between Timotheus and Pasio's son also permitted an analysis of the way to confirm accounts of the recent past, by calling for jurors' testimony, a strategy that involves a game with the public (*thorybos*). Even if, in the Assembly, the *thorybos* can work as a way to reinforce the sovereignty of the *dēmos* upon the skills of the orators,⁷⁰ Apollodorus seems here able to take into

---

67 Canevaro 2019, 151–157. See also Kapellos 2018.
68 For instance, And. 2.26, Ant. 5.71, 74, Dem. 20.68, 77, 57.60, 59.30, Aesch. 2.150, Isae. 7.13, Isocr. 6.52, 7.64, 66, 8.12, 14.56, 16.4, Lys. 2.72. See Bonner 1979, 85 and Wolpert 2003, 550.
69 The influence of the *thorybos* is similar in the Assembly after Nicias' speech (Thuc. 6.24): "And so, on account of the exceeding eagerness of the majority, even if anyone was not satisfied, he held his peace, in the fear that if he voted in opposition he might seem to be disloyal to the state". Tacon 2001, 186 comments: "Ecclesiastic *thorubos* generated by a large section of those present was allegedly such a powerful influencing force as to cow the few opponents to Nicias into submission".
70 Villacèque 2013, 296–304. On how the speakers incite *thorybos*, on the contrary, see Bers 1985, 6–15.

account the diversity of his audience and to play with its differentiated knowledge in order to win his case, as he did.[71]

Timotheus' indictment by Apollodorus soon became itself a part of the recent past, since the orator, possibly inspired by his reference to an *eisangelia* against Timotheus, launches four *eisangeliai* between 362 and 360, including one against Timotheus.[72] Even if the outcome of this trial is not known, it is certain that Timotheus suffered once again an *eisangelia* in 356 and was sentenced this time to pay a large fine: he had to go into exile.[73]

Bibliography

Bers, V. (1985), "Dikastic *Thorubos*", in: P.A. Cartledge/F.D. Harvey (eds.), *Crux: Essays in Greek History Presented to G. E. M. de Ste. Croix on his 75th Birthday*, London/Exeter, 1–15.
Blass, F. (1893), *Die attische Beredsamkeit*, III, 1: *Demosthenes*, Leipzig [1877].
Bonner, R.J. (1979), *Evidence in Athenian Courts*, Chicago [1905].
Canevaro, M. (2019), "Memory, the Orators, and the Public in Fourth-Century BC Athens", in: L. Castagnoli/P. Ceccarelli (eds.), *Greek Memories. Theories and Practices*, Cambridge, 136–157.
Carey, C. (ed.) (2007), *Lysiae Orationes cum Fragmentis*, Oxford.
Cargill, J. (1981), *The Second Athenian League: Empire or Free Alliance?*, Berkeley.
Davies, J.K. (1971), *Athenian Propertied Families. 600-300 B.C.*, Oxford.
Dover, K.J. (1968), *Lysias and the Corpus Lysiacum*, Berkeley/Los Angeles.
Gauthier, P. (1985), *Les cités grecques et leurs bienfaiteurs*, Bulletin de Correspondance hellénique, Suppl.12, Paris.
Gernet, L. (ed.) (1957), *Démosthène. Plaidoyers civils*, II, Paris.
Gernet, L. (ed.) (1959), *Démosthène. Plaidoyers civils*, III, Paris.
Gray, V.J. (1980), "The Years 375 to 371 BC: A Case Study in the Reliability of Diodorus Siculus and Xenophon", *CQ* 30/2, 306–326.
Hamel, D. (1998), *Athenian Generals: Military Authority in the Classical Period*, Leiden.
Hansen, M.H. (1975), *Eisangelia. The Sovereignty of the People's Court in Athens in the Fourth Century B.C. and the Impeachment of Generals and Politicians*, Odense.
Hansen, M.H. (1983), "*Demos*, *Ecclesia* and *Dicasterion* in Classical Athens", in: M.H. Hansen, *The Athenian Ecclesia: A Collection of Articles, 1976-1983*, Copenhagen, 139–160 [1978].
Harris, E.M. (1988), "The Date of Apollodorus' Speech against Timotheus and its Implications for Athenian History and Legal Procedure", *AJP* 109, 44–52.
Harrison, A.R.W. (1971), *The Law of Athens*, II: *Procedure*, Oxford.
Hesk, J. (2000), *Deception and Democracy in Classical Athens*, Cambridge.

---

71 Plut. *Dem.* 15.
72 See Hansen 1975, 95–98 (nos. 90–93) and Trevett 1992, 131–138, from Dem. 36.53.
73 See Hansen 1975, 101 (no. 101).

Kapellos, A. (2018), "Lysias Interrogating Eratosthenes on the Murder of Polemarchus (Lys. XII 25)", *Erga-Logoi* 6, 51–64.

Kapparis, K.A. (ed.) (1999), *Apollodoros 'Against Neaira' [D.59]*, Berlin/New York.

Kapparis, K.A. (ed.) (2017), "Narrative and Performance in the Speeches of Apollodoros", in: S. Papaioannou/A. Serafim/B. da Vela (eds.), *The Theatre of Justice. Aspects of Performance in Greco-Roman Oratory and Rhetoric*, Leiden/Boston, 283–303.

Kirchner, J.E. (1901–1903), *Prosopographia Attica*, I/II, Berlin.

Leisi, E. (1907), *Der Zeuge im Attischen Recht*, Frauenfeld.

MacDowell, D.M. (1978), *The Law in Classical Athens*, Ithaca/London.

MacDowell, D.M. (2009), *Demosthenes the Orator*, Oxford.

Mossé, C. (1974), "Les procès politiques et la crise de la démocratie athénienne", *DHA* 1, 207–236.

Nouhaud, M. (1982), *L'utilisation de l'histoire par les orateurs attiques*, Paris.

Ober, J. (1989), *Mass and Elite in Democratic Athens. Rhetoric, Ideology, and the Power of the People*, Princeton.

Ober, J. (1996), *The Athenian Revolution: Essays on Ancient Greek Democracy and Political Theory*, Princeton.

Pearson, L. (1941), "Historical Allusions in the Attic Orators", *CP* 36, 209–229.

Perlman, S. (1961), "The historical example, its use and importance as political propaganda in the Attic orators", *Scripta Hierosolymitana* 7, 150–166.

Queyrel Bottineau, A. (2010), *Prodosia. La notion et l'acte de trahison dans l'Athènes du Ve siècle*, Bordeaux.

Rhodes, P.J. (ed.) (1981), *A Commentary on the Aristotelian Athenaion Politeia*, Oxford.

Rice, D.G. (1997), "Litigation as a Political Weapon: The Case of Timotheos of Athens", in: C.D. Hamilton/P. Krentz (eds.), *Polis and Polemos. Essays on Politics, War, and History in Ancient Greece in Honor of Donald Kagan*, Claremont, 227–240.

Roberts, J.T. (1982), *Accountability in Athenian Government*, Madison.

Rubinstein, L. (2000), *Litigation and Cooperation. Supporting Speakers in the Court of Classical Athens*, Stuttgart (Historia Einzelschriften, 147).

Sato, N. (2020), "Inciting *thorubos* and narratives strategies in attic forensic speeches", in: M. Edwards/D. Spatharas (eds.), *Forensic Narrative in Athenian Courts*, London/New York, 102–118.

Scafuro, A.C. (ed.) (2011), *Demosthenes. Speeches 39–49*, Austin.

Scafuro, A.C. (2018), "*Epicheirotonia* and the so-called '*euthynai* of generals", in: B. Biscotti (ed.), *Kállistos Nómos. Scritti in onore di Alberto Maffi*, Turin, 199–219.

Schaefer, A. (1856), *Demosthenes und seine Zeit*, II, Leipzig.

Sealey, R. (1956), "Callistratos of Aphidna and his Contemporaries", *Historia* 5, 178–203.

Sinclair, R.K. (1993), *Democracy and Participation in Athens*, Cambridge [1988].

Siron, N. (2019), *Témoigner et convaincre. Le dispositif de vérité dans les discours judiciaires de l'Athènes classique*, Paris.

Steinbock, B. (2013), *Social Memory in Athenian Public Discourse. Uses and Meanings of the Past*, Ann Arbor.

Stylianou, P.J. (ed.) (1998), *A Historical Commentary on Diodorus Siculus Book 15*, Oxford.

Tacon, J. (2001), "Ecclesiastic *Thorubos*: Interventions, Interruptions, and Popular Involvement in the Athenian Assembly", *G & R* 48/2, 173–192.

Tod, M.N. (1962), *A Selection of Greek Historical Inscriptions*, II, Oxford [1948].

Todd, S.C. (1993), *The Shape of Athenian Law*, Oxford.

Todd, S.C. (ed.) (2007), *A Commentary on Lysias. Speeches 1–11*, Oxford.
Trevett, J. (1991), "The Date of [Demosthenes] 49: A Re-examination", *Phoenix* 45, 21–27.
Trevett, J. (1992), *Apollodoros the Son of Pasion*, Oxford.
Tuplin, C. (1984), "Timotheos and Corcyra: Problems in Greek History, 375–373 B.C.", *Athenaeum* 62, 537–568.
Usher, S. (1999), *Greek Oratory: Tradition and Originality*, Oxford.
Villacèque, N. (2013), "Θόρυβος τῶν πολλῶν : le spectre du spectacle démocratique", in: A. Macé (ed.), *Le Savoir public. La vocation politique du savoir en Grèce ancienne*, Besançon, 287–312.
Wolpert, A.O. (2003), "Addresses to the Jury in the Attic Orators", *AJP* 124/4, 537–555.

Brad L. Cook
Family Portraits in Demosthenes' Inheritance Speeches: Between Rhetoric & History

Abstract: This chapter shows how Demosthenes in his inheritance speeches, then in his early twenties, speaks of his family at the time of his father's illness and death, over a decade earlier, and the repercussions of that loss. Because of the nature of the estate and Demosthenes' later fame, historians have much mined these speeches. Demosthenes does not, however, tell all that we would like but offers only glimpses within the house, carefully framed to serve his immediate rhetorical goals. This essay articulates the design and purpose of these glimpses to showcase the orator's nascent rhetorical skill in fashioning character portraits, and to qualify, and nuance, the uses that some studies have made of these glimpses into Demosthenes' household.

When we want to study Demosthenes' background, to learn about his personal, intellectual, and political roots, it seems practical to examine the five speeches related to his inheritance, delivered in three trials from 364/3 to 362/1, when he was only twenty to twenty-two years old (Dem. 27–31). Surely he would talk about his family, about the death of his father when he was only seven or eight and how his mother managed to raise him and his younger sister over the next ten years. We might well begin to question such an expectation if we consider that over three decades later, when responding to Aeschines' slander about his supposedly traitorous grandfather and barbarian grandmother, Demosthenes chose to attack Aeschines' parents and say nothing about his own family history.[1] What we find in the inheritance speeches is scarcely more than his silence over thirty years later, in 330. Throughout the five speeches, Demosthenes provides only that information about his family that serves the immediate case, certain details of family happenings within the house and also of business and

---

I thank A. Kapellos, G. Martin, and D. Mirhady for helpful comments in the last stages of writing and I especially thank Kerri J. Hame for reading and improving this essay from its inception to its current form.

---

1 Aesch. 2.22, 78, 93, 127, 180, 183, 3.171–172; Dem. 19.199, 281, 287, 18.129–130, 259–260.

fiscal matters of public knowledge and significance.² Otherwise, the door to further details is kept closed. In our eagerness to learn more about these actual ancient persons, so interesting in their own right, we need to keep the rhetoric of each of these portraits in the foreground before attempting to say more about the history of their lives and their era.

Previous scholars have sought to draw on Demosthenes' inheritance speeches for their research on a variety of topics. The influence of Isaeus, the master of inheritance disputes, has been examined, as well as the old notion that Isaeus wrote Demosthenes' inheritance speeches himself.³ Much ink has been spent studying Demosthenes' description of his father's estate, some questioning his accounting.⁴ Studies on economic and social topics have mined these speeches,⁵ on developments in socio-economic norms,⁶ and on the status and role of Athenian women.⁷ Rhetorical analysis of them is found in MacDowell's masterful book on the Demosthenic corpus, in Mirhady's analysis of the role of documentary evidence in them, and in Usher's stylistic survey of the extant speeches of the Attic orators.⁸ With these rhetorical analyses in mind, I assemble and assess what Demosthenes says in these speeches about the members of his family. Framed within the rhetorical role that he gives them in these speeches, these family portraits can be appreciated for what they originally are, carefully crafted glimpses of his family members, limited to serve his argument. Such limitation calls, in turn, for greater nuance in their use in historical studies.

I begin chronologically with his maternal grandfather Gylon. Demosthenes first mentions him in the second of his two speeches in the prosecution of Aphobus, at the very opening: "Aphobus' lies to you are numerous and immense, but I will attempt to refute first the thing he said that particularly pained

---

2 Carlier 1993, 47. Though small, the body of basic data on Demosthenes' family is occasionally misstated, e.g., Aphobus and Demophon, the nephews of Demosthenes' father, are called his "brothers" in every edition of the *OCD*, from Dobson 1949 to Cawkwell 2012, so too Brun 2015, 82 (though correct elsewhere); Onetor, the (former) brother-in-law of Aphobus is called "his sister's husband", Hunter 1994, 48, so too Brun 2015, 82; that his mother's sister is married to Demochares is said to be unknown by Badian 2000, 14 n. 14, though even her name, Philia, is known from a marble funerary lekythos (*IG* II² 6737a; see Humphreys 2018, 2.931).
3 Usher 1999, 171–183 and note Schaefer 1885–1887, 1.304.
4 Jaeger 1938, 24–25; cf. MacDowell 2009, 30–36.
5 Finley 1952, esp. 17, 39, 67–68, 116; on *eisphora*, Christ 2007 and, still, Ste Croix 1953.
6 Burke 1998, but note Johnstone 2003, 265 n. 86.
7 Hunter 1989a; 1989b; 1994; Foxhall 1996; Cox 1998.
8 MacDowell 2009, 30–58; Mirhady 2000b, 186–198; Usher 1999, 171–183; see also Daix & Fernandez 2017; Ghiggia 2007; Pearson 1972 (and also Pearson 1976, 40–47); and Gernet 1954.

me. He said that my grandfather was in debt to the public treasury" (Dem. 28.1).⁹ Demosthenes' pain over this statement about Gylon, however rhetorically strategic, is presented as an emotional response, a rare occurrence in these speeches,¹⁰ but one guaranteed surely to strike a chord with the jurors. Aphobus actually made two interconnected claims, one about Gylon and one about Demosthenes' father: that Gylon "was in debt (ὤφειλε) to the public treasury", and presumably died in debt, and that Demosthenes' father, because of his father-in-law's supposedly unpaid debt, did not want the guardians to lease the estate, "so as not to put it at risk" (Dem. 28.1), whether some imagined or actual liability would pass from Gylon to the younger Demosthenes.¹¹ The failure of the guardians to lease the estate is the real issue, but Demosthenes' expression of personal pain serves to sharpen attention on his refutation of this distracting and insulting claim about his grandfather and to make the fiscal failure of his guardians even clearer, and thus worthy of condemnation.

Demosthenes questions first the imperfect tense of ὤφειλε, "was in debt", and the implied on-going aspect of his grandfather's debt. The context of the verb is unknown, since Aphobus has not presented any documentation, at least in his first speech. Demosthenes warns the jurors that if Aphobus presents such documentation in his second speech, they must pay close attention to the tense of the verb in that document. That his grandfather *had* been in debt to the public treasury is not disputed by Demosthenes. What he disputes is Aphobus' claim that Gylon was still in debt when he died.¹² The implication is that the documentation presented by Aphobus at the arbitration said only that Gylon "owed" (ὤφλεν) a debt, which proves nothing about his financial status at his death. Demosthenes could not introduce the relevant documentation that the debt had been paid, that "all his (Gylon's) obligations to the city had been settled", because he had "been ambushed" (ἐνηδρεύθημεν) by Aphobus' last minute action (Dem. 28.2). With this rare, dramatic word Demosthenes recalls his initial admission of inexperience "of affairs", as opposed to the guardians' verbal skill and insidious plotting (Dem. 27.2). This bit of self-portraiture enhances the presentation of Aphobus as conniving but, particularly effective here, it creates a pause so that his two counterproofs sound all the more effective,

---

9 Translations are my own.
10 Usher 1999, 176.
11 On inheritance of state debt, even maternally, see Harrison 1968, 127–130, esp. 128 n. 3; Gernet 1918; and Hunter 2000, 29–30; Kapparis 1994, 116.
12 Their arguments assume that Gylon predeceased his father (contra any such "possibility" as Davies 1971, 122).

proofs that require no documentation whatsoever: first, that Demochares, the husband of his grandfather's other daughter, never feared putting his estate "at risk"; second, that the guardians have already publicly admitted to and documented having received four and half talents from his father's estate upon his death. Aphobus' red herring dispelled, we would still like to hear something more about Gylon from his own grandson, but he limits himself to proving that he died debt-free.

Of his father, Demosthenes tells us more. The key, and frequently repeated point, is the first thing that we hear: "Demosthenes, my father, men of the jury, left behind (κατέλιπεν) an estate worth about fourteen talents, as well as me, then seven years old, my sister, age five, and also our mother, who had brought fifty minas into the household" (Dem. 27.4). He then describes how his father "took thought for us" and entrusted them and the estate to three guardians, Aphobus, Demophon, both his nephews, and Therippides, a friend since childhood (Dem. 27.5). He entrusted seventy minas to Therippides for him to use until Demosthenes came of age, at which time he would return the seventy minas. To Demophon, he immediately entrusted two talents (120 minas) to be the dowry for his daughter, whom Demophon was to marry when she came of age. To Aphobus was given Demosthenes Sr.'s widow to marry, with a dowry of 80 minas, and the use of the family's house until Demosthenes came of age. His intent for Therippides, Demosthenes explains, was "that he not manage my affairs at all poorly out a desire for gain", and, for the two nephews, that "if he should make these men even more closely related to me, I would not be treated poorly by guardians who have these additional family connections" (Dem. 27.5). Through this detailed account, describing and explaining his father's intentions, Demosthenes assures the jurors that his father did everything imaginable to safeguard his family's future.

In spite of his careful intentions, ten years later Demosthenes was given an estate valued at seventy minas, consisting of the house, fourteen slaves, and somewhat more than thirty minas cash (Dem. 27.6, 37).[13] That sum is one twelfth the value of the estate at his father's death and less than four percent of thirty talents, the value at which the estate should be after ten years, as will be accepted by the jury. Pointing, then, at this relatively small sum of seventy minas, Demosthenes tells the jurors the most important fact about his father: "he did not leave me (κατέλιπεν) poor" (Dem. 27.8). Variants of this verb, of what his

---

[13] How the fourteen slaves, the remnants of the original thirty-some slaves in the ironworks — half, or so, had been sold as soon as the guardians acquired control (Dem. 27.13, 18, 61) — and house are currently valued at only forty minas is not made clear; see MacDowell 2004, 22 n. 9.

father "left" him or the estate that was "left" him, appear over forty times in the first speech against Aphobus, forming verbally the most prominent feature of Demosthenes' portrait of his father, through which he fashions him as a veritable co-plaintiff.

The majority of Demosthenes' uses of "he left" have the estate as object. The "he did not leave me poor" variant is rare, and that rarity is all the more marked by its strategic placement. It appears in the opening of the speech and again two-thirds of the way through, where Demosthenes presents a summary of the undisputed four and a half talents entrusted to the guardians (Dem. 27.8, 45). This second use of the phrase is poignant and pointed: my father "certainly did not want to leave me, his son, poor, while his heart was set on making these men, who were already rich, richer still" (Dem. 27.45). Then, near the end of the speech, rather than repeat the word "poor", he describes what that poverty will mean: "But I am the most wretched of all people, twice over, at a loss how to dower my sister and by what means to manage the rest of my affairs. The city is insistent on having me pay an *eisphora*, and rightly so, since my father left me (κατέλιπεν) sufficient wealth for doing so, but these man have taken all the money that was left me (καταλειφθέντα)" (Dem. 27.65–66). The jurors now see that they too were to be beneficiaries of his father's good intentions.[14] This private family history has public significance.

Demosthenes closes his first speech not with a recollection of his father but a veritable reviving of him: "I think that my father would groan loudly if he should realize that the very dowries and gifts that he himself gave these men have put me, his own son, at risk of a fine" (Dem. 27.69). This striking *prosopopoeia* may seem overly dramatic, especially with its "groaning", but his one other use of the verb suggests otherwise. In *Against Aristocrates*, written over a decade later to oppose the granting of special status to the Athenian general Charidemus, Demosthenes invokes the Athenian warriors of the past "who died for glory and freedom and left behind memorials of many fine deeds", who, if they knew of this proposal, "would groan greatly indeed" (Dem. 23.210).[15] His reuse of this *prosopopoeia* shows that he did not consider it too dramatic, but something, rather, to be reserved for the right moment. This paternal *prosopopoeia* is particularly effective, because he bases the intensity of his father's groaning on the backfiring of his own plans: rather than restrain their greed, his

---

14 Cf. Dem. 28.19 and MacDowell 2009, 17 and n. 14.
15 Blass 1887–1898, 3.1.177–180, esp. 178 n. 2; Usher 1999, 175; on terms, Lausberg §§ 820–825, 826–829.

efforts enflamed it. The jurors hear yet again key aspects of the injustices against the family in an unexpected, unforgettable form.

After spending most of the first speech on repeating essential financial details and documentation, in his second speech he takes time for an extended account of his father on his deathbed. Here the numbers and details of the will, instead of being listed and relisted as in the first speech, are enacted. Realizing his death was at hand, his father summoned the guardians and, with his brother Demon seated beside him,[16] "he physically placed us in their hands and spoke of us as a deposit;" then, after listing the terms of the will, his father now "placed me on Aphobus' knees" (Dem. 28.15–16). Though Demosthenes frequently uses the plural of himself, in the first action, the clasping of hands, the "us" includes his sister; then, in the final action, the focus is on Demosthenes, as he is placed on Aphobus' knees. The father, whose ghost was about to groan at the end of the first speech, is all but visible to the jurors, embodying the terms of the will, his trust of the guardians, and his intentions for his two small children.

After this portrait of a father, who uses what little time and strength left him to lavish such care on his children, we wonder what Demosthenes can say of his mother.[17] His first mention of her is rather financial, the gloss about her "bringing fifty minas into the household" (Dem. 27.4).[18] She appears again briefly in this financial role in Demosthenes' inventory of the estate: "also a house worth 3.000 drachmas, and furniture, cups, gold jewelry (χρυσία), and clothes, my mother's trousseau (κόσμον), all of which was together worth about 10.000 drachmas" (Dem. 27.10). Out of this total, "in accordance with the will", Aphobus "took my mother's gold jewelry (τὰ χρυσία) and the cups that had been left behind", valued at 50 minas, and kept them as part of the dowry for the intended marriage (Dem. 27.13). Moments later we are told that Aphobus was failing to maintain the house and that his excuse is that there was "a little issue (μικρόν) to be discussed with my mother about some small items of jewelry (περὶ χρυσιδίων), after which Aphobus claims that, everything "would be fine for Demosthenes" (Dem. 27.15). This continued presentation of his mother in financial terms fulfills Demosthenes' need to be objective about the value of the estate,

---

16 On Demon's role see MacDowell 1989.
17 He never uses her name, per custom (Gagarin 2001; see still Schaps 1977); its earliest appearance is in [Plut.] *Mor.* 844A.
18 On dowries, and their size, see Schaps 1979, 74–84, 99; her dowry is sizable but not such as to suggest, as Will 2013, 22, and others, any peculiar significance, relative to Gylon or otherwise.

while illustrating Aphobus' greed. Whether, reminded by his mother, Demosthenes was recalling Aphobus' exact language for the compounding of "little", μικρόν, and the diminutive "bits of jewelry", χρυσίδια, such language makes Aphobus sound like the sophist that Demosthenes later calls him, especially since Demosthenes leaves the jurors to conclude that things did not go "fine" for Demosthenes.[19]

Throughout the initial accounting of the estate his mother is presented as passive. Even in his account of the dispute over the pieces of jewelry, it is Demochares, his mother's brother-in-law, who intervened and called on Aphobus to support the family properly. We are told nothing further of this confrontation, or of his mother's role in it. Only once in the speech are we given a glimpse of the otherwise seemingly silent role of his mother. Just over halfway through the speech, Demosthenes pauses and observes that the jurors have learned by then enough about the extent of the guardians' thefts. He adds, though, that they would have even fuller knowledge if the guardians would hand over the will, "in which had been written, as my mother tells me, all that my father left behind" (Dem. 27.40). It is, then, his mother's indirect testimony about the will that forms the foundation of his case. He has acquired and presented an abundance of documentation for an army of details, but the specific claims that prompted him to acquire that documentation arose from the stories about his father and the will, told him by his mother.

Except for this citation of his mother as the verbalized source of the will's content, Demosthenes has described no action of his mother's in the past. The only time that he parts the curtains to show her active is for a very recent action. After he was found guilty, Aphobus brought a suit for false witness against a certain Phanus, who had testified for the first case that Aphobus had admitted that Milyas, the supervisor of the family's ironworks, had been set free by Demosthenes' father on his deathbed, and so could not be subject to judicial torture, βάσανος, with regard to a question about the workshop's income in the two years following his father's death.[20] Demosthenes delivers a supporting speech for Phanus,[21] in which, as a *synegoros*, he makes arguments for which he

---

[19] Hunter 1989b, 42, has mislabeled Demosthenes' focused use of his narrative here as being "immensely evasive"; moreover it is not Demosthenes who is "dismissive" with the use of the diminutive χρυσίδια but rather Aphobus.
[20] On βάσανος in general see Mirhady 2000a, 53–55. For a detailed investigation of Aphobus' inconsistent claims about Milyas' status see Thür 1972.
[21] Dem. 29, *Against Aphobus for Phanus*, confusingly labeled often as *Against Aphobus 3*; see MacDowell 2009, esp. 45–47 and n. 31 for discussion of any questions about the speech's age and authorship.

has particular knowledge, spending most of the speech reviewing details already presented in the original trial against Aphobus. One passage, however, is wholly new, since the scene described occurred in preparation for this new trial, and his mother plays the central role.

Near the midpoint of his speech, to reinforce the fact that Milyas had been set free by his father, Demosthenes reports that he gave Aphobus the opportunity to subject to *basanos* the slave women in his household who "remember that he had been set free at that time", when his father was dying (Dem. 29.25). To reinforce the significance of that challenge, he narrates how: "my mother was willing, having stood me and my sister beside her, her only children, for whose sake she remained a widow, to swear by us a pledge that he had been set free by my father as he lay dying and was considered among us as free" (Dem. 29.26).[22] He speaks again of this scene only minutes later in the speech, using this same vivid participle, "having stood me and my sister beside her", though there the point of the pledge was that Aphobus was in possession of the dowry (Dem. 29.33). In his closing review, he speaks again of the proposed pledge in regard to Milyas' status (Dem. 29.56). This repeated scene of his mother placing her now adult children beside her to swear this pledge calls to mind the scene of her dying husband not simply freeing Milyas but also entrusting his then small children into the care of these ruthless guardians. The weight of this pledge is made even greater by an additional glimpse into his mother's life, a glimpse not of a recent, brief action but of her life ever since her husband died, some thirteen years prior. With that brief clause, "for whose sake she lived as a widow", Demosthenes declares that it was his mother's choice not to remarry. That she offers to make this pledge is in itself a very serious matter, but the addition of this detail of her remaining a widow bespeaks her dedication of more than a decade to raise her children. The cumulative portrait of his mother, spoken of only briefly when a young widow but now seen offering a most solemn oath in defense of her children, fulfilled traditional expectations and was rhetorically effective.[23]

If Demosthenes has been discrete about his mother, observing Pericles' classic advice,[24] he says even less of his sister, but she was only five years old at the time of their father's death (Dem. 27.4). In listing the essential terms of the

---

22 On such oaths Konstantinidou 2014, 41–42.
23 Though Hunter 1989b, 41 finds this to be "not even effective rhetoric".
24 Thuc. 2.45.2; tradition attributes to Demosthenes an extraordinary interest in and knowledge of Thucydides' text, especially the speeches; see Fromentin and Gotteland 2015, 19–20; Westwood 2019, 183–184.

will he says that she was affianced by their father to his nephew Demophon, to whom immediate control of her two-talent dowry was granted (Dem. 27.5, 45).²⁵ Otherwise, though some of his first-person plural vocabulary may include her, it is only at the end of the speech that she appears again. In a variation on the customary use of wife and children to draw sympathy from the jurors for a person being prosecuted, Demosthenes calls to mind the jurors' merciful custom of leaving a guilty litigant with enough resources to maintain a pitiable family and sets that in stark contrast to how their guardians have treated them: they feel no shame, no pity "for my sister, if she, who was thought worthy of two talents by our father, gets not a drachma of what she deserves" (Dem. 27.65). In the end of his second speech, Demosthenes brings the family together to appeal to the jurors not to overlook "my mother and me and my sister" in their unjust suffering (Dem. 28.19). He adds a closing vignette about his mother, sitting at home and waiting to hear that he has won the case so he can "take care of her and give my sister in marriage" (Dem. 28.21). All the fathers and brothers in the jury now knew that they would, if they so voted, be aiding not just Demosthenes, and his mother, but also his sister, of whom they, and we, only know two things, that she was just then of marriageable age and that her father intended her to have a dowry of two talents, which was quite large.²⁶

There is one later occasion when Demosthenes speaks about these trials, and there he makes mention of both his mother and sister. In his speech *Against Meidias*, written for a trial in 347/6, though Demosthenes is charging Meidias with "acting unjustly in regard to the festival" of Dionysus of the previous spring (Dem. 21.1), he weaves in mention of the conflict with his guardians over fifteen years prior. Just after he finishes the main narration of the events relevant to the case, he pauses to explain to the jurors the origins of the hatred that had developed between Meidias and him, which dates back to the legal conflicts with his guardians (Dem. 21.77). He describes how young and inexperienced he was, calling himself "an absolute kid" (μειρακύλλιον ὢν κομιδῇ, Dem. 21.78), which would sound comical, if the risks, particularly financial, were not so great.²⁷ He narrates how,²⁸ only days before the trial against Aphobus was to

---

25 Cf. Dem. 28.15, 19; 29.43, 45.
26 How large a dowry Demosthenes was able to give he when she was married to her cousin Laches, son of Demochares and her mother's sister, sometime in the 350s, is unknown; like her mother, she had a son who became a prominent Athenian orator, Demochares, but of her we know nothing else (MacDowell 2009, 17).
27 Cf. νέος at Dem. 21.80; on the *topos* of calling oneself ἄπειρος, as at Dem. 27.2, see Daix and Fernandez 2017, 46–47, 124–125; though he was only twenty years old in that first speech, the text already manifests his perspicacious analysis of the situation at hand and his effective

take place, Meidias' brother, Thrasylochus, and Meidias "barged into "Demosthenes' house and demanded that Demosthenes either take on a joint-trierarchy with which Thrasylochus was charged, costing 20 minas, or to exchange properties, by the curious procedure of *antidosis* (Dem. 21.78).[29] Demosthenes, "not at all realizing the implications of these actions" (Dem. 28.17) — with the exchange of properties would go his ability to sue his guardians — initially agreed to the *antidosis*. Thrasylochus immediately, then and there, attempted to start taking stock of the house and its contents before Demosthenes could, presumably, hide anything: "First they broke open the doors into the rooms of the house, treating them as already belonging to them in accordance with the exchange of properties" (Dem. 21.79). As Thrasylochus and Meidias started forcing doors open, they, unsurprisingly, came upon Demosthenes' sister, who "was still then at home, a young maiden" all the while mouthing foul, unrepeatable things "in front of her", and, he adds, "they let loose against my mother and me and all of us every kind of abuse" (Dem. 21.79). These unsavory details are discreetly avoided in the earlier speeches; their shock value would have distracted the jurors too much from the main villain in the 360s, Aphobus.[30]

The way Demosthenes ends his list of people insulted by Thrasylochus and Meidias, "and all of us", appears to include the slaves, and perhaps even Milyas, who, as supervisor (ἐπίτροπος, Dem. 27.19) of the ironworks, which was in or attached to the house, likely still lived in the house, even though he had been

---

deployment of courtroom rhetoric (any *youthful* speech impediment, per the embroidered tales in the biographical tradition, was well in hand by then, and the early difficulties in delivery, as reported, were an issue in some early effort in the Assembly, not in the courtroom).

28 For my reconstruction of the events see Kennedy (1852–1863) 4.116 n. 1; cf. MacDowell 1990, 295–299 and 2009, 38–40 (despite Harris 2008, 114 n. 132 and 2005, 137–138; Badian 2000, 17 uses the difference in accounts as part of his invalid claim that Dem. 27 and 28 were not written by Demosthenes).

29 Gabrielsen 1987.

30 Usher 1999, 177. As for the rest, Demosthenes got them out of the house, assuming that Thrasylochus would initiate a *diadikasia* — in which the court would decide in his favor — but for the present he was expecting that a *diadikasia* would put the exchange of properties in limbo so that the prosecution of his guardians could proceed. Thrasylochus, however, did not initiate a *diadikasia* but did something "most shocking", far worse than their verbal assault on the household: he declared that he was terminating the legal proceedings against Demosthenes' guardians since now "the suits were their business" (Dem. 21.79). Demosthenes immediately responded by reversing his initial agreement to accept the exchange of property, mortaged his house to get the necessary twenty minas, and handed the money to Thrasylochus, which amount he had *already* paid as his portion of the joint-trierarchy (Dem. 21.80), all of this taking place within a day or two, perhaps three, before the trial against Aphobus took place.

manumitted by Demosthenes Sr. on his deathbed. Milyas unexpectedly became a key figure in the trial of 362/1 when Aphobus sued one of Demosthenes' witness, Phanus, for false witness in the original trial against him, since he had testified, along with others, that Aphobus had previously admitted that Milyas had been manumitted. Demosthenes insists that Aphobus had constructed a legal attack merely to try to rouse pity for himself because he now owed Demosthenes ten talents (Dem. 29.2). Milyas, and his status over the past dozen years, may have been the only thing that Aphobus could think to attack, but one wonders whether there was some prejudice against freedmen that he sought to rouse in the jurors.[31] But the quantity and character of the written testimony mustered by Demosthenes, which includes Aphobus' earlier admission that Milyas had been freed, seems legally unassailable. Above all, his mother's current offer to swear on the head of her two children shows that Milyas' status had been and was an on-going family concern (Dem. 29.26, 56).

This presentation of the family's concern for Milyas may initially seem to be in bizarre contrast to how he speaks of those still enslaved in the household. Foremost is the literate slave whom Demosthenes takes with him as a transcriber on many occasions, including when Aphobus admitted that Milyas had been manumitted (Dem. 29.11–12, 17–21, 52, 55). He speaks also of serving women who were in the household fifteen years earlier and who, "while my father was dying, remember that he then set this man free" (Dem. 29.25). Third, he speaks of another set of similarly long-serving household slaves who know that Aphobus was selling raw materials, ivory and iron, from the workshop (Dem. 29.38, 56). Demosthenes mentions these slaves at different points in this speech but all for the same reason, to offer them all to Aphobus to verify under torture their respective claims. Of the first slave he becomes quite detailed, delineating how this slave, who knows his letters, was "ordered by us not to do anything corruptly, not to write down part and leave out part of what this man said about these matter, but simply to write down the whole truth, whatever he said" (Dem. 29.11). Demosthenes provocatively asks, "What better way, then, was there to convict us of lying than by torturing this slave?" (Dem. 29.12). Do we conclude from this passage, and from his offering of other slaves for *basanos*, that Demosthenes was "blithely" offering up any and every household slave for torture?[32] No. His question, "What better way ...?", is how he highlights what this slave has accomplished, the original documenting of Aphobus' statement

---

[31] Cf. the disputed status of Cittus, a slave of the banker Pasion, Isocr., *Trap.* (17), esp. 11–17.
[32] Sternberg 2006, 172.

and now, by Aphobus' refusal to subject him to *basanos*, that what he wrote really is what Aphobus admitted. Such is the case with the other slaves as well.

These three examples of proposed slave torture fall into the category of what Mirhady has called "a rhetorical tactic without any intention on the part of the challenger to have a *basanos* carried out."[33] The slave-scribe would only be confirming what documented witnesses have already said (Dem. 29.30–33); the serving women would likewise be supporting that same testimony, though from their own experience of the original event (Dem. 29.26); and the other household slaves would be supporting the documentation that Demosthenes already had about materials in the workshop (Dem. 27.33, 28.13). They were not at any risk of torture, and Demosthenes knew that. The effect is to show that the entire household stands with Demosthenes to prove his case, and to save the household. Their presence in these speeches is as supporting players in Demosthenes' carefully planned marshalling of evidence and argument.

These glimpses of family portraits are all that Demosthenes reveals about his family history. The slightness of these glimpses results from his focus on the rhetorical needs of these speeches. But this reticence about his family has left openings that scholars have too often filled with problematic interpretations. Of Gylon, some moderns persist in treating as historical evidence the slanderous attacks stirred up by Aeschines decades later,[34] in which Aeschines was likely attempting to drawn on suspicions as old as these very inheritance trials. Failing to appreciate Aeschines' ingeniousness, these moderns have not heeded Clinton's comment on this very issue made at the dawn of modern, critical historiography: "Some deduction ought in reason to be made from the charges of an adversary, which are not to be considered as containing strict historical truth."[35] The only thing that Demosthenes' reticence about his maternal grandfather proves is his efficient and effective rhetoric to refute Aphobus' claim by spotlighting two very different sums of money: what the guardians admittedly took from the estate and what his uncle, married to Gylon's other daughter, had expended on public liturgies. Demosthenes' father has, in turn, been labeled by

---

[33] Mirhady 2000a, 55.
[34] E.g., Cohen 2000, 76, citing Davies 1971, 121; Badian 2000, 13–14, on Aesch. 3.171–172, cf. 2.78, 93, 127, 171, 180, 183; cf. the same attempt by Dinarchus in the 323 trials over the Harpalus affair, esp. Din., *Ag. Dem.* 15, 95.
[35] Clinton 1834–1851, 2^3.432 note f, originally in response to Mitford's extraordinary account of Gylon; cf. Thirlwall 1855, 5.355 n.1, and, more recently, MacDowell 2009, 15–17; Carey in Waterfield and Carey 2014, vii, esp. n. 2. On affairs in the Crimea, note Minns 1913, 561 and, at length, Moreno 2007, 166–167, 174–176 (though he states without qualification that Gylon married "into the Scythian nobility", 167).

some scholars, just as illegitimately, a tax evader.[36] Of his mother, rather than what have been mistakenly called rhetorical flaws in his careful portrait of her,[37] we should recognize Demosthenes' praise of her,[38] which makes us want to know more about her, and her sister and any family ties back to the Black Sea.[39] Of Milyas, Demosthenes does not merely insist that he had become free and had been so since his father's death, he delineates repeatedly his many efforts and arguments to prove that.[40]

However much some historical interpretations need to be adjusted, or corrected, what I insist readers of Demosthenes should not miss is the opportunity to observe the slight glimpses that Demosthenes gives of his family. But just as these courtroom speeches are not objective, transparent source texts for historians, so they are not pages from a diary or youthful memoir. They are rhetorical portraits composed by a young man who has lived since the age of seven in the aftermath of his father's death and the resentment at the economic abuse of his guardians, two of whom were his first cousins. This is not simply a fight for his inheritance but a response to the attacks over an entire decade against his father's dying requests, careful plans, and written directions to safeguard his business and investments for the future of his son, daughter, and widow. As courtroom speeches, they are rhetorical documents that Demosthenes had been developing not just since coming of age in 366/5 but since that first disagreement between his mother and Aphobus about some jewelry, over a decade earlier.[41] Out of those years of experiences, he offers these glimpses of his deceased father, his mother, sister, and freed and enslaved members of the household, all of historical interest, but all serving the rhetorical needs of the moment.

---

[36] Following a suggestive footnote in Ste. Croix 1953, 55 n. 105, this notion became almost a fact in Davies 1971, 128–129, and was turned into a "long tradition of tax avoidance" by Cohen 1992, 200–201 (cf. 2000, 76); and Cohen's claim that "Demosthenes *père* seems systematically to have kept his property 'invisible'" is not to be attributed, as his n. 63 implies, to Korver 1941, who concludes, rather, since Demosthenes could earn 12% or as much as 17% on his investments, "it is likely that he deliberately scorned investment in real estate" (1941, 201); cf. Brun 2015, 77 tendentiously of Demosthenes' silence regarding "la générosité ou plutôt la pingrerie de son père."
[37] Hunter 1989b, discussed above; cf. Hunter 1994, 30 n. 43.
[38] Foxhall 1996, 144 calls her "the real heroine of this social drama" (though "nagged", 144, is inappropriate).
[39] So Mathieu 1948, 8–9; cf. Burke 1998, 63–64 and esp. Moreno 2007, 251–260, but see Kremmydas 2012, 244–245.
[40] Contra Cohen 2000, 140 n. 51 (as Cohen 1992, 93 n. 155), followed by Kamen 2013, 24, though with the admission of ambiguous uncertainty.
[41] As Jaeger 1938, 26: "Probably the affair had cast its shadow on his family life for a long time."

Bibliography

Badian, E. (2000), "The Road to Prominence", in: I. Worthington (ed.), *Demosthenes, Statesman and Orator*, London, 9–44.
Blass, F. (1887–1898), *Die Attische Beredsamkeit*, 2nd ed., 3 vols. in 4 parts, Leipzig.
Boegehold, A.L. et al. (1995), *The Lawcourts at Athens: Sites, Buildings, Equipment, Procedure, and Testimonia* (The Athenian Agora 28), Princeton.
Brun, P. (2015), *Démosthène : rhétorique, pouvoir et corruption*, Paris.
Burke, E.M. (1998), "The Looting of the Estate of the Elder Demosthenes", *C & M* 49, 45–65.
Carlier, P. (1993), "Démosthène par lui-même", in: M.-F. Baslez/P. Hoffmann/L. Pernot (eds.), *L'invention de l'autobiographie d'Hésiode à Saint Augustin*, Paris, 47–53.
Carlier, P. (2006), *Démosthène*, 2nd ed., Paris.
Cawkwell, G.L. (2012), "Demosthenes", in: S. Hornblower/A. Spawforth, with E. Eidinow (eds.), *Oxford Classical Dictionary*, 4th ed., Oxford, 439–441.
Christ, M. (2007), "The Evolution of the *Eisphora* in Classical Athens", *CQ* 57, 53–69.
Clinton, H.F. (1834–51), *Fasti Hellenici: The Civil and Literary Chronology of Greece*, 3 vols., 1st ed. (vol. 1), 3rd ed. (vols. 2–3), Oxford.
Cobetto Ghiggia, C. (2007), *Demostene, Orazioni XXVII–XXXI. Introduzione, testo rivisto, traduzione e note*, Alessandria.
Cohen, E.E. (1992), *Athenian Economy and Society: A Banking Perspective*, Princeton.
Cohen, E.E. (2000), *The Athenian Nation*, Princeton.
Cox, C.A. (1998), *Household Interests: Property, Marriage Strategies and Family Dynamics in Ancient Athens*, Princeton.
Daix, D.-A./Matthieu, F. (2017), *Démosthène, Contre Aphobos I & II suivi de Contre Midias*, Paris.
Davies, J.K. (1971), *Athenian Propertied Families, 600–300 B.C.*, Oxford.
Dobson, J.F. (1949), "Demosthenes", in: M. Cary et al. (eds.), *The Oxford Classical Dictionary* (1st ed.), Oxford, 268–269.
Finley, M.I. (1952), *Studies in Land and Credit in Ancient Athens, 500–200 B.C.: The Horos-Inscriptions*, New Brunswick.
Foxhall, L. (1996), "The Law and the Lady: Women and Legal Proceedings in Classical Athens", in: L. Foxhall/A.D.E. Lewis (eds.), *Greek Law in its Political Settings: Justifications not Justice*, Oxford, 133–152.
Fromentin, V./Gotteland, S. (2015), "Thucydides' Ancient Reputation", in: C. Lee/N. Morley (eds.), *A Handbook to the Reception of Thucydides*, Chichester, 13–25.
Gabrielsen, V. (1987), "The *Antidosis* Procedure in Classical Athens", *C & M* 38, 7–38.
Gagarin, M. (2001), "Women's Voices in Attic Oratory", in: A. Lardinois/L. McClure (eds.), *Making Silence Speak: Women's Voices in Greek Literature and Society*, Princeton, 161–176.
Gernet, L. (1918), "Note sur les parents de Démosthène", *REG* 31, 185–196.
Gernet, L. (1954), *Démosthène, Plaidoyers civils*, vol. 1, Paris.
Harris, E.M. (2005), "Feuding or the Rule of Law? The Nature of Litigation in Classical Athens", in: R.W. Wallace/M. Gagarin (eds.), *Symposion 2001: Vorträge zur griechischen und hellenistischen Rechtsgeschichte*, Vienna, 125–142.
Harris, E.M. (2008), *Demosthenes, Speeches 20–22*, Austin.
Harrison, A.R.W. (1968–1971), *The Law of Athens*, 2 vols., Oxford.

Humphreys, S.C. (2018), *Kinship in Ancient Athens: An Anthropological Analysis*, 2 vols., Oxford.
Hunter, V. (1989a), "The Athenian Widow and Her Kin", *Journal of Family History* 14, 291–311.
Hunter, V. (1989b), "Women's Authority in Classical Athens: The Example of Kleoboule and her Son (Dem. 27–29)", *Echoes du Monde Classique* 33, 39–48.
Hunter, V. (1994), *Policing Athens: Social Control in the Attic Lawsuits, 420–320 BC*, Princeton.
Hunter, V. (2000), "Policing Debtors in Classical Athens", *Phoenix* 54, 21–28.
Jaeger, W. (1938), *Demosthenes: The Origin and Growth of His Policy*, Berkeley.
Johnstone, S. (2003), "Women, Property, and Surveillance in Classical Athens", *CA* 22, 247–274.
Kamen, D. (2013), *Status in Classical Athens*, Princeton.
Kapparis, K. (1994), "Was *atimia* for Debts to the State Inherited Through Women", *RIDA* 41, 113–121.
Kennedy, C.R. (1852–63), *The Orations of Demosthenes*, 5 vols., London.
Konstantinidou, K. (2014), "Oath and Curse", in: A. Sommerstein/I.C. Torrance (eds.), *Oaths and Swearing in Ancient Greece*, Berlin, 6–47.
Korver, J. (1941), "Demosthenes gegen Aphobos", *Mnemosyne* 10, 8–22.
Lausberg, H. (1973), *Handbuch der literarischen Rhetorik*, 2 vols., 2nd ed., Munich. (repr. 1990 as "3rd ed."; repr. 2008 as "4th ed."; Engl. trans. 1998 uses same reference §§)
MacDowell, D.M. (1989), "The Authenticity of Demosthenes 29 (*Against Aphobos III*) as a Source of Information about Athenian Law", in: G. Thür (ed.), *Symposion 1985: Vorträge zur griechischen und hellenistischen Rechtsgeschichte*, Cologne, 253–262.
MacDowell, D.M. (1990), *Demosthenes, Against Meidias*, Oxford.
MacDowell, D.M. (2004), *Demosthenes, Speeches 27–38*, Austin.
MacDowell, D.M. (2009), *Demosthenes the Orator*, Oxford.
Mathieu, G. (1948), *Démosthène, l'homme et l'œuvre*, Paris.
Minns, E.H. (1913), *Scythians and Greeks: A Survey of Ancient History and Archaeology on the North Coast of the Euxine from the Danube to the Caucasus*, Cambridge.
Mirhady, D.C. (2000a), "The Athenian Rationale for Torture", in: V.J. Hunter/J. Edmondson (eds.), *Law and Social Status in Classical Athens*, Oxford, 53–74.
Mirhady, D.C. (2000b), "Demosthenes as Advocate: The Private Speeches", in: I. Worthington (ed.), *Demosthenes: Statesman and Orator*, London, 181–204.
Moreno, A. (2007), *Feeding the Democracy: The Athenian Grain Supply in the Fifth and Fourth Centuries BC*, Oxford.
Pearson, L. (1972), *Demosthenes, Six Private Speeches*, Norman.
Pearson, L. (1976), *The Art of Demosthenes*, Meisenheim.
Ste Croix, G.E.M. de (1953), "Demosthenes' TIMHMA and the Athenian *Eisphora* in the Fourth Century", *C & M* 14, 30–70.
Schaps, D.M. (1977), "The Woman Least Mentioned: Etiquette and Women's Names", *CQ* 27, 323–330.
Schaps, D.M. (1979), *Economic Rights of Women in Ancient Greece*, Edinburgh.
Schaefer, A. (1885–87), *Demosthenes und seine Zeit*, 2nd ed., vols. 1–3; (1858), 1st ed., vol. 4, Leipzig.
Sternberg, R.H. (2006), *Tragedy Offstage: Suffering and Sympathy in Ancient Athens*, Austin.
Thirlwall, C. (1855), *The History of Greece*, 2nd ed., 8 vols., London.
Thür, G. (1972), "Der Streit über den Status des Werkstätten Leiters Milyas (Dem. or. 29)", *RIDA* 19, 151–177.

Usher, S. (1999), *Greek Oratory: Tradition and Originality*, Oxford.
Waterfield, R./Carey, C. (2014), *Demosthenes, Selected Speeches*, Oxford.
Westwood, G. (2019), "Views of the Past", in: G. Martin (ed.), *The Oxford Handbook of Demosthenes*, Oxford, 178–189.
Will, W. (2013), *Demosthenes*, Darmstadt.
Worthington, I. (2013), *Demosthenes of Athens and the Fall of Classical Greece*, Oxford.

Gunther Martin
Reusing Invective: Demosthenes on Androtion's Past

Abstract: Androtion, a prominent politician and historian, was twice attacked by Demosthenes on account of his political record, at an interval of roughly two years, and in largely identical terms. The paper examines the differences between the two passages. It shows how the orator adapts his tactics to the changed setting and circumstances of the second trial and discusses what the changes and the unchanged parts of the text may suggest about Demosthenes' (or his client Diodorus') strategy in the trial.

There can be little doubt that Androtion was a respectable person. He excelled both in politics and as a historian. However, no speech and no extended quote have survived.[1] Even worse, not once but twice is he the victim of vilification in Demosthenes' surviving speeches: in *Against Androtion* (Dem. 22, about an illegal honorary decree) from 355/4 and *Against Timocrates* (Dem. 24, about an 'unsuitable' law allowing public debtors to be saved from imprisonment if they gave sureties) from 353/2,[2] both composed for a certain Diodorus.[3] The most vicious attacks are launched towards the end of the speeches (22.47–78, 24.160–186), in one of the most extensive examples of reuse of text in the orators.[4] The section is concerned with two episodes from Androtion's record as officeholder: as a collector of tax arrears and as a supervisor of the melting down of old crowns in the treasury of Athena.

---

1 Baiter & Sauppe 1850, 245, BNJ 324, translations in Harding 1994.
2 On the dates cf. Dion. Hal. *Amm.* 1.4 and Harris 2008, 168; 2018, 109–110.
3 In the following I shall use Demosthenes' name, except where delivery or the prosecutorial role in the trial is concerned. There is a question mark behind the sole authorship of 24.110–159, but for the present purpose I shall be content to assume the presence of Demosthenes' hand throughout (on the matter see e.g. Dover 1968, 161–163; Worthington 1993, 71; MacDowell 2009, 195–196).
4 It is surpassed only by Dem. 8.38–67~10.11–27, 55–70. This case, however, has long aroused suspicions that Dem. 10 is not an authentic speech: cf. Hajdú 2002, 44–49; MacDowell 2009, 354–355.

https://doi.org/10.1515/9783110791877-016

There are some variations between the two versions. Scholars are content to state that Demosthenes makes some adaptations and implicates Timocrates in Androtion's history of abuse of office.[5] He thereby extends the attack to the nominal target of the second lawsuit, Timocrates, the proposer of the 'unsuitable' law.[6] He also strengthens his claim that the two were long-standing accomplices – ultimately lending credibility to his story that Timocrates proposed his law to rescue Androtion and his friends from an impending prison sentence (e.g. 24.2–3, 9, 130, 187). We shall see that the references to Timocrates cover only part of the differences. Instead, the account of Androtion's past actions is adapted to the speaker's strategy in more subtle and strategically advanced ways.

1 Androtion's political activity

It appears that Demosthenes goes out of his way to denigrate Androtion's political record, besmirching his conduct in office in two special commissions, both of which the politician seems to have initiated himself.

1.1 Collector of tax arrears

In the 370s, or possibly at the time of the Social War,[7] when Athens' public funds were depleted, the Assembly voted for a proposal by Androtion that a board be appointed to collect outstanding *eisphora*. Androtion was one of ten elected officials (Timocrates being another), and fulfilled his duty, collecting five or seven[8] talents. If Demosthenes is to be believed on the basic facts, he shamed people in public (22.61–64, 67, 24.124) and forced his entry to people's houses. The people in question, who had not been bothered about their debts before, were suddenly asked to come up with sizeable sums of money. It would not be surprising if Androtion's shock and awe tactics really led some, as Demosthenes suggests, to hide or flee. Whatever the truth, Androtion acted in the

---

5 E.g. Schaefer[2] 1885, 383; Vieze 1885, 41; MacDowell 2009, 195.
6 The best explanation of the procedure is given in Canevaro 2016 and 2018.
7 The majority of scholars now prefers the later date: cf. Harding 1976, 193; MacDowell 2009, 177; but Moscati Castelnuovo 1980, 255 points to 24.175, which sounds pointless if events were fairly recent. She is largely followed by Bearzot 2011.
8 24.162 vs 22.63.

public interest, on the Assembly's order, and assisted by the Eleven and other officials (24.162). Demosthenes claims that the means he used were excessive. That assessment may be acceptable, but if there had been any formal complaints of or public resistance against Androtion's discharge of his office, we can be sure that Demosthenes would not pass over that fact silently.

1.2 Supervisor in the Treasury of Athena

According to Demosthenes' account, at some time Androtion moved a decree to melt down gold crowns that had showed signs of age (metal leaves had fallen off) and rework the material into processional vessels; again Androtion had himself elected to oversee the works. Demosthenes insinuates that he embezzled some of the gold but saves most of his indignation for the fact that the crowns had borne inscriptions honouring the Athenians:[9] these dedications disappeared with the crowns and were replaced by inscriptions stating that the new vessels had been produced "under the supervision of Androtion". Not only is this substitution for a public honour of an individual's name disgraceful, Demosthenes says, but Androtion had defiled and thus disqualified himself from any contact with the sanctuary (22.73~24.181): the melting down of crowns dedicated to the gods was thus a sacrilege in itself.

There may be some external evidence: D. Lewis linked the story to an inscription from 365/4 (*SEG* 14:47), moved by Androtion, which mentions a decree on processional vessels, and to the disappearance of crowns from the annual inventory lists after 366.[10] We know neither whether the cited decree is the one leading to Androtion's commission nor whether it was Androtion who was in charge of the removal of these specific crowns. What is clear, however, is that Androtion's actions were not out of the ordinary: crowns did indeed lose leaves and were molten; as long as the gold did not leave the sanctuary, no sacrilege was committed.[11]

Demosthenes obviously scandalises normal actions — partly claiming that they were excessive, partly intimating that the actions were offences even when they were not. He throws a number of other accusations into the mix:[12] that he

---

9 The inscriptions cited by Demosthenes are mostly unlikely to be authentic, as Lewis 1954, 45 has shown; they illustrate the kind of text to be found on such crowns.
10 Lewis 1954, 39–47, similarly Moscati Castelnuovo 1980, 258; *contra* Harding 1976, 191–192.
11 Linders 1987, 116 n. 13; 1989–1990, 281 n. 4–6, 282–283, Harris 1995, 33; cf. Martin 2009, 129–130.
12 McDowell 2009, 177–178.

was part of an anti-democratic elite and behaved in an inappropriate way towards others in the Assembly, but also that Androtion was disqualified from entering sanctuaries, because he had prostituted himself in his youth (22.73, 78~24.181, 186) and that he let his father, a debtor to the state, avoid paying up and escape from prison (22.56~24.168, 22.68).

The fact that we cannot be sure when the two main incidents took place is revealing about Demosthenes' or Diodorus' strategy of large-scale decontextualisation. The board of special tax collectors was appointed when the financial situation of the city was dire (22.48–9~24.160–1). Demosthenes, however, does not state that fact explicitly nor which circumstances created that situation, but only that Androtion denounced Euctemon, who was in charge of the war tax (εἰσφορά). This has led to different datings,[13] just as we are not able (at least from the speech alone) to date the production of the processional vessels. While Demosthenes mentions the political activity of Androtion, he chooses not to connect these with broader policies and a general political outlook — just as we are left under the impression that Timocrates' law is the service of a hireling or part of a coup rather than a purposeful measure responding to the demands of the time at the end of the Social War (see below). It is hence not surprising that Androtion's political alignment is still controversial.[14] Demosthenes'/Diodorus' aims, by contrast, seem clear: not to alienate any sympathisers of Androtion's political stance by explaining his (probably reasonable) actions, but to ascribe to him the most sinister motives possible.

2 The two versions of the attack

The two trials took place more than a year apart. Some in the audience of the later trial may have noticed that the attack against Androtion was being repeated (24.159). The attack runs as follows:

---

13 Cf. n. 7
14 For three very different takes cf. Harding 1994, 24–25; Bearzot 2011, esp. 128–129; Rowe 2000.

Tab. 2: Synopsis of Dem. 22.47–78 and 24.160–86.

Dem. 22	Dem. 24	Content	Changes[15]
47b–69	160–175	**Androtion as collector of tax arrears**	
47b–51a	160–162	preparation of the tax collection in the Assembly; eventual ineffectiveness of the enterprise	- the section serves to assess Androtion's acts and prevent being deceived by his bluster (160) - Androtion did not exact money from Euctemon but from "you" (162) + Timocrates' nomination by Androtion (160) and his participation in the operation (160, 161, 162) + attendance of *apodektai* and attendants (162)
51b–58	16316–9	excessive behaviour	
51b–53	163–165	cruelty of entering private houses; comparison with oligarchy	plurals for singulars (164) - details of people hiding and disgracing themselves before their families + houses being as unsafe as marketplaces
54–58	166–169	indignity and unfairness of imprisonment	plurals for singulars (166, 167) + address to Timocrates (166) - absence of physical punishment for free men (slightly shortened, 167)
{56b–58}			- specific cases of overstepping competences; lawlessness of the action; Androtion, lacking the right character, should have turned on his father
	{169}		+ contrast between Timocrates' mercilessness in demanding payments and the proposed law
59–69	170–175	refutation of the argument that the action benefitted the Athenians	plurals for singulars (172–173)

---

15 I do not list minute changes (e.g. 163: omitted ἐστίν, added εὖ οἶδ' ὅτι). "+" marks short additions, "-" short omissions in *Against Timocrates*. Braces indicate entire paragraphs unique to one speech.

Dem. 22	Dem. 24	Content	Changes[15]
{59–64}			– hostility against Androtion is the result of his cruelty and abusiveness; comparison with Satyrus
	{170–171}		+ Athenians ought to dispute that they benefited; leniency is only appropriate if the accused share Athens' character, i.e. mercifulness
{67b–68}			– Androtion never accused anyone because he thinks people are worthless and insults them like slaves
	{174–175}		+ Androtion and Timocrates never accused anyone because of collusion with others in stealing from people; need to punish them despite the interval since their deeds
69–78	176–186	Androtion as supervisor for the melting down of crowns	
69–70a	176–177	*indignatio*: evilness of Androtion's actions	plurals for singulars (176–177) + Timocrates chosen as accomplice (177)
70b–71	178–179	Androtion acting without witnesses	
72–73	180–181	loss of honorary inscriptions	+ inscription on Chabrias
	{182}	*indignatio*	+ criminality of Timocrates' and Androtion's actions; their arrogant confidence
75–77	183–185	Androtion's lack of understanding for meaning of crowns	
78	186	criticism of the Athenians	

The most frequent type of change concerns no more than the use of the plural instead of the singular, to include Timocrates. Several times it is stated that Timocrates joined Androtion as his colleague in collecting the arrears[16]— five times in 24.160–162 alone —, and once for the melting down of gold crowns (only § 177). All these additions, however, are short, not more than one or two

---

[16] On Timocrates' role cf. 24.111: ἦρχεν αὐτὸς μετ' Ἀνδροτίωνος, 162: μόνος τῶν συναρχόντων δέκ' ὄντων, 199: μόνος δέκα τῶν συναρχόντων ὄντων.

lines each in the Oxford text. The most substantial changes do not concern this fact: two sections are substituted completely (24.169–171 for 22.56b–64, 24.174–175 for 22.67b–68) and one paragraph is inserted (24.182).[17] Changes are much more frequent and substantial in 24.160–175 than in 176–186, and while we cannot know whether any motifs or formulations were replaced because they failed on first delivery,[18] there emerges a rationale behind the changes.

One major trend is to excise details of Androtion's transgressions in collecting the money owed to the state. In *Against Androtion* Demosthenes details (22.53) how a debtor,

> οὐκ εὐπορῶν ἀργυρίου, ἢ τέγος ὡς τοὺς γείτονας ὑπερβαίνοι, ἢ ὑποδύοιθ' ὑπὸ κλίνην ὑπὲρ τοῦ μὴ τοσῶμ' ἁλοὺς εἰς τὸ δεσμωτήριον ἕλκεσθαι, ἢ ἄλλ' ἀσχημονοίη ἃ δούλων, οὐκ ἐλευθέρων ἐστὶν ἔργα, καὶ ταῦθ' ὑπὸ τῆς αὑτοῦ γυναικὸς ὁρῷτο ποιῶν, ἣν ὡς ἐλεύθερος ἠγγυήσατο καὶ τῆς πόλεως πολίτης, ὁ δὲ τούτων αἴτιος Ἀνδροτίων εἴη.

> when he had no silver at hand, went over the roof to his neighbours' house or slipped under his bed lest his body be caught and dragged to prison or disgraced himself in a way befitting slaves, not free men, and was seen doing so by his own wife, whom he had wed as a free man and a citizen of the polis. And it was Androtion who was responsible for this.

For *Against Timocrates* Demosthenes takes out these vignettes and replaces them with a less drastic impression of the consequences of Androtion's actions (24.165):

> οὐκ εὐπορῶν ἀργυρίου, μὴ μόνον εἰς τὴν ἀγορὰν φοβοῖτ' ἐμβαλεῖν, ἀλλὰ μηδ' οἴκοι μένειν ἀσφαλὲς ἡγοῖτο, ὁ δὲ τούτων αἴτιος Ἀνδροτίων εἴη.

> when he had no silver at hand, not only was he afraid to enter the Agora, he did not even consider it safe to stay at home. And it was Androtion who was responsible for this.

Demosthenes does not suppress the transgressive aspect of Androtion's actions, i.e. the fact that he invaded people's private space. But the disgracefulness is now left unmentioned. Demosthenes also does not individualise: the focus is on the feeling that is the same for all debtors alike, while in the earlier speech he had mentioned specific reactions.

The trend to cut out concrete details can also be found elsewhere. In a longer section of *Against Androtion* Demosthenes aims to refute Androtion's ex-

---

[17] It appears that in two places, 22.67 and 74, the text of Dem. 24 has been copied into Dem. 22. Most editors follow these deletions by Funkhaenel and Sauppe.
[18] For example, Demosthenes cuts references to Androtion's verbal insults in the Assembly. The reason is unclear, especially since he mentions them in 24.124.

pected claim that he incurred hatred when acting in the interest of the people (22.59–69). He contests both parts of the claim and states that a) Androtion did not benefit the people significantly and b) the hatred arose from Androtion's abusive language in the Assembly. He mentions Androtion's unlawful and unacceptable use of force in the seizure of Sinope and Phanostrate, two notorious hetairai, whose owner presumably owed money to the treasury (22.56–57). The owner himself remains unnamed but may have been known to many in the jury.[19] Other victims of Androtion are not given the same anonymity: Leptines, Theoxenos, Callicrates, and the son of Telestes are listed with the petty amounts retrieved from them (22.60). And Satyrus is mentioned as a positive foil to Androtion (22.63), because as superintendent of the dockyards he had collected money with far greater success than Androtion and without negative consequences for his personal standing.

In the corresponding section of *Against Timocrates* (24.170–175) Demosthenes retains only one half of the argument: that Androtion's actions did not benefit Athens and the Athenians. He could easily have mentioned Androtion's and Timocrates' victims or Satyrus. The argument would fit into this speech just as well as into *Against Androtion*. But he omits these cases, along with several paragraphs about Androtion insulting honourable citizens (unnamed, for obvious reasons) in the Assembly and calling them slaves, whores, and sons of whores (22.61–63). The reduction of specifics is thus the overarching trait of these passages. Everything that smacks of individual cases is removed, and what is left from the *Androtiana* are generalities (24.172):

> ὅτι τοίνυν οὐδὲ τὴν εἴσπραξιν αὐτὴν ὑπὲρ ὑμῶν πεποίηνται, καὶ τοῦτ' αὐτίκα δὴ μάλ' ὑμῖν δῆλον ποιήσω. εἰ γάρ τις ἔροιτ' αὐτοὺς πότερ' αὑτοῖς δοκοῦσ' ἀδικεῖν μᾶλλον τὴν πόλιν οἱ γεωργοῦντες καὶ φειδόμενοι, διὰ παιδοτροφίας δὲ καὶ οἰκεῖ' ἀναλώματα καὶ λῃτουργίας ἑτέρας ἐλλελοιπότες εἰσφοράν, ἢ οἱ τὰ τῶν ἐθελησάντων εἰσενεγκεῖν χρήματα καὶ τὰ παρὰ τῶν συμμάχων κλέπτοντες καὶ ἀπολλύντες, οὐκ ἂν εἰς τοῦτο δήπου τόλμης, καίπερ ὄντες ἀναιδεῖς, ἔλθοιεν, ὥστε φῆσαι τοὺς τὰ ἑαυτῶν μὴ εἰσφέροντας μᾶλλον ἀδικεῖν ἢ τοὺς τὰ κοίν' ὑφαιρουμένους.

> In a moment I shall also make very clear to you that they have not even done the very tax collection for your benefit. For if someone asked them who, in their minds, acted more unjustly towards the city, the thrifty farmers, who may have missed to pay the wealth tax due to childrearing, private expenditures, or other liturgies or those who steal and waste the money of those willing to pay the tax or of the allies – surely, even though they are

---

19 Sinope was a notorious prostitute (Papachrysostomou 2016, 154–155 on Amphis *PCG* 23). Apparently, the two were slaves who were seized as sureties.

shameless, they would not be so bold as to say that those who do not pay their own tax act more unjustly than those who take away public funds.

Demosthenes' changes lead to a concentration on more generalised thoughts. His thinking here is by no means highly conceptual and refined, but it centres on more abstract considerations about guilt and punishment: it asks whether Androtion's (and Timocrates') treatment of citizens is commensurate with the spirit of the law at issue, which spares some debtors to the state imprisonment. The issue of the trial, as Demosthenes frames it, is discussed on the level of principle: what are the state's priorities and what is its attitude towards justice? While the passages that Demosthenes cuts from *Against Androtion* may have had some rhetorical effect and would not have been alien to the new context, he dispenses with them and adapts the argument to a more elevated level of discussion. This is appropriate for a γραφὴ νόμον μὴ ἐπιτήδειον θεῖναι: this type of trial concerns a constitutional issue in that it deals with the questions of whether the law endangers the consistency of the legal corpus and whether it meets the standards of legislation in general. Laws are not supposed to concern individual cases.[20]

On the other hand, when Demosthenes adds new material, it strengthens the connection to the case and contributes to those aspects of the new case that were not present in the one against Androtion. This is done most obviously in 24.169, where Demosthenes points to the apparent inconsistency between the mercilessness in collecting the arrears and Timocrates' law that allows a moratorium for debtors to the state.

In §182 Demosthenes inserts a piece of *indignatio* that sticks out inorganically from the surrounding passages as it interrupts the continuous treatment of Androtion's handling of the crowns and the seriousness of his removing the inscriptions on them (24.181, 183~22.73, 75).[21] He complains that although Androtion and Timocrates in melting the vessels committed multiple offences, they feel untouchable by the court: Timocrates trusts that Androtion's support will save him, and Androtion himself stands his ground. By this insertion Demosthenes attacks the co-operation between the two in the trial. He goes beyond associating Timocrates in Androtion's misconduct in office and decries the "fact" that members of a corrupt political class act in each other's favour: Timocrates hopes to profit from the backing of an influential orator — after he

---

[20] Hansen 1991, 171–173.
[21] The text of 182 is also found as 22.74, but the allusion to Timocrates reveals that it has been interpolated.

himself proposed his law to save Androtion and his friends from going to prison.

Sleaze, in which politicians collude to the detriment of the state, is a motif that pervades the argument of the entire second half of the speech. The point is made by Demosthenes in another departure from the *Androtiana*, when he asks why Androtion throughout his political career never prosecuted any political delinquent (22.66–24.173). The answer in *Against Androtion* was that Androtion is guilty himself and full of contempt for the people (67b–68). In *Against Timocrates*, by contrast, he turns it into a more general opposition between Androtion and Timocrates as part of a colluding political class and the mass who are taken advantage of (174):

> μετέχουσιν ὧν ἀδικοῦσιν ὑμᾶς τινες, ἀπὸ δὲ τῶν εἰσπραττομένων ὑφαιροῦνται· δι' ἀπληστίαν δὲ τρόπων διχόθεν καρποῦνται τὴν πόλιν. οὔτε γὰρ ῥᾷον πολλοῖς καὶ τὰ μίκρ' ἀδικοῦσιν ἀπεχθάνεσθαι ἢ ὀλίγοις καὶ μεγάλα, οὔτε δημοτικώτερον δήπου τὰ τῶν πολλῶν ἀδικήμαθ' ὁρᾶν ἢ τὰ τῶν ὀλίγων.

> They share in the unjust acts that some commit against you, and they take some of the money they have collected: because of their insatiable nature they use two ways of reaping profit from the state. For neither is it easier to incur the hatred of many who err on a small scale than of few who err on a large scale, nor, surely, is it more democratic to regard the misdeeds of the many than those of the few.

Androtion is cast as a symptom of a general problem in Athenian society, signalling a divide between a treacherous elite and the abused mass of the people. This fits the scenario that Demosthenes draws throughout the speech: Timocrates' law is described as a ploy to remove the impending imprisonment from the necks of Androtion, Melanopus, and Glaucetes. A clique of politicians enrich and empower themselves, undermining the state. Demosthenes lifts the problem of their behaviour from one of mere greed and personal advantage to the constitutional level: the group of self-serving politicians act as an undemocratic elite.

The same tactics of tying Androtion's past acts to a wider constitutional issue and to construct a clash between the two is also visible in the last passage that Demosthenes inserts into the earlier version of his character attack (170–171):

> ἀλλὰ μισεῖν ὀφείλετε τοὺς τοιούτους, ὦ ἄνδρες Ἀθηναῖοι, μᾶλλον ἢ σῴζειν. τὸν γὰρ ὑπὲρ τῆς πόλεως πράττοντά τι καὶ πρᾴων ὑμῶν τευξόμενον τὸ τῆς πόλεως ἦθος ἔχοντα δεῖ φαίνεσθαι. τοῦτο δ' ἐστὶ τί; τοὺς ἀσθενεῖς ἐλεεῖν, τοῖς ἰσχυροῖς καὶ δυναμένοις μὴ ἐπιτρέπειν ὑβρίζειν, οὔτους μὲν πολλοὺς ὠμῶς μεταχειρίζεσθαι, κολακεύειν δὲ τὸν ἀεί τι δύνασθαι δοκοῦντα. ὃ σὺ ποιεῖς, ὦ Τιμόκρατες· δι' ἃ πολλῷ μᾶλλον ἂν εἰκότως μὴ θελήσαντες ἀκοῦσαι σοῦ θάνατον καταψηφίσαινθ' οὗτοι ἢ δι' Ἀνδροτίων' ἀφεῖησαν.

You, men of Athens, are obliged to hate such men rather than to save them. For someone who acts on behalf of the state and wants to find your mercy needs to appear to have the state's character. What is that? To pity the weak, not to allow the strong and powerful to abuse them, not to treat the many cruelly while flattering whoever seems powerful. That is what you do, Timocrates, and why they shall naturally sentence you to death — unwilling to listen to you — rather than release you for Androtion's sake.

The text combines and extends two sections of *Against Androtion* (22.57, 64):

τὸ πρᾶγμά γ' οὐκ ἐπιτήδειον γίγνεσθαι, τηλικοῦτό τινας φρονεῖν διὰ καιρὸν ὥστε βαδίζειν ἐπ' οἰκίας καὶ σκεύη φέρειν μηδὲν ὀφειλόντων ἀνθρώπων. πολλὰ γὰρ ἄν τις ἴδοι πολλοὺς ἐπιτηδείους ὄντας πάσχειν καὶ πεπονθέναι. ἀλλ' οὐ ταῦτα λέγουσιν οἱ νόμοι, οὐδὲ τὰ τῆς πολιτείας ἔθη, ἃ φυλακτέον ὑμῖν· ἀλλ' ἔνεστ' ἔλεος, συγγνώμη, πάνθ' ἃ προσήκει τοῖς ἐλευθέροις. [...]

ἀλλὰ μισεῖν δικαιότερον διὰ ταῦτά σ' ὀφείλουσιν ἢ σῴζειν. τὸν γὰρ ὑπὲρ πόλεως πράττοντά τι δεῖ τὸ τῆς πόλεως ἦθος μιμεῖσθαι, καὶ σῴζειν ὑμῖν τοὺς τοιούτους, ὦ ἄνδρες Ἀθηναῖοι, προσήκει, καὶ μισεῖν τοὺς οἵουσπερ οὗτος.

It is not right that this took place, that some were so puffed up by the opportunity as to go into houses and carry away furniture from people who were free from debt. For one can see many people deserving to suffer or have suffered many things. But that is not what the laws say nor is it the customs of our state, which you have to preserve: instead, there is pity in it, forgiveness, everything that becomes free men. [...]

They are therefore obliged by justice to hate you than to save you. For someone who acts on behalf of the state needs to imitate the state's character, and it befits you, men of Athens, to save such men, and to hate such people as him.

In 22.64 Demosthenes does not speak of Androtion's violent intrusion into other people's houses, but about the insults he heaps on others in the Assembly. So the ἦθος of the state is not directly related to the ἔθη in § 57. Still the idea of pity shows that Demosthenes was thinking of both passages when he composed 24.170–171, where the issue is again the merciless exaction of arrears and the imprisonment of debtors. By describing Athens' nature he tries to establish a constitutional and judicial principle on which the judges are to base their decision. Linking the character to the sentence against Timocrates once again extends the role of abstract ideas while diminishing the link to examples (in the case of 22.57: Sinope and Phanostrate). To the leniency of the state he adds in 24.171 the people's resilience against the power of the few: the Athenian disposition towards the many is fundamentally democratic, while the elite, who does not expect to be held accountable, is deeply undemocratic.

The focus on abstract principles and the "populist"[22] tactics of pitting an elite against the people illustrate two ways in which Demosthenes adapts the section he takes from *Against Androtion* to the present case beyond making Timocrates Androtion's accomplice. On the one hand, the tone and substance of the argument is made to conform with the nature of the charge, the γραφὴ νόμον μὴ ἐπιτήδειον θεῖναι.[23] By contrast, the *Androtiana* was delivered in a γραφὴ παρανόμων about an honorary decree, in which Androtion, as part of the Council, is also an honorand. On the other hand, the passage is aligned with the strategy of casting the entire struggle about Timocrates' law as a fight against a corrupt elite. Timocrates in legislating serves the interest of a group that operates against the Athenian values of kindness and democracy. While the first type of change responds to the institutional framework in which the trial takes places, the latter aspect reflects a strategical decision on how to frame the events.

3 The connection to the rest of the speech

The integration of the invective into the new speech is facilitated by the fact that the effects of Timocrates' law are in many respects contrary to Androtion's behaviour as Demosthenes had (incidentally) portrayed it in the first speech: the law that gives debtors a chance to escape prison seems so obviously incoherent with the merciless and dehumanising exaction of debts that Demosthenes had his argument cut out for him. There are, however, further motifs in the section, even in the version of the *Androtiana*, that are relevant for the speech as a whole.

Let us start with another "constitutional" issue that Androtion's allegedly unlawful and undemocratic pressure campaign against debtors raises: for, Androtion introduces new customs into the πολιτεία, i.e. the community but also the constitution (24.162). The idea of new laws undermining the constitution and the legal system is exactly what one expects in a γραφὴ νόμον μὴ ἐπιτήδειον θεῖναι (cf. e.g. 24.1, 5, 38 and 20.17, 108, 155). For Demosthenes, this is only the starting point for a disturbing comparison (24.163–164~22.51–52):

> εἰ γὰρ θέλετ' ἐξετάσαι τίνος εἵνεκα μᾶλλον ἄν τις ἕλοιτ' ἐν δημοκρατίᾳ ζῆν ἢ ἐν ὀλιγαρχίᾳ, τοῦτ' ἂν εὕροιτε προχειρότατον, ὅτι πάντα πραότερ' ἐν δημοκρατίᾳ. [...] παρ' ἡμῖν πότε

---

22 For the concept see e.g. Mudde/Kaltwasser 2018, 498–504.
23 Hansen 1991, 170–174.

πώποτε δεινότατ' ἐν τῇ πόλει γέγονεν; εὖ οἶδ' ὅτι ἐπὶ τῶν τριάκοντα ἅπαντες ἂν εἴποιτε. Τότε τοίνυν, ὡς ἔστιν ἀκούειν, οὐδεὶς ἔστιν ὅστις ἀπεστερεῖτο τοῦ σωθῆναι, ὅστις ἑαυτὸν οἴκοι κρύψειεν, ἀλλ' αὐτὸ τοῦτο κατηγοροῦσι τῶν τριάκοντα, ὅτι τοὺς ἐκ τῆς ἀγορᾶς ἀδίκως ἀπῆγον.

If you wish to examine why someone may choose to live in a democracy rather than in an oligarchy, you should very easily find that it is because everything is more lenient in a democracy. [...] When did the most terrible things happen here in your city? Obviously, you would all say under the Thirty. But look, then, as we can hear, nobody was robbed of his chance to be saved if he hid at home, but what they accuse the Thirty of is that they took people away from the Agora.

Bizarre as the juxtaposition of Androtion (teaming up with Timocrates) and the Thirty may sound,[24] Demosthenes refers to the latter, or oligarchy in general, six times in the rest of the speech (57, 59, 76, 90, 154, 206). Timocrates' law is described as no less than a plot to bring the entire legal system down, a step towards a new constitution (in addition to the above, e.g. 5, 76, 91, 101, 152). When Androtion is characterised as worse than an oligarch because of his conduct while collecting tax arrears, it perfectly matches the idea that Timocrates' law exempting debtors from prison took the first step towards overthrowing the constitution. That Androtion and Timocrates treat free men as if they were slaves (167) is only a variation of this idea, though one which also has parallels earlier in the speech (124, 143).

Another element emerging from the quote above is the leniency characteristic of democracy. We have already seen Demosthenes' more extended version (24.171), but the idea of Athenian leniency originally derived from this passage that is almost identical in both speeches. The orator found it useful enough to make the point several times (24, 51–52, 69, 123, 192–193, 197–198).

One could point to other recurring themes: the father as debtor (24.125, 168, the same about Timocrates' father: 200–201) or greed as motivation (65, 200). Suffice it here to mention one other motif that is central to Demosthenes' attacks: the impiety that is constituted by Androtion's acts in particular. For Demosthenes, taking away crowns that had been dedicated to Athena is temple-robbery, impiety, and theft (177 ἱεροσυλίᾳ καὶ ἀσεβείᾳ καὶ κλοπῇ καὶ πᾶσι τοῖς δεινοτάτοις εἴσ' ἔνοχοι). The religious accusations are aggravated by the "fact" that Androtion was not permitted to enter the sanctuary, due to his past as a prostitute. Not only did he enter, he even secured his lasting symbolic presence by leaving his name on the new processional vessels produced "under the su-

---

24 Cf. Nouhaud 1982, 310–311.

pervision of Androtion" (181 Ἀνδρωτίονος ἐπιμελουμένου). This line of argument culminates in the following words, practically the same as the final climax of *Against Androtion* (24.186~22.78):

> τοῦτ' ἀσέβημ' ἔλαττον τίνος ἡγεῖσθε; ἐγὼ μὲν γὰρ ἡγοῦμαι δεῖν τὸν εἰς ἱερ' εἰσιόντα καὶ χερνίβων καὶ κανῶν ἁψόμενον, καὶ τῆς πρὸς τοὺς θεοὺς ἐπιμελείας προστάτην ἐσόμενον οὐχὶ τακτὸν ἡμερῶν ἀριθμὸν ἁγνεύειν, ἀλλὰ τὸν βίον ἡγνευκέναι τοιούτων ἐπιτηδευμάτων οἷα τούτῳ βεβίωται.

> Is there any impiety greater than this one? For I believe that the man who is going to enter the sanctuary and dip his hand into the lustral basins and baskets and who will be head of the service to the gods must not abstain for a set number of days but have abstained his entire life from such act activities as this person has spent his life pursuing.

This is the end of the passage, followed in the *Timocratea* by a peroration. The idea that Androtion defiled the sanctuary by his presence and robbed and destroyed sacred objects again ties in with his portrayal in the speech. His alleged indecency in his youth is brought up when Demosthenes denies that he did not deserve to go to prison (24.126). More importantly, Demosthenes repeatedly frames Androtion's non-payment and the law that lets him avoid prison as temple-robbery and robbery of the goddess's money (82, 111, 119–120, 122, 125, 129–130, 137). By linking the melting of the crowns and not giving the goddess her due Demosthenes creates continuity in Androtion's ἱεροσυλία, and this reinforces the characterisation of the law as entailing a serious breach of religious norms.

It is worth repeating that all the passages from § 160–186 cited in this section appear without significant differences in *Against Androtion*. They were thus composed before Timocrates even moved the law that Diodorus and Euctemon tried to repeal. Nevertheless, the passage is rich in motifs that are essential to the case in the new speech or contribute substantially to the arguments regarding the case against Timocrates. It dovetails so well with the *ad rem*-parts of the speech that one would not suspect that it pre-dates the affair about Timocrates. That raises the question of how a pre-written section can fit so well into the speech.

In that context a suggestion last made by E. Harris becomes particularly intriguing: that Demosthenes has concocted the story that Timocrates wrote his law to benefit Androtion.[25] Harris presents a number of serious arguments for this idea and in particular points to inconsistencies and gaps in Demosthenes'

---

25 Harris 2018, 117, but see already Libanius *arg. D.* 23.6, Roisman 2006, 103–114.

version. Such a scenario would have interesting consequences for the inclusion of the two episodes from Androtion's (and Timocrates') past. For, the contradictoriness between Timocrates' law and Androtion's severity in collecting debts – and generally the excellent match between Androtion's past and the present case – would likely have been one of the main reasons for Demosthenes' fabrication of the story. Timocrates' previous involvement in Androtion's dealings, while probably coincidental, would lend strong credibility to the invention of a sinister motive behind his proposal.

Harris' theory, however, leaves itself some questions unanswered.[26] It is, moreover, possible to find alternative explanations for the good match of the passage and the general strategy of the speech. The good match would then be the reason for reusing it in the first place. In part, it may merely have been good luck on Diodorus'/Demosthenes' part that Androtion's past actions, the collection of tax in particular, lent themselves to the construction of a contradiction. We must not forget, though, that Demosthenes distorts Androtion's action. Androtion followed the orders of the people; and it is not clear how representative the instances of cruelty against citizens were. Demosthenes comes up with the most negative interpretation of events – and that interpretation is useful for the new trial.

In addition, Timocrates' law does not open the gates of prisons or cause lawlessness, as Demosthenes wants, but it allows for the suspension of prison sentences if debtors provide securities. The spirit behind the two measures may even be the same: at the end of the Social War Athens needed additional funds more than ever, and the two proposals, each in its way, provided or secured income. For, those who wanted to make use of Timocrates' law would guarantee payment: the city, in turn, would weaken her own financial power if she ruined financially potent debtors by imprisonment.

Demosthenes, once he had decided to reuse the passage against Androtion, may have included some motifs in the earlier parts of the speech or made them

---

[26] For example, he fails to give a reason for why Diodorus should have been interested in the sentence against Timocrates, as his personal motivation for the trial was revenge against Androtion, not Timocrates (24.6–8). That the two did indeed have some sort of relationship is also suggested by the fact that Androtion (and "many other politicians": 24.157) is prominently present at the trial and expected to speak in support of Timocrates. A speaker may not have anticipated this unless the two were actually politically aligned. (Demosthenes never suggests that the defendants have been elected by the Assembly, as in the case of *Against Leptines*: cf. 24.36, Rubinstein 2000, 165). Some kind of political relationship is also suggested by Timocrates' membership of the board of tax collectors – a fact Demosthenes could hardly make up entirely; cf. also Sealey 1993, 120.

more prominent, to prepare their recurrence in the reused section.²⁷ They become more compelling if they fit into the overall narrative. A case in question is the repeated reference to the "sacrilegious" aspect of Timocrates' law, which allegedly forfeits tax that is due to the goddess. The repeated reference to these 10% and the 2% for the heroes may have resonated with parts of the audience, but on their own they remain weak. The passage in which Demosthenes tells the jurors to condemn Timocrates to death "so that he give this law in Hades to the impious" (104) seems over the top, but it can stand if it forms part of a narrative that — untypically for Demosthenes' speeches —²⁸ casts the opponents as religious enemies of the gods.

Finally, some elements of the invective concern stock accusations against major politicians. Accusations of greed and of objectionable private conduct are smears that opponents often face.²⁹ For men like Androtion, who stood in the public eye and who were not afraid to take on official duties, it is also common to be portrayed as elitist, even beyond what is acceptable for a democrat. In Aeschines' speeches, for example, Demosthenes gets a taste of his own medicine.³⁰

Under the hands of a gifted orator, an opponent's past political activity was a source of malleable material for attacks. Already in *Against Androtion*, Demosthenes had extracted some ambivalent traits in Androtion's — publicly spirited and mostly unobjectionable — actions to turn them against the public servant. Thus the passage can probably serve as an illustration of the precariousness of a politician's reputation. Exposed to scrutiny by a not at all benign enemy, one's actions were bound to be described out of context. The accusations are so manifold and diverse that they can be combined and put in parallel with many other issues to create the image of a villain and be adapted to new situations and contexts without much effort.³¹

---

27 Most obviously the collection of tax arrears and the melting down of the crowns in 24.8, 197.
28 Martin 2009, 134–136.
29 Süß 1910, 249–250; Dover 1974, 171–172; Roisman 2005, 173–176.
30 Aesch. 1.173, 3.168.
31 A recent contribution by Zilong Guo 2021, which discusses similar questions as this paper, appeared after my manuscript had been submitted.

Bibliography

Baiter, J.G./Sauppe, H. (1850), *Oratores Attici. Pars posterior. Scholia Fragmenta Indices*, Zurich.
Bearzot, C.S. (2011), "La testimonianza di Demostene su Androzione", in: F. Gazzano/G. Ottone/L. Santi Amantini (eds.), *Ex fragmentis/per fragmenta historiam tradere*. Atti della Seconda Giornata di studio sulla storiografia greca frammentaria (Genova, 8 ottobre 2009), Tivoli, 107–129.
Canevaro, M. (2016), "The Procedure of Demosthenes' *Against Leptines*: How to Repeal (and Replace) an Existing Law", *JHS* 136, 39–58.
Canevaro, M. (2018), "Laws against laws: the Athenian ideology of legislation", in: C. Carey/I. Giannadaki/B. Griffith Williams (eds.), *Use and Abuse of Law in Athenian Courts*, Leiden, 271–292.
Dover, K.J. (1968), *Lysias and the Corpus Lysiacum*, Berkeley.
Dover, K.J. (1974), *Greek Popular Morality in the Time of Plato and Aristotle*, Berkeley.
Guo, Z. (2021), "Republished Texts in the Attic Orators", *Journal of Ancient Civilizations* 36.2, 139–172.
Hajdú, I. (2002), *Kommentar zur 4. Philippischen Rede des Demosthenes*, Berlin.
Hansen, M.H. (1991), *The Athenian Democracy in the Age of Demosthenes*, Oxford.
Harding, P. (1976), "Androtion's Political Career", *Historia* 25, 186–200.
Harding, P. (1994), *Androtion and the Atthis. The Fragments*, Oxford.
Harris, D. (1995), *The Treasures of the Parthenon and Erechtheion*, Oxford.
Harris, E.M. (2008), *Demosthenes, Speeches 20–22*, Austin.
Harris, E.M. (2018), *Demosthenes, Speeches 23–26*, Austin.
Lewis, D.M. (1954), "Notes on Attic Inscriptions", *ABSA* 49, 17–50.
Linders, T. (1987), "Gifts, Gods, Society", in: T. Linders/G. Nordquist (eds.), *Gifts to the Gods: Proceedings of the Uppsala Symposium 1985*, Uppsala, 115–122.
Linders, T. (1989–1990), "The Melting Down of Discarded Metal Offerings in Greek Sanctuaries", in: *Scienze dell'antichità: Storia archeologia antropologia* 3–4, 281–285.
MacDowell, D.M. (2009), *Demosthenes the Orator*, Oxford.
Martin, G. (2009), *Divine Talk. Religious Argumentation in Demosthenes*, Oxford.
Moscati Castelnuovo, L. (1980), "La carriera politica dell'Attidografo Androzione", *Acme* 33, 251–278.
Mudde, C./Rovira Kaltwasser, C. (2013), "Populism", *The Oxford Handbook of Political Ideologies*, Oxford, 493–511.
Nouhaud, M. (1982), *L'utilisation de l'histoire par les orateurs attiques*, Paris.
Papachrysostomou, A. (2016), *Amphis. Introduction, Translation, Commentary*, Heidelberg.
Roisman, J. (2005), *The Rhetoric of Manhood. Masculinity in the Attic Orators*, Berkeley.
Roisman, J. (2006), *The Rhetoric of Conspiracy in Ancient Athens*, Berkeley.
Rowe, G.O. (2000), "Anti-Isocratean Sentiment in Demosthenes' Against Androtion", *Historia* 49, 278–302.
Rubinstein, L. (2000), *Litigation and Cooperation: Supporting Speakers in the Courts of Classical Athens*, Stuttgart.
Schaefer, A. (²1885), *Demosthenes und seine Zeit. Erster Band*, Leipzig.
Sealey, R. (1993), *Demosthenes and his Time. A Study in Defeat*, New York/Oxford.
Süß, W. (1910), *Ethos. Studien zur älteren griechischen Rhetorik*, Leipzig/Berlin.

Vieze, H. (1885), *De Demosthenis in Androtionem et Timocrate morationibus*, PhD thesis Halle.
Worthington, I. (1993), "Once More, the Client/Logographos Relationship", *CQ* 43, 67–72.

Jeremy Trevett
A Tale of Two Sea-battles: Demosthenes' Praise of Chabrias in the Speech *Against Leptines*

Abstract: This chapter explores Demosthenes' presentation in his early public speech *Against Leptines* (Dem. 20) of the career of the Athenian general Chabrias. It argues that Demosthenes' arrangement is loosely chronological, from Chabrias' early successes to the battle of Naxos to his death at Chios, but that the coverage is uneven. The early years are dealt with briskly and without appeal to any supporting evidence: Demosthenes assumes knowledge of Chabrias' manoeuvring at Thebes, his defeat of Gorgopas, and his service in Cyprus and Egypt. Unsurprisingly he devotes more space to the battle of Naxos in 375 B.C., where he both appeals to the memories of older members of his audience and provides documentation in the form of the decree honouring Chabrias and his own list of his achievements. However, when Demosthenes turns to the recent Athenian defeat at Chios, in which Chabrias lost his life, he makes a vague and eulogistic account of the latter's death serve to minimize his responsibility for a humiliating military reverse.

1 Introduction

Demosthenes' speech *Against Leptines* of 355/4 B.C. was delivered as part of a legal challenge to a recent law, proposed by Leptines, that removed from the Athenian Assembly the right to award grants of financial exemption (*ateleia*) as a civic honour.[1] The purpose of Leptines' law, passed at a time of crisis in Athens' public finances, was to close a perceived loophole which, its proponents argued, allowed some wealthy men to evade the performance of liturgies. Demosthenes and his co-plaintiffs challenged the law using the procedure of a public prosecution against an inexpedient or illegally proposed law. His speech focuses on the consequences of Leptines' law. His central point is that it is both dishonourable and political inept to take away honours that have already been granted, since recipients and their descendants will be insulted, potential bene-

---
[1] Date: Dion. Hal. *ad Amm.* 1.4. On Athenian civic honours see Henry 1983; Liddel 2016; Domingo Gygax 2016.

factors will be deterred, and Athens will lose a lot of goodwill for little if any financial gain.²

The speech is rich in references to the past, since Demosthenes devotes fully a third of it to a series of examples of men whom the Athenians have honoured with grants of *ateleia* (§§ 29–84). The recipients whom he discusses include various non-Athenians as well as two Athenian generals, Conon and Chabrias. In each case, Demosthenes gives an account of the benefits to Athens that made the honorands deserving of the honours that they received. Of his examples, the majority fall within the period of the Peloponnesian and Corinthian Wars.³ But pride of place is given to the final honorand he discusses, Chabrias, whose career extended into the very recent past: first serving as a general in the Corinthian War, he had died in battle just a couple of years before the speech was delivered.⁴

In this paper I examine Demosthenes' presentation of Chabrias' career (§§ 75–86), with a focus on how he shapes and, in some cases, distorts the historical record to suit his rhetorical purpose.

2 Chabrias' early successes

Demosthenes starts by acknowledging that the jurors are already knowledgeable about his subject, whose recent death no doubt prompted considerable reflection on and commemoration of his career: "Perhaps you realize without me telling you that Chabrias was an excellent man." He then undertakes to remind (ἐπιμνησθῆναι) them briefly of some of his achievements (§ 75):

> The manner in which he positioned you for the battle against all the Peloponnesians at Thebes, how he killed Gorgopas on Aegina, the number of trophies that he erected on Cyprus and later in Egypt, and how he traveled over almost the entire world without ever bringing disgrace on the city's name or on himself, these are topics to which it would not be at all easy to do justice. It would also be very shameful for my words to make his actions appear inferior to what everyone thinks of them today. (§ 76).

---

2 On what exactly Leptines' law stipulated see Canevaro 2018.
3 Peloponnesian War: Epicerdes of Cyrene (§§ 41–46); Corinthian war: pro-Athenians in Corinth, Thasos and Byzantium (§§ 51–63) and Conon (§§ 68–74). The one other recipient of *ateleia* discussed in the speech is Leucon of Bosporus (§§ 29–41), whose service to Athens (supplying grain) was of a different character.
4 On Chabrias' career see Pritchett 1974, 72–77; Bianco 2000.

The first allusion is to Chabrias' role in the defence of Theban territory from Spartan attack in the early 370s, when Athens and Thebes were allied to each other. Demosthenes' reference to the manner in which (ὃν μὲν τρόπον) Chabrias deployed the Athenians ("you") for battle (§ 76) seems to allude to the "at ease" stance that he ordered his troops to adopt, with their spear extended and their shield placed on the ground leaning against their knee, and in which he himself was depicted in the statue that was voted him a few years later.[5] According to Diodorus, however, he was in command not of Athenians but of mercenaries (τῶν μισθοφόρων ἀφηγούμενος) when he ordered his soldiers to await the enemy's advance.[6] Whilst mercenaries employed by Athens could in a sense be regarded as Athenian, Demosthenes' use of the second person plural would naturally be taken to mean that citizens were involved, which according to Diodorus was not the case.

Our one other source for the defeat of the Spartan general Gorgopas on Aegina is Xenophon, who narrates how in 388 Athenian hoplites were used to lure him into an ambush, where his force was attacked by Chabrias and his peltasts and he was killed.[7] Demosthenes' choice of words ("how he killed") might suggest that the manner in which victory was achieved, by means of a craftily laid ambush, had caught the popular imagination.[8] As for the remaining two exploits, Chabrias was despatched by Athens in 388 to support Evagoras, the pro-Athenian ruler of Salamis, who was in revolt from Persian rule.[9] His victories in Egypt, described as "later" than those on Cyprus, refer to his service under the pharaoh Akoris, who was at war with Persia, in the period immediately after the King's Peace, c. 386–380.[10] Diodorus and Nepos both claim that he went to Egypt in a private capacity, but a passage of Aristophanes' *Plutus* of 388 refers to a recent alliance with Egypt,[11] and the fact that Athens rapidly recalled Chabrias in 380, under pressure from Persia to do so, led Hornblower to conclude that he "cannot be regarded as wholly independent of the Athenian state."[12]

---

5 Diod. 15.32; Nepos *Chabr.* 1. On the connection between the pose in which Chabrias was depicted and the stance which he ordered his soldiers to adopt see Nepos *Chabrias* 1.2. See further Buckler 1972.
6 Diod. 15.32.5.
7 Xen. *Hell.* 5.1.10–12.
8 Other examples of Chabrias' use of ambush: Polyaen. 3.11.3 and 9.
9 Xen. *Hell.* 5.1.10.
10 See Diod. 15.29.1–4 and Nepos *Chabr.* 2–3.1 (though the latter has confused Chabrias' two spells in Egypt).
11 Alliance: Aristoph. *Plutus* 178 with *schol.* (= Bengtson [1962] no. 236); see too Ruzicka 2012, 75.
12 Recall: Diod. 15.29.3–4, Nepos *Chabr.* 3.1. Not wholly independent: Hornblower 2002, 227.

Three of these episodes belong to the 380s, but the action at Thebes from the early 370s is pulled out of chronological sequence and placed first, presumably because it was the most famous of his early exploits.[13]

3 The battle of Naxos

Demosthenes follows with a section on Chabrias' most celebrated achievement: his command of the Athenian fleet that defeated the Spartans in the battle of Naxos in 376:

> Well now, he defeated the Spartans in a naval battle, captured forty-nine triremes, conquered most of the nearby islands and brought them over to your side, making former enemies into your friends. He brought 3,000 prisoners here and paid in a sum of more than 110 talents taken from the enemy. The older men among you are my witnesses for these events. In addition, he captured more than twenty other triremes, taking one or two at a time, all of which he brought back into your harbours ... (§ 77).

These figures he supports by means of a detailed document that he asks the clerk to read out: "So that I do not omit any of his achievements from my account, there will be read a list of the number of ships that he captured and the place where each was taken, as well as the number of cities, the amount of money, and the location of his trophies." (§ 78). After the list has been read, he summarizes as follows: "he took seventeen cities, captured seventy ships and 3,000 prisoners, paid in 110 talents, and set up so many trophies." (§ 80). Most of this is repeated from before: the seventy ships consist of the forty-nine from Naxos and the "more than twenty" additional others. But the number of cities that were taken is new information. This document is eventually followed by the reading of the decree honouring Chabrias, which is introduced by a piece of mock improvisation intended to ensure that he has the jurors' attention (§ 84): "In fact, get the decree that was voted for Chabrias. Go and look for it. It must be here somewhere."

The battle of Naxos was a major Athenian success.[14] Demosthenes' treatment of it, however, is curiously oblique. He says nothing about the context or the course of the battle, which indeed he does not name, perhaps because it was

---

13 Nepos also places this episode first, out of chronological order, in his biography of Chabrias (1.1). For the possibility that he had either direct or indirect knowledge of Dem. 20 see p. 284 below.
14 Sources: Diod. 15.34.3–35.2; Xen. *Hell.* 5.4.61; Plut. *Phoc.* 6.2–3; Polyaen. 3.11.11.

so well known.¹⁵ His focus is entirely on the profits that accrued to Athens, about which he supplies a series of precise numbers (of ships, prisoners, money, as well as of cities taken). Clearly, he wishes his audience both to be impressed by these numbers and to regard them as accurate. The correct information would presumably have been accessible from the archives, from such records as Chabrias' reports and financial accounts. And yet, in the one instance where we have other information, the result is to cast doubt. Specifically, there is a substantial discrepancy between the numbers that Demosthenes and Diodorus give for the enemy ships captured at Naxos. Diodorus says that eight Spartan ships were captured and twenty-four destroyed, out of a total fleet of sixty-five ships. Xenophon deals very briefly with the battle but confirms the approximate size of the Spartan fleet: its admiral Pollis had been allocated sixty ships.[16] If twenty-four of sixty-five Spartan ships were destroyed, and others escaped, Demosthenes' claim that forty-nine were captured cannot be correct. Some of the discrepancy might conceivably be due to disagreement whether wrecked ships, which may have been mostly recoverable, should be counted as destroyed or captured, but even so Demosthenes claims a larger number of ships captured than Diodorus' total of enemy ships sunk and captured.

On the face of it, Demosthenes is guilty of egregious "rhetorical" exaggeration in order to make Chabrias' achievement seem all the greater.[17] The list of ships, etc., does not correspond to any known form of official document, even if some of the information in it could have been taken from official records, and was surely compiled by Demosthenes himself.[18] In other words, nobody would have checked that the information was accurate, nor will the jurors have been in a position to know whether or not it was. Since we do not know what either the list or the decree contained, we cannot be sure what if any manipulation of the numbers there has been, but there is, at the least, grounds for suspicion about the number of ships captured. About the other numbers all that can be said is that they are not obviously implausible.

The most striking honour that Chabrias received in connection with the victory at Naxos was the award of a bronze portrait statue, which was prominently

---

15 See Nouhaud 1982, 340. Demosthenes does not name Conon's victory at Cnidus either (§ 68).
16 Diod. 15.35.2; Xen. *Hell.* 5.4.61.
17 "C'est à propos de la bataille de Naxos que l'exagération dans l'éloge est manifeste." (Nouhaud 1982, 340).
18 So Kremmydas 2012, 325. One plausible documentary source is the records of the Naval Commissioners: entries in a naval catalogue of the mid-370s (*IG* ii² 1606 and 1607) identify several ships as "captured from those with Chabrias".

situated in the Agora.[19] Aeschines expressly says that among recipients of awards and statues was Chabrias "for the battle of Naxos" (3.243). Fragments of the inscribed base of the statue show that it was decorated with no less than seven carved wreaths, visual representations of crowns that had been awarded to Chabrias, each with a short inscription naming the donors. Although Chabrias is not named on any of the surviving fragments, the fact that one crown was given by "the soldiers on the ships from the sea-battle at Naxos" makes the identification of the base certain. The other inscriptions refer to Syros, Mytilene (twice) and the Hellespont. The mention of soldiers on Syros supports Demosthenes' statement that Chabrias won over the nearby islands; the references to Mytilene and the Hellespont suggest that he campaigned in those areas in the following year or years.[20] The grant of *ateleia* which is at issue in this speech was presumably — though Demosthenes never says — made at much the same time as the statue was awarded, soon after the battle.

It is surprising, then, that Demosthenes makes no mention of the statue, which was distinctive in appearance and would have made a fine subject for rhetorical elaboration. It is possible that his reference to the manner in which Chabrias disposed his forces at Thebes is intended as an implicit allusion to the statue, which depicted him in the stance that he ordered his troops to adopt in that engagement. But this would be an oddly roundabout way of proceeding, when it would have been easy, as in the case of Conon's statue (§ 70), to refer to it directly. Demosthenes was not obliged to mention the statue, and we can only speculate about the reason why he does not. Perhaps, having just singled out Conon as the first recipient of an honorific statue since the tyrannicides, he thought that Chabrias' later statue might seem by comparison less impressive. Or perhaps the statue was too closely connected in the popular mind with the optimistic early years of the Second Athenian League, a sore subject at the time of the Social War.[21]

---

19 On the date see Burnett and Edmonson 1961. They conclude (p. 91) that: "The vote of public recognition for the victory at Naxos, granting Chabrias a crown and a statue, was most likely passed in the fall or winter of 376/5, soon after the return of the fleet. In the following spring Chabrias was sent to gather the fruits of that victory, and by the time he returned at the end of the summer the statue would have been finished or very nearly so, and the base could be cut."
20 The fragments of the statue base are discussed by Burnett and Edmonson 1961. See too Geagan 2012, 83–86 (C148).
21 Burnett and Edmonson 1961, 91 conclude that the honours recorded on the statue base "symbolized the strength and popularity of the new Athenian League" and suggest that the statue was placed near the inscription recording the establishment of the league.

4 The battle of Chios and the death of Chabrias

Demosthenes says nothing at all about Chabrias' later career and jumps directly from the victory at Naxos to his recent death in battle in the defeat at Chios, about which he speaks as follows:

> Men of Athens, everyone saw that during his lifetime Chabrias always acted in your interest and ended his life fighting for no one else. As a result, it would be right to show your appreciation to his son not only for his achievements during his lifetime but also for the way he died. (§ 80) ... Now, men of Athens, here is something else worth thinking about: we should avoid looking worse than the Chians in the way we treat our benefactors. Although he attacked these men as an enemy in arms, they have not taken away any of the rewards that they previously gave him, but they have placed more weight on his past services than on their recent complaints. You, the men he died to protect while fighting them are about to be seen taking away one of the rewards you gave him for his past services ... (§ 81) His devotion to the city was in my opinion truly unshakable. He had a reputation for being the most cautious (ἀσφαλέστατος) of all your generals.[22] When in command, he used this quality to protect you, but as for himself, when he was assigned to a dangerous position, he showed no concern for it and chose to lose his life rather than pour shame on the honors that he had received from you ... (§ 82)

Chabrias lost his life during the opening engagement of the Social War, an unsuccessful Athenian land and sea attack on the rebel ally Chios.[23] Diodorus, our main source for the battle, describes it as follows:

> The Athenians chose Chares and Chabrias as generals and dispatched them with an army. The two generals on sailing into Chios found that allies had arrived to assist the Chians from Byzantium, Rhodes, and Cos, and also from Mausolus, the tyrant of Caria. They then drew up their forces and began to besiege the city both by land and by sea. Now Chares, who commanded the infantry force, advanced against the walls by land and began a struggle with the enemy who poured out on him from the city; but Chabrias, sailing up to the harbour, fought a severe naval engagement and was worsted when his ship was shattered by a ramming attack. While the men on the other ships withdrew in the nick of time and saved their lives, he, choosing death with glory instead of defeat, fought on for his ship and died of his wounds. (16.7.3–4).

Nepos gives a broadly similar account of the battle itself, albeit with differences of detail. According to him, Chabrias ordered his steersman to sail into the har-

---

[22] It is hard to say whether Chabrias' military career as a whole supported Demosthenes' characterization of him as "most cautious". Pritchett 1974, 31–32 saw a reference to his decision not to pursue the defeated Spartan fleet at Naxos.
[23] The chronology of the Social War is a notoriously vexed problem: see Peake 1997.

bour of Chios, but the other ships did not immediately follow him. Surrounded and under attack, he refused to abandon his trireme and swim back to the nearby Athenian ships, as others of the crew did, but stayed to fight and be killed (*Chabr.* 4.2–3).[24]

As with Naxos, Demosthenes says nothing about the circumstances leading to the battle: there is no mention of the Social War, no explanation of why Chabrias was attacking the Chians, and no account of the engagement itself, even though the details must have been well known. He does not even say that Chabrias died aboard ship rather than on land. His focus instead is on the manner of his death (§ 80), his exceptional patriotism (§ 81), his desire to protect others, lack of concern for his own safety, and wish to avoid dishonour (§ 82). The lack of detail about the battle is hardly surprising: the jurors had no need or wish to be given a full account of a disaster which they could remember all too well. But an additional reason for Demosthenes' reticence, I believe, is that he wished to gloss over any responsibility that might have attached to Chabrias for the result of the battle, and by extension of the war.

A much-debated question, of central importance for the issue of responsibility, is whether Chabrias took part in the battle as a private citizen or as general in command of the fleet. The problem is as follows. Nepos makes a point of saying that Chabrias was serving in a private capacity but adds that he exceeded the generals in authority and the soldiers looked up to him more than to them.[25] Diodorus, as we have seen, states in his account both of the despatch of the expedition and of the fighting at Chios that Chabrias was, with Chares, one of the two generals appointed to command. Either he or Nepos must be wrong. Bradley, in his discussion of Nepos' sources, reasonably doubts whether the biographer would have invented "out of whole cloth" the claim that Chabrias served as a private citizen and was held in higher regard than the generals.[26] But it is no less implausible to suppose that Diodorus twice states that Chabrias was general if this was not what he found in his source (perhaps Ephorus), or that the historian he was following would have been wrong on this point.

One important, though frustratingly inconclusive, piece of evidence is an inscription of 357/6 from the Athenian acropolis recording an alliance between Athens and the Euboean city of Carystos (*IG* ii² 124 = Rhodes and Osborne [2003]

---

24 Bradley (1991) argues that Nepos made use of fourth-century Greek historians, and that his and Diodorus' accounts of Chabrias are both based on Ephorus.
25 *Chabr.* 4.1. Since Chabrias was in command of the ship, he would in this case have been serving as trierarch. On his wealth and record of liturgical service see Davies 1971, 560–561.
26 Bradley 1991, 69–70.

no. 48). It contains a list of the generals who were to swear the oaths, from which the name of Chabrias has been deliberately erased. Different explanations of the erasure have been advanced. One is that Chabrias, having initially been appointed general, was then deposed over his recent unsatisfactory dealings with the mercenary commander Charidemus in Thrace (Dem. 23.171–178 and see below). Another is that, subsequent to the inscribing of the stone, news was received at Athens that he had died in battle, and for that reason his name was removed. A third is that the letter-cutter erroneously entered his name twice (the next name, of which only the first two letters can be read, begins Cha-) and then corrected his mistake.[27] Of these explanations, only the first, for which there is no direct evidence, would have prevented Chabrias, having been elected general, from serving in that capacity at Chios. Unfortunately, the chronology of the Social War is very uncertain, and neither the inscription nor the battle of Chios is securely dateable. But if the war broke out in summer 357, and the battle took place in 357/6, then Chabrias should have been available to command.

Although Demosthenes does not say explicitly in what capacity Chabrias fought at Chios, his use of the passive voice (ἐπειδὴ τὸ καθ' αὑτὸν ἐτάχθη κινδυνεύειν) could reasonably be taken to suggest that he had been assigned to a position of danger, in the van of the Athenian fleet, by someone other than himself, i.e. that he was not general.[28] But Demosthenes' words do not require this interpretation, and I suspect that the ambiguity is in fact deliberate and is intended to obscure the fact that Chabrias had, as Diodorus reports, been general.[29] Why Demosthenes would wish to do so is not hard to explain. Defeated Athenian generals were routinely criticized and often prosecuted for their failures, and, although Chabrias was no longer alive, it would undermine Demosthenes' praise of him to reveal that he had been in charge of the fiasco.[30] His performance as general would surely have given rise to posthumous criticism. People might have said, for instance, that not only did he have overall responsibility for the conduct of the battle, but that it was his rash decision to make an unsupported attack on the enemy ships that precipitated the defeat; moreover, his refusal to swim to the safety of a nearby ship, from where he could have

---

[27] See Rhodes and Osborne (2003) *ad loc.*, with reference to earlier scholarship.
[28] Canevaro 2016, 324 takes the words in this sense: "Demostene sembra sostenere che Cabria fu schierato da altri in posizione pericolosa."
[29] On what follows see in detail Bearzot 1990, who argues that the discrepant traditions about Chabrias to be found in our sources reflect contemporary controversy about his record.
[30] On trials of Athenian generals see Pritchett 1974, 4–33; Hansen 1975; Roberts 1982.

resumed command, left the Athenian fleet without effective leadership.[31] Maybe indeed, to speculate a little further, Chabrias chose to fight to the death precisely because he feared the consequences for himself if he were to return to Athens as a defeated general.[32] Be that as it may, it was safer for Demosthenes to focus on his noble death and say nothing about his role in what had gone wrong. There is a parallel in a slightly later speech of Demosthenes: Hornblower has persuasively argued that the orator engages in similar misdirection in the speech *On the Liberty of the Rhodians*, where behind his emphasis on the responsibility of Mausolus for the outbreak of the Social War (Dem. 15.3) lies not just an obvious wish to downplay the role of the allies — obvious because he is seeking to persuade the Athenians to go to the aid of their former enemies the Rhodians — but also "perhaps invisibly present — the desire to exonerate the generals whose conduct had lost the Social War."[33] If this is the case, then a plausible explanation for Nepos' error (if such it be) is that he, or his source, had read Demosthenes' speech and been misled by it into supposing, not unreasonably, that Chabrias had not been general. His statement that Chabrias exceeded the general(s) in authority might then represent an attempt on his part to explain why, although not (so he believed) general, he played such a prominent in the battle.

5 Demosthenes' rhetorical strategy

To understand Demosthenes' presentation of Chabrias, we need to consider the rhetorical task he has set himself in this section of the speech, and the factors that he needed to take into account in crafting it. As we have seen, his broad purpose is to provide examples of men who received grants of *ateleia* as rewards for actions which were of value to Athens. Chabrias, the victor of a major sea-battle among other feats of arms, clearly fitted the bill. But the circumstances of Demosthenes' involvement in the case obliged him not just to include Chabrias

---

[31] Plutarch makes exactly this claim in his life of Phocion, that Chabrias' habitual rashness led him to throw his life away (6.1). Bearzot 1990, 109–110 suggests that at Chios he was desperate to recover his lost prestige by means of a brilliant *coup de main*.

[32] Diodorus claims that he was afraid to pursue the fleeing Spartans at Naxos, being mindful of the trial and execution of the generals at Arginusae (15.35.1). Theopompus implies that (like other leading generals) he was often absent from Athens in part because of the Athenians' harshness towards their generals (BNJ 115 F 105).

[33] Hornblower 1982, 211, who adduces Dem. 20 as a parallel case.

but to feature him prominently. For he was, on his own account, speaking not just against Leptines' law but also, albeit secondarily, in support of Chabrias' son Ctesippus, who stood to be stripped of the hereditable *ateleia* awarded to his father (§ 1). As a result, Chabrias is mentioned right at the start of the speech and then given the culminating place of honour among the recipients of *ateleia*. Demosthenes was therefore obliged to make his achievements seem particularly impressive. How does he do so?

First, he concentrates on the early part of Chabrias' career. This made sense, both because it was for his successes in this period that he had been awarded *ateleia* and because the final twenty years of his life offered significantly less material for the orator to work with. Our knowledge of Chabrias' later career is incomplete, but what we know of his record is uneven at best. His last success was the effective resistance that he offered to the Thebans at Corinth in the early 360s. Thereafter he and Callistratus were prosecuted for treason over the loss of Oropus to the Thebans (both were acquitted). After a further, abortive, spell of mercenary service in Egypt, he undertook a mission to negotiate with the mercenary commander Charidemus in Thrace which ended with his agreeing terms that were promptly repudiated by the Athenian Assembly.[34] And then came the battle of Chios. It is, therefore, unsurprising that Demosthenes concentrates on his earlier career. This decision also fits with his broad focus on examples of grants of *ateleia* from the period c. 395–375.[35] Through his description of the circumstances occasioning these awards, he presents a version of Athens' history in the first quarter of the fourth century that emphasizes military success against the Spartans and the loyalty of her supporters in other cities. The story that he tells is one in which the restoration of democracy was followed by the victories of Conon and Thrasybulus, which in turn led to the triumphant peace of Antalcidas and the humbling of Sparta (*sic*). When war broke out again, the Athenians steadfastly opposed the Spartans on land and for a second time defeated them at sea. Although this version of the past is one which the jurors were no doubt delighted to hear,[36] especially at a time when good news was in short supply, it also served Demosthenes' purpose to show not only that the awards were deserved by the individuals who received them, but also that the

---

[34] Corinth: Diod. 15.68–69; Oropus: Dem. 21.164 and Ar. *Rhet.* 1364a with discussion by Hansen 1975, 92–93; Egypt: Diod. 15.92.2, Plut. *Ages.* 37; Charidemus: Dem. 23.171–172.

[35] I.e. the grants to pro-Athenians in Corinth, Thasos and Byzantium, to Conon, and to Chabrias himself.

[36] Westwood 2020, 84 sees this speech as already showing Demosthenes' characteristic "strategic deployment of the Athenian past as a continuum of excellence."

activities for which they were awarded contributed to a period of sustained Athenian success. Such glorification of the earlier fourth century was not uncommon in Demosthenes' time. For example, Dinarchus wrote that: "Our city was great, renowned in Greece, and worthy of our forebears, apart from the well-known exploits of the past, at the time when Conon triumphed, as our elders tell us, in the naval battle at Cnidus; when Iphicrates destroyed the Spartan company, when Chabrias defeated the Spartan triremes at sea off Naxos, when Timotheus won the sea battle off Corcyra." (1.75). By contrast, about the more recent past, the period of a further twenty years between the Battle of Naxos — in retrospect a high point of Athens' revival — and the present day, during which Athens had suffered a series of military, diplomatic and economic woes, Demosthenes has understandably little to say.[37]

Demosthenes then has the problem of how to deal with the battle of Chios which, whatever the precise degree of Chabrias' responsibility, was a humiliating reverse for Athens. He does so by glossing over the battle itself and instead focusing on Chabrias' gallant death, an emotionally charged moment which encouraged reflection on his career as a whole. Demosthenes treats Chabrias in a manner that he would surely not have employed had he either died much earlier or been still alive. In short, his account of Chabrias' career is eulogistic in tone and epideictic in style. This can be seen in the heavy use of pathos, hyperbole, antithesis, and superlatives and all-or-nothing language. The numerous emotive references to the injustice inflicted by Leptines' law on Chabrias' son make much of the fact that his father's death has left him an orphan, and as such deserving of sympathy. Demosthenes also refers repeatedly and in the most general terms to Chabrias' trophies as indices of his military success, often with heavy antithesis: "there is no trophy erected by your enemies from spoils taken from you under his command, but there are many that you erected over numerous foes when he was general" (§ 78); "what are we going to say … when the entire world sees standing the trophies that he set up when serving as general for you, yet the rewards that he received for them are being taken away?" (§ 83). Chabrias' service abroad is used to portray him as a global ambassador for the city: "he traveled over almost the entire world without ever bringing disgrace on the city's name or on himself" (§ 76). The hyperbolic assertions that he "has been the only one out of all our generals who did not lose a city, a fortress, a ship, or a soldier when he was your leader" (§ 78) and "never caused

---

37 Since our knowledge of grants of *ateleia* depends heavily on this speech, it is difficult to say how many such grants Demosthenes could have cited from the recent past.

anyone's child to become an orphan" (§ 82) are obviously not true.[38] The latter claim seems to have been introduced merely to draw a contrast with the orphaning of Chabrias' own son. Again, Demosthenes' claim that "If he had lost one city or only ten ships, these men [i.e., supporters of Leptines' law] would indict him for treason" (§ 79) reads oddly in light of the fact that Chabrias *had* been prosecuted on precisely such a charge over the loss of Oropus. Demosthenes also uses some of the tropes of epideictic oratory, such as the speaker's inadequacy to do justice to his subject (§ 76) and the concern to omit nothing (§ 78). Indeed, the fourth-century prose texts to which this passage has the closest affinities are both to be found in epideictic speeches: Isocrates' praise of his pupil Timotheus in *Antidosis* and, with the particular point of resemblance that it also addresses the recent death in battle of an Athenian general, Hyperides' praise of Leosthenes in his *Epitaphios*.[39]

6 Conclusion

It is hardly surprising that Demosthenes is selective in his handling of Chabrias' career and includes only what suits his purpose. His arrangement is loosely chronological, from Chabrias' early successes to the battle of Naxos to his death at Chios, but the coverage is uneven. The early years are dealt with briskly and without appeal to any supporting evidence: Demosthenes assumes knowledge of Chabrias' manoeuvring at Thebes, his defeat of Gorgopas, and his service in Cyprus and Egypt. Unsurprisingly he devotes more space to the battle of Naxos, where he both appeals to the memories of older members of his audience and provides documentation in the form of the decree honouring Chabrias and his own list of his achievements. But there are grounds for thinking that his claims to accuracy are at least partially fraudulent. He also says nothing about the battle itself, or about possible allegations that Chabrias let a decisive victory slip away out of an excess of caution. Chabrias' less glorious recent past is passed over in silence, and his death is presented in a strongly emotional style which obscures his culpability for Athens' defeat.

---

38 The Athenians certainly suffered losses at Naxos, and there must have been other casualties in so long a career. Westwood 2020, 106 aptly refers to the "virtual heroizing of Chabrias" in this passage.
39 Isoc. 15.101–139; Hyp. 6 (*Epitaph.*) *passim*. Herrman 2009, 61–62 writes *ad* Hyp. 6. (*Epitaph.*) 3 that "The focus on the individual is unique to this epitaphios" (p. 61) and suspects the influence of prose encomia.

Everything in this passage is carefully composed to serve Demosthenes' rhetorical purpose, to present Chabrias in the best possible light. The numbers given for the aftermath of Naxos suggest that accurate and detailed information was regarded as desirable, but, since they may be exaggerated, we need to be alive to the possibility that the precision is bogus and serves a purely rhetorical purpose, to give the impression that the speaker values accuracy and is therefore reliable. Exaggeration that does not advance Demosthenes' case seems to be almost a reflex. As Nouhaud asked: was it necessary for him to cheat in this way in order to prove that Chabrias' son should not be deprived of the privileges that he inherited from his father?[40] Finally, Demosthenes' handling of the recent past is not more reliable or straightforward than his treatment of earlier events. His account of Chabrias' death may be literally true, so far as can be judged, but it is overblown and deliberately misleading on the critical question of whether Chabrias was general at the time. On this point, although Demosthenes is writing so soon after the event, the argument that he is for that reason more credible than Diodorus is not cogent. Diodorus, whatever his faults as a historian, was concerned to tell what happened, whereas the orator's brief is simply to persuade.

Bibliography

Bearzot, C. (1990), "L'orazione demostenica 'Contro Leptine' e la polemica sulla morte di Cabria", in: M. Sordi (ed.), *Dulce et decorum pro patria mori: la morte in combattimento nell'antichità*, Milan, 95–110.

Bengtson, H. (1962), *Die Staatsverträge des Altertums II: Die Verträge der griechisch-römischen Welt von 700 bis 338 v. Chr.*, Munich.

Bianco, E. (2000), "Chabrias Atheniensis", *RSA* 30, 47–72.

Bradley, J.R. (1991), *The Sources of Cornelius Nepos: Selected Lives*, New York/London.

Buckler, J. (1972), "A second look at the monument of Chabrias", *Hesperia* 41, 466–474.

Burnett, A./Edmonson, C. (1961), "The Chabrias Monument in the Athenian Agora", *Hesperia* 30, 74–91.

Canevaro, M. (2018), "What was the law of Leptines' really about? Reflections on Athenian public economy and legislation in the fourth century BCE", *Constitutional Political Economy* 29, 440–464.

Canevaro, M. (2016), *Demostene Contro Leptine*, Berlin/Boston.

Davies, J.K. (1971), *Athenian Propertied Families 600–300 BC*, Oxford.

---

40 "Était-il nécessaire de tricher de la sorte pour prouver que le fils de Chabrias ne devait pas être privé par la loi de Leptine des privilèges hérités de son père?" (Nouhaud 1982, 340).

Domingo Gygax, M. (2016), *Benefaction and Rewards in the Ancient Greek City: The Origins of Euergetism*, Cambridge.
Geagan, D.J. (2012), *Inscriptions: The Dedicatory Monuments* (The Athenian Agora XVIII), Princeton.
Hansen, M.H. (1975), *Eisangelia: The Sovereignty of the People's Court in Athens in the Fourth Century B.C. and the Impeachment of Generals and Politicians*, Odense.
Harris, E.M. (2008), *Demosthenes, Speeches 20–22*, Austin.
Harris, E.M. (2018), *Demosthenes, Speeches 23–26*, Austin.
Henry, A.S. (1983), *Honours and Privileges in Athenian Decrees*, Hildesheim.
Herrman, J. (2009), *Hyperides: Funeral Oration*, Oxford.
Hornblower, S. (1982), *Mausolus*, Oxford.
Hornblower, S. (2002), *The Greek World 479–323 BC^3*, London/New York.
Kremmydas, C. (2012), *Commentary on Demosthenes* Against Leptines, Oxford.
Nouhaud, M. (1982), *L'Utilisation de l'histoire par les orateurs attiques*, Paris.
Peake, S. (1997), "A note on the dating of the Social War", *G & R* 44.2, 161–164.
Pritchett, W.K. (1974), *The Greek State at War*, vol. II, Berkeley/Los Angeles.
Rhodes, P.J./Osborne, R. (2003), *Greek Historical Inscriptions 404–323 BC*, Oxford.
Roberts, J.T. (1982), *Accountability in Athenian Government*, Madison/London.
Ruzicka, S. (2012), *Trouble in the West: Egypt and the Persian Empire 525–323 BCE*, Oxford/New York.
Westwood, G. (2020), *The Rhetoric of the Past in Demosthenes and Aeschines*, Oxford.

Nathan Crick
The Rhetoric of Deflection: Demosthenes's *Funeral Oration* as Propaganda

Abstract: This chapter argues that when Demosthenes was chosen by the Athenians to deliver the funeral oration for those who had died fighting Philip II of Macedonia at the battle of Chaeronea in 338, he was given an unenviable task. Not only had the Athenians been decisively defeated, but Demosthenes had been an outspoken advocate for the disastrous campaign. His solution was to craft what Max Goldman has called a "rhetoric of defeat" whereby the Athenians could claim that "true victory is in the excellence of the city itself that produced the citizens who fought nobly." This chapter explores the rhetorical nuances of this type of rhetoric in more detail. Using Kenneth Burke's *War of Words*, Crick argues that Demosthenes combines strategies of *reversal* and *spiritualization* in order to reverse victory into defeat by changing the register of a valuation from a materialistic to an idealistic standard that produces emotional satisfaction at the expense of realistic evaluation.

The soldiers representing the alliance formed between the Athenians and the Thebans met the forces of Philip of Macedon at Chaeronea in the late summer of 338 B.C. The clash, for the alliance, was to be a mighty battle that would redeem the policy advocated by Demosthenes for years to confront the rising power of Macedon before it was too late. But by 338, it was too late — if indeed the Greeks ever had a timely opportunity. The Greek forces were routed: "Perhaps as much as half of the Greek army was killed or captured. In complete shock and disarray the survivors (including Demosthenes) managed to struggle over the Kerata Pass ... to their homes."[1] Yet the Athenians did not immediate fall to the Macedonian army. A negotiated peace was declared, the price for the Greeks being partial occupation and giving up their freedom to direct their own foreign policies. The long-term practical result, of course, was that Philip would bring all of mainland Greece under his control. As I. Worthington writes, "even though the polis as an entity continued to exist, the Greeks now had to contend with the

---

I would like to thank Aggelos Kapellos for keen editorial guidance and always positive spirit.

---

1 Worthington 2014, 88.

practical rule of Macedonia."² But in the immediate aftermath, this fate was as yet unwritten; as Athenians still dreamed that their freedom might yet be won. Philip had not destroyed Athenian democracy and subsequent actions by the Athenians, such as offering "asylum to anyone fleeing Philip's purges," showed they had not fully accepted their subordination to his rule.³ As W. Jaeger narrates this moment, "inwardly, the time was one of dull pressure and smoldering distrust, flaring up to a bright flame at the least sign of any tremor or weakness in Macedonia's alien rule," an "excruciating state of affairs [that] continued as long as any hope remained."⁴ It was within this tense moment that Demosthenes was entrusted to deliver the *Funeral Oration* for those who had died in a failed effort to fulfill the aims of Demosthenes's own campaign, aims which he continued to defend in 330 B.C. in his oration *On the Crown* when he boasted that it was he alone who "saw Philip reducing all mankind to servitude, I opposed him, and without ceasing warned and exhorted you to make no surrender" (18.72). The task after the collapse of this policy was straightforward if daunting — to reinterpret a defeat as a victory, redeem his foreign policy, make the deaths of the soldiers meaningful, give hope to the Athenians, and finally refute the accusation by his political rival Aischines that "Demosthenes broke ranks and ran away" during the battle.⁵

The text of the speech that has come down to us, Demosthenes 60, the *Funeral Oration*, has not historically enjoyed a good reputation; indeed, its apparent flaws led Dionysius of Halicarnassus, writing three centuries later, to deny Demosthenes's authorship based on the fact that it was "vulgar, empty, and childish" and, "utterly defective in composition."⁶ Jaeger agrees, arguing that in light of the orator's past genius, the speech would have shown that "the strength of his soul somehow seems to have been paralyzed," which Jaeger refuses to contemplate.⁷ However, the text has more recently been championed as being both authentic and, if not great, at least not wholly deficient. D. MacDowell argues that to criticize the speech for its lack of "fiery vigour and spirited defiance of the Macedonians" is out of place, for "this is not a political speech but a funeral oration, in which fiery vigor would have been inappropriate."⁸ Worthington also emphasizes that, given the context, one could not expect a

---

2 Worthington 2014, 90.
3 Worthington 2013, 257.
4 Jaeger 1938, 192.
5 MacDowell 2009, 372.
6 Cited in MacDowell 2009, 377.
7 Jaeger 1938, 192.
8 McDowell 2009, 377.

high level of eloquence: "While the speech may not be on par with Demosthenes' other speeches, we should not forget how hard a task it must have been for him to write against the background of this failed anti-Macedonian policy."[9] Furthermore, as J. Roisman has shown, the logic of the speech adapts perfectly to the contours of the rhetorical situation. Traditionally, Athenian funeral orations proclaimed "that the highest honors are to be attained in war" to the extent that Demosthenes even lamented, at one time, that in peace, Athens "squandered its wealth and lost allies won at war."[10] It is hardly surprising that he would continue to celebrate the "martial virtues" of Athenians even in defeat.[11] N. Loraux, for instance, writes that Demosthenes's "eulogy ultimately tries, then, to identify the dead of Chaeronea with their mythical ancestors; in order to be faithful to their progenitors, the citizens of the ten tribes have only to die glorious deaths, and this death is a return to the sources of Athens. Through death the destiny of the city is fulfilled: history is abolished, the past justifies the present, and the present returns to the distant past."[12] Furthermore, any flaws can be accounted for by the contradictory demands placed upon the orator.[13] As a representative of the epideictic genre, the speech thus represents a fitting rhetorical response to a complex political situation in a way that makes it worthy of analysis.[14]

For our purposes, what makes the speech relevant in our time is less the way he bolsters Athenian pride and more the way it exemplifies how the rhetorical strategy of deflection can deny reality and encourage an audience to operate under false illusions of its own grandeur. In this case, the rhetoric of deflection responds to a situation marked by defeat, failure, and impending catastrophe by scapegoating opponents, deflecting from uncomfortable reality, and the mystifying an audience through the myth of heroism. A familiar rhetoric of deflection in the context of United States history is the "Myth of the Lost Cause" that arose after the defeat of the Confederacy by the Union forces. As E. Bonekemper writes, "the myth was developed during Reconstruction as shell-shocked and impoverished Southerners tried to rationalize the institution of slavery and the heroic performance of Confederate leaders and soldiers."[15] According to A. Nolan, "the purpose of the legend was to hide the Southerners

---

9 Worthington in Demosthenes 2006, 25; see also Worthington 2003.
10 Roisman 2005, 113.
11 Roisman 2005, 113.
12 Loraux 1986, 127.
13 See Roisman 2014, 277–293.
14 See Herrman 2008, 171–178 and Rung 2018, 76–83.
15 Bonekemper 2015, 2.

tragic and self-destructive mistake... The victim of the Lost Cause legend has been *history*, for which the legend has been substituted in the national memory."[16] Although the specific situations of the American and Greek confederacies were hardly analogous, the rhetoric of deflection that arose in the wake of catastrophic defeats shared similar characteristics. Indeed, I wish to argue that what we see in Demosthenes 60 captures many of the intuitive rhetorical strategies that people can use to mask the true nature of their situation so that they can live as heroes in their imagination even as they ignore the true nature of suffering and neglect the pressing demand for leadership. In other words, the *Funeral Oration* attributed to Demosthenes, whether authentic or not, remains useful to us as a warning against the temptation to mask painful reality with flattering delusion.

1 The Rhetoric of defeat

What I am calling Demosthenes's rhetoric of deflection builds on the concept of the "rhetoric of defeat" conceptualized by M.L. Goldman to interpret the same oration. For Goldman, the *Funeral Oration* by Demosthenes, although largely following the epideictic conventions of its age, was different from previous funeral oration, such as that of Pericles, by having to "reframe the defeat at Chaeronea as a species of victory."[17] Hence, the rhetoric of defeat persuades an audience to reinterpret a decisive and devastating military loss as a kind of victory when evaluated by different standards than strictly martial strategy. In the case of Demosthenes, Goldman argues that he "accomplishes this reframing in two main ways: first, he emphasizes the role of fate and divinity in determining the outcome of any battle, and second, he redefines victory in terms of individual hoplite valor."[18] For Demosthenes, to wonder about the cause of defeat is to needlessly inquire into the mind of a fickle divinity who determines the loser in winner of any battle. However, in Goldman's words, "true victory is the excellence (*arete*) displayed by the soldier who fought and the politicians who directed the policy of the city. True victory is in the excellence of the city itself that

---

16 Nolan 2000, 12.
17 Goldman 2017, 124.
18 Goldman 2017, 123.

produced the citizens who fought nobly."[19] To put it another way, better to lose with honor then win through base trickery[20] or brute force.

The present interpretation of the *Funeral Oration* differs from Goldman's analysis largely in terms of tenor rather than specific facts. Goldman accurately identifies each of the primary strategies Demosthenes uses to translate defeat into victory, and his insights will be subsequently drawn upon in this analysis. Where I differ is reading the speech more explicitly as a variant of propaganda that can have both devastating consequences in both the short-term, in terms of political decision-making, and the long-term, in terms of enduring sociological attitudes. Goldman strives to maintain an even tone throughout his analysis, arguing that "both the funeral oration and the defense speech *On the Crown* provide precious insight into how a society and a political leader could deal with the decisive and devastating defeat."[21] There is an implication here that Demosthenes set the model that might be usefully imitated by contemporary political orators, an interpretation bolstered by Goldman's effort to defend the quality of the oration. In his conclusion, he writes that "the very conventionality of the speech, so often criticized, provides Demosthenes and his audience with a ready-made rhetoric for addressing disruptive defeat by minimizing faults through the continuity of Athenian exceptionalism."[22] Although it is unclear whether Goldman is recommending this as an adequate strategy, he nonetheless spares Demosthenes any criticism of his rhetorical choices; the speech emerges as a reasonable and, indeed, underappreciated oration that displays an innovative way to persuade Athenians to believe what history proved to be completely untrue.

To be clear, I do not find fault with the absence of ethical or instrumental evaluation in Goldman's analysis; an important component rhetorical criticism is evaluating a speaker on his or her own terms and I shall consequently freely draw from his insights. I simply wish to draw the contrast between the rhetoric of defeat, which follows a neo-Aristotelian method, and the rhetoric of deflection inspired by a dramatistic and propagandistic approach. The subsequent analysis will thus draw from two theoretical sources. The work of K. Burke will provide the tools for dramatistic interpretation, specifically rhetorical devices defined in his book, *The War of Words*. For Burke, words can always be used as

---

19 Goldman 2017, 140.
20 Cf. Piovan in this volume about Lys. 2 and his interpretation of the Athenian defeat at Aegospotami as a conspiracy theory.
21 Goldman 2017, 141.
22 Goldman 2017, 141.

instruments of war, and finding devices by which wars are instigated, won, lost, transformed, deferred, or continued indefinitely can help us, perhaps, avoid war in the future. Then the work of J. Ellul, specifically his book *Propaganda*, will point out the consequences that propaganda, particularly when it exploits the resources of myth, can have on a culture when it becomes embedded in its sociological fabric. Both of these resources will then show how the *Funeral Oration* of Demosthenes helped establish a model of rhetoric whose primary function was to mask reality through an attractive delusion.

2 The Rhetoric of deflection

All rhetorical performances involve some quality of deflection. As language is by nature selective even when it attempts to reflect reality, it will naturally deflect from certain aspects of it, particularly those that the speaker wishes to avoid and an audience does not desire to confront, such as the name of the place of a defeat.[23] Burke acknowledges that "since even the most imaginative, intelligent, virtuous, and fortunate of men must err in their attempts to characterize reality, some measure of deflection is natural, inevitable," particularly when "special interests can gain advantage by deflections in the vocabulary of criticism."[24] The prevalence of deflection is particularly characteristic of epideictic genres of rhetoric when people attend orations *desiring* to hear words that mask uncomfortable realities, reminiscent of Socrates's observation in Plato's *Menexenus* that it is easy to flatter Athenians among Athenians (235a2–b2). Speaking of the context of Demosthenes's speech, for instance, Carey notes that any funeral oration of this type "becomes an act of collective self-definition and self-assertion," meaning that the speaker "must present that collective self-image in a way that is inherently convincing and so conducive to the general sense of identity and of shared purpose."[25] Consequently, a speaker like Demosthenes must depart from the literal transcription of facts and construct a "narrative which combines events from the mythic past with events from (predominantly fifth century) history, both told to create a coherent image and therefore both in essence mythical, since not only is the historical past filtered from suitable events but those events in turn are told in a way which by selective treat-

---

23 See Kapellos 2022, 1–27.
24 Burke 2018, 68.
25 Carey 2007, 243.

ment conforms with the message of the encomium."[26] Not only, therefore, is deflection a natural characteristic of rhetoric, but it is so integral to funeral orations that an audience who did not properly get "carried away" from harsh reality by the orator would leave dissatisfied and perhaps even offended.

Deflection as a rhetorical device is something other than distraction. To distract from one thing to another is simply to call attention to a different, sometimes totally unrelated object, event, or person. Had Demosthenes flatly ignored the loss to Phillip and discoursed instead about his brilliant plans for an upcoming battle this would have been simply a distraction, bolstered by the device of what Burke calls "the quietus," which amounts to a strategy of refutation by which an event is denied or an idea is rejected by the collective agreement by leaders of public opinion to simply stop talking about it.[27] Deflection, by contrast, does not seek to turn our attention *away* from something or just plug our ears to bad news; indeed, it purports to direct our attention precisely *to* the issue at hand. The difference is that "deflection is got by a changing of the terms in which a question is considered."[28] Consider, for example, how both Demosthenes in On the Crown and Lycurgus in Against Leocrates attempted to deal directly with the consequences of the loss at Chaeronea while at the same time deflecting from the facts that might have caused panic.[29] In other words, deflection changes our view of something by altering the context of its surroundings, the direction of our approach, the terms by which we describe it, and the questions that we ask of it, and the principles we use in its evaluation. In the rhetoric of defeat, deflection might be a matter of asking the audience to consider "in what ways was this battle a victory?" But there are many other, more subtle deflections that can be far more effective and long-lasting.

The strategy of deflection that Demosthenes relies on most heavily, and which is characteristic of these types of orations, is deflection by widening the circumference of the scene. The strategy uses what Burke calls "the most typical convenience of reasoning, the use of wider terms that subsume narrower terms," such as when you attack or defend "an individual in the name of his class or nation."[30] In its aggressive forms, Burke notes that this strategy is almost like getting back at an enemy "vicariously by kicking his dog."[31] But one

---

26 Carey 2007, 243.
27 Burke 2018, 182.
28 Burke 2018, 71.
29 See Roisman in this volume.
30 Burke 2018, 70.
31 Burke 2018, 70.

can also do the opposite, which is to say to praise a man by complimenting his dog and indeed all the pets he has ever owned. Demosthenes wastes no time pursuing this latter strategy. After his formulaic introduction that acknowledges the inability of any speech to praise such glorious dead, he immediately deflects attention from the specific context of the battle by inviting his audience to think about the entire land of Athens and the many generations of descendants stretching back far into history. In fact, Demosthenes goes to almost absurd lengths to deflect attention away from the immediate crisis by making the virtually nonsensical claim that "from the dawn of time, everyone has acknowledged the nobility of these men's birth" (60.4). Having extended time to infinity, Demosthenes then expands the circumference of space to include all of the land of Athens. The dead soldiers, he says, "can trace their heritage not only to a human father but also to this entire land, which they all share in common in which they are recognized as indigenous. For they alone of all people lived in this land from which they were born and handed it on to their descendants." (60.4). As Worthington notes, Demosthenes here refers to the common belief that these soldiers "were born of the land itself (autochthonous)" and thus identified completely with the place of their birth from which they grew like native fauna.[32] Through this first deflection, therefore, the audience is invited to see the bones of the soldiers as a mere reflection or expression of the beauty of the land and the nobility of the descendants that sprung from it.

As the *Menexenus* showed, the purpose of funeral speeches was not so much to honor the dead but to flatter the living (235a5–7). Accordingly, Demosthenes transitions effortlessly into proving the racial superiority of the Athenians by stressing what Burke calls "inborn dignity." This is a strategy of deflection whereby the actual successes or failures of particular actions are largely bypassed in order to stress the innate virtue of the actors that is earned simply by being born of a certain "blood" of a certain "race." In this sense, if one has inborn dignity, one can really do no wrong. Burke sees the strategy, for instance, in the use of Hitler's rhetoric, "whereby the 'Aryan' is elevated above all others by the innate endowment of his blood, while other 'races,' in particular Jews and Negroes, are inherently inferior."[33] In the funeral oration, Demosthenes seeks to "prove" this inborn dignity by ignoring deeds "regarded as myths" and focusing only on "those events which have each been the subject of so many honorable stories that the poets compose in regular meters or in song" (60.9). In an interesting turn, Demosthenes uses the fact that a deed appears

---

[32] Worthington 2006, 26.
[33] Burke 1989, 218.

within a classical poem as proof of its empirical fact. The most ready-to-hand stories, of course, are drawn from the histories and legends of the Persian wars, which tell respectively how "our ancestors alone twice repelled by land and by sea the horde which invaded from the whole of Asia" (in contrast to the heroes at Troy who "captured only one place in Asia with great difficulty after besieging it for ten years") (60.10). The use of the term "hordes" to describe the Persians is a convenient devil-term with which to contrast the virtuous Greeks and only heightens the effect of this strategy and brings him in closer proximity to Hitler's rhetoric by comparison, especially when one takes into account that, as Burke explains, "after the defeat of Germany in the [First] World War, there were especially strong emotional needs that this compensatory doctrine of an *inborn* superiority could gratify."[34] But as Isaac has shown, the Athenians in many ways established the rhetorical foundations of racism in the Western world, in part through their "novel association of the elements of Athens nourishing and serving as fatherland for all other Greeks."[35] To be clear, Demosthenes had very little else in common with Hitler. I only wish to point out that he used the same logic in appealing to inborn quality.

Yet a rhetoric of deflection for a sophisticated civilization like that of Athens cannot rely on earthly appeals alone, as if their virtue simply grew from the soil and was lodged in blood. Demosthenes had to balance them with an equal, if not greater emphasis on the strength of its *ideals*. For Burke, this would call for "a rhetoric of deflection got by the shuttling between two orders of terms, one 'worldly,' one 'spiritual.'"[36] This device is called "spiritualization," or what Burke calls the "Nostrum" because "where mine and thine (the *meum* and the *tuum*) are distinct, they must be spiritually merged in an idea of 'ours' (the *nostrum*.)"[37] The Nostrum allows a speaker to move back and forth between the realms of the body and the mind, the material in the ideal, and the individual and the collective. As a deflection device, it is particular useful when uncomfortable empirical realities press against the senses and demand to be counted; when the last thing one wishes to do in confront such realities, spiritualization comes to the rescue. Burke is worth quoting at length here:

> Are things disunited in the "body"? Then unite them "in spirit." Would a nation extend its physical dominion? Let it talk of spreading its "ideals." ... Is an organization in disarray? Talk of its overall "purpose." Are there struggles over means? Celebrate agreement on

---

34 Burke 1989, 218.
35 Isaac 2013, 121.
36 Burke 2018, 103.
37 Burke 2018, 92.

"ends." Would you sanction expedience? Speak of the corresponding principles. Praise conditions in the name of "freedom."[38]

This set of instructions could have been written for Demosthenes. Here he encountered an Athenian state in disarray, struggling over the means to reestablish its dominion, and seeking to validate its actions in the name of higher principles. Demosthenes, after praising the valor and lineage of the soldiers, then found it necessary to praise their upbringing and, most importantly, the cause for which they were fighting — democratic freedom. Unlike oligarchies which "being run by a few produce fear in their citizens, but do not foster a sense of duty," democracies like that of Athens "have many noble and just qualities, to which sensible people must be loyal, and in particular freedom of speech, which cannot be prevented from showing the truth because it is based on speaking the truth" (60.27). The soldiers did not die because (the gods forbid!) of an ill-planned venture against a stronger enemy; they died in defense of democratic freedom "to avoid the shame of future reprimands, they stalwartly faced the danger coming from our enemies, and chose a noble death rather than a disgraceful life" (60.27). Born from the earth with dignity, these men now ascend to the spiritual Nostrum where they glory in the shared ideals that make Athens superior.

As final evidence that everything he claimed was true, Demosthenes concludes by recourse to a "Spokesman" device by which he claims to speak on behalf not only of the dead but of the living. For Burke, "the Spokesman, as a rhetorical device of deflection, enters when, under the guise of speaking *for* another, we in reality speak *to* him. The spokesman device, in this sense, is designed to induce in an audience an attitude which the audience is supposed to have already, and which the rhetorician is ostensibly but expressing in their behalf."[39] Demosthenes makes use of this device insofar as he purports to be simply stating what everyone knows. Addressing each of the ten tribes of Athens, Demosthenes connects each tribe with the deeds of a mythic hero who "inspired the men in each tribe to be brave" (60.27). For instance, one tribe was inspired to defend their homeland: "The Acamantidae remembered the epics in which Homer says that Acamas failed to Troy for the sake of his mother Aethra. So if Acamas faced every danger to save his own mother, how could these men not decide to brave every danger to save all their parents at home?" (60.29). Another tribe, says Demosthenes matter-of-factly, felt they should die nobly

---

38 Burke 2018, 92.
39 Burke 2018, 77.

rather than accept a lesser prize as dictated by the gods: "The Aeantidae were aware that after Ajax was robbed of the spoils of valor, he considered his own life unlivable. Thus, when the divinity gave the spoils of bravery to another, they thought they should die while warding off the enemy and so not suffer ignominy themselves" (60.31). In each case, Demosthenes imparts motives to each of the soldiers in each tribe under the flatly absurd notion that they went to their deaths inspired by heroic tales rather than the dictates of the state.

The rhetorical use of myth in the closing of the speech provides a powerful way of deflecting from grim details in the present and encouraging his audience to dwell in the misty but attractive realm of imagined origins and destinies. By claiming that Demosthenes made rhetorical use of myth, I do not refer to the fact that he simply told stories of Greek gods and heroes like Theseus, Orpheus, or Dionysus in a somewhat ham-handed effort to argue that each tribe died in order to live up to the virtuous standards established by their actions. Rather, I use myth as defined by J. Ellul, which is to say as a specific strategy of deflection. By "myth" he does not mean a false or fantastic story; he means "an all-encompassing, activating image: a sort of vision of desirable objectives that have lost their material, practical character have become strongly colored, overwhelming, all-encompassing, and which displace from the conscious all that is not related to it. Such an image pushes man's action precisely because it includes all that he feels is good, just, and true."[40] Myth in propaganda has more to do with political utopia; it is "an explanation for all questions in an image of a future world in which all contradictions will be resolved."[41] Consequently, it is the myth of Athens itself that is the dominant myth in Demosthenes's speech that energizes the entire speech. The pale reflection of this political mythology in the form of heroic legends shows Demosthenes at his weakest; the power of his speech lay rather in the Nostrum that sanctioned and glorified the death of thousands of young men on the field of battle.

The power of myth should not be understated, for it is its unique capacity to translate every loss into a victory and to dissolve all particular realities into the fog of collective origins and destinies. Observe, for instance, the rhetorical magic by which Demosthenes translates horrific death in a catastrophic military loss into not just a victory but a blessing.[42] Not only will they receive a "public burial" and "ageless glory in which their children will be raised in honor" in ex-

---

40 Ellul 1965, 21.
41 Ellul 1965, 117.
42 Similarly, Kapellos 2013 argues that Xenophon and the orators do not describe the slaughter of the Athenian captives at Aegospotami in order to avoid offending their audiences.

change for their short life, but their bodies will be "free of sickness in their souls know no pain" (60.32). Indeed, Demosthenes speculates that they "have the same position in the islands of the blessed as the brave men of earlier times" (60.34). Although he admits that it is difficult "to lighten present misfortunes with his speech," he suggests everyone should take great consolation that "it is a majestic thing to see that they have immortal honor and a public memorial of their virtue and are thought to deserve sacrifices and games in perpetuity" (60.35). With such evidence before them, "how can we not consider them fortunate?" (60.34). In fact, for those caught up in the thrall of mythic deflection, there is no pain, suffering, torture, or disaster that can befall an audience that is not considered fortunate, for myth paralyzes all thought and directs attention to the hazy beauty of an imaginary other-world.

3 Conclusion

When interpreting funeral orations and other representatives of the epideictic genre of rhetoric, one must of course account for the fact that the audience *wishes*, to a great degree, the consolations of myth and dreamy imagery. Especially when faced with suffering and death, people naturally wish to have their thoughts deflected toward sunnier conclusions. Who wants to look at the bones of their loved ones and think that they died for nothing? As MacDowell writes, "the audience for the speech consisted primarily of bereaved relatives, who wanted not stimulation but consolation of a traditional kind. They will have been glad to be told that their loved sons and fathers are now free from trouble and enjoy the greatest honor, and will not have found this 'vulgar, empty, and childish.'"[43] And they would have liked to have heard, as Goldman puts it, that "the defeat at Chaeronea was not a defeat at all but proof of continuing Athenian exceptionalism."[44] In dying gloriously they proved their superiority; they are dining at the right hand of the gods who will undoubtedly turn history toward Athenian glory.

But Athens did not achieve glory; within two years it was absorbed within the new Macedonian hegemony of the League of Corinth, which "forever altered the face of Greek politics and brought to an end the centuries-long period of

---

43 MacDowell 2009, 377.
44 Goldman 2017, 133.

Greek autonomy."[45] Consequently, the problem with this sort of interpretive approach is that it denies reality. Just because people desire to be flattered and consoled does not mean that anything goes. Furthermore, attempting to place a bell jar over the epideictic genre, in effect isolating it from the wider situational context, denies the clear political and deliberative aspects of the speech insofar as it occurred at a *public* funeral led by the *politician* who advocated for the military campaign. What Demosthenes asserts in the funeral oration leaves a residue in the public mind that carries over into other judgments and attitudes.

Ellul refers to this impact as a kind of "sociological propaganda," similar to what Goldman refers to in his references to Athenian exceptionalism. Sociological propaganda uses more diffuse cultural forms of communication, such as rituals, festivals, entertainment, athletics and the like, "to integrate the maximum number of individuals into itself, to unify its members' behavior according to a pattern, to spread its style of life abroad, enough to impose itself on other groups."[46] Sociological propaganda does not tell people specifically what to do in any case, but what it does is establish the ground for further action. Ellul writes: "Sociological propaganda can be compared to plowing, direct propaganda to sowing; you cannot do one without doing the other first."[47] In other words, the myth that Demosthenes uses to console an audience in a specific funeral oration reaffirms the basic prejudices, stereotypes, and worldviews that can be drawn upon for future campaigns — such as the fruitless effort Demosthenes led to resist Phillip. In Burke's words, sociological propaganda establishes a myth whereby "the essential 'All' becomes divided into a 'We' and a 'They,' with 'Us' invited to cleanse ourselves by assigning the unwanted elements to 'Them,' culminating in "ritual purging by use of enemy as scapegoat."[48] As there is, in short, nothing innocent about Demosthenes's funeral oration.

The most disastrous aspect of the rhetoric of deflection when used in such contexts is that it effectively eliminates the possibility for critical thought. Once the myth it propagates is in place, it pushes out the possibility for detachment, attention to individual facts, the weighing of alternatives, and prediction of consequences. As Ellul writes, "through the myth it creates, propaganda imposes a complete range of intuitive knowledge, susceptible of only one interpreta-

---

45 Worthington 2014, 100.
46 Ellul 1965, 62.
47 Ellul 1965, 15.
48 Burke 2018, 126.

tion, unique and one-sided, and precluding any divergence."⁴⁹ The final proof of this effect in Demosthenes is his complete mystification of the actual battle. This happens in two ways. First, just as Lysias had said in his funeral oration that the defeat was the result of a god's plan (2.58) Demosthenes blames the reason for the loss on the fickle whims of the gods, as in the story he told of Ajax. He writes that "in cases where the divine spirit, the master of all men, decides the outcome as he wishes, all others, being human, must be acquitted of the charge of cowardice" (60.21). But he reveals his political bias when he notes that if anyone is to blame, it is the Theban generals for not making proper use of the "unconquerable spirit" of their forces (60.32).⁵⁰ As Goldman accurately concludes, "the multiple causes for defeat effectively cut off a search for the causes of the defeat and focuses on the excellence of Athens."⁵¹ Second, Demosthenes claims that the loss was actually a victory because their hard fighting led to a negotiated peace, claiming that the Macedonians "did not wish to face the relatives of those men in battle once again" (60.19). Goldman writes that, for Demosthenes, "as long as Athens maintains its institutions, there can be no real defeat, no lasting diminution of Athenian leadership".⁵² And this was the point – to reaffirm the status quo. By a strategy of deflection, the Athenians were invited to simply ignore the defeat altogether and assume their usual posture of confidence in their mythic destiny that would allow Athens to rise again.

The funeral oration by Demosthenes, whether actually penned by him or not, nonetheless stands as a representative of the rhetoric of deflection and sociological propaganda. It deserves to be read and studied because it reveals, in absolutely clear logic, the way in which a speaker can satisfy the immediate emotional needs of an audience who has suffered defeat in a way that leaves a lasting impression of their unearned cultural superiority. The impact of this impression should not be underestimated, for it establishes a flattering mythology that denies the reality of their larger world and sets the stage for scapegoating violence and inevitable disaster as they move forward with false confidence of their own excellence in an ever-changing world. This essay has made casual reference to the American Confederacy and Nazi Germany as examples of cultures which have left a mythic residue in contemporary life that remains as

---

49 Ellul 1965, 11.
50 This conforms to a typical Athenian strategy of scapegoating others for their defeats. It is reminiscent of the way the Athenians scapegoated Adeimantus after their defeat at Aegospotami, explored in Kapellos 2009. Piovan also argues in this volume that Lysias accuses the general at Aegospotami as conspiring with the Spartans.
51 Goldman 2017, 133.
52 Goldman 2017, 134.

powerful and dangerous and seductive as ever; but these are just to make a point. We hear this kind of mythic rhetoric of deflection in every culture and at every time, each confident in its own cause. For, unfortunately, it is human nature to seek solace primarily by being reassured of one's special excellence, whether that is racial supremacy, religious doctrine, national glory, or simply the random placement of a certain grouping of people on the globe. There is no limit to the ways human beings can distort the meaning of their situation to make themselves feel superior even as they deny all responsibility for making good judgments. Demosthenes performed the task he was called to perform by the Athenians; by their standards and that of the genre, he performed admirably. But perhaps with the gift of distance we might begin to question rhetorical strategies that allay our fears through deflection and rationalize our flaws and failures through myth.

Bibliography

Bonekemper, E.H. (2015), *The Myth of the Lost Cause: Why the South Fought the Civil War and Why the North Won*, New York.
Burke, K. (1989), *On Symbols and Society*, J.R. Gusfield (ed.), Chicago.
Burke, K. (2018), *The War of Words*, A. Burke/K. Jensen/J. Selzer (eds.), Berkeley.
Carey, C. (2007), "Epideictic Oratory", in: I. Worthington (ed.), *A Companion to Greek Rhetoric*, Malden, 236–252.
Ellul, J. (1965), *Propaganda: The Formation of Men's Attitudes*, New York.
Goldman, M.L. (2017), "Demosthenes, Chaeronea, and the rhetoric of defeat", in: J.H. Clark/B. Turner (eds.), *Brill's Companion to Military Defeat in Ancient Mediterranean Society*, Leiden, 123–143.
Herrman, J. (2008), "The Authenticity of the Demosthenic Funeral Oration", *Acta Ant. Hung.* 48 (1–2), 171–178.
Jaeger, W. (1938), *Demosthenes: The Origin and Growth of his Policy*, Berkeley.
Isaac, B. (2013), *The Invention of Racism in Classical Antiquity*, Princeton.
Kapellos, A. (2009), "Adeimantos at Aegospotami: Innocent or Guilty?", *Historia* 58, 257–275.
Kapellos, A. (2013), "Xenophon and the Execution of the Athenian Captives at Aegospotami", *Mnemosyne* 66.3, 464–472.
Kapellos, A. (2022), "Xenophon and the Orators on the Topography of Arginousae and Aegospotami", *Mnemosyne* (on line) 1–27.
Loraux, N. (1986), *The Invention of Athens: The Funeral Oration in the Classical City* (trans. Alan Sheridan), Harvard.
McDowell, D.M. (2009), *Demosthenes the Orator*, Oxford.
Nolan, A.T. (2000), "The Anatomy of the Myth", in: G.W. Gallagher/A.T. Nolan (eds.), *The Myth of the Lost Cause and Civil War History*, Bloomington, 11–34.
Roisman, J. (2014), "Persuading the People in Greek Participatory Communities", in: D. Hammer (ed.), *A Companion to Greek Democracy and the Roman Republic*, Malden, 277–293.

Roisman, J. (2005), *The Rhetoric of Manhood: Masculinity in the Attic Orators*, Berkeley.
Rung, E.V. (2018), "Remembering the Athenian Defeat at Chaeronea", *Revista San Gregoria* 23, 76–83.
Worthington, I. (2003), "The Authorship of the Demosthenic 'Epitaphios'", *MH* 60, 152–157.
Worthington, I. (2006), *Demosthenes, Speeches 60 and 61, Prologues, Letters*, Austin.
Worthington, I. (2013), *Demosthenes of Athens and the Fall of Classical Greece*, Oxford.
Worthington, I. (2014), *By the Spear: Phillip II, Alexander the Great, and the Rise and Fall of the Macedonian Empire*, Oxford.

Patrice Brun
Demosthenes, between Fake News and Alternative Facts

Abstract: The decision of the Athenians to accept the Peace of Philocrates in 346 and the formation of a military alliance with Thebes in 339 help us learn from the way Demosthenes had re-invented recent history in his favour. In 346 Athens had no other choice but sue for peace with Philip and Demosthenes agreed with this position. Three years later, he tried to make the Athenians believe that they could have continued the war, showing that the Peace was faulty and trying to make Philocrates and Aeschines responsible for the situation. In 18.168–216, about the alliance with Thebes in 339, Demosthenes recalls that the speech he delivered on that occasion as ambassador prompted the Thebans to become allies to Athens. However, if Demosthenes only talks about himself and never about the others, Hyperides' *Against Diondas* puts him back in his right place since the latter's version is rather different from the one given by Demosthenes.

In the work of Demosthenes, two particular historic moments illustrate how orators shed light on what could be called recent events; they are defined as a narration of facts which most of the audience had been directly aware of, either because they had taken part in the debates occurring in the Assembly of the People or because they had had an indirect representation through conversations with friends or relatives. These two moments, one concerning the decision to accept the so-called Peace of Philocrates in 346 and, the other about forming a military alliance with Thebes in 339, have been selected because they can be analyzed through different versions: Demosthenes *vs* Aischines for the events of 346 with cross-analysis of the protagonists in 343 about the embassy that had negotiated the alliance, Demosthenes *vs* Aeschines and *vs* Hyperides (through the fragments of his recently published *Against Diondas*) for the alliance with Thebes. These two examples help us learn from the way Demosthenes had re-invented recent history in his favour, as well as the manner in which the listeners perceived history re-written by the orator.

1 Athens at the time of the Peace of Philocrates

To understand the words of Demosthenes when he accused Aeschines of treason, we have to go back five years in time. These events are well-known but they are worth recalling.

In the year 348 Olynthus, an ally of Athens, surrendered after being besieged for several months by Philip's armies. To understand the insufficient and delayed aid brought to Olynthus by Athens, we also have to keep in mind that at the same time, the city had to confront a rebellion of the Euboean cities, determined to leave the Second Confederation. We tend to forget this war in Euboea, so close to Athens, because Demosthenes acts as though this war did not ever happen. This position is rather paradoxical at first sight but can be accounted for by the fact that this intervention had been suggested by his bitter enemy Meidias.[1] This vision can seem quite strange today but in ancient Athens, personal and political oppositions often derived from one another. Personal differences brutally came in addition to this strategic confrontation, because during the March 348 Dionysia, in the midst of tension about Olynthus, an incident occurred during which Meidias, attacked him during the celebration; this triggered off a judicial imbroglio which ended with a financial arrangement between both parties.[2]

Much later Demosthenes (10.8) accused Philip of starting the popular uprising of the cities of Euboea, using his agents to distract the Athenians. But we first have to remember the responsibilities of the Athenian people who could not care less about the desire of the Euboeans to live in full autonomy and who were not particularly upset about supporting tyrants entirely devoted to them on the island; and among them was Demosthenes although he constantly praised how excellent their democratic regime was and how ideal it was to defend freedom everywhere.[3] Whether the Euboean rebels had taken advantage of the earlier Athenian forces in Chalcidice to revolt or not, or whether the Thebans had encouraged the Euboeans to do so in one way or another, this is highly likely. But Philip at the time did not have the diplomatic tools to interfere so far

---

[1] In fact, Meidias was the *proxenos* of Plutarchus, tyrant of Eretria (Dem. 21.110). On this enmity see Rhodes 1998, esp. 150–152, 158–160; MacDowell 2002, 5–9.
[2] Dem. 21.13–18. Cf. MacDowell 2002, 1–13; Sealey 1993, 143; Mossé 2010, 76–85. It will be recalled that the origin of mutual hatred between the two men has its origins in the trials relating to the inheritance of Demosthenes. See Cook in this volume.
[3] "Oligarchic regimes know that no one other than us aims to restore freedom": Dem. 15.19 (351/0). Cf. also 8.42; 9.70 (341).

from his own bases. Only after 348, probably around 342 or 341,⁴ did he intervene in Euboea more directly.

To the Athenians, waging a war on the two fronts being set was a complete failure: Euboea was lost for the Athenians and during the summer 348, the Athenians were forced to recognize the independence of the cities of the island that were leaving the Confederation, now reduced to an alliance with more modest islands.

The situation did not get any better in the following years: indeed, the Third Sacred War opposing the Phocians and the Thebans, was dragging on. Weakened after several years of conflict, in 347 the Thebans asked for Philip's help to vanquish the "sacrileges"; the latter was quick to accept. For the Athenians, this meant troops being present in Phocis, south of the Thermopylae, which strategically defended the access to central Greece and thus leading to Attica.⁵ From the Phocian side, various possibilities had emerged: the new leader, Phalaikos, Onomarchos' nephew, prohibits the Athenians from accessing the Thermopylae and, the situation became quite unfavorable for them. So, they decided to organize a rebellion front particularly in the Peloponnese in the name of Hellas' freedom. But the potential alliances were not formally established, and Athens did not impress the Greek cities that were unwilling to help a city still determined to exert its power for its own benefit. Furthermore, the Athenians had neither human nor material means to save Phocis and the peace with Philip, whatever its lawful aspect, was eventually in everybody's minds. Philocrates had succinctly summarized the diplomatic situation: there is no chance at all for Athenians to seek victory because most of the Greeks are hostile to the city and many strike up a friendship with Philip.⁶ In the sources still available, only one *politeuomenos*, Aristophon of Azenia, clearly declared he was opposed to a peace treaty that he found unfair.⁷

---

4 Cawkwell 1978, 50.
5 Ober 1989, 73–74.
6 Theopompus, *FGrHist*, 115, F. 164 (= BNJ 115, F 164). Cf. Shrimpton 1991, 84; Harding 2006, 95–96.
7 Theopompus, *FGrHist*, 115, F. 166 (= BNJ 115, F 166). Cf. Shrimpton 1991, 84. It is noted that these two passages are set like an antilogy, the first in favour of the peace, the second against it (Harding 2006, 195–197, 254–255). Probably Theopompus wished to condensate the various arguments exchanged on that occasion and Demosthenes' absence in this debate is worth noting. As the fragments originate from a papyrus with Didymus' comments Περὶ Δημοσθένους, it is likely that Didymus would not have failed to mention Demosthenes' probable position hostile to peace.

In this context we have to understand why embassies had been dispatched between the city and Philip and neither Demosthenes nor Aeschines, like all the other Athenian ambassadors sent to Pella twice, seem to oppose a peace rapidly concluded. As a matter of fact, it was the wisest decision to make. Libanius, with access to sources unavailable today, sums up the situation in one sentence: "The Athenians wanted peace because the military situation was unfavorable to them".[8]

However, Athens soon lost hope: the peace did not stop Philip from spinning his web and finding new alliances in the Peloponnese; the Phocians, former allies of Athens, were fiercely treated by Philip and the Thebans were in a closer-than-ever alliance with the king. All the advantages that the Athenians thought they might gain from the war faded away and their fury turned against Philocrates who had led the embassies. Charged in 343 by Hyperides for treason and corruption by *eisangelia*,[9] he fled into exile before his trial, convinced that he could not prove his good faith. All the envoys who had taken part in the embassy, Demosthenes and Aeschines in the first place, raged against their former colleague who had become so disruptive.[10] Indeed, since the peace was concluded, Philip had made remarkable progress and the Athenians' position, both diplomatic and military, had become weaker, thus leading us to think that the peace was just a fool's bargain. It is known that Demosthenes, with Timarchus' help, wanted to accuse Aeschines of colluding with Philocrates but Aeschines counter attacked by turning popular anger against his prosecutor: this was the suit *Against Timarchus*. Demosthenes fought back directly and, and rare as it may be, we have the cross speeches of Demosthenes and Aeschines. It is also known that Demosthenes, as well as Aeschines in their respective speeches try on the one hand to show how treacherous Philocrates was, he who had sold the city to the Macedonian and on the other hand attempt to convince the jurors that "the other one" had been accomplice to the *traitor* Philocrates.

But what is interesting here lies in the rhetorical strategy chosen by Demosthenes in 343 during the trial. It was indispensable for him to deny any collusion with Philocrates and so three years after the events, and against all likelihood he had to show that he had always been hostile to this treaty which proved to be so unfavorable to the Athenian interests. Hence his rather awkward attempt to pretend that he had been kept away from the real negotiations which had apparently taken place while he was away. In his argument, he goes

---

[8] Dem. 5. *Hyp.*, 1.
[9] Hyp. 3.28–30.
[10] Dem. 19.116; Aesch. 2.6.

as far as to assert that concluding such an early peace in 343 was of no interest for Athens, adding that only Philip was compelled to it. For Demosthenes' line of argument, omissions and lies become necessary.

Omissions in Demosthenes' way of thinking are very clearly echoed in a passage of the speech delivered by Philocrates and kept in Theopompus' fragment quoted above: Athens has no reliable allies and Demosthenes willingly forgets to draw up the list of the enemies or those who distrust Athens. The neighbouring cities are hostile to it: Thebes, a long-time enemy and now an undisputed ally to Philip but also Megara, a city against which the Athenians had led an expedition in 349.[11] Since the Social War (357–355) the East Aegean large cities had become the enemies of Athens. The situation in the Peloponnese was so complicated that the Athenians could not rely on anyone at all because of the alliance they had developed with Sparta, most unanimously hated in the peninsula, whereas on his side Philip had forged strong friendly ties with those who openly opposed Sparta. For Peloponnesian cities, nobody was fearful of Philip and Athens as well as Sparta were hated by almost everybody, as the past and the present testified to it. Lastly, Demosthenes again "fails" to mention the plight of many Athenians who had been held prisoners when Olynthus was besieged — a good trade-off. And of course, Demosthenes never speaks about the financial situation of the city; indeed, to support an aggressive position, Aristophon evokes public incomes up to 400 talents, a figure corroborated by Demosthenes who gives the same figure for the same period of time.[12] But the costs of a campaign were high and the unbalance between the wealth of the city and Philip's was obvious, given that it took him ten years before taking control of the mines of Pangaion. Once again Demosthenes kept silent.[13]

There are lies too in Demosthenes' words when it comes to the Phocians. In his line of argument, he asserts — somehow daringly — that Philip had obtained the right to negotiate the peace, then among the reasons why the peace could not be concluded according to the predicted conditions (to which he himself had agreed though), he claims that Philip had become weaker, unable to have supplies and that the Phocians were in a position to defend themselves (19.123). This is totally untrue: as soon as the king of Macedonia waged the war against

---

11 Dem. 13.32; 3.20. See above, n. 6.
12 Dem. 10.37–38.
13 Even if he tries to make believe in the discourse *On the Peace*, by appealing to the memory of the Athenians (5.10) — artificial expression because, in such a short period of time, there is no doubt that there were still several "collective memories", that he has always been suspicious of this peace. Cf. MacDowell 2009, 327–328. For using of citizens' memory, see below n. 45.

the Phocians, the war which the latter led against the Thebans to control the Sanctuary of Delphi had taken a decisive turn and had shown the incapacity of the Athenians to help their Phocian allies.

Omissions and lies here is a genuine and perfect example of how history is re-invented, less than three years after the facts and of course Demosthenes' assertions were totally false. The Athenians were the ones who were forced into peace, Philip was not and he was not threatened in any way, unlike what Demosthenes indicated. He was defeated on the legal ground (Aeschines was cleared of the charge of treason brought by Demosthenes), but does it mean that the Athenians had taken this biased argument into account? That, in other words they refused to condemn Aeschines because the vast majority of them had understood that Demosthenes was not telling the truth? Because they had not forgotten the real situation of the year 346? Or only because they did not believe Aeschines guilty of treason as Demosthenes claimed?

2 Demosthenes and the Theban alliance in 339

Another example of how Demosthenes distorted the truth is shown in the embassy sent by the Athenians in 339 to the Thebans to convince the latter to abandon the Macedonian allegiance which became a burden against the friendship and the alliance of the Athenians. Demosthenes gives his own side of the story describing the role he played on that occasion and more generally after Philip besieged Elateia: everyone has in mind the renowned episode in which he showed himself the "supreme (or divine) savior", and where, according to Slater's fortunate formula, he acted out his own epiphany.[14] In the complicated diplomatic round which led the Thebans to leave Philip, Demosthenes played a key role, other orators such as Hyperides or Hegesippus of course have also supported this idea, though Demosthenes does not quote their names in his writings about the course of events and yet they had opposed Macedonia for much longer.[15] So, in these conditions, it is hard to agree with Ian Worthington that "Demosthenes was the only one person with a plan to rescue Athens".[16] Thus, how the delegation of ten ambassadors sent to Thebes was composed remains unknown: Demosthenes does mention ten ambassadors designated on

---

[14] Dem. 18.123; Slater 1998, formula taken over by Westwood 2020, 297.
[15] Sawada 2019, 342–346; Gallo 2019, 357–358.
[16] Worthington 2013, 243.

that occasion.[17] But, he does not mention any of them, almost pretending that he was alone whereas that of 346, he names every single person, obviously to water down his own responsibility.

Indeed, in 18.153, in order to account for the shift of the Thebans, he unhesitatingly asserts that "it was thanks to the favour of some god and also, as it depended on one man only, thanks to me", establishing a perfect union of speech and action. As P. Hunt underlines it, "he is far from modest".[18] This is the least we can say. And what about the way he presented, a little further in the speech, his action at the Assembly when the Athenians learned of the capture of Elateia by Philip? In this solemn passage, in probably the most stirring moment of the speech, where emotion and *pathos* prevail,[19] he speaks only of himself and suggests, against all likelihood, that he alone spoke — which is of course impossible.

In his long account of this embassy,[20] Demosthenes reports that, on arriving in Thebes, a Macedonian embassy was already present and that the speech he delivered in front of the Assembly made the Thebans turn to the Athenian alliance. This side of the story is corroborated by Theopompus:[21] inspired by his words, the Thebans rejected fear, thoughtfulness and gratitude to Philip for the noble cause.

It can be noted that for Theopompus, Demosthenes' speech to the Thebans, his powerful style is what changed the situation and even more after he spoke in

---

17 Dem. 18.178, 211.
18 Hunt 2019, 117. Yunis 1996, 268 speaks about "a tour de force of rhetorical artistry".
19 E.g. Kennedy 1994, 76–80; Yunis 1996, 268–277; Roisman 2004, 274–275; MacDowell 2009, 369–371, 391; Worthington 2013, 241–243; Brun 2015, 247–250; Katula 2016, 141. Contrary to what the absolute defenders of Demosthenes' thought (Glotz et al. 1938, 207–209; Treves 1933, 127–128), one should not imagine the whole Greece hanging on the decision of the Athenian justice. It was undoubtedly a great moment of eloquence (cf. Aesch. 3.56, Theophr. *Char.* 8) where the hatred between Demosthenes and Aeschines bursts, where the lies multiply on both sides, but there was no political stake: Athens does not come out of this trial more aggressive against Macedonia than before, and had left Sparta the year before alone against the troops of Antipatros (Din. 1.34–35; Aesch. 3.133. Cf. Brun 2015, 246.
20 18.168–216.
21 Plut. *Dem.* 18.2–3 (= Theopomp., *FGrHist.*, 115, F. 328 = BNJ 115, F 328); for Philoch., *FGrHist.*, 328, F. 56a (= BNJ 328, F 56a; *Dion. Hal.* 10.11,6) and 56b (= BNJ 328, F 56b; *Didymus*, col. XI, 37), see below. Guth 2014, 160–163 rightly notices that Theopompus' version dwells only on the orator's speech, with whom he somehow overlaps. It is clear, however, that Theopompus does not validate the action of Demosthenes, which led Thebes and Athens to their loss. The rhetorical power of the speaker is shown here as harmful: Flower 1994, 144–145; Pownall 2001, 67–68.

front of Philip's ambassadors. Impressed as he had been by the impact of the speech, the king is said to have sought to conclude the peace. This is quite unlikely but echoes the idea that Demosthenes had tried to defend some years earlier: that Philip needed peace (cf. *supra*). But Theopompus reports the orator's words, only because he has a strong interest in enhancing Demosthenes' position in order to accuse him of acting unfairly.

For his part, Diodorus reports the very same events as Demosthenes describes them, going as far as to quote a passage from the orator's speech and rephrase it, unequivocally proving that his direct source when it comes to relating events, is noone else but Demosthenes himself.[22] Consequently, using historians to confirm the orator's version is the sort of circular argument which it is necessary to mistrust.

The recent publication of extracts of Hyperides' *Against Diondas*[23] allows to put things and Demosthenes to a fairer place, for the version brought by this orator is somehow rather different from the one given by Demosthenes. To begin with, of the new manuscript by L. Horváth and particularly the comparison between this manuscript and Demosthenes' *On the Crown* shows a great similarity in words and expressions.[24] Of course, this does not entail that Demosthenes had obviously borrowed extracts from his friend. Horváth is quite right to favour the idea of a shared vision of both orators who cooperated politically.[25] Nonetheless this similarity, as it is shown, points out the differences in the very course of the embassy itself and I will insist here on one of them, which seems significant to me in the way in which Demosthenes treated a contemporary history, of nine years earlier.[26]

This is how we learn that Hyperides was part of the embassy (which Demosthenes had concealed, as he wished to keep to himself the honour of success)

---

[22] Diod. 16.84.
[23] The speech was made shortly after the destruction of Thebes, as proved by the presence of Theban exiles in the city (Hyp. *Diondas*, 173v 25–28). For the date, cf. Carey *et al*. 2008, 3. Rhodes 2009, 226 favors May-June of this year, just after the first Alexander's victory at the River Granicus and the dedications made to Athens, a moment that Diondas thought favorable to a *graphê*.
[24] Horváth 2014, 165–173. See also the extensive study of numerous similarities in the two speechs by Todd 2009, 168–174.
[25] Horváth 2014, 175.
[26] Among other differences between the two texts, Todd 2009, 167 emphasizes that, according to Hyperides (*Diondas*, 137r 13), Thebes had three choices (alliance with Athens, with Macedonia or neutrality) while Demosthenes (18.213), for rhetorical purposes, reduces them to a simple alternative.

and above all he makes a clear distinction between Demosthenes' speech and the Thebans' decision to shift to the Athenian side. But after the orator intervened, the Thebans still hesitated, sending an embassy to Philip, showing that becoming an ally to him could not be precluded yet. Only when their own embassy came back did the Athenians decide to send an army to Thebes from Eleusis where it had gathered, to show how real their military involvement was at a time when the alliance had neither been concluded nor formalized as he clearly indicates.[27] Again, this version seems to be corroborated by other sources independently of one another, Philochorus and Aeschines.[28] These sources had been reduced to mere controversies for long, Aeschines of course for comprehensible reasons, but especially Philochorus.

The fragments of the Atthidographer Philochorus are somewhat different: if one of the two fragments summarizes Demosthenes' version, by associating the embassy led by Demosthenes to the Theban decision to break the Macedonian alliance, (56a), another fragment is both more explicit and contradictory with this pre-Demosthenian version.[29] This presentation does not exclude Demosthenes from the diplomatic circle and does not question his probably prominent role in the embassy. On the other hand, it cannot be contentious for in 334 Hyperides was still a close friend of Demosthenes whom he supports in his speech against Diondas. And precisely this bond of trust between the two orators is essential because the words of Hyperides greatly put into perspective the impact of the speech delivered in Thebes by Demosthenes and give the latter a more modest role than the one he attributed to himself later. By compressing chronology and simplifying events, he made his listeners believe in 330 that only the magic of his orations persuaded the Thebans, as he wanted to bring out *his* political victory which was easy for him to oppose to the military defeat that was not his own and thus was side-lined.

---

27 Hyp. *Diondas*, 137r 2–8. Cf. Carey *et al.* 2008, 12; Westwood 2020, 71.
28 Aesch. 3.140; Philochor. *FGrHist.*, 328, F. 56 a–b (= BNJ 328, F 56a–b).
29 Philochor. *FGrHist.*, 328, F. 56 a (= BNJ 328, F 56a): "After Philip had captured Elateia and Kytinion and had sent to Thebes ambassadors from the Thessalians, the Aenianians, the Aetolians, the Dolopians and the Phthiotians, and was demanding that they give Nikaia back to the Locrians in contravention of the resolution of the Amphiktyons that the Thebans themselves had taken, after expelling Philip's garrison that was holding it when he was in Scythia, they (the Thebans) replied that an embassy would be sent to Philip to negotiate about all issues". Cf. Harding 2006, 82–84, text and translation.

3 The fake news at the Assembly

In these two examples we also have to learn from the way the Athenian citizens perceive these false assertions and these true lies spoken at the Pnyx. At that time how did the Athenians feel about this re-interpretation of recent history, of this abundance of fake news launched at the Assembly? And in what way did *the logos* allow to free itself from the very notion of truth? These are the questions which need answering.

In the first place it is necessary to remind the reader that lies were commonly spread on the Pnyx and the orators took liberties with the truth, to say the least. As political speeches under the name of Demosthenes outnumber by far those of other orators, we can be under the impression that he lied more than anybody else: this is highly unlikely. But lying is part of the rhetorical arsenal. The well-known example of Aeschines' origins seen by Demosthenes is a good illustration.[30] Scholars like H. Yunis have realized that Demosthenes' demonstrations produced "an utterly compelling version of reality in which his policy, whatever its inherently unconvincing and disagreeable features, appears as the only realistic one".[31] But in the same way we understand the limits of Demosthenes' *logos* in seeking the truth. Thus Demosthenes, through his rhetorical skills, can turn the defeat of Chaeronea, into a personal victory: Athens was not defeated, insofar as he is representative of it.[32] One shall admire Demosthenes' rhetorical skill which consists in first recalling that the defeat was military and not political and that in this matter he had no responsibility.[33] Then considering the defeat of Chaeronea, the thousands of fallen citizens, the loss of the Thracian Chersonese and the disappearance of what was left of the Confederation equally to a moral victory is quite daring and Demosthenes' talent is here brought into the open, since, with arguments the validity of which can be disputed, he finally carried the decision of the jury. It could be said that he led his demonstration with absurd excess if we ignored the Athenians' greed for such high feelings, again similar to the tone and content which can be found in Lycurgus who also mentions the deaths of those who fell in Chaeronea as men fallen victoriously.[34] So, for Lycurgus, the Athenians who had died at war were

---

[30] See Dem. 19.281 and 18.129. Cf. Keaney 2016, 68. For the real life of Atrometus, as we can reconstruct it from the information given by his son, see Fisher 2001, 8–11.
[31] Yunis 1996, 260–261.
[32] Dem. 18.244–247. Cf. Demont 1990, 373–375; Keaney 2016, 87–88.
[33] See Crick in that volume.
[34] Lyc. 1.49 and Roisman in this volume.

the real victors of Chaeronea, just like Demosthenes could boast he had outpowered Philip.

Once this distinction is set, it is useless to insist on the reality as it comes to us: Athens showed defiance towards establishment and orators specifically[35] (and they knew all about it), but Demosthenes' warnings were more violent than they were sincere. Then, one should ask oneself whether they are credible or not. Let us come back to Demosthenes and his way of distorting history described above: were the Athenians as a whole sensitive to such biased arguments? Answering this question is no easy task. It is well known that the *epitaphioi*, are monuments of historical invention. And yet obviously the Athenians were sensitive to the excitement and thrill of their city. Demosthenes, like his colleagues at the Assembly, infinitely praises the political and social values of the "good citizen" who could serve as a model to each Athenian. This shows how strongly eager the Athenians were to take comfort in the words of glory, and how they could not careless about the truthfulness of the words they could hear at the Assembly.

Therefore, undoubtedly it was easy for Demosthenes to re-invent the past to their benefit, without totally fearing the indignant response from their fellow citizens. It is quite understandable that the Athenians who had listened to Demosthenes' and Aeschines' opposed cross speeches in 343 about the embassy had much difficulty in forming their own opinions. Had they forgotten that Demosthenes, now quite hostile to Philip of Macedon, had supported the approach of the embassy, the desire for peace and its conclusions? In fact, maybe they had not. As sixty votes made the difference (thirty switch votes would have been necessary for Demosthenes to win), we can possibly imagine that some Athenians had not believed that Aeschines could be charged of corruption, but at the same time it may not be precluded that others, among those opposed to Demosthenes, remembered his former positions. But this, we shall never be sure of.

As for the issue of the embassy to Thebes, it was even more difficult for the Athenians to form their own opinions. What had really occurred in Thebes remained unknown to most Athenians: who had spoken? how and when had the Thebans shifted their allegiance? Fortunately, the manuscript of *Against Diondus*, even partially, has been re-discovered: otherwise never would we have had an objective testimony of the accurate way the embassy took place.

Nevertheless, easy as it was for orators to report events of recent history after modifying them a lot, it does raise questions about democracy, and democratic practice: a climate of mistrust towards the orators, as a tradition in Athens

---

35 The title of Carey's 2016 communication is "Bashing the establishment".

through the previous decades had definitely developed on a larger scale. The abolition of democracy in 322 in favour of a census system was certainly not due to this lack of trust. But no doubt this attitude has to be taken into account. "All corrupt, all liars", many Athenians may have thought, as they watched these rhetorical debates at the Assembly, which could be partially held responsible for the final defeat in front of the Macedonian army. If the Athenians had any confidence in their democratic system, they did not grant it to their politicians, who were always accused of lying, of enriching themselves, of prioritizing their personal interests, speaking of general interest to settle their personal accounts.[36] There is a contradiction between the faith shared by the greatest number in a democratic regime led by the art of rhetoric and a general distrust towards speakers in charge of representing it.

We can (and we must) ask ourselves: where can we find the slightest trace of this "free speech", of this *parrhêsia*, "a fundamental ideal of democratic politics",[37] which the Athenians were so proud of? On the contrary, we must think that *parrhêsia* does not always mean, as Demosthenes himself repeatedly asserts in his speeches in the *bêma*, the search for truth,[38] but is an essential part of the struggle for political power and, sometimes, the right to lie for one's own interests. In this sense, Demosthenes confirms the thought of Plato, not a staunch defender of democracy as we know, who, associated *parrhêsia* and frankness in the context of his dialogues[39] to equate *parrhêsia* to thoughtless and reckless comments often made by drunken men.[40] In other words, this misuse of *parrhêsia* as a political tool by Demosthenes in particular, and by speakers in general, could also play a role in the disintegration of democracy: never indeed, when democracy was reborn in the years and decades after 322, did democracy see the same operating methods: Stratocles was never a Demosthenes nor was he a Hyperides.

So, we come to this final question: what was the state of the individual and collective memory of the Athenians, three or nine years after the events recalled by the *On the False Embassy* and *On the Crown* trials? This is of course an unsolvable question, of course (cf. *supra* n. 13). But, in either case, it can be as-

---

36 Johnstone 2011, 168–169.
37 Monoson 1994, 174.
38 Dem. 4.51; 6.31 and especially 60.26.
39 eg. *Charm.* 156a; *Lach.* 178a etc.
40 *Rep.* 8.557b; *Laws* 10.908c, 1.649b; 2.671b. Two different kinds of *parrhêsia* must be distinguished in Plato's dialogues: the "Socratic *parrhêsia*", "the freedom to speak the truth, however unwelcome it may be to the audience" and the democratic one, which pursuits an inferior goal, "to please the audience, rather improve its condition" (van Raalte 2004, 309).

sumed that the events had been reshaped by the awareness that the Athenians had subsequently developed from them. In 343, Demosthenes may have thought that anger born from a disappointing peace would allow him to defeat his intimate enemy and by a narrow margin of thirty votes he could have succeeded in making believe that Athens had been wrong in 346 in swearing a peace that he himself approved of at that time. In 330, Aeschines estimated that the policy of Demosthenes which had led to Chaeronea would be condemned by the people. But he had neglected what the collective memory had wanted to preserve: a defeat, certainly, but which had nothing to do with the catastrophe experienced by the Thebans. It is on this collective memory that Demosthenes could consolidate his argument, fueled by omissions and lies, that the Athenians were willing to hear.

Lies, alternative facts, fake news, delivered from the *bêma* at the Pnyx by orators keen on developing them had a detrimental impact on Athenian democracy: while they still believed that the *logos* was important in the democratic process, perhaps the Athenians came to see it as a dead end, precisely because the orators on the *bêma* had misused it. The fall of democracy could not well be the sole result of the military process, even if it cannot be discarded of course. It is also partly the consequence of how the *logos* aiming at a collective decision was progressively diluted by the personal interests of the *politeuomenoi* who had the upper hand at the Pnyx. In this sense, intentionally distorting the truth in speeches and multiplying fake news bears a huge responsibility in the collapse of Athenian classical democracy. For democracies do not always fall under tyrants' yokes: they can also kill themselves or give their enemies the weapons to get killed.

Bibliography

Azoulay, V./Ismard, P. (eds.) (2011), *Clisthène et Lycurgue d'Athènes: autour du politique dans la cité classique*, Paris.
Brown, D. (1974), *Das Geschäft mit dem Staat: Die Überschneidung des Politischen und des Privaten im Corpus Demosthenicum*, Hildesheim.
Brun, P. (2013), "Y avait-il vraiment des anti-Macédoniens à Athènes entre 338 et 323 ? A propos d'un nouveau fragment d'Hypéride *Contre Diondas*", *ZPE* 187, 87–92.
Brun, P. (2015), *Démosthène. Rhétorique, Pouvoir et Corruption*, Paris.
Canevaro, M. (2019), "Memory, the Orators and the Public in the Fourth Century Athens", in: L. Castagnoli/P. Ceccarelli (eds.), *Greek Memories: Theories and Practices*, Cambridge, 136–157.
Canevaro, M./Gray, B. (eds.) (2018), *The Hellenistic Reception of Classical Athenian Democracy and Political Thought*, Oxford.

Carey, C. (2016), "Bashing the Establishment", in: Sanders/Johncock 2016, 27–39.
Carey, C. et al. (2008), "Fragments of Hyperides' *Against Diondas* from the Archimedes Palimpsest", *ZPE* 165, 1–19.
Cartledge, P./Millet, P./von Reden, S. (eds.) (1998), KOSMOS. *Essays in Order, Conflict, and Community in Classical Athens*, Cambridge.
Castagnoli, L./Ceccarelli, P. (eds.) (2019), *Greek Memories Theories and Practices*, Cambridge.
Cawkwell, G.L. (1978), *Philip of Macedon*, London.
Demont, P. (1990), *La cité grecque archaïque et classique et l'idéal de tranquillité*, Paris.
Demont, P. (2011), "Les nouveaux fragments d'Hypéride", *REG* 124, 21–45.
Efstathiou, A. (2004), "The 'Peace of Philocrates': The Assemblies of 18th and 19th Elaphebolion 346 BC. Studying History through Rhetoric", *Historia* 53, 385–387.
Engels, J. (1993), *Studien zur politischen Biographie des Hyperides. Athen in der Epoche der lykurgischen Reformen und des Makedonischen Universalreiches*², München.
Faraguna, M. (1992), *Atene nell'età di Alessandro. Problemi politici, economici, finanziari*, Roma.
Euben, P.J./Wallach, J./Ober, J. (eds.) (1994), *Athenian Political Thought and the Reconstruction of American Democracy*, Ithaca.
Fisher, N. (2001), *Aeschines. Against Timarchos*, Oxford.
Flower, M.A. (1994), *Theopompus of Chios: History and Rhetoric in the Fourth Century B.C.*, Oxford.
Gallo, L. (2019), "Allies and Foes (II): Politicians without Transmitted Speeches", in: G. Martin, (ed.), *The Oxford Handbook of Demosthenes*, 353–362.
Glotz, G./Roussel, P./Cohen, R. (1938), *Histoire grecque*, IV, Paris.
Guth, D. (2014), "Rhetoric and historical narrative: the Theban-Athenian alliance of 339 B.C.", *Historia* 63, 151–165.
Harding, P. (2006), *Didymos: On Demosthenes*, Oxford.
Harris, E.M. (2019), "Speeches to the Assembly and in Public Prosecutions (Dem. 1–24)", in: Martin 2019, 365–388.
Horváth, L. (2008a), "Dating Hyperides' *Against Diondas*", *ZPE* 166, 27–34.
Horváth, L. (2008b), "Hyperides' *Against Diondas* (addenda)", *ZPE* 166, 35–36.
Horváth, L. (2014), *Der "Neue Hyperides": Textedition, Studien und Erläuterungen*, Berlin.
Hunt, P. (2019), "Diplomacy", in: G. Martin (ed.), *The Oxford Handbook of Demosthenes*, 115–125.
Katula, R. (2016), "Crafting Nostalgia: *Pathos* in *On the Crown*", in: J.J. Murphy (ed.), *Demosthenes' On the Crown. Rhetorical Perspectives*, Carbondale, 130–147.
Keaney, J.J. (2016), "Demosthenes' *On the Crown*. A Translation", in: J.J. Murphy (ed.), *Demosthenes' On the Crown. Rhetorical Perspectives*, Carbondale, 46–101.
Kennedy, G.A. (1994), *A New History of Classical Rhetoric*, Princeton.
Lape, S. (2019), "Political Elites", in: G. Martin (ed.), *The Oxford Handbook of Demosthenes*, 101–113.
Loraux, N. (1997) [2005], *La cité divisée. L'oubli dans la mémoire d'Athènes*, Paris.
Luraghi, N. (2018), "Stairway to Heaven: The Politics of Memory in Early Hellenistic Athens", in: Canevaro/Gray, 21–43.
MacDowell, D.M. (2002), *Demosthenes. Against Meidias*, Oxford.
Maltagliati, G. (2020), "Persuasion through Proximity (and Distance) in the Attic Orator's Historical Examples", *GRBS* 60, 68–97.
Martin, G. (ed.) (2019), *The Oxford Handbook of Demosthenes*, Oxford.

Monoson, S.S. (1994), "Frank Speech, Democracy and Philosophy: Plato's Debt to a Democratic Strategy of Civic Discourse", in: P.J. Euben/J. Wallach/J. Ober (eds.), *Athenian Political Thought and the Reconstruction of American Democracy*, Ithaca, 172–197.
Mossé, C. (2010), *Au nom de la loi*, Paris.
Netz, R./Noel, W./Tchernetska, N./Wilson, N. (2011), *The Archimedes Palimpsest*, Cambridge.
Ober, J. (1989), *Fortress Attica. Defense of the Athenian Land Frontier 404–322 B.C.*, Leiden.
Perlman, S. (1963), "The Politicians in the Athenian Democracy of the Fourth Century B.C.", *Athenaeum* 41, 324–355.
Pownall, F. (2001), "Theopompus' View of Demosthenes", in: M. Joyal (ed.), *In Altum: Seventy-Five Years of Classical Studies in Newfoundland*, Saint John, 63–72.
Rhodes, P.J. (1998), "Enmity in Fourth Century Athens", in: Cartledge *et al.* 1998, 144–161.
Rhodes, P.J. (2009), "Hyperides' *Against Diondas*: two Problems", *BICS* 52, 223–228.
Rhodes, P.J. (2019), "Athenian Foreign Policy", in: G. Martin (ed.), *The Oxford Handbook of Demosthenes*, 129–141.
Roisman, J. (2004), "Speaker Audience Interaction in Athens: A Power Struggle", in: Sluiter/Rosen 2004, 261–278.
Sanders, E./Johncock, M. (eds.) (2016), *Emotion and Persuasion in Classical Antiquity*, Stuttgart.
Sawada, N. (2019), "Allies and Foes (I): Aeschines, Hyperides, Lycurgus", in: G. Martin, (ed.), *The Oxford Handbook of Demosthenes*, 337–351.
Sealey, R. (1993), *Demosthenes and his Time: A Study in Defeat*, New York.
Shrimpton, G.S. (1991), *Theopompus the Historian*, Montréal.
Siron, N. (2019), *Témoigner et convaincre. Le dispositif de vérité dans les discours judiciaires de l'Athènes classique*, Paris.
Slater, W.J. (1988), "The Epiphany of Demosthenes", *Phoenix* 42, 126–130.
Tchernetska, N. (2005), "New fragments of Hyperides", *ZPE* 154, 1–6.
Todd, S.C. (2009), "Hyperides *Against Diondas*, Demosthenes *On the Crown*, and the Rhetoric of Political Failure", *BICS* 52, 161–174.
Treves, P. (1933), *Demostene e la libertà greca*, Bari.
Ucciardello, G. (2009), "Hyperides and the transmission on Attic Oratory", *BICS* 52, 229–252.
Van Raalte, M. (2004), "Socratic *Parrhêsia* and its Afterlife in Plato's *Laws*", in: I. Sluiter/M.R. Ralph (eds.), *Free Speech in Classical Antiquity*, Leiden/Boston, 279–312.
Westwood, G. (2020), *The Rhetoric of the Past in Demosthenes and Aeschines. Oratory, History and Politics in Classical Athens*, Oxford.
Will, W. (1983), *Athen und Alexander. Untersuchungen zur Geschichte der Stadt von 338 bis 322 v. Chr.*, München.
Worthington, I. (ed.) (2000), *Demosthenes, Statesman and Orator*, London/New York.
Worthington, I. (2013), *Demosthenes of Athens and the Fall of Classical Greece*, Oxford.
Yunis, H. (1996), *Taming Democracy: Model of Political Rhetoric in Classical Athens*, Ithaca/London.

Peter A. O'Connell
Facts, Time, and Imagination in Demosthenes and Aeschines

Abstract: This chapter considers two ways that Demosthenes tries to make the version of the recent past he presents in his speech *On the False Embassy* seem factual. First, he treats the second embassy, when he maintains Aeschines was working on Philip's behalf, as though it belongs to the distant past. This lets him present his argument as a search for facts about Aeschines's behavior that time has made hard for other people to obtain or recall. Second, through a strategy of enactive narration, he encourages the judges to imagine experiencing one of the events he describes, a symposium in Pella where he claims Aeschines got violently drunk. O'Connell also briefly considers similar rhetorical strategies in Demosthenes 18 and Aeschines 2 and 3.

Aeschines's trial in 343 B.C. for accepting a bribe from Philip II of Macedon to betray Athens[1] exemplifies the challenge of learning facts about the recent past from Attic oratory. The peace that Athens had made with Philip in 346, called the Peace of Philocrates after its lead Athenian supporter, had quickly turned out badly for Athens. Demosthenes sought to blame the peace on Aeschines's treachery, even though both men had supported it, at least initially, and had served on the embassies that negotiated it.[2] His prosecution speech and Aeschines's defense give starkly different accounts of what happened on these embassies and at the debates about peace in the Athenian assembly. Besides the central issue of whether Philip paid Aeschines to promote his interests, the two orators disagree about what they each said privately and publicly, about when pivotal events happened, and about which of them was more closely associated with Philocrates, who had been condemned as a traitor earlier in 343 and was in exile from Athens.[3] Although each insists on his own honesty and brands the

---

I am grateful to Joseph Roisman and Matthew Simonton, who critiqued earlier versions of this chapter, to Dániel Bajnok, who shared a pdf of an inaccessible text, and to Aggelos Kapellos, who invited me to participate in the volume, shared bibliography and pdfs, and improved my argument with generous, thoughtful advice.

---

1 Dem. 19.8 and 178 paraphrase the charges against Aeschines.
2 Buckler 2000, 115–132 is a short account of the historical background to the embassy trial.
3 Dem. 19.116; Aesch. 2.6; Hyp. 3 *Eux.* 20–30; *Agora* 19 P26.455–460.

other a liar,⁴ neither is interested in the truth unless it helps his case.⁵ Modern scholars who try to reconstruct the facts from their speeches have to grapple with bias, inaccuracy, and outright falsehoods.⁶ The original audience of judges, all of whom had lived through the events they were being asked to evaluate, may have had as much trouble telling fact from fiction as modern scholars do. Aeschines was acquitted, but his slim margin of victory reveals that neither litigant's account won the support of an overwhelming majority of the judges.⁷

This chapter will consider two ways that Demosthenes tries to make the version of the recent past he presents in his prosecution speech, *On the False Embassy*, seem factual. First, he treats the second embassy, when he maintains Aeschines was working on Philip's behalf, as though it belongs to the distant past. This lets him present his argument as a search for facts about Aeschines's behavior that time has made hard for other people to obtain or recall. Demosthenes is especially concerned with ways that Aeschines has failed to act consistently.⁸ Second, he encourages the judges to imagine experiencing one of the events he describes, a symposium in Pella where he claims Aeschines got violently drunk. In presenting himself as a truth teller, Demosthenes tries to convince the judges to adopt his view of how Athens should respond to Philip. At the same time that they were weighing disputed facts to determine Aeschines's guilt, the judges also were considering whether Athenian foreign policy should be guided by the belligerence of Demosthenes or the accommodation of Aeschines and Eubulus.

Although Demosthenes's *On the False Embassy* will be my main case study, I will briefly consider the use of similar tactics in Aeschines's defense speech, also called *On the False Embassy*, and in the prosecution and defense speeches from the crown trial of 330, Aeschines's *Against Ctesiphon* and Demosthenes's

---

4 E.g. Dem. 19.8, 80–82; Aesch. 2.2, 54, 92, 98, 126, 153.
5 Buckler 2000, 114–115. On Demosthenes's misleading account of the Peace of Philocrates see Brun's chapter in this volume.
6 Cf. Cawkwell 1969, 163: "In 343 both Demosthenes and Aeschines in discussing the events of a mere three years past denied all responsibility for the making of the Peace of Philocrates; one, at least, was lying, confidently." For possible ways of dealing with such flawed sources, see Harris 1995, 7–16 and Efstathiou 2004, especially his concluding remarks on 401–405.
7 Idomeneus BNJ 338 F 10=Plut. *Vit. Dem.* 15.5–6. Cf. [Plut.] *Vit. X Or.* 840c.
8 For the idea that inconsistently upright behavior cloaks an evil nature, see Dem. 24.133 with Dover 1974, 88–95 on Greek ideas about the persistence of character traits. For forensic arguments based on consistency of character, see Roisman 2005, 199–203; Lanni 2006, 60–61; Gagarin 2012, 305; Kapellos 2014b, 41–42.

On the Crown.[9] These two speeches address whether, in light of Athens's defeat at the Battle of Chaeronea in 338,[10] Demosthenes deserved to be honored with a crown for his service to the *polis*.[11] What happened in the recent past is one of the central questions in the long-running quarrel between Demosthenes and Aeschines, and they address it in complementary ways.

1 Making the recent past seem distant

In Attic oratory, the passage of time can be a rhetorical construct rather than a standard of measurement. Depending on the context, four years can be a long time and one-hundred years can be a short one.[12] When orators choose to present recent events as though they happened long ago, they can either suggest that it is easy to know facts about them because they are part of common knowledge[13] or that it is hard because they happened a long time ago.[14] The second option is fundamental to Demosthenes's rhetorical strategy in *On the False Embassy*. To encourage the judges to doubt their own memories of the second embassy and the roles that he and Aeschines played in it, he treats the not quite four years that have passed since then[15] as a long time. Chronological manipulation allows Demosthenes to pose as an expert guiding the judges through an obscure subject they could never understand on their own. It also justifies his interpreting the embassy in light of more recent events rather than on its own terms.

---

9 Translations of Dem. 18 and 19 and Aesch. 2 and 3 are adapted from Yunis 2005 and Carey 2000.
10 Cf. Crick, Roisman, and Cooper in this volume on the battle of Chaeronea.
11 Aesch. 3.49–50.
12 Cf. Maltagliati 2020 on the importance of "framing expressions" in the orators that can make events seem near or far away in time regardless of the actual number of years that have passed since they happened.
13 E.g. Aesch. 3.53: "My fear is that your response may be to feel that what I say is true but ancient and all too generally acknowledged [ἀρχαῖα καὶ λίαν ὁμολογούμενα]. And yet, Ctesiphon, when the worst of a man's disgraceful acts are so certain and familiar to the hearers [πιστὰ καὶ γνώριμα τοῖς ἀκούουσιν] as to give the impression that the accuser is not telling lies but talking of matters that are old and all too readily acknowledged from the start [παλαιὰ καὶ λίαν προωμολογημένα], does he deserve a golden crown or a reproach?"
14 See Kapellos, Introduction in this volume.
15 MacDowell 2000, 205.

From the outset of the speech, Demosthenes is confident that he will prove Aeschines's guilt. "But in spite of my assurance," he says to the judges:

> I am troubled — I tell you openly and shall not hide it: every case tried before you, Athenians, seems to depend as much on the circumstances of the moment as on the facts of the matter; and I fear that because the embassy took place a long time ago you may have forgotten Aeschines's crimes or become inured to them.[16]

Demosthenes tries to undermine Aeschines's defense by presenting the central conflict in the trial as between facts and the judges' memories. The judges must guard against any tendency towards acquitting Aeschines, because it comes from their own incorrect way of remembering what happened "a long time ago." What Demosthenes calls Aeschines's crimes are the touchstone for determining whether memories are accurate. Those who accept Aeschines's guilt are remembering correctly, and those who do not are remembering wrongly. Demosthenes presents this claim as the consequence of a supposed general rule that judges are influenced by their immediate situation as much as by actual facts. A scholion points out that the effect of this argument is to make whatever Demosthenes puts forward believable and whatever Aeschines says suspect,[17] especially if it coincides with what the judges remember now. A central feature of Aeschines's defense will be that Demosthenes himself had been a political ally of Philocrates, had supported the peace, and had even praised Aeschines's work on the second embassy.[18] Demosthenes does not address this so early in his speech, lest he weaken his own case, but he is subtly instructing the judges in how they should think about it. If the judges remember him supporting peace, they ought to question that memory as biased or incomplete.

The memory of the embassy is a problem, but Demosthenes is a problem-solver. He constructs a scenario where the judges can reach a just decision if they do what he says.[19] To make-up for their supposed inability to remember, Demosthenes provides them with five standards for judging Aeschines: his report, his advice, the instructions he was given, his use of time, and whether he was corrupt.[20] In laying out the case under these headings, Demosthenes presents himself as an authority imposing order on the judges' haphazard recollec-

---

[16] Dem. 19.3.
[17] Schol. 20c Dilts to Dem. 19.3.
[18] Aesch. 2.12–19, 56, 121–123.
[19] Dem. 19.4. See O'Connell 2020, 91–92 on the tactic of speakers presenting themselves as guides for judges in confusing situations.
[20] Dem. 19.4.

tions. He is offering, as the scholiast writes, "some measurements [κανόνας], as it were," for the judges to "look at."[21] The measurements seem to be impartial, but there is no question that they will support Demosthenes's case. They also contribute to his self-characterization as the judges' instructor, the provider of facts as a counterweight to their incorrect memories.

Demosthenes has a dilemma. There is no fact he can point to as proof that Philip actually bribed Aeschines. Instead, he bases his arguments on circumstantial evidence dressed up in the language of memory and fact. Aeschines was initially conspicuous as Philip's enemy and as an opponent of peace, but then he became an enthusiastic supporter of the Peace of Philocrates. Such a change of heart, Demosthenes reasons, is evidence of a bribe.[22] Sidestepping the question of whether gift-giving is a custom of Macedonian diplomacy,[23] he implies that Aeschines has not only violated Athens's laws against bribery by accepting a gift from Philip but has also entered into a reciprocal relationship that places Philip's interests above Athens's.[24] As Demosthenes presents it, anyone who remembers Aeschines's policies correctly — with Demosthenes's help, of course — will reach this conclusion. "I wish to remind you," he says to the judges, "though most of you surely need no reminder."[25]

More damning for Aeschines than his early opposition to Philip is that the peace he advocated has left Athens isolated and threatened by enemies. According to Demosthenes, Aeschines had promised the Athenians that Philip would help the Phocians and oppose the Thebans in the endgame of the Third Sacred War.[26] Since Thebes, the preeminent power in central Greece, was a threat to Athenian influence, Athens had been favoring Phocis. Philip may have intended to settle the war in such in a way that checked Theban power,[27] but in the end he

---

21 Schol. 25c Dilts to Dem. 19.4.
22 Dem. 19.9–16. Bribery was fundamental to Philip's diplomacy, as Worthington 2008, 23–25 shows. Cf. Diod. 16.53.3, 16.54.3–4. On bribery in Athens, see Taylor 2001 and, with specific reference to Demosthenes's rhetoric, Nichols 2019.
23 Perlman 1976, 226–228; Lape 2016, 98. Dem. 19.167 calls "gifts of hospitality" just a "pretext." As Harvey 1985, 106–107 points out, accepting even a ritualized gift still "entailed doing something in return." On Philip's manipulation of Greek expectations about reciprocal gift exchange, see Mitchell 1997, 148–166, 181–186.
24 Dem. 19.248, 314. Nichols 2019, 173–174. Cf. Cooper 2007. On the Greek conception of bribery as accepting a gift from an outsider contrary to the interest of the *polis*, see Herman 1987, 73–81.
25 Dem. 19.9. Cf. 19.27. On the rhetorical effect of telling the judges what it is that they remember, see Siron 2019, 243.
26 Dem. 19.19–22, 26, 35, 49, 74.
27 Worthington 2008, 97.

did the opposite of what Aeschines promised. He conquered Phocis, promoted the interests of the Thebans, and posed a direct threat to Athenian security by gaining control of the pass at Thermopylae.[28] Philip had sought to control Thermopylae since 352, when he retreated in the face of an Athenian force,[29] and now he used a combination of diplomacy, threats, and half-truths to seize it before the Athenians had a chance to stop him.[30] Demosthenes claims that Aeschines's promises were part of Philip's plan to keep the Athenians from defending it a second time.[31] All of this Demosthenes presents as evidence of a bribe, especially since Aeschines has never claimed he misunderstood Philip or was duped by him into making misleading statements to the Athenians. Demosthenes even disingenuously offers to forgive Aeschines, if he really had been fooled.[32] "The facts themselves clearly make the case," he says, that Aeschines acted out of corruption and not naivete.[33] In arguing that the judges can know what happened on the embassy because of what happened after it, Demosthenes continues to rely on his characterization of the embassy as "a long time ago." He can illuminate this allegedly distant event through the lens of the more recent past. Aeschines seems to have appreciated the appeal of Demosthenes's argument. He complains near the end of his defense speech that he is being tried not for what he actually did on the embassy but for his failure to anticipate its consequences.[34]

Demosthenes's *ex hoc propter hoc* reasoning is based on probability: since Aeschines promised that the peace would further Athens's interests, and since in fact it has benefited Philip more than Athens, then it is likely that Aeschines was bribed by Philip to trick the Athenians into accepting peace.[35] Avoiding the language of *eikos*, Demosthenes insists throughout the speech that it is the facts and not probability that guarantee Aeschines's guilt.[36] For instance, when he

---

[28] Dem. 19.53–66, 83–85. Brun 2015, 182–185.
[29] Diod. Sic. 16.38.2; Justin 8.2.8–12; Dem. 19.84. Hammond and Griffith 1979, 279–281; Worthington 2008, 66–68.
[30] Worthington 2008, 98–101; 2013, 177.
[31] Dem. 19.43, 58.
[32] Dem. 19.98–110.
[33] Dem. 19.101. On the rhetorical tactic of asserting that the facts themselves are proving a point see Siron 2019, 270–275.
[34] Aesch. 2.178.
[35] Demosthenes's logic is consistent with the argument in Conover 2014, 75–76 that the Athenians conceptualized bribery in terms of outcome, not intent.
[36] On *eikos* arguments in general see Schmitz 2000. Gagarin 2014, 25, 28–29 argues that implicit *eikos* arguments become more common in the fourth century than ones that actually use the word *eikos*. Furthermore, Gagarin contends, as speakers such as Demosthenes come to

imagines Aeschines asking, "Yet who testifies that I took bribes?" Demosthenes answers:

> The facts, Aeschines, which are the most trustworthy of all witnesses, for the facts cannot be impugned or blamed for being what they are because they've been seduced or are doing a favor for someone; rather, what you've done through betrayal and corruption determines what the facts turn out to be when examined.[37]

Demosthenes strategy is consistent. He is the source of facts, and his argument is based on facts. He conceals, however, that the facts he adduces, even if they are true, are not actually about Aeschines's bribe-taking. They are facts about more recent events that he interprets to portray Aeschines's actions on the embassy in the worst possible light. Demosthenes pretends to be so sure that the judges will accept the interpretation he offers that he claims they "already know" it.[38]

Demosthenes's narrative choices contribute to his argument. He could have told his story in the order it happened, but instead he postpones his description of the second embassy to the very end of his narrative, after using most of it, sections 15–153, to describe how the events after the embassy were the consequence of Aeschines's treachery.[39] When the judges finally hear Demosthenes's selective version of the embassy in sections 154–176, they have already been primed to think of Aeschines as Philip's henchman.[40] Mixing up the order of events also frees Demosthenes from having to discuss the peace negotiations as a response to what happened before them, namely Athens's inability to entice other cities into an anti-Philip alliance and lack of funds to pay for the necessary military operations. He ends his narrative with the claim that Aeschines was seen leaving Philip's tent at night and spent an extra day and night with him in Pella after the other ambassadors left.[41] Aeschines will deny ever being

---

frame factual evidence through *eikos* arguments, there ceases to be a firm distinction between the two.
37 Dem. 19.120. Cf. Dem. 19.279.
38 Dem. 19.216–220 with Pearson 1976, 170–171. Cf. Dem. 19.72. On the "you all know" *topos* see Ober 1989, 149–151; O'Connell 2017, 110; 2020, 86; Canevaro 2019, 151–155; Siron 2019, 225–240; Maltagliati 2020, 90–92. Cf. Lys. 21.6 with Kapellos 2014a, 80, where the speaker relies on Alcibiades being "known to everyone."
39 Cf. Pearson 1976, 161. On the persuasive effects of how speakers choose to tell stories in the Attic courts, see Gagarin 2003. Edwards 2007 discusses how Demosthenes's stories do not always follow chronological order but move backwards and forwards in time.
40 Cf. Roisman 2006, 122 on Demosthenes's portrayal of Aeschines as Philip's accomplice.
41 Dem. 19.175.

away from his messmates at night,⁴² but Demosthenes has placed this at the culmination of the narrative for maximum rhetorical effect. It is a perfect opportunity for Philip to have given Aeschines instructions or paid him off.

In *On the Crown*, Demosthenes reprises the strategy of portraying recent history, in this case the events of the past ten years, as ancient history. Aeschines has waited to prosecute, Demosthenes claims, because he could not have misrepresented facts to the judges "when events were recent and the memory of them was still fresh." Now that the truth is no longer evident, Aeschines can approach the trial as a "competition between public speakers" where *logoi* are being judged rather than what is best for Athens.⁴³ As Demosthenes presents it, events of the distant past lend themselves to rhetorical tricks that benefit Aeschines and not to straightforward evaluation of the facts, which, he implies, would support his own case. Aeschines preemptively responds to this argument in *Against Ctesiphon* by ignoring the distinction Demosthenes makes between the recent and distant past and introducing another way of thinking about time. Presenting delay as a sign of prudence, Aeschines notes that he does not speak every day like a speaker who hires himself out but only at the right times. This is the hallmark of the truly democratic citizen, who volunteers to speak when the situation demands it.⁴⁴

Behind this debate over whether the right time to speak is immediately or when circumstances demand it lies a familiar assessment of how the Athenian democracy makes its decisions. Demosthenes's criticism of Aeschines recalls Thucydides's Cleon accusing the Athenians of being "spectators of *logoi* and hearers of *erga*" who treat the Assembly as a place for rhetorical competition rather than political deliberation.⁴⁵ As part of his analysis, Cleon speaks specifically about how the Athenians evaluate claims about the recent past, asserting that they deem what they have heard more credible than what they have actually seen being done. Cleon's speech draws on the tactics of forensic rhetoric,⁴⁶ and his analysis is relevant for judges who have to make decisions about recent events as well as for Assemblymen. The judges in the embassy and crown trials

---

42 Aesch. 2.124–127.
43 Dem. 18.225–226. In the immediate context, the events Demosthenes is referring to are Aeschines's failures to prosecute first Aristonicus and then Demomeles and Hyperides for proposing that Demosthenes be crowned, but, as Yunis 2001, 235 notes, he also "castigates Aeschines's entire prosecution for its lateness."
44 Aesch. 3.220.
45 Thuc. 3.38.4–7; Yunis 2001, 236.
46 Harris 2013.

were considering both political and legal issues.⁴⁷ Aeschines and Demosthenes frequently accuse each other of putting on rhetorical shows and avoiding serious debate in the courts in similar language to Cleon's.⁴⁸ Cleon makes two related arguments about hearing and seeing: the Athenians paradoxically value hearing over seeing as a source of knowledge, and they confuse the two senses and experience words as though they carry the authority properly belonging to *erga*. Through Cleon, Thucydides shows a sensitive awareness of how the mind can be led through language to accept as facts things that it does not know and may be false. The next section of this chapter will consider an example of how Demosthenes tries to manipulate his audience into doing just that in one section of *On the False Embassy*.

2 Imagined presence and the recent past

In his defense speech at the embassy trial, Aeschines accuses Demosthenes of making lies seem like facts.⁴⁹ He says:

> In my political life I have become enmeshed to an extreme degree with a charlatan and a criminal, a man who could not speak the truth even by accident. When he is telling a lie, he first swears an oath by his shameless eyes, and he not only presents imaginary events as fact but even gives the day when he claims they happened. And he falsely adds someone's name, claiming he happened to be there, in imitation of people telling the truth.⁵⁰

Aeschines is referring to Demosthenes's scurrilous story that he got drunk and had a captive Olynthian woman whipped at a symposium in Pella while both men were there on the second embassy.⁵¹ In making Aeschines's victim an Olynthian, Demosthenes portrays Aeschines as indifferent to what Athens's ally Olynthus suffered after falling to Philip's soldiers.⁵² Support for a free Olynthus

---

47 Cf. Yunis 1988, with particular reference to *graphai paranomōn*.
48 Aesch. 1.173–176, 3.16, 202; Dem. 18.225–227, 19.246; Harris 2013, 103.
49 Cf. Schmitz 2000, 63–64.
50 Aesch. 2.153. On using names of imaginary witnesses to bolster false stories, see Theophr. *Char.* 8.4 with Diggle 2004, 282. Siron 2019, 73–87 describes how witness testimony serves to support the truthfulness of what a litigant says.
51 Dem. 19.196–198.
52 Hobden 2013, 136; Spatharas 2019, 111. On the fall of Olynthus in 348 see Worthington 2008, 74–83. In turning the judges' minds to northern Greece, Demosthenes may also be subtly reminding them of Athens's claim to Amphipolis, which, in 19.253–254, he will explicitly accuse Aeschines of giving to Philip in exchange for the bribe.

had been a cornerstone of Demosthenes's Macedonian policy, and he may include the episode of the abused Olynthian woman to prove to the Athenians that they should have followed his advice and funded an expedition to defend the city.[53] Like Olynthus itself, the woman should be free but is treated as though she is a slave. Aeschines's criticism of Demosthenes's story is not fully consistent with the version in Demosthenes's speech, which includes the names of people who "happened to be there" but does not provide a date. Since Demosthenes proudly declares that he wasn't at such a shameful spectacle, which he claims was hosted by the son of one of the Thirty,[54] these witnesses are vital to his credibility.

Demosthenes has carefully constructed the story so that a range of details can excite the judges' patriotic anger at Aeschines and pity for the abused woman.[55] By associating Aeschines with an exiled oligarch that he himself went out of his way to avoid, Demosthenes encourages the judges to view Aeschines as an antidemocratic elite who joins other antidemocratic elites in aping the barbarous drinking habits of the Macedonians — even when he is supposed to be representing Athens.[56] Athenian sources consistently portray Macedonian symposia as drunken and chaotic, contrasting them with their own more orderly symposia and ignoring the way that Philip used competitive drinking as a male bonding ritual to secure loyalty to himself.[57] Demosthenes revisits Aeschines's disregard for captive Olynthian women later in his speech, ensuring it remains in the forefront of the judges' minds.[58] Aeschines maintains that he made the whole thing up.[59] Comparing Demosthenes's account with Aeschines's denial of it will reveal on a small scale some of the ways the two speakers try to make their audiences believe they are learning facts about the recent past.

---

[53] I am grateful to Aggelos Kapellos for this point. On Demosthenes's policy towards Olynthus and his rhetoric about it see Pearson 1976, 127–135; Worthington 2013, 132–144. Cawkwell 1962, 134–140 argues that Demosthenes's policy was strategically flawed and the Athenians were right to reject it.

[54] Dem. 19.196 with MacDowell 2000, 287. Aesch. 2.157 denies this, saying the host was a Macedonian. On the self-interested motives of exiles engaging in informal diplomacy with residents of their home cities see Loddo 2019.

[55] Spatharas 2019, 114–116.

[56] Hobden 2013, 134–135; Spatharas 2019, 112–113.

[57] Pownall 2010, 61–65.

[58] Dem. 19.306–309.

[59] Aesch. 2.153–158.

A scholion notes that Demosthenes's narrative of the assault on the woman is persuasive because of *enargeia*,[60] usually translated as "vividness." At first glance, the claim seems strange, since the narrative has few of the concrete details generally associated with making the reader or listener feel like a spectator[61] and no tell-tale directives that the audience should "look" or "imagine." However, Demosthenes's tactics are consistent with the concept of *enargeia* as a multisensory imaginative experience rather than one focused on sight alone. Dionysius of Halicarnassus, in one of the earliest discussions of *enargeia*, insists that it appeals to "the senses," not only to sight, and he emphasizes the feeling of presence it encourages.[62] Along these lines, Demosthenes makes his listeners feel present at the symposium he describes by appealing to their sense of hearing through direct speech and their experience of movement in physical space through verbs of motion. In Cleon's terms, as I discussed, he encourages them to experience these events as *erga* rather than merely as *logoi*. In Aeschines terms, he "presents imaginary events as fact." Aeschines tries to turn these same rhetorical techniques against Demosthenes.

Demosthenes begins by contrasting Aeschines's behavior with that of the comic actor Satyrus at an earlier symposium. When Philip offered to grant Satyrus whatever he desired, the actor asked Philip to free the unmarried daughters of his murdered friend Apollophanes, who were among the prisoners captured at Olynthus.[63] Since Demosthenes presents Satyrus's request in direct speech,[64] the judges in court seem to hear it at the same time as Philip and the other guests in the story. This shared listening experience encourages the judges to imagine that they are not merely hearing a story but actually experiencing something at first hand. The guests' boisterous approval of Satyrus's request serves as a model for the judges and leaves them with a high opinion of Satyrus as Demosthenes moves on to Aeschines.[65] His account of Aeschines's *hybris*[66]

---

60 Schol. 399 Dilts to Dem. 19.196.
61 Plut. *De glor. Ath.* 3 347a.
62 Dion. Hal. *Lys.* 7. Webb 2016, 213; 2020.
63 Dem. 19.192–195. Cf. Diod. 16.55.3–4.
64 Since there is no explicit verbal transition to direct speech (Bers 1997, 189–190), Demosthenes must have relied on performance to present the unusual solemnity of Satyrus's tone.
65 See O'Connell 2017, 150–152 on how an internal audience's reaction to quoted speech can be a model for the external audience of judges.
66 Ironically, Aeschines and Phyrnon accuse the woman of *hybris* (Dem. 19.197) when their own behavior exemplifies "insulting, brutal, or sexually shaming behaviour" (Hobden 2013, 136, following the definition at Fisher 1992, 115). By associating Aeschines with *hybris* without

gains plausibility by following a temporal sequence structured around simple physical movements and featuring direct speech at its climax. When the company went [ἐπειδὴ ἧκον] to drink, the host led in [εἰσάγει] the Olynthian woman. At first [πρῶτον], they gently urged her to drink and eat, but as the affair progressed [προῄει] and they grew warm from wine, they ordered her to recline and sing. When the anguished woman didn't cooperate, Aeschines and another Athenian named Phrynon grew enraged and said, "Call a slave," and, "Have someone bring a whip." A slave came [ἧκεν] with a strap, and ripping [περιρρήξας] the woman's clothes he thrashed [ξαίνει] her.[67] Jumping up [ἀναπηδήσασα], she fell [προσπίπτει] on Iatrocles's knees and overturned [ἀνατρέπει] a table. Iatrocles snatched her away [ἀφείλετο] just in time to save her from being murdered.[68] Although Demosthenes gives no details of the physical space of the symposium besides the table and the implied couches,[69] the verbs of motion and the temporal markers give his account a strong sense of place and time. He begins with simple verbs of movement that establish the basic topography of the space, allowing the judges to imagine who is where at what time based on their own experiences of symposia or just of the arrangement of homes.[70] The verbs become more specific as the narrative progresses, with the tearing, the flogging, and finally the woman's frantic starting up and collapsing that knocks the table over and leads Iatrocles to rescue her. This culminating action is a quick sequence of up, down, and away, highlighted by the ἀνα-, προσ-, and ἀπο- prefixes.[71]

The verbs of movement and the prefixes of direction make it easier for the listeners to imagine the actions occurring sequentially within a space. They also appeal to what Ruth Webb has called "kinaesthetic imagination."[72] Listeners can imagine being present in such a scene because they know instinctively what it is like to enter a room, what it is like to jump up, what it is like to knock a table over. What J. Grethlein and L. Huitink call the "imageability" of the scene

---

formally accusing him of it, Demosthenes may be trying to excite the judges' outrage. He had used such a strategy on a larger scale in *Against Meidias* (MacDowell 1990, 16–17).
67 "Thrash" is the translation of Harris 2017, 234.
68 Dem. 19.197–198.
69 Cf. de Bakker 2012, 394, which analyzes the way that Demosthenes creates a sense of space in the narrative of *Against Zenothemis* (Dem. 32.4–9) while describing only the most important physical details.
70 On audiences supplying details from their own experience see Theophr. fr. 696 (Fortenbaugh) with O'Connell 2017, 129–130.
71 Cf. Webb 2020, 165–166.
72 Webb 2020, especially 166.

comes not from detailed descriptions of things, of which there are none, but from the way the "enactive narration" appeals to the listeners' own embodied experience of the world. In their terms, we "perceive our surroundings in terms of actual and potential bodily interactions," and so a narrative that is structured around those interactions gives an audience "the feeling of being right on the spot."[73] The table and the whip are central details of Demosthenes's account because they are linked with actions: he does not say, "there was a table," but, "she overturned a table,"[74] nor does he say, "there was a whip," but, "a slave brought a whip and thrashed her." The verb "thrash" appeals to the judges' kinaesthetic imaginations more than a more neutral verb for whipping would, since, as E. Harris points out, it conveys "the image of the sharp whip lacerating the woman's flesh."[75] A focus on actions helps to make Demosthenes's story plausible because it encourages the judges to feel like witnesses experiencing it as it happens.[76] Demosthenes is preparing them to accept his claim that the incident was infamous even in Arcadia and to believe the testimony of Diophantus, the witness he is about to produce.[77] *Enargeia* is linked with emotions in ancient rhetorical theory, and Demosthenes's enactive narration is also designed to arouse emotions in the judges. As D. Spatharas shows, the judges who evaluate the woman's movements and gestures in terms of the values and norms of fourth-century Athens recognize signs of how pitiably she is being treated. For instance, the fact that the woman reclines only under duress highlights that she is a free woman being forced to act like a slave, and her overturning the table emphasizes the affront to the basic rules of hospitality caused by Aeschines's behavior.[78]

The direct quotation of Aeschines and Phrynon's command to the slave contrasts with the earlier quotation of Satyrus and further contributes to the listeners' sense of physical presence. Grethlein and Huitink call direct speeches an

---

[73] Grethlein and Huitink 2017. The quotation in this sentence is from page 75.
[74] Schol. 415 Dilts to Dem. 19.198 may be correct that the table being knocked over ironically recalls Aeschines's taunt that Demosthenes cared nothing for the table-fellowship shared by the ambassadors (Dem. 19.189).
[75] Harris 2017, 234–235.
[76] MacDowell 2000, 28 notes that, even if the story is untrue or exaggerated, Demosthenes "makes it seem real by the vivid details of his narration." Many of the details he lists at page 286 are actions: "coaxing the woman to eat, telling her to recline and then to sing, her bewilderment, the orders to a slave, and so on."
[77] Dem. 19.198. He gives the story further plausibility by saying he heard about it from Iatrocles himself (19.197), although Iatrocles does not testify on his behalf. Paulsen 1999, 208.
[78] Spatharas 2019, 114–115.

example of "dynamic veracity." This means that it takes the same amount of time to hear the speech within the narrative as it would take to hear it in the real world. This helps create a sense of presence because the listeners are not just hearing a paraphrase of the speech but are given the illusion of hearing the speech itself being delivered in real time.[79] As the scholiast notes, the direct speech is also an imitation of the way that drunken, libidinous men speak. Through *ēthopoeia*, it adds a further element of plausibility.[80] Portraying Aeschines as a plausible drunk is consistent with Demosthenes's broader strategy of attacking his character and making him seem like the kind of person who would betray his polis.[81]

Although Aeschines accuses Demosthenes of attempting to suborn a witness,[82] the heart of his rhetorical strategy is to turn Demosthenes's enactive narrative against him. Through verbs of movement, Aeschines tries to conjure unlikely images that will stick in the judges' minds and replace the ones generated by Demosthenes. For instance, Aeschines claims that Demosthenes accused him of dragging [ἕλκομαι] a female prisoner by the hair, grabbing [λαβών] a strap, and whipping [μαστιγοίην] her.[83] In transforming Demosthenes's charge that he encouraged the maltreatment of a free Olynthian into the charge that he personally did the whipping, Aeschines turns it into an object of mockery. How preposterous to think that he, "the adviser of the greatest city, the counsellor of the Ten Thousand in Arcadia," could have done such a thing![84] Aeschines's strategy is risky, since it calls attention to the possibility that he was a violent maniac for the sake of dismissing it. This is consistent with Aeschines's general approach to Demosthenes in *On the False Embassy*. He exaggerates Demosthenes's allegations to make them seem ridiculous and Demosthenes's performance to make it seem inappropriate.[85] In Aeschines's telling, Demosthenes wept on the *bēma* and strained his "shrill, vile voice" making ridiculous allega-

---

[79] Grethlein and Huitink 2017, 73, 83. See Bers 1997, 223–226 for a cautious assessment of how direct speech might contribute to the sense that the quoted speaker is being made present. Cf. Paulsen 1999, 209 on the dramatic effect of direct speech here.
[80] Schol. 408 Dilts to Dem. 19.197. Cf. Schol. 403 Dilts to the same paragraph. On the way that direct speech contributes to characterization, see Trevett 1995, 126–132.
[81] Pearson 1976, 169–170; MacDowell 2000, 285; Pasini 2011, 349–350. Gagarin 2005, 371–375 argues that the Attic orators tend to use violence as a sign of their opponent's character rather than as a topic to be emphasized for its own sake.
[82] Aesch. 2.154–155.
[83] Aesch. 2.157.
[84] Aesch. 2.157.
[85] Cf. Harris 1995, 178 n. 6; 2017, 235–236.

tions.⁸⁶ He also mocks Demosthenes for being interrupted by the judges while describing the alleged assault. Aeschines uses verbs of violent action, "you threw him out" [ἐξεβάλετε] and "he was tossed out by you" [ὑφ' ὑμῶν ἐξερρίφη].⁸⁷ By implying that all the judges took part in this interruption, Aeschines suggests that any judges who support Demosthenes are in the minority and should change their minds. Enactive narration complements the mockery, as the verbs of throwing help create the sense that Demosthenes was under a sustained attack and not simply being hissed by some of the judges.

In this one clash between Demosthenes and Aeschines, the two orators appeal to their listeners' sense of hearing and bodily experience of the world to recreate a version of Aeschines's encounter with the Olynthian woman, either to lend it plausibility, in Demosthenes's case, or to mock it, in Aeschines's. Where Demosthenes tries to instill a sense of presence in his audience that makes them feel like they are experiencing *erga* and not simply hearing *logoi*, Aeschines tries to make those *erga* seem so preposterous that the jury will dismiss them out of hand. Mockery is appropriate only for certain situations, but direct speech, references to sound, and enactive narrations structured around verbs of movement are all techniques that Demosthenes and Aeschines employ in other speeches as well to make their audiences accept their accounts of the recent past.

In *On the Crown*, Demosthenes uses all three techniques to encourage the judges to experience in their minds his version of the Assembly held in 338 after Philip unexpectedly changed the direction of his advancing army and seized Elatea. From this town just north of Boeotia, the Macedonian army could be at Athens within days, and Philip was pressuring the Thebans to help him attack it.⁸⁸ Demosthenes evokes the news arriving in Athens with verbs that create a sense of movement in the familiar space of the agora and with a reference to the uproar that filled the city.⁸⁹ Then he focuses on the sounds of the Assembly, as he compares the herald's announcement, "Who wishes to speak?" to the voice

---

86 Aesch. 2.157. On Aeschines's mocking comparison of Demosthenes's voice to his own in this section, see Easterling 1999, 163; Hall 2006, 372–373.
87 Aesch. 2.4, 153; Schol. 411 Dilts to Dem. 19.197. These may be metaphors from booing theatrical performances (Dem. 19.337). Athenian audiences regularly showed their approval or disapproval of speakers with cheers or interruptions. Bers 1985; Tacon 2001; Villacèque 2013, 296–309; Sato 2020. Harris 2017, 236 argues that the judges, like Aeschines himself, objected to Demosthenes's breaches of courtroom decorum.
88 Dem. 18.213. Cf. Arist. *Rh.* 2.23.6. Worthington 2013, 241–242.
89 Dem. 18.169.

of the nation calling out for a savior.[90] Finally, he quotes, or pretends to quote, his own speech advocating an anti-Philip alliance with Athens's rival Thebes, ending it with the claim that everyone approved and no one spoke in opposition.[91] Demosthenes recreates the Assembly in a selective way. Focusing on himself and eliding the contributions of others, he influences the judges to remember him as the clear-sighted leader Athens needed, a leader who deserves a crown.[92] He also makes himself solely responsible for the alliance with Thebes that successfully held off Philip until Chaeronea.[93] Direct speech and references to sound also characterize Aeschines's accounts of Demosthenes's behavior on the two embassies to Philip in *On the False Embassy*.[94] On the first embassy, when all the Macedonians were looking forward to hearing Demosthenes, Aeschines claims that Demosthenes was overcome with cowardice and fell silent when he tried to speak.[95] Later, Aeschines claims to describe a meeting of the ambassadors during the second embassy, quoting both his own speech and the speech he says Demosthenes delivered at a yell.[96] Finally, he paraphrases the flattering speech Demosthenes addressed to Philip, quotes what he claims was its culmination, and notes that it was followed by laughter and then silence, modeling a reaction for the judges.[97]

Creating a sense of bodily presence is a technique consistently used by Demosthenes and Aeschines in both small-scale and large-scale accounts of the recent past. Its unique power comes from the way that it coopts the audience's imaginations and makes them participants in the versions of events they hear about.

---

[90] Dem. 18.170.
[91] Dem. 18.174–179.
[92] Yunis 1996, 275–276; Brun 2015, 209–210.
[93] See Guth 2014 for reasons the Thebans may have accepted the alliance besides Demosthenes's advocacy. Cf. Brun 2015, 211 on his likely cooperation with Hyperides and Hegesippus.
[94] Direct speech is vital to the embassy speeches of both Demosthenes and Aeschines, since the case depended on convincing the judges of exactly who said what and when they said it. Trevett 1995, 140, 142. On the rhetorical strategies of ambassadorial teams see Rubinstein 2016.
[95] Aesch. 2.34. Demosthenes never responds to this, perhaps out of embarrassment. Sealey 1993, 150–151, 304 n. 70 doubts Aeschines's story. Cf. Guth 2015, 340 n. 11.
[96] Aesch. 2.103–107.
[97] Aesch. 2.109–113. Worman 2008, 255–260 shows how Demosthenes's allegedly poor oratorical skills contribute to the degenerate persona that Aeschines constructs for him. Cf. Easterling 1999, 163–164.

3 Conclusions

In Book II of *Rhetoric*, Aristotle insists that to make an argument you have to know the facts, or at least some of them.[98] Through the techniques I have discussed in this chapter, Demosthenes and Aeschines suggest not only that they know the facts but that their judges know them too. More than just an accurate understanding of what happened in the recent past was at stake in these trials. The orators were tussling over Athens's relations with Philp and its place in a rapidly changing Hellas. People who let Demosthenes influence their memories of the Peace of Philocrates or who experienced in their imagination the crack of a whip on a free woman's back would have been primed to follow his views about how Athens should handle Macedon and about the Athenians' responsibility to their city and the other Greeks.

Bibliography

Bers, V. (1985), "Dikastic Thorubos", in: P.A. Cartledge/F.D. Harvey (eds.), *Crux: Essays in Greek History Presented to G.E.M. de Ste. Croix on his 75th Birthday*, London, 1–15.
Bers, V. (1997), *Speech in Speech*, Lanham, MD.
Brun, P. (2015), *Démosthène : Rhétorique, pouvoir et corruption*, Paris.
Buckler, J. (2000), "Demosthenes and Aeschines", in: I. Worthington (ed.), *Demosthenes: Statesman and Orator*, London, 114–158.
Canevaro, M. (2019), "Memory, the Orators, and the Public in Fourth-Century BC Athens", in: L. Castagnoli/P. Ceccarelli (eds.), *Greek Memories: Theories and Practices*, Cambridge, 136–157.
Carey, C. (trans.) (2000), *Aeschines*, Austin.
Cawkwell, G. (1962), "The Defence of Olynthus", *CQ* 12, 122–140.
Cawkwell, G. (1969), "The Crowning of Demosthenes", *CQ* 19, 163–180.
Conover, K.M. (2014), "Rethinking Anti-corruption Reforms: The View from Ancient Athens", *Buffalo Law Review* 62, 69–117.
Cooper, C. (2007), "Rhetoric of Philippizing", in: W. Heckel/L. Tritle/P. Wheatley (eds.), *Alexander's Empire: Formulation to Decay*, Claremont, 1–12.
de Bakker, M.P. (2012), "Demosthenes", in: I.J.F. de Jong (ed.), *Space in Ancient Greek Literature*, Leiden, 393–412.
Diggle, J. (2004), *Theophrastus: Characters*, Cambridge.
Dover, K.J. (1974), *Greek Popular Morality in the Time of Plato and Aristotle*, Berkeley.
Efstathiou, A. (2004), "The 'Peace of Philokrates': The Assemblies of 18th and 19th Elaphebolion 346 B.C.: Studying History through Rhetoric", *Historia* 53, 385–407.

---

98 Arist. *Rhet.* 2.22.4–9 1396a3–33.

Easterling, P. (1999), "Actors and Voices: Reading between the Lines in Aeschines and Demosthenes", in: S. Goldhill/R. Osborne (eds.), *Performance Culture and Athenian Democracy*, Cambridge, 154–166.

Edwards, M.J. (2007), "Demosthenes", in: I.J.F. de Jong/R. Nünlist (eds.), *Time in Ancient Greek Literature*, Leiden, 337–342.

Fisher, N.R.E. (1992), *Hybris: A Study in the Values of Honour and Shame in Ancient Greece*, Warminster.

Gagarin, M. (2003), "Telling Stories in Ancient Greek Law", *TAPA* 133, 197–207.

Gagarin, M. (2005), "La violence das les plaidoyers attiques", in: J.-M. Bertrand (ed.), *La violence dans les mondes grec et romain*, Paris, 365–376.

Gagarin, M. (2012), "Law, Politics, and the Question of Relevance in the Case On the Crown", *CA* 31, 293–314.

Gagarin, M. (2014), "*Eikos* Arguments in Athenian Forensic Oratory", in: V. Wohl (ed.), *Probabilities, Hypotheticals, and Counterfactuals in Ancient Greek Thought*, Cambridge, 15–29.

Grethlein, J./Huitink, L. (2017), "Homer's Vividness: An Enactive Approach", *JHS* 137, 67–91.

Guth, D. (2014), "Rhetoric and Historical Narrative: The Theban-Athenian Alliance of 339 BCE", *Historia* 63, 151–165.

Guth, D. (2015), "The King's Speech: Philip's Rhetoric and Democratic Leadership in the Debate over the Peace of Philocrates", *Rhetorica* 33, 333–348.

Hall, E. (2006), *The Theatrical Cast of Athens: Interactions between Ancient Greek Drama and Society*, Oxford.

Hammond, N.G.L./Griffith, G.T. (1979), *A History of Macedonia, Volume 2, 550–336 B.C.*, Oxford.

Harris, E.M. (1995), *Aeschines and Athenian Politics*, Oxford.

Harris, E.M. (2013), "How to Address the Athenian Assembly: Rhetoric and Political Tactics in the Debate about Mytilene (Thuc. 3.37–50)", *CQ* 63, 94–109.

Harris, E.M. (2017), "How to 'Act' in an Athenian Court: Emotions and Forensic Performance", in: S. Papaioannou/A. Serafim/B. da Vela (eds.), *The Theatre of Justice: Aspects of Performance in Greco-Roman Oratory and Rhetoric*, Leiden, 223–242.

Harvey, F.D. (1985), "Dona Ferentes: Some Aspects of Bribery in Greek Politics", in: P.A. Cartledge/F.D. Harvey (eds.), *Crux: Essays in Greek History Presented to G.E.M. de Ste. Croix on his 75th Birthday*, London, 76–117.

Herman, G. (1987), *Ritualized Friendship and the Greek City*, Cambridge.

Hobden, F. (2013), *The Symposion in Ancient Greek Society and Thought*, Cambridge.

Kapellos, A. (2014a), *Lysias 21: A Commentary*, Berlin.

Kapellos, A. (2014b), "*In Defense of Mantitheus*: Structure, Strategy, and Argumentation in Lysias 16", *BICS* 57, 21–46.

Lanni, A. (2006), *Law and Justice in the Courts of Classical Athens*, Cambridge.

Lape, S. (2016), "The State of Blame: Politics, Competition, and the Courts in Democratic Athens", *Critical Analysis of Law* 3, 87–113.

Loddo, L. (2019), "Political Exiles and Their Use of Diplomacy in Classical Greece", *Ktèma* 44, 7–21.

MacDowell, D.M. (1990), *Demosthenes:* Against Meidias, Oxford.

MacDowell, D.M. (2000), *Demosthenes:* On the False Embassy (Oration 19), Oxford.

Maltagliati, G. (2020), "Persuasion through Proximity (and Distance) in the Attic Orators' Historical Examples", *GRBS* 60, 68–97.

Mitchell, L.G. (1997), *Greeks Bearing Gifts: The Public Use of Private Relationships in the Greek World, 435–323 BC*, Cambridge.
Nichols, R.J. (2019), "Corruption", in: G. Martin (ed.), *The Oxford Handbook of Demosthenes*, Oxford, 167–178.
Ober, J. (1989), *Mass and Elite in Democratic Athens: Rhetoric, Ideology, and the Power of the People*, Princeton.
O'Connell, P.A. (2017), *The Rhetoric of Seeing in Attic Forensic Oratory*, Austin.
O'Connell, P.A. (2020), "The Story About the Jury", in: M. Edwards/D. Spatharas (eds.), *Forensic Narratives in Athenian Courts*, Abingdon, 81–101.
Pasini, G. (2011), "The ἐξεταστικὸν εἶδος of the *Rh. Al.* and Parallels in Aeschines' *Against Timarchus* and Demosthenes' *On the False Embassy*", *Rhetorica* 29, 336–356.
Paulsen, T. (1999), *Die Parapresbeia-Reden des Demosthenes und des Aischines: Kommentar und Interpretationen zu Demosthenes, or. XIX, und Aischines, or. II*, Trier.
Pearson, L. (1976), *The Art of Demosthenes*, Meisenheim am Glan.
Perlman, S. (1976), "On Bribing Athenian Ambassadors", *GRBS* 17, 223–233.
Pownall, F. (2010), "The Symposia of Philip II and Alexander III of Macedon: The View from Greece", in: E. Carney/D. Ogden (eds.), *Philip II and Alexander the Great: Father and Son, Lives, and Afterlives*, Oxford, 55–65.
Roisman, J. (2005), *The Rhetoric of Manhood: Masculinity in the Attic Orators*, Berkeley.
Roisman, J. (2006), *The Rhetoric of Conspiracy in Ancient Athens*, Berkeley.
Rubinstein, L. (2016), "Envoys and *Ethos*: Team Speaking by Envoys in Classical Greece", in: P. Derron (ed.), *La rhétorique du pouvoir: Une exploration de l'art oratoire délibératif grec*, Vandoeuvres, 79–128.
Sato, N. (2020), "Inciting *Thorubos* and Narrative Strategies in Attic Forensic Speeches", in: M. Edwards/D. Spatharas (eds.), *Forensic Narratives in Athenian Courts*, Abingdon, 102–118.
Sealey, R. (1993), *Demosthenes and His Time: A Study in Defeat*, Oxford.
Schmitz, T.A. (2000), "Plausibility in the Greek Orators", *AJP* 121, 47–77.
Siron, N. (2019), *Témoigner et convaincre: Le dispositif de vérité dans les discours judiciaires de l'Athènes classique*, Paris.
Spatharas, D. (2019), *Emotions, Persuasion, and Public Discourse in Classical Athens*, Berlin.
Tacon, J. (2001), "Ecclesiastic *Thorubos*: Interventions, Interruptions, and Popular Involvement in the Athenian Assembly", *G & R* 48, 173–192.
Taylor, C. (2001), "Bribery in Athenian Politics", *G & R* 48, 53–66, 154–172.
Trevett, J. (1995), "The Use of Direct Speech by the Attic Orators", in: F. De Martino/A.H. Sommerstein (eds.), *Lo spettacolo delle voci*, Bari, 2.123–145.
Villacèque, N. (2013), "Θόρυβος τῶν πολλῶν: Le spectre du spectacle démocratique", in: A. Macé (ed.), *Le savoir public: La vocation politique du savoir en Grèce ancienne*, Besançon, 287–312.
Webb, R. (2016), "Sight and Insight: Theorizing Vision, Emotion, and Imagination in Ancient Rhetoric", in: M. Squire (ed.), *Sight and the Ancient Senses*, Abingdon, 205–219.
Webb, R. (2020), "As If You Were There: *Enargeia* and Spatiality in Lysias 1", in: M. Edwards/D. Spatharas (eds.), *Forensic Narratives in Athenian Courts*, Abingdon, 157–170.
Worman, N. (2008), *Abusive Mouths in Classical Athens*, Cambridge.
Worthington, I. (2008), *Philip II of Macedonia*, New Haven.
Worthington, I. (2013), *Demosthenes of Athens and the Fall of Classical Greece*, Oxford.
Yunis, H. (1988), "Law, Politics, and the *Graphe Paranomon* in Fourth-century Athens", *GRBS* 29, 361–382.

Yunis, H. (1996), *Taming Democracy: Models of Political Rhetoric in Classical Athens*, Ithaca.
Yunis, H. (2001), *Demosthenes: On the Crown*, Cambridge.
Yunis, H. (trans.) (2005), *Demosthenes, Speeches 18 and 19*, Austin.

Dániel Bajnok
Peace and War with Philip: Aeschines' *Against Ctesiphon* on the Recent Past

Abstract: This chapter examines how Aeschines presented the peace of Philocrates and the battle of Chaeronea in 330. He tried to convince the judges to prefer his interpretation of events over that of Demosthenes. In general, Aeschines seems to have tried to turn Demosthenes into a scapegoat responsible for all the mishaps of Athens. As for the peace, Aeschines decided to omit his own service as envoy, to turn back a number of Demosthenes' previous charges (used in 343) against his opponent, and not to blame the disadvantageous peace on Philip II. Concerning Aeschines' presentation of the antecedents and the aftermath of Chaeronea, Philip played again a more positive role than Demosthenes. Aeschines expected that the Athenian attitude towards the Macedonians had been adapted to the political realities, therefore using the sorrowful memories of a historical disaster and turning his opponent a scapegoat might prove to be a successful strategy again.

When Aeschines brought his indictment against Ctesiphon to trial in August 330, he expected the hearing to be a great showdown with Demosthenes in their political debate aggravated by personal animosity, which had lasted for at least sixteen years, starting during the negotiations of the Peace of Philocrates (346). The trial provided the audience with a panoramic view of the past fiercely contested by two excellent orators, ultimately weighing Demosthenes' anti-Macedonian policy in the balance of Athenian history.[1] This view allows us to analyse Aeschines' perception of the most significant landmarks of their recent past, therefore the following chapter examines two turning points in the relations of Athens and Macedonia that retrospectively proved to be decisive in the public lives of both Aeschines and his adversary: the negotiations of the peace of Philocrates and the battle of Chaeronea.

I am grateful to Aggelos Kapellos, Edward Harris, Joseph Roisman, Gunther Martin, and Guy Westwood for a number of suggestions on various drafts of this chapter.

[1] For a recent overview on how Aeschines and Demosthenes utilized the past to prevail at the court see Westwood 2020.

I will argue that Aeschines' strategy included an attempt to turn Demosthenes into a scapegoat by reminding the Athenians of the bitter consequences of Chaeronea and by proving that it was not Philip or Alexander who was responsible for their fate but rather Demosthenes. Aeschines believed that the general Athenian attitude to the Macedonians (and to Demosthenes) had recently adapted to political realities.[2] After filing the indictment in 336, he waited for six years to bring his case against Ctesiphon to court,[3] and during this time he saw that the Macedonian kingdom was not only victorious in Hellas but also conquered the inhabited world, and all those (Thebans, Spartans, Persians) who tried to stand against it failed.[4] This experience may have confirmed his political approach to Macedon: as they never attempted to subjugate Athens but treated her with respect,[5] Athens needed to be at peace with Philip and Alexander under the best terms available. Since Aeschines participated in negotiating the treaties in 346 and in 338, he believed that his policy of peace was constantly threatened by the warmongering of Demosthenes. During the years from 346 to 330, though he soon distanced himself from Philocrates and may have seen the imperfections of the peace, he never said a word of harsh criticism against Philip.[6]

Aeschines had three main charges against Ctesiphon, who had proposed in 336 that Demosthenes be rewarded with a golden crown. First, he asserted that Ctesiphon's motion was illegal because it offered the crown to Demosthenes while he was still subject to audit for the office he held as *teichopoios*. Second, the crowning of Demosthenes was proposed to take place in the theatre of Dionysus, which, according to Aeschines, was prohibited by law. These two legal objections did not extend beyond one-fifth of the speech (until Aesch. 3.48),[7] thus leaving ample room for the third and main charge against Ctesiphon's proposal: the decree for crowning contained a false statement in so far as Demosthenes was "constantly speaking and acting in the best interests of the Athenian people."[8] This rather conventional phrase[9] provided Aeschines with

---

[2] Worthington 2013, 257.
[3] Recently Carawan, 2019 has argued that Demosthenes and his supporters forced Aeschines to bring the case to court in 330 by reviving the decree of Ctesiphon, but see the detailed refutation by Harris 2019.
[4] See esp. Aesch. 3.132–133, 163–166.
[5] Psoma 2014, 141–144.
[6] Carey 2005, 94.
[7] Both of Aeschines's legal charges were weak, see Harris 2017 (for the first) and Canevaro 2013, 290–293 (for the second).
[8] Aesch. 3.49, 101, 237, cf. Dem. 18.57, 59.
[9] Cook 2009, 42.

an excuse to open a lengthy critical narrative on the entire political career of Demosthenes (Aesch. 3.49–167), which, Aeschines hoped, would prove that his opponent's speeches and actions, promoting either peace or war, were to the detriment of Athens. The account of Demosthenes' career and his seemingly misguided policy against Macedonia was meant to be the strongest argument in the indictment.

Aeschines divided his opponent's political crimes (3.54) into four periods, which were not discussed evenly or given equal weight. The first phase, for example, would incorporate the early public activity of Demosthenes, including his efforts for a more interventionist foreign policy that he pursued in the late 350s. Still, Aeschines omitted this entire period and concentrated here only on the negotiations of the "earlier peace" (starting with preliminaries in 348) and on Demosthenes' hypocritical cooperation with Philocrates. Details of the subsequent periods are also selective, which was dictated both by time constraints and rhetorical considerations, but a reader of the speech may have the impression (as some have noted) that Aeschines predominantly based his accusation on the consequences of a single historical event that proved to be decisive in the life of Athens (and of many other *poleis*): the battle of Chaeronea.[10]

The actions surrounding the peace and the battle are all linked to the king of Macedon, with whom the treaty was made and against whom the battle was fought. Aeschines' attitude towards Philip certainly had an impact on his political movements during these years in general and also in reference to the mentioned key events. How did Aeschines' relationship with Philip change, if it changed at all, while the king bested the Athenians first in diplomacy, and then on the battlefield as well?

1 The Peace

Macedonian expansion in the northern Aegean coastline under Philip II posed a serious threat to Athens, because losing the Chersonese and other strategic bases would have deprived Attica not only of timber and metals in the north, but also of a secure route for the grain imported from the Black Sea region.[11] At the same time, Athenian attempts to control Euboea in 348 proved futile, and

---

10 Yunis 2001, 13; Worthington 2013, 296–297; and Alexiou 2020, 226.
11 Dem. 20.31–32 with Canevaro 2016, 244–251.

the prospect of a two-front war was more than alarming to Athens.[12] For different reasons, Philip also wanted peace with Athens.[13]

As for the Peace of Philocrates,[14] Aeschines and Demosthenes were both members of the embassy that visited Pella twice in early 346, but their relationship deteriorated quickly due to their different perceptions of Philip's intentions, and their quarrel had a lasting effect on Athenian policies against Macedon.[15] In 330, Aeschines chose an interesting strategy to address the issue of the peace negotiations with Philip: he completely omitted his role in the embassies and put all the blame for the imperfections of the treaty on Demosthenes and Philocrates.[16] The final agreement should have been much more advantageous for the Athenians, but "you were robbed of this opportunity by Demosthenes and Philocrates and the bribes they took for plotting against your collective interests".[17] Therefore Aeschines accused Demosthenes with the following main charges concerning the peace: collaborating with Philocrates (3.57, 60, 62–64, 72–74), fawning upon Philip and his envoys (3.61, 76), taking bribes (3.58, 66, 69),[18] changing his policy when speaking against the joint resolution of the allies on the second day of the Assembly (3.71–73), and causing the destruction of the Phocians and Cersebleptes (3.73–74, 80). These accusations were all part of Demosthenes' arsenal against Aeschines at the trial on the Embassy, but in 330 the latter felt confident enough to insert a condensed reflection of his opponent's previous prosecution into his speech.[19] Although Aeschines highlighted Demosthenes' repeated service as envoy to Philip (Aesch. 3.73), he curiously "forgot" to mention his own role in forging the peace.[20] The only passage referring to Aeschines' activity in this period (348–346) is his alleged support of the

---

12 See Brun in this volume.
13 Harris 1995, 43–50; Buckler 2003, 430–443.
14 See Brun in this volume.
15 Instead of becoming an effective team, the group of Athenian envoys failed to work optimally, mainly due to lack of cooperation on the part of Demosthenes; see Rubinstein 2016, 90.
16 See esp. Aesch. 3.73.
17 Aesch. 3.58. All translations of Aeschines are adapted from Carey 2000. Cf. Aesch. 1.173: "the peace that was brought about through me and Philocrates."
18 Accepting bribes from Philip and thus betraying Athenian interests during the second embassy was a major charge against Aeschines in 343 (see O'Connell in this volume). Aeschines' similar countercharge against Demosthenes was also taken up by e.g. Dinarchus (see Worthington in this volume).
19 Some of these charges had been also used against Demosthenes in 343; see Harris 1995, 70–71, 117, 145–146.
20 Aeschines also skips over the events after Elaphebolion 346 in his speech of 330, especially the Second Embassy.

joint resolution of the allies at the Assembly, where ultimately Philocrates' motion was accepted.[21] Otherwise, Aeschines kept silent about his actions, and even asserted that the general dissatisfaction caused by this imperfect treaty provoked severe criticism against the makers of the peace: Philocrates and Demosthenes.[22] The prosecution of Aeschines in 343 has no trace in *Against Ctesiphon*.

The activity of Aeschines in 348–346 and his attitude to Philip is much better documented in his earlier orations and in Dem. 19. Demosthenes narrated that Aeschines had started his public career as a fervent opponent of Philip, and in accordance with the decree of Eubulus he was sent to the Peloponnese to gain support for a joint military venture against Philip in 348/7.[23] "In his speeches, he repeatedly labelled Philip a barbarian and an evil fury." (Dem. 19.305.) However, Aeschines' efforts to unite the Peloponnese and Attica proved futile, and his failure made him realize that Athens needed to sheathe the sword and make the best possible peace with Macedon. Therefore, instead of denying the above words of Demosthenes, Aeschines revealed his decisive political turn in the speech *On the Embassy*:

> While the war lasted, I tried to the best of my ability to unite the Arcadians and the rest of Greece against Philip. But when no one in the world was supporting our city but some were idly watching what would befall us while others joined the fight against us, while the public speakers in Athens were looking to the war to underwrite their daily living costs (χορηγόν), I admit that I advised the Assembly to come to terms with Philip and conclude the peace. (Aesch. 2.79)

The details implied by this passage are intentionally vague: no enemies are named, not even the Athenian politicians who outrageously profited from the war. Nevertheless, in this section Aeschines openly reflected on his change of mind concerning Philip, and claimed he had used to see the king as an enemy to destroy, yet hard political experience taught him to treat Philip now as an opponent to negotiate with. Or did he cherish, at least for a while, an even more positive image of the king?

---

[21] "I admit that I spoke in support of this resolution, as did all those who addressed the people in the first of the Assemblies." (Aesch. 3.71, cf. 2.61, but see Efstathiou 2004, 390 highlighting that the position of the allies was stated twice.)

[22] Aesch. 3.80. Aeschines claimed that this alleged attack (and also their disagreements over profits of treason) accounted for the quarrel of Demosthenes and Philocrates, and also for Demosthenes' change of political sides (Aesch. 3.81–82).

[23] Dem. 19.9–14, 302–307. For the Athenian embassies to the Greeks between 348 and 346, see Harris 1995, 158–161.

In *Against Timarchus* (346/5), only a few months after the peace was concluded, Aeschines predicted that Demosthenes, supporting Timarchus, would try to involve Philip in the defence in order to divert the case: "Philip will be there in plenty; and the name of his son Alexander[24] will be thrown in, too." (Aesch. 1.166) Speaking against Philip, as Aeschines claimed, was ignorant and ill-timed, because the king deserved praise for his auspicious words and for the generous promises he made to them (1.169). Here Aeschines portrayed the Macedonian ruler as a noble friend of Athens, because he still wanted the Athenians to believe that Philip would deliver on the promises that he had made during the peace negotiations.[25]

Such enthusiasm for Philip is absent from the speech *On the Embassy*, which is no surprise if we consider the substantial change in Athenian public opinion on the peace in the intermittent years;[26] however, the way Aeschines presented the king in 343 was still markedly favourable. Far from the image of the barbarian king enjoying drunkenness and lewd dancing,[27] Aeschines depicted Philip as an affable (albeit cunning) ruler with an impressive appearance and stunning oratory (highlighting his excellent memory), who repeatedly emphasized his commitment to making peace, but he certainly did his best to make it most beneficial to him.[28] "And if Philip deceived our city, his purpose in lying was to gain the peace that was to his advantage" (Aesch. 2.123), as opposed to Demosthenes, who was lying against the interests of Athens. We can note that Aeschines did not attribute generous promises to Philip any more, yet he was ready to accept that the king deceived them, because in a diplomatic negotiation both sides naturally seek benefits for themselves. He tried to influence Philip with the power of his speeches: on the first embassy, he criticized him for continuing war against Athens and came up with shifty arguments to regain Amphipolis (2.30–33), and on the second he tried to persuade him not to punish the Phocians too harshly but to prevent Thebes becoming master of Boeotia

---

24 This is the first recorded reference to Alexander the Great. See also Aesch. 1.167–169 with Fisher 2001, 312–313.

25 For the unfulfilled promises, see Dem. 19.20, 40–41, 220, 326 with Harris 1995, 87–88, 199–200. Aesch 1.169 may also indicate a touch of doubt.

26 For the details (failed amendment of the peace, the fall of Philocrates, etc.), see Harris 1995, 107–116; Worthington 2013, 179–200.

27 This was a stereotypical image of Philip beyond the circles of the common anti-Macedonian propaganda, see e.g. Dem. 2.18–19, Diod. 16.55 and 87, Theopompus BNJ 115 F27 and F282. Cf. Worthington 2014, 19–20; Alexiou 2015, 15–16.

28 Passages characterizing Philip in Aesch. 2: 21, 38–39, 41–43, 47–48, 51–52. Philip is committed to making peace: Aesch. 2.12–13, 16–17, 82.

again (2.113–117). But it was all in vain, since "Fortune and Philip were responsible for what was done" (Aesch. 2.118).

Despite his fruitless efforts as an envoy to control events, which, as we could see, are completely concealed in the trial of 330, and despite his expressed disappointment, there is not a shred of grudge against Philip in Aeschines' words. On the contrary, Aeschines takes great delight in narrating the scene where Philip was first confronted by Demosthenes in Pella (Aesch. 2.34–35), and used it to elevate the one and debase the other at the same time.[29] The veracity of the well-prepared (cf. 2.21), vivid and amusing rendition of Demosthenes' unsuccessful speech in front of Philip and their fellow envoys is still disputed,[30] but it was certainly a forceful way of highlighting Philip's superiority over Demosthenes in matters of speaking: while the mighty orator was paralyzed by stage fright, lost his words, and abandoned his speech, Philip kindly encouraged him to calm down and start over again. The 'barbarian' king is presented here almost as a tolerant teacher of oratory instructing a beginner, so that Aeschines could humiliate the great Demosthenes even more in the eyes of the Athenian audience at court.[31]

There is a final point to make about Philip as a kind ruler in Aeschines' presentation. Philip's behaviour was often described by various later sources with the term φιλανθρωπία and its cognates, designating benevolence, generosity, and humane feeling. After conquering Amphipolis, Diodorus reported that Philip treated neutral citizens φιλανθρώπως, and the same adverb is used to describe how he dealt with the Athenian garrisons in Potidaea.[32] Plutarch asserted that the sacrifices the Athenians offered to the gods on Philip's death were not honourable, since the king had treated them so mildly and humanely (φιλανθρώπως).[33] The *Suda* recorded that Philip "accomplished more through the fairness and humanity of his character (διὰ ... φιλανθρωπίας τῶν τρόπων) than through force of arms".[34]

---

[29] For Aeschines' heavy reliance on narrative, see Edwards 2004, 349.

[30] Harris 1995, 57–60 concludes that since Aeschines had the testimony of numerous witnesses to support him, we can accept the essentials of his account. Worthington 2020, 23–24 considers Aeschines' effective tale 'fake news'. See also Worthington 2017, 24–25.

[31] Cf. Roisman 2005, 143–144 and Alexiou 2015, 16. For Philip as a competent orator, see Diod. 16.3.1, 16.95.3–4. Demosthenes denied Philip's rhetorical skills, see Guth 2016.

[32] Diod. 16.8.2 and 5, see also 16.4.3, 16.55.3. For Philip in Diodorus see McQueen 1995, 14–16.

[33] Plut. *Dem.* 22.4, see also Plut. *Phoc.* 16.5, where Phocion expressed that the Athenians should accept Philip's friendly policy and kindly overtures (φιλανθρωπίαν) to them; see Várzeas 2009, 335–336.

[34] Suda phi 354, transl. T. Natoli.

Philanthropia, however, was a value-term conspicuously often used by Demosthenes as well.[35] Before him, it was usually (though not exclusively) applied to refer to generous, friendly, or humane attitude of rulers, aristocrats or generals towards their people, as it is attested in e.g. the works of Xenophon and Isocrates.[36] It was not a specifically Athenian term, though in some cases this virtue was attributed to certain Athenians.[37] The coherent and programmatic use of this (originally aristocratic) virtue by Demosthenes may have been an attempt to turn it into a democratic ideal, i.e. the way how the Athenian people treat each other and even their foreign relations.[38] For Demosthenes (and for some of his allies),[39] while the Athenian demos truly possessed this virtue, Philip's φιλανθρωπία was only feigned, and the king was never a true φιλάνθρωπος, as all such occurrences are ironical.[40] Aeschines, on the other hand, seemed to stick to the 'old' meaning of the term: he used it nine times in his extant speeches, but only once connected to the Athenian people (2.30), while four of the occurrences are references to Philip: (1) Before the peace negotiations started, a certain Ctesiphon[41] reported to the Athenian Assembly about Philip's intention to make peace and about his great kindness (φιλανθρωπίαν, 2.13). (2) Aristodemus, the actor was elected envoy to Philip because the king knew him and was fond of his acting talents (φιλανθρωπίαν τῆς τέχνης, 2.15). (3) When Philip addressed the first embassy in Pella, he emphasized his goodwill (φιλανθρωπίαν, 2.39) towards Athens, which, according to Aeschines, refuted Demosthenes' earlier concerns that Aeschines' first speech enraged the king (2.36–37). (4) Finally,

---

35 There are 18 occurrences of the term and its cognates in Dem. 18 and 19, and 72 occurrences in the whole *corpus Demosthenicum*. For the relative frequency of the concept see Bajnok 2019, 9–22.

36 *Cyr.* 1.2.1, *Ages.* 1.22, Isoc. 5.114, 9.43, etc. For further examples, see Christ 2013, 203–204. On the development of the term in general, see Sulek 2010; for its special significance in Athenian democratic ideology, see also Barbato 2020, 118–126. There is a single extant contemporary Attic inscription (*IG* II² 1186) using the term, see Veligianni-Terzi 1997, 216.

37 E.g. Euryptolemus, speaking in defence of the Arginusae generals (406), claimed that they acted with *philanthropia* when they tried to take care of the shipwrecked (Xen. *Hell.* 1.7.18), see Kapellos 2019, 180–181.

38 Christ 2013; Low 2007, 182. *Epitaphioi* frequently refer to Athens being just and helpful towards others, which formed part of the Athenian notion of *philanthropia*; see Barbato 2020, 63–64.

39 The speaker of [Dem.] 7.31, probably Hegesippus (see Wang in this volume), also used the term in reference to the people of Athens.

40 Dem. 18.231, 298, 19.39, 102, 139, 140, 315; see Christ 2013, 206–207.

41 This Ctesiphon (*PA* 8893) is probably not identical with the proposer of the crown (*PA* 8894); see Carey 2000, 159–160.

Aeschines used this term once more in 330: "the responsibility for the city's survival lies with [...] the individuals who have treated the city's situation with humanity (φιλανθρώπως) and moderation, while the responsibility for all our misfortunes lies with Demosthenes." (Aesch. 3.57)

It is self-evident (and it is also confirmed by a *scholion*) that the individual who had treated Athens with humanity after Chaeronea was Philip.[42] In all the above passages of Aeschines, the king is attached to the traditional, 'aristocratic' virtue of *philanthropia*, and not to its democratized counterpart favoured by Demosthenes; moreover, the term was never applied ironically to Philip by Aeschines.[43] A passage in *Against Ctesiphon* (Aesch. 3.247–248) indicates that Aeschines may have been fully aware of Demosthenes' intent to appropriate *philanthropia* (among other terms) for a 'democratic' discourse, and he was not willing to cede it to his opponent.[44] Therefore, he kept using the concept in the 'old-fashioned' way in reference to Philip, who was undoubtedly an enemy of Athens, but a more humane and dignified one than Demosthenes, at least in the eyes of Aeschines. It was possible to make peace with Philip, but never with Demosthenes.

2 The Battle

From Aeschines' point of view, another crucial landmark in the career of Demosthenes (and also in the history of Greece) was the Battle of Chaeronea, which Aeschines considered an irreparable catastrophe, but it is still iterated again and again: "a disaster befell the city – I am sorry to mention it so often" (3.252).[45] Aeschines admitted that the memory was painful, but he may have believed that he could focus this pain and anger towards Demosthenes by reminding the Athenians that his opponent has sole responsibility for the events. After all, in 330, when the situation of Athens proved to be secure and the rela-

---

42 Sch. Aesch. 3.57 [125]: διὰ τὸν Φίλιππον λέγει. εἰ γὰρ μὴ φιλανθρώπως ἡμῖν προσηνέχθη, τί ἐκώλυε κρατήσαντα ἐν Χαιρωνείᾳ πιθέσθαι τῇ πόλει;
43 However, Aeschines used the term ironically when referring to Demosthenes, who invited the young Aristarchus into his well-known generosity (εἰς τὴν φιλανθρωπίαν ταύτην, Aesch. 1.171). The allusion is made to Demosthenes' erotic pretensions, see Fisher 2001, 318.
44 Cook 2009, 39; Bajnok 2019, 10.
45 Cf. Lyc. 1.16. Orators were reluctant to mention events that were unpleasant to their audience; see Kapellos 2014, 95. The toponym 'Chaeronea' became a symbol of defeat, therefore Demosthenes and Hyperides avoided uttering it; see Kapellos 2022, 18–21.

tionship with the Macedonians was solid (thanks to abstaining from the Spartan revolt),[46] Aeschines considered the time was ripe for bringing a public speaker to court and claiming that his political activities were all leading to the disaster.[47]

In August 338 at Chaeronea, Philip and Alexander defeated the allied forces of Athens and Thebes by means of superior military leadership and personal valour: a thousand Athenian citizens were killed, and twice that number were taken as captives.[48] Aeschines did not dwell on details of the battle at all, except for one that seemed important to him: Demosthenes played the coward and deserted the battlefield. This particular detail is stated or alluded to 12 times in the speech, although Chaeronea itself is mentioned only twice.[49] The trial in 330 was not the first time Aeschines questioned the personal courage and masculinity of Demosthenes,[50] but here the cowardly-deserter frame was specifically built to denigrate and ridicule his entire political and private character, which may have been a well-conceived rhetorical strategy.[51]

Beside the battle itself, Aeschines invested much more in highlighting Demosthenes' responsibility for the situation that led Athens to Chaeronea.[52] He claimed that the alliance with the Thebans in 339, which enabled Athens to fight the battle in Boeotian territory instead of Attica, was not a merit of Demosthenes: Thebes was drawn into alliance with Athens by their fear caused by the military movements of Philip (e.g. the seizure and fortification of Elatea).[53] "What brought you to Thebes was the crisis, their fear, and their need for an alliance, not Demosthenes." (Aesch. 3.141).[54] On the other hand, he also be-

---

[46] Worthington 2013, 290–293.
[47] *Pace* Carawan 2019. For the delay and the timing of the trial of Ctesiphon see Harris 2019, 93 and Westwood 2020, 277.
[48] Dem. 18.264, Diod. 16.86.4, Ellis 1976, 198; Hammond 1994, 154; Worthington 2014, 88.
[49] Desertion of Demosthenes: Aesch. 3.7, 148, 152, 155, 159, 170, 175, 176, 181, 187, 244, 253. (Cf. Worthington 1992, 148 with a slightly different list of passages.) Chaeronea: Aesch. 3.55, 187. Pytheas (Plut. *Dem.* 20.2) added that Demosthenes even abandoned his shield, which was never explicitly stated by Aeschines.
[50] Aesch. 1.131, 181, 2.22, 79, 88, 99, 106, 139, 151, 177. For masculinity on the battlefield, see Roisman 2005, ch. 5, esp. 118–119 and Christ 2006, 134–141.
[51] Cook 2012. For Demosthenes' desertion, see Worthington in this volume.
[52] Demades' dictum on Demosthenes' responsibility for the war (Arist. *Rhet.* 1401b.32–34) might refer to the same situation.
[53] Aeschines also listed a number of former Athenian ambassadors and *proxenoi* to Thebes to show that none of them managed to draw the Thebans into friendship with the Athenians, Aesch. 3.137–141.
[54] Demosthenes tried to take all credits for the alliance (18.178), but see Brun 2015, 211 and Guth 2014.

lieved that a single Demosthenes, acting alone to the detriment of Athens, was a suitable subject to be blamed for everything, as we will see in the following.

One of the greatest crimes of Demosthenes, according to Aeschines, was that he misrepresented Philip's attitude to Athens. Aeschines indeed had an easy task to show from hindsight in 330 that Philip hated Thebes and preferred Athens: "Though Philip, while ostensibly at war with you, in reality was much more hostile to Thebes, as events themselves have shown (need I say more?), Demosthenes concealed this fact, which is of fundamental importance, by pretending that the alliance was about to be concluded not because of the crisis but because of his diplomacy." (3.141) In reference to Aeschines' comment on Philip's intentions towards Athens, we need to remark that ancient orators and all Athenians tried to fill in the gap about the real motives of the Macedonian king on the basis of the results. However, these results were still open to endless debate. Philip did not destroy the city after Chaeronea, but why did he not? Demosthenes allegedly claimed that the omens were not favourable for him (Aesch. 3.131),[55] but Aeschines asserted that the king did not want to harm Athens. Obviously, none of them could predict what Philip would do, and in their interpretation of recent events, they also contradicted each other, as neither they themselves nor their listeners were informed about the true motives and thoughts of Philip.[56]

Aeschines also reported Philip's peace offer some time before the battle. "Philip had no slight regard for the Greeks and was well aware (he was no fool) that in a small portion of a day he would risk all he possessed in battle. For this reason he wanted to make peace and was proposing to send envoys."[57] The destination of the envoys is vague: Aeschines continues by saying that the Thebans hesitated whether to undertake the dangers of war, thus they were certainly approached by Philip's ambassadors, but we can assume that Athens was also offered peace in this situation.[58] Demosthenes thwarted the offer, because, as Aeschines implied, he wanted a share of the bribes that Demosthenes believed the Boeotarchs received from Philip. Aeschines wished to show that Philip was still open to discussion amid the greatest tensions (yet another positive trait of the king!), but he also asserted that Demosthenes, "suspecting that the Boeotarchs were about to make a separate peace in exchange for money from Philip with no share for him, decided that life was not worth living if he was left

---

55 Cf. also Dem. 60.20.
56 Cf. Harris 1995, 5 and see Roisman in this volume.
57 Aesch. 3.148.
58 This is confirmed by Plut. *Dem.* 18.2 and *Phoc.* 16; see Harris 1995, 132–133. Cf. Dem. 18.174.

out of any chance of bribery (3.149)."[59] Aeschines tried to prop up his slander by claiming that Demosthenes imitated the warmongering of Cleophon (3.150), as if it was a message to the Boeotarchs that he would stop opposing Philip if they give him a share of the bribe. The claim, however, is at odds with Aeschines' earlier assertion that Demosthenes did little to influence Thebes.[60] Despite this inconsistency, the overall message of Aeschines is simple here: Philip was still ready to make peace, but it was Demosthenes alone who ultimately drove Athens (and Thebes) to war.

However, beyond discussing the antecedents, Aeschines tried to benefit even more from the battle itself and its consequences. In spite of their fears,[61] Attica was not stormed by Macedonian troops, and no garrison was deployed on the Acropolis. Unlike Thebes, Athens was treated lightly:[62] the captives were sent home and a new peace was negotiated with Philip by an embassy that again included Aeschines himself, which indicates his activity in the aftermath of the battle.[63] The Athenians could give a proper funeral to their citizens killed at Chaeronea, and the orator entrusted by the people to deliver the funeral speech was — Demosthenes. Though he later he took great pleasure in reminding Aeschines of this moment,[64] the task of speaking at the tombs of those who died fighting Philip was obviously not easy. Dem. 60 (if authentic) was the first one to exhibit the battle not as a disaster but as a heroic exploit to satisfy the emotional needs of the audience and to present sociological propaganda by means of 'rhetoric of deflection':[65] Athens chose the right path, and the failure was caused by the Theban generals (Dem. 60.22). This funeral oration may have turned the tables in the interpretation of the event: regardless of the outcome, fighting for freedom at Chaeronea was the best option to do in the given circumstances.[66]

In early 331, Lycurgus prosecuted Leocrates for deserting Athens at the time of the battle at Chaeronea (Lyc. 1.8).[67] Lycurgus devoted much space to the sor-

---

[59] This is one of the few exceptional cases where bribery was suggested on the basis of intent as opposed to outcome, cf. Conover 2014.
[60] Carey 2000, 215 n. 168.
[61] Cf. Hyperides' proposal, see Cooper in this volume.
[62] Diod. 16.87.3, Justin *Epitome*, 9.4.4–5.
[63] Aesch. 3.227 and Dem. 18.282 with Worthington 2013, 256–257.
[64] Dem. 18.285–288.
[65] The rhetoric of deflection attempts to reframe a subject by altering the audience's approach to it; see Crick in this volume.
[66] Hyp. *Diond*. 19 (Horváth 2014, 77).
[67] For dating see Harris 2001, 159 n. 1 and Roisman and Edwards 2019, 2 n. 2.

rowful memories of 338, as he evoked the moments when the news of the battle arrived at Athens: women cowering in fear, old men preparing for the defence of the city, and the people voting for granting arms to slaves and foreigners (Lyc. 1.39–42).[68] The case is referred to also by Aeschines, who informs us that the votes of the judges were equal, therefore Leocrates narrowly escaped the death penalty.[69] If someone like Leocrates was almost convicted only because he "sailed to Rhodes and ... did not handle his fear like a man" (Aesch. 3.252), then how could Demosthenes, who is to blame for all the troubles of Greece, ever deserve a crown? While carefully planning his strategy against his opponent, Aeschines may have decided that portraying Chaeronea as a terrible disaster again and making Demosthenes solely responsible for it was an acceptable presentation of recent past in front of an Athenian audience.

He considered Demosthenes an ideal subject for scapegoating in a situation which can be set in parallel with the case of Adeimantus, the Athenian general spared by Lysander after the decisive Spartan victory over the Athenian fleet at Aegospotami in 405.[70] His fellow general Conon, who managed to flee the battle and then returned to Athens after 393, had Adeimantus convicted and executed for betraying the city.[71] There are several parallels to note between Adeimantus and Demosthenes. First, both were attacked by some Athenians after the fatal battle of Aegospotami / Chaeronea: Adeimantus was accused of betraying the fleet (Xen. *Hell.* 2.1.32), and Demosthenes claimed that in the period following the battle he was prosecuted almost every day (Dem. 18.249).[72] These accusations, however, did not destroy the defendants. Second, several years later both of them were challenged again by another plaintiff (Conon / Aeschines) and were held accountable for all the misfortunes of their city. Since the witnesses were either dead or supporting Conon in this second prosecution, Adeimantus was effectively turned into a scapegoat for surviving a disastrous battle that sealed the fate of Athens in the Peloponnesian war, regardless whether he was actually guilty or not.[73] Aeschines may well have had the same rhetorical strate-

---

[68] Cf. Worthington in this volume, who claims that Lycurgus (and Aeschines) may have made the mistake of overemphasizing the tragic aspect of Chaeronea.
[69] On the interpretation of Aesch. 3.252; see Bianchi 2002.
[70] Xen. *Hell.* 2.1.32.
[71] Lys. 14.38, but the case had been recently mentioned in 343 (Dem. 19.191), which may have given a hint for the strategy of Aeschines.
[72] Cf. Hyp. *Diond.* 9 (Horváth 2014, 73).
[73] For the reconstruction of the case of Adeimantus, see Kapellos 2009, 266–275.

gy in mind when he decided to take the prosecution to trial and put all the blame on Demosthenes.[74]

When Aeschines addressed the consequences of Chaeronea, he used the event as a disaster in the common memory of all Athenians, but said almost nothing about the direct aftermath of the battle, except for the passing reference to Philip, who did not attack Athens when he had the chance (Aesch. 3.131). However, in a very curious section of the speech (3.152–158), Aeschines used powerful images to remind the Athenians to what happened. He started with mentioning the brave men whom Demosthenes sent to their death in spite of the bad omens he received, "yet he had the nerve (mounting the dead men's tomb with those runaway feet that deserted their post) to speak in praise of their courage."[75] These words refer to Demosthenes' funeral speech over the victims of the battle, which Aeschines naturally could not approve, so in the following section he composed a strange blending of four scenes into one sequence, as if it was his own version of commemorating the heroes of Chaeronea.

This strong passage of *enargeia*[76] imagines a setting in the theatre ("please imagine yourselves … in the theatre", 3.153), where the audience first sees the herald coming forward to announce the decree of Ctesiphon crowning Demosthenes before the premiere of the new tragedies. Then Aeschines switches focus to the relatives of the Chaeronea heroes by asking the listeners: "will they shed more tears over the tragedies […] or at the city's insensitivity" (i.e. crowning the culprit)? Drawing the attention of the audience to mourning relatives of the dead, some of them probably present at the hearing, may have been an effective move. Because one thousand citizens lost their lives in the battle (see above), Aeschines could expect to make a strong case by mentioning their relatives, which he does repeatedly in his speech to revive the sense of loss in his audience.[77] There is a parallel strategy to that of Aeschines which is known to us from Xenophon's *Hellenica*: at the trial of the Arginusae generals (406), Theramenes instructed certain persons to wear black clothes and to have their hair cut so that they might appear to be the mourning relatives of those whom the generals had allegedly failed to save after the battle of Arginusae. These fake mourners, evoking the recent loss and also stirring a hunger for revenge, proved

---

74 Cf. Koulakiotis 2018, 44, who claims that in 345 Demosthenes searched for a scapegoat for the political situation after the peace of Philocrates, and therefore he had Timarchus prosecute Aeschines for *parapresbeia*. Implicitly, Aeschines might have intended to turn the tables in 330.
75 Aesch. 3.152.
76 See O'Connell in this volume.
77 Indirect references to relatives of the dead: Aesch. 3.211, 225, 235.

to be powerful props in the prosecution and condemnation of the victorious generals.[78]

After the rhetorical question, Aeschines continues with a second scene (3.154) that he claimed was once set in the theatre: the treatment of the sons of the war dead. These young people, dressed in full hoplite armour, were also exhibited to the demos, and a ceremonial proclamation was made that the orphans would be reared to adulthood by the people of Athens.[79] This announcement of the orphans' public care may have been another allusion to funeral speeches, as it is an element we can find in the *epitaphios logos* of Pericles (Thuc. 2.46) and Socrates/Aspasia (Plat. *Menex.* 248e), but not in Dem. 60. Then Aeschines bitterly admits that the orphans are not honoured in the theatre any more, and thus he moves on to a third scene (3.155), which is parallel with the first one, where he invites the audience to imagine again how the herald announces the honorary decree of Demosthenes. In this scene, however, the Athenians are not presented with a sight (as it is usual in *enargeia*) but rather with a voice: if the herald proclaims the crown, "Shame prompted by the truth will not stay silent", but will speak out against the herald, countering all his claims and revealing that Demosthenes is the worst of men (if he is a man at all), and a coward, who deserted his post.[80] The 'divine' intervention of Shame is followed by a short intermezzo, where Aeschines begs the audience "not to set up a trophy of your own defeat" in the theatre, i.e. not to make Demosthenes a crowned memorial of Chaeronea. Finally, Aeschines turns to the fourth scene, the destruction of Thebes:

> But since you were not there in person, witness their disasters with your mind's eye and imagine that you can see their city being captured, the demolition of the walls, the burning of the houses, the women and children being led away to slavery, old men, old women learning late in life to forget their freedom, weeping, begging you, angry not at the people who were taking revenge on them but at the men responsible for these events. (Aesch. 3.157)

The terrible fate of Thebes was treated by Diodorus in an equally dreadful description (Diod. 17.13–14). Over six thousand Thebans were killed, more than thirty thousand captured, and the city was piled high with corpses.[81] The Athe-

---

[78] Xen. *Hell.* 1.7.8 with Kapellos 2019, 151–153. For a similar though less elaborated rhetorical use of mourning relatives, see Lyc. 1.142.
[79] The children of the war dead exhibited in the theatre: Isoc. 8.82. The raising of these children was financed by public money: Arist. *Pol.* 1268a, [Arist.] *Ath. Pol.* 24.3, Diog. Laert. 1.55.
[80] Cook 2012, 234.
[81] Bosworth 1988, 33.

nians were shocked to hear the news (Diod. 17.15.1), and Aeschines now recalled memories of this recent event through the audience's imagination. Still, evoking the disaster of the Thebans is in many respects out of place here. First, the destruction of Thebes was not a direct consequence of Chaeronea but that of their revolt in 335, following the death of Philip and the accession of Alexander.[82] This kind of chronological manipulation is necessary to conceal the second problem, namely that the Thebans were angry not at the Macedonians and Alexander, who annihilated their city, but at Demosthenes, whose inactivity in the post-Chaeronea years is notorious.[83] (Aeschines expected it could work, because Demosthenes encouraged and helped the Thebans to rebel before he reversed policy.)[84] Third, the vivid *enargeia* in this scene (with burning houses, enslaved people weeping) presented the fate of the Thebans in such a horrific and disturbing way that was probably inappropriate during the recollection of the dead heroes of Chaeronea, where the sequence of scenes started.[85] Though we need to keep in mind that the orator maintained a certain distance between the above painful scenes (after all, the suffering Thebans are not Athenians), we can also trace the role of suffering in his underlying strategy. Aeschines did not seem to be concerned with offering any relief for the battle, but instead he hoped to stir up the vengeful emotions of the listeners against Demosthenes by recalling their worst memories of war and destruction.[86]

Until the last moment, Aeschines may have believed that his view of the past would prevail over that of Demosthenes. However, the result of the trial in 330 showed that Aeschines' hopes of exploiting the memories of his kinsmen concerning Chaeronea were vain, to say the least: he failed to gain one fifth of the judges' votes, lost his right to file public charges, and left Athens for the rest of his life.[87] The anecdote, in which his Rhodian audience was surprised how he could have been defeated with such a marvellous speech, is evidence that his strategy and performance in 330 was strong and effective, but it also highlights

---

[82] Worthington 2014, 131–135.
[83] Worthington 2000.
[84] Worthington 2013, 279.
[85] The description of the fate of Thebes can be compared to Demosthenes' earlier evocation of the destruction of Phocis in Dem. 19.64–65; see Webb 2009, 141–143.
[86] Yunis 2001, 16–17. Cf. O'Connell 2017, 242, who believes that Aeschines' exaggerated *enargeia*-scene may have backfired.
[87] Plut. *Dem.* 24.2 and numerous ancient *vitae* of Aeschines. On the information in the lives of Aeschines about events after 330 see Harris 2019, 96–97.

the reason why he lost: "You would not marvel thus, if you had heard Demosthenes in reply to these arguments."[88]

3 Conclusion

Looking back in 330 to the recent past of Athens, Aeschines was convinced that it was possible to live in peace with Macedon. In his view, the policy of Philip (and Alexander) was not hostile against Athens, because after Chaeronea the city was not treated the way Thebes was punished, and he also hoped that his fellow Athenians would share his opinion. However, had everything depended on Demosthenes, the battle would have had much worse consequences, but fortunately Philip was acting with friendliness and moderation (Aesch. 3.57). On the other hand, Aeschines' insistence on friendly terms with Philip led to a contradiction in his arguments that weakened his interpretation of recent events. Aeschines seems to have had two mutually irreconcilable views, which undermined each other. First, he assumed that Chaeronea was a terrible disaster for Athens that should have never happened and that the only person responsible for this disaster was Demosthenes, whom he tried to turn into a scapegoat. Second, he also asserted that events could have turned out to be much worse for the city, but Philip and Alexander were fortunately not hostile to Athens. A disastrous event that might have been even more catastrophic was a far less appealing story than the one Demosthenes presented.

Bibliography

Alexiou, E. (2015), *Ρητορική και ιδεολογία: Ο Φίλιππος Β΄ της Μακεδονίας στον Ισοκράτη και σε συγχρόνους του*, Thessaloniki.
Alexiou, E. (2020), *Greek Rhetoric of the 4th Century BC: The Elixir of Democracy and Individuality*, Berlin/Boston.
Bajnok, D. (2019), *Appropriation of Language: Some Value-terms in the Oratory of Aeschines*, Budapest.
Barbato, M. (2020), *The Ideology of Democratic Athens: Institutions, Orators and the Mythical Past*, Edinburgh.
Bianchi, E. (2002), "Ancora su Eschine, III 252", *Dike* 5, 83–94.
Bosworth, A.B. (1988), *Conquest and Empire: The Reign of Alexander the Great*, Cambridge.

---

[88] Philostr. *V.S.* 1.510. (Transl. W.C. Wright).

Brun, P. (2015), *Démosthène: Rhétorique, pouvoir et corruption à Athènes*, Paris.
Buckler, J. (2003), *Aegean Greece in the fourth century BC*, Leiden.
Canevaro, M. (2013), *Documents in the Attic Orators. Laws and Decrees in the Public Speeches of the Demosthenic Corpus*, Oxford.
Canevaro, M. (2016), *Demostene, "Contro Leptine". Introduzione, Traduzione e Commento Storico*, Berlin/Boston.
Carawan, E. (2019), "How the 'Crown Case' Came to Trial and Why", *GRBS* 59, 109–133.
Carey, C. (2000), *Aeschines*, Austin.
Carey, C. (2005), "Propaganda and Competition in Athenian Oratory", in: K.A.E. Enenkel/I.L. Pfeijffer (eds.), *The Manipulative Mode: Political Propaganda in Antiquity: A Collection of Case Studies*, Leiden/Boston, 65–100.
Christ, M.R. (2006), *The Bad Citizen in Classical Athens*, Cambridge.
Christ, M.R. (2013), "Demosthenes on Philanthrôpia as a Democratic Virtue", *CP* 108, 202–222.
Conover, K. (2014), "Rethinking Anti-Corruption Reforms: The View from Ancient Athens", *Buffalo Law Review* 62, 69–117.
Cook, B.L. (2009), "Athenian Terms of Civic Praise in the 330s: Aeschines vs. Demosthenes", *GRBS* 49, 31–52.
Cook, B.L. (2012), "Swift-boating in Antiquity: Rhetorical Framing of the Good Citizen in Fourth-Century Athens", *Rhetorica* 30, 219–251.
Edwards, M. (2004), "Aeschines", in: I. de Jong et al. (eds.), *Narrators, Narratees, and Narratives in Ancient Greek Literature: Studies in Ancient Greek Narrative*, Volume One, Leiden/Boston, 349–353.
Efstathiou, A. (2004), "The 'Peace of Philokrates': The Assemblies of 18th and 19th Elaphebolion 346 B.C. Studying History through Rhetoric", *Historia* 53, 385–407.
Ellis, J.R. (1976), *Philip II and Macedonian Imperialism*, London.
Fisher, N.R.E. (2001), *Aeschines: Against Timarchos*, Oxford.
Guth, D. (2014), "Rhetoric and Historical Narrative: The Theban-Athenian Alliance of 339 BCE", *Historia* 63, 151–165.
Guth, D. (2016), "The king's speech: Philip's rhetoric and democratic leadership in the debate over the Peace of Philocrates", *Rhetorica* 33, 333–348.
Hammond, N.G.L. (1994), *Philip of Macedon*, London.
Harris, E.M. (1994), "Law and Oratory", in: I. Worthington (ed.), *Persuasion: Greek Rhetoric in Action*, London/New York, 130–150.
Harris, E.M. (1995), *Aeschines and Athenian Politics*, Oxford.
Harris, E.M. (2001), "Lycurgus", in: I. Worthington/C. Cooper/E. Harris (trans.), *Dinarchus, Hyperides, and Lycurgus*, Austin, 153–218.
Harris, E.M. (2017), "Applying the Law about the Award of Crowns to Magistrates (Aeschin. 3.9–31; Dem. 18.113–117): Epigraphic Evidence for the Legal Arguments at the Trial of Ctesiphon", *ZPE* 202, 105–117.
Harris, E.M. (2018), "The Stereotype of Tyranny and the Tyranny of Stereotypes: Demosthenes on Philip II of Macedon", in: M. Kalaitzi et al. (eds.), Βορειοελλαδικά: *Tales from the lands of the ethne. Essays in honour of Miltiades B. Hatzopoulos*, Athens, 167–178.
Harris, E.M. (2019), "The Crown Trial and Athenian Legal Procedure in Public Cases against Illegal Decrees", *Dike* 22, 81–111.
Horváth, L. (2014), *Der Neue Hypereides. Textedition, Studien und Erläuterungen*, Berlin.
Kapellos, A. (2009), "Adeimantos at Aegospotami: Innocent or Guilty?", *Historia* 58, 257–275.
Kapellos, A. (2014), *Lysias 21: A Commentary*, Berlin/Boston.

Kapellos, A. (2019), *Xenophon's Peloponnesian War*, Berlin/Boston.
Kapellos, A. (2022), "Xenophon and the Orators on the Topography of Arginousae and Aegospotami", *Mnemosyne* (online), 1–27.
Koulakiotis, E. (2018), "Attic Orators on Alexander the Great", in: K.R. Moore (ed.), *Brill's Companion to the Reception of Alexander the Great*, Leiden/Boston, 41–71.
Low, P. (2007), *Interstate Relations in Classical Greece: Morality and Power*, Cambridge.
McQueen, E.I. (1995), *Diodorus Siculus: The Reign of Philip II: The Greek and Macedonian Narrative from Book XVI: A Companion*, Bristol.
O'Connell, P. (2017), "*Enargeia*, Persuasion, and the Vividness Effect in Athenian Forensic Oratory", *Advances in the History of Rhetoric* 20, 225–251.
Psoma, S. (2014), "Athens and the Macedonian Kingdom from Perdikkas II to Philip II", *REA* 114, 133–144.
Roisman, J. (2005), *The Rhetoric of Manhood: Masculinity in the Attic Orators*, Berkeley/Los Angeles/London.
Roisman, J. and Edwards, M.J. (2019), *Lycurgus: Against Leocrates*, Oxford.
Steinbock, B. (2013), "Contesting the Lessons from the Past: Aeschines' Use of Social Memory", *TAPA* 143, 65–103.
Sulek, M. (2010), "On the Classical Meaning of Philanthrôpía", *Non profit and Voluntary Sector Quarterly* 39, 385–408.
Várzeas, M. (2009), "Tragedy and *Philanthropia* in the *Lives of Demosthenes and Cicero*", in: J.R. Ferreira et al. (eds.), *Symposion and Philanthropia in Plutarch*, Coimbra, 333–340.
Veligianni-Terzi, C. (1997), *Wertbegriffe in den attischen Ehrendekreten der Klassischen Zeit*, Stuttgart.
Wankel, H. (1976), *Demosthenes: Rede für Ktesiphon über den Kranz*, vols. 1–2, Heidelberg.
Webb, R. (2009), "Eschine et le passé athénien: narration, imagination et construction de la mémoire", *CEA* 46, 129–147.
Westwood, G. (2020), *The Rhetoric of the Past in Demosthenes and Aeschines: Oratory, History, and Politics in Classical Athens*, Oxford.
Worthington, I. (1992), *A Historical Commentary on Dinarchus: Rhetoric and Conspiracy in Later Fourth-Century Athens*, Ann Arbor.
Worthington, I. (2000), "Demosthenes' (in)activity during the reign of Alexander the Great", in: I. Worthington (ed.), *Demosthenes: Statesman and Orator*, London/New York, 90–113.
Worthington, I. (2013), *Demosthenes of Athens and the Fall of Classical Greece*, Oxford/New York.
Worthington, I. (2014), *By the Spear: Philip II, Alexander the Great, and the Rise and Fall of the Macedonian Empire*, Oxford.
Worthington, I. (2017), "Audience Reaction, Performance and the Exploitation of Delivery in the Courts and Assembly", in: S. Papaioannou et al. (eds.), *The Theatre of Justice: Aspects of Performance in Greco-Roman Oratory and Rhetoric*, Leiden/Boston, 13–25.
Worthington, I. (2020), "*Fake News*: The Greek Orators' Rhetorical Presentation of The Past", *Roda da Fortuna* 9, 15–31.
Yunis, H. (2001), *Demosthenes: On the Crown*, Cambridge.

Joseph Roisman
Lycurgus and the Past

Abstract: This chapter deals with Lycurgus' attempt to shape the memory and historical record of the recent past in his sole surviving speech *Against Leocrates*. Beginning with events roughly twenty years prior to Leocrates' trial (371–331 B.C.), the paper discusses how Lycurgus uses the recent past for examples and precedents that he hopes will sway the court to convict the defendant and sentence him to death. He makes purposeful and creative use of the past for his other mission: to inspire citizens with uncompromising patriotism and strong adherence to traditional values and practices. These goals affected Lycurgus' treatment of the battle of Chaeronea, the Athenians' frame of mind aftermath, the measures they took to defend themselves and the Macedonian perceived threat to the city. The result is a "history", which, though credible in its substance, is highly imbalanced, at times even bordering on invention.

Lycurgus, son of Lycophron, 390/80–324 B.C., was a prominent Athenian leader whose career peaked in 340's–320's, during which time he was much involved in, and even dominated, the city's politics, finances, administration, and religious and cultural affairs. Lycurgus is widely considered to have been responsible for Athens' recovery from its defeat to Macedonia in the battle of Chaeronea (338) and even its growth in power.[1] Lycurgus was also an active public speaker, who used his rhetorical skills in diplomacy and in Athens' deliberative and judicial institutions. His rhetorical distinction was evinced by his inclusion in the canon of ten Attic orators. It is regrettable, then, that of all of his speeches only *Against Leocrates* survives *in toto*, together with a number of fragments from other speeches. This paper focuses on Lycurgus' treatment of recent history in *Against Leocrates*.[2]

In 331 Lycurgus prosecuted the Athenian citizen Leocrates for treason, using the *eisangelia* (impeachment) procedure. He charged Leocrates with desert-

---

[1] On Lycurgus see e.g., Faraguna 1992, Humphreys 2004, 77–129; Azoulay and Ismard 2011; Hanink 2014; Roisman 2019, esp. 10–24. All dates are B.C. I wish to thank the editor and Peter O'Connell for their valuable comments on an earlier draft of the paper.
[2] Lycurgus the orator: Roisman and Worthington 2015, 189–211, and the previous note. For an analysis of Lycurgus' fragments see Conomis 1961; Oranges 2015. Henceforth all unattributed citations are to Lycurgus 1, *Against Leocrates*, and all translations of the speech are by Edwards in Roisman 2019.

ing and betraying Athens after the battle of Chaeronea, because he left the *polis* when it mobilized its male population in anticipation of a Macedonian invasion. Lycurgus supplemented or integrated these charges with other crimes, including overthrowing democracy, sacrilege, impiety, abuse of parents and additional misconducts. Leocrates argued in his defense that he left the city on a prearranged business trip, and that he violated no law. Lycurgus' hope of condemning Leocrates to death was frustrated by an evenly split jury that resulted in Leocrates' acquittal.[3] Yet he aimed beyond convicting the defendant. Lycurgus used the prosecutor's podium to indoctrinate and reaffirm for the Athenians their traditional virtues, collective identity, civic duties and cardinal values such as patriotism, solidarity, piety, courage and similar public and private expectations. He tried, not always successfully, to link his ideological mission to the case by presenting Leocrates as violator of these virtues and as someone who represented an internal danger to the state. His punishment would serve as a deterrent to others and as validation of Athenian ideals and legacy.[4]

For Lycurgus, the past, both recent and more distant, was an important resource that he could use in the service of his legal and ideological agendas. He mined it for proofs in the form of legal precedents and historical circumstances that placed the defendant in the wrong. In addition, he used the past to illustrate Athenian ideals and habits that shaped, or ought to have done, Athens' present. The many references to the past and the important role that it plays in *Against Leocrates* make the speech stand out among other forensic speeches.[5] However, we should expect neither Lycurgus nor the jurors to adhere to strict chronological boundaries between the recent and more distant past. The speaker makes no such temporal distinction, and although he refers a number of times to the "old days", which in the speech stretch from mythical times to the end of the fifth century, he otherwise lumps the recent and more distant past together. He uses this strategy to show that throughout history the Athenians unfailingly kept customs and ideas that Leocrates offended and that they severely punished men like him.[6] Accordingly, his many attributions of laws, acts or thoughts to the ancestors of the Athenians or Greeks are too nebulous to be

---

[3] Aesch. 3.252 with Hansen 1975, 108, n. 121; Bianchi 2002. See Harris 2013, 175–176 for Lycurgus' and Leocrates' different interpretations of Leocrates' trip.
[4] Lycurgus' mission: Allen 2000; Azoulay 2011; Steinbock 2011; Roisman 2019, 24–41 (on the darker side of his ideology).
[5] Lycurgus and the past: Azoulay 2009; Lambert 2018, 113–131; Grethlein 2014; Volonaki 2019; Westwood 2020, 47–49.
[6] Old days: 61, 62, 75, 80, 84, 98. See Azoulay 2009.

securely dated.⁷ In addition, he, with his audience's acquiescence, might regard a story's didactic quality more important than its authenticity. Thus, he prefaced a legend about a Sicilian youth who saved his father from hot lava with "even if the story is somewhat fantastic, it is nevertheless worth all the younger men hearing it even now" (95–96; cf. 10).

When the purpose of history was to teach a lesson or support a legal point, it did not always matter whether it was recent or not. In Lycurgus' speech, the didactic and the pattern-setting function of the past privileged ancient, including mythical, history over recent history because it was richer in examples and precedents that could support his case.⁸ It also formed part of the Athenians' shared knowledge and thus resonated with the audience better than recent history, that did not always enter their collective memory.⁹ Moreover, defining what constituted 'recent past' in the speech is problematic because Lycurgus, as we have seen, showed little awareness of the concept. The nearest he comes to it is in his introduction of Callistratus' trial in the 350's as an event that the elders remember and the young know of (93 and below). The memory span of the old jurors is unknown, not to mention that appeals to memory and shared knowledge in Attic oratory can serve other purposes than authentication.¹⁰ Nevertheless, in light of the periodization of the oratorical past suggested in the Introduction to this volume, I set the limits of recent past in *Against Leocrates* to around twenty years before Leocrates' trial, that is, 350's–331.¹¹

Lycurgus used this period up to the battle of Chaeronea only sparingly. The recent past assumes a significantly greater role in his treatment of the battle and especially of what happened in Athens in its immediate aftermath, about seven to eight years before Leocrates' trial. Lycurgus reconstructed these historical events in a way that contrasted Leocrates' behavior with the Athenians' cherished conduct and ideals both through the ages and after the battle, and which together made his acts impeachable. This chapter, accordingly, examines the character of Lycurgus' depictions of the recent past and whether they can be verified. Excluded from the discussion is the personal history of Leocrates that,

---

7 E.g. 1, 12, 27, 75–76, 107, 129.
8 Grethlein 2014 argues that forensic and deliberating oratory favored more recent history over early history, but points out Lycurgus' exceptions. See also Maltagliati 2020 on the appeal to "recency" and familiarity in the orators' use of historical examples.
9 Athenian common knowledge: Ober 2008, 183–191, with the reservations of Hesk 2012 and Roisman 2019, 34–36.
10 See Maltagliati 2020, esp. 89–92; Siron in this volume.
11 See Kapellos Introduction, in this volume. Assmann 2011, 36, suggests 40-year generational memory of the recent past.

in spite the prosecution's claims, had little impact on the history of Athens or Greece.

Within his engagement with the recent past, Lycurgus mentions only one historical example that is not linked to the battle of Chaeronea, but that like many other of his examples was designed to destroy the defense's argument. Leocrates claimed that he would not have returned to Athens and risked a death sentence if he were not innocent. Lycurgus seized the claim as an opportunity to enlist the gods to the prosecution's case. He argued that Leocrates came back because the gods confounded his mind in order that the man who wronged the city would face justice in the city he had harmed.[12] He then offered proofs from both the ancient and more recent past. He cited an unknown ancient poet to the effect that the gods harmed people by causing them to make unintentional mistakes. This, hopefully, took care of Leocrates' assertion that it did not make sense for him to return to Athens if he was guilty of treason. Lycurgus' more recent example demonstrated the poet's verses. It concerned the politician Callistratus, who c. 361, was impeached for that, as a rhetor, he did not speak in the people's best interest. Callistratus left for exile and a few years later he returned to the city as a suppliant after an oracle said that he would get fair treatment from the laws. Callistratus, however, was put to the death, which, Lycurgus explained, was a fair punishment for doing wrong. He added that the gods thus enabled the people to punish the man who was guilty of doing them harm (90–93).

Lycurgus authenticates Callistratus' story by invoking the elders' memory, and the young's knowledge, of it (above). This may seem insufficient to verify his tale, but because no other source reports on Callistratus' fate, it is fairer to accept than reject the essence of the account. More questionable is the religious framing of the story, which obscures the differences between Callistratus' and Leocrates' cases, and so weakens Lycurgus' proof from the past. He made Leocrates as guilty as Callistratus even before the jurors decided Leocrates' case. Indeed, unlike Callistratus, Leocrates was not a fugitive from justice. Lycurgus' religious reading of the episode also reshapes history because it is highly doubtful that when Callistratus came back, many regarded it as the gods' gift to popular, retributive justice. It is likelier than not, however, that these issues did not bother the speaker or the court, for whom the point was that history showed

---

[12] For a similar claim in a ca. 400 trial against the returned exile Andocides, and his response, see [Lys.] 6.19–20, 27, 32; And. 1.137–39; Roisman 2019, 175.

how the gods helped to bring criminals to justice and that it instructed the jurors to sentence the defendant to death.[13]

Lycurgus' use of history to condemn the defendant and educate the citizens also affected his treatment of the battle of Chaeronea (46–51).[14] He turned the battlefield into a display ground of civic ideals, which Leocrates betrayed and shamed, but that the Athenians, and especially their fallen, heroically followed. They fought there for freedom and showed courage, self-sacrifice, solidarity and local and Hellenic patriotism in the face of danger (46–51; 144). The Athenian tradition of the *epitaphios logos*, or funeral oration, that was delivered at the public burial of the war dead, gave Lycurgus a ready-made model of describing the battle and the valor of the Athenian dead.[15] That is why his account of Chaeronea is only partly historically specific while the rest can be applied with few modifications to other battles. When the Athenians were defeated in battle, this rhetorical genre articulated a collective wish to turn a loss into a moral victory, and Lycurgus offered his own version of the topos. He ranked highest, and clearly above the battle results, the fighters' noble aims and spirit, and claimed that those who died free and valorous were actually victorious.[16] There is little doubt that the jurors willingly shared Lycurgus' counter-factual, or paradoxical (his word), interpretation of history that many Athenians had lived through only seven or eight years before the trial. They were also probably reluctant to dispute his granting Athens alone the glory of fighting for freedom at Chaeronea, while ignoring other Greeks who fought there by their side. The historical value of Lycurgus on Chaeronea, then, is in how the battle was perceived and its memory shaped. Lycurgus deals more extensively with recent history in relation to Athens' reactions to the defeat. In many (though not all) respects, his report of what happened is credible, but his selective and slanted presentation challenges the authenticity of his account.

The Athenians feared that Philip would follow his victory at Chaeronea with a march on Attica and a siege of the city and its harbor. Lycurgus' aim in describing the Athenian reactions to the prospective invasion was to show that, by

---

[13] Callistratus was impeached for treason earlier in 366, but was acquitted. His trials: Hyperides 1.4; Arist. *Rhet.* 1.7.13 1364a 19–23; Plut. *Dem.* 5; Hansen 1975, 92, no. 83; Hochschultz 2007, 185–195, who, based on [Dem.] 50.48–50, speculates a second treason trial for Callistratus.
[14] Compare Lycurgus' prosecutorial use of the battle to Hyperides' use of it in his defense: Cooper, in this volume.
[15] For the genre see Loraux 1986; Prinz 1997. Lycurgus' use of it in 46–51: Sullivan 2002, 122–125; Engels 2008, *ad loc.*; Roisman 2019, 132–138.
[16] The rhetoric of defeat: Roisman 2005, 67–71. Demosthenes preceded Lycurgus in denying defeat at Chaeronea: Dem. 60; 18.208; Goldman 2017.

leaving Athens, Leocrates violated the laws and his patriotic duty to contribute to the polis' defense and share in its difficulties.

In actuality the danger never materialized, for the Athenians found out, maybe even in a matter of days, that Philip was not going to invade Attica.[17] Lycurgus never acknowledged what in reality made Leocrates' departure and its impact on the city relatively inconsequential. Instead, he painted for the audience vivid pictures of the Athenians' troubles and fear guided by the idea that the greater the distress, the greater was Leocrates' culpability. The way Lycurgus put it, his goal was "to remind you (the jurors) about the critical times and the great dangers the city faced when Leocrates betrayed it" (36). His historical reminders often involved Athens' defensive measures that Lycurgus described as acts of desperation. We should not, however, allow his historical perspective to dominate our view of post-Chaeronea Athens. The Athenians' fear was not all-consuming, as suggested by Demosthenes, who claimed that the city recovered from its defeat and took necessary steps to protect itself within three days (Dem. 18.195). Indeed, what for Lycurgus were regrettable and shameful acts (below), could be equally viewed as testimonies of Athens' resolve to fight the enemy and of its resourcefulness. The speaker, however, had to steer the audience away from such a view in order to emphasize that Athens' reactions showed its miserable state.

He led the audience in several ways, such as recalling a decree proposed by the politician Hyperides that recommended radical measures for the defense of Athens (36–38, 41).[18] Lycurgus has the decree read to the court just as depositions of witnesses' testimonies are used to support and authenticate the prosecution's charges. The decree also represents the people's will, which the defendant allegedly defied. Although the text of the decree is now lost, it can be said that its main value for Lycurgus is less in providing a legal ground for conviction, (which it barely did), and more as a historical account of difficult times. This is why his annotations on the decree are more important than its language. An example is the decree's instructing the Council to go in arms to the Piraeus in order to discuss its defense and other security matters. Lycurgus says nothing

---

[17] The sources are unclear about when exactly the Athenians found out about Philip's peaceful intentions, which, at the earliest, was a few days after the battle: Dem. *Epist.* 3.11; Diod. 16.87.1–3; Plb. 5.10.1–5; Just. 9.4.4–5; Plut. *Phoc.* 16; [Plut.] *Mor.* 849a; cf. Plut. *Dem.* 21; [Demades] *On the Twelve Years* 9–10. For Philip-Athens' negotiations see Ellis 1976, 198–200; Worthington 2008, 156–157; 2013, 255–259.

[18] For the decree see, in addition, Hyp. fr. 27–39; [Dem.] 26.11; [Plut.] *Mor.* 848f–849b, 851a; Photius 495b; Dio of Prusa 15.21; Engels 1989, 99–102; Roisman and Worthington 2015, 252–253; Cooper in this volume.

about the Council's actions or decisions. Instead he pictures for the jurors the anomalous sight of the Councilmen, who were exempt from military service, marching as if they were soldiers. Clearly the Councilmen's deliberations or actions in defense of the harbor and the city outweighed in importance their taking up arms, yet Lycurgus had nothing to say about the former. Instead he focused the court's attention on their march under arms as an antithesis to Leocrates' flight and because it better supported his contention that Leocrates left the city when the Athenians' fear for their safety following their defeat was, as he said, not trivial and ordinary (37).

The Athenians' fear was just one manifestation of the misfortune of the polis that Lycurgus wished the jurors to remember or learn. He also adduced the city's humiliation at that time. In an effort to supplement and refill the ranks of the city's defenders that were thinned after Chaeronea, Hyperides' decree promised freedom to slaves and state debtors and full citizenship to metics and the disenfranchised. Lycurgus presented the enfranchisement as a painful wound to Athens' pride and its autochthonian identity (41). One may assume that when the decree was proposed, many Athenians did not regard it as shameful, and even if they did, they ranked this concern below Athens' security. The jurors who acquitted Hyperides in a later trial on proposing the decree seemed to share this view. Lycurgus, however, interpreted the defensive measure solely in terms of an insult to Athens' honor. Conveniently, he failed to mention that none of Hyperides' proposed measures were implemented because, with no invasion, there was no need for them.[19]

The speaker noted other forms of national disgrace. As in the case of the Councilmen in arms, he turned the jurors into spectators (and so virtual witnesses) of scenes that showed the breakup of norms. One involved free women, who were supposed to stay modestly indoors and avoid interacting with strangers, crouching frightened at their doors and enquiring if their male relatives survived the battle. Lest some in his audience found the sight pitiful, Lycurgus defined it as shameful (40).[20] This scene in the speech followed another with a similar message. Around the time of the trial, male residents of Athens at the age of 18–59 were eligible for hoplite and other services. Indeed, one could

---

[19] Hyperides' acquittal: Hansen 1974, 36–37, no. 27. Fate of his measures: Roisman 2019, 124.
[20] For the scene see Tandoi 1970, 157–160, who links it to the elite notion of *sophrosyne*; Castro 1975–1976, who discusses its tragic element, as does O'Connell 2017, 136–139 on the rhetoric of the visual.

expect a kaleidoscope of age groups in the army or on guard duty.[21] Lycurgus, however, insists dwelling on just the elderly defenders of the city. He claims that the "people placed their hopes of safety in the men over fifty," and describes how weak and old men, who were normally exempted from service, wandered around, and, somewhat pathetically, readied themselves for battle (39–40). The description was factually correct but also misleading. Firstly, the elderly who came to the defense of Athens showed their patriotism, not their weakness, but Lycurgus, who elsewhere commended the Athenians of every age on their patriotism in spirit and action under crisis (44 and below), made the elders illustrative of the city's low point. Secondly, Athens trusted its defense not just to the old, but also, if not even more, to younger and fitter men. Lycurgus and the jurors knew it, but the speaker focused their minds on the unusual and somewhat peripheral sight of wandering old men that better portrayed the city's misfortune. A selective, partial perspective characterizes Lycurgus' rewriting of history here and elsewhere.

Lycurgus' lament over Athens' misfortune after Chaeronea includes contrasting it with its golden past in a way that is relevant to his rhetorical use of history. According to him, Athens fought in the past for other Greeks' freedom, but after Chaeronea it could barely protect its own safety. In the past it ruled barbarian land, but after Chaeronea it struggled against the Macedonians to protect its own land. In the past Spartans, Peloponnesians and Asian Greeks came to Athens to ask for help, but now Athens asked Andros, Ceos, Troezen and Epidaurus for aid (42). At the basis of the historical comparison was the construct of the recent past as time of decline and hitting rock bottom. The viewpoint was not from past to present but the opposite, where the role of the more distant and glorified past, mostly of fifth-century Athens, was to illuminate the sorry and shameful state of the present. Lycurgus' choice of historical examples was thus constrained by their function as mirror images and by their general familiarity to his audience, although it's anybody's guess how well informed they were of Athens' requests for aid from Andros, Ceos, Troezen and Epidaurus. It hardly mattered, however, because the orator's point was clear: Athens was shamefully reduced to needing aid from, and being grateful to,

---

21 Draft by age groups and exemptions: *Ath. Pol.* 53.4, 7; Plut. *Phoc.* 24; Christ 2001, esp. 404, 1410–1411. Old and young in the army and on guard: Thuc. 2.13.7; Xen. *Hell.* 6.1.5. Cf. Burkhardt 1996; Oliver 2007, 138–147, 173–191.

poleis that had historically looked up to Athens, and were weaker than that glorious *polis*.²²

Athens' distress called upon male Athenians to come to its rescue, and Lycurgus depicted them as eager to fulfill their patriotic duties. They displayed civic solidarity and willingness to help the polis when they showed up for guard duties, or built fortifications. Although Leocrates was hardly the only citizen who left the city at this time (below), we may take Lycurgus at his word that the Athenians responded to the call to defend the land with enthusiasm and en masse. He described an all-out effort to which everyone and everything contributed. Even the land sacrificed its trees, the dead their tombs, and the temples their arms (16, 43–44).²³ The language was metaphoric and was understood as such. But it can be safely assumed that till Lycurgus' speech only a few Athenians regarded the use of tombstones and trees for fortifications and dedicated weapons for arming the defenders as the dead's, land's and temples' patriotic contribution to the polis. Lycurgus changed the perception of the recent past without changing its substance.

So far Lycurgus' efforts amplified the Athenians' difficulties and extolled their patriotism in order to place Leocrates' departure in a historical context and make it treasonable and deplorable. In addition, he found in the recent past legal cases and a popular decision that justified, in his mind, a conviction and death penalty for the defendant. The instances he cited happened shortly after Chaeronea and involved the Areopagus' arrest and execution of men who tried to flee the country; a conviction in a jury court of one Autolycus, who sent his family abroad to safety; and an Assembly's decree that turned the offence of cowardice into treason punishable by death (52–54; cf. 144). Many scholars believe, present writer included, that Leocrates left Athens before the Assembly voted on the decree, which freed him from the charge of disobeying it.²⁴ Lycurgus' other two cases are presented as legal precedents. In the Athenian judicial system, precedents had no binding power, and speakers offered them as guidance to the jurors, who were urged to follow them for the sake of social and institutional consistency and stability.²⁵ To give his precedents more compelling power Lycurgus engaged in creative synchronization of two different trials. He

---

22 Rhetorical contrasting of past and present: Yunis 2000; Hobden 2007; Rhodes 2011, 24–29; Hesk 2012, 207. See Roisman 2019, 127–129, for a discussion of Lycurgus' historical examples.
23 For the Athenian defensive measures see Faraguna 1992, 257–258; Roisman 2019, 130–131.
24 E.g. Hansen 1975, 108 n. 121; Liddle 2007, 114; Ober 2008, 185.
25 Lanni 2004; Rubinstein 2007; Harris 2013, 248–273, esp. 262–263 (arguing for effective legal power of precedents).

addressed the jurors in Leocrates' trial as "you yourselves condemned and punished Autolycus," even though the chances that some of Leocrates' jurors sat on Autolycus' trial around 338 were quite slim.[26] He could take such an anachronistic leap thanks to a common rhetorical appeal to jurors as representatives of the demos across different institutions and even history.[27] In this case, the rhetorical "you" bridged the temporal gap between the two panels of jurors and created a shared identity and an impossible self-contradiction if the "same" jurors who found Autolycus guilty were to acquit Leocrates. Yet the case for conviction was not as strong as Lycurgus pretended. He took three individual legal decisions that involved three different institutions, i.e. the Areopagus, the court and the Assembly, and suggested that they had a common purpose that likely never existed. Moreover, when Lycurgus mentioned the Areopagus' action, he provoked interruptions and protest from his listeners, which he tried to hush by praising the Areopagus for its judicial excellence. There were Athenians who regarded the Areopagus as an enemy of democracy, and its arrest and execution of men charged with desertion appeared to be both controversial and counterproductive as a precedent. The hostile reaction to Lycurgus' use of it indicates the problems of bringing up recent historical examples.[28]

Finally, the most striking use of the recent past in *Against Leocrates* involved what might be called an imagined invasion of Attica. In fact, Philip never marched on Athens. Athenian patriots took credit for his decision when they explained that he feared meeting brave Athenians again in battle, or that he made concessions thanks to Athens' countermeasures, or that he gave up on the invasion because of bad omens.[29] Lycurgus came close to doing the same when he praised the Athenian dead at Chaeronea for preventing the destruction and torching of their land (47). He also stressed that, unlike Leocrates, the men who remained in Athens and faced the danger at their posts, saved it (142). Aeschines, however, suggests a recognition, less appealing to the people, that Athens owed its survival to Philip himself (Aeschin. 3.57). Yet while all other sources acknowledged that no invasion took place or made no mention of it, Lycurgus was exceptional in speaking about a nearly-happened, or virtual, Macedonian

---

[26] Autolycus' trial, in which Lycurgus was the prosecutor: Lyc. F 3; [Plut.] *Mor.* 843d–e; Harpocration, s.v. Ἀυτόλυκος; Hansen 1975, 104; Roisman and Worthington 2015, 206–207; Roisman 2019, 139–141.
[27] Wolpert 2003; Siron in this volume.
[28] For suspicions of the Areopagus and its controversial actions see Rhodes 2011, 23; Wallace 2000, 583; Harris 2016, 78–79.
[29] Respectively, Dem. 60.20; [Plut.] *Mor.* 849a; Aeschin. 3.131, and the sources cited in the n. 17. See also Bajnok in this volume.

attack.[30] He repeatedly charged Leocrates with betraying or surrendering the *polis* into the enemy's hands (8, 18, 59, 71, 78, 85, 89, 133, 147). In response to Leocrates' claim that he left on a trading mission, Lycurgus proclaimed that no imported goods were as important as reporting to duty and repelling the attackers (57). He accused Leocrates of betraying his parents to the enemy (97), and that he abandoned a statue that his father put in the temple of Zeus Soter to the enemy to loot and deface (136). Lycurgus' goal was obvious: the case for treason was much stronger when presented against a background of an enemy at the gates. He could strengthen his case in this way because throughout the speech he blurs the difference between a threat to the city and its realization. He also warned the jury that the values of Athens and the preservation of the polis itself were at stake (e.g. 150), which made the ramifications of Leocrates' action more significant than its actual effect. Judging by the vote count, half of the jurors imagined along with the orator a devastating Macedonian invasion, not a bad outcome for an invented piece of recent history.

Plutarch tells an anecdote about the Alexander historian Onesicritus that is relevant to the topic. Sometime after 306/5 Onesicritus read out to king Lysimachus, who was one of Alexander's Successors and formerly his close friend, a description of Alexander's meeting with the queen of the Amazons. Lysimachus smiled gently and asked "And where was I then?"[31] Although the authenticity of the story is uncertain, it suggests that fear of protest by contemporaries, who knew an account to be false, did not deter its invention and promulgation. Lycurgus did not invent history, but came pretty close to doing so with his partial, at times distorted, account of the recent past.

Bibliography

Assmann, J. (2011), *Cultural Memory and Early Civilization: Writing, Remembrance, and Political Imagination*, Cambridge.
Azoulay, V. (2009), "Lycurgue d'Athènes et le passé de la cité: entre neutralisation et instrumentalization", *Cahiers des études anciennes* 46, 149–80 =
https://etudesanciennes.revues.org/175 [last access date September 8th, 2022].
Azoulay, V. (2011), "Les métamorphoses du koinon athénien: autour du Contre Léocrate de Lycurgue", in: V. Azoulay/P. Ismard (eds.), *Clisthène et Lycurgue d'Athènes: autour du politique dans la cité Classique*, Paris, 191–217.

---

30 See Crick in this volume for a similar alternate history in Dem. 60, *Funeral oration*.
31 Plut. *Alex*. 46 = Onesicritus BNJ 134 T 8.

Azoulay, V./Ismard, P. (eds.) (2011), *Clisthène et Lycurgue d'Athènes: autour du politique dans la cité Classique*, Paris.
Bianchi, E. (2002), "Ancora su Eschine III 252", *Dike* 5, 83–94.
Burkhardt, L.A. (1996), *Bürger und Soldaten: Aspekte der politischen und militärischen Rolle athenischer Bürger im Kriegswesen des 4. Jahrhunderts v. Chr.*, Stuttgart.
Castro, O. (1975–1976), "Le donne ateniensi non devono imprecare. Licurgo, Contro Leocrate 40", *Annali Della Facoltà di lettere e Filosofia di Lecce* 7, 25–30.
Christ, M. (2001), "Conscription of Hoplites in Classical Athens", *CQ* 51, 398–422.
Conomis, N.C. (1961), "Notes on the Fragments of Lycurgus", *Klio* 39, 72–152.
Ellis, J.R. (1976), *Philip II and Macedonian Imperialism*, London.
Engels, J. (1989), *Studien zur politischen Biographie des Hypereides: Athen in der Epoche der lykurgischen Reformen und des makedonischen Universalreiches*, Munich.
Engels, J. (2008), *Lykurg: Rede gegen Leokrates*, Darmstadt.
Faraguna, M. (1992), *Atene nell'età di Alessandro: problem politici, economici, finanziari*, Rome.
Goldman, M. (2017), "Demosthenes, Chaeronea, and the Rhetoric of Defeat", in: J.H. Clark/ B. Turner (eds.), *Brill's Companion to Military Defeat in Ancient Mediterranean Society*, Leiden, 123–143.
Grethlein, J. (2014), "The Value of the Past Challenged: Myth and Ancient History in the Attic Orators", in: J. Ker/C. Pieper (eds.), *Valuing the Past in the Greco-Roman World*, Leiden, 326–354.
Hanink, J. (2014), *Lycurgan Athens and the Making of Classical Tragedy*, Cambridge.
Hansen, M.H. (1974), *The Sovereignty of the People's Court in Athens in the Fourth Century BC and the Public Actions against Unconstitutional Proposals*, Odense.
Hansen, M.H. (1975), *EISANGELIA: The Sovereignty of the People's Court in Athens in the Fourth Century B.C. and the Impeachment of Generals and Politicians*, Odense.
Harris, E.M. (2013), *The Rule of Law in Action in Democratic Athens*, Oxford.
Harris, E.M. (2016), "From Democracy to the Rule of Law? Constitutional Changes in Athens during the Fifth and Fourth Centuries BCE", in: C. Tiersch (ed.), *Die athenische Demokratie im 4. Jahrhundert: zwischen Modernisierung und Tradition*, Stuttgart, 73–88.
Hesk, J. (2012), "Common Knowledge and the Contestation of History in Some Fourth-Century Athenian Trials", in: J. Marincola/L. Llewellyn-Jones/C. MacIver (eds.), *Greek Notions of the Past in the Archaic and Classical Eras: History without Historians*, Edinburgh, 207–226.
Hobden, F. (2007), "Imagining Past and Present: A Rhetorical Strategy in Aeschines 3, *Against Ctesiphon*", *CQ* 57, 490–501.
Hochschultz, B. (2007), *Kallistratos von Aphidnai: Untersuchungen zu seiner politischen Biographie*, Munich.
Humphreys, S.C. (2004), *The Strangeness of Gods: Historical Perspectives on the Interpretation of Athenian Religion*, Oxford.
Lambert, S.D. (2018), *Inscribed Athenian Laws and Decrees in the Age of Demosthenes: Historical Essays*, Leiden.
Lanni, A.M. (2004), "Arguing from 'Precedent': Modern Perspectives on Athenian Practice", in: E.M. Harris/L. Rubinstein (eds.), *The Law and the Courts in Ancient Athens*, London, 159–171.
Liddel, P. (2007), *Civic Obligation and Individual Liberty in Ancient Athens*, Oxford.

Loraux, N. (1986), *The Invention of Athens: The Funeral Oration in the Classical City*, A. Sheridan, trans., Cambridge, MA.

Maltagliati, G. (2020), "Persuasion through Proximity (and Distance) in the Attic Orators' Historical Examples", *GRBS* 60, 68–97.

Ober, J. (2008), *Democracy and Knowledge: Innovation and Learning in Classical Athens*, Princeton.

O'Connell, P.A. (2017), *The Rhetoric of Seeing in Attic Forensic Oratory*, Austin.

Oliver, G.J. (2007), *War, Food, and Politics in Early Hellenistic Athens*, Oxford.

Oranges, A. (2015), "Anti-Macedonian Feelings on Trial: Lawsuits Against Lycurgus", in: C. Bearzot/F. Landucci (eds.), *Alexander's Legacy. Atti del Convegno Università Cattolica del Sacro Cuore Milano 2015*, Milan, 257–277.

Prinz, K. (1997), *Epitaphios Logos: Struktur, Funktion und Bedeutung des Bestattungsreden im Athen des 5. und 4. Jahrhunderts*, Frankfurt.

Rhodes, P. (2011), "Appeals to the Past in Classical Athens", in: G. Herman (ed.), *Stability and Crisis in the Athenian Democracy*, Stuttgart, 13–30.

Roisman, J. (2005), *The Rhetoric of Manhood: Masculinity in the Attic Orators*, Berkeley.

Roisman, J. (2019), *Lycurgus, Against Leocrates*, trans. M. Edwards, Oxford.

Roisman, J./Worthington, I. (2015), *Lives of the Attic Orators: Texts from Pseudo-Plutarch, Photius and the Suda*, transl. R. Waterfield, Oxford.

Rubinstein, L. (2007), "Arguments from Precedent in Attic Oratory", in: E.M. Carawan (ed.), *Oxford Readings in Classical Studies: The Attic Orators*, Oxford, 359–371.

Steinbock, B. (2011), "A Lesson in Patriotism: Lycurgus' *Against Leocrates*, the Ideology of the Ephebeia, and Athenian Social Memory", *CA* 30, 279–317.

Sullivan, J. (2002), "An Historical Commentary on Lykourgos' Against Leokrates", Diss. University of Leeds. Available at <http://etheses.whiterose.ac.uk/11264/1/410588.pdf>.

Tandoi, V. (1970), "Le donne ateniensi che non devono piangere", *SIFC* 42, 154–178.

Volonaki, E. (2019), "Performing the Past in Lycurgus' Speech Against Leocrates", in: A. Markantonatos/E. Volonaki, (eds.), *Poet and Orator. A Symbiotic Relationship in Democratic Athens*, Boston, 281–301.

Wallace, R.W. (1989), *The Areopagus Council to 307 B.C.*, Baltimore.

Westwood, G. (2020), *The Rhetoric of the Past in Demosthenes and Aeschines. Oratory, History, and Politics in Classical Athens*, Oxford.

Wolpert, A. (2003), "Addresses to the Jury in the Attic Orators", *AJP* 124, 537–555.

Worthington, I. (2008), *Philip II of Macedonia*, New Haven.

Worthington, I. (2013), *Demosthenes of Athens and the Fall of Classical Greece*, Oxford.

Yunis, H. (2000), "Politics as Literature: Demosthenes and the Burden of the Athenian Past", *Arion* 8, 97–118.

Craig Cooper
Remembering Chaeronea in Hyperides

Abstract: This chapter treats the issue of Hyperides' proposal of a series of emergency measures in the Assembly in the aftermath of Chaeronea in 338 B.C. that involved evacuating women and children to the Peiraeus, arming the Boule, restoring all exiles and disenfranchised citizens, granting citizenship to metics, and freeing and arming slaves for a possible attack on Athens by Philip. Although the proposal was approved, it was never implemented given Philip's conciliatory attitude towards Athens. Still Hyperides was indicted for introducing an illegal decree, but successfully defended himself, arguing that Macedonian arms obstructed the words of the laws prohibiting his proposal. In the many trials that followed Athens' defeat, Hyperides justified the city's involvement in the battle by recasting the memory of Chaeronea into a critical moment in Athens' history, like epic struggles of the past. This chapter, then, examines how he recalls and uses the memory of Chaeronea rhetorically in his forensic speeches to attack his political opponents and assist his clients in court.

In the aftermath of Chaeronea in 338 B.C., Hyperides proposed a series of emergency measures in the Assembly that involved evacuating women and children to the Peiraeus, arming the Boule, restoring all exiles and disenfranchised citizens, granting citizenship to metics, and freeing and arming slaves for a possible attack on Athens by Philip.[1] Although the proposal was approved, it was never implemented given Philip's conciliatory attitude towards Athens, largely through the diplomatic efforts of Demades.[2] Still Hyperides was indicted for introducing an illegal decree, but successfully defended himself, arguing that Macedonian arms obstructed the words of the laws prohibiting his proposal.[3] Although Chaeronea was a decisive defeat for Athens, resulting in the death of

---
[1] Hyp. frs. 27–39a; Lyc. 1.16, 36–37, 41; [Dem.] 26.11. Unless specified otherwise, I follow Jensen's Teubner text of Hyperides.
[2] Diod. 16.87.1–3; Demad. 1.9; Dem. 18.285; For an account of the aftermath of Chaeronea, Demades' role and the lenient terms of the settlement see Dmitriev 2021, 15–16, 21–22, 28, 126–127; Worthington 2008, 152–157; Sealey 1993, 198–201; Hammond 1994, 155–157; Hammond and Griffith 1979, 604–610; Schaefer 1887, 18–31. For a critical evaluation of the sources describing Demades' address to Philip see Dmitriev 2021, 126–154.
[3] Hyp. fr. 27; [Plut.] *Vit. X Orat.* 849a.

https://doi.org/10.1515/9783110791877-023

one thousand Athenian soldiers and the capture of two thousand more,[4] politicians who advocated war with Philip, as Hyperides had, suffered little in the way of political consequences over the ensuing period, as they were repeatedly successful in court.[5] Only the general Lysicles was condemned to death, prosecuted by Lycurgus.[6] In the trials that Hyperides faced following Athens' defeat, he justified that enterprise by recasting the memory of Chaeronea into a critical moment in Athens' history along the lines of epic struggles of the past. This chapter, then, exams how he recalls and uses the memory of Chaeronea rhetorically in his forensic speeches to attack his political opponents and assist his clients in court.

1 Fragmented memory

At some point Aristogeiton brought a *graphê paranomôn* against Hyperides for the measures he introduced following Chaeronea.[7] Only fragments remain from Hyperides' defense (frs. 29–39a), and in some cases, only single words, preserved by Harpocration. So, for instance, Hyperides mentions the tribes Cercopis (fr. 36) and Oineis (fr. 38); we do not know in what context they were mentioned, but the coastal trittys of Oineis bordered on Boeotia, and Hyperides did mention how news of the battle of Chaeronea was heard at Oinoe (fr. 31), which sat on the border with Boeotia within Hippothontis.[8] It is possible that Hyperides narrated how the news of the disaster spread quickly through Attica to Athens, creating the same kind of dramatic scene of panic as we see in Lycurgus.[9] This point is suggested by fr. 39, where Hyperides describes, in similar language to Lycurgus (1.39),[10] "the city being on edge at the news" (ὀρθῆς δε τῆς πόλεως

---

4 On the battle of Chaeronea see Diod. 16.85.2–86.6; Just. 9.3; Paus. 7.10.5 with Worthington 2008, 147–151; Sealey 1993, 196–198; Ellis 1976, 197–201; Hammond 1994, 151–154; Hammond and Griffith 1979, 596–603.
5 Horváth 2009, 189; 2008, 28; Sealey 1993, 201.
6 Diod. 16.88.1; [Plut.] *Vit. X Orat.* 843d.
7 Hansen 1974, no. 26. [Plut.] *Vit. X Orat.* 849a; [Dem.] 26.11. Harris 2018, n. 145 questions the value of this ancient testimonia on Aristogeiton's role. The trial perhaps occurred soon after peace with Philip was secured: Poddighe 2004, 48.
8 See Traill 1975, Tables VI to VIII & Maps 1–2.
9 Lyc. 1.39–43 with Roisman in this volume.
10 Lyc. 1.39: ὀρθὴ δ' ἦν ἡ πόλις ἐπὶ τοῖς συμβεβηκόσιν.

οὔσης ἐπὶ τούτοις).[11] Photius' comment is instructive: he notes that Hyperides used this expression in place of describing the city as "having become agitated and fearful" (ἀντὶ τοῦ κεκινημένης καὶ πεφοβημένης). Perhaps in this context Hyperides also stated that "another time (*tempus*) is appropriate for debate and advice; but when an armed enemy is present, he must be resisted not with words but with arms" (fr. 39a).[12] If *tempus* is Rutilius' translation of *kairos*,[13] then Hyperides was already exploring a theme that would become prominent in his later speeches.[14] In the present context he argued the critical situation of Chaeronea called for action, not debate.

Was it in this context that Hyperides also mentioned the Eurysakeion, the temenos to Eurysakes, the son of Ajax, located in the city deme Melite (fr. 35)?[15] Melite was part of the tribe Cercopis, but its connection with the rapidly spreading news of Chaeronea is unknown. Perhaps Hyperides noted (fr. 32) in the same context "the money both sacred and public" (καὶ τὰ χρήματα τά τε ἱερὰ καὶ τὰ ὅσια), which either needed to be moved to safety or used to finance Athens' defence.[16] In either case Hyperides was clearly attempting to recall the panic that followed Chaeronea to justify his action: as he stated, it was not he, who "proposed the decree but the battle of Chaeronea" (fr. 28). Athens' defeat and the anticipated invasion of Attica by Philip prompted his various measures. And here, like Lycurgus (1.16), Hyperides criticizes Aristogeiton for forcing him to bring up these frightening memories: "you cannot not even learn from the proverb: 'don't stir up an evil happily resting'" (fr. 30).

In his speech (fr. 29) Hyperides first discussed the 150,000 slaves in the mines and the countryside, which he proposed freeing; then the state debtors, the disenfranchised (*atimoi*) and those voted off the deme registries, to whom he proposed restoring their rights, and finally the metics to whom he proposed granting citizenship.[17] His justification (fr. 27) came in a brilliant *sermocinatio* in

---

11 Photius (*Lex. s.v.* ὀρθῆς) does not explicitly assign this fragment to the speech against Aristogeiton.
12 Rut. Lup. 2.12: *nam disputandi aut suadendi est aliudido neum tempus: cum quidem adverarius armatus praesto est, resistendum est huic non verbis sed armis*. The fragment was assigned by Babington to the speech.
13 Lewis and Short 1980, 1851, s.v. *tempus*.
14 For a discussion of *kairos* in fourth-century Attic oratory, with specific reference to Isocrates and Demosthenes, see Usher 2004.
15 For a history of the Eurysakeion see Ferguson 1938, 15–18.
16 On the meaning of this phrase see Maffi 1982 and Connor 1988.
17 On the categories of *atimoi* covered in Hyperides' decree, with parallels to previous grants of amnesty, see Poddighe 2006; cf. Poddighe 2004.

which Hyperides answers Aristogeiton's questions on each point of his proposal:

> 'Did you propose in the decree to grant freedom to slaves?' I did to prevent free man from experiencing servitude. 'Did you propose to restore exiles?' I did, to prevent anyone else from suffering exile. 'Now then, did you not read the laws that prohibited this?' I couldn't, because Macedonian arms stood in the way and obstructed their words.[18]

The looming prospect of a Macedonian invasion and the panic that critical moment created became Hyperides' defense.

2 Chaeronea on the offense

At some point following Chaeronea (August 338), either before or soon after Philip's death (July/August 336),[19] a *graphê paranomôn* was brought against Philippides for proposing to commend the *Proedroi* (4.4), who had illegally introduced in the Assembly a decree or series of decrees by Philippides and his associates honouring certain Macedonians, including Alexander (fr. 8).[20] Hyperides was only one of several speakers involved in the prosecution. What remains of his speech is extremely fragmentary, with only the epilogue preserved in full. In the epilogue (4.6) Hyperides sums up the two legal points on which the jurors must decide the legality of Philippides' decree honouring the *Proedroi*: that "they behaved justly toward the Athenian people and because they carried out their duties according to the law". In the surviving fragments Hyperides focuses his argument on the first point and defines just behaviour toward the people as voting "honours reserved for benefactors". At 4.5 Hyperides asks rhetorically whether the jurors "intend to punish those who propose illegal decrees or intend to award *Proedroi* who violate the law with honours reserved for benefac-

---

[18] The last line was also attributed to Demades, when he was indicted: Diels 1874, 108 no. 1 = Marzi 1995, 640 no. 5. This fact may undercut the value of the attribution to Hyperides: Dmitriev 2016, 941.
[19] That Philip was still alive at the time of the trial might be suggested by use of the perfect tense at Hyp. 4.7: καὶ ἐν μὲν σῶμα ἀθάνατον ὑπείληφας ἔσεσθαι: Engels 1993, 137 n. 254; Whitehead 2000, 29–30; Bernhardt 2012, 267 n. 20; Cooper 2001, 84 n. 11, but contrast Horváth 2009, 203 and Horváth 2004, who dates the speech to the winter of 336, after Philip's death.
[20] Hansen 1974, n. 32. On the legal issue see Whitehead 2000, 31–32. Cooper 2001, 80 suggests the *Proedroi* had introduced the decree(s) without prior vetting by the Boule. For the *probouleuma* and whether all motions had to go to the Boule first see Rhodes 1972, 52–57.

tors". Thus, part of his argument leading up to the epilogue centres on a comparison between true benefactors of the past, who were deserving of Athens' gratitude, and the certain Macedonians and their supporters, whose actions merit no praise. At the heart of that argument is Chaeronea.

At fr. 6 Hyperides describes a past benefactor, who was responsible for actions that did honour to Athens and the rest of Greece, and for which he was rightly honoured by Athens and other communities.[21] This contrasts with fr. 8 where we have a reference to Alexander, who is sarcastically thanked for those who died at his hands.[22] Here we have a reference to Chaeronea and to Alexander's role in breaking the Greek lines. As Whitehead notes, Hyperides continued ("but I think ...") with a description of what happened.[23] Did that description describe the battle as we find in historical accounts, in which Alexander turned the Greek center and in so doing annihilated the Theban Sacred Band on the Greek right?[24] Ironically, it was Philp who broke the Athenian lines.[25] But it served Hyperides' rhetorical purposes to credit Alexander with Athens' loses as he was the one being honoured and had been present with Antipater in Athens. A report of Alexander's exploits in the battle may have been circulating at the time, making Hyperides' description that more effective rhetorically.

Hyperides also questions the motives of Philip's supporters, whose actions are characterized as treasonous. In fr. 1 there is a reference to those in a free city (Athens?) working in the interests of tyrants and towards slavery.[26] The whole intent behind Philippides' actions is to enslave a free city, and this point is picked up in the epilogue (4.10), where Hyperides asks rhetorically of the jurors why they should acquit Philippides: "Because he is a democrat? But you know

---

21 The reference may be to Conon, who is thus characterized in Attic oratory: see Dem. 20.68–74; Din. 1.14 with Worthington 1992, 21–23, 148–155. Cf. Whitehead 2000, 40 and Cooper 2001, 81 n. 3.
22 Fr. 8: δεῖ χάρι[ν ἡμᾶ]ς ἀ[ποδιδ]όναι Ἀλεξ[άνδ]ρῳ [διὰ τοὺ]ς τελευτή[σαντ]ας [ὑπ' αὐτοῦ]... ἐγὼ δὲ οἶμαι. "We must thank Alexander for all those who died at his hand; but I think ..." The expression, δεῖ χάριν, may allude to the decree honouring Alexander: Whitehead 2000, 41; Carey et al. 2008, 16. For the grant of honorary citizenship to Alexander see Osborne 1983, T69.
23 Whitehead 2000, 41.
24 Diod. 18.86.2–3; Plut. Alex. 9.3 with Worthington 2008, 150–151; cf. Hammond and Griffith 1979, 600–601. For a cautionary tale on the historical reliability of later historians who were rhetorically trained see Dmitriev 2016, but contrast Kucharski in this volume. On this so-called "rhetorical history" see Kremmydas 2013, 141; Marcincola 2001, 111; Woodman 1988, 198.
25 Polyaen. Stratag. 4.2.2, 7; Front. 2.1.9.
26 Fr. 1: ἐν ἐλευθέρᾳ πό[λει τὰ τ]οῖς τυράννοις [συμφέρ]οντα πραττοντ[ες ... ν] εἰς δουλεία[ν ...

that he chose to be a slave of tyrants". Earlier at fr. 11, Hyperides characterizes the actions of pro-Macedonians,[27] who work on Philip's behalf, as treason:

> ... democracy. <I will pass over> most of his actions, but I will clearly show the times <he pleaded> Philip's cause and campaigned with him against our country, <which is his most serious offence> In fact, he did campaign on Philip's side against us and our allies ... precisely. (fr. 11)

The restoration of Philip's name, though not certain, is generally accepted.[28] But who is the unnamed individual who has advocated on Philip's behalf and campaigned with him? There are various possibilities: Alcimachus or Antipater mentioned by Hyperides (fr. 77) in his prosecution of Demades through a *graphê paranomôn*,[29] or the Olynthian Euthycrates, who was the beneficiary of Demades' proposal of *proxenia* (fr. 76).[30] In the case of Alcimachus and Antipater at the time (337/6) he delivered his speech against Demades, Hyperides speaks of their grant of citizenship and *proxenia* as something in the past, and *IG* ii² 239 records the honouring of a certain Alcimachus in the 6th prytany of the archonship of Phyrnichus (337/6), possibly the same,[31] and perhaps one of the beneficiaries of Philippides' proposals.[32] Both Alcimachus and Antipater, along with Alexander, are said to have been despatched by Philip to Athens after Chaeronea.[33] In the case of Euthycrates Hyperides rhetorically challenges

---

[27] I use the phrase "pro-Macedonian" cautiously, as positions taken by politicians on both sides of the Macedonian question shifted: see Engels 1993, 51–56; Brun 2013; Sawada 2019, 337–338.
[28] See Whitehead 2000, 42–43.
[29] Hansen 1974, n. 28.
[30] The trial took place before Philip's assassination in July/August 336: Engels 1993, 137; Horváth 2009, 203. Dmitriev 2021, 29–35 questions the authenticity of fr. 76 and considers' Hyperides' speech against Demades a rhetorical fiction.
[31] Lambert 2012, 126 n. 103; Cf. Heckel 2006, 9–10; Bosworth 1980, 134. Cf. Cawkwell 1969, 168 n. 2; Engels 1993, 129 n. 237; Horváth 2009, 205 n. 76.
[32] The name of the proposer is not preserved in *IG* ii² 239 (Tod 180: Lambert 126 no. 55: Schwenk no. 4), but in *IG* ii² 240 (Tod 181: Lambert 118 n. 33: Schwenk no. 7), which was passed in the 10th prytany of the same year, Demades' name is preserved: he proposed *proxenia* for someone who assisted the Athenians visiting Philip, and so may also have been behind the proposal to grant *proxenia* to Alcimachus, earlier in the year. The preserved letters of the honorand's name in *IG* ii² 240 indicates the recipient was not Antipater. In any case, citizenship and proxeny were never granted together: Osborne 1983, 70. Cf. Dmitriev 2021, 18–19.
[33] Schaefer 1887, 31–32; Hammond 1994, 157; Worthington 2008, 155; Cawkwell 1978, 167; Hammond and Griffith 1979, 606; Marzi 1986, 280 n. 4. Justin (9.4.6) mentions Alexander and Antipater, whereas Diodorus (16.87.3) does not name the envoys. There is no mention of Alcimachus, but the fact that he was granted honorary citizenship and/or *proxenia* along with

Demades (fr. 76) to submit in writing the real reasons behind making the Olynthian *proxenos*, to which Hyperides responds with his usual wit and sarcasm by presenting a "mock-honorific decree" outlining Euthycrates "beneficial" contributions: he spoke and acted in the interests of Philip; when he was hipparch, he betrayed the Olynthian cavalry to Philip; his action caused the destruction of the Chalcidians; after the capture of Olynthus he assessed the value of the prisoners; he opposed the city over the matter of the Delian temple; after the city's defeat at Chaeronea, he neither buried any of the dead or ransomed any of the prisoners. Euthycrates' actions at Chaeronea, among other things, disqualified him for the honour. In fact, his behaviour there was part of a pattern of perfidy.

To return to the Philippides speech, if indeed Euthycrates is the subject of fr. 11, then Hyperides is characterizing his actions at Chaeronea, as campaigning with Philip against Athens and her allies. And the fragment fits nicely with fr. 15a, where Hyperides provides a blacklist of traitors: "one in Thebes, another in Tanagra and another in Eleutherae, doing everything in the service of the Macedonians".[34] All the names point to southern Boeotia and may represent the fallout from Chaeronea, as one by one, pro-Macedonians began to betray their cities by making friendly overtures to Philip. Eleutherae falls on the border between Boeotia and Attica, and we can surmise that Hyperides continued his list of traitors by turning to Athens and the actions of Philippides and his associates, whose proposals to honour certain Macedonians resemble the treasonous behaviour of Euythcrates and others.[35] And this is suggested by fr. 15b: "Or do they not pray for the overthrow of all the rest of Greece, since they reap the benefits from the cities destroyed? They always want you to live in fear and danger." Here Hyperides alludes to the fears that gripped the demos following Athens' defeat at Chaeronea. As Whitehead notes, Hyperides uses a startling metaphor drawn from cultic imagery: these pro-Macedonian traitors, scattered throughout various cities, help themselves to the first fruits of the cities offered up as sacrifices to Philip.[36]

Antipater might suggest this. But see, however, Osborne 1983, 70–71 (T 70–71), who suggests that Alcimachus may have received his grant as result of a visit in 337/6.

34 Fr. 15a: [προδί]δωσιν ἕκαστος αὐτῶν, ὁ μὲν ἐν Θήβαις, ὁ δ' ἐν Τανάγρᾳ, ὁ δ' ἐν τῇ ἐλευθε[ρίδι, πάντ]α τὰ τῶν [Μακεδόνων πράτ]των. The third name in the list is restored. As Whitehead 2000, 44 notes the singular article indicates it should be Eleutheris, but argues it is a periphrasis for Eleutherae.

35 A similar list of traitors is presented at *Dion.* 173r 31–175r8 with the clear implication that those in Athens working on Philip's behalf are disloyal.

36 Whitehead 2000, 44–45 citing Oplet 1982.

Among these pro-Macedonians Hyperides undoubtedly includes Philippides and his associates, as his comments are directed to the Athenian jury, who are being kept in constant fear and danger. Indeed, this point is picked up in the epilogue (4.7–8) where Hyperides expressly accuses Philippides and his associates of thinking only of flattering those who strike fear in the people, assuming Philip would be immortal and thereby condemning Athens to death. They are described as "opportunity-watchers" (καιροφυλακοῦντες), who "dare to speak about opportunities" (περὶ καιρῶν), but in fact "are on guard for critical moments to act against the city" (τοὺς κατὰ τῆς πόλεως καιροὺς παραφυλάξαντες). "When others took pity on the city for its misfortunes, Philippides and his associates exalted" (4.9). This line of attack seems directed at Philippides' argument that the critical situation, the *kairos* of Chaeronea, demanded honours for Alexander and other Macedonians. We find a similar argument being made by Diondas, who repeatedly drafts decrees "in the name of *kairos*" to gratify Alexander against the interests of the city (*Dion.* 144v 28–31). In the present case Hyperides' turns Philippides' argument on its head: the opportunity of Chaeronea was less about flattering than about harming. He and his associates watched to see how the winds of fortune would blow, and their decision to flatter Philip was not out of character as they always court whomever has the power to harm the Athenians (4.1). In the past it was the Spartans, but "now since that power has passed to Philip, they chose to flatter him" (4.1). As in the case of Euthycrates, Philippides' response to Chaeronea is symptomatic of something deeper, a latent hostility toward Athens. As Hyperides puts it at 4.1, "whenever they spoke on behalf of the Spartans, it was not because they were their friends, but because they hated Athens and wanted to court those who always used their power against you". Philippides' flattery of Philip is motivated by a long-standing hatred and not out of any concern for Athens' safety, unlike those who fought at Chaeronea, who "chose to save Greece and despite their good intentions suffered an underserved fate" (4.9).

Now we turn to a private suit: the prosecution of Athenogenes through a *dikê blabês*.[37] The plaintiff, Epicrates, has accused the defendant of defrauding him in the sale of three slaves and their perfume business, by not fully disclosing the debts owed by the slaves. Epicrates had agreed to assume any debts that the slaves had accumulated in running the business, assured by Athenogenes that they were insignificant and would be easily covered by the wares of the shop, and signed an agreement to that effect (5.4–9). After taking possession of

---

[37] On the type of suit see Whitehead 2000, 267–268; Cooper 2001, 88–89, 96 n. 27; Cooper 2003, 61; Phillips 2009, 90–93; Todd 1993, 266; Thür 2013, 4–6.

the slaves, he soon discovered that they owed 5 talents. Athenogenes will argue from the law of *homologia* that "any agreement made by two parties is binding" (ὅσα ἂν ἕτερος ἑτέρῳ ὁμολογήσῃ κύρια εἶναι), whereas Epicrates maintains that such agreements are only binding if they are fair (5.13). It seems that there were no clauses in the law limiting what made an agreement binding or not,[38] and Epicrates' insistence that agreements need to be τὰ δίκαια was his own gloss on the law and not an actual provision.[39] Consequently, he must argue that he was materially damaged by the agreement[40] and cites (5.14–22) various, analogous laws to shore up his position.[41] The arguments based on these laws perhaps mask the inherent weakness of Epicrates' case,[42] requiring him to make an appeal to Chaeronea to prejudice the jurors against Athenogenes.

Although the case came to court several years after Chaeronea, between 330 and 324,[43] the memory of that event still ran deep and proved a powerful rhetorical device, with which to attack the character of the defendant and underscore Epicrates' early assertions that the defendant had schemed to defraud him, making their agreement unfair. The essential point of Epicrates' argument is that as a metic, Athenogenes' decision to abandon Athens in time of need represented a breach in the social contract between the city and the metic.[44] Epicrates

---

38 Namely, the agreement was made in front of witnesses (Dem. 42.12; 47.77; 48.11; Din. 3.4); was entered into willingly (Dem. 48.54; 56.2); or the thing agreed upon was just or fair (Hyp. 5.13; [Dem.] 44.7). All these restrictions seem to be glosses by litigants on the law: Phillips 2009, 89–106; Whitehead 2000, 305–306; Carawan 2006, 344–349; Cohen 2006, 74; Cohen 2005, 296; Thür 2013, 7; Cooper 2001, 93 n. 18. Contrast MacDowell 1978, 140; Pringsheim 1950, 34–44; Todd 1993, 257; Harris 2013, 200–201. Gagliardi 2015 argues that consensual agreements, *homologiai*, like the one concluded by Epicrates were vitiated by consensual defects, like fraud or duress. Consequently, Epicrates repeatedly argues that Athenogenes plotted to defraud him (5.7, 11, 18, 26, 27). See Thür 2013, who argues against interpreting these as consensual contracts.
39 Whitehead 2000, 305.
40 Carawan 2006, 346; Gagliardi 2015, 387.
41 Epicrates cites six laws for analogy: the law against misrepresenting goods sold in the Agora (5.14); the law requiring the seller of a slave to disclose any physical defects (5.15); the law on betrothal (5.16); the law on wills (5.17); a law holding owners responsible for damages and loses by their slaves (5.22); and the law that no decree justly drafted (δικαίως ἔγραψεν) has greater authority (κυριώτερον) than the laws (5.22). In each case Epicrates uses parallel language to recall his point on validity and fairness. See Phillips 2009, 106–114 on the deceptive nature of Epicrates' interpretation of these laws, and as a counterpoint Harris 2013, 198–205.
42 So, Phillips 2009, 106–117, but contrast Harris 2013, 198–205 and Arnaoutoglou 2019, 190–191.
43 On the date of the trial see Whitehead 2000, 266–267; Cooper 2001, 89.
44 Cooper 2003, 77.

sets the stage (5.26–28) for this argument by creating a sharp dichotomy between himself, the naïve citizen, and Athenogenes, the tricky metic. Though the text is fragmentary, we can get some sense of his thought: Epicrates is no perfume seller but a farmer who works a small plot of land left to him by his father. It is more likely that Athenogenes had designs on his property than Epicrates desired his trade. The jury thus has good reason to empathize with Epicrates for being deceived and for falling in with a fellow like Athenogenes (5.26). On top of this misfortune, Epicrates now runs the risk of being disenfranchised by Athenogenes (5.27).[45] The result would be terrible for Epicrates: he simply made a mistake, whereas Athenogenes committed an injustice; the one a citizen and the other a metic (5.28).[46] Now Epicrates invokes the memory of Chaeronea (5.29–30), heightening his attack on Athenogenes' character. Some of his comments recall Hyperides' attack on Philippides, whose long-standing hatred of Athens prompted his disloyalty. In Athenogenes' case, it was his persistent self-interest. Unlike others, who stood by Athens in its moment of need, Athenogenes abandoned Athens: "In the war with Philip, he left the city just before the battle and did not serve with you at Chaeronea but moved to Troezen contrary to the law" (5.29).[47] Cleverly, Epicrates has identified the jurors trying the case with the men who fought at Chaeronea. Their bravery is set in contrast to Athenogenes' self-serving actions. According to Epicrates, Athenogenes acted as he did because he thought Troezen would survive, but he condemned Athens to death (5.29), just as Philippides' flattery of Philip had (4.7). Like Philippides, Athenogenes watched to see how the winds of fortune blew. The latter raised his daughters, we are told, in the prosperity which Athens provided, but when misfortune befell the city, he married them off elsewhere (5.29). His intention was always to return to Athens to take up his business once peace was restored (5.30). At this point the text becomes extremely fragmentary but enough remains to suggest a contrast between Athenogenes and other metics, who in times of peace shared in Athens' prosperity but in times of danger worked for the collective safety. Whereas in the past, as at Plataea, good metics stood by Athens, Athenogenes

---

45 On how Epicrates could suffer *atimia* see Whitehead 2000, 331–332 and Cooper 2001, 98 n. 33.

46 5.28 is extremely fragmentary and the sense is far from clear: see Whitehead 2000, 332–333; Cooper 2001, 98 tries to make some sense of the text.

47 The law, which forbade metics from migrating from Athens in time of war, is cited at 5.33. If someone committed this offense, he was subject to *endeixis* and *apagôgê* upon his return to Athens. This is precisely the offense committed by Leocrates but nowhere does Lycurgus (1.53, 144) mention the law, suggesting that it applied only to metics. On this point see Whitehead 2000, 335–336; Cooper 2001, 99 n. 36.

had abandoned the city in its recent crisis.[48] These comments describe the social contract into which metics enter, when they take up permanent residency in Athens: the city provides them the opportunity to prosper but in turn demands of them the obligation to defend the city. Athenogenes' actions at the time of Chaeronea has violated that social contract, thus voiding the private agreement with Epicrates: "having transgressed the common agreements with the city, he insists on the private ones with me, as if anyone would be convinced that the man who held in utter contempt fair dealings with you, that this same man would consider fair dealings with me" (5.31).

3 Chaeronea on defense

We now turn back to a public suit, Diondas' indictment of Hyperides for his proposal to crown Demosthenes. In 338 Hyperides, along with Demomeles, proposed to crown Demosthenes over his efforts to secure the Theban Alliance.[49] Diondas responded with a *graphê paranomôn*.[50] A portion of Hyperides' defence speech has been recovered from the Archimedes Palimpsest.[51] Hyperides made his proposal before Chaeronea, and Diondas brought his indictment after news of Athens' defeat reached the city. But the case did not come to court until four years later in 334.[52] If as Horváth suggests the case against Philippides was the direct antecedent, some of the arguments presented by Hyperides in that case are picked up and fleshed out further in his defence against Diondas.[53] In particular, the *kairos* of Chaeronea becomes an even more important theme, used

---

48 In the preserved text at 5.30 there is a reference to peace, dangers, Plataea, and Athenogenes. See Whitehead 2000, 338, and Cooper 2001, 99 for a reconstruction. Cf. Schroeder's 1922, 453 for a restoration of the text.
49 [Plut] *Vita X Orat.* 846a; 848e–f; Dem. 18.222–223. Worthington 2013, 244–245, and Roisman and Worthington 2015, 229, 251 suggest the indictment was against Demomeles, who was successfully defended by Hyperides. Cf. Todd 2009, 163. Demosthenes 18.223 speaks of decrees of Demomeles and Hyperides; and Yunis 2001, 235 suggests the plural because of a rider was added by Hyperides to Demomeles' decree.
50 Hansen 1974, no. 26.
51 For the Greek text see Horváth 2014; Carey *et al.* 2008 provide an English translation, which I have adapted. On the transmission of this text in the Byzantine period see Ucciardello 2009; cf. Easterling 2008.
52 Horváth 2009, 196 and 2014, 20 dates the case between January and March 334, whereas Rhodes 2009, suggests May/June 334.
53 Horváth 2009, 203–205.

not only against Diondas, but also to defend Hyperides' proposal. The stunning success of Hyperides' defense is attested by the fact that he was acquitted ([Plut.] *Vit. X Orat.* 848f), with Diondas receiving less than one-fifth of the vote (Dem. 18.222).

I focus on sections 137r–136v to 145v–144r, where Hyperides engages in an extended word play on *kairos*.[54] This clever rhetorical argument is meant to address the current political climate where Diondas and other pro-Macedonians repeatedly draft proposals to gratify Alexander under the name of *kairos*:[55]

> And yet isn't it terrible if it's possible for those who draft shameful things against the city to repeatedly invoke the name of the 'critical situation' (τὸ τοῦ καιροῦ ὄνομα) when they draft whatever they think will gratify Alexander ([Ἀ]λεξάνδρωι χαριεῖσθαι), but those who at that time adopted policies which were advantageous to the demos are not even permitted to mention the period. (144v 28–145v 2)

This is essentially the argument used by Philippides, when proposing honours for certain Macedonians including Alexander. The situation, Athens' defeat at Chaeroena, called for it, he claimed. In response Hyperides argued that Philippides and his associates were opportunity-watchers, looking out for critical moments to harm the city. Here we are told that Diondas and his associates keep invoking *kairos* when they draft proposals to gratify Alexander; this is a reference to the decree granting honorary citizenship to Alexander, when he came to Athens following Chaeronea.[56] Such decrees are characterized as shameful, below Athens' dignity, particular when Diondas and his associates refuse to allow those, who have always advocated in the best interests of the demos, to mention those times: that is the events leading up to and following Chaeronea. They instead respond with indictments. If we go back a few lines (145r–144v9–22), Hyperides has just characterized Diondas as a sycophant, accusing him of initiating fifty indictments;[57] in all he has never once brought an indictment against those working politically in Philip's interests (κατὰ μὲν τῶ[ν] ὑπὲρ Φιλίππου πολιτευομένων), nor verbally abused them, but those who

---

[54] Carey *et al.* 2008, 16: "Hyperides throughout this section plays with the word *Kairos*, which at different points refers to the situation before Chaeronea and the situation at the time of the trial". Cf. Demont 2011, 40–41.

[55] On the political context of the trial see Horváth 2009, 197–211 and Horváth 2014, 24–32.

[56] Osborne 1983, T 69. Carey *et al.* 2008, 16; Horváth 2014, 141; Hamond and Griffith 1974, 609–610; Schaefer 1887, 31–33.

[57] Cf. Dem. 18.249 for the multiple suits against Demosthenes, including that of Diondas.

pursue polices that opposed Philip, he constantly abuses at their trials.⁵⁸ Diondas initiated indictments, we are told, against Charedimus, Lycurgus, Demosthenes and Hyperides himself, who faced three in a single day. As Horváth suggests, these likely included the present case initiated by Diondas, but also the indictment brought under Aristogeiton's name with the assistance of Diondas.⁵⁹ At 174r. 30–32 we are told that Diondas (?) prosecuted Hyperides over his proposal to free the slaves.⁶⁰

As we noted above, in defence of his proposals for Athens' safety, if our understanding of Rutilius is right, Hyperides already characterized Chaeronea as the *kairos*, the critical situation, that demanded armed resistance, not debate; though he elaborates on the theme of *kairos* in his attack on Philippides, it is here that he explores it most fully. After describing all the indictments initiated by Diondas, Hyperides then (144v 23–28) accuses him of reaching such a level of shamefulness that he prevents the jurors from following (χρῆσθαι) those whom the demos have agreed upon or Hyperides has proposed (προεβούλευσα),⁶¹ or who have been confirmed by a judgment of the court.⁶² Besides this, he prevents the jurors "from listening to anyone speak about the critical situation, without which there is nothing at all useful (to say)" (πρὸς δὲ τούτο[ι]ς οὐδ' ὑπὲρ τοῦ καιροῦ ἀκούειν λέγοντ(ος) οὗ χωρὶς οὐδὲν τῶν πάντ(ων) χρήσιμόν ἐστιν). This attack prefaces his statement about Diondas' monstrous behaviour of repeatedly invoking the name of *kairos* when proposing measures against the city to gratify Alexander. The present trial, Hyperides suggests, will determine whether the jurors will be allowed to adopt the leaders the Assembly has already voted to honour, namely Demosthenes. If there is ever a time, it is this moment, the critical situation of the present trial, in which Hyperides must defend his motion to have Demosthenes crowned, that it is appropriate (χρήσιμον) to recall the memory of Chaeronea. This seems to be the import of Hyperides' words, before

---

58 Later (175v 1) Hyperides expressly calls Diondas a sycophant in the context of his fifty indictments. Cf. Dem. 18.249 with Herrman 2009a, 176.
59 Horváth 2009, 200 and Horváth 2014, 163.
60 Dion. 174r. 30–32: ἀλλ' ὅμως ἐμοῦ κατηγόρει, ὅτι τοὺς δούλους τοὺς συναγωνιουμένους τῶι δήμωι ἔγραψα ἐλευθέρους εἶναι κτλ. Flórez 2012, 69–71 sees a reference to Aristogeiton in the anonymous associate mentioned at 174r 25–32 and suggests that Aristogeiton and not Diondas is the subject here.
61 Hyperides was likely a member of Boule at the time of Chaeronea. On the question of whether προεβούλευσα is used in a technical sense here see Carey 2008, 16; Demont 2011, 34 n. 46 (non-technical); Flórez 2012, 67–68 and Horváth 2014, 2 (technical).
62 Earlier (145r 2–3) Hyperides comments that he is on trial for things which the jurors have previously decided. Cf. Dem. 18.223 for a similar accusation, with Horváth 2014, 136.

turning and attacking Diondas' own insistence on invoking the name of the *kairos* to justify his proposals against the city but disallowing others who work in the interests of the demos from doing the same.

After making his accusation against Diondas for inappropriately invoking the name of the *kairos*, Hyperides again speaks of the usefulness of *kairos* both in terms of present situation, the trial, and of recalling the memory of Chaeronea (145v 2–11):

> But I would have wished, men of the jury, just as the critical moment (ὁ καιρός) is important (χρήσιμος), that you would be able just as easily to recognize it, and I think the exact opposite is appropriate to what Diondas says, who states that anger irrespective of the situation (ὀργὴν ἄκαιρον),[63] not defence speeches, actually destroys those brought to trial, though in his accusation he himself appeals to a known situation (εἰς καιρὸν ἀναφερόμενος ἐγνωσέμ(ον)).[64] Now naturally, Diondas rejects the importance of the situation (τὸν καιρὸν), while he himself does nothing (appropriate) in the (present) situation (οὐδὲν αὐτὸ(ς) ἐν καιρῶι πράττων), the one who accuses me that the alliance was not on equal terms, and we contributed twice as much as the Thebans to the war, in money, horses and soldiers.

In this passage Hyperides provides an extended play on the word *kairos*, shifting from the present situation of the trial to the past situation of Chaeronea, an appropriate understanding of which is crucial for determining the outcome of the *graphê paranomôn*. Since Diondas keeps invoking the name of *kairos*, Hyperides takes as a given that the *kairos* of Chaeronea is important (χρήσιμος), but the jury need to know when it is important to invoke its memory. Certainly, at the present trial, which is over decrees stemming from that critical moment, is as important a time as any; with the adjective χρήσιμος Hyperides recalls what he said a moment ago when he accused Diondas of preventing the jury "from listening to anyone speak about the critical situation (of Chaeronea), without which there is nothing at all useful (to say)" (οὗ χωρὶς οὐδὲν τῶν πάντ(ων) χρήσιμόν ἐστιν). That is, if Hyperides cannot speak about the critical moment of Chaeronea, there is no point in saying anything at all. Obviously, Hyperides is addressing Diondas' warning to the jury not to listen to what Hy-

---

[63] Carey et al. 2008, 13 translate ὀργὴν ἄκαιρον as "anger not fitting the situation"; Horváth 2014, 84 "von den Umständen unabhängige Zorn"; Demont 2011, 40 "un pathos inapproprié à la situation présente".
[64] Carey et al. 2008, 13 translate the phrase κατηγορεῖν εἰς καιρὸν ἀναφερόμενος ἐγνωσέμ(ον) as "while addressing his accusations to a specific situation"; Horváth 2014, 84 as "wobei er nicht die Verteidigung, sondern die Anklage auf einebestimmte Situation bezieht", who, however, restores the text as κατηγορεῖν εἰς καιρὸν ἀναφερόμενος. ἴσως μὲν οὖν εἰκότως.

perides will say about that moment.⁶⁵ But Hyperides' argument here is an appeal to the jury to give an impartial hearing. If Diondas can speak of Chaeronea, the *kairos*, as he calls it, so can Hyperides in his defence. As Hyperides remarks, he takes a different position from Diondas as to when it is appropriate to speak of that *kairos*. Although Diondas claims that it is the jury's anger at wrongdoing, regardless of the situation in which it was committed,⁶⁶ and not what defendants say about the situation, that will lead to their conviction, Diondas, nonetheless, appeals to a specific *kairos* (Theban alliance/Chaeronea) in his accusations against Hyperides. Though Diondas rejects the importance of *kairos* in the case of the defendant, he says nothing appropriate to the current situation of the trial, when he alleges that the alliance with Thebes was imbalanced. And here (145v 12–144r 24), as a counter-argument, Hyperides points to historic battles, like Salamis where Athens provided 220 out of 360 ships, Marathon where the Athenians fought alone against the Persians, and Artemisium, where other Greeks contributed only one-fifth the triremes, to justify the terms of the alliance.⁶⁷ As he says, among its many virtues, the city does not quibble over numbers "at such critical situations to ensure each one contributes the same" (ἐν τ[οῖ]ς τοιούτοις καιροῖς, ὅπως ταὐτὰ ἕκαστοι συμβαλοῦνται), but accepts what each state contributes and assumes leadership of the whole giving all it has for the common safety of Greece. Though Marathon and Salamis were common historical *exempla* in Attic oratory,⁶⁸ here they purposely serve to underscore both the importance and rightness of the Theban Alliance and the ensuing battle. Chaeronea now ranks among the great historic battles of the past, in which Athens assumed a leadership role and contributed accordingly.

Earlier in his speech (137r –136v) Hyperides lays out clearly for the jury how critical it was to secure an alliance with Thebes.⁶⁹ He presents a counterfactual argument to make his point: Thebes had three choices: to join Philip, to join Athens or to remain neutral; if they had joined Philip, they would have invaded Attica with Philip; if they had remined neutral, Athens would have fought alone against Philip in their own territory. But since Thebes sided with the Athenians,

---

65 Carey *et al.* 2008, 16.
66 So Horváth 2014, 142.
67 Cf. Dem. 18.208 for a similar comparison between Chaeronea and the historic battles of Salamis, Marathon and Artemisium, with Herrman 2009a, 177. For other similarities between *On the Crown* and *Against Diondas* in terms of language, detail and arguments see Carey *et al.* 2009, 3; Herrman 2009, 178–179; Todd 2009; Martinis 2012, 51–59; cf. Guth 2014 for differences in their narratives of the Theban Alliance.
68 Efstathiou 2013, 184.
69 On the Theban Alliance see Guth 2014.

Athens faced the danger in Theban territory with their support. Having thus stated the critical nature of the alliance, Hyperides next (136v 20–25) poses a rhetorical question to Diondas: "Of the three choices consider which one did not happen? And I would even be pleased to learn from the accuser himself whether the alliance with Thebes at those critical moments (κατὰ τοὺς καιροὺς ἐκείνους) seemed advantageous to the city and to the Greeks or not". Hyperides responds with another rhetorical question: "if this (the alliance) is acknowledged by all, who were responsible for these outcomes"? To this he answers: first the demos, who sounded the call to battle; next individual citizens who joined the fight with conviction; and finally, Hyperides himself, who showed more enthusiasm than anyone else for the cause.[70] Even though the jurors, were tripped up in the battle,[71] nothing in itself remarkable, what is remarkable, he argues, is their "choosing the noble cause and believing it necessary to risk danger to free the Greeks as in the past". Here Hyperides anticipates his later argument against Diondas' assertion that the alliance was unequal: the leadership role, which Athens assumed at Chaeronea, emulates the historic roles that it played at Marathon and Salamis, and in making this epic history the jurors themselves were active participants.

4 Conclusion

I have tried to show that Chaeronea loomed large in Hyperides' thinking: it was a politically important event in his life; in many ways it defined him, even if Lamia became the defining moment of his career.[72] His rhetoric on Chaeronea, as the critical moment, which shaped the responses of various politicians to the Macedonian question and against which one's loyalty to Athens was measured, became the filter through which the memory of Chaeronea was recalled. Any wavering in one's commitment to that memory, as a defining moment in Athens' history, like Marathon and Salamis, in which Athens fought sacrificially for Greek freedom, was regarded by Hyperides as disloyalty. By comparing Chaero-

---

[70] This suggests Hyperides served on the embassy: Guth 2011, 155 n. 12.
[71] With the verb ἐσφάλητε Hyperides might be using a wrestling metaphor, which would be appropriate for his subsequent argument that the outcome of Chaeronea was a matter of Tyche (137v 2–8). Dem. 18.192–194, 300 and Dem. 60.19–21 likewise attribute the defeat at Chaeronea to Tyche. See Todd 2009, 170–171 and Crick in this volume for Dem. 60.
[72] When he delivered the funeral oration over the fallen dead (Hyp. 6): for which see Herrman 2009b; Cooper 2001, 128–136; Worthington 1999; Bracessi 1970.

nea to the epic struggles of the past, Hyperides immortalized those who died there and comforted the survivors among the jury, by drawing their memory away from the bitter aspects of defeat and the obvious failure of policy, toward a reimagined history. Those who proposed measures to garner Philip's favor, even if their motivation was genuine concern for Athens' safety, were represented as working for Philip against the best interests of Athens and thereby desecrating the memory of Chaeronea.

Bibliography

Arnaoutoglou, I. (2019), "Twisting the Law in Ancient Athens", in: C. Carey/I. Giannadaki/ B. Griffith-Williams (eds.), *Use and Abuse of Law in the Athenian Courts*, Leiden/Boston, 181–197.
Bernhardt, J. (2012), "Rhetorische Strategie und politischer Standpunkt bei Hypereides", *Hermes* 140, 263–283.
Bosworth, A.B. (1980), *A Historical Commentary on Arrian's History of Alexander*, Volume 1: Books I–III, Oxford.
Bracessi, L. (1970), "L'epitafio di Iperide come fonte storica", *Studi Periodici di Litteratura e Storia* 48, 276–301.
Brun, P. (2013), "Y avait-il vraiment des anti-Macédoniens à Athènes entre 338 et 323? A propos d'un nouveau fragment d'Hypéride 'Contre Diondas'", *ZPE* 187, 87–92.
Burtt, J.O. (1954), *Minor Attic Orators II: Lycurgus, Demades, Dinarchus, Hyperides*, Cambridge, MA.
Carey et al. (2008), "Fragments of Hyperides 'Against Diondas' from the Archimedes Palimpsest", *ZPE* 165, 1–19.
Carawan, E. (2006), "The Athenian Law of Agreement", *GRBS* 46, 339–374.
Cawkwell, G.L. (1969), "The Crowning of Demosthenes", *CQ* 19, 163–180.
Cawkwell, G.L. (1978), *Philip of Macedon*, London/Boston.
Cohen, E.E. (2005), "Commercial Law", in: M. Gagarin/D. Cohen (eds.), *The Cambridge Companion to Ancient Greek Law*, Cambridge, 290–302.
Cohen, E.E. (2006), "Consensual Contracts at Athens", in: E. Cantarella/J.M. Modrzejewski/ G. Thür (eds.), *Symposion 2003*, Wien, 73–84.
Colin, G. (1968), *Hypéride Discours*, Paris.
Connor, W.R. (1988), "'Sacred' and 'Secular': Ἱερὰ καὶ ὅσια and the Classical Athenian Concept of the State", *AncSoc* 19, 161–188.
Cooper, C.R. (2001), *Hyperides*, in: I. Worthington/C.R. Cooper/E.M. Harris, *The Oratory of Classical Greece Volume 5: Dinarchus, Hyperides, and Lycurgus*, Austin, 57–151.
Cooper, C. (2003), "Worst of All He's an Egyptian", *Syllecta Classica* 14, 59–81.
Deils, H. (1874), "Δημάδεα", *RhM* 29, 107–117.
Dmitriev, S. (2016), "Killing in Style: Demosthenes, Demades, and Phocion in Later Rhetorical Tradition", *Mnemosyne* 69, 931–954.
Dmitirev, D. (2021), *The Orator Demades: Classical Greece reimagined through Rhetoric*, Oxford.

Demont, P. (2011), "Les nouveaux Fragments d'Hypéride", *REG* 124, 21–45.
Easterling, P. (2008), "*Fata Libellorum*: Hyperides and the Transmission of the Attic Orators", *Acta Ant. Hung.* 48, 11–17.
Efstathiou, E. (2013), "The Historical Examples of Marathon as used in the Speeches *On the False Embassy*, *On the Crown*, and *Against Ctesiphon* by Demosthenes and Aeschines", C. Carey/M. Edwards (eds.), *Marathon – 2,500 Years: Proceedings of the Marathon Conference 2010, BICS* Supplement 124, London, 181–198.
Ellis, J.R. (1976), *Philip II and Macedonian Imperialism*, Princeton.
Engels, J. (1993), *Studien zur politischen Biographie des Hypereides: Athen in der Epoch der lykurgischen Reformen und des makedonischen Universalreiches*, München.
Ferguson, W.S. (1938), "The Salaminioi of Heptaphylai and Souion", *Hesperia* 7, 1–74.
Flórez, J.M. (2012), "Seis Comentarios al texto del nuevo 'In Diondam' de Hiperides", *ZPE* 180, 67–71.
Gagliardi, L. (2015), "The Athenian law on 'homologia' and the Regulation of Duress and Fraud in Contractual Bargaining", *RIDA* 93, 375–391.
Guth, D. (2014), "Rhetoric and Historical Narrative: The Theban Alliance of 339 BCE", *Historia* 63, 151–165.
Hammond, N.G.L. (1994), *Philip of Macedon*, London.
Hammond, N.G.L./Griffith, G.T. (1979), *History of Macedonia II 550–336 B.C*, Oxford.
Hansen, M.H. (1974), *The Sovereignty of the Peoples' Court in Athens in the Fourth Century B.C. and the Public Actions against Unconstitutional Proposals*, Odense.
Harris, E.M. (2013), *The Rule of Law in Action in Democratic Athens*, Oxford.
Harris, E.M. (2018), *The Oratory of Classical Greece Volume 15: Demosthenes, Speeches 23–26*, Austin.
Heckel, W. (2006), *Who's Who in the Age of Alexander the Great*, Oxford.
Herrman, J. (2009a), "Hyperides' *Against Diondas* and the Rhetoric of Revolt", *BICS* 52, 175–185.
Herrman, J. (2009b), *Hyperides: Funeral Oration*, New York.
Horváth, L. (2004), "Eine fragwürdigieLesart (Hyp. IV. Kol. V.8)", *Acta Ant. Hung.* 44, 163–170.
Horváth, L. (2008), "Dating Hyperides' 'Against Diondas'", *ZPE* 166, 27–36.
Horváth, L. (2009), "Hyperidea", *BICS* 52, 187–222.
Horváth, L. (2010), "Hyperidis Contra Diondas: Editio Critica", *Acta Ant. Hung.* 50, 389–400.
Horváth, L. (2014), *Der Neue Hyperiedes*, Berlin/Boston.
Janko, J. (2009), "Some Notes on the New Hyperides (Against Diondas)", *ZPE* 170, 16.
Kremmydas, C. (2013), "Hellenistic Oratory and the evidence of Rhetorical Exercises", in: C. Kremmydas/K. Tempest (eds.), *Hellenistic Oratory: Continuity and Change*, Oxford, 139–163.
Lambert, S. (2012), *Inscribed Athenian Laws ad Decrees 352/1–322/1 BC*, Leiden/Boston.
MacDowell, D.M. (1978), *The Law in Classical Athens*, Ithaca.
Maffi, A. (1982), "Τὰ ἱερα καὶ τὰ ὅσια: Contributo allo Studio dellaTerminologia giuridico – sacrale Greca", in: J. Modrzejewski/D. Liebs (eds.), *Symposion 1977: Vortrage zur griechischen und hellenistischen Rechtsgeschichte*, Wien, 34–53.
Marincola, J. (2001), *Greek Historians*, Cambridge.
Martinis, L. de (2012), "I democratici Ateniesi dopo Cheronea alla luce del nuovo Iperide", *Aevum* 86, 39–62.
Marzi, M. (1977: repr. 1986), *Iperide*, in: M. Marzi/P. Leone/E. Malcovati (eds.), *Oratori Attici Minori* Vol. 1, Torino, 1–328.

Marzi, M. (1995), "Demade", in: M. Marzi/S. Feraboli (eds.), *Oratori Attici Minori*, Vol. 2, Torino, 601–689.
Poddighe, E. (2006), "Ateniesi infami (*atimoi*) ed ex ateniesi senza i requisiti (*apepsephismenoi*)", *Annali della Facoltà di Lettere e Filosofia* 24, 5–24.
Poddighe, E. (2004), "I termini giurdici del decreto di Iperide sulla concessione di privilegi in cambio della disponibilità a combattere per Atene", *Annali della Facoltà di Lettere e Filosofia* 21, 43–68.
Oplet, I. (1982), "Die Polemik des Redners Hypereides", *Koinonia* 6, 7–13.
Osborne, M.J. (1983), *Naturalization in Athens*, Volumes III and IV, Brussel.
Phillips, D.D. (2009), "Hypereides 3 and the Athenian Law of Contracts", *TAPA* 139, 89–122.
Pringsheim, F. (1950), *The Greek Law of Sale*, Weimar.
Rhodes, P.J. (2009), Rhodes, "Hyperides 'Against Diondas': Two Problems", *BICS* 52, 223–228.
Rhodes, P.J. (1972), *The Athenian Boule*, Oxford.
Rosiman, J./Worthington, I./Waterfield, R. (2015), *Lives of the Attic Orators: Texts from Pseudo-Plutarch, Photius and the Suda*, Oxford.
Sawada, N. (2019), "Allies and Foes (I): Aeschines, Hyperides, Lycurgus", in: G. Martin (ed.), *The Oxford Handbook of Demosthenes*, Oxford, 337–351.
Schaefer, A. (1887), *Demosthenes und seine Zeit 3^2*, Leipzig.
Schroeder, O.J. (1922), "Beiträge zur Wiederherstellung des Hyperides–Textes", *Hermes* 57, 450–464.
Schwenk, C.J. (1985), *Athens in the Age of Alexander: The Dated Laws and Decrees of 'the Lykourgan Era' 338–322 B.C.*, Chicago.
Sealey, R. (1993), *Demosthenes and His Time: A Study in Defeat*, New York/Oxford.
Thür, G. (2013), "The Statute on Homologein in Hyperides' Speech Against Athenogenes", *Dike* 16, 1–10.
Tod, M. (1985), *Greek Historical Inscriptions*, Two Volumes in One, Chicago.
Todd, S.C. (2009), "'Against Diondas', Demosthenes 'On the Crown', and the Rhetoric of Political Revolt", *BICS* 52, 161–174.
Todd, S.C. (1993), *The Shape of Athenian Law*, Oxford.
Traill, J.S. (1975), *The Political Organization of Attica*, Hesperia Supplement XIV, Princeton.
Ucciardello, G. (2009), "Hyperides in the Archimedes Palimpsest: Palaeography and Textual Transmission", *BICS* 52, 229–252.
Usher, S. (2004), "*Kairos* in Fourth-century Greek Oratory", in: M. Edwards/C. Reid (eds.), *Oratory in Action*, Manchester, 52–63.
Whitehead, D. (2000), *Hypereides: The Forensic Speeches*, Oxford.
Woodman, A.J. (1988), *Rhetoric in Classical Historiography*, London/New York.
Worthington, I. (1992), *A Historical Commentary on Dinarchus: Rhetoric and Conspiracy in Later Fourth-Century Athens*, Ann Arbor.
Worthington, I. (1999), *Greek Orators 2, Dinarchus 1 and Hyperides 5 and 6*, Warminster.
Worthington, I. (2008), *Philip II of Macedonia*, New Haven/London.
Worthington, I. (2013), *Demosthenes of Athens and the Fall of Classical Greece*, Oxford.
Yunis, H. (2001), *Demosthenes. On the Crown*, Cambridge.

Janek Kucharski
Hyperides, Diondas, and the First Ascendancy of Demades

Abstract: This chapter deals with the recently deciphered Hyperidean speech Against Diondas (22–23 Horvath), which provides a glimpse into the early period of Demades' ascendancy in the 330s. Hyperides deplores the fact that Demades and his clique monopolized Athens' policy, and seems to impute to him a tyrannical attempt to enslave the city paired with embarrassing flattery towards his Macedonian sponsors. These accusations provide a clear illustration of the rhetorical distortions to which events from recent history are subjected in ancient Athens: treachery may be a label given to prudence, while rational appeasement of a much stronger enemy could be misconstructed as a case of debased fawning. Traitor and flatterer were indeed the two principal shades with which the image of Demades was painted in later authors. The preserved fragment of Against Diondas is one of the earliest known testimonies in which these unflattering traits are outlined in crisp detail.

Demades' rise to prominence begins after Chaeronea. This is at least what the sources tell us. From 338 B.C. until his death at the hands of Cassander in 319 B.C. he was a major player in Athenian politics, and at times even the *de facto* leader of the city. During these two decades he earned a well deserved — to judge from the grudging praises of Plutarch and many others — reputation as an excellent orator, second to none, including Demosthenes, and a much less flattering label of a sycophant (in every possible meaning), as well as a backstabbing traitor who sold his country along with its best men to the Macedonian despots, and then in turn tried to sell them as well. The modern view of Demades has to a large extent followed the picture bequeathed by the ancient sources. Only the last couple of decades have brought about a reappraisal of his

---

My sincerest thanks go to Aggelos Kapellos for inviting me to contribute to this volume and for his continued support in my work on this chapter. I also owe a great debt of gratitude to the late P.J. Rhodes and to Gunther Martin for reading this piece and offering several perceptive suggestions and corrections. The dubious credit for all remaining errors is entirely mine.

political allegiances and decisions.[1] It has been proven beyond any doubt that he was not an unflinching supporter of Macedon at the expense of his country,[2] and plausibly argued that the policy of appeasement he advocated stemmed more from a rational assessment of Athens' abilities than from corruption and treachery.

The bulk of the available information about Demades comes from much later sources. The few contemporary remarks and a handful of epigraphic documents can only delineate his policy and its perception in very broad outlines (though clearly enough to debunk some excesses of later tradition). Quite obviously Demades has little to say about himself, given that he did not put his speeches into circulation, and most if not all of the apophthegms attributed to him are forgeries. As for his fellow-orators and politicians, Dinarchus frequently complains about his influence, corruption and venality, but he says the same of Demosthenes (Din. 1.7, 11, 89, 101) and once even concedes that both did great services to their country (2.15). Demosthenes himself acknowledges his successful negotiation of the peace with Philip (18.285). Hyperides by contrast mercilessly mocks one of his honorific decrees, but the extant fragment focuses primarily on the honorand and not on the proposer (F 76 Jensen). Lycurgus and Polyeuctus have cast the most aspersions on him, insinuating sycophancy and treachery on his part (F 9.1 Conomis; F 1.1 Sauppe), but abuse like this was too common in the Athenian courts to allow the drawing of any specific conclusions.

To this rather modest selection of contemporary oratorical sources the newly discovered fragments of Hyperides' defence speech *Against Diondas* have provided a substantial, perhaps even game-changing addition. The speech was delivered after Alexander's request for triremes was sent to Athens (see below); the only secure *terminus ante quem* is 330 B.C. (Dem. 18.222). An early date within this timespan seems more likely,[3] and therefore plausible suggestions have been made to place the trial either in the spring or in the summer of 334 B.C. The relevant passage, near the end of the speech, begins with a denunciation of Diondas' "wickedness" (*kakia*) and "lunacy" (*aponoia*) in his criticism of the anti-Macedonian policies predating Chaeronea (*Dion.* 20 Horváth). Hyperides

---

[1] This unflattering image of Demades has been challenged throughout the last three decades or so by Mitchel 1970, 14–18; Williams 1989, Brun 2000 and Dmitriev (BNJ Biographical Essay) and his recent (2021) monograph among others; cf. recently Gallo 2019, 360–361.
[2] See *IG* II² 1623.160–188 (BNJ 227 T 21) and 1631.605–606 (BNJ 227 T 24) with Brun 2000, 44–45, 108–109 and Dmitriev's commentaries.
[3] Thus Horváth 2009, 187–197 and Rhodes 2009, 223–226.

then goes on to list several politicians from abroad who, like Diondas, work for Philip against their own countries (*Dion.* 20). In the end, he returns to Athens with a pessimistic assessment of the city's current policy-making (*Dion.* 22):

[22] ἀλλά, οἶμαι, τὰ πράγμα(τα) τῆι πόλει οὕτως νῦν περιέστηκεν, ὡς οὐκ ἂν ἐβουλόμην. ἐπεὶ τίς οὐκ ἂν ἀλγήσειεν, ὅταν ἐν τῆι ἐκκλησίαι ὑμῶν κελευόντων ἀπαλεῖψαί τι τῶν γεγραμμένων μὴ ἐθέληι Δημάδης — ἄλλο γράψουσιν αὖ ὑμ(ῖν) φήσει ἀπιέναι ἐκ τῆς πόλεως — παρελθὼν δέ τις τῶν κοινωνῶν αὐτοῦ εἴπηι ὅτι ὑμεῖς, [ὡς] ἂν ἔχηι, ψηφιεῖσθε ταῦτα, ὅπω[ς] ἂν δουλείαν ὑπάγειν ὑπὸ Δημάδου ἔχητε. [23] τοῦτο γὰρ τῶν πάντων παραλογώτατόν ἐστιν, ὅτι ἐν μὲν τοῖς ἔμπροσθε[ν χρόνοις οἱ] ἰδιῶται, εἰκότως, οἶμαι, ἐδεδοίκεσαν μὴ τιμ[ωρί]αν ὑπὸ τοῦ δήμου ἔχωσι, νυνὶ δὲ τοὐναντίον· ὁ δῆμ(ος) ἐδέδιεν, μὴ ὑπὸ τῶν ἰδιωτῶν αἰτίαν λάβηι. [24] [καὶ] γὰρ νῦν τὰ μὲν ἄλλα ἐ[ά]σω τῆς ἀσελγείας αὐτοῦ, ἔλεγε δὲ ἐν τῆι πρώιην ἐκκλησίαι δεῖν ἡμᾶς τὴν Πάραλον πέμψαντας ὡς Ἀλέξανδρον μέμφεσθαι αὐτῶι, ὅτι ὑστάτοις ὑμῖν ἐπέστειλεν περὶ τῶν τριήρων. οὕτως δῆλον, ὅτι τὸ λοιπὸν πρώτοις ἡμῖν ἐπιτάττ[ει] καὶ ἃ [οὐ]δ' ἀναγκαζομένους καλῶς ἔχει ποιεῖν, ταῦ(τα) [ἀ]γανακ[τ]εῖ, εἰ μὴ πρῶτοι ποιήσομεν. [25] ἢ πάλιν, ἐπειδὰν Διώνδας ἐπὶ τῶν δικαστηρίων σεμνύνηται λέγων ὅτι πεντήκον(τα) γραφὰς ἐγράψατο, εἰ δέ τις αὐτὸν ἐρωτῆσαι· 'ἔστιν οὖν ἥντινα τούτων ᾕρηκας;', οὐδεμίαν φανήσεται. (text after Horváth 2014)

[22] But — I think — the city's situation has now turned out in a way I would not have wished. For who would not be pained, whenever in the Assembly despite your call to expunge a clause in a written proposal Demades refuses (furthermore he will tell you when you intend to draft otherwise that he will leave the city), and one of his collaborators comes along and says that you will vote for this regardless, so that you can endure (*hypagein*) servitude (*douleian*) under Demades (*hypo Dēmadou*)? [23] For this is the most amazing thing of all, that in former times individuals — rightly, I think — were afraid that they would be punished by the demos, while now it's the opposite: the demos is afraid that it may be held responsible by some individuals. [24] Just now ([*kai*] *gar nun*) I shall omit the rest of his outrageous behaviour (*aselgeias autou*). But in the Assembly the other day (*prōēn*) he said (*elege*) that you should send the Paralus to Alexander and complain that he wrote to you last of all about the warships. Clearly this means that in other matters he gives his requests to us first, and is displeased when we do not do first what otherwise would be dishonourable to do, even under duress. [25] Or again (sc. who would not be pained) when Diondas puffs himself up in the lawcourts saying that he brought fifty indictments, and someone asks him: 'Is there any one of them you've won', it will be evident that there isn't one. (Carey *et al.* 2008; adapted to the text in Horváth 2014)

1 Demades' outrageous behaviour?

I would like to begin from the end: with the "outrageous behaviour" (*aselgeia*) deplored by Hyperides, and exemplified by the embarrassingly obsequious "complaint" addressed to Alexander. This is the only explicit reference to the recent past in the passage quoted, underscored both grammatically (indicative imperfect: *elege*), lexically (*prōēn*), and most likely pinned on a concrete historical event: Alexander's request for the Athenian contingent of triremes. The exact date of this event — which, as noted above, also provides the *terminus post quem* of the entire speech — is still a matter of conjecture. Only two sources place it more securely in the beginning of 333 B.C. (before the battle of Issus),[4] but they explicitly refer to a subsequent request from the king.[5] The remaining testimonies provide no clues regarding their date,[6] and therefore it can also be pinned on Alexander's preparations for the invasion of Asia (334 B.C.), as plausibly argued by Horváth,[7] or even on one of his earlier campaigns.[8]

The grovelling complaints about Alexander's request for triremes were voiced at the Assembly, most likely the one on which the request itself was under debate. In the end the Athenians resolved to send twenty ships, along with a contingent of ground troops, as mandated by the treaty of Corinth (though perhaps with one significant alteration). But the discussion was far from one-sided. According to pseudo-Plurtarch, the king's message was opposed — unsuccessfully — by Demosthenes and Hyperides. Plutarch himself adds to this that the orators' objections (he does not provide any names) were quashed — in the Council, and not in the Assembly[9] — by Phocion, who reminded them about their and Athens' place in the new world order.[10] Ridiculous and humiliating as it may seem, the protest itself, however, is not nearly as preposterous as the manner of conveying it to the king. To this end, as Hyperides tells us, it was suggested that the Athenians send the state ship, the sacred trireme Paralus, and that — if we accept Horváth's precise dating of the debate — during winter. In other words, the message berating Alexander for sending his demands to

---

[4] Arr. 2.2.3; Curt. 3.1.19; cf. Gehrke 1976, 75–76, who argues that the remaining sources also refer to this request.
[5] Ἡγελόχωι, ὅτωι προσετέτακτο ὑπ' Ἀλεξάνδρου αὖθις ξυναγαγεῖν δύναμιν ναυτικήν (Arr. 2.2.3); *copiis autem praefecit Hegelochum* (Curt. 3.1.19); this request may not have had anything to do with Athens whose contingent (unlike those of other Greek cities) was not disbanded by Alexander; see Diod. 17.22.5; cf. Horváth 2009, 197.
[6] Plut. *Phoc.* 21.1; [Plut.] *Vit. X Orat.* 847c, 848e; [Mor.] 188c; Diod. 17.22.5.
[7] Horváth 2009, 194–196; 2014, 18–20; endorsed by Rhodes 2009, 225.
[8] Roisman – Worthington – Waterfield 2015, 239, 249 link them to Alexander's campaign against the Triballi (336 B.C.).
[9] Cf., however, Rhodes 1972, 46.
[10] Plut. *Phoc.* 21.1; [Mor.] 188c; cf. Gehrke 1976, 75–76.

Athens last was to be considered as one of paramount importance to Athens as a state.¹¹

For all the attention Hyperides lavishes on the absurd details of the motion in question, he seems surprisingly vague when it comes to one important point: its authorship. In earlier scholarship, beginning with the *editio princeps* of the speech, the consensus was: Demades.¹² This is undoubtedly an attractive solution: not only does it provide yet another contemporary piece of evidence as to Demades' political hyperactivity in the 330s, but also it falls in line with the later tradition of his arrogance towards his fellow citizens and flattery towards his Macedonian sponsors.¹³ More recently an alternative understanding of the passage in question has gained traction: the "outrageous behaviour" is pinned not on Demades, but on Diondas himself.¹⁴ Throughout the entire speech he is represented as an overenthusiastic supporter of Macedon, and a person consistently working in the interests of its kings, both in the lawcourts and in the Assembly.¹⁵ Whatever the validity of these accusations, they seem to provide an adequate context for casting Diondas into the role of a parasitic flatterer.¹⁶

Neither grammatical nor stylistic analysis can provide a definite answer to this question, although it seems to me that more can be said in favour of Diondas on these grounds (see appendix). Furthermore, the speech itself seems to provide a hint towards such an attribution, although admittedly in a badly mutilated part of the text. The debate concerning Alexander's request for triremes is also (most likely) mentioned earlier on, where it said that "Diondas is not indignant" about the fact that the Athenians are to send "twice as many triremes... but even proposes (*graphei*)..." (*Dion.* 14). The actual content of his motion is, unfortunately, illegible, but Horváth's suggestion, that it consisted in offering even more forces voluntarily, has much to commend it, as it places this sentence in a clear antithetical relationship with the directly following one. There Diondas is said to be indignant about Athens devoting greater effort than

---

11 Cf. Plut. Mor. 811c (ὥσπερ ἡ Σαλαμινία... καὶ ἡ Πάραλος οὐκ ἐπὶ πᾶν ἔργον, ἀλλ' ἐπὶ τὰς ἀναγκαίας καὶ μεγάλας κατεσπῶντο πράξεις); see also *RE* s.v. Paralos (8) and more recently Bubelis 2010, 393–395.
12 Carey et al. 2008, 18; Horváth 2009, 193–194; Rhodes 2009, 225; de Martinis 2012, 56; Bernhardt 2012, 276; Dmitriev BNJ 227 T 120 (2016).
13 Plut. *Dem.* 31.4 (ἐκολάκευεν αἰσχρῶς); *Phoc.*1.3 (ἀσελγῶς βιώσας); cf. also Polyeuctus F 1.2 Sauppe.
14 Herrman 2009, 179; Brun 2013, 90 n. 20; Horváth 2014, 17–18 (an updated and translated version of Horváth 2009), 159; Liddell 2020, 1.936–7.
15 E.g. *Dion.*7, 11, 25, 27.
16 Cf. καρπούμενο(ς) ὧν ἐνθάδε ὑπὲρ αὑτοῦ ἠγωνίζετο; Dion. 27.

its allies to the war against Philip; here by contrast, he "is not annoyed if for the sake of following others [we provide] twice *as many ships*, but he actually proposes *to offer more voluntarily* [LH]."[17]

Could this particular motion be somehow related to the fawning message to Alexander? We know nothing of the details of this letter. In fact, we do not even know if the "complaint" ever materialized into an actual decree on the basis of which the message would be drafted.[18] The imperfect *elege* (as opposed to the formulaic aorist: *eipe*) may simply denote a proposal that was eventually discarded. In any case, its actual meaning may very well have been entirely different, with Hyperides deliberately misrepresenting it as a specimen of subservient and ridiculous pandering. It would not be the first time he was guilty of such distortion. In a public prosecution speech *Against Philippides*, most likely delivered not long before the defense against Diondas (336–335 B.C.), he attacks a run-of-the-mill motion to praise the *proedroi* of the Council as a specimen of humiliating flattery towards the Macedonian hegemon.[19] That such misrepresentation was a strategy frequently deployed in the Athenian courts is evident also from the speech *On Behalf of Euxenippus*, where the prosecutor accuses the defendant of fawning (*kolakeia*) over Olympias and the Macedonians, because he allowed the queen mother to send a votive offering to an Attic shrine.[20] Thus, for all the absurd detail with which Hyperides furnishes his remark about the complaints to Alexander (and regardless of who the person actually is), the proposal itself in all probability was not nearly as embarrassing and outrageous as he would have us believe.

2 Servitude to Demades?

The remark about servitude (*douleia*) by contrast, seems to have nothing to do with a deliberate attempt to rewrite the recent past. Grammatically couched in a sequence of generalizing subjunctives, it is set up not as a comment on a particular historical event, but an appraisal of contemporary political situation. A

---

17 Horváth 2009, 214, 219–220; 2014, 50, 58.
18 Cf. Liddell 2020, 1.936–937.
19 *Phil.* 1.7 (κολακεύειν), 10 (τὴν πόλιν εἰς τὰς ἐσχάτας αἰσχύνας καθιστάς); it is assumed that the true reason for launching the lawsuit were pro-Macedonian honorific decrees put to the vote by the *proedroi*; see Whitehead 2000, 32.
20 3.19 (κολακείαν), 3.20 (κόλακα) (Jensen); Hyperides may of course be guilty here of undue trivialization of such charges; cf. Worman 2008, 220 and 232 for similar accusations.

negative one, to be sure. Unlike the point about the "outrageous behaviour," it is also explicitly linked to Demades, which however makes it no less difficult to understand, on the level of the text, the syntax and the context. The key phrase *douleian hypagein hypo Demadou* is usually taken to mean "to endure servitude under Demades" (as in the translation quoted above),[21] and therefore to represent the orator as a tyrannical figure who managed to "enslave" the Athenian people. Given what we are told in the first part of this sentence, about Demades' autocratic antics in the Assembly, his use of threats and lackeys to force his way, this seems the only logical inference. And the topsy-turvy topos, with the *dēmos* fearing the displeasure of individuals, which follows it directly, can only serve as its fitting ideological conclusion.

There is of course no denying that throughout the 330s Demades was a politician of considerable stature in Athens. Several sources attest this both directly and indirectly, beginning with the exceptional honours awarded to him (free meals in the Prytaneion and a bronze statue in the agora),[22] most likely after the eponymous peace (338 B.C.) was concluded through his intervention. Plutarch states explicitly that in the aftermath of the destruction of Thebes (335 B.C.) and his second diplomatic success, this time with Alexander, Demades — along with Phocion — was considered the "big man" (*megalos*) in his country.[23] Some time later, during the Harpalus trial (324 B.C.),[24] Dinarchus casually remarks that it is not safe to cross him — and Demosthenes — and applauds the Areopagus council for not caving in to their power (*dynamis*).[25] The sheer number of decrees enacted on the initiative of Demades in these years,[26] along with the aforementioned honours, and offices held (treasurer of the Military Fund) is also a revealing, if indirect, testimony to his political influence.[27]

Demades' ascendancy in the 330s was nevertheless a democratic phenomenon (unlike that after the Lamian War). Thus Hyperides' remark about his ty-

---

[21] See also Demont 2011, 37; Bernhardt 2012, 276; Brun 2013, 87–88; Dmitriev (BNJ 227 T 120); this was also the case with Horváth's earlier contributions (2009, 193).
[22] Dmitriev attempts to discount this piee of information as a later invention; his solution to the fact that it is mentioned in Din. 1.101 is to declare this speech inauthentic as well (2021, 256).
[23] Plut. *Dem.* 24.1.
[24] For which see Worthington in this volume.
[25] Din. 1.7, 11; on the Areopagus and the Harpalus affair see Wallace 1989, 198–202.
[26] For the 330s: seven preserved as epigraphic documents (a list is given in Brun 2000, 177) along with another seven known from literary sources (Liddell 2020, 1.620–676); see also Hansen 1989, 40 and Lambert 2012, 268–271.
[27] For which see Brun 2000, 55–83; cf. also de Falco 1954, 93–95.

rannical dealings with the people cannot be approached otherwise than as a case of glaring misrepresentation. The strongest conclusions from this observation are drawn by Sviatoslav Dmitriev in his monumental BNJ entry on Demades and his recent monograph dedicated to this orator. According to him, the account in *Against Diondas* cannot be reconciled in any possible way with the historical reality of the 330s, and therefore betrays the inauthenticity of the speech (which he takes it to be a later, possibly Hellenistic forgery).[28] Much more plausible is the suggestion of P. Brun: while not denying that Hyperides' account is quite at odds with what the contemporary sources tell us about Demades, he considers it a violent hyperbole, a case of hostile repackaging of the orator's political authority.[29] Turning a champion into a despot was not an unfamiliar trope to the ancient Athenians, and Demades was not the only prominent politician to suffer from this dialectic. In the old days of democracy this was the principle behind the institution of ostracism. The great Pericles was also mocked as a tyrant by Cratinus (*PCG* 258). In later times we find a similar "repackaging" of Demosthenes' policy — with striking similarities to the Hyperidean passage — by his political and personal enemy Aeschines (Aesch. 3.145–146):

> He fashioned for himself a tyranny (*dynasteian*) of such a sort that when going up to the speaker's platform he said that he will go on an embassy wherever he deems it fit, even if you will not send it. As he enslaves (*katadouloumenos*) all the magistrates and thus accustoms them never to oppose him, if one of the generals did speak against him, he said he would make a challenge (*diadikasian*) for the speaker's platform against the generals' office over who had the better claim.

Aeschines is, in fact, much more precise in misrepresenting his opponent as a despot than Hyperides. Which has nothing to do with the latter's style or argument, but with the poor state of the text of the relevant passage. Even the phrase "endure servitude" (*douleian hypagein*) itself is nothing but a conjecture based on traces of single letters (most notably delta and gamma). It also raises objections when it comes to semantics, as the sense "endure" is nowhere attested for

---

28 He argues that Demades at that time was recognized "a partisan of his city and of democracy, which was incompatible with slavery and tyranny," and suggests that this reference is influenced by the later tradition stemming from the period after the Lamian war when democracy in Athens was abolished, and Demades (along with Phocion) became the de facto ruler of the city (BNJ 227 T 120, comm.); cf. Dmitriev 2021, 238–250.
29 Brun 2013, 87–88; cf. Horváth 2014, 158 (sardonischer Hohn).

hypagein.³⁰ One might suggest the meaning "undergo," but this would still require a passive form of the verb, and preferably accompanied by a preposition (e.g. *eis douleian hypagesthai*). Furthermore, the assumption — shared by most recent studies — that the servitude here should be understood as Demades' tyranny can also be legitimately questioned. In ancient Greek as we know it, the clause *hypo Dēmadou* is highly unlikely to mean "under Demades". Only rarely does the preposition *hypo* take the genitive to signify a purely spatial relationship of being "under," and never to denote subjection.³¹ The latter sense, by contrast, is regularly expressed with the dative. In this light, a much more plausible understanding of *hypo Dēmadou* is "through the agency of Demades" or "by Demades," which has been adopted in the more recent edition of *Against Diondas* by Horváth.³² In other words, the servitude mentioned in the speech is not tantamount to subjection to Demades: he is presented only as an agent of its infliction. In whose interest? Who will the Athenians be enslaved to as a result of Demades' antics in the Assembly? Without committing themselves to an answer, Horváth and Maehler seem to imply that the subjugation in question is nothing more than a general idea opposed to democratic freedom. In other words, it is still nothing more than a sweeping comment on the state of Athenian politics, as noted in the beginning of this section, and not a remark stemming from Hyperides' attempt to rewrite the recent past. In the following section, however, I explore a different possible understanding of this passage.

3 Demades and Alexander?

While the recasting of Demades as a tyrant in *Against Diondas* may be legitimately questioned, the distorted picture of Athenian policy-making which Hyperides paints is quite securely grounded both in terms of text and of grammar. We are told that Demades forces his way in the Assembly by blackmailing the people. What he threatens the Athenians with is own departure from the city

---

30 Carey et al. 2008, 18 rightly note that ὑπέχειν (suggested by E. Handley) instead of ὑπάγειν would be a much better alternative; unfortunately gamma is one of the few letters in this place discernible even to the untrained eye.
31 ὑπό with the genitive to denote spatial relationship ("under"): *LSJ* s.v. A I.2 (note "the Orators have only ὑ[πὸ] μάλης" as in Lys. F 87 (Carey); with the dative, to denote spatial relationship: *LSJ* s.v. B I; to denote subjection: B II.2.
32 "[I]hr *mit Demades' Hilfe* [JK] die Knechtschaft werdet einführen können" Maehler in Horváth 2014, 86, cf. ibid. 158.

(the passage is fairly well preserved in the palimpsest and legible even to the untrained eye). This remark is probably the most surprising one among Hyperides' recriminations. The Demades emerging from it, far from being a despot, is actually presented as a politician whose presence and services are considered by the people as essential for the well-being of the city, which would rank him among other outstanding political figures whose help was actively coveted in periods of crises such as Pericles, Alcibiades, and Demosthenes.[33]

There can be little doubt that the primary qualities which made Demades into a politician of fundamental importance to the Athenians at that time were his relations with the Macedonians. This is what the later tradition tells us,[34] and what his contemporaries — perhaps grudgingly — acknowledge.[35] Such is the context in which, I believe, Hyperides' account of Demades' blackmail should be approached. Although the orator seeks to present it as a generic example illustrating the lamentable state of Athenian politics, it is hardly conceivable that Demades, despite his popularity throughout the 330s, would have had the leverage to use such threats in any matter other than a diplomatic crisis with Macedon. In other words, despite the generalizing tone of Hyperides' account, this particular detail must be pinned on one such episode. By 334 B.C. Athens had already witnessed three critical situations of this kind: the first, after the battle of Chaeronea (338 B.C.), the second, after Philip's death and Alexander's accession to the throne (336 B.C.), and the third, after the destruction of Thebes (335 B.C.).[36]

After Chaeronea the Athenians expected an imminent attack on their city followed by a siege and a possible destruction, testimony to which are the emergency measures passed by Hyperides and Lycurgus.[37] Instead Philip (who had no such intentions to begin with) sent Demades with a reassuring message followed soon by a very generous peace offer and a release of all Athenian prisoners of war.[38] For the Athenians this was undoubtedly an "unexpected deliver-

---

[33] Pericles: Plut. *Per.* 37.1–2 (cf. Thuc. 2.65.4); Alcibiades: Plut. *Alc.* 32.1–3 (cf. Xen. *Hell.* 1.4.18–19) with Kapellos 2019, 39–65; Demosthenes: Plut. *Dem.* 27.6–8; Demades' services were again solicited by the Athenians after the defeat in the Lamian war; cf. Diod. 18.18.1–2 (BNJ 227 T 49); Plut. *Phoc.* 26.3.
[34] Plut. *Phoc.* 1.1; Arr. 1.10.3; cf. also Diod. 18.48.1 — this testimony however refers to the last year of Demades' career (319 B.C.).
[35] As Polyeuctus (F 1.1 Sauppe).
[36] Cf. Squillace 2003, 760.
[37] Lyc. 1.41; [Plut.] *Vit. X Orat.* 849a; [Dem.] 26.11; see also Hyp. *Dion.* 28; cf. Cooper in this volume and Kucharski 2017.
[38] Polyb. 5.10.4; 22.16.2; Diod. 16.87.3; Iust. 9.4.4.

ance", as Aeschines puts it (3.159), and therefore there seems to have been little ground for disagreement when it came to ratifying the peace treaty in the Assembly.[39] Two years later, after Philip's death, when the young Alexander made his way south to reassert his authority, Athens (among several other states) sent a delegation to the king with an apology for not recognizing his hegemony quickly enough.[40] Trouble was already brewing in Greece, and therefore the apology was well judged, but the lack of any further details regarding its drafting makes it impossible to consider this event reliably as the basis for Hyperides' recriminations.[41] When it comes to the situation after the destruction of Thebes, the sources are much more generous. As the Greek world witnessed in horror the annihilation of one of its most important and most powerful states, the other cities supporting the anti-Macedonian rebellion, Athens included, quickly lost heart. An embassy was sent to Alexander, probably on Demades' motion, with grovelling congratulations for punishing Thebes. The king, however, was not impressed: he demanded the extradition of several leading politicians and generals, including Demosthenes, Charidemus, Lycurgus and Polyeuctus of Sphettos. The king's ultimatum was brought back to Athens, and during the Assembly which followed, among much bickering, Demades proposed a skilfully written decree authorizing yet another delegation to the young king, with a promise that the persons previously requested by him would be duly punished in Athens.[42] The embassy was successful, largely owing to Demades' rhetorical skills: Alexander remained adamant only about Charidemus, who went into exile.

Of these three diplomatic crises with Macedon, the last is therefore the most likely candidate as the basis for Hyperides' invective. This identification has been already suggested by Horváth, who compares the passage in *Against Diondas* to Diodorus' extended account of the Assembly debate on Alexander's ultimatum.[43] I do remain somewhat skeptical about certain conclusions drawn from this comparison, for instance the suggestion that the comprehensive de-

---

39 Plutarch *Phoc.* 16.4 reports an objection by Phocion; cf. Tritle 1988, 114, but see Will 1983, 14.
40 It is possible that Demades was part of this embassy, cf. [Demades] *On the Twelve* 14; see also Brun 2000, 72; Engels 1993, 157; Hansen 1974, 39 (not mentioned in Hansen 1989, 40).
41 Will (1983, 36) asserts that the decree was supported by the anti-Macedonians as well, which he probably concludes from Demosthenes' (initial) presence among the ambassadors sent to Alexander; cf. Aesch. 3.161; Diod. 17.4.7; Plut. *Dem.* 23.3 (who confuses this embassy with the one in 335 B.C.).
42 Diod. 17.15.4 (περιεῖχε γὰρ [τὸ ψήφισμα] ... ἐπαγγελίαν τοῦ κολάζειν κατὰ τοὺς νόμους); cf. Sch. Aesch. 3.159; see also Marzi 1991, 70–83.
43 Horváth 2009, 192, 193; endorsed by Rhodes 2009, 225; cf. Diod. 17.15.3–4.

scription in the *Historical Library* depends on Hyperides' brief and passing remark. As noted above, I believe the orator's goal is not to present one particular event in crisp historical detail, but a more general example highlighting the problem with Athenian politics. The blackmailing episode itself, however, seems viable only under a very particular set of circumstances, and these circumstances have been ingeniously – and to my mind, rightly – pinned by Horváth on the fateful debate after the destruction of Thebes.

And what of the servitude encroaching upon Athens? If indeed what Hyperides says about Demades can be linked to the tough negotiations in the Assembly which followed Alexander's ultimatum, his rational, perhaps cynical propositions, like the provision about punishing the persons on the extradition list, could easily be misrepresented as acts of humiliating subjection. And, as a result, the person behind them could easily be cast into the unenviable role of the agent of encroaching servitude. Which, incidentally, is precisely the meaning stipulated by the syntax of that difficult passage. This would make *Against Diondas* into yet another of the few contemporary sources where Demades is (mis)represented as a traitor working in the interests of Macedon. Given that an extended list of such "traitors" in other Greek cities is mentioned in the directly preceding chapter of the speech,[44] it might seem only fitting that the pride of place, Athens itself, goes to the politician who devoted his political skill and influence to maintaining proper relations with the powerful and dangerous hegemon from the north.

4 Conclusion

Athenian rhetoric always had an uneasy relationship with history.[45] The more recent the past, the more violent the distortions to which it was subject at the hands of the orators. This applied in particular to periods of crisis, such as the 330s in Athens, when the city faced not only existential threats but also the daunting task of re-defining itself and its role in a completely new world order. In those times, to travesty the haunting ruminations of Thucydides, prudence was easily misconstrued as treachery, and rational appeasement as debased fawning. Such is the spirit behind Hyperides' casual remarks about Demades in the recently deciphered fragments of *Against Diondas*. The poor state of the

---

44 *Dion.* 21; cf. Dem. 18.295 for a similar list.
45 See Kapellos' Introduction to this volume.

preserved text precludes certainty on a number of issues that were the subject of this discussion. Demades may have been made into an outrageous flatterer, although I have argued that Diondas could be the more likely candidate for this unenviable role. His undeniable influence over Athenian politics in the 330s was an easy target of distortion into tyrannical aspirations, although I have suggested that catchword "servitude" might also refer to Athens' subjection to Macedon. He may indeed have frequently forced his way during the meetings of the Assembly, although the key detail of his antics seems to belong to one particular and fateful debate. What is certain is that Hyperides places him at the heart of what he sees as the nadir of Athenian politics. To be sure, Demades himself was more than capable of countering such manipulations with even more violent distortions of his own. Had he only chosen to publish his work, the subsequent tradition might have been more favourable towards him. As it turned out, however, history was on the side of Hyperides, as it always is — on that whose voices are better heard.

5 Appendix: who is the "he" in "his outrageous behaviour" (*aselgeias autou*)?

Demades. It is more natural to refer the pronoun "his" (*autou*) to the last person mentioned before, i.e. Demades. Moreover, the particle *gar* used in the opening of this sentence seems to bind it causally with the preceding one. Finally, a more suitable pronoun referring to Diondas, i.e. Hyperides' opponent, would be a deictic one, perhaps even with the added emphasis: *toutoui*.[46]

Diondas. It should be noted that Demades is mentioned in the speech only as a case in point within a larger argument about the lamentable political situation in Athens. This argument begins with Hyperides' complaints about the "city's situation" (22), and seems to find a fitting conclusion in the topsy-turvy topos about the *dēmos* fearing the disapproval of individuals (24). After this a new topic should be expected, one no longer dealing with Demades. Indeed, the next four chapters (25–28) are explicitly focused on Diondas, which may suggest that "his outrageous behaviour" proleptically refers to him as well. Furthermore, the phrase opening this lengthy invective "or again (*ē palin*) whenever Diondas puffs himself up" (25), is clearly positioned in parallel relationship with

---

[46] I owe both these observations to Gunther Martin.

a preceding thought,[47] which is most likely the remark about the kowtowing complaints. If so, both should have Diondas as a subject — or else the expected analogy breaks down.[48] Ascribing them to Demades on the other hand, requires the correspondence to be found somewhere else. In the *editio princeps* it is suggested that it hinges on the idea expressed in "who would not be pained" (22), which, as a result, must be understood in the "or again" clause. But while the point made about Demades having his way in the Assembly (22) does indeed provide a good reason for distress, the one about Diondas does so much less. Here we are simply told about his boasts concerning his fifty prosecutions, which are quickly and in an almost comic manner dismissed as empty fanfaronade (25). To be sure, sykophantic abuse of the lawcourts can still be considered a reason for distress. But such an accusation fits much better the character assassination of Diondas, which follows it directly, than the reflection on the lamentable state of Athenian politics.

Bibliography

Bernhardt, J. (2012), "Rhetorische Strategie und politischer Standpunkt bei Hypereides", *Hermes* 140.3, 263–293.
Brun, P. (2000), *L'orateur Démade. Essai d'histoire et d'historiographie*, Bordeaux.
Brun, P. (2013), "Y avait-il des anti-Macédoniens à Athènes entre 338 et 323 ? A propos d'un nouveau fragment d'Hypéride Contre Diondas", *ZPE* 187, 87–92.
Bubelis, W.S. (2010), "The Sacred Triremes and Their Tamiai at Athens", *Historia* 59, 385–411.
Carey, C., *et al.* (2008), "Fragments of Hyperides' *Against Diondas* from the Archimedes Palimpsest", *ZPE* 165, 1–19.
De Falco, V. (1954), *Demade oratore. Testimonianze e frammenti*, Napoli.
De Martinis, L. (2012), "I democratici ateniesi dopo Cheronea alla luce del nuovo Iperide", *Aevum* 86.1, 40–62.
Demont, P. (2011), "Les nouveaux fragments d'Hypéride", *REG* 124.1, 21–45.
Dmitriev, S. (2015), *Brill's New Jacoby* 227: Demades (https://referenceworks.brillonline.com/entries/brill-s-new-jacoby/demades-of-athens-227-a227).
Dmitriev, S. (2021), *The Orator Demades: Classical Greece Reimagined through Rhetoric*, Berlin.
Engels, J. (1993²), *Studien zur politischen Biographie des Hypereides. Athen in der Epoche der lykurgischen Reformen und des makedonischen Universalreiches*, München.

---

47 As in Aesch. 1.162; Din. 1.43; cf. *LSJ* s.v. III.
48 As in: "other examples of [Demades'] insolence I will omit (...) or again whenever Diondas puffs himself up;" the two clauses here are logically disconnected and cannot be understood in an antithetical relationship.

Gallo, L. (2019), "Allies and Foes (II): Politicians without Transmitted Speeches", in: G. Martin (ed.), *The Oxford Handbook of Demosthenes*, Oxford, 351–362.
Gehrke, H.-J. (1976), *Phokion. Studien zur Erfassung seiner historsichen Gestalt*, München.
Hansen, M.H. (1974), *The Sovereignty of the People's Court in Athens in the Fourth Century B.C. and the Public Action against Unconstitutional Proposals*, Odense.
Herrman, J. (2009), "Hyperides' *Against Diondas* and the Rhetoric of Revolt", *BICS* 52, 175–185.
Horváth, L. (2009), "Hyperidea", *BICS* 52, 187–222.
Horváth, L. (2014), *Der Neue Hyperides. Textedition, Studien und Erläuterungen*, Berlin.
Kapellos, A. (2019), *Xenophon's Peloponnesian War*, Berlin.
Kucharski, J. (2017), "Hyperides' Hypophora. Against Diondas 28 (174r 21–32): A Suggestion," *ZPE* 203, 56–64.
Lambert, S. (2012), *Inscribed Athenian Laws and Decrees*, Leiden.
Liddel, P. (2020), *Decrees of Fourth-Century Athens (403/2–322/1 BC)*, V. 1–2, Cambridge.
Marzi, M. (1991) "Demade politico e oratore", *Atene e Roma* 36.2–3, 70–83.
Mitchel, F.W. (1970), *Lykourgan Athens: 338–322*, Cincinnati.
Rhodes, P.J. (1972), *The Athenian Boule*, Oxford.
Rhodes, P.J. (2009), "Hyperides' Against Diondas: Two Problems", *BICS* 52, 223–228.
Roisman, J./Worthington, I./Waterfield, R. (2015), *Lives of the Attic Orators. Texts from Pseudo-Plutarch, Photius and the Suda*, Oxford.
Squillace, G. (2003), "La figura di Demade nella vita politica ateniese tra realtà e invenzione", *MedAnt* 6.2, 751–764.
Tritle, L.A. (1988), *Phocion the Good*, London.
Wallace, R.W. (1989), *The Areopagos Council to 307 B.C.*, Baltimore.
Whitehead, D. (2000), *Hyperides. Forensic Speeches*, Oxford.
Will, W. (1983), *Athen und Alexander. Untersuchungen zur Geschichte der Stadt von 338 bis 322 v.Chr*, München.
Williams, J.M. (1989), "Demades' Last Years, 323/2–319/8: A 'Revisionist' Interpretation", *AncW* 19, 19–30.
Worman, N. (2008), *Abusive Mouths in Classical Athens*, Cambridge.

Zhichao Wang
Hegesippus and his Treatment of the Recent Past

Abstract: As an orator with an anti-Macedonian stance, Hegesippus' speech tended to use the recent past as an argument, but he showed a tendency to distort, invent, and interpret facts in a way that favored Athens. But, when compared with Demosthenes, Hegesippus' interpretation of the recent past tends to be factual, and rarely rises to the general principle; his attack on Philip was intended only to prove that Philip was dishonest, not to portray him as a tyrant; his use of the recent past and his attacks on Philip seem to be confined to words rather than the call to action.

Hegesippus of Sunnion, born into a wealthy family around 400 B.C., was an active Athenian politician in the fourth century.[1] His career in public affairs extended from the 360s to the 320s, but its apex was in the 340s. From the sources available, we know six decrees that were proposed by Hegesippus[2] or thirteen deeds that are connected with him.[3] Records show that Hegesippus appeared early on in the guise of a passionate Athenian patriot, but it is difficult to know when he began to take an anti-Macedonian stand. However, it is certain that in 346 B.C. he was one of the leading men who firmly opposed the signing of the Peace of Philocrates. Presumably, his anti-Macedonian stance will have

---

I am grateful to Dr. Aggelos Kapellos, Prof. Ian Worthington, Prof. P.J. Rhodes, Prof. Gunther Martin, Prof. D.F. McCabe, Dr. Daniel Bajnok and Dr. Janek Kucharski for their valuable help. For the Attic oratory, the texts I am using are all Texas translations.

---

1 Life and political careers: Ian Worthington and John Davies have endeavoured to collect literary sources and inscriptions to benefit our research (Roisman, Worthington and Waterfield 2015, 36–37; Worthington 2013, 96, 170, 192, 198, 211–212; Davies 1971, 209–210; Davies 2011, 11–23; Gallo 2018, 7–22).
2 Hansen 1989, 47.
3 Davies 2011, 19–20.

been formed earlier, but not later, than Demosthenes'. However, the only text he left was *On Halonnesus*, which was included in the corpus of Demosthenes.[4]

Two pieces of evidence enable most modern scholars to achieve a consensus on its authorship: the speaker claimed he had prosecuted a man named Callippus (7.43),[5] and the speaker said he was one of the ambassadors to Philip in 343 (7.2).[6] McCabe analysed the prose rhythm of the speech and demonstrated that it is not the work of Demosthenes.[7] As far as Hegesippus' political affiliation was concerned, he was a radical anti-Macedonian politician and probably an ally of Demosthenes.[8] Demosthenes also participated in the debate of Halonnesus[9] and opposed the acceptance of Philip's offer.[10] However, this speech has not survived, and Hegesippus' speech was mistaken for that of Demosthenes. In this case, we can study how Hegesippus treated the recent past in this speech, which helps us understand the Attic orators' approach to the recent past.[11] Moreover, by comparing how Hegesippus and Demosthenes dealt with the re-

---

4 It means I have accepted the point that was debated in antiquity, namely, Hegesippus, not Demosthenes, is the author of *On Halonnesus*. For ancient debate about the author, see Dion. Hal. *Demosth*.13; Libanius *Hypothesis* to Demosthenes 7. Furthermore, Milns 2000, 205 suggests that Hegesippus may also have been the author of Dem. 17, but Herrman 2009, 180–183 suggests that the author of Dem. 17 was Hyperides.
5 Libanius said the prosecutor is Hegesippus, not Demosthenes.
6 MacDowell 2009, 344 noted that, according to Dem. 19.331, Demosthenes was not in that embassy.
7 McCabe 1981, 186–199. Moreover, the ending of the speech in *On Halonnesus* was very famous for its vulgarity (Dem. 7.45). This impressive ending was regarded by Libanius as proof of Hegesippus' style.
8 Davies 2011, 15 thinks Hegesippus is 'a man whose agenda, even in the 340s and 330s, was the re-creation and defence of the fifth-century Empire and the full works, too, not just the renewed "League" which Aristoteles and Callistratus had pushed to the limits of prudence in the 370s and 360s'.
9 Halonnesus is a small island off the coast of Thessaly between the two islands of Lemnos and Scyros, but it is debatable whether ancient Halonnesus is the same as the island now called Halonnesus (MacDowell 2009, 343 n. 1).
10 Aesch. 3.93; Hammond and Griffith 1979, 510–516; Worthington 2013, 211–212.
11 On the Attic orators' treatment of the past, Pearson 1941 analysed their historical allusions and thought they respected the prejudices and sensitivity of their audiences but not the truth; Perlman 1961 claimed that the Attic orators used historical examples as political propaganda and 'they are primarily an expression of contemporary history and also of the political opinions of the orators and their audience brought up the real effect'; Milns 1995 investigated the historical paradigms in Demosthenes' public speeches and concluded that the number of historical events used paradigmatically is fairly limited; Westwood 2018 examines how versions of the past, particularly the Athenian past, figure and are deployed rhetorically in the public part of Demosthenes' texts.

cent past, this may, in turn, provide circumstantial support for denying that Demosthenes is the author of *On Halonnesus* as well as helping us better understand their widely different styles.¹² This chapter will provide an analysis of Hegesippus' speech and his treatment of the treaty with Philip, and the last section of the chapter will compare Demosthenes' speeches with Hegesippus'.

1 Hegesippus' partiality to the recent past

Unlike modern people, the ancient Greeks paid enough attention to the past to show that they thought it helped solve problems of the present. In van Groningen's words, the Greeks were in the 'grip of the past'.¹³ By the fourth century B.C., the Athenians seemed more inclined to use recent past or contemporary events for persuasion. In the Assembly and courtroom, Attic orators of the fourth century seldom mentioned distant history. When they needed to refer to the past to increase their cogency, most of what they mentioned were historical events that occurred in the last 20 years.¹⁴ Hegesippus is not an exception.

At the beginning of this speech, Hegesippus highlights the starting point of the whole discussion, namely, Philip's letter. In his letter, Philip answered the Athenians' complaints and made two proposals: first, he would give the island of Halonnesus to the Athenians; second, Athens should establish a bilateral judicial agreement with Macedonia and take joint action to suppress piracy in the Aegean Sea.¹⁵ These two proposals, among other issues, angered Hegesippus and prompted him to respond, which means that Hegesippus tells the audience to focus on a recent letter and a speech.¹⁶ In the following discussion, and in addition to the letter mentioned at the beginning of this speech, Hegesippus

---

12 Westwood 2018a, 186 mentions the advantages of comparing Demosthenes with Hegesippus but does not go into detail on this point ('may be an extreme, but at the same time instructive, way to close').
13 van Groningen 1953.
14 On the definition of 'recent past', see Kapellos' Introduction in this volume.
15 This letter is not the one preserved in Dem. 12, which dates to 340 B.C. These two points are summed up by Hegesippus' accusation. On the use of letters by Attic orators, see Ceccarelli 2013, 83–104 and Sickinger 2013, 125–140.
16 The speech is dated by Dionysius of Halicarnassus to 343/2, see *First Letter to Ammaeus* 10. Trevett 2011, 114 claims it probably belongs in the first half of 342.

also mentions Philip's invasion of Potidaea (7.10),[17] Philip's ambassadors to Athens, led by Python of Byzantium, to negotiate for the revision of the Peace of Philocrates (7.18–23),[18] another letter from Philip (7.27),[19] Philip's invasion of Ambracia and Cassopia (7.32)[20] and Philip's gift of the land of Chersonese to the Cardians (7.39). His point is that Philip supported the Cardians to encroach on land that belonged to Athens, but it is difficult to judge which side the land belonged to.[21] When Hegesippus spoke in the Assembly, these events had taken place some months previously and, without doubt, belonged to the recent past. These events serve the same purpose: to show Philip's cunning, impudence and deceit. Only in one place does Hegesippus feel a need to strengthen his case by evoking a historical episode that is a little more distant: 'The Macedonians have no need of judicial agreements with the Athenians, as history shows: for neither Amyntas, the father of Philip, nor the other kings ever made judicial agreements with our city' (7.11). Still, this is a special case, and Hegesippus rarely mentions the distant past.

In their public speeches on territorial disputes, the orators used to justify ownership of a piece of land, a city or a temple by referring to quite distant history and even mythical events to enhance the historical legitimacy of such own-

---

17 After a considerable siege in the summer of 356, Philip captured Potidaea, sold the Potidaeans as slaves and handed over the city to the Olynthians: Diod. 16.8.5; Plut. *Alex.* 3.8. See also Hammond and Griffith 1979, 246–247 and Worthington 2013, 64–65.

18 Except for Hegesippus' speech, some other sources refer to Python of Byzantium and his embassy to Athens in 343 B.C.: Dem. 18.136; Plut. *Dem.* 9 (Cawkwell 1963, 123–126). Some sources refer to Philip's sending an embassy to Athens to renegotiate some terms of the Peace of Philocrates with which the Athenians were not satisfied: Dem. 12.18; Libanius, *Hypothesis* to Demosthenes 6; *Didymus: On Demosthenes*, col. 8.8.

19 In 357 B.C., when Philip was besieging Amphipolis, he sent a secret letter to the Athenians offering to give it to Athens in exchange for Athens' support. The Athenian ambassadors proposed giving the nearby city, Pydna, to Philip in return for Amphipolis (Brill's New Jacoby, 76F4; Dem. 2.6; Diod. 16.8.3). For detailed discussion of this secret, see Hammond and Griffith 1979, 238–244; Cawkwell 1978, 73–75; Worthington 2008, 41; de Ste. Croix 1963, 110–119.

20 In the summer of 342 B.C., Philip led his forces against Molossia and Cassopia (near to Ambracia), drove out the King of Molossia, Arrybas, (who fled to Athens), and attacked four independent cities that were colonies of Elis (Justin 8.6.4–18; Diod. 16.72; Theopomp. BNJ 115F 284; Hammond 1994, 120–122). However, it is debatable whether or not Philip attacked the Ambracians: Cawkwell (1978, 116) claimed 'nothing happened to Ambracia. Philip clearly had no intention of attacking it', but Hammond and Griffith 1979, 508–509 think Philip intended to conquer Ambracia and retreated because he was not prepared to engage in a general war.

21 After Philip's return to Macedon, the Thracian campaign had begun by the end of June in 343 B.C. (Diod. 16.71 and 74, Dem. 8.14 and 35). Also, see Hammond 1994, 122–125; Cawkwell 1978, 116; Worthington 2008, 122–125.

ership or claim.²² For example, when Aeschines went to Philip as ambassador in 346 B.C. to defend the Athenian claim to Amphipolis, he argued that Athens should have ownership of Amphipolis because Acamas, one of Theseus' sons, received the city as a dowry for his marriage to the Thracian princess Phyllis.²³ Thus, if he had followed the general habit of the Attic orators when Hegesippus referred to diplomatic affairs (7.9–13), like the ownership of Potidaea, which was now possessed by Philip, he should have appealed to a more distant history or an illusory myth as an argument that, along with other arguments, would have constructed complete historical justification. However, Hegesippus did not invoke any myth or the distant past but took a legalist line of argument, like a lawyer.²⁴ He mentioned Philip's father and other Macedonian kings to prove that Athens had never entered into a judicial agreement with Macedonia in an attempt to prove that Athens would never bargain with the Macedonians over the sovereignty of Potidaea. After all, Philip's father lived at a time that was more recent than the distant past.²⁵

Why did Hegesippus not, like the other orators, use ancient examples or myths to increase his power of persuasion when expressing territorial claims in diplomatic negotiations? In other words, why did he prefer the argumentative value of the recent past? I think there are two reasons.

First, most of the Attic orators in the fourth century, including Hegesippus, were more likely to use the recent past as a more convincing and safer example than distant history or mythical events when addressing the Assembly and courts. Taking into account the peculiarities of speaking at such a public Assembly, the orator needed to give examples that were known and familiar to the audience rather than examples that were unfamiliar and incomprehensible to them. For example, 'Very good, but these events are ancient and long past. As for events that you have all seen, you know that recently you...' (Dem. 22.14); 'I will remind you of one incident from the distant past that all of you know better than I do' (Dem. 22.15).²⁶ As we can see from this citation, familiarity is the key to

---

22 For related discussions, especially on the use of myth in diplomatic negotiations see Perlman 1961, 159 and Parker 1996, 223–235.
23 Aesch. 2.31.
24 Schaefer 1886, 439 said the Dem. 7 speech has the character of an advocate's argument rather than a statesman's oration.
25 Amyntas III was King of Macedonia from ca. 393 to 370 B.C. For Amyntas III, see Hammond and Griffith 1979, 172–180; Errington 1990, 29–35; Worthington 2008, 223–224. For his alliance with Athens see Tod 1948, no. 129.
26 As Prof. Gunther Martin privately has pointed out to me, there is a difference between public speeches, forensic speeches and funeral speeches when it comes to dealing with the

illustrating a problem with historical examples. This was also summed up by an ancient rhetorician: 'One has to take the paradigms that belong to the topic itself and are as close as possible to the audience regarding time and place; if such are missing, then the grandest and best known of the others'.[27] As a result, it is understandable that orators tend to refer apologetically to the distant past or ancient history, even going so far as to exclude mythological events.[28] Clearly, Hegesippus followed this tradition. For him, a speech on a topic that was familiar to the audience not only made a valid argument but also avoided arousing the audience's resentment against an educated elite man who always referred to events or figures from the remote past that were not familiar to them.[29]

Second, Hegesippus was a more radical anti-Macedonian politician than Demosthenes, and his nickname, Krobylos[30] (top-knot or hair bun), reflects his relatively fierce character (and, perhaps, stance).[31] His objective in this speech was to refute every word of Philip and his ambassador, Python of Byzantium. On the one hand, the style of the speech was methodical, trivial and delicate, and on the other hand, very violent and vulgar. To make his point, he had to capture the mood of the audience and gradually excite them by concentrating on Philip's letter and his ambassador, not by giving the audience a moment's hesitation, but by following his train of thought closely so that analysis and discussion of the recent past were preferable to those of the distant past or obscure myths. But how does Hegesippus present the recent past when he prefers to make use of it as a valuable argument?

---

distant past. The former is even more strict in their handling of the distant past. However, in the case of Demosthenes' *Against Androtion*, although it is a speech in court, it is well known that it has a strong political background that deals with a subject that is not purely private, so I think its handling of the past, when it needs to cite history, supports the point made in this paragraph. On the different standards in different oratorical genres, see also Westwood 2020, 38–58.

27 Anaximenes, *Ars rhetorica*, 32.3.
28 Isoc. 3.26; 4.28; 5.42; Din. 1.37. See Grethlein 2014, 329–330 and Kapellos' Introduction in this volume.
29 Ober 1989, 179, 181.
30 Aesch. 1.64.
31 For similar views see Davies 2011, 14–15.

2 Hegesippus' distortion of the recent past

In the fourth century B.C. the Athenians believed that more recent events were closely related to the present. In *Archidamus*, Isocrates expressed negative views of mythical events: 'Perhaps I would seem to be discussing ancient events (ἀρχαῖα) and speaking far from the present circumstances'.[32] Moreover, in *Panegyricus*, when he mentioned the myth of Demeter who gave the gifts of corn and Eleusinian Mysteries to the Athenians, Isocrates anticipated that the audience might find Demeter's story too old to be believed: 'for because many have told and all have heard the story which describes them, it is reasonable to regard this not, to be sure, as recent (καινά), yet as worthy of our faith'.[33] Presenting and explaining the recent past to a public gathering of thousands was an important skill for an orator, a skill that reflected an orator's character, style, political stance and political status. Hegesippus' treatment of the recent past represents the radical style of some Athenian politicians, that is, with less attention to the logic and grace of persuasion, whose main purpose is to pander to and stir up the emotions of the Assembly.[34] For this purpose, he presents the recent past with varying degrees of distortion.

First, whenever circumstances required, he would deliberately muddle the facts and explain the recent past in Athens' favour. At the beginning of the speech, when pointing out the subject (Philip's letter and his messenger's speeches), Hegesippus immediately accused Philip of making a ridiculous offer to Athens to **give** it the island of Halonnesus, which had been seized by pirates. Why is it ridiculous? The first reason, he explained, was that the island originally belonged to Athens, and the second was that Philip wanted to humiliate Athens by the act of **giving**. 'He insists on this term not to gain credit for doing you a favour, since it would be a ridiculous favour, but to demonstrate to all of Greece that the Athenians are happy to receive places on the coast from the hands of a Macedonian' (7.6). Philip wanted to **return** or **give** a small island that was not controlled by Athens to Athens, which could be regarded as goodwill shown by Philip after cracks had already appeared in the Peace of Philocra-

---

32 Isocr. 6.42.
33 Isocr. 4.30.
34 In the *Hellenica*, Xenophon represented Lyciscus as a politician who was in line with Theramenes, intimidated those who intended to defend the generals of Arginousai and urged the assemblymen to regard the supporters of the generals as supporters of the conspiracy against the democracy (1.7.13). The main task of these politicians was to create uproar to support their leader politician (see Kapellos 2019, 172–173).

tes. However, Hegesippus, on the one hand, emphasised major differences between **return** and **give**, and on the other hand, judged the motive of Philip's offer as a malicious move.³⁵

Under such a premise, Hegesippus vaguely explained the proposal for arbitration in Philip's letter. 'Whenever he says that he wishes to submit these matters to arbitration, he is simply mocking you ... if you follow this policy, how will it not amount to an admission on your part that you have abandoned the entire mainland of Greece ... if indeed you do not fight for the places on the sea, where you claim to be strong, but go to law instead?' (7.7–8). However, Philip's proposal did not go beyond the common practice of the city-state world in ancient Greece of settling disputes between two city-states by agreeing to invite a third party to arbitrate.³⁶ Hegesippus goes on to say that if the Athenians and Philip had reached a judicial agreement, the agreement would be valid not when it was ratified by an Athenian court, as Athenian law prescribed, but only when it was taken back to Philip.³⁷ According to current research, the judicial agreements signed between the ancient Greek city-states were mainly to provide a legal basis for citizens of one city to sue and be tried in the courts of another city. This right was mutual, not unilateral.³⁸ Therefore, we do not know the exact point of Hegesippus' accusation here. However, it is possible that Hegesippus maliciously and unfairly suggested that the *symbola* would not be ratified in Athens and that Athens would be at the mercy of judgements in Macedon,

---

35 Brun 2015, 192 discusses the problem of 'give' (*donner*) and 'return' (*restituer*) and notes that its background is the Athenians' hope for cities like Amphipolis that had been captured by Philip.

36 In ancient Greece, the use of third-party arbitration to settle disputes between countries originated in the Ionian region in sixth century B.C. This practice continued into the fifth and fourth centuries B.C. (Westermann 1907, 197–201; Low 2007, 105–108; Magnetto 2016, 192–215).

37 Dem. 7.9. In the mid-fifth century B.C., with the formation of the Athenian empire, many cases belonging to the subject states were brought before the Athenian courts. By the middle of the fourth century B.C., although the Athenian empire had ceased to exist, Athens created maritime legal procedures to protect commerce at sea, resulting in most Aegean trade disputes going to Athenian courts for justice. This is the context in which Hegesippus speaks, and it has to be said, in a definite Atheno-centric context (Lanni 2006, 17, 150–155; MacDowell 1978, 220–234).

38 The fact that the anti-Macedonian group, represented by Demosthenes, had so many false reports about Philip and the Macedonian kingdom, and was increasingly able to win the support of the citizens' assembly, seemed to prove that Athenians' knowledge of the Macedonian system of government remained at the level of hearsay, so the orators could play with this and be persuasive. On justice in Macedonia in the fourth century, see Hammond and Griffith 1979, 392–395.

while *symbola* actually had to be ratified by both parties. Philip, in his offer of *symbola*, had mentioned ratification by him but had not mentioned ratification by Athens.[39]

Second, Hegesippus, in various passages of his speech, deliberately distorts recent events to make the Athenians suspicious of Philip's motives and character. When the issue of revising the peace treaty was mentioned, Hegesippus insisted that Philip's embassy had promised to accept the Athenians' proposal: 'Each party should have what belonged to it' (7.18). But now, Philip denied that he had promised to accept the Athenians' proposal. He is quite sure that Philip's representatives had said this in the Athenian Assembly: 'Python, therefore, urged those who speak in the Assembly not to find fault with the peace, saying that it is wrong to do away with peace. But (he said) if any clause of it had been badly drafted, it should be revised, and he would do whatever you might vote' (7.22).[40] Moreover, some Athenian politicians had persuaded Philip to make the offer because the Athenian citizens would not remember what had been said in the Assembly: '… he disputes that he made this offer or that his ambassadors said this to you, being quite simply persuaded by these men here, whom he treats as his friends, that you do not recall what was said in the Assembly' (7.18). Hegesippus also suggests another piece of evidence: 'Since the reading of the decree followed immediately after the speeches, it is impossible that you voted for a resolution that gave the lie to the ambassadors' (7.19). This evidence is still a construction in nature, belonging to what Aristotle calls *entechnoi pisteis* (artistic proofs).[41] Such details are likely to be remembered (but hard to remember accurately) only by the citizens who were present at that Assembly; however, not all of the citizens now faced by Hegesippus were present. Therefore, he is putting forward an argument based on what few people remember.[42] To enhance the effect of this depiction, Hegesippus also evokes an imaginative scene: 'The ambassadors themselves, to whom the decree gave the lie, when you read out your answer to them and invited them to enjoy our hospitality, did not dare to come forward and say, "You are telling lies about us, men of Athens,

---

39 Such judicial agreements are probably not retroactive; thus, it did not acknowledge the *fait accompli* of Philip's capture of Potidaea and the like (Harrison 1960, 248–252).
40 In 344/3 B.C., Philip sent an embassy to Athens led by the orator Python of Byzantium to propose negotiations on the revision of the Peace of Philocrates (n. 14).
41 Arist. *Rhet.* 1355b30–1356b15.
42 In a series of important studies, Ober argued that Athenian democracy and its knowledge system were founded not on a set of reference-based, empirical or objectively verifiable truths but on collective opinion and a politically constructed 'regime of truth' (Ober 1993, 81–89; see also Mader 2006, 367–386).

and are accusing us of saying something that we did not say." Instead, they went off in silence and departed' (7.20). As we can see, Hegesippus went to great lengths to paint Philip as a dishonest man by promising to accept Athens' proposals for revising the Peace of Philocrates,[43] but in failing to keep his promise, he deceived the Athenians. Is this really the case? Clearly, Hegesippus' words are incredible; that Philip should have promised to accept whatever the Athenians came up with was contrary to the most basic common sense of diplomacy. Philip could not have made such a promise.

Third, Hegesippus often invented 'the past' and used fabricated facts to serve his central purpose. In different passages, Hegesippus insisted that Philip had accepted the revisions of the Peace of Philocrates proposed by the Athenians and acknowledged that Amphipolis belonged to the Athenians in a letter that was written during the siege of Amphipolis in 356 B.C. (7.19–23, 26). In terms of revising the Peace of Philocrates, the Macedonian embassy could not have had the same ideas as the Athenians, and Philip could not have promised to accept any of the proposals that might be put forward by the Athenians. Regarding Amphipolis, given the strategic position of the city and its history over the past one hundred years, it would not have been sensible for him to admit that it belonged to Athens because, on the one hand, Amphipolis is near the mouth of the Strymon River and is rich in mineral and timber resources. On the other hand, Athens lost control of that city as early as 422 B.C. and had enjoyed almost independent status until Philip captured it in 356 B.C.[44] If Philip had admitted that to the Athenians, it would have required a reasonable explanation. By inventing the past in such a way, Hegesippus portrays a completely dishonest Macedonian king. Moreover, he seems to remind the Athenians of their once-dominant position on the sea and of the numerous colonies they once had. Halonnesus and Amphipolis are symbols of those colonies Athens once had but subsequently lost.[45]

Hegesippus distorts the recent past in *On Halonnesus* to present an unreliable Philip who is dishonest, spiteful and even vicious. Through such rhetoric, Hegesippus shows a fierce, uncompromising anti-Macedonian stance. Fisher said, 'It gives a good impression of a vigorous and belligerent style in support of a very strong anti-Philip line'.[46] This is where Demosthenes distanced himself from Hegesippus.

---

43 On Demosthenes and the Peace of Philocrates, see Brun in this volume.
44 Heskel 1997, 19–52; Hammond and Griffith 1979, 351–355; de Ste Croix 2008, 236–237.
45 Hammond 1994, 31–35; Cawkwell 1978, 69–90.
46 Fisher 2001, 204.

3 The contrast between Hegesippus and Demosthenes in the treatment of the recent past

There is no doubt that Hegesippus, like Demosthenes, belonged to a group of anti-Macedonian politicians. Two (and perhaps more) politicians of the same political stance spoke on the same issue and gave similar (or the same) advice to the Assembly.[47] However, if we can attribute the authorship of this speech to Hegesippus, there is a degree of difference between him and Demosthenes that is reflected in the way they deal with the recent past.[48]

3.1 Similarities

First, they both prefer the recent past to the distant past or mythical events. As mentioned above, a preference for the recent past was a common feature of Attic orators in fourth-century B.C. It is especially true of those politicians, such as Demosthenes and Hegesippus, who were radical anti-Macedonian politicians who devoted much of their energy to attacking Philip. Naturally, in the past seventeen years (since the accession of Philip), diplomatic events relating to Philip or Macedonia, namely, the recent past, dominated their public speeches. In *On Halonnesus*, all of the historical events mentioned by Hegesippus belong to the recent past, except for the reference in 11–12 to Philip's father Amyntas and the alleged tribute paid by the Macedonians to Athens at that time. Demosthenes used historical examples from the remote past relatively often in different speeches, especially when it was necessary to unite with other Greek city-states against Macedonia. For example, the *Third Philippic*'s central theme is advocating the joint resistance of the Greek city-states against Macedon, so it refers to the hegemony that Athens and Sparta once enjoyed as well as the battle of Leuctra (371 B.C.).[49] In contrast, *On the Chersonese*, written in the same context and devoted to the interests of Athens, makes little mention of any distant past. On the one hand, references to the distant past are limited to a few

---

47 Libanius, Hypothesis to Demosthenes, 7.
48 Westwood 2018, 186–187 notes the difference in their use of the past to serve rhetorical ends between Demosthenes and the author of *On Halonnesus*, but he does not say what the difference is.
49 Dem. 9.21–5.

paradigms,⁵⁰ and their argumentative role is secondary to the recent past. On the other hand, the recent past is the subject and main argument of most of his speeches. For example, the *Second Philippic*, composed around the same time as *On Halonnesus*, refers to the recent past, not the distant past. In Athenian foreign policy discussions of late 340 B.C., Grethlein suggests that recent events provide stronger proof because they are more familiar and relevant to the audience.[51]

Second, their descriptions and interpretations of the recent past concentrated on attacking Philip and portraying him in a negative light. Hegesippus' speech was inundated with words that aimed to portray Philip as a fraud who had deceived the Athenians and other Greeks in the Peace of Philocrates and other diplomatic matters[52] and whose purpose was to humiliate the Athenians, who would never trust him. For example, he reveals Philip's contempt for Athens by referring to the recent past: 'Whenever he says that he wishes to submit these matters to arbitration, he is simply mocking you' (7.7). He also revealed Philip's deceit of the Athenians by referring to the recent past: 'You all know that he granted this revision but now denies it' (7.26); 'he remembers the decree of Philocrates but has forgotten about the letter he sent you when he was besieging Amphipolis,[53] in which he admitted that Amphipolis is yours' (7.27). Demosthenes held a similar view of Philip in depicting his character by referring to the recent past. In the *Second Philippic*, probably written in the same year as *On Halonnesus* (343 B.C.), Philip was accused of being a liar who did not keep his promises: 'watch Philip dispensing gifts and promises. Yet, if you are prudent, you should pray that you do not find yourselves being tricked and deceived by him' (6.23). Most of the references to the recent past in the speech served this aim, even to exaggerate, distort or invent the facts for it. For instance, Demosthenes said: '… whereas Philip … would rebuild Thespiae and Plataea, and put an end to Thebes' arrogance, and dig through the Chersonese at his own expense, and would give you Euboea and Oropus in return for Amphipolis. I know you recall all these claims being made from the speaker's platform…' (6.30). Here, Demosthenes takes a very vague look at the recent past; 'I know you recall…' was a positive psychological suggestion, leading the audi-

---

50 The list contains the names and virtues of the founders and restorers of the democracy, of the deeds that secured the freedom of Athens and Hellas from foreign conquest and of the period of Athens' greatest power and fame (Milns 1995).
51 Grethlein 2014, 328–333.
52 See Brun in this volume.
53 357/6 B.C.

ence to believe that Philip had indeed made that promise. However, Demosthenes did not provide any hard evidence, and most of the audience probably could not remember whether it had happened. As we have seen, Hegesippus used similar rhetorical devices when referring to the recent past.

3.2 Differences

First, Hegesippus' interpretation of the recent past is often merely proof of some right belonging to Athens or of Philip's contempt (or deceit) for Athens, while Demosthenes tends to summarise using an aphoristic sentence or general principles after making a narrative about the recent past. In *On Halonnesus*, Hegesippus describes at great length the situation of Python of Byzantium who came to Athens to negotiate the treaty (7.18–23), only to say that Philip, who had accepted the Athenians' proposal, had cheated the Athenians by going back on it. When he refers to Philip's successive conquests of Olynthus, Apollonia and Pallene and the pillage of Pandosia, Bouches and Elateia, it is only to prove that Philip despised Athens and did not care about the Greeks' autonomy and freedom (7.28–32). These conclusions from the recent past never go beyond the matter of fact. However, when Demosthenes also refers to the fact that Philip continued to lay siege to 'Pydna, Potidaea, Methone, Pagasae and the other places', he concludes with a more abstract principle: 'We always abandon any opportunity that presents itself and hope that the future will turn out well of its own accord' (1.9). After he said that, Philip set about seizing Serrium and Doriscus and expelling the Athenian troops and generals from Fort Serrium and the Sacred Mountain, but some Athenians thought these places were unimportant. He continued, 'whether these places were small, or whether any of them concerned you, are different matters', and he immediately proposed a general principle: 'Piety and justice are equally important, whether someone transgresses over a small or a large matter' (9.15–16).[54] Thus, we can see that Hegesippus, in his interpretation of the recent past, is limited to detail, while Demosthenes tends to derive an aphorism from it that does not just apply to the present. Of course, these principles or aphorisms serve to illustrate the ambitions of Philip and the Athenians' inaction.[55]

---

[54] See also Dem. 6.20–25; 8.64–67; 4.4–8, 9–12.
[55] On the style of Demosthenes' public speeches see Milns 2000, 209–218; on the development of Demosthenes' public speeches see Pearson 1964, 95–109. However, neither of them points out the rhetorical features of Demosthenes generalising with an aphorism or general principle from the narrative of the recent past.

Second, they did not paint exactly the same picture of Philip. Demosthenes described Philip as close to a tyrant, while Hegesippus described him only as an unfaithful king. A theme that runs through Hegesippus' speech is that Philip cheated the Athenians by not keeping his word on the Peace of Philocrates. Furthermore, he sought naval supremacy under the guise of fighting with pirates. Hegesippus quipped, '...This man who has no naval ambitions is building triremes, and constructing the docks, and wishes to send out naval squadrons, and...' (7.16).[56] However, in explaining Philip's character and behaviour, Demosthenes, influenced by the traditional political discourse of Athens,[57] often used information provided by the recent past to describe Philip as a typical tyrant (or barbarian).[58] In Demosthenes' speeches, apart from his failure to keep his word, Philip's characteristics included distrusting men of talent and virtue, often killing or banishing them;[59] relying on mercenaries to support his rule;[60] alcoholism, violence, indecency and abuse of women.[61] Thus, Philip was not only a tyrant but a barbarian tyrant. Obviously, the image of Philip constructed by Demosthenes is richer in content and more in line with the traditional cognitive structure[62] of the Athenians than Hegesippus' Philip, so it is more persuasive for Athenian citizens to believe that Macedon, under Philip, must be hostile to the Athenians and their democracy.[63]

Third, Demosthenes' interpretation of the recent past is directed towards action, whereas Hegesippus seems to be confined to words alone and lacks strong motivation for action. In *On Halonnesus*, the accusations against Philip focus on his dishonesty and broken promises as well as his deception of the Athenians. To prove this, Hegesippus provides not moral evidence, such as Philip's misdeeds, but very specific evidence of his impudence and untrustworthiness. The

---

56 Sanders 2016, 61 claims that the aim of 7.14–16 was to create a fearful atmosphere for Athenians by raising the spectre of Macedonians becoming a sea power.
57 Hdt. 5.92; Arist. *Pol.* 3.8.3, 5.9.6–7; Xen. *Hier.* 5.1–2.
58 Harris 2018, 167–178.
59 Dem. 2.18–19.
60 Dem. 1.22; 2.17; 6.15; 9.16, 49; 19.81, 87.
61 Dem. 19.196–198.
62 To the Athenians, tyrants were the mortal enemy of their democracy. They believed that tyrants abroad were hostile to their democracy at heart and were plotting to overthrow their government because they could not coexist with a constitutional government that upheld the rule of law. For Demosthenes, the Athenians did not seek to rule others but resisted invaders and liberated those who were oppressed. As long as the Athenians were democratic, Philip was their mortal enemy (Dem. 1.5; 8.40–43; 10.13–17).
63 In the fourth century, the tyrant's original ideological role is ignored, and his negative personality traits are emphasised instead (Rosivach 2014, 56–57).

past evoked in the oration is not just close to but in the immediate run-up to the events in question. In that sense, they are not an example or parallel nor a distant justification of a present state but a direct cause and legal basis. Not surprisingly, some scholars have suggested that Hegesippus thought like a lawyer, even a legalist,[64] and wrote in a trivial and prosaic way. In the end, he even put aside Philip's record of deceiving the Athenians and attacking traitors in Athens. From beginning to end, he did not, as Demosthenes had done, reflect on recent events and appeal to the Athenians to take action. Demosthenes' account of the recent past and his attack on Philip shows a definite direction of action. However, in the *Second Philippic*, Demosthenes urged the Athenians to action: 'But you...if you do not act promptly, will find, I think, that without realising it, you have submitted to everything — so much stronger are immediate gratification and idleness than any consideration of future benefit. You may deliberate later by yourselves about what we need to do if you are sensible: but now I shall tell you what response you should vote for' (6.27–28). At the end of *On the Chersonese*, Demosthenes even theorises the relationship between words and actions: 'Timotheus spoke these words, and you acted, but the success arose from these two things together: his words and your action' (8.75).[65] Beginning with the series of *Olynthiac* speeches in 349/8 B.C., he constantly urged the Athenians to pay taxes, build warships, serve themselves and send troops. In Demosthenes' public speeches, it can be said that action was always a theme. The tendency became stronger in 343 B.C., the year of *On Halonnesus* and *Second Philippic*, until the final battle between Athens and Macedonia at Chaeronea.

4 Conclusion

Hegesippus, like other Attic orators, prefers to refer to the recent past rather than the distant past or mythical events. However, like other speakers, his references to the past serve not to establish the truth but to persuade audiences and influence public opinion and political propaganda. Therefore, he could also distort or even fabricate historical facts to express his political position. There are similarities and differences between his speeches and Demosthenes'

---

64 Davies 2011, 14.
65 See also Dem. 3.14: 'You must also know, men of Athens, that a decree is worthless if it is not accompanied by the will to carry out the decision with enthusiasm', and 4.9, 'You see the situation, men of Athens: how insolent that man is, who does not even allow you to choose between taking action and living quietly...'.

speeches in their treatment of the recent past.⁶⁶ Hegesippus was a comrade of Demosthenes in his rhetoric of anti-Macedonia and anti-Philip, but the difference in the concrete way in which he dealt with the recent past and the simplicity of the structure of his speeches made him a second-rate orator. Hegesippus, as MacDowell pointed out, lacked a full understanding of the complexity of the conflict between Athens and Philip as well as the broader vision of Demosthenes, so he was more like a lawyer than a statesman.⁶⁷

Bibliography

Brun, P. (2015), *Démosthène: Rhétorique, pouvoir et corruption*, Paris.
Cawkwell, G.L. (1978), *Philip of Macedon*, London.
Cawkwell, G.L. (1963), "Demosthenes' Policy after the Peace of Philocrates", *CQ* 13, 123–126.
Ceccarelli, P. (2013), "The Use (and Abuse) of Letters in the Speeches of the Attic Orators", in: U. Yiftach-Firanko (ed.), *The Letter: Law, State, Society and the Epistolary Format in the Ancient World*, Wiesbaden, 83–104.
Clarke, K. (2008), *Making Time for the Past: Local History and the Polis*, Oxford.
Davies, J.K. (1971), *Athenian Propertied Families: 600-300 B.C.*, Oxford.
Davies, J.K. (2011), "Hegesippos of Sounion: An Underrated Politician", in: S.D. Lambert (ed.), *Sociable Man: Essays on Ancient Greek Social Behaviour in Honour of Nick Fisher*, Swansea, 11–23.
de Bakker, M.P. (2012), "Demosthenes", in: I.J.F. de Jong (ed.), *Space in Ancient Greek Literature: Studies in Ancient Greek Narrative*, Leiden, 393–412.
de Ste Croix, G.E.M. (2008), "The Character of the Athenian Empire", in: P. Low (ed.), *The Athenian Empire*, Edinburgh, 232–276.
Errington, R.M. (1990), *A History of Macedonia*, California.
Fisher, N.R.E. (2001), *Aeschines Against Timarchus* (translation with introduction and commentary), Oxford.
Gabriel, R.A. (2010), *Philip II of Macedonia*, Washington D.C.
Gallo, L. (2018), "Un politico 'minore' di età demostenica: Egesippo *misophilippos*", *Erga-Logoi* 6, 7–22.
Goldman, M.L. (2018), "Demosthenes, Chaeronea, and the Rhetoric of Defeat", in: A. Richlin (ed.), *Brill's Companion to Military Defeat in Ancient Mediterranean Society*, Leiden, 123–143.
Grethlein, J. (2010), *The Greeks and Their Past: Poetry, Oratory and History in the Fifth Century BCE*, Cambridge.
Grethlein, J. (2014), "The Value the Past Challenged: Myth and Ancient History in the Attic Orators", in: J. Ker/C. Pieper (eds.), *Valuing the Past in the Greco-Roman World*, Leiden, 326–353.

---

66 Perhaps the difference is also indirect or less obvious evidence that Demosthenes was not the author of *On Halonnesus*.
67 MacDowell 2009, 345–346.

Hammond, N.G.L. (1994), *Philip of Macedon*, London.
Hammond, N.G.L./Griffith, G.T. (1979), *A History of Macedonia*, vol. 2, Oxford.
Hansen, M.H. (1987), *The Athenian Assembly in the Age of Demosthenes*, Oxford.
Hansen, M.H. (1989), *The Athenian Ecclesia II: A Collection of Articles 1983-89*, Copenhagen.
Hansen, M.H. (1991), *The Athenian Democracy in the Age of Demosthenes*, Oxford.
Harris, E.M. (2018), "The Stereotype of Tyranny and the Tyranny of Stereotypes: Demosthenes on Philip II of Macedon", in: M. Kalaitzi/P. Paschidis/C. Antonetti/A.-M. Guimier-Sorts (eds.), *Βορειοελλαδικά: Tales from the Lands of the Ethne: Essays in Honour of Miltiades B. Hatzopoulos*, 167–178.
Harrison, A.R.W. (1960), "[Demosthenes] De Halonneso 13", *CQ* 10, 248–252.
Harding, P. (2006), *Didymus: On Demosthenes*, translated with introduction, texts and commentary, Oxford.
Herrman, J. (2009), "Hyperides' Against Diondas and the Rhetoric of Revolt", *BICS* 52 (1), 135–148.
Heskel, J. (1997), *The North Aegean Wars: 371-360 B.C.*, Stuttgart.
Kapellos, A. (2019), *Xenophon's Peloponnesian War*, Berlin/Boston.
Kremmydas, C. (2013), "The Discourse of Deception and Characterization in Attic Oratory", *GRBS* 53, 51–89.
Kremmydas, C. (2016), "Demosthenes' Philippics and the Art of Characterisation for the Assembly", in: P. Derron (ed.), *La Rhétorique du Pouvoir: Exploration de L'art Oratoire Délibératif Grec*, 41–70.
Lanni, A. (2006), *Law and Justice in the Courts of Classical Athens*, Cambridge.
Leopold, J.W. (1981), "Demosthenes on Distrust of Tyrants", *GRBS* 22, 227–246.
Low, Polly (2007), *Interstate Relations in Classical Greece*, Cambridge.
Magnetto, A. (2016), "Interstate Arbitration and Foreign Judges", in: E.M. Harris/M. Canevaro (eds.), *The Oxford Handbook of Ancient Greek Law*, Oxford, 192–215.
McCabe, D.F. (1981), *The Prose-Rhythm of Demosthenes*, New York.
MacDowell, D.M. (1978), *The Law in Classical Athens*, Cornell.
MacDowell, D.M. (2009), *Demosthenes the Orator*, Oxford.
Mader, G. (2005), "Pax Duello Mixta: Demosthenes and the Rhetoric of War and Peace", *CJ* 101, 11–35.
Mader, G. (2006), "Fighting Philip with Decrees: Demosthenes and the Syndrome of Symbolic Action", *AJP* 127, 367–386.
Milns, R.D. (1995), "Historical Paradigms in Demosthenes' public speeches", *Electronic Antiquity*, Vol. 2, Issue 5.
Milns, R.D. (2000), "The Public Speeches of Demosthenes", in: I. Worthington (ed.), *Demosthenes: Stateman and Orator*, Routledge, 205–223.
Nouhaud, M. (1982), *L'utilisation de l'histoire par les orateurs attiques*, Paris.
Ober, J. (1989), *Mass and Elite in Democratic Athens: Rhetoric, Ideology and the Power of the People*, Princeton.
Ober, J. (1993), "Thucydides' Criticism of Democratic Knowledge", in: R.M. Rosen/J. Farrell (eds.), *Nomodeiktes. Greek Studies in Honor of Martin Ostwald*, Michigan, 81–89.
Parker, R. (1996), *Athenian Religion: A History*, Oxford.
Pearson, L. (1941), "Historical Allusions in the Attic Orators", *CP* 36, 209–229.
Pearson, L. (1964), "The Development of Demosthenes as a Political Orator", *Phoenix* 8, 95–109.

Perlman, S. (1961), "The Historical Example, It's Use and Importance as Political Propaganda in the Attic Orators", *Scripta Hierosolymitana* 7, 151–166.
Rhodes, P.J. (2009), "Hyperides' *Against Diondas*: two Problems", *BICS* 52, 223–228.
Roisman, J./Worthington, I./Waterfield, R. (2015), *Lives of The Attic Orators: Texts from Pseudo-Plutarch, Photius, and The Suda*, trans. and comment, Oxford.
Roisman, J./Worthington, I. (eds.) (2010), *A Companion to Ancient Macedonia*, Oxford.
Rosivach, V.J. (1988), "The Tyrant in Athenian Democracy", *QUCC* 30.3, 43–57.
Sanders, Ed (2016), "Persuasion through emotions in Athenian deliberative oratory", in: E. Sanders/M. Johncock (eds.), *Emotion and Persuasion in Classical Antiquity*, Stuttgart, 57–73.
Sealey, R. (1993), *Demosthenes and His Time: A Study in Defeat*, Oxford.
Schaefer, A. (1886), *Demosthenes und seine Zeit*, vol. 2, Leipzig.
Sickinger, J. (2013), "Greek Letters on Stone", in: U. Yiftach-Firanko (ed.), *The Letter: Law, State, Society and the Epistolary Format in the Ancient World*, Wiesbaden, 125–140.
Trevett, J. (2011), *Demosthenes, speeches 1-17*, Austin.
Tod, M.N. (1948), *Selection of Greek Historical Inscriptions*, vol. 2, Oxford.
Todd, S.C. (1990), "The Use and Abuse of the Attic Orators", *G & R* 37, 159–178.
Todd, S.C. (1993), *The Shape of Athenian Law*, Oxford.
van Groningen, B.A. (1953), *In the Grip of Past: Essay on an Aspect of Greek Thought*, Leiden.
Westermann, W.L. (1907), "Interstate Arbitration in Antiquity", *CJ* 2, 197–211.
Westwood, G. (2017), "Demosthenes and the Islands: On Organization 34", *Mnemosyne* 70, 501–511.
Westwood, G. (2018a), "Views on the Past", in: G. Martin (ed.), *The Oxford Handbook of Demosthenes*, Oxford, 179–190.
Westwood, G. (2018b), "Philocrates and the Orgas", *Hermes* 146, 349–357.
Westwood, G. (2020), *The Rhetoric of the Past in Demosthenes and Aeschines: Oratory, History, and Politics in Classical Athens*, Oxford.
Worthington, I. (1994), "History and Oratorical Exploitation", in: I. Worthington (ed.), *Persuasion: Greek Rhetoric in Action*, London, 109–129.
Worthington, I. (2008), *Philip II of Macedonia*, Yale.
Worthington, I. (2013), *Demosthenes of Athens and the Fall of Classical Greece*, Oxford.
Yunis, H. (2007), "Politics as Literature: Demosthenes and the Burden of the Athenian Past", in: E. Carawan (ed.), *Oxford Readings in The Attic Orators*, Oxford, 372–390.

Ian Worthington
Dinarchus, the 'Recent' and the 'Very Recent' Past: Lessons from Aeschines, Demosthenes and Lycurgus?

Abstract: In this essay, I discuss how the orators handled the 'distant past' and 'recent past' by considering aspects of Dinarchus 1, and more briefly, Lycurgus 1 and Aeschines 3. In doing so, I suggest there was another 'past' that shaped the orators' narrative, which I call the 'very recent past', referring to things that were still fresh in an audience's mind. Dinarchus' speech shows that he treated this 'very recent past' less cavalierly than the 'recent past' of even a decade previously when his audience's memory might have started to dim.

In early 323, Demosthenes and several other Athenians (including the general Philocles) were put on trial for taking bribes from Harpalus, Alexander's fugitive imperial treasurer, who had fled to Athens the previous year with 6,000 mercenaries, 5,000 talents of stolen money, and thirty ships to incite a revolt against the king.[1] Denied entry, he left most of his force at Taenarum and returned to Athens; this time he was admitted, sparking what modern scholars refer to as the Harpalus affair.[2] Demosthenes persuaded the Athenians to imprison him and to send an embassy to Alexander for his decision.[3] The money Harpalus had brought with him (allegedly 700 talents) was put under armed guard on the Acropolis, but at a later point Harpalus fled, after which only half of that amount could be found (Hyp. 5.9–10; cf. [Plut.] *Mor.* 846b).

It was thought that Harpalus had bribed his way out of the city, and people suspected Demosthenes of taking money to arrange Harpalus' escape. He immediately issued a challenge (*proklesis*), demanding that the Areopagus produce the necessary proof for the allegations made against him on pain of death, and many of the others implicated in the affair followed suit.[4] The Areopagus

---

[1] Theopompus BNJ 115 F 244, 245, Diod. 17.108.6, Curt. 10.2.1; cf. Plut. *Dem.*25.1. Philocles the general had probably admitted Harpalus: Din. 3.1, Plut. *Dem.* 25.3, [Plut.] *Mor.* 846a.
[2] Badian 1961; Goldstein 1968, 37–94; Worthington 1992, 41–77; Blackwell 1998; Worthington 2000, 102–106; Lehmann 2004, 206–216; Gottesman 2015.
[3] Din. 1.70 and 89 (cf. 90); cf. Hyp. 5.9 and [Plut.] *Mor.*846b.
[4] Din. 1.1, 18, 40, 61, 63, 83–84, 86, 104, 108, 3.2, 5, 16, 21; cf. Hyp. 5.1, 34, Plut. *Dem.* 26.1.

https://doi.org/10.1515/9783110791877-026

accordingly began a formal investigation into the issue (*apophasis*).⁵ After a six-month enquiry (Din. 1.45) that body issued its report (*apophasis*), accusing various men of taking bribes (*dorodokia*) from Harpalus; next to each man's name was the suspected amount — in Demosthenes' case, twenty talents — but citing no evidence.⁶ As was the legal custom in the *apophasis* procedure, the Areopagus did not need to furnish proof of its findings; nevertheless, Demosthenes issued a second *proklesis* for total transparency (Din. 1.6, Hyp. 5.3), but in vain. He and others were formally indicted and tried before a jury of 1,500 men.⁷

In addition to the furor over Harpalus and the inevitable strain in Athens' relations with Alexander was the latter's Exiles Decree.⁸ This unilateral measure was intended to ease problems in the eastern part of the Macedonian empire by sending home tens of thousands of exiles to their native Greek cities — and empowering Antipater to use force if need be. By the time of Harpalus' arrival in Athens in mid-324, the Athenian general Leosthenes had transported eight thousand exiles to Taenarum in Greece; at least 20,000 gathered at the Olympic Games (1 July to 4 August) to hear Alexander's envoy Nicanor of Stageira, proclaim the directive, and Athenian exiles were grouping at Megara (Din. 1.58, 94 Curt. 10.2.6–7). The exiles' return would cause enormous political and economic upheaval in Greece, and numerous cities sent embassies to Alexander at Babylon to protest the decree.

While Harpalus was incarcerated, Demosthenes went to Olympia to discuss the decree with Nicanor.⁹ That conversation may have prompted Demosthenes to arrange Harpalus' escape from Athens to bolster the embassy's chances of success over the decree, as was Demosthenes' move to recognize Alexander as the thirteenth god on Olympus under the name of Dionysus and erect a temple to him.¹⁰ Since Demosthenes had previously stated that only traditional gods should be worshipped, Dinarchus and Hyperides attributed his change of heart to bribery (Din. 1.94, 103, Hyp. 5.31–32). In the end, Alexander rejected all the embassies' pleas; the Athenian embassy's return, about six months later, was

---

5 Din. 1.4, 6, 68, 82–83, 86, Hyp. 5.1, 2, 8, 34.
6 Din. 1.6, 45, 53, 69, 89, Hyp. 5.2, 7, 10; Dem. *Let.* 2.1, 15 and 3.42; cf. Plut. *Dem.* 25.4–5, with Worthington 1992, 54–56.
7 Jury: Din. 1.105–106; cf. 113, Hyp. 5.6–7, Dem. *Let.* 2.14; cf. Plut. *Dem.* 26.2.
8 Hyp. 5.18, Diod. 17.109.1, 18.8.2–7, Curt. 10.2.4–7, [Plut.] *Mor.* 221a, 845c, Justin 13.5.2–6, Rhodes and Osborne 2003, no. 83, Dmitriev 2004, Worthington 2012.
9 Din. 1.81, Hyp. 5.18, Plut. *Dem.* 9.1, [Plut.] *Mor.* 845c.
10 Val. Max. 7.2, Ael. *VH* 5.12, Athen. 6.251b, Diog. Laert. 6.63; cf. Hyp. 6.8. Hyperides 1.21 and 6.21 suggest statues of Alexander and shrines and altars to him in Athens; cf. [Demades] *On the Twelve* 48.

when the Areopagus released its *apophasis*, a coincidence that did not go unnoticed, for Hyperides commented that Demosthenes walked around the city 'speaking and making accusations that the Council was seeking Alexander's favor and so wanted to destroy him' and that he did not take money from Harpalus as a bribe but for the Theoric Fund (5.12–14).[11]

The Athenians appointed ten prosecutors at Demosthenes' trial (whether the others accused faced all ten is not known).[12] Only Dinarchus' speeches against Demosthenes (1), Aristogeiton (2), and Philocles (3), Hyperides' speech against Demosthenes (5), and probably that of Demades against Demosthenes (1) are extant,[13] although Dinarchus 1 contains three lacunae, Dinarchus 2 and 3 are incomplete as they lack endings, and Hyperides 5 and Demades 1 are badly fragmented.[14] We also have a small amount of a speech by Stratocles, who was first in the prosecution line up.[15] Because of the fragmentary nature of our speeches I will draw on only Dinarchus 1 in this essay, as it is our most complete speech to have survived.

*

Dinarchus was faced with a major challenge: how to write a prosecution speech that would get Demosthenes convicted when there was no actual evidence against him. There was also the issue of Demosthenes' two *prokleseis* to the Areopagus to produce its evidence against him and his willingness to submit to the death penalty– those who had something to hide would not be expected to demand an investigation into their conduct, and after such a lengthy enquiry the Areopagus' refusal to cite evidence in this high-profile public enquiry is bewildering.[16] That he was victimized was plausibly shown by his condemnation,[17] along with Philocles (Dem. *Let.* 3.31–32), and possibly also Demades (Din. 1.29, 104, 2.14), yet at least Aristogeiton, Hagnonides and Polyeuctus were ac-

---

11 On taking money for the fund see Worthington 1992, 69–73.
12 Number: [Plut.] *Mor.* 846c. On the prosecutors see Worthington 1992, 52–54; Dinarchus' client was either Himeraeus or Menesaechmus: Worthington 1992, 53–54.
13 Demades' speech: Worthington 1991a.
14 Commentary on Dinarchus: Worthington 1992 and (on Din. 1 and Hyp. 5–6) Worthington 1999; on Hyperides: Whitehead 2000.
15 Blass 1898, 302–304 and Worthington 1992, 54.
16 Demosthenes the victim of a political trial connected to the immediate background of the Exiles Decree: Worthington, 1992, 58–69; 2013, 320–324.
17 Plut. *Dem.* 26.2, Dem. *Let.* 2.2, 14–16, 21, 26, 3.37–8 and 43. He returned during the Lamian War: Worthington 2013, 331–332.

quitted.[18] Since no proof was submitted against any of the accused men, the jury at their trials ought to have either condemned or acquitted all of them — a fact that the prosecutors stressed (Din. 1.113, 2.21, Hyp. 5.5–7).

The central, legal argument to Dinarchus' speech (likewise that of Hyperides) was that the report of the Areopagus should be accepted without question, as I have shown in my analysis of the detailed ring structuring of the speech.[19] Although there was rhetorical exploitation of the laws in oratory, the actual specifics of the law were grounded in fact, which the jurors recognized, hence Dinarchus was on firm ground in speaking of the Areopagus' judicial function.[20] In support, he constantly reminds the jurors of Areopagus' integrity, lack of bias, and its long history, and he clearly expected Demosthenes to argue that the council's report was flawed as it cited no evidence against him (1.1.1.7, 12).[21] Dinarchus (and Hyperides) also took pains to remind the jury that Demosthenes was willing to suffer execution if the Areopagus found him guilty (Din. 1.1,40, 61, 63, 83–84, 86, especially 104, 108, Hyp. 5.1). That Dinarchus should resort to these tactics is unsurprising; as we noted above, there was not a shred of evidence against Demosthenes to justify the accusation leveled against him, let alone proceed to trial, hence Dinarchus could fall back only on the standing of the Areopagus to convince the jury to accept its *apophasis* (see further below).[22]

Dinarchus, therefore, had his work cut out for him. But as well as appealing to the standing of the Areopagus he could resort to standard rhetorical techniques of manipulation of the past and character denigration, often similar in fashion to Aeschines.[23] I am less concerned with the latter (which peppers his

---

18 Dem. *Let.* 3.37, 42 [Plut.], *Mor.* 846c–d, Plut. *Phoc.* 29.3.
19 Especially Din. 1.48–63; at 55, the absolute central component of the ring structuring, and hence of the entire speech, is that the Areopagus imply issues a report against someone. As I said in my commentary (Worthington 1992, *ad loc.*): 'By extension, the identification of the central structure of the speech and Dinarchus' handling of the Areopagus enables us to realize two things: the basis Dinarchus envisaged for his case against Demosthenes, and the necessity of exploiting the reputation of the Areopagus, given the lack of actual evidence'.
20 Law and rhetoric: Sickinger 2006.
21 Cf. Aristogeiton's stance against the Areopagus' results, truth, and justice at Din. 2.1–3; cf. 17–19 and 20–21.
22 On the judicial role of the Council of the Areopagus see Worthington 1992, *ad* 1.6, citing bibliography.
23 Din. 1.31: 'When he began to advise the people, and would he had never done so — I will pass over his private affairs, for time does not allow me to speak at length — is it not true that absolutely no good has come to the city and that not only the city but all Greece has fallen into danger, misfortune, and disgrace?'. Dinarchus also often accuses the defendants of taking bribes against the city (Demosthenes: 11, 13, 15, 26, 29, 40, 46–47, 53, 60, 64, 67, 88, 108; cf.

speech) as it is a form of attack that was expected in oratory to prejudice an audience, no different from casting aspersions on, or making belittling comments about, opponents today, and can largely be shown to be groundless. In terms of history, though, the imposition of Macedonian hegemony, under which the Greeks were forced to live and work, would appear to work in Dinarchus' favour. Even if the youngest juror at Demosthenes' trial in 323 was at the minimum age to serve, hence thirty, he would have been fifteen in 338, and so able to remember that fateful day when Philip II defeated a coalition Greek army at Chaeronea to become master of Greece.[24] It had been Demosthenes' jingoistic rhetoric that had constantly defied Philip and eventually persuaded Athens to ally with Thebes and face the king in that battle.[25] And eight years after the battle, in 330, Aeschines anchored his famous prosecution speech *Against Ctesiphon* (3) in the argument that Demosthenes' entire policy towards Philip was flawed and ultimately led to the Greek defeat and the end of centuries of Greek autonomy (see below).

Freedom and autonomy were ideals that the Greeks cherished the most, and for which they had always fought. Yet in 331, when Agis III of Sparta attempted to rally the Greeks to war against Macedonia, Demosthenes persuaded the Athenians otherwise (see below). And in 324, when Harpalus arrived with men, ships, and money urging the Athenians to revolt against Macedonian hegemony, Demosthenes (who surely would have embraced this offer in the days of Philip) counselled the people to reject his support and not even admit him into the city.[26] All of these events were fresh in the jurors' minds in 323, especially those of the previous year. We would presume that Dinarchus' strategy to counteract the dearth of evidence was to create prejudice by bringing up the recent past and contrasting it with the "good old days" of Greek freedom, and so motivate the jury to condemn him.[27]

The problem, however, was that two equally high profile (we may presume) cases in the city, also within the jurors' memory, had employed a similar use of history and anti-Macedonian bias, but failed. In 330, Lycurgus prosecuted Ly-

---

Hyp. 5.13, 21, 38; Aristogeiton: 2.1–2, 6, 15, 20, 22–23, 26; Philocles: 3.2, 6, 18, 22) as part of a general character assassination.

24 Battle: Diodorus 16.86, Plut. *Alex.* 9, *Pelop.* 18.7, Justin 9.3.4–11, Polyaen. *Stratag.* 4.2.2, 7 with Worthington, 2013, 248–251, citing bibliography.

25 Alliance: Worthington 2013, 241–245.

26 Demosthenes during Alexander's reign: Cawkwell 1969; Worthington 2000; 2013, 275–293, 310–325.

27 Jury: Din. 1.105–106; cf. 113, Hyp. 5.6–7, Dem. *Let.* 2.14; cf. Plut. *Dem.* 26.2.

curgus for desertion after the battle of Chaeronea,[28] and in the same year Aeschines rekindled his charge (from 336) against Ctesiphon who, among other things, had proposed that Demosthenes be awarded a gold crown in the theatre of Dionysus for his recent civic activities and 'because he consistently speaks and acts in the best interests of the people'.[29] We have only Lycurgus' speech from the former trial (1) but both speeches of Aeschines (3) and Demosthenes (18) from the latter, although they were revised after oral delivery, hence the veracity of historical information in them is compromised.[30]

True, Lycurgus had never properly made the case that Leocrates' offence, deserting Athens in its hour of need (Lyc. 1.68), was an act of treason (*prodosia*); his manufacture of the recent past was questionable, as J. Roisman argues in this volume.[31] However, he had contrasted Leocrates' alleged cowardice with the Athenians' ancestors patriotically fighting for freedom at Chaeronea, and claimed that Leocrates' action made the city vulnerable to Philip after his victory, even including quotations from Homer, Tyrtaeus, and Euripides for dramatic and moral effect.[32] In response, Leocrates could only weakly state that he had not fled the city but had been travelling on business.[33] Yet, despite Lycurgus' impassioned speech and the rhetorical exploitation of life under Macedonian rule, Leocrates was acquitted (Aes. 3.252).

Aeschines in his prosecution speech had attacked Demosthenes' anti-Macedonian stance throughout his career (3.49–167), especially the alliance with Thebes in 339 (3.140–151) that led to Chaeronea. Demosthenes responded to Aeschines' assertion at length (18.160–226), acknowledging the terrible defeat at Chaeronea, which he then rhetorically turned into victory because the Greeks had fought it for the sake of their *eleutheria*, thus matching the patriotic standard of their ancestors in the Persian Wars (18.63, 66–68, 192–195, 199, 206, 245–246, 208, 270–275). His policy, Demosthenes argued, had thus given the

---

28 See now Roisman and Edwards 2019, citing bibliography.
29 Aesch. 3.49; other charges: Aesch. 3.11, 32–48. Discussion of the background and the case, see Burke 1977; Sawada 1996; Atkinson 1981; Worthington 2013, 294–306. Aeschines' speech: Blass 1898, 182–193, Worthington 2013, 296–298. Demosthenes' speech: Blass 1898, 364–383, Wankel 1976, Lehmann 2004, 197–203, MacDowell 2009, 382–397, Worthington 2013, 299–306.
30 Wankel 1976, 48–51, Buckler 2000, 148–154. I have argued elsewhere that manifest historical errors in our surviving speeches may well be the product of the revised speech, for at the stage the outcome of a trial is no longer a concern: Worthington 1991b.
31 See Roisman in this volume.
32 Lyc. 1.46–51, 59–62; Homer (1.103), Tyrtaeus (1.107), Euripides (1.100), with Roisman and Edwards 2019, *ad locc*.
33 He spent time in Rhodes and Megara: Lyc. 1.14–15, 16–19, 21–27.

Athenians another glorious episode in their history to make their ancestors proud. Demosthenes therefore neatly moved from the gloomy historical presentation of the battle and its aftermath, as Lycurgus and Aeschines had portrayed, and made the symbolism of the battle its most important aspect. He crafted, then, a 'rhetoric of defeat' extolling the excellence of the city and its people, as N. Crick argues in this volume.[34]

Lycurgus and Aeschines failed because they had gone about reminding the Athenians of the recent past in the wrong way — especially in making Chaeronea too centre stage when their audience still did not want to face the truth of the battle. After all, shortly after it Lysicles, the Athenian general at Chaeronea, was condemned to death as 'a living monument of our country's shame and disgrace' (Diod. 16.88.1–2). Leocrates was acquitted not because he was innocent, but because of a reaction against Lycurgus for how he rubbed salt into the wound of lost autonomy. Demosthenes was acquitted because he had presented his version of the truth; unlike Aeschines, he reversed the defeat at Chaeronea in a near-epideictic style by claiming that the Greeks had won a moral and patriotic victory, and so could hold up their heads high.

That the jury was so swayed by Demosthenes' presentation of the battle is evidenced, I suggest, by his being selected shortly after to give the *epitaphios* for those who fell at Chaeronea (Dem. 60).[35] Thucydides tells us (and surely the same is true of the fourth century), only the man 'most endowed with wisdom and preeminent in public esteem' was selected for this high civic honour (2.34). Hence, we would hardly expect a traitor who had never served his city well, as Aeschines described Demosthenes, to deliver this solemn speech unless his audience realized Demosthenes' stance had been the right one.

Dinarchus must have been influenced by the outcomes of the two cases of 330 that had encompassed the loss to Macedonia, not to mention well aware of Demosthenes' rhetorical prowess and ability to turn the tables on a prosecutor. Although as a metic he was not as personally involved in the case, as a *logographos* whom the state had hired to write speeches for the prosecution he was clearly very much invested in it for his business and reputation.[36] Therefore, he could not present a recent past, something the people had lived through, in an unpalatable manner that would cause the jurors to react against him — or play into Demosthenes' hands. In composing his speech, he needed to stress the reputation of the Areopagus, and, to support his case further, allude to Demos-

---

34 See Crick in this volume. See too Worthington 2013, 302–304, 306.
35 See Worthington 2013, 259–262.
36 Dinarchus' life and works: Worthington 1992, 3–12.

thenes' role in historical events that proved detrimental to the city. To this end, he presented a view of historical events anchored in when they took place and what he perceived to be the jurors' recollection of them.

*

As mentioned above, Dinarchus refers frequently to the *apophasis* and reputation of the Areopagus, as well as to Demosthenes' launch of the enquiry and willingness to submit to the death penalty if it declared against him, which he folds into a narrative of events after Harpalus' arrival in Athens and his escape. His tone is a matter-of-fact one, largely un-sensational, and certainly devoid of the rhetorical flourishes that we find in Aeschines and Demosthenes. For example:

> Athenians, your popular leader has pronounced a sentence of death on himself if it be proved that he took any sum from Harpalus ... as for the actual report the Council of the Areopagus has published fair and true findings (1.1)

> When the Assembly voted in favour of a lawful decree and when all of the citizens wanted to determine which of the politicians dared to take money from Harpalus to the disgrace and danger of the city, and, further, when you and many others, Demosthenes, proposed in the decree that the Areopagus should investigate these men – as is its traditional right – to see if any have taken gold from Harpalus, the Council of the Areopagus began its enquiry (1.4).

> But of all those ever reported, you alone of your own volition requested that these men be your judges and examiners, and you proposed the decree against yourself, and made the people witnesses of what was agreed, laying down the death penalty on yourself if the council should report that you had taken any of the money brought into the country by Harpalus (1.61).

> Demosthenes himself proposed in the Assembly to guard for Alexander the money brought into Attica with Harpalus, clearly showing how this was a just measure. Well, my good friend, tell me how we are to guard it, when you have taken twenty talents for your own pocket, someone else fifteen, Demades six thousand gold staters and others the amounts attributed to them? Sixty-four talents have been discovered, for which you must see that the guilt must be placed on these men (1.89).

Elsewhere, the Areopagus 'made the right decision and it did not wish to subvert the truth and its own prestige because of you' (1.5) and it was not been swayed by the influence of either Demosthenes or Demades, but has deemed justice itself and truth of more consequence' (1.11), while the jurors are challenged to abide by the report because of the power of the council (1.6):

> Shall the Council, which is sufficiently trustworthy to establish justice and truth in cases of wilful murder, and which has the right to pass life and death judgments on each citizen,

and to champion those who died a violent death, and to expel or punish by execution those who have transgressed any law in the city, shall it now be powerless to exact justice over the money shown to have been taken by Demosthenes?

The Areopagus' report is one of the major subjects of the speech, which is not surprising as Dinarchus must anchor his case in its reputation and the need to accept its findings. The ring structuring shows that the judicial powers and process of the council take up chapters 48–63, and the justification of the report chapters 5–11 and 104.[37] There are no rhetorical flourishes, but simple, straightforward appeals. Dinarchus was simply stating what everyone already knew, and challenging the jury to defy the Areopagus by not accepting its report — an undemocratic action for sure.

There is little of the rhetorical embellishment or indignation to which Aeschines, for example, resorted in his survey of Demosthenes' career. Granted, we could put this down to Dinarchus being a stylistically inferior oratory; however, I think it more likely that he is presenting these events without fabrication because they came from a very recent past, literally the previous several months, and so still very fresh in Athenian minds.

*

Once we move, however, from this very recent past to further back in time, even only a few years, such as Agis III of Sparta's war of 331–330 or the razing of Thebes in 335, it is a different matter. Let us begin with the former. In 331, Agis had attempted to rouse the Greeks to unite under him against Macedonian rule.[38] Most of the Peloponnese and some northern Greeks responded positively, especially as Antipater was busy with a revolt in Thrace.[39] Demosthenes may have initially urged the Athenians to support Sparta, but then persuaded them to stand aloof and true to the League of Corinth.[40] In 330 Antipater defeated and killed Agis in battle at Megalopolis; after fining his allies heavily, he had the Spartans surrender fifty noblemen to him, and Alexander imposed more punitive measures.[41]

Demosthenes, rightly recognizing that resistance to Macedonian rule was futile, and wanting to prevent Alexander from moving against Athens should he

---

[37] Worthington 1992, 329 for the primary-level of the speech.
[38] Aesch. 3.165–166, Diod. 17.48.1, 62.6–63.4, 73.5, Curt. 6.1; cf. Arr. 2.13.4, 3.6.3 and 16.10, with Cawkwell 1969, 170–180, Badian 1994, Worthington 2013, 287–291.
[39] Diod. 17.62.7, McQueen 1978, 52–59.
[40] Aesch. 3.165–166, Din. 1.34–35, Diod. 17.62.7, [Plut.] *Mor.* 818e–f; cf. Plut. *Dem.* 24.1.
[41] Diod. 17.63.1–3, 73.5–6, Curt. 6.1.19–21.

so decide, thus gave his fellow citizens prudent advice.⁴² Nevertheless, Aeschines and Dinarchus seized on this *volte face* to accuse him of bringing discredit to Athens and misery to Sparta. How they did so is significantly different. Thus, Dinarchus has this to say about Agis' war (1.34):

> Is it not necessary for us to raise up another force such as we had in the time of Agis, when all the Spartans had taken the field, joined by the Achaeans and Eleans and ten thousand mercenaries? Alexander, so they said, was in India, and because of traitors in each city, the whole of Greece was unhappy with the situation and was hoping for some relief from misfortunes?

Contrast Aeschines' lament at 3.133:

> And the poor Spartans ... who once claimed to be leaders of Greece, are about to be sent to Alexander as hostages and make an exhibition of their calamity, to suffer, both individually and as a country, whatever he chooses, and to have their fate decided by the mercy of a victory they have wronged.

Aeschines is more accurate than Dinarchus, which ought not surprise us as Aeschines' speech was delivered in the same year as Megalopolis – in other words, the recent past, when memories of Agis' abortive action would still have been vivid. It is possible that Demosthenes' flip-flopping over supporting Agis might have made him vulnerable to prosecution, hence Aeschines revived his earlier charge against Ctesiphon at this time.⁴³ Indeed, not long after Agis' defeat, Macedonian sympathizers in Athens were indicted, including Euxenippus for giving bad advice to the people, taking bribes, and flattering Macedonians.⁴⁴

This apparent background betrays reality. After Agis' war ended, the Athenians, including the jurors at Ctesiphon's trial, would have been well aware that they had escaped the king's wrath (had they supported Sparta) thanks to Demosthenes. Hence, Aeschines could not blame Demosthenes for missing the opportunity to end Macedonian rule, a fabrication his jury would have immediately seen through, but instead chose to address the wretched fate of Sparta to rouse the jury's pity.

Seven years later, Dinarchus could deal with Agis very differently as memories began to fade. He claims that the Athenians had already mobilized a force and that there were traitors in every city eager to end Macedonian rule. We can

---

42 *Contra* Cawkwell 1969, 176–180, but see Worthington 2000, 94–100; 2013, 290–291.
43 See Wankel 1976, 18–25.
44 The prosecution speech by Polyeuctus has not survived, but fragments exist of Euxenippus' defense speech, written by Hyperides: Blass 1898, 54–58.

well imagine that the Greeks would have relished the opportunity to end Macedonian rule (they had revolted on Philip's death in 336 and would do so again on that of Alexander in 323), but we have no idea whether an actual force was raised or who these traitors were.[45] What we can say with certainty is that Alexander was not in India at the time of Agis' war: he was at Persepolis, where the destruction of the palace might also have been intended as a warning shot to the Greeks about supporting Agis.[46]

Alexander did not invade India until 326. Dinarchus covers his apparent chronological error with the oratorical catch-phrase 'so they said', but why bother making the king out to be in India when he knew he was not? A plausible answer is that Dinarchus does not see events of eight years ago as 'recent past', still vivid in juror's memories, and hence by locating Alexander even further away in India he can create prejudice against Demosthenes for a missed opportunity to liberate Greece. But again, we note that he can only level insinuations against Demosthenes, not actual charges.

We see Dinarchus similarly exploit a less recent event when he accuses Demosthenes of betraying Thebes to its destruction in 335 (1.24):

> But thanks to [Demosthenes], the children and wives of the Thebans were divided among the tents of the barbarians, a neighboring and allied city has been torn from the middle of Greece, and the city of Thebes, which shared the war against Philip with you, is being ploughed and sown. I repeat: it is being ploughed and sown!

Thebes had defied Alexander in that year, forcing the king to besiege it.[47] When it capitulated, he massacred the surviving male population, enslaved the women and children, seized the treasury, and then razed the city to the ground. Stratocles also connected Demosthenes to Thebes' fate,[48] as had Aeschines in 330 (3.133). Our sources claim that Persian King sent as many as 300 talents to Greece to induce a Greek revolt and assist Thebes, but that Demosthenes kept all of it, hence Thebes fell to Alexander.[49] However, as I have argued, there is no truth to this allegation that he kept, let alone received, money from Persia; the confusion of our sources on the amount of money and Demosthenes' circum-

---

45 Revolts: Worthington 2013, 273–274, 277–278 (336) and 329–334 (the Lamian War of 323–322).
46 Worthington 2004, 69–70.
47 Diod. 17.8.2–14.1, Arr. 1.7–9, Plut. *Alex*.11.6–13, *Dem*. 23.1–3, Justin 11.3.6–4.8; see Worthington 2013, 279–280, citing bibliography.
48 A fragment of his speech says 'the city of the Thebans, which fought on the same side in the war against Philip with you, is being ploughed and sown': Blass 1898, 302–304.
49 Aesch. 3.239, Din. 1.10 and 18, Diod. 17.4.8, Plut. *Dem*. 14.2 and 20.4–5, Justin 11.2.7.

stances point to a popular topos against him likely fashioned by Aeschines in 330.⁵⁰

Yet when the jurors exonerated Demosthenes in the Crown trial, they were also confirming that they did not believe, or at least were not swayed by, all the slander (including the accusation about Thebes) that Aeschines had thrown against his opponent. Why, then, did at least two, and possibly more, of Demosthenes' prosecutors in 323 still accuse him of betraying Thebes to destruction? Certainly, the razing of that city had an impact on the Greeks, and rhetorical accounts of the tragedy abounded,⁵¹ but then again — and this is an important point — Greeks were hardly without sin when it came to their treatment of enemy cities and populations, and Thebes' medizing history hardly earned it widespread popularity.

Since Demosthenes was on trial for betraying his own city, Dinarchus could exploit the fate of Thebes, now twelve years in the past, to emphasize the horrors befalling a city from the treachery of its leading citizens. That Thebes was doomed from the moment it had defied Alexander was overlooked, and perhaps even largely forgotten; instead its destruction was tied to the (alleged) venality of Demosthenes. Likewise, his taking a bribe from Harpalus had placed the city in similar peril, according to Dinarchus, which is vividly expressed at 1.68:

> And what if — for let us imagine this scenario — Alexander sends an envoy and, in accordance with Demosthenes' decree, demands from us the gold brought into the country by Harpalus, and, relying on the fact of the report of the Areopagus, sends us the slaves, recently returned to him, expecting us to find out the truth from them? By the gods, gentlemen, what shall we say?

Dinarchus' scare tactic rhetoric was that since Athens was in no position to repay Alexander the money Harpalus had stolen, something the jurors would be well aware of from only a year ago, the king might punish the city in similar fashion to Thebes: if he had done this once, he could do so again — and again, it would be Demosthenes' fault. Even if Demosthenes could rebut his role in Thebes' downfall, could he rebut the report of a body as venerated as the Areopagus? Dinarchus knew he could not — especially as it did not need to cite evidence. Perhaps, even, some jurors reconsidered Demosthenes' alleged betrayal of Thebes, in which case Dinarchus' argument borders on *eikota*: if Demosthenes took money once to a city's detriment (Thebes), he would do so again (that time from Harpalus) against Athens.

---

50 Worthington 1992, *ad* 1.10 and 18–21; 2010.
51 For example, Hegesias of Magnesia, BNJ 142 T 3, FF 7, 10–12, 16, 17, 20.

The battle of Chaeronea was, interestingly, differently treated. Taking place fifteen years before Demosthenes' trial, we would expect Dinarchus to manipulate that pivotal battle for rhetorical effect, given the elapsed time. But not so, and for a very good reason. We have noted above how the presentation of Chaeronea by Lycurgus and Aeschines worked against them, and how Demosthenes resoundingly turned the battle and the Greek defeat into a noble victory. Dinarchus treads very carefully when bringing up the battle, given how Demosthenes had rewritten it into Athenian mythology. Instead of focusing on the actual battle he follows a line that Aeschines had used to cast aspersions on Demosthenes' character by dramatically claiming he fled the battlefield as a coward (1.12):[52]

> Demosthenes nevertheless goes around both slandering the council and speaking about himself, tales that he will perhaps presently tell you in an effort to deceive you ... I brought everyone into line at Chaeronea.' No again; on the contrary, you yourself and no one else fled from the line there.

> Compare 1.71 ('Is it fitting that ... [you] are ordering others to take the field when you yourself deserted the battle-line?') and 1.81 ('Is it right to entrust and turn over the city to this man as danger threatens, who, when it was necessary to fight the enemy with his fellows, deserted the rank and went off home')

Dinarchus' attack is manifestly untrue, for Demosthenes would have been charged with desertion and would have lost his civic rights, which clearly never happened.[53] That the remnants of the Greek army, Demosthenes included, fled when defeated by Philip was enough of a kernel of truth for Dinarchus (and Aeschines) to use against Demosthenes, but unlike Aeschines, Dinarchus does not make explicit that the battle ended Greek freedom. Only on two occasions does he speak of the aftermath of the battle, and then it is to denigrate Demosthenes' character further: at 1.78: 'Athenians, listen also to that decree proposed by Demosthenes, which this democrat proposed after the battle of Chaeronea when the city was in dire straits', and at 1.80: 'For when he heard that Philip was intending to invade our land after the battle of Chaeronea he appointed himself envoy in order that he might escape from the city'.[54]

---

52 Aesch. 3.151–152, 159, 175–176, 181, 187, 244, and 253; see too Plut. *Dem.* 20.2 and [Plut.] *Mor.* 845f.
53 Andoc. 1.74 for the law.
54 Decree of Demosthenes and Hyperides enacting a wide range of emergency measures: Lyc. 1.16, 36–37, 41, Dem. 18.248, [Dem.] 26.11, [Plut.] *Mor.* 848f–849a, 851a; Envoy (to procure grain from abroad): Lyc. 1.42, Aesch. 3.159, 259, Dem. 18.248.

Dinarchus might well have exploited the level of historical memory of the jury, as that battle is not from the very recent past, but he was careful not to defy the 'new normal' of Chaeronea that Demosthenes had created.

Further, as the style of his entire speech shows, he was acutely aware of not only when but also, even more importantly, *how* to exploit previous eras, which he does not view as one continuum but distinguishes between the very recent and not so recent past. In doing so, his audience's memory clearly plays a deciding role.

Bibliography

Atkinson, J.E. (1981), "Macedon and Athenian Politics in the Period 338 to 323 BC", *Acta Classica* 24, 37–48.
Badian, E. (1961), "Harpalus", *JHS* 81, 16–43.
Badian, E. (1994), "Agis III: Revisions and Reflections", in: I. Worthington (ed.), *Ventures into Greek History. Essays in Honour of N.G.L. Hammond*, Oxford, 258–292.
Blackwell, C.W. (1998), *In the Absence of Alexander. Harpalus and the Failure of Macedonian Authority*, New York.
Blass, F. (1898), *Die attische Beredsamkeit*^{2}, 3, Leipzig.
Buckler, J. (2000), "Demosthenes and Aeschines", in: I. Worthington (ed.), *Demosthenes: Statesman and Orator*, London, 114–158.
Burke, E.M. (1977), "*Contra Leocratem* and *De Corona*: Political Collaboration?", *Phoenix* 31, 330–340.
Cawkwell, G.L. (1969), "The Crowning of Demosthenes", *CQ*^{2} 19, 163–180.
Dmitriev, S. (2004), "Alexander's Exile's Decree", *Klio* 86, 348–381.
Goldstein, J.A. (1968), *The Letters of Demosthenes*, New York.
Gottesman, A. (2015), "Reading the Arrivals of Harpalus", *GRBS* 55, 176–195.
Lehmann, G.A. (2004), *Demosthenes von Athen: ein Leben für die Freiheit*, Munich.
MacDowell, D.M. (2009), *Demosthenes the Orator*, Oxford.
McQueen, E.I. (1978), "Some Notes on the Anti-Macedonian Movement in the Peloponnese in 331 B.C.", *Historia* 37, 52–59.
Nouhaud, M. (1982), *L'Utilisation de L'Histoire par les Orateurs Attiques*, Paris.
Pearson, L. (1941), "Historical Allusions in the Attic Orators", *CP* 36, 209–229.
Perlman, S. (1961), "The Historical Example, Its use and Importance as Political Propaganda in the Attic Orators", *Scripta Hierosolymitana* 7, 150–166.
Rhodes, P.J./Osborne, R. (eds.) (2003), *Greek Historical Inscriptions, 404–323 BC*, Oxford.
Roisman, J./Edwards, M. (2019), *Lycurgus, Against Leocrates*, Oxford.
Sawada, N. (1996), "Athenian Politics in the Age of Alexander the Great: A Reconsideration of the Trial of Ctesiphon", *Chiron* 26, 57–82.
Sickinger, J. (2006), "Rhetoric and the Law", in: I. Worthington (ed.), *A Companion to Greek Rhetoric*, Malden, 286–302.
Wankel, H. (1976), *Demosthenes, Rede für Ktesiphon über den Kranz*, 2 vols., Heidelberg.
Whitehead, D. (2000), *Hyperides, The Forensic Orations*, Oxford.

Worthington, I. (1991a), "The Context of [Demades], *On The Twelve Years*", *CQ*² 41, 90–95.
Worthington, I. (1991b), "Greek Oratory, Revision of Speeches and the Problem of Historical Reliability", *C & M* 42, 55–74.
Worthington, I. (1992), *A Historical Commentary on Dinarchus. Rhetoric and Conspiracy in Later Fourth-Century Athens*, Ann Arbor.
Worthington, I. (1994), "History and Oratorical Exploitation", in: I. Worthington (ed.), *Persuasion: Greek Rhetoric in Action*, London, 109–129.
Worthington, I. (1999), *Greek Orators 2, Dinarchus 1 and Hyperides 5 & 6*, Warminster.
Worthington, I. (2000), "Demosthenes' (In)activity During the Reign of Alexander the Great", in: I. Worthington (ed.), *Demosthenes: Statesman and Orator*, London, 90–113.
Worthington, I. (2004), "Alexander the Great and the Greeks in 336? Another Reading of *IG* ii² 329", *ZPE* 147, 59–71.
Worthington, I. (2010), "Intentional History: Alexander, Demosthenes and Thebes", in: L. Foxhall/H-J. Gehrke (eds.), *Intentional History: Spinning Time in Ancient Greece*, Stuttgart, 239–246.
Worthington, I. (2012), "From East to West: Alexander and the Exiles Decree", in: E. Baynham (ed.), *East and West in the World of Alexander: Essays in Honour of A.B. Bosworth*, Oxford, 93–106.
Worthington, I. (2013), *Demosthenes of Athens and the Fall of Classical Greece*, New York.

Joshua P. Nudell
Remembering Injustice as the Perpetrator? Athenian Orators, Cultural Memory, and the Athenian Conquest of Samos

Abstract: Timotheus' conquest of Samos in 366 and the alleged expulsions of the Samian demos that followed came to be remembered as one of the worst excesses of Athenian imperialism. Despite the hostile memory of Athenian overreach in the wider Greek world, however, the Attic orators universally characterize Timotheus' conquest as the "liberation" of Samos. Rhetorical manipulation of facts is well established; the question is whether the orators could shape the collective memory about a gross violation of Greek interstate norms to create a collective amnesia about an event from the recent past. An analysis of four speeches from three Attic orators (Isoc. 15; Dem. 15; Din. 1 and 3) suggests that they could not, which, in turn, casts doubt on the orthodox interpretation of this period in the history of Samos.

War between Athens and Alexander seemed inevitable in 323. Negotiations had broken down and both sides prepared to fight, with members of Alexander's court such as Gorgus of Iasos pledging enormous amounts of military equipment (Ephippus, BNJ 126 F5). The crux of this conflict sat squarely on Athenian ownership of Samos. According to popular memory in the Greek world, the Athenians had notoriously dissolved the Samian polity after conquering the island in 366 and expelling the population. By the 320s, an estimated 6,000 to 12,000 Athenian families lived on Samos.[1] Alexander had deferred ruling on an appeal from displaced Samians early in his reign (Plut.

I would like to thank Aggelos Kapellos, Christine Plastow, and Ian Worthington for reading early drafts of this paper and giving me invaluable feedback.

---

1 For an estimate of the overall size of the cleruchy see Shipley 1987, 14–15, 141.

https://doi.org/10.1515/9783110791877-027

Alex. 28.1),² but this time he came down in their favor. When combined with the near-contemporary Exiles Decree, this decision was too much for the Athenians and they prepared to face the consequences of their impertinence.³

The Athenians were clearly outraged by the prospect of giving Samos back to the exiled Samians, but the process by which the island became an integral Athenian territory is less clear. Evidence from the 320s suggests that the rest of the Greek world felt empathy for the plight of the Samians such that even long-time rivals like Erythrae and Priene set aside their traditional hostility in order to offer aid.⁴ And yet, with one possibly apocryphal exception, Attic sources are vague about both Timotheus' capture of the island and the subsequent treatment of its inhabitants. None of the four extant invocations in the corpus of the Athenian orators, the most direct references to the event in contemporary written sources, even mentions the Samians! In each instance, Isocrates (15.106–28), Demosthenes (15.9) and Dinarchus (1.14; 3.17), the logographer elides the circumstances of the conquest. My question, therefore, is whether omitting the historical context reflects and, indeed, helped create a cultural amnesia about this historical moment or whether it merely represents the memory of a past that was less severe than the tradition from outside of Athens leads us to believe. Put another way, which memory of the conquest of Samos is more accurate?

---

2 This chronology is generally accepted, but the date and context are controversial because Plutarch connects it to Alexander's divine pretensions. Hammond 1993, 379–382 argues that the letter belongs in the period 334–332, meaning that Plutarch mistook its meaning, while Hamilton 1953, 151–157 and 1969, 74, puts it in 323, accusing Plutarch of being mistaken about the date. Rosen 1978, 9–21 questions its authenticity, suggesting that it holds parallels to Alexander's *hypomnema*, which was an early Hellenistic forgery. Plutarch's quotation reads like a response in an ongoing exchange, but too little is preserved to know whether it confirmed Athenian possession of Samos (as Hammond) or revoked it (Hamilton). On the authenticity of Alexander's letters in Plutarch generally cf. Hamilton 1961.
3 Part of this preparation included operations against Samos, resulting in the capture of prisoners who Antileon of Chalkis ransomed, probably after the battle of Crannon in 322, Habicht 1957, no 1. On the date of Antileon's intervention see Errington 1975, 51–57.
4 Both communities, as well as many others that received thanks in the early Hellenistic period, were within the Carian sphere of influence at the time of the exile, but it is also notable that many of these decrees specify individual honorands, as Cargill 1983, 331 points out, e.g. Sosistratus of Miletus extended a personal loan of three talents to the returning Samians, (*IG* XII 37), Habicht 1972, no. 4; Cf. Shipley 1987, 161–163.

1 Historical example and historical memory

Before turning to the event in question, a brief methodological note.

The crucial role of the historical example in classical oratory is familiar ground, but a recent turn has begun to consider oratory as part of a broader "memory community," rather than perpetuating an accurate record of events, received *topoi*, or naked politics.[5] Exemplary of this turn is B. Steinbock, who rehistoricized the historical example as one of several vectors of social memory in Athenian public discourse by bringing classical oratory into dialogue with the modern study of memory.[6] In the ancient world as much as the modern, social memory is a complex tangle of remembering, misremembering, and forgetting woven into the physical, monumental landscapes, with memories subject to continual restructuring in their transmission. In classical Athens, physical monuments and state institutions formed a loom on which orators wove a richly contoured tapestry of collective memory.[7]

Equally important to collective memory is forgetting. In *The Divided City*, N. Loraux sought to explain why the Athenians swore an oath during the reconciliation of 403 to not remember (οὐ μνησικακεῖν) crimes committed by anyone other than the thirty, the ten, and the eleven (Andoc. 1.90; [Arist.] *Ath. Pol.* 40.3).[8] "To not remember" has a different force than "to forget," but aims at the same end. Loraux casts the *polis* as an ideology that created an underlying unity and erases the possibility of division, which, in turn, underpinned the destructiveness of *stasis* and demanded reconciliation by forgetting past injustices.[9]

---

[5] On this transition, see particularly Canevaro 2019. Pearlman 1961 offered the classic labels for the categories of analysis, with recent discussion in Steinbock 2013, 38–47. Recent studies have rightly focused on persuasive potential of the historical example, see e.g. Maltagliati 2020, who examines how orators manipulated the proximity of examples to affect audiences.
[6] Steinbock 2013, particularly 1–96. Steinbock is hardly the only scholar to evaluate social memory in antiquity (see e.g. Wolpert 2002a), but reviewers praised his methodological contributions while critiquing aspects of his case study such as the relationship between Athens and Thebes, see e.g. Pownall 2014, 366–368 and Kucharsky 2014, 170–172.
[7] This process is particularly prominent in the *epitaphios logos*, see Loraux 2006a and Shear 2013, but is evident elsewhere in Attic oratory, see for instance Hobden 2007. For "how Athens built its brand" with appeals to history, cf. Hanink 2017, 32–55.
[8] Loraux 2006b; cf. Wolpert 2002a, 76–99. On the context for the reconciliation see Ober 2002; Rubinstein 2018; Wolpert 2002a, 29–47 and 2002b.
[9] Loraux 2006b, 30; cf. 43–44, where she discusses the altar to Lêthê in the Erechtheion on the Acropolis that served as a primary locus of reconciliations (Plut. *Mor.* 741b). Attic oratory preserves evidence of reconciliation in action, particularly in Lysias' prosecutorial speeches in the wake of the Thirty, where he addresses the jurors as though they uniformly supported the

The events on Samos involved a different set of circumstances. Its capture was clearly a point of pride in the way that the trauma at the end of the fifth century was not, so the question remains whether it is possible to simultaneously invoke a historical event and erase it from the collective memory without the unity, either real or imagined, created by the *polis*.

Considering Timotheus' conquest of Samos along these lines offers not insignificant obstacles. The capture of Samos appears only four times across the extant collection of epideictic, deliberative, and forensic speeches, and two of those Dinarchus deploys nearly verbatim. Although there are examples from each type of oratory, this is a deep dive into a shallow pool. Moreover, the extant corpus of speeches from the Attic orators hardly represents a comprehensive record. Most of the few surviving deliberative speeches, for instance, come from the Demosthenic corpus and focus on the conflict with Macedonia.[10] Ionia, including Samos, by contrast, only receives oblique mention in the extant materials.[11] Thus, while the Athenian Assembly must have debated Samos in the years Timotheus was active and lost forensic speeches may have provided insight into the makeup of the population, only trace evidence remains. The only extant reference to a speech dedicated to Samos appears in Aristotle's *Rhetoric*, where he says Kydias implored his countrymen to vote on sending a cleruchy to Samos as though the rest of Greece stood around, watching (Arist. *Rhet.* 1384b).[12] Other references mark Samos as an Athenian possession, reflecting Athenian interest in the island as a dominated space,[13] while Timotheus' conquest remained on the fringes of memory.

---

democracy (e.g. 12.47) and tries to conscript them in defense of the democracy in the rare instance where he acknowledges the division (e.g. 13.92); see Wolpert 2002a, 91–95, 122–123 and 2003, 543–545.

10 This selective survival may have stemmed Demosthenes' unusual habit of writing down his Assembly speeches for publication even though deliberative oratory required improvisation; see Herrman 2019, 20–26, cf. Rubinstein 2009, 512–513.

11 See Nudell 2018.

12 The name "Kydias" is rare but appears in a comic fragment of Eubulus (F 67) that may suggest that he was a navarch. Edmonds dates the fragment to c. 363, which leads Develin 1989, 261 to connect the office to his intervention in 365, but this is highly speculative. Inscriptions testify to the name on Samos, including on lists of magistrates from the Athenian cleruchy (*SEG* 45.1162 col. I line 19) and on a list of citizens from the Hellenistic period (*SEG* 37.725 col. IV line 188 and McCabe *Samos* 179). However, when Aristotle describes Athens as being censured (ψέγουσιν) for reducing the Greeks to slavery (κατεδουλόντων), he names Aegina and Potidaea, not Samos (*Rhet.* 1396a7).

13 Nudell 2018, 178–179.

2 Conquests, cleruchs, and exiles

In 366 the Athenian *strategos* Timotheus besieged Samos under ambiguous circumstances. Officially he had sailed to the eastern Aegean with a mandate to support the rebel Persian satrap Ariobarzanes but instead landed on Samos where a Persian hyparch by the name of Tigranes had installed a garrison commanded by Cyprothemis.[14] Reconstructing the details of the siege is beyond the scope of this paper, but Timotheus conducted the ten-month operation largely without support from Athens (Isocr. 14.111), making-do instead with what resources he could extort from nearby poleis and by having his soldiers harvest the local crops to sell back to the besieged at a markup ([Arist.] *Oec.* 2.1350b; cf. Polyaen. 3.10.9–10).[15]

Timotheus' defenders framed the campaign as an Athenian defending Greek liberty against barbarian aggression, but the circumstances are anything but clear. The name Tigranes is probably Persian, but which of the satraps he worked for, if indeed he worked for a Persian satrap, is unknown. Demosthenes implies that Tigranes operated independently as *hyparch* of the king (15.9), but most scholars choose to point the finger at Mausolus as the primary instigator because he was expanding his influence in Ionia at about this time.[16] In 480, Isocrates warned that the *poleis* near to the Anatolian coast were susceptible to Persian influence (4.120), but there is neither any indication of either constitutional change at Samos nor an appeal from a disempowered faction. The absence of evidence is not evidence of absence, though, and Athenians like Timotheus, whose father Conon had built close family relationships with Ionia, kept abreast of events.[17] The pages of Herodotus and Thucydides are filled with personal diplomatic appeals so, while there is no surviving evidence for any com-

---

14 Shipley 1987, 137; cf. Hornblower 1982, 187, with n. 36.
15 Polyaenus records that Timotheus installed regulations that demanded provisions be sold at quantity to limit the amount sold and omits a buyer, likely because [Aristotle's] story seemed implausible.
16 Polyaenus preserves a story about one Aegyptus who Mausolus dispatched to capture Miletus by deception (6.8). He was unsuccessful, but Mausolus nevertheless succeeded in drawing Miletus into his orbit, see Hornblower 1982, 76, 111. At 198–199, Hornblower notes Mausolan coins on the island. Buckler 2003, 353 suggests that Tigranes acted on orders from Autophradates, who Diodorus names as satrap of Lydia (15.90).
17 Conon received honorary statues at Erythrae (*RO* 8), Ephesus, and Samos (Paus. 6.3.16) and had commissioned Isocrates to establish a new constitution on Chios ([Plut.] *Mor.* 837b). On the statue at Erythrae see Ma 2006; for the campaign more generally see Dem. 20.69; Diod. 14.39.3; Nepos *Conon* 5.

munication, Timotheus probably counted on local support.[18] Indeed, despite Polyaenus' comment that Timotheus took the city by force (κατὰ κράτος, 3.10.9), the surviving sources do not offer the same portrait of high-intensity fighting that Thucydides does for Pericles' campaign in 440 (Thuc. 1.115–17; cf. Plut. Per. 25–26).

However, it was not the capture of Samos, but the subsequent developments that shaped how the conquest was remembered: the Samian *polis* dissolved and some number of the original inhabitants went into exile.[19]

The overwhelming weight of modern scholarship accepts the wider Greek memory of the conquest, namely that the expulsion of the Samians and creation of Athenian cleruchies marked a grotesque violation of interstate norms.[20] Thus C. Habicht declares that if the expulsion of the Persian forces "could have been laudable from the Greek point of view, the sequel could not"[21] and S. Hornblower characterizes the Samians as people "who had been put on the streets of Greece by Athens" and "walking mementoes of the power of Fortune, τύχη, no less than πλεονεξία, the Greed, of the Athenians."[22] Other scholars are equally sharp, if less poetic, in their criticisms. Shipley notes that some of cleruchs were the descendants of Samians exiled in Athens since 403 and that the total number sent were enough "to occupy all the houses and farms,"[23] with the implication that ancestral Athenians mingled with ancestral Samians in the new *demos*. Even J. Cargill, who later offered an apology for the cleruchy that deserves further consideration, initially defended it not by questioning the nature of the conquest, but on the grounds that it did not violate the prohibition against cleruchies in the charter of the Second Athenian Confederacy. After all, Samos was not a signatory (*IG* II² 43; Diod. 15.28.3 cf. Dem. 15.9).[24]

---

18 Shipley 1987, 140 suggests that "the neutralization of democratic elements in 403 may never have been seriously put to rights even in 394 or 391."
19 Rubinstein 2004, 1098 notes that the cleruchic polity is not called a *polis*, lending weight to the interpretation that it was absorbed by Athens. The number of exiles is unknown and estimates vary widely.
20 E.g. Buckler 2003, 354; Habicht 1996, 398; Hornblower 1982, 199; Kebric 1977; Shipley 1987, 141.
21 1996, 398.
22 Hornblower 1982, 199.
23 Shipley 1987, 141.
24 Cargill 1981, 148–149. The prospectus included promises to prospective members that Athens would not repeat the unpopular policies of earlier Athenian and Spartan hegemonies (ll. 15–46) but specifies that these benefits only applied to league members. The membership list of the Second Athenian League found principally on the fragmentary Aristoteles Decree (*IG*

Contemporary evidence underpinning the explicit narrative of conquest, expulsion, and cleruchy is slim. Most ancient sources collapse the Athenian decision about Samos to a single moment, such as Aristotle's example of a rhetorical appeal to shame (Arist. *Rhet.* 1384b). However, other evidence testifies to waves of Athenian cleruchs, concluding with some two thousand who arrived in 352/1, more than a decade after Timotheus' conquest (Philochorus BNJ 328 F 154 and Strabo 14.1.18).[25] A common assumption is that these cleruchs displaced the entire population of Samos because of a declaration by the contemporary philosopher Heraclides Ponticus that Aristotle quoted in the *Samian Politeia* (οἱ δὲ ἐλθόντες πάντας ἐξέβαλον, Arist. Fr. 611.35 (Rose)), but this is far from certain.[26] Moreover, the limited evidence for the composition of the cleruchs makes it possible that most of them were in fact ancestral Samians.

In an article subsequent to *The Second Athenian League*, Cargill argued that the cleruchs, most of whom he identifies as descendants of Samians naturalized as Athenian citizens, occupied estates confiscated from wealthy Samians, while the majority of the population never went into exile, instead becoming absorbed by the cleruchic state.[27] Shipley rejects Cargill's thesis, principally on onomastic grounds. There are only sixty or so names known for the Athenian cleruchs and about a third of those have parallels among the names known to be Samian, but in each case the attestation comes in the early Hellenistic period, leading him to conclude that many of the cleruchs chose to stay on after the regime change.[28]

II[2] 43) is not without controversy (see e.g. Baron 2006; Dmitriev 2011, 381–390; Fauber 1998; Woodhead 1957 and 1962), but no reconstruction of the inscription includes Samos.
25 Shipley 1987, 141 suggests a minimum of three waves of cleruchs. See Cargill 1983 for a synopsis of the epigraphic evidence.
26 Hornblower 1982, 199 with n. 132, Shipley 1987, 132–133, 141 and Zelnick-Abramovitz 2004, 330 are skeptical of the "total expulsion" from an island with the population of Samos. The quotation is exceedingly terse, Thomas 2019, 313 takes it to refer to a fifth-century cleruchy. Cf. Diod. 18.8.7.
27 Cargill 1983, particularly 326–329. Cargill advances a more sophisticated position from Griffith 1978, 139–140, who imagines a bifurcated state on Samos with the Samian *demos* initially enjoying a symbiotic relationship with Athens, only to end up oppressed or in exile after 352. There is no evidence of a Samian *polis* after 365 until Alexander's decision in 324/3. Shipley 1987, 141–142 suggests many now-disenfranchised citizens retreated to the mountains and lived on the fringes of society. All scholars accept that *some* of the cleruchs were ancestral Samians and that the exiled population centered on those who had resisted Athens. Thus Shipley 1987, 140: "Only the ruling oligarchs had anything to fear." The differences of opinion come from where one sits on the sliding scale of the two extremes. The larger the ancestral Samian component, the smaller the number of exiles, and vice-versa.
28 Shipley 1987, 141, with endnote 2.

Moreover, he argues that the grant of Athenian citizenship expired, using as evidence a single case where a Samian, Meidon, was a metic in the Peiraeus during the 320s, unable to claim the privileges of citizenship. Shipley's objections provide important counterpoints to a straightforward narrative of peaceful symbiosis, but his vision of extreme disruption is based not entirely on his own fragmentary evidence, but because "what tells against [Cargill's] main argument, however, is that Kydias thought that the Athenians were doing something to be ashamed of."[29] If this Aristotle passage reflects a particular strand of cultural memory about the Athenian behavior rather than fact, then this objection similarly fails to hold up to scrutiny.

Where the later Samian outrage implies a singular traumatic expulsion, the chronology of events actually shows a slow-unfolding political crisis. The initial Athenian mandates probably included expulsions only for those people who had collaborated with the Persian agents, but the number of exiles may have grown in time as critics vocalized their opposition to the new regime. Those who remained must have been accommodated by a cleruchic state that operated semi-independently of Athens.[30]

Against this tumultuous backdrop we have the appearance of Timotheus' campaigns in the surviving corpus of the Attic orators: too many to condemn the episode to irrelevance, but too few to give a complete picture of the public debate. The question, then, is the relationship between how these invocations received and how they shaped the memory of the capture of Samos.

3 Remembering injustice?: Timotheus' conquest in extant speeches of the Attic orators

Samos appeared only six times in extant speeches from the fourth century, and one third of the references (Dem. 21.71 and Aesch. 1.53) mention it only in the context of the cleruchy. The four remaining invocations approach Samos through the lens of Timotheus, thereby entwining the memory of the conquest

---

29 Shipley 1987, 142, n. 77.
30 Rubinstein 2004, 1098 characterizes the cleruchy as a dependent *polis* with elected officials and a demos characterized as "Athenian" such as on an inscription from 334/3 where Ἀθηναίων ὁ δῆμος ὁ ἐν Σάμωι dedicated a gold crown at Delphi, *Syll.*³ 276A, cf. Cargill 1995, 62, with n. 24. Some residents also maintained Athenian citizenship such that they enrolled in the ephebeia (e.g. Epicurus: Strabo 14.1.18; Diog. Laert. 10.1), but this need not have been universal.

with a referendum on the historical memory of the conqueror, who fled into exile in Chalcis in 356/5 after being unable to pay the fine levied from a conviction on the charge of taking bribes.[31]

The earliest of the four is Isocrates' defense of his former student in the course of his *Antidosis* of 354/3, an epideictic speech in the form of a defense against the charges of sophistry and corrupting the youth (15.15, 101).[32] The imaginary accuser implicates Isocrates with the crimes of Timotheus,[33] so Isocrates sets about to clear his name by exonerating his former pupil. He declares that the accuser is utterly shameless in slandering a dead man to whom Athens owes a debt (15.101) and claims that he would ask to share the blame should his defense fail and Timotheus be proved a bad man (15.106), even while asserting that he bears no culpability for his protégé's actions. What follows is an extended section where Isocrates rehabilitates Timotheus' memory on two grounds: service to Athens (15.106–115) and qualities as a leader (15.116–128).[34] The second quality is also the more abstract, attributing a leadership *topos* that Timotheus had followers who others looked to as leaders (15.116) and his judgement in action that preserved the reputation of Athens among the other Greeks (15.121–124). In contrast, the first and primary argument for Timotheus' virtue is that he captured more *poleis* by force than anyone else, bringing them into the Athenian sphere without spending either allied tribute or Athenian *eisphora* (15.107–113; cf. 118).

Samos receives special mention in this list, coming close to having what Isocrates laments being unable to provide overall: context (15.114). Isocrates opens by invoking the public memory of Pericles, praising the titan of the previous century for excelling above all others in wisdom, justice, and self-control (ὁ

---

31 Isaeus 6.60 invokes a battle off Chios during an unspecified campaign that was probably Timotheus' expedition in 366/5, but does not mention Samos; see Schweigert 1940, 198. Ferrucci in this volume notes that the lack of historical context was typical of Isaeus' historical references. Timotheus was reportedly acquitted in an *eisangelia* trial in 373/2, but removed from office anyway, see Xen. *Hell.* 6.2.13; [Dem.] 49.9–10; Diod. 15.47.3; Hamel 1998, 150. Since only Apollodorus [Dem.] 49.9–10 mentions the specific charge, Siron in this volume questions its historicity. Following the battle of Embata in 356/5, Timotheus, along with Iphicrates and Menestheus, was again put on trial for failing to have adequately aided Chares. The jury acquitted Iphicrates and Menestheus, both of whom retired from public life, but convicted and fined Timotheus. Sealey 1955, 74 suggests that this trial took place before the end of the Social War.
32 On the form of the *Antidosis* see Papillon 1997, 54–57; 2006, 60–62; Too 2008, 137.
33 The fictionalized sycophant in the *Antidosis* is named Lysimachus, but Isocrates (15.5) says he was prompted to create this work after losing a liturgy trial; see Too 2008, 1–4.
34 Of course, one need not look beyond the invocations of Timotheus to see the same evidence deployed in the opposite purpose, see below with Dinarchus.

μεγίστην ἐπὶ σοφίᾳ καὶ δικαιοσύνῃ καὶ σωφροσύνῃ), and then noting that Pericles was only able to reduce Samos with a fleet of two hundred ships and the expenditure of a thousand talents (15.111). Timotheus, by contrast, required no financial support and a smaller force that he funded with the spoils of war.

Of course, Isocrates is disingenuous. He holds a common line regarding Timotheus' character, implying here what he states plainly at the end of this section, namely that Timotheus' crime lies not in malicious intent, but in his unwillingness to flatter the demos (132–134). Yet, Isocrates simultaneously flattens the memory of Pericles into his positive qualities, overstates the cost of the expedition to Athens, and glosses the relative prominence of Samos in 440 versus Samos in 366[35] in order to equate the achievements of his pupil with the heyday of Athens. That Isocrates did not deliver his treatises before a public audience makes it unlikely that his account shaped the memory of the conquest of Samos, but its presence in a nominal defense speech properly reflects Athenian memory even before the final wave of cleruchs arrived in 352. Each of these campaigns was publicly remembered as a service to Athens and suggests that the Athenians held Samos in particular esteem as an extension of Athenian territory.

Omission is also a powerful tool. Isocrates' rhetorical purpose is to shape the memory about Timotheus, not Samos, so the Samians appear nowhere outside of the implication that they were worthy, if ultimately defeated, adversaries. Perhaps Isocrates glossed over the resolution on Samos in order to disassociate his subject from the subsequent events, but the unambiguously positive presentation here more likely implies that Isocrates did not see anything that needed to be hidden.

This tension also emerges from the deliberative oratory of Demosthenes where his *On the Freedom of the Rhodians* in 351 follows the same general pattern.[36] His purpose in this deliberative speech is to prompt an Athenian intervention on Rhodes, and so he provides more context than does Isocrates. After a brief introduction and laying out his position, Demosthenes begins his argument by invoking the campaign to Samos (15.9):

---

[35] Samos in 440 may have possessed the largest navy in the Delian League after Athens but had suffered severely from the conditions of the treaty that ended the war with Athens and then from the Peloponnesian War. The war between Athens and Samos was grievously expensive, with a final bill of more than 1400 talents that the Samians repaid in annual instalments of 50 talents (ML 55=*IG* I³ 363), see Blamire 2001, 101–103; Fornara and Lewis 1979, 9–12; Marginesu and Themos 2014, 171–184; Shipley 1987, 117–118.

[36] On the context of *On the Freedom of the Rhodians* see Worthington 2013, 123–126.

ὅτι δ' οὐδὲν καινὸν οὔτ' ἐγὼ λέγω νῦν κελεύων Ῥοδίους ἐλευθεροῦν, οὔθ' ὑμεῖς, ἂν πεισθῆτέ μοι, ποιήσετε, τῶν γεγενημένων ὑμᾶς τι καὶ συνενηνοχότων ὑπομνήσω. ὑμεῖς ἐξεπέμψατε Τιμόθεόν ποτ', ὦ ἄνδρες Ἀθηναῖοι, βοηθήσοντ' Ἀριοβαρζάνῃ, προσγράψαντες τῷ ψηφίσματι "μὴ λύοντα τὰς σπονδὰς τὰς πρὸς τὸν βασιλέα." ἰδὼν δ' ἐκεῖνος τὸν μὲν Ἀριοβαρζάνην φανερῶς ἀφεστῶτα βασιλέως, Σάμον δὲ φρουρουμένην ὑπὸ Κυπροθέμιδος, ὃν κατέστησε Τιγράνης ὁ Βασιλέως ὕπαρχος, τῷ μὲν ἀπέγνω μὴ βοηθεῖν, τὴν δὲ προσκαθεζόμενος καὶ βοηθήσας ἠλευθέρωσε.

I will remind you of some of the things you have accomplished to show that neither my proposal regarding the freedom of the Rhodians, nor your action if I should persuade you, are novel. You, men of Athens, once dispatched Timotheus to aid Ariobarzanes, appending to the decree "provided that it not dissolve the treaty with the king." [Timotheus], seeing that Ariobarzanes was in open revolt from the king and that Samos was garrisoned by Cyprothemis, who Tigranes, hyparch of the king stationed there. Reneging on the promise of aid for [Ariobarzanes], [Timotheus] besieged and liberated [Samos].

Demosthenes presents Samos as a clear precedent for Athenian intervention at Rhodes and Timotheus as a liberator who acted after learning of the Persian presence on the island. Owing to his lack of interest in Timotheus, Demosthenes emphasizes the context while erasing the details of the campaign even more than did Isocrates. All that remains is the reminder that once upon a time Athenians were willing to exert themselves for the good of other Greeks — a model that they ought to again emulate. Demosthenes thus invokes a long-held tradition about Athenian self-identity, that they stood as the defenders of Hellas. This self-styled reputation stemmed from Athenian claims to the victories of Marathon and Salamis during the Persian Wars and from fifth-century imperial propaganda, but Demosthenes inserts the example of Samos into the pre-existing narrative template.[37] Once he finished burnishing Timotheus' decisions with altruistic motivations, the conquest of Samos offered a directly and obviously applicable model for intervention in the eastern Aegean.

However, *On the Freedom of the Rhodians* was a failed speech with multifarious causes for its failure. Intervention was expensive and could have provoked a war. Some Athenians surely saw the Rhodians as traitors who, along with the people of Chios and Byzantium, had waged war against Athens less than a decade earlier. But could Demosthenes use of Samos as a positive exemplum for Athenian intervention have also been seen as hypocritical?

---

37 Aristotle *Rhet.* 1396a6 describes Marathon and Salamis as essential examples for praising Athens; see Efstathiou 2013 on the renewed valence of Marathon in fourth-century oratory. On the importance of narrative templates for creating collective memory see Wertsch 2008, 120–135.

Demosthenes delivered *On the Freedom of the Rhodians* within a year of the final wave of cleruchs arriving on Samos. If, on the one hand, the cleruchies marked an egregious transgression of interstate norms, then one might expect Demosthenes to omit Samos because it would undermine his claim that the campaign was for the cause of Greek liberty. On the other hand, if, as Cargill has argued, the waves of cleruchies were largely composed of the descendants of Samian democrats who had supported Athens during the Peloponnesian War, then Timotheus' campaign would have marked an important point in his favor. The aftermath of the proposed campaign to Rhodes would not have lined up so neatly with the one on Samos, but Demosthenes here elides those events because they are extraneous to his argument and counts on the recent reminder about Samos to sway the audience toward the broader conception of the Athenian custom of defending Greeks against barbarians. In other words, Demosthenes is not trying to whitewash Athenian actions, but expecting a positive memory to strengthen his argument.

Finally, three decades after Demosthenes' speech, Dinarchus invoked Timotheus' memory twice in two different forensic speeches (1.14; 3.17). In his prosecution of Demosthenes in 324, Dinarchus declares (1.14):

> καὶ Τιμοθέῳ μέν, ὦ Ἀθηναῖοι, Πελοπόννησον περιπλεύσαντι καὶ τὴν ἐν Κερκύρᾳ ναυμαχίαν νικήσαντι Λακεδαιμονίους καὶ Κόνωνος υἱεῖ τούτους Ἕλληνας ἐλευθερώσαντος καὶ Σάμον λαβόντι καὶ Μεθώνην καὶ Πύδναν καὶ Ποτείδαιαν καὶ πρὸς ταύταις ἐτέρας εἴκοσι πόλεις, οὐκ ἐποιήσασθ' ὑπόλογον, οὐδὲ τῆς τότ' ἐνεστώσης κρίσεως οὐδὲ τῶν ὅρκων, οὓς ὀμωμόκοτες ἐφέρετε τὴν ψῆφον, ἀντικατηλλάξασθε τὰς τοιαύτας εὐεργεσίας, ἀλλ' ἑκατὸν ταλάντων ἐτιμήσατε, ὅτι χρήματ' αὐτὸν <Ἀριστοφῶν> ἔφη παρὰ Χίων εἰληφέναι καὶ Ῥοδίων.

> With regard to Timotheus, men of Athens, who sailed around the Peloponnese and emerged victorious in a naval battle against the Spartans near the Corcyra, and being the son of Conon, the liberator of Greece, and capturing Samos, Methone, Pydna, Potidaea, and twenty cities more, you did not account for these services in his trial or in the oaths you swore about casting your votes. But rather, you fined him a hundred talents because Aristophon said he took money from the Chians and the Rhodians.

Dinarchus' invocation to the conquest of Samos in a speech prosecuting Demosthenes more than two decades after Demosthenes had used the same exemplum to show how Athenians ought to act is a nice parallel but is most likely coincidence, since he repeats the phrase in *Against Philocles* of 323 (3.17), another prosecution delivered for similar effect. Contrasted with both Isocrates and Demosthenes, Timotheus' importance for Dinarchus lay in his conviction, not his service. Dinarchus only invokes the campaign therefore in order to demonstrate that it was *despite* his benefactions (*euergesia*) that the jury convicted Timotheus; the greater the service, the more significant the conviction.

Mention of Samos required no illusion of proximity. Demosthenes' trial took place during the fallout from the Harpalus affair in 324/3 and thus at a time when the loss of the island was imminent.[38] But if Dinarchus invokes the memory of Timotheus' conviction in light of the contemporary political situation that had not yet have become a memory, what does he say about the expulsion of the Samians? The answer, of course, is nothing. Dinarchus indicates neither who Timotheus fought in 366 nor who would be coming back to recover the island. By the time Dinarchus prosecuted Demosthenes, the cultural memory surrounding the conquest had already been flattened and Samos incorporated into the Athenian conception of space. Thus, Samos appears in the surviving corpus of Athenian forensic oratory in the intervening years as the setting for events mentioned in legal disputes (Dem. 21.71; Aesch. 1.53) and as defining characteristic of the titular character in Menander's *Samia*, but Timotheus' conquest of the island is conspicuously absent, albeit with the same result: the expulsion of the Samians is nowhere in Athenian cultural memory.[39] By 324, though, the new context featuring the imminent return of the displaced Samians further complicated the memory of events surrounding the acquisition of Samos.

4 Conquest, displacement, and memory

The evidence for Timotheus' conquest of Samos reveals not one, but two memories. In the one that is widely followed by modern historians, Athens conquered the island and displaced its population, creating a wave of displaced persons

---

38 Maltagliati 2020, 80–81 has evaluated Dinarchus' other references to Timotheus in Dinarchus 1 in terms of how they create the appearance of chronological proximity. On this passage in particular, see Worthington 1992, 151. There is an extensive bibliography on the Harpalus Affair. The most recent treatment, Gottesman 2015, offers a good survey of the older work, among which, see particularly Badian 1961, 16–43; Blackwell 1999, 134–144; Worthington 1992, 41–77 and 1994. Scholars frequently link Alexander's decision about Samos with the Exiles Decree as though it demanded the return of Samos, following Diod. 18.8.7 (e.g. Blackwell 1999, 123), but although the displaced Samians presented themselves as exiles (*RO* 90, l. 6) it was a separate ruling, Ephippus BNJ 126 F 5; cf. Dmitriev 2004, 366–370; Worthington 2015.

39 Demosthenes was even said to have married a Samian woman (Plut. *Dem.* 15.4; [Plut.] *Mor.* 847c), which complicated the status of his children. Roisman and Worthington 2015, 240 suggest that she was Samian rather than a cleruch with Athenian citizenship, since the proposals for his recall and honorific statue came from his cousin and nephew, respectively, rather than his children.

through the eastern Mediterranean. In the other, the Athenians liberated Samos and incorporated it into the Athenian *polis*. An old adage holds that when one person says 'black' and the other says 'white,' the person hearing assumes that the truth is somewhere on the spectrum of gray even when one or the other position is correct. One might be inclined to say the same about competing cultural memories, but here there is reason to locate the truth in the gray.

Without question, the Athenians drove oligarchic Samians into exile and the cleruchs disrupted life on the island, but, despite a series of honorific decrees in the early Hellenistic period thanking individuals and cities for their support during the period of exile, there is no evidence for the cascading consequences that mass expulsion from a *polis* the population of Samos would have caused. The seemingly-widespread hostility toward Athens in 323 most likely reflects a bias in the surviving sources. Exaggerating the collective trauma was a powerful political tool for Samian elites who had been in exile since the 360s. When returnees such as Duris ascended to power, they squashed any indication that their sympathies might not have been shared by all Samians because the narrative of oppression and exploitation at the hand of Athens helped create a unified identity in the previously fragmented *polis*.[40]

The corpus of speeches from the Attic orators is an important reflection of Athenian memory, but these few instances did not shape that trajectory. From the perspective of the Athenian orators, there *was* an underlying unity between Athens and Samos, with a tradition from the end of the fifth century that was inscribed not once, but twice, delivering Athenian citizenship to the people of Samos. In this sense, these speeches were part of a broader shaping of cultural memory that was successful, but only in Athens. Beyond this ideological ecosystem, the memory of Athenian imperialism festered, giving rise to the narratives used to restore Samos as a viable *polis* in the early Hellenistic period.

---

40 The best contemporary Samian source is the historian Duris (BNJ 76), who dominated political life in the restored community, but none of the surviving fragments of his work mentions Timotheus or the exile. Duris' account of the war in 440/39 (F 65–67) oozes with vitriol toward Pericles, sentiments often read as a reflection of Duris' youth spent in exile; see Gattinoni 1997, 233 n. 46; Pownall 2016, F 96 commentary. Hau 2020, 52–53, also interprets this account as a product of cultural memory but suggests that it was the "history of the victims." However, Duris' anti-Athenian agenda is better explained as part of a program to legitimize the new regime; see Thomas 2019, 283–294. Duris' brother Lynceus probably studied under Theophrastus at Athens, but the evidence for Duris is more suspect; see Dalby 1991; Pownall 2016, T 1 commentary.

Bibliography

Badian, E. (1961), "Harpalus", *JHS* 81, 16–43.
Baron, C.A. (2006), "The Aristoteles Decree and the Expansion of the Second Athenian League", *Hesperia* 75, 379–395.
Blackwell, C.W. (1999), *In the Absence of Alexander: Harpalus and the Failure of Macedonian Authority*, New York.
Blamire, A. (2001), "Athenian Finance, 454–404 B.C.", *Hesperia* 70, 99–126.
Buckler, J.M.H. (2003), *Aegean Greece in the Fourth Century*, Leiden.
Cargill, J. (1981), *The Second Athenian League*, Berkeley/Los Angeles.
Cargill, J. 1983), "*IG* II2 1 and the Athenian Kleruchy on Samos", *GRBS* 24, 321–332.
Cargill, J. (1995), *Athenian Settlements of the Fourth Century B.C.*, Leiden.
Dalby, A. (1991), "The Curriculum Vitae of Duris of Samos", CQ^2 41, 539–541.
Develin, R. (1989), *Athenian Officials, 684–321 B.C.*, Cambridge.
Dmitriev, S. (2004), "Alexander's Exiles Decree", *Klio* 86, 348–381.
Dmitriev, S. (2011), *The Greek Slogan of Freedom and Early Roman Politics in Greece*, Oxford.
Efstathiou, A. (2013), "The historical example of Marathon as used in the speeches *On the false embassy*, *On the crown*, and *Against Ctesiphon* by Demosthenes and Aeschines", in: C. Carey/M. Edwards (eds.), *Marathon–2,500 Years* (Bulletin of the Institute of Classical Studies Supplement, 124), 181–198.
Errington, R.M. (1975), "Samos and the Lamian War", *Chiron* 5, 51–57.
Fauber, C.M. (1998), "Was Kerkyra a Member of the Second Athenian League?", CQ^2 48, 110–116.
Fornara, C.W./Lewis, D.M. (1979), "The Chronology of the Samian War", *JHS* 99, 7–19.
Gattinoni, F.L. (1997), *Duride di Samo*, Rome.
Griffith, G.T. (1978), "Athens in the Fourth Century", in: P.D.A. Garnsey/C.R. Whittaker (eds.), *Imperialism in the Ancient World*, Cambridge, 127–144.
Gottesman, A. (2015), "Reading the arrivals of Harpalus", *GRBS* 55, 176–195.
Habicht, C. (1957), "Samische Volksbeschlüsse der hellenistischen Zeit", *MDAI(A)* 72, 152–274.
Habicht, C. (1972), "Hellenistische Inschriften aus dem Heraion von Samos", *MDAI(A)* 87, 191–228.
Habicht, C. (1996), "Athens, Samos, and Alexander the Great", *PAPhS* 140, 397–405.
Hamel, D. (1998), *Athenian Generals: Military Authority in the Classical Period* (Mnemosyne Supplements 182), Leiden.
Hamilton, J.R. (1953), "Alexander and His 'So-Called' Father", CQ^2 3, 151–157.
Hamilton, J.R. (1961), "The Letters in Plutarch's Alexander", *Proceedings of the African Classical Associations* 4, 9–20.
Hamilton, J.R. (1969), *Plutarch, Alexander: A Commentary*, Oxford.
Hammond, N.G.L. (1993), "Alexander's Letter concerning Samos in Plut. 'Alex.' 28.2", *Historia* 42, 379–382.
Hanink, J. (2017), *The Classical Debt: Greek Antiquity in an Era of Austerity*, Cambridge, MA.
Hau, L. (2020), "Tragedies of War in Duris and Phylarchus: social memory and experiential history", in: J. Klooster/I.N.I. Kuin (eds.), *After the Crisis: Remembrance, Re-anchoring and Recovery in Ancient Greece and Rome*, London, 49–64.
Herrman, J. (2019), *Demosthenes, Selected Political Speeches*, Cambridge.

Hobden, F. (2007), "Imagining Past and Present: A Rhetorical Strategy in Aeschines 3 'Against Ctesiphon'", *CQ²* 57, 490–501.
Hornblower, S. (1982), *Mausolos*, Oxford.
Kebric, R. (1977), *In the Shadow of Macedon: Duris of Samos* (Zeitschrift fur alte Geschichte: Einzelschriften, 29), Wiesbaden.
Kucharski, J. (2014), "Review: Steinbock, *Social Memory in Athenian Public Discourse*", *Phoenix* 68, 170–172.
Loraux, N. (2006a), *The Invention of Athens: The Funeral Oration in the Classical City*, A. Sheridan (trans.), New York.
Loraux, N. (2006b), *The Divided City: On Memory and Forgetting in Ancient Athens*, C. Pache with J. Fort (transl.), New York.
Ma, M. (2006), "A Gilt Statue for Konon at Erythrae?", *ZPE* 157, 124–126.
Maltagliati, G. (2020), "Persuasion through Proximity (and Distance) in the Attic Orators' Historical Examples", *GRBS* 60, 68–97.
Marginesu, G./Themos, A.A. (2014), "Ἀνέλοσαν ἐς τὸν πρὸς Σαμίος πόλεμον: A New Fragment of the Samian War Expenses (*IG* I³ 363+454)", in: A.P. Matthaiou/R.K. Pitt (eds.), *Athenaion Episkopos: Studies in Honour of H.B. Mattingly*, Athens, 171–184.
Nudell, J. (2018), "'Who Cares About the Greeks Living in Asia?,' Ionia in Fourth-Century Attic Oratory", *CJ* 114, 163–190.
Ober, J. (2002), "Social Science History, Cultural History, and the Amnesty of 403", *TAPA* 132, 127–137.
Papillon, T. (1997), "Mixed Unities in the 'Antidosis' of Isocrates", *RSQ* 27, 47–62.
Papillon, T. (2006), "Isocrates", in: I. Worthington (ed.), *The Blackwell Companion to Greek Rhetoric*, Malden, MA, 58–74.
Perlman, S. (1961), "The Historical Example: Its use and importance as propaganda in Attic Orators", *Scripta hierosolymitana* 150–166.
Pownall, F. (2014), "Review: Steinbock, *Social Memory in Athenian Public Discourse*", *CJ* 109, 366–368.
Pownall, F. (2016), "Duris of Samos (76)", in: I. Worthington (ed.), *Brill's New Jacoby*, Leiden.
Roisman, J./Worthington, I. (2015), *Lives of the Attic Orators*, Oxford.
Rosen, K. (1978), "Der 'göttliche' Alexander, Athen und Samos", *Historia* 27, 20–39.
Rubinstein, L. (2004), "Ionia", in: M.H. Hansen/T.H. Nielsen (eds.), *Inventory of Archaic and Classical Poleis*, Oxford, 1053–1107.
Rubinstein, L. (2009), "Oratory", in: B. Graziosi/P. Vasunia/G. Boys-Stones (eds.), *The Oxford Handbook of Hellenic Studies*, Oxford, 505–517.
Rubinstein, L. (2018), "The Athenian Amnesty of 403/2 and the 'Forgotten' Amnesty of 405/4", in: W. Riess (ed.), *Colloquia Attica: Neuere Forschungen zur Archaik, zum athenischen Recht und zur Magie* (Hamburger Studien zu Gesellschaften und Kulteren der Vormoderne, 4), Stuttgart, 123–144.
Schweigert, E. (1940), "The Athenian Cleruchy on Samos", *AJP* 61, 194–198.
Sealey, R. (1955), "Athens after the Social War", *JHS* 75, 74–81.
Shear, J. (2013), "'Their Memories Will Never Grow Old': The Politics of Remembrance in the Athenian Funeral Orations", *CQ²* 63, 511–536.
Shipley, G. (1987), *A History of Samos: 800–188 BC*, Oxford.
Steinbock, B. (2013), *Social Memory in Athenian Public Discourse: Uses and Meanings of the Past*, Ann Arbor.
Thomas, R. (2019), *Polis Histories, Collective Memories and the Greek World*, Cambridge.

Too, Y.L. (2008), *A Commentary on Isocrates' Antidosis*, Oxford.
Wertsch, J.V. (2008), "The Narrative Organization of Collective Memory", *Ethos* 36, 120–130.
Wolpert, A. (2002a), *Remembering Defeat: Civil War and Civic Memory in Ancient Athens*, Baltimore.
Wolpert, A. (2002b), "Lysias 18 and Athenian Memory of Civil War", *TAPA* 132, 109–126.
Wolpert, A. (2003), "Addresses to the Jury in the Attic Orators", *AJP* 124, 537–555.
Woodhead, A.G. (1957), "*IG* II^2 and Jason of Pherae", *AJA* 61, 367–373.
Woodhead, A.G. (1962), "Chabrias, Timotheus, and the Aegean Allies, 375–373 B.C.", *Phoenix* 16, 258–266.
Worthington, I. (1992), *A Historical Commentary on Dinarchus*, Ann Arbor.
Worthington, I. (1994), "The Harpalus affair and the Greek response to the Macedonian hegemony", in: I. Worthington (ed.), *Ventures into Greek History*, Oxford, 307–330.
Worthington, I. (2013), *Demosthenes of Athens and the Fall of Classical Greece*, Oxford.
Worthington, I. (2015), "From East to West: Alexander and the Exiles Decree", in: P. Wheatley/E. Baynham (eds.), *East and West in the World Empire of Alexander: Essays in Honour of Brian Bosworth*, Oxford, 93–105.
Zelnick-Abramovitz, R. (2004), "Settlers and Dispossessed in the Athenian Empire", *Mnemosyne* 57, 325–345.

James Sickinger
State Inscriptions from the Recent Past in the Attic Orators

Abstract: This chapter examines how the Attic orators integrated recent inscriptions — ones set up within a few decades of the date of the speeches in which they are mentioned — into their speeches in order to support and enhance their arguments. He notes that scholars have often discussed the fourth-century practice of citing older, fifth-century documents, especially inscribed documents, for the moral exempla and models of behavior that they provide for their audiences. Nevertheless, less often explored are how and why the Attic orators turned to more recently inscribed texts to support their cases and reinforce specific arguments. Several speeches include references to recent inscriptions and requests to have their texts read out, but unlike the fifth-century *stelae* cited by the orators, these citations are not meant to illustrate behavior of a distant era or provide models that an audience should emulate. Instead, their texts provide specific evidence in support of some aspect of a speaker's case. Sickinger shows that the orators and their audiences recognized that inscriptions of different dates could serve different functions, and that ones close to their own time were a potentially valuable source for information more immediately relevant to the issue at hand.

This chapter examines how the Attic orators make use of inscriptions from the recent past,[1] ones set up in the decade or two before the delivery of the speeches that mention them. References to older state documents, usually ones dating to the fifth century, are well known. Fourth-century speakers in both the Assembly and lawcourts appeal to their texts in trials and debates concerning contemporary issues for their persuasive and paradigmatic value, and they often use them to fashion positive images of a bygone era that contrast with present-day decline.[2] Contemporary or near-contemporary inscriptions also attract attention,

---

[1] For a definition of the time-span of the recent past see Kapellos' Introduction in this volume.
[2] Andoc. 1.95–96, Lycur. 1.124–126 (decree of Demophantus); Dem. 9.41–44, 19.271–272, Din. 2.24–25 (decree condemning Arthmius of Zelea); Dem. 20.69 (decree of Conon); Dem. 20.127–130 (decree for descendants of Harmodius and Aristogeiton); [Dem.] 59.94–106 (decree granting citizenship to the Plataeans); Lyc. 1.117–119 (decree condemning Hipparchus son of Charmus). For discussion see now Liddel 2020, 2:109–158 (especially Table 3, p. 147), focusing primarily on decrees.

but the orators refer to them and their texts differently. Newer *stelai* are cited because their contents preserve specific texts or details that a speaker cites to support of an argument or to comment on the character of an opposing party, or both. Some of these references are brief and amount to little more than a passing mention. Others are more substantial and tie in more directly to subject matter of a speech. What the orators do not do is ascribe broader didactic or exemplary value to recently-inscribed texts or construct from them idealized images of the recent past. They cite and treat them primarily as documents that provide written evidence of matters of interest to them.

A good starting point is a decade-old inscription cited in Andocides' *On the Peace*.[3] The ostensible occasion of the speech was a meeting of the Assembly in 391, in which Andocides presented terms of a proposed peace treaty that would end the Corinthian War. Andocides cites several historical *exempla* to support this proposal throughout the speech, but he also compares its provisions explicitly to the inscribed terms of the treaty ending the Peloponnesian War just over a decade before (And. 3.10–12). He prefaces this comparison by addressing concerns over the aftermath of that treaty and by characterizing it as a truce (σπονδαί), as opposed to the "peace" (εἰρήνη) that he is now proposing. But his actual comparison between the two is direct and focused: he quotes directly from the *stele* on which the treaty was published, and he compares some of its terms explicitly to corresponding ones in his own proposal (Andoc. 3.12). He does not describe the inscription or its text as a paradigm (παράδειγμα) or reminder (ὑπόμνημα), as other orators do when citing inscriptions from the more distant past.[4] Instead, he mentions the *stele* simply as the source on which the text of the earlier treaty with Sparta was published, and he cites portions of its inscribed text to support his own proposal.[5]

The authenticity of *On the Peace* is disputed, and so its rhetorical practices may not reflect ones actually used in speeches given before the Assembly.[6] And in fact, other symbouleutic speeches do not cite recently-inscribed treaties, decrees, or other documents with the same degree of specificity. But they do not ignore them either, and references to *stelai* in deliberative oratory suggest that debate in the Assembly sometimes did take the contents of recently-published

---

[3] On the speech see Harris and Pownall in this volume; cf. Grethlein 2010, 126–146 on Andocides' use of historical *exempla*.
[4] Inscription as reminder: Dem. 9.41; Lyc. 1.126; as paradigm Lyc. 1.119, 124, Dem. 9.41; Din. 2.24.
[5] On the passage see also Sickinger 2002, 157–158.
[6] For arguments against authenticity see Harris in this volume, building on Harris 2000; arguments against authenticity are advanced by Rhodes 2016, 182–186; cf. also Pownall in this volume.

inscriptions into consideration. In 418 an Argive embassy came to Athens and complained of Spartan violations of "what was written in the treaty" (Thuc. 5.56.1–2), an allusion to a clause in the recent alliance between Athens, Argos, Mantinea, and Elis, concluded in 420 (Thuc. 5.47.5); inscribed copies of it stood at Athens, Argos, Mantinea, and Olympia (Thuc. 5.47.11). This complaint prompted the Athenians, on the urging of Alcibiades, to append a statement to the "Laconian" *stele*, stating that the Spartans had violated their oaths (5.56.3). This *stele* was probably the inscription recording the Peace of Nicias, concluded between Athens and Sparta in 421, just three years earlier (Thuc. 5.18).[7] The specifics of this debate are beyond recovery, but the references to two treaties, both recently published on stone, and the addition made to one of their inscribed texts, suggest that Andocides was not the first speaker in the Assembly to cite the contents of a relatively new inscription. Fourth-century deliberative speeches do not mention *stele* quite as explicitly, but some passages point to a familiarity with the inscribed copies of treaties. Demosthenes alludes to the potential destruction of recent *stelai* in the speech *For the Megalopolitans*, delivered in 353. He notes that previous speakers had called upon the Megalopolitans to tear down the inscriptions recording their treaty with Thebes if they wanted to secure alliance with Athens (Dem. 16.27); that treaty was just over a decade old at the time of this debate.[8] What those speakers actually said is also impossible to say, but Demosthenes' mention of their demand reveals that even the contents of non-Athenians inscriptions were known to some Athenians. Suggestive also are some references to the Peace of Philocrates, concluded in 346. It too was published on stone, and its terms were a frequent subject of debate in the years following its ratification.[9] In one speech Demosthenes actually observes that its written text was visible (Dem. 8.5), and the Athenians later voted to tear down its *stele* when they declared war on Philip in 340 (Philoch. BNJ 328 F 55a). Removal of the inscribed copies of treaties was not automatic when they became obsolete or were cancelled, and both Demosthenes, who introduced the motion to destroy the *stele*, and other speakers may well have

---

[7] See Bolmarcich 2007, 481–482, on this incident.
[8] See Bolmarcich 2007, 482 on this passage. The Theban-Megapolitan alliance could not have been earlier than 370, when Megalopolis was founded; on the date see Hornblower 1990; Buckler and Beck 2008, 135–136.
[9] The *stele* is mentioned by Philochorus BNJ 328 F 55a (cf. F 161); see also [Dem.] 12.8; Aesch. 3.70; on the decree ratifying the peace see Liddel 2020, 2:477–487.

discussed the inscription and its text when the Athenians decided that their treaty with Philip was no longer in force.[10]

References to inscriptions from the recent past appear with greater frequency in forensic speeches, where state documents play a more prominent role in orators' rhetorical strategies. Litigants rarely mention the sources from which they obtained the documents they cite or refer to the physical media on which their texts were recorded, but they and their audiences knew that inscriptions preserved authentic texts of state documents, and a passage of the Demosthenic *Against Evergus and Mnesibulus* ([Dem.] 47) illustrates their accessibility. The unnamed speaker relates how, when an elderly freed women living in his household died after an altercation with his opponents, he sought advice from the *exegetai*, interpreters of Athenian law, on his legal remedies ([Dem.] 47.67–68). He then inspected the law of Dracon on homicide "from the *stele*" ([Dem.] 47.71).[11] No other speech describes the direct consultation of an inscribed document so explicitly, and a desire to connect himself with one of Athens' ancient lawgivers may explain why this speaker alludes to this specific inscription.[12] But there is no hint that the speaker was doing anything unusual, and allusions to specific *stelai*, including ones closer in time to the speeches themselves and not associated with well-known legislators, show that still others knew of and consulted their texts.

Andocides, for example, relates in his speech *On the Mysteries*, delivered in 400 or 399, how one inscribed document came up in the course of discussion over his alleged violation of a sacred regulation. According to him, Callias, a priest of the Eleusinian cult, claimed at a meeting of the Council that Andocides had placed a suppliant's branch on an altar in the Eleusinium during the celebration of the Mysteries (Andoc. 1.110–116).[13] That was prohibited, and Callias cited an interpretation of an ancestral, and evidently unwritten, law requiring immediate execution of the perpetrator, whom he identified as Andocides (Andoc. 1.115). But Cephalus immediately objected and pointed to a nearby *stele* whose text specified a fine of 1000 drachmas for the same offense; its text was then read out (Andoc. 1.116). The preference for a written rule over an ancestral, unwritten law is noteworthy, but also significant is that Cephalus knew the

---

10 See Bolmarcich 2007, on the removal of inscribed treaties (esp. 483 on the Peace of Philocrates).
11 A copy of Dracon's law was republished on stone *stele* in 409 (*IG* 1³ 104) and may be the inscription that the speaker examined.
12 On appeals to Athenian lawgivers see Hansen 1989; Thomas 1994; Johnstone 1999, 25–33.
13 On the date of the speech see MacDowell 1961, 204–205; Loening 1987, 140.

penalty recorded on the inscription before he cited it; he did not have search for a relevant statute. Moreover, the inscription cited by Cephalus was not necessarily ancient or associated with a famous lawgiver. Its date is uncertain, but estimates range from the 470s to 403/2, only a few years before Andocides' speech.[14] Whatever its date, the episode shows that Athenians recognized inscriptions as reliable sources of legal information and that they were ready to appeal to their written contents when appropriate.

Reliance on specific details derived from recently-inscribed texts is illustrated in the Lysianic *Against Nicomachus*, delivered in the early 390s.[15] Nicomachus had been one of the *anagrapheis* responsible for reviewing the laws of Athens at the end of the fifth century. The *anagrapheis* served two terms in office, and during their second term, lasting from 403 to 399, they published a new sacrificial calendar, fragments of which survive.[16] Their work, however, proved controversial, and Nicomachus was accused of misconduct when his time in office came to end. The speaker of Lysias 30 alleges that he had exceeded the mandate given to the *anagrapheis* and inserted more sacrifices into the new sacrificial calendar than their original instructions prescribed (Lys. 30.4, 19). As a result the costs associated with the new calendar cost six more talents per year than was necessary, so that older, traditional sacrifices valued at three talents per year had gone unperformed in each of the past two years (Lys. 30.17–20).

The speaker cites *kyrbeis*, pillar-like objects often associated with Solon and recording his laws, as the source of the older sacrifices left neglected because of the work of the *anagrapheis* (Lys. 30.17, 18, 20).[17] He argues that if the *anagrapheis* had simply worked from the *kyrbeis*, as they were supposed to do, enough funds were available to perform all the sacrifices recorded on them. By contrast, the new sacrificial calendar recently published by Nicomachus and his

---

14 The inscription is sometimes identified with *IG* 1³ 6, which records regulations on the Eleusinian Mysteries: see Osborne and Rhodes 2017, 41; Scafuro 2010, 35–37; Lambert 2020, 30 note 125. It is dated to c. 475–450: see Lambert 2020, 28. Ostwald 1986, 165, suggests that the inscription cited by Cephalus may have been more recent and a product of the revision of Athens' laws completed in 403/2.
15 For date and background see Carawan 2010; Todd 1996.
16 See Lambert 2002 for a new edition, to which add Gawlinski 2006. Dow 1953–7 remains essential. On the work of the *anagrapheis* see also Shear 2011, 70–111; Volonaki 2001; Rhodes 1991; Robertson 1990.
17 The physical form of the *kyrbeis* remains controversial; see Stroud 1979, Davis 2011, and Meyer 2016.

colleagues was displayed on *stelai* (Lys. 30.21).[18] Nowhere does he cite specific details from these *stelai*, but he calls upon witnesses to confirm his calculations of the excessive costs of the new sacrificial calendar (Lys. 30.20), and the figures he provides depend on knowledge of their contents and those of the *kyrbeis*. In addition, although he ties the past prosperity of Athens to the faithful performance by earlier generations of the sacrifices recorded on the *kyrbeis*, he ascribes no such significance to the more recent *stelai* of Nicomachus. He mentions them simply as the physical objects on which the new sacrificial calendar, and its allegedly unauthorized additions, were recorded.

Many Athenian officials set up inscriptions displaying details of their financial activities when their time in office came to an end.[19] The *stelai* of the *anagrapheis* were not precisely parallel to these inscribed accounts and inventories, but the recourse that the prosecutor of Nicomachus had to the inscriptions that he and his fellow *anagrapheis* had set up raises the question of how often others may have turned too the newly-inscribed financial documents for evidence of official misconduct. The speeches of the orators offer no answer to this question, as they preserve only a single reference to an inscribed official account or inventory. It occurs in the Demosthenic *Against Evergus and Mnesibulus* ([Dem.] 47), where the speaker relates how, when appointed to serve as trierarch and overseer of a naval symmory in 357/6, he and other incoming trierarchs learned that many of their predecessors had failed to return naval gear they had borrowed from the dockyards in Peiraeus. The new trierarchs were authorized to recover the missing equipment from those who had it in their possession, and the speaker was assigned Demochares and Theophemus, who had previously served together as co-trierarchs. He received their names from dockyard officials, but he also points out that they had been "written on the *stele*" as "owing equipment to the city" ([Dem.] 47.22). That *stele* was a naval inscription, one of a class of inscribed documents set up by the superintendents of the dockyards. They listed both naval gear stored in the dockyards and the names of individuals who had borrowed certain items each year; fragments, dating from the fourth century, survive in large numbers.[20] The specific *stele* to which the speaker refers was only a few years old at the time of his speech, and its mention of Demochares and Theophemus as debtors was not something that some-

---

18 Editors emend the text of Lys. 30.17 to create another reference to *stelai*, but that emendation should be rejected: see Nelson 2006
19 On these inscribed accounts and inventories see Davies 1994; cf. also Aleshire 1989, 103–108.
20 See Gabrielsen 1994, 13–19.

one could pick out easily from casual observation.²¹ It derived from close examination of the inscription itself.

No other speech mentions an inscribed account or inventory in this or any other way, and this neglect may suggest that accounts and inventories was largely ignored once they were published.²² It is worth noting, however, that our extant speeches were not composed for suits involving financial misconduct by state officials or ones in which published accounts of officials' activates were relevant. Even the naval inscription cited in this speech was not directly related to the suit of false testimony for which the speech was delivered; the speaker mentions it only in passing and primarily to disparage Theophemus, with whom he had a longstanding quarrel. But that quarrel, and the failure of Theophemus to return items of naval gear in his possession, had been the subject of other, previous litigation mentioned briefly in the speech.²³ Those earlier proceedings, and similar ones involving other state officials accused of malfeasance, may have provided more opportunities for consult and citing recently-erected inscriptions than the speeches of the orators imply.²⁴

More explicit use of details recorded in an inscription appears in the Lysianic *Against Agoratus*, delivered some time around 400.²⁵ Agoratus had denounced Dionysodorus, the brother-in-law of the speaker, for subverting the democracy in the final months of the Peloponnesian War. Dionysodorus was arrested and later executed by the Thirty, but after the democracy was restored, the speaker and other relatives of Dionysodorus charged Agoratus with homicide. The events leading up to his death occupy the first half of the speech (Lys. 13.5–48), while the second half addresses several arguments that Agoratus was expected to make in his own defense (Lys. 13.49–97). One of those involved a claim to Athenian citizenship by Agoratus for his supposed role in the assassination of Phrynichus (Lys. 13.70).²⁶ The speaker rejects this claim and cites an

---

21 The inscription was standing in the year of the speaker's trierarchy, 357/6. The speech itself was delivered a year or so later; MacDowell, 2009 140, suggests 356/5; Scafuro 2011, 297–298, puts it no earlier than 354/3. A record of the equipment owed by Demochares and Theophemus survives: *IG* 2² 1612.313–316.
22 So Davies 1994, 211–212; cf. also Liddel 2020, 2:146–148.
23 See Rhodes 1972, 154–156 and Gabrielsen 1994, 164–166, for the speaker's initial quarrel with Theophemus and his attempts to retrieve missing naval gear.
24 For one example see *SEG* 51.1001 (= Chankowski 2001).
25 The date of the speech is disputed. Todd 2000, 138–139 and Gernet and Bizos 1924, 186 n. 1 place it in the early 390s, but Loening 1987, 74; Bearzot 1997, 74–76; and Carawan 2013, 119–125 argue convincingly for a date before 400.
26 On Phrynichus see Rhodes in this volume.

inscribed decree granting citizenship to Thrasybulus, one of the killers of Phrynichus, to rebut it. He has a court clear read out its text, and he observes that the *stele* recording it did not make Agoratus a citizen, as it did Thrasybulus. He further alleges that some individuals contrived to have their names added to this *stele* by bribing the proposer of its decree, an allegation he supports by having a second decree read out (Lys. 13.72). Although he does not say so explicitly, the implication is that Agoratus was one of those false benefactors.

An inscription of 409 (*IG* 1³ 102) sheds some light on the speaker's arguments. It records a decree honoring several individuals for their involvement in the killing of Phrynichus, and its contents resemble closely several features of the inscribed decree described by Lysias, including a citizenship grant to Thrasybulus (lines 14–22), mention of Agoratus as a benefactor (lines 25–29) and allusions to bribery (lines 39–44). But there are also discrepancies, and the speaker appears to be quoting selectively and possibly overlooking other relevant decrees, such as one by which Agoratus was made an Athenian citizen.[27] What matters for our purposes is how the speaker makes use of a decade-old inscription. His references to it are brief and direct, and he does not attach broader meaning or significance to it. The *stele* functioned as a writing support whose contents he cited as evidence to support his own claims about the status of Agoratus.

A similar and even simpler reference to a *stele* occurs in the Demosthenic *Against Theocrines* ([Dem.] 58), delivered around 340. Its speaker, Epichares, had charged Theocrines with initiating several public prosecutions illegally because, as a state debtor, he was ineligible to do so.[28] Epichares devotes much of the speech to those prosecutions and the alleged debts incurred by Theocrines, but he also attacks several supporters of Theocrines, including a certain Moerocles. This Moerocles had proposed a decree meant to protect merchants on sea voyages from harm, but, Epichares points out, he is now defending Theocrines, whose malicious prosecutions have harmed those very same merchants in Piraeus ([Dem.] 58.53–56).[29] As Ephichares concludes his attack on both Moerocles and Theocrines, he asks the court clerk to "read the *stele*" (58.56), meaning a text recorded on an inscription and probably the decree of Moerocles

---

27 On the relationship between the inscription and the account of Lysias see Osborne and Rhodes 2017, 500–505; cf. also Scafuro 2009.

28 On the speech and its date see MacDowell 2009, 293–298; Bers 2003, 129–131; Gernet 1960, 40–41.

29 On the decree see Ampolo 1981, 197–198. Liddel 2020, vol. 1: 739–742. Lambert 2007, 111–113, finds a reference to the decree in *IG* 2² 543 (now *IG* 2³ 1.414), dating from c. 340, based on his new reading of its text.

itself.³⁰ Why Epichares asks for the *stele* to be read out and not the decree is unclear, and he does not comment any further on the inscription.³¹ The decree of Moerocles was, however, recent: scholars normally date its passage to the few years immediately preceding the prosecution of Theocrines.³² One wonders whether that recent approval and publication played a role in the decision of the Epichares to mention its *stele*. Possibly, Epichares knew of the Moerocles' decree from attending a meeting of the Assembly at which it was ratified. But the inscribing of decrees on stone was also selective, and he may have wanted to enhance its status in the minds of his audience by calling attention to its physical copy.

References to several inscriptions in Demosthenes' *Against Leptines* offer further insights into the rhetorical use of inscriptions and how their age could affect descriptions of them. The speech was delivered in 355/4 in a suit challenging the legality of a law, proposed by Leptines, cancelling exemptions from liturgies granted by the Athenians in the past and prohibiting similar exemptions in the future.³³ Demosthenes argued that the law damaged the interests of Athens, and he devotes a large portion of his speech to its impact on previous benefactors (Dem. 20.29–87). His first example is Leucon, ruler of the Cimmerian Bosporus, whom the Athenians had rewarded with a number of privileges, including exemptions from liturgies, for his assistance in ensuring an adequate grain supply for the city (Dem. 20.30–33). He describes the benefits that the Athenians have received from Leucon, notes the privileges granted by him to Athenian merchants, and asks the judges how they think Leucon will react when he learns that they have revoked their previous honors to him (Dem. 20.34–35).

Demosthenes has the decrees conferring honors on Leucon read out to the judges, and he observes that copies of them stood on *stelai* in Peiraeus, Bosporus, and Hierum (Dem. 20.35–36). Those inscriptions probably dated as far back as the early 380s, more than thirty years before the date of the speech, when

---

30 Bers 2003, 147 n. 59, and Liddel 2020, 1:741 think that the *stele* mentioned at section 56 carried a law or laws related to the case, but that seems unlikely, given the focus of the preceding sections on Moerocles' decree. In addition, the speaker discusses several laws related to the case earlier in the speech and has their texts read out; but nowhere does he indicate that any of their texts existed on *stelai*.
31 See Boegehold 1991, 151–152, for the citation of physical objects (e.g., *stelai*) instead of their texts (e.g. a *psesphismata*).
32 On the date of the decree see Ampolo 1981, 196–204; Lambert 2007, 112.
33 For historical and legal background see Canevaro 2016, 3–100; Kremmydas 2012, 2–60.

Leucon became sole ruler of the Bosporan kingdom.[34] That time frame puts them just beyond a recent past of twenty years, and Demosthenes describes them in such a way that their meaning was ambiguous, caught between a recent and more distant past. He instructs his audience to think of the inscribed *stelai* as *synthekai*, terms of a mutual agreement between two parties, as if the services rendered by Leucon and the honors given to him by the Athenians formed a binding contract.[35] Viewed in this way, those *stelai* will show that Leucon is living up to his obligations by continuing to offer his assistance to Athens, while Athenians, because the law of Leptines takes away some of his privileges, will be exposed as failing to keep up their end of the bargain, even though its terms (the *synthekai* recorded on *stelai*) remain standing. That contradiction, Demosthenes suggests, "is much worse than simply tearing down" the *stelai*, because their visibility will provide "proof to those wanting to slander the city that their words are true" (Dem. 20.37).[36]

Demosthenes is speaking metaphorically when he equates the *stelai* recording the decrees honoring Leucon with *synthekai*, but his discussion highlights how the meanings attached to were fluid. He works from the assumption that inscriptions should reflect accurately, for as long as they stand, the relationship between Leucon and Athens; they should function as documents and supply evidence of their mutual obligations. Their failure to do so meant that they now risked assuming a new, more sinister meaning, as signs or symbols of Athenian ingratitude. He puts that shift in meaning, however, in the future, and the implication of his argument is that cancellation of the law of Leptines would allow the inscribed *stelai* to resume their original, documentary purpose.[37]

Demosthenes raises questions about the meaning of these inscriptions because of the (supposed) ambiguity caused by the passage of Leptines' law and his own suit against its legality. He does not address their age, but in a later section of the speech he suggests that the passage of time also affected the function of inscriptions. After discussing Leucon he turns to other foreign benefactors of Athens whose exemptions were threatened by the law of Leptines. He recalls their services and has the decrees rewarding them read out (Dem. 20.41–69). He does not mention any inscribed *stelai* at first, although his language

---

34 For the date see Werner 1955, 415–417; Tuplin 1982, 125–127; Liddel 2020, 1:188.
35 On this meaning of *synthekai* see Carusi 2006, 21; Mirhady 2004, 57–58; Kussmaul 1969, 15–20; on the passage in general, see Canevaro 2016, 258–262; Kremmydas 2012, 259–262.
36 On the relevance of this passage to the removal of inscribed treaties see Bolmarcich 2007, 482–483.
37 Note the future verbs: φανεῖται (20.35); ἑστήξουσιν (20.36).

does recall that of surviving honorary decrees, and a stone copy of at least one of the ones he cites does survive.³⁸ But as he concludes this section he raises the possibility that some of the foreign benefactors he has mentioned may no longer be alive, so that cancellation of their exemptions by the law of Leptines was moot. Nonetheless, the results of their actions live on, and so their *stelai* should be allowed to stand "in force for all time."³⁹ He continues by explaining that while honorands are alive, they are protected by those inscriptions from unjust treatment at the hands of the Athenians, presumably because the inscriptions safeguarded their privileges by providing written evidence of them.⁴⁰ We might say that they fulfilled a sort of police function and protected the interests of the individuals named on them.⁴¹ After their honorands died, those inscriptions did not lose meaning but acquired a new purpose. They would then become "a reminder of the character of Athens and stand as illustrations, for those who want to do you some favor, of how many persons who have done good for our city it has rewarded in return."⁴² That is, they would someday serve as visible reminders of the generosity of Athens and as incentives for prospective benefactors, by showing the number of individuals the Athenians had recognized for their services in the past. This latter notion recalls the "hortatory intention," a type of clause found in the inscribed copies of Athenian honorary decrees from the middle of the fourth century. It is expressed in a variety of ways, but one formulation explains the purpose behind passing and inscribing honorary decrees in terms of both rewarding benefactors for their actions and encouraging

---

38 On the similarities between the language Demosthenes and the motivation formulae of inscribed decrees see West 1995. The decree for Epicerdes of Cyrene, described at 20.41–48 and read out at 44, is preserved in *IG* 1³ 125; on their relationahip see Nouhaud 1982, 127–128; Canevaro 2016, 216. The decree honoring Thasian supporters of Athens, described by Demosthenes at 20.59, 61–63 is sometimes identified with *IG* 2² 33: see Canevaro 2016, 292; Kremmydas 2012, 295; *contra* Liddel 2020, 1:190–191. Demosthenes also mentions a decree honoring a certain Heraclides (Dem. 20.60, read out at 63), which is sometimes identified with *IG* 1³ 227. But that connection is disputed: see Canevaro 2016, 293–294 for competing views.
39 Dem. 20.64: προσήκει τοίνυν τὰς στήλας ταύτας κυρίας ἐᾶν τὸν πάντα χρόνον.
40 Dem. 20.64: ἵν' ἕως μὲν ἄν τινες ζῶσι, μηδὲν ὑφ' ὑμῶν ἀδικῶνται.
41 For the phrase "police function" see Finely 1986, 40–42, who applies it primarily to inscribed financial records; cf. also Lambert 2011, 205 who speaks of "tangible guarantees." Apollodorus makes a similar point in *Against Neaera* ([Dem.] 59.105) about the *stele* recording the grant of citizenship to the Plataeans and its list of the original recipients.
42 Dem. 20.64: ἐπειδὰν δὲ τελευτήσωσιν, ἐκεῖναι τοῦ τῆς πόλεως ἤθους μνημεῖον ὦσι, καὶ παραδείγμαθ' ἑστῶσι τοῖς βουλομένοις τι ποιεῖν ὑμᾶς ἀγαθόν, ὅσους εὐποιήσαντας ἡ πόλις ἀντ' εὖ πεποίηκεν.

or promoting similar behavior from others in the future.⁴³ Demosthenes' words show that this sentiment was not restricted to epigraphic culture but was more widely shared in Athenian society.

Important for our purpose is that Demosthenes divides the function of inscribed *stelai* into two temporally distinct phases: at first they had evidentiary value and documented the decisions recorded on them; later they acquired more symbolic meaning.⁴⁴ Because Demosthenes links their shift in purpose to the lifespans of their honorands, we cannot fix the amount of time that honorary inscriptions served their original purpose in terms of a specific number of years, which would naturally vary according to individual cases. But his formulation does allow a general estimate: given ancient life spans most honorands would not be alive more than twenty or thirty years after receiving their honors, and most honorary inscriptions would lose their practical value within two or three decades. That estimate, in fact, accords roughly with the examples cited by Demosthenes in the immediately preceding chapters. He has just had read out decrees rewarding citizens of Thasos and Byzantium for their loyalty to Athens in the late 390s and early 380s (Dem. 20.59–63), some thirty-five years before the date of the speech, and many of their honorands had almost certainly passed away by the time of the speech.⁴⁵ His explanation of the temporally distinct functions of honorary inscriptions also helps to explain his earlier comments about the *stelai* honoring Leucon (Dem. 20.36–38).They too were more than 30 years old, and so they should have already assumed paradigmatic and symbolic value. But Leucon was still alive, and Demosthenes argues that the law of Leptines was altering their function, as written evidence of the honors granted to Leucon, prematurely. The artificial shift was also endowing the inscriptions with meanings at odds with their intended future purpose: instead of testifying to Athenian gratitude and providing incentives to potential, future benefactors, they might now bring disgrace and disrepute upon the city.

The *stelai* to which Demosthenes refers in *Against Leptines* displayed honorary decrees, but his remarks about their changing meaning have broader application, because they can also be applied to the ways in which he and other orators treat older and newer inscriptions. Inscriptions from the distant past are

---

43 On the hortatory intention in honorific decrees see especially Henry 1996, Hedrick 1999, and Miller 2016. For its use to explain the inscribing of honorary decrees see especially Lambert 2011; cf. also Luraghi 2009, 248–252; Liddel 2020, 2:126–127, 166–167. Note that not every statement of the hortatory intention applies to publication: Sickinger 2009.
44 See also the comments Lambert 2011, 205–206.
45 On the dates see Liddel 2020, 2: 169–172, 189–192.

normally invoked for the paradigmatic or symbolic value of their texts. But when the orators cite inscriptions dating from the decades immediately preceding their speeches (i.e., from the recent past), their references see them primarily as objects supplying written evidence of a specific fact, detail, or piece of information. In some cases, these recently-inscribed *stelai* receive only passing notice, like those associated with Theophemus ([Dem.) 47.22) and Moerocles ([Dem.] 58.56), and the details that they mention have only a tangential connection to the primary issue under consideration. In other cases speakers refer to newer inscriptions as sources of information for specific points that support an argument more closely related to the matter at hand, as in Andocides' *On the Peace* and Lysias's *Against Nicomachus* and *Against Agoratus*. Both sets of cases suggest that, at least in the decades immediately after a document was inscribed and publicly displayed, they saw *stelai* primarily as source for their texts and written evidence of the details recorded in them.

It must be admitted that the orators cite recent inscriptions only rarely. But their appeals to inscribed *stelai* of any age are also small in number, and they presumably relied primarily on other sources when they sought out documents to incorporate into their arguments.[46] Nonetheless, the ways in which they exploit documents inscribed relatively recently are significant, because they may shed light more on the intentions and motives for inscribing state documents in general. The fact that the Athenians (and other Greeks) saw inscriptions as reliable, authoritative sources for the texts displayed on them is widely acknowledged, as I noted at the start of this chapter. But practical aims tend to take a back seat to honorific, religious, and other motives in in.[47] Those considerations were certainly important, and it is not my intention to deny their significance. But it may be that those purposes only became more fully realized as inscriptions grew older. If the small number of references to recent inscriptions in the orators are any indication of broader attitudes and practices, in the years immediately following the publication of state documents, their stone copies were valued just as more for their written contents, especially when they concerned living individuals. Just how far that was that case will require further study, but it is a topic on which inscriptions themselves have much more to say.[48]

---

[46] On these sources, and especially the archives housed in the Metroon, see Sickinger 1999, especially 160–189; cf. also Liddel 2020, 2: 116–120, 155–158.
[47] See, e.g., Liddel 2020, 2: 127–132; Meyer 2013; Lambert 2011; Thomas 1989, 45–60.
[48] See especially Lambert 2012, discussing references to the past, sometimes in the form of older inscriptions, appearing in inscribed Athenian laws and decrees of the fourth century.

Bibliography

Aleshire, S.B. (1989), *The Athenian Asklepieion. The People, Their Dedications and Their Inventories*, Amsterdam.

Ampolo, C. (1981), "Tra finanza e politica. Carriera e affari del signor Moirokles", *RFIC* 109, 187–204.

Bearzot, C. (1997), *Lisia e la tradizione su Teramene: Commento storico alle orazioni XII e XIII del corpus Lysiacum*, Milano.

Bers, V. (2003), *Demosthenes. Speeches 50–59*, Austin.

Boegehold, A. (1990), "Andokides and the Decree of Patrokleides", *Historia* 39, 149–162.

Bolmarcich, S. (2007), "The Afterlife of a Treaty", *CQ* 57, 477–489.

Buckler, J./Beck, H. (2008), *Central Greece and the Politics of Power in the Fourth Century BC*, Cambridge.

Canevaro, M. (2016), *Demostene, Contro Leptine. Introduzione, Traduzione e Commento Storico*, Berlin.

Carawan, E. (2010), "The Case against Nikomachos", *TAPA* 140, 71–95.

Carawan, E. (2013), *The Athenian Amnesty and Reconstructing the Law*, Oxford.

Carusi, C. (2006), "Alcune osservazioni sulle *syngraphai* ateniesi del V e del IV secolo a.C", *ASAA* 84 Ser. 3a 6 (1), 11–35.

Chankowski, V. (2001), "Un nouveau procès délien : les comptes des naopes de Délos et la procédure athénienne au IVe Siècle", *BCH* 125, 175–193.

Davies, J.K. (1994), "Accounts and Accountability in Classical Athens", in: R. Osborne/S. Hornblower (eds.), *Ritual, Finance, Politics: Athenian Democratic Accounts Presented to David Lewis*, 201–212, Oxford.

Davis, G. (2011), "*Axones* and *Kurbeis*: A New Answer to an Old Problem", *Historia* 60, 1–35.

Dow, S. (1953–1957), "The Law Codes of Athens", *Proceedings of the Massachusetts Historical Society* 71, 3–36.

Finley, M.I. (1986), *Ancient History. Evidence and Models*, New York.

Gabrielsen, V. (1994), *Financing the Athenian Fleet: Public Taxation and Social Relations*, Baltimore.

Gawlinski, L. (2007), "The Athenian Calendar of Sacrifices: A New Fragment from the Athenian Agora", *Hesperia* 76, 37–55.

Gernet, L. (1960), *Démosthène. Plaidoyers civils. Tome IV (Discours LVII-LIX)*, Paris.

Gernet, L./Bizos, M.I. (1924), *Lysias. Discours. Tome I (I-XV)*, Paris.

Grethlein, J. (2010), *The Greeks and Their Past: Poetry, Oratory and History in the Fifth Century BCE*, Cambridge.

Hansen, M.H. (1989), "Solonian Democracy in Fourth-Century Athens", *C&M* 40, 71–99.

Harris, E.M. (2000), "The Authenticity of Andokides' De Pace: A Subversive Essay", in: P. Flensted-Jensen/T. Heine (eds.), *Polis & Politics: Studies in Ancient Greek History Presented to Mogens Herman Hansen on His Sixtieth Birthday*, August 20, 479–505, Copenhagen.

Hedrick, C.W. (1999), "Democracy and the Athenian Epigraphical Habit", *Hesperia* 68, 387–439.

Henry, A.S. (1996), "The Hortatory Intention in Athenian State Decrees", *ZPE* 112, 105–119.

Hornblower, S. (1990), "When Was Megalopolis Founded?", *ABSA* 85, 71–77.

Johnstone, S. (1999), *Disputes and Democracy: The Consequences of Litigation in Ancient Athens*, Austin.

Kremmydas, C. (2012), *Commentary on Demosthenes against Leptines: With Introduction, Text, and Translation*, Oxford.
Kussmaul, P. (1969), *Synthekai. Beiträge zur Geschichte des attischen Obligationsrechtes*, Basel.
Lambert, S.D. (2002), "The Sacrificial Calendar of Athens", *ABSA* 97, 353–399.
Lambert, S.D. (2007), "Athenian State Laws and Decrees, 352/1-322/1: III Decrees Honouring Foreigners. B. Other Awards", *ZPE* 159, 101–154.
Lambert, S.D. (2010), "Connecting with the Past in Lykourgan Athens: An Epigraphical Perspective", in: L. Foxhall/H.-J. Gehrke/N. Luraghi (eds.), *Intentional History: Spinning Time in Ancient Greece*, 225–238, Stuttgart.
Lambert, S.D. (2011), "What was the Point of Inscribed Honorific Decrees in Classical Athens?", in: S.D. Lambert (ed.), *Sociable Man: Essays on Ancient Greek Social Behaviour in Honour of Nick Fisher*, 193–214, Swansea.
Lambert, S.D. (2012), "Inscribing the Past in Fourth-Century Athens", in: J. Marincola/L. Llewellyn-Jones/C. Alasdair (eds.), *Greek Notions of the Past in the Archaic and Classical Eras: History without Historians*, 253–275, Edinburgh.
Lambert, S. (2016), "The Selective Inscribing of Laws and Decrees in Late Classical Athens", *Hyperboreus* 22, 217–239.
Lambert, S. (2020), *Attic Inscriptions in UK Collections British Museum Decrees of the Council and Assembly*, AIUK vol. 4.2. (https://www.atticinscriptions.com/papers/aiuk/).
Liddel, P. (2020), *Decrees of Fourth-Century Athens (403/2-322/1 BC)*, 2 vols., Cambridge.
Loening, T.C. (1987), *The Reconciliation Agreement of 403/402 B.C. in Athens: Its Content and Application*, Wiesbaden.
Luraghi, N. (2010), "The Demos as Narrator: Public Honors and the Construction of Future and Past", in: L. Foxhll/H.-J. Gehrke/N. Luraghi (eds.), *Intentional History: Spinning Time in Ancient Greece*, 247–263, Stuttgart.
MacDowell, D.M. (1962), *Andocides. On the Mysteries*, Oxford.
MacDowell, D.M. (2009), *Demosthenes the Orator*, Oxford.
Meyer, E.A. (2013), "Inscriptions as Honors and the Athenian Epigraphic Habit", *Historia* 62, 453–505.
Meyer, E.A. (2016), "Posts, Kurbeis, Metopes: The Origins of the Athenian 'documentary' *stele*", *Hesperia* 85, 323–383.
Miller, J. (2016), "Euergetism, Agonism, and Democracy: The Hortatory Intention in Late Classical and Early Hellenistic Athenian Honorific Decrees", *Hesperia* 85, 385–435.
Mirhady, D.C. (2004), "Contracts in Athens", in: D.L. Cairns/R.A. Knox (eds.), *Law, Rhetoric, and Comedy in Classical Athens: Essays in Honour of Douglas M. MacDowell*, 51–63, Swansea.
Nelson, M. (2006), "The Phantom *stelai* of Lysias, *Against Nicomachus* 17", *CQ* 56, 309–312.
Osborne, R./Rhodes, P.J. (2017), *Greek Historical Inscriptions, 478-404 BC*, Oxford.
Ostwald, M. (1986), *From Popular Sovereignty to the Sovereignty of Law. Law, Society, and Politics in Fifth-Century Athens*, Berkeley.
Rhodes, P.J. (1972), *The Athenian Boule*, Oxford.
Rhodes, P.J. (1991), "The Athenian Code of Laws, 410–399 B.C.", *JHS* 111, 87–100.
Rhodes, P.J. (2016), "Heraclides of Clazomenae and an Athenian Treaty with Persia", *ZPE* 200, 177–186.
Robertson, N. (1990), "The Laws of Athens, 410–399 BC: The Evidence for Review and Publication", *JHS* 110, 43–75.

Scafuro, A.C. (2009), "Eudikos' Rider (*IG* I³ 102.38–47)", in: A.A. Themos/N. Papazarkadas (eds.), *Αττικά Επιγραφικά: Μελέτες προς τιμήν του Christian Habicht*, 47–66, Athens.

Scafuro, A.C. (2010), "Conservative Trends in Athenian Law: IE 138, a Law Concerning the Mysteries", in: G. Thür (ed.), *Symposion 2009. Vorträge zur griechischen und hellenistischen Rechtsgeschichte* (Seggau, 25.-30. August 2009) 21, 23–46, Vienna.

Scafuro, A.C. (2011), *Demosthenes. Speeches 39–49*, Austin.

Shear, J.L. (2011), *Polis and Revolution: Responding to Oligarchy in Classical Athens*, Cambridge.

Sickinger, J.P. (1999), *Public Records and Archives in Classical Athens*, Chapel Hill.

Sickinger, J.P. (2002), "Literacy, Orality, and Legislative Procedure in Classical Athens", in: J.M. Foley/I. Worthington (eds.), *Epea and Grammata: Oral and Written Communication in Ancient Greece*, 147–169, Leiden.

Sickinger, J.P. (2009), "Nothing to Do with Democracy: 'Formulae of Disclosure' and the Athenian Epigraphic Habit", in: L. Mitchell/L. Rubinstein/J.K. Davies (eds.), *Greek History and Epigraphy*, 87–102, Swansea.

Stroud, R.S. (1979), *The Axones and Kyrbeis of Drakon and Solon*, Berkeley.

Thomas, R. (1989), *Oral Tradition and Written Record in Classical Athens*, Cambridge.

Thomas, R. (1994), "Law and the Lawgiver in the Athenian Democracy", in: R. Osborne/S. Hornblower (eds.), *Ritual, Finance, Politics: Athenian Democratic Accounts Presented to David Lewis*, 119–133, Oxford.

Todd, S.C. (1996), "Lysias against Nikomachos: The Fate of the Expert in Athenian Law", in: L. Foxhall/A.D.E. Lewis (eds.), *Greek Law in Its Political Setting: Justifications Not Justice*, 101–131, Oxford.

Todd, S.C. (2000), *Lysias*, Austin.

Tuplin, C.J. (1982), "Satyros and Athens. *IG* II² 212 and Isokrates 17.57", *ZPE* 49, 121–128.

Volonaki, E. (2001), "The Re-Publication of the Athenian Laws in the Last Decade of the Fifth Century B.C.", *Dike* 4, 137–167.

Werner, R. (1955), "Die Dynastie Der Spartokiden", *Historia* 4, 412–444.

West, W.C. (1995), "The Decrees of Demosthenes' Against Leptines", *ZPE* 107, 237–247.

Pierre Chiron
The *Rhetoric to Alexander* and its Political and Historical Context: The Mystery of a (Quasi-) Occultation

Abstract: Technical treatises as *tekhnai rhetorikai* have suffered what philologists call "fluid transmission". It means that their content may have been adapted to their various contexts of use or fraudulous attributions. In the case of *Rhetoric to Alexander*, if we admit the testimony of Quintilian (3., 4., 9.) describing under the name of Anaximenes a doctrine very close of that of the treatise in its current state but not identical to it, we have the proof of such adaptations and a quite clear motive for them: accrediting the attribution of the text to Aristotle. This is why, examining the scarce echoes left on the *Rhetoric to Alexander* by contemporary events, Chiron begins with textual hypotheses. But he examines other possibilities too: political reasons (the links of Anaximenes to Macedonian power, the bad image of logography), communicational reasons (addressing a larger audience than democratic Athens), or "philosophical" reasons, linked to the influence of Isocrates on the treatise and the preeminence of personal imitation on the transmission of models or experiences.

Examining the traces left by immediate or more distanced current events in the *Rhetoric to Alexander*[1] is a delicate task, especially since this treatise and Aristotle's *Rhetoric* differ significantly on this point. In addition, comparing them to other works is impossible since they are the only systematic treatises left from the classical period.

While the contrast with Aristotle's *Rhetoric* is striking, this is not to say that the latter is a direct — or might we venture, innocent — reflection of its context of production. It is riddled with astounding silences, studied choices that are probably linked to the proximity between Aristotle and the Macedonian monarchy at a time when the latter regime was attacking Athens and its democratic values, and eventually eradicated them. But the fact remains that Aristotle's *Rhetoric* fits within the framework of Athenian democracy in fourth century B.C. It is filled with quotes, constantly referencing recent or contemporary texts and protagonists. The *Rhetoric to Alexander*, on the other hand, only includes a

---

[1] Ed. Fuhrmann 1976; Chiron 2002; Mirhady 2011.

single citation from a text that was already older[2] at the time: the lost Euripidean *Philoctetes*.[3] Current events and recent history are almost completely left untold.

1 Review of hypothesis

Such silence can be interpreted through a certain number of hypotheses.

We have the proof that the treatise was textually altered, probably at the time of its fraudulent inclusion in the Aristotelian corpus. If we are to admit that Quintilian[4] was in fact referring to the *Rhetoric to Alexander* when he attributed its doctrine to Anaximenes of Lampsacus, while Syrianus reproduced the same doctrine three centuries later and attributed it to Aristotle, and if we are to compare these reports with the text that is currently available, we can conclude that modifications were made to the text on the essential point of the number of genres of political speeches (for the same number – seven – of species, Quintilian and Syrianus used two, and three are mentioned in the current text of the *Rhetoric to Alexander*). In light of such reconditioning, we can be led to think that some of the text's allusions may have been removed at a later date, after Quintilian, at a time when rhetoricians found the political conflicts of the classical period to be less relevant.

To stay in the realm of pure speculation, if we admit that Anaximenes is the author of the treatise's first textual stratum, and in light of the historian's close relationship with the young Alexander – according to the *Suda* he may have been Alexander's teacher of rhetoric – in light also of Aristotle's prudence regarding aspects of the news that were embarrassing to him,[5] we can imagine that the technographer wanted to sell his treatise in a hostile environment and, therefore, "neutralized" it, in a way.

A third hypothesis should also be considered. As a technical treatise covering all oratory varieties, the *Rhetoric to Alexander* does not fully align with Isocrates' orientations in terms of education to culture (*paideia*).[6] As we know, Isoc-

---

[2] If we admit the dating of the first textual stratum of the *Rhetoric to Alexander* to be *circa* 340 B.C. On this point, see our edition, Chiron 2002, XL–CVII.
[3] Fr. 797 Nauck[2] (1433 b 11–14).
[4] 3, 4, 9; all elements of the case can be found in Chiron 2002, XLII–XLV.
[5] Aristotle is almost completely silent about Demosthenes, for example.
[6] Starting with his inclusion of judicial rhetoric, an activity which Isocrates practiced but which he later disavowed cf. *infra*. For a precise study of the links (few divergences, countless convergences) between the *Rhetoric to Alexander* and Isocrates, see Chiron 2002, CXXXI–

rates placed a lot of importance in his students' natural abilities. While he recognized the need for technical training,[7] he favored tireless practice, sports-related exercise,[8] all of which led to fully assimilating the forms of expression and — paradoxically — acquiring full expressive freedom and improvisational abilities in all circumstances.[9] His position may have served as an answer to the criticism that Alcidamas[10] directed towards the proponents of written discourse. Incidentally, the *Rhetoric to Alexander* teems with points of view, crypto-quotes, pieces of advice resembling Isocrates precepts, including a recommendation to exercise. The first rhetorical attestation of the word *progymnasmata*[11] is in fact found in the treatise. As we know, this word was later destined to a great future.

However, there is a relatively clear breach between Isocrates and the philosophical tradition imparted by Socrates regarding the teacher's place and role.[12] Socrates is *atopos*, "nowhere", therefore unpredictable.[13] He uses feigned naiveté to be critical and, in so doing, acts as a catalyst. He tracks the contradictions in his interlocutors' comments without revealing his own position. While the listener must assimilate his own thought, he must do so in a depersonalized way, ordered by a rational norm of coherence and truth, through demanding intellect but without alienation. This paradigm is, of course, that of philosophical dialectics. In this context, the only assimilation that justifies asceticism is the assimilation with God (*homoiôsis theôi*).

Strangely, Isocrates was fascinated by Socrates. His great midlife to later works — *Antidosis* and, to an even greater extent, *Areopagiticus* — are literally obsessed with the sacrificial figure of Socrates. However, either due to a sense of

---

CXLVIII. Most of Isocrates's pedagogical options (his "philosophy") after opening his school *ca* 390 can be found in *Against the Sophists* and in the *Antidosis*. For a particularly clear and innovative presentation of Isocratic thought, see Noël 2008, 91–101.

7 The *tekhnè* conserved under his name is a compilation of which he is not the author. Specialists tend to refuse the idea that Isocrates even thought of writing one since his precepts were entertwined with practice or took the form of meta-discursive remarks in his "philosophical" works. See *Against the Sophists*, 12, 19–20; Mathieu & Brémond 1929, 228–234; Noël 2008, 153–155 and *passim*.
8 See the famous comparison between the "philosopher" and the paedotribe, *Antidosis*, 183–184.
9 *Against the Sophists*, 16–18.
10 Author of *On those who write written Speeches* or *On the Sophists* (ed. Avezzu 1982; French translation by M. Patillon in Pradeau 2009, 93–101; English translation by LaRue van Hook 1919, 91–94). See Trédé 1992, 255–260; Noël 2008, 119–120, 135.
11 1436 a 25.
12 See Noël 2008, 154–155.
13 See, in particular, Vlastos 1991; French translation by Dalimier 1994, 37–68.

competition between rival schools training the elites or due to egotism or authorial pride, or — once more — because of a skeptical refusal to acknowledge the possibility of a science of the Being and an absolute trust in the powers of the *doxa*, Isocrates did not accept the erasure of the figure of the teacher behind reason or truth. In his school, his own texts were presented as models to be imitated. They were obsessively drafted and re-drafted to reach the perfect alignment between form and content and to be delivered as models for imitation. Such work, or asceticism, was in itself the making of a form of intellectual and moral progress. In a similar way, the use of outside models seems to be banned in the *Rhetoric to Alexander*, favoring instead examples that the technographer, and only him, a.k.a Isocrates, creates for the needs of the moment. The fact that the crypto-quotes in the *Rhetoric to Alexander* often originate from Isocrates does not seem to be a coincidence.

If one accepts this dichotomy, the abundance of varied examples in Aristotle's *Rhetoric* would concur with an adaptation of the Socratic model[14] enabled by initiatives that are specific to the Stagirite in relation to Plato: there is the impersonality of the teacher but there is also a recognition of the *endoxa*. This means that the principles that stem from experience are seen as seeds of truth through a cumulative documentary and scientific approach,[15] through pragmatism that leads to politics, and therefore to rhetoric, wherein the abstract model adapts to particular geographical, economical and, of course, cultural, conditions. Culture, paradigms, would therefore have the status of precedents on a path that leads to a philosophical rhetoric.

Historically, these two archetypes melded into the previously mentioned tradition of the *progymnasmata*: reading (*anagnôsis*)[16] transmits a diversified heritage and covers all possible cases, while the teacher-student relationship, as seen by Isocrates, is imbued with strong affects and can be found in the works of Aelius Theon and Quintilian. But what interests us here is the disconnected aspect of the *Rhetoric to Alexander*. The absence of quotes and of allusions to other oratory practices may have originated from Isocrates following his view that technique needed to give way to a lively and personal mode of transmission.

---

14 This model may be seen in the last sentence of the treatise, which seems to be relaying the importance of the reader's initiative rather than imitation through a quote that may be borrowed from the last sentence of Lysias' *Against Eratosthenes* (12.100): "I spoke, you heard, the decision is in your hands; you judge."
15 In regard to the dialectics, also see the last chapter of the *Sophistical Refutations*.
16 Aelius Théon, *Progymnasmata*, ed. Patillon/Bolognesi 2007, 102–105.

2 Back to the text

It is now time to move away from assumptions and delve into the text of the treatise to detect the remains of current events or recent history.

The number of proper nouns in the *Rhetoric to Alexander* is very low. While an index of Greek terms appears in the edition David Mirhady gave to the LCL in 2011, there is no index of nouns. In our edition, we recorded between 25 and 30 proper nouns[17] — the variation is due to the inclusion or exclusion of a diverse range of names for a given geographical reality (for example: Syracuse and [the] Syracusans).

This list becomes a third shorter when the nouns from the apocryphal letter are excluded, since the letter is foreign to the treatise and is meant to mislead the reader into believing in a false attribution. These nouns are as follows: Aristotle, Alexander, the Greeks, Theodectes (from Phaselis), Corax, Nicanor (close to Alexander), and, in a proverbial expression, the residents of Paros.

The remainder of the treatise is composed of fewer than twenty names. The number of nouns of place and inhabitants can be further reduced to seven entities (Athens, Carthage, Corinth, Greece, Thebes, Syracuse and Sparta). While some of these nouns of place are attached to significant historical events, they are not numerous. The reason the city-states of Carthage and Corinth are mentioned is because of the unexpected victory of the latter on the former — an event that historians situate around 341 and which is the *terminus post quem* for dating the treatise. Other than that, the Phyle episode (late 404) and the Theban victory in the battle of Leuctra (371) are mentioned, the former having been the first step towards democratic restoration in Athens, consecutive with the Thirty Tyrants, the latter the beginning of the short Theban hegemony in the fourth century, both events belonging to the remote past, not the recent years.[18]

These nine mentions form an extremely limited reserve of widely known geographical and historical realities. In a development on the argument of advantageous in international politics, the rhetorician describes the opportunities for alliances between Athens, Sparta and Thebes, in a conjuncture that is reminiscent of the period after Leuctra.[19]

---

17 Chiron 2002, 203–205.
18 Cf. Kapellos, Introduction in this volume.
19 The "three-headed monster" (*Tricaranos*), according to the title of the anti-Athenian pamphlet that Anaximenes circulated under the name of Theopompus (Chiron 2002, LXXXV). Regarding these alliances, see 1422 b 40–1423 a 8 and the *ad loc.* notes.

Names of men are also rare in the *Rhetoric to Alexander*, but they are a little less neutral: we found the names of Dionysius and Dion of Syracuse (1429 b 15–17). The victory of the latter on the former in 357 BC[20] serves as a paradoxical example. The process that is described is simple: if the wish is to defend a thesis that conforms with common or plausible opinion (*eikos*) — such as the idea that numerical superiority is a factor of victory —, then examples featuring the strong beating the weak should be used. But if the aim is to make people accept the reverse opinion, then the strategy consists of multiplying the number of paradoxical cases, of victories won by weaker parties. This is what the rhetorician does, since he enumerates at least four historical episodes that appear surprising at first glance.[21] We will not venture to view these references as an allusion to Plato based on the philosopher's visits to the Syracuse court and his close relationship with Dion. However, if this were the case, this allusion would be particularly bold since the rhetorician describes without condemnation a sophistic use of illusionism made possible by the *doxa*.

To illustrate the heightened use of the legal argument by the authority of an allegedly uncontested personality, the author of the *Rhetoric to Alexander* cites, or rather invents, a sentence in which the noun Lysitheides appears ("I am not alone in asserting that the lawmaker enacted this law with this intention; already in the past, the jurors — when Lysitheides developed arguments that are very close to those I am defending now — voted in the same way regarding this law" 1422 b 20–24). In the absence of demotics, we must be cautious, but we cannot help but think of Lysitheides of Kikynna,[22] who was mentioned several times as a rich man in charge of important archonships and liturgies in the Demosthenic corpus. A significant detail emerges: Isocrates, who opened his school around 390, refers to him as one of his first students (*Antidosis*, § 93). J.K. Davies[23] adds several other elements: "at some date before 353, he had received a crown from the City for 'having spent much from his own property on the City' (Isocr. 15.94), and a few years later was serving as eponym of a symmory (...). His name occurs frequently in the mining leases as that of a landowner in the mining area, from the middle of the fourth century onwards (...); he was still alive in 342/1 (...) and perhaps also in 338/7". In sum, this mention *could* allude to recent years, that is to a man still alive in the time span of twenty years after the writing of the Treatise, but is also to vague to allow any firm conclusions.

---

20 On this event see Finley 1968, I, 74–94.
21 Phyle episode and so on, see above.
22 Lysitheides 3 (*RE* Bd. XIV, 1 [J. Miller]).
23 Davies 1971, 356–357 (n° 9461).

The list reveals itself to be very short. The rhetorician often proposes what we can refer as "patterns" or standard phrases. These were probably close to that which Isocrates named *ideai*, and to a typology of two different types of alternatives, known as a two-term expression (*eis duo legein*). It can be presented almost mathematically, despite a lack of confirmed precision. We have agents (me, person[1], person[2]); we have the ability to perform an action, either one or two action(s), a and/or b; we have the *and / or* relation whereby the patterns are as follows: 1) I can do a and b; 2) person[1] cannot do a but person[2] can; 3) person can do a and b; 4) neither I nor anyone can do a; 5) person can do a but not me; 6) I can do a but person cannot do b. For the first specific case, the rhetorician cites the name of Timotheus in the function of *strategos*. This reminds us greatly of the conqueror of Kerkyra (375 BC), one of the founders of the Second Athenian Confederacy. The quote does not necessarily reflect well on the protagonist: "Not only was I the cause of these advantages for you, but I also stood in the way of Timotheus who was about to lead a charge against you" (1435 a 13–15). When looking back on the career of Timotheus, a famous and controversial war chief,[24] the choices are almost limitless when it comes to identifying a potential protagonist, including Ariobarzanes, a Persian opponent to the great King Timotheus fought in 366.[25] The only indication that is truly consistent is that this person was another student of Isocrates.[26]

The name Lysicles is also mentioned once — it competes with the name Callicles in the other part of the manuscript tradition — an example of a surreptitious testimony (1432 a 4) as seen in Davies's prosopography:[27] these two names were common in the fourth century B.C. The second name is reminiscent of *Gorgias*, Plato's character. The other name does not elicit such famous reminders. Many interrogations remain: what is the meaning of this variation? Which name served to correct, or to elucidate the other? What is the connection between the two names and the deception described in the sentence in which they appear?

Apart from the quote taken from Euripides's *Philoctetes*, we have stated that there were no other explicit quotes (none that featured identifiable beginnings and endings or indications of the names of the cited authors). However, there

---

24 On Timotheus see in particular: Carlier 1995, 49–51 and Siron's paper in this volume. In the *Against Timotheus* (Demosthenes corpus, n° 49), we can follow the financial troubles that went hand in hand with the general's career.
25 See Demosthenes XV, *On the Liberty of Rhodians*.
26 [Plut.] *Vies des dix orateurs. Isocrate*, 9 (Mathieu/Brémond 1929, XXVIII). Isocrates praises Timotheus in *Antidosis*, 15.101–139.
27 Davies 1971.

are crypto-quotes that are devoid of source identifiers and textual markings. We would love to identify them with a high degree of plausibility by confronting them word for word with the source text or with the parallel text, while also leaving open the possibility that the two available versions may not depend on each other but on another shared model. However, that cannot be. Most of the parallels can only be coarsely established, leaving a significant place for uncertainty. The most convincing connections are those between the model statements given for the *procatalepsis* (1432 b 15–19) and the beginning of the *Archidamus*, between the rebuttal against an orator's young age (1437 a 39 sq.) and the § 3 sq. of the *Archidamus*; a sentence on the orator's moral preparation (1445 b 32–34) is reminiscent of the *Antidosis*, 278. The summarizing modes described in 1433 b 33 sq. are echoed in the works of Isaeus, Isocrates, Demosthenes and Aeschines,[28] but these encounters are more methodological than they are literal and they rely more on terms than on full syntagms.

After having examined the rare nouns and the crypto- or pseudo-quotes in the treatise, we can also ask ourselves whether historical or political clues might transpire in the seemingly technical presentation of processes or topics. We must first broadly state that, while such clues do exist, they always remain vague. Let us examine the example of war financing. This is one of the topics of deliberation discussed in chapter 2 (1425 b 18–35). In regard to the lack of credits, the rhetorician provides the solution of rallying poor citizens, thus showing that the democratic citizen-soldier model is in crisis and that mercenary activity has become widespread. Such an indication does little more than to confirm that the treatise is anchored in the fourth century, which is something that we already knew. In the same passage, wealth tax is used as another form of financing. This measure is viewed by the rhetorician as an exceptional war tax, which was the case until the year 347/346, at which point such a tax became ordinary, with an annual fixed price of ten talents. The problem is that, while the rhetorician's formulation points toward an exceptional tax, it does not formally exclude the two systems from coexisting.

In the same way, the deliberative genre is presented as a common address to the people (1421 b 12), without giving details on the contours of the *kurion* that is being discussed and on whether the framework is explicitly that of the

---

28 See Chiron 2002, notes 386–389 *ad loc*. It is important to underline that these echoes show and only show that the author of the *Rhetoric to Alexander* knew very well the rhetorical practices and judicial rules of the fourth Century BC Athens, not that the treatise was known or read there at that moment. On these convergences, see the Special Issue of *Rhetorica* we published with M.-P. Noël and especially Pasini's paper (2011, 336–365); see also Pasini 2012, 139–181.

polis (1422 a 2). We do not know if this city-state is democratic in the Athenian sense or if it follows another model. If we were to yield to instinctive athenocentrism, a sentence illustrating the argument of the just supported by authorities would be enough to show the extent of the difference in points of view: "We are not the only ones to hate our enemies and to harm them, the Athenians and the Lacedemonians also consider it just to chastise enemies" (1422 a 39–41). This "we" is unequivocally Greek, but that is all that we know.

Another example touches upon the colors of the "moderate" democracy, one that is selective and elective, as upheld by Isocrates against the proponents of a hard and pure democracy and of random selection. To illustrate the extension of the argument of advantageous through an analogy, the rhetorician writes: "Therefore, as it is useful to put the most valiant warriors at the front row during combats, it is similarly advantageous to have the most sensible and probative people take precedence over the mass in governments" (1422 b 30–33). Since this sentence praises both democracy and elitism through the image of the phalanx, we think of the *Areopagiticus* (21–23) Isocrates wrote in 357, but we must admit once more that we have not moved beyond vague generalities.

In the same spirit, we will refrain from overinterpreting the sentence where philosophy is coined as the origin of progress in intellectual ability (*deinoteron einai peri phronèsin*, 1426 a 11), in a typology of the different causalities, the latter of which serving to diversify the arguments of praise: the example is set in a series (the health of the body stems from assiduous exercise, an aversion to effort leads to weakness), thus making philosophy into a form of hygiene, following Isocrates's view. The same trivialization occurs in investigation species (1427 b 12–30) wherein the method — detecting contradictions in the words or actions of examined speech or detecting deviances from given standards — could be reminiscent of the Socratic method, but without its ambition or rigor.

We are provisionally led to conclude that, through its historical, geographical and political references, the *Rhetoric to Alexander* gives us a glimpse of the vague silhouette of Greek city-states probably before Chaeronea, but without any prints of the political climate at this time,[29] in any case before the time when, after the Lamian war, democratic institutions were suppressed in Athens.[30]

Such vagueness is due to the nature of the systematic manual: the *pro* and *con* arguments for each thesis must be covered and, in the case of open ques-

---

[29] See Sealey 1993 and Worthington 2004, 2008.
[30] On the complex history of the end of democracy in Athens, see Habicht 2000. Cf. the rhetorical treatment of the battle of Chaeronea by Aeschines, Hyperides, Lycurgus and Dinarchus with Bajnok, Cooper, Roisman and Worthington in this volume.

tions, the whole range of possible ideas must be discussed. When the rhetorician considers the various possible proposals that can be made at the Assembly in terms of cult, he limits the description — and that is to be expected — to three logical formulas: he talks about the increase, the maintenance or the decrease of spending without expressing a personal preference (1423 a 29–b 32).

But the rhetorician is more forward in his views when it comes to legislative deliberation (1424 a 8–b27). He fails to state all options and only formulates the principles for the perpetuation of two — and only two — political regimes: the democratic and the oligarchic models. In other words, while the rhetorician presents a vague silhouette of the socio-political framework in which the precepts exist, he does draw its contours. It is both too much, and too little. It is now time to return to all of the hypotheses we formulated in light of the changes in our interrogations.

3 Assessment

By reexamining these hypotheses one by one — and recalling the constitutional weakness of the *a silentio* argument to which we are often reduced — we can say that the first hypothesis (a text that was modified over the course of its transmission) cannot be verified. The oldest textual source, the *PHib.* 26,[31] is too incomplete for us to measure the degree of the transformation, apart from a passage of two to three oratory genres which was probably the result of the "new" author confronting the treatise's doctrine.

The second hypothesis regards Anaximenes's self-censorship, as he feared that his treatise would be poorly received in Athens, where he was viewed as politically hostile. Although this theory is just as difficult to support, it could find a paradoxical form of reinforcement in the fact that the monarchical regime is absent from the treatise. We know that this type of regime is not generally in favor of developing the technique of rhetoric, but subsequent political history has shown that enlightened monarchs needed to master it. This paradigm owes a lot to Isocrates and counts shining examples such as Marcus Aurelius. By avoiding alluding to despotism, Anaximenes may have wanted to hide his ties with the Macedonian dynasty. Such cautious impersonality could also be linked to the bad reputation of the social role of the treatise's addressees. Speech pro-

---

[31] See Chiron 2002, CLXI. This exceptional document, which is dated in the middle of the third century B.C. comes a century after the Treatise.

fessionals, and especially those specializing in judicial discourse — the logographers — were often viewed suspiciously: by heightening the abilities of some and not of all, they could "limit the *isegoria* of common citizens",[32] a capital feature of democracy when shared. From our perspective, there has not been enough perceptiveness around the difficult math of allying two aspects of the treatise. If we admit a dating *circa* 340 and if we look at the references and context, the treatise can be identified as, and attributed to, a protagonist in the political and judicial world of Athens, during the city-state's last moments of freedom. And yet, we have also shown that the treatise is composed of precepts that are morally questionable to the point of perhaps being used for the contemptible activity of the sycophant.[33] There is also advice meant to exonerate the act of taking hold of public discourse instead of exercising the function as a naive citizen in the context of an authentic democracy that isn't monopolized, even distorted, by professionals.

One could object that the same goes for Aristotle's *Rhetoric*. But the status of the latter treatise is different: the text was meant for the internal use of the School. And Aristotle had a distanced position as a philosopher, theorizing oratory activity in the context of a vast political and ethical project in which, he included the choice of the right political system, the right legislation and management of affairs.[34] All of this exempted him from using precautions that other rhetoricians, closer to daily life and not shying away from more morally dubious precepts, may have needed to take.

The reserve displayed by the treatise may therefore only be a strategy meant to ensure its distribution in professional circles that were unwilling to show their inner workings other than in an impersonal way. We must add that such caution is compatible with the third hypothesis formulated above, since Isocrates himself sought to hide his career as a logographer; he shared these techniques only in the context of an internal use in his school. The fact that the treatise only speaks of two regimes and two regimes only — democracy and oligarchy — may in fact be the sign that he was reaching out to a Panhellenic audience, one that was not exclusively Athenian, as is the case for the open

---

32 We quote here Ober 1989, 172 (commenting Aesch. 1.175). Cf. also Hansen 1991, 230. To refute the preventions against logographers and rhetoricians, the *Rhetoric to Alexander* offers a detailed set of arguments; see, in particular 1444 a 16–b 7.
33 Therefore, in the chapter on plausibility as "applied to men": "if the one whom you accuse is young, say that he did what people of his age do; due to the resemblance, accusations against him will be taken into account" (1428 b 26–29).
34 See Pellegrin 2017.

letters distributed by Isocrates. This may have been another reason to prune the treatise and rid it of specific elements.

The paradox, of course, is that the treatise's attribution to Aristotle gave it a publicity that his author may not have wanted. We could express some irony when looking at this betrayed secret, given the fact that the *Rhetoric to Alexander* is not exceptionally brilliant. But that would be forgetting the coincidence of the treatise with the practices of the orators of its time. This manual therefore becomes a true key for us to understand Attic eloquence. For all time periods, it is a first class *vademecum* for practitioners, much more so than Aristotle's treatise — the latter of which is conceptually richer but less directly applicable.

Bibliography

Avezzù, G. (1982), *Alcidamante: Orazioni e frammenti. Testo, introduzione, traduzione e note*, Roma.
Carlier, P. (1995), *Le IVe siècle grec jusqu'à la mort d'Alexandre*, Paris.
Chiron, P. (2002), *Pseudo-Aristote, Rhétorique à Alexandre*, Paris.
Davies, J.K. (1971), *Athenian Propertied Families, 600-300 B.C.*, Oxford.
Finley, M.I. (1968), *A History of Sicily*, I, London.
Fuhrmann, M. (1976), *Anaximenis Rhetorica ad Alexandrum*, Leipzig.
Habicht, C. (2000), *Athènes hellénistique. Histoire de la cité d'Alexandre à Marc Antoine*, traduit de l'allemand par M. et D. Knœpfler, Paris.
Hansen, M.H. (1991), *Athenian Democracy in the Age of Demosthenes*, Oxford.
Mathieu, G./Brémond, É. (1929–1962), *Isocrate, Œuvres*, I–IV, Paris.
Mirhady, D. (2011), *Rhetoric to Alexander* (LCL 317), London.
Noël, M.-P. (2008), *Silves grecques 2008-2009* (Isocrate, Sept discours), Neuilly.
Ober, J. (1989), *Mass and Elite in Democratic Athens*, Princeton.
Pasini, G. (2011), "The *exetastikon eidos* of the *Rh. Al.* and Parallels in Aeschines' *Against Timarchus* and Demosthenes' *On the False* Embassy", *Rhetorica* 29/3, 336–365.
Pasini, G. (2012), "Questioni di diritto attico nella *Rhetorica ad Alexandrum*", *Rivista di Diritto Ellenico* 2, 139–181.
Patillon, M./Bolognesi, G. (2007), *Aelius Théon, Progymnasmata*, Paris.
Pellegrin, P. (2017), *L'Excellence menacée. Sur la philosophie politique d'Aristote*, Paris.
Pradeau, J.-F. (2009), *Les Sophistes* II, Paris, GF-Flammarion.
Sealey, R. (1993), *Demosthenes and his Time: A Study in Defeat*, Oxford.
Trédé, M. (1992), *Kairos. L'à-propos et l'occasion*, Paris.
Van Hook, LaRue (1919), "Alcidamas versus Isocrates; the Spoken versus the Written Word", *The Classical Weekly* 12, 89–94.
Vlastos, G. (1991), *Socrates Ironist and Moral Philosopher*, Cambridge.
Vlastos, G. (1994), *Socrate. Ironie et philosophie morale*, French translation by C. Dalimier, Paris.
Worthington, I. (2004), *Alexander the Great, Man and God*, London.
Worthington, I. (2008), *Philip II of Macedonia*, Yale.

List of Contributors

Thomas G.M. Blank is Professor of Cultural History of the Ancient World at Mainz University and author of *Logos und Praxis. Sparta als politisches Exemplum in den Schriften des Isokrates* (Berlin: De Gruyter 2014). His recent research focuses the demarcation of social spaces in Roman Religion (*Esoterisch-exoterische Kommunikation und ihre Effekte. Eine Untersuchung zu separater Religion und 'religiösem' Konflikt in der römischen Republik*, Stuttgart: Steiner tbp 2021). He co-edited volumes on truth in post-classical historiography (*Die symphonischen Schwestern*, Stuttgart: Steiner 2018) and on the cliché of the 'Mad Emperor' in ancient and modern public culture (*Caesarenwahn. Ein Topos zwischen Antiwilhelminismus, antikem Kaiserbild und moderner Populärkultur*, Köln: Böhlau tbp 2021).

Michael Gagarin is Professor of Classics Emeritus at the University of Texas in Austin. He has written widely on Greek law, Greek rhetoric, and the Sophists. Among his books is *Antiphon the Athenian: Oratory, Law, and Justice in the Age of the Sophists* (Austin, TX 2002).

Peter Rhodes was Professor of Ancient History, Emeritus Professor and Honorary Professor in the University of Durham. He was interested particularly in both the formal and the informal aspects of Greek politics, and in the literary and epigraphic sources for our knowledge of Greek history. His books include editions of Thucydides, I–V. 24 (1988–2014) and of Herodotus V (2019); *Greek Historical Inscriptions, 404–323* and *478–404 B.C.* (with R.G. Osborne, 2003–2017), and *A History of the Classical Greek World, 478–323 B.C.* (2nd edition 2010).

Frances Pownall is Professor of Classics at the University of Alberta. She has published widely on Greek historiography. Her publications include *Lessons From the Past: The Moral Use of History in Fourth-Century Prose* (Ann Arbor 2004), *Ancient Macedonians in the Greek and Roman Sources* (co-edited with T. Howe, Swansea 2018), *Lexicon of Argead Macedonia* (co-edited with W. Heckel, J. Heinrichs, and S. Müller, Berlin 2020), and *Affective Relations & Personal Bonds in Hellenistic Antiquity* (co-edited with E.M. Anson and M. D'Agostini, Oxford and Philadelphia 2020).

Edward M. Harris is Emeritus Professor of Ancient History at Durham University. He is the author of *Democracy and the Rule of Law in Classical Athens* (Cambridge University Press 2006) and The *Rule of Law in Action in Democratic Athens* (Oxford University Press 2013). He has co-edited *The Ancient Greek Economy: Markets, Households, and City-States* (Cambridge University Press 2016) and *Skilled Labor and Professionalism in Ancient Greece and Rome* (Cambridge University Press 2020). He has translated *Demosthenes, Speeches 20–22* (University of Texas Press 2008) and *Demosthenes, Speeches 23–26* (University of Texas Press 2018).

Cinzia Bearzot is Professor of Greek History in the Catholic University of Milan. Her main interests focus on political and institutional history of ancient Greece, on history of ancient political thought, and on history of ancient historiography (Thucydides, Xenophon, fragmentary historians). She has published many books and papers on these topics. Among them: *Federalismo e autonomia nelle Elleniche di Senofonte* (2004); *Come si abbatte una democrazia. Tecniche di* *colpo di stato nell'Atene antica* (2013); *Manuale di Storia greca* (2015); *Studi su Isocrate, 1980–2020* (2020); *Alcibiade* (2021).

Dino Piovan obtained the National Scientific Qualification as associate professor in Greek Language and Literature in 2013, after studying in Italy (Universities of Padua and Pisa, Italian Institute for Historical Studies in Naples) and abroad (LMU of Munich in Bayern, UCL London). He is currently working as adjunct professor of Ancient Greek at the University of Verona. His publications include a commentary on Lysias' speech 25: *Defence Against a Charge of Subverting the Democracy* (Padua/Rome 2009) and two monographs: *Memoria e oblio della Guerra civile. Strategie giudiziarie e racconto del passato in Lisia* (Pisa 2011); *Tucidide in Europa. Storici e storiografia greca nell'età dello storicismo* (Milan 2018). He is also co-author of *Con parole alate*, a three-volume history of Ancient Greek literature, with translated and commented texts (Bologna 2020), and co-editor of *Brill's Companion to the Reception of Athenian Democracy* (Leiden/Boston 2021).

Markus Zimmermann is assistant professor of ancient history at the University of Bayreuth (Germany). His research focuses on Imperial Rome and the history of Classical Athens. He has published a book on the Romanisation of Noricum and is currently writing his second book on decision making in Classical Athens.

Aggelos Kapellos has written the books *Lysias 21: A Commentary* (De Gruyter-Trends in Classics, Berlin 2014) and *Xenophon's Peloponnesian War* (De Gruyter-Trends in Classics, Berlin 2019). He has edited the volume *Xenophon on Violence* (De Gruyter-Trends in Classics, Berlin 2019). Moreover, he has written a string of papers on Xenophon's *Hellenica* I–II and the Attic orators. He is presently working on a new commentary on Hyperides' *Funeral speech* for which he was a visiting fellow at the CHS-Harvard, Washington D.C. in 2014, and a monograph called *The Arginousai trial in Greek and Latin literature*.

David Whitehead is Emeritus Professor of Ancient History at Queen's University, Belfast, and a Member of the Royal Irish Academy. After early monographs on Athenian metics (1977) and Athenian demes (1986) he has specialised in commentaries, with introduction and translation. These include *Hypereides: The Forensic Speeches* (2000), *Philo Mechanicus: On Sieges* (2016), *Xenophon: Poroi* (2019), and – in two volumes, with a new text – *Isokrates: The Forensic Speeches (nos. 16-21)* (2022).

Yun Lee Too is an independent scholar who writes on Greek literature and intellectual history. She is the author of *The Rhetoric of Identity in Isocrates: Text, Power, Pedagogy* (Cambridge: 1995) and *A Commentary on Isocrates' Antidosis* (Oxford: 2008). Her latest book is *Xenophon's Other Voice: Irony as Social Criticism in the 4th Century BCE* (Bloomsbury: 2021). She is working with Thomas Blank on a project entitled *Self Matters*.

Stefano Ferrucci is Associate Professor of Ancient Greek History at the University of Siena. His fields of research include Isaeus and the attic orators, Athenian democracy and ancient Greek historiography. He is the author of *L'Atene di Iseo* (Pisa 1998), Iseo, *La successione di Kiron* (critical edition, with introduction, translation and commentary, Pisa 2005), *La democrazia diseguale* (Pisa 2013), *Plutarco, vita di Artaserse* (introduction and notes, Milan 2020).

Nicolas Siron is a Doctor in Ancient History from Université Paris 1 Panthéon-Sorbonne, middle school teacher of History and Geography and adjunct professor of Greek History at Université Paris 1 Panthéon–Sorbonne and at Université Paris Sciences et Lettres. He is associate member of the ANHIMA Research Center (Anthropologie et histoire des mondes antiques, Paris). He has published *Témoigner et convaincre. Le dispositif de vérité dans les discours judiciaires de l'Athènes classique* (2019) about witnesses and other means of persuasion in Attic Oratory. His current work focuses on the cultural history of the Greek world.

Brad L. Cook is an Associate Professor of Classics at the University of Mississippi. He writes on Demosthenes in contemporary sources ("Athenian Terms of Civic Praise in the 330s B.C.," *GRBS* 2009, and "Swift-boating in Antiquity: Rhetorical Framing of the Good Citizen in Fourth-Century Athens," *Rhetorica* 2012), and in ancient and Byzantine biographies, on which he has a chapter in *The Oxford Handbook of Demosthenes* (2019). He also publishes on biographical texts relating to Philip II, Alexander, and Cicero, from antiquity to the Renaissance.

Gunther Martin is a lecturer at the Universities of Zurich and Bern. His dissertation was published as "Divine Talk. Religious Argumentation in Demosthenes" (Oxford 2009). Since then he has edited "The Oxford Handbook of Demosthenes". Other works include a commentary on Euripides' Ion (Berlin 2018) and the first edition of the new Dexippus palimpsest.

Jeremy Trevett is Associate Professor of ancient history at York University, Toronto. His research focuses on Athenian oratory and on the history of classical Athens. He is the author of *Apollodoros the Son of Pasion* (1992) and of *Demosthenes: Speeches 1–17* (2011).

Nathan Crick is a professor of communication at Texas A&M University. He explores the relationship between rhetoric and power both philosophically and as they manifest in different periods of political and social change. His books *Democracy and Rhetoric: John Dewey on the Arts of Becoming* and *Dewey for a New Age of Fascism: Teaching Democratic Habits* constructs a view of rhetoric, logic, and aesthetics that is consistent with an ethics of democracy that promotes creative individuality. His books *Rhetoric and Power: The Drama of Classical Greece* and *The Keys of Power: The Rhetoric and Politics of Transcendentalism* explore how major historical figures conceptualize the function of rhetoric in history.

Patrice Brun is senior Professor of Greek History in Bordeaux Montaigne University. His researchs focuses on Asia Minor, the Cyclades and especially on Athens during the classical period. He has published several works on the latter subject including *Eisphora, Syntaxis, Stratiotika. Recherches sur le financement de la guerre à Athènes au Ive siècle* (1983) and biographies of Demades (2000) and Demosthenes (2015).

Peter A. O'Connell is an Associate Professor of Classics and Communication Studies at the University of Georgia. He is the author of *The Rhetoric of Seeing in Attic Forensic Oratory* and of articles on Greek oratory and poetry.

Dániel Bajnok is a senior lecturer teaching Ancient History at Eszterházy University, Eger, Hungary. His main topics of interest include politics, religion, and oratory in classical Athens.

He is author of *Appropriation of Language: Some Value-terms in the Oratory of Aeschines* (Budapest, 2019). His project on 'Aeschines' *Against Ctesiphon* is supported by the János Bolyai Research Scholarship of the Hungarian Academy of Sciences.

Joseph Roisman is a Professor Emeritus of Classics, Colby College. His recent monographs include *Lycurgus, Against Leocrates*. Introduction and Commentary by Joseph Roisman. Translation by Michael Edwards. Clarendon Ancient History Series, Oxford University Press. 2019; *The Classical Art of Command: Eight Greek Generals Who Changed the History of Warfare*. Oxford University Press. 2017; *Lives of the Attic Orators: Texts from Pseudo-Plutarch, Photius and the Suda*. Introduction and Commentary by Joseph Roisman and I. Worthington, Translation by Robin Waterfield. Clarendon Ancient History Series, Oxford University Press. 2015; *Alexander's Veterans and the Early Wars of the Successors*. University of Texas Press. Austin, TX. 2012.

Craig Cooper is Professor of Classics in the Department of History at the University of Lethbridge, where he previously served as Dean of Arts and Science. Professor Cooper's research and teaching focuses on Greek History, Athenian Law, Greek Oratory and Rhetoric, Ancient Biography and Plutarch. Important contributions include: his 2008 edited volume, *Epigraphy and the Greek Historian* (University Toronto Press); 2007 article, "Making irrational myth plausible history: Polybian intertextuality in Plutarch's Theseus," (*Phoenix* 61); 2002 article, "Aristoxenus, Περὶ Βίων and Peripatetic Biography," (*Mouseion* 2), and his 2001 translation of Hyperides in *The Oratory of Classical Greece: Vol. V: Dinarchus, Hyperides, Lycurgus* (University of Texas Press).

Janek Kucharski is assistant professor at the University of Silesia in Katowice. His main research interests are classical Greek oratory and Athenian tragedy though he has also published on Homer, ancient rituals, and the reception of antiquity in Byzantium. He is the author and co-author of annotated Polish translations of Hyperides, Antiphon and Dinarchus, as well as several papers dealing with the above-mentioned subjects.

Zhichao Wang is associate professor in the Department of History, Shanxi Normal University, China and he has been a visiting scholar in the Department of Ancient History, Macquarie University of Sydney (2018–2019). His academic interests mainly focus on the Attic Orators and Athenian Democracy. He has published the monograph *Demosthenes and the Atheinan Foreign Policy* (Beijing, 2012, in Chinese).

Ian Worthington is Professor of Ancient History at Macquarie University (Sydney), and specializes in Greek history and oratory, on which he has written extensively. His most recent books are *Athens after Empire: A History from Alexander the Great to the Emperor Hadrian* (OUP 2021); *Ptolemy I: King and Pharaoh of Egypt* (OUP 2016); *By the Spear. Philip II, Alexander the Great, and the Rise and Fall of the Macedonian Empire* (OUP 2014); and *Demosthenes of Athens and the Fall of Classical Greece* (OUP 2013). He co-authored *Lives of the Attic Orators: Pseudo-Plutarch, Photius and the Suda* with J. Roisman and R. Waterfield in the Clarendon Ancient History Series (OUP 2015), and he is also Editor-in-Chief of *Brill's New Jacoby* (2003–). He founded the *Orality and Literacy in Ancient Greece* conference series, and is a Fellow of the Royal Historical Society.

List of Contributors — **497**

Joshua P. Nudell is an Assistant Professor of History at Truman State University. His current research centers on Classical Ancient Ionia. In addition to several articles on this topic, first monograph, *Accustomed to Obedience? Classical Ionia and the Aegean World, 480–294 BCE*, is under contract with the University of Michigan Press.

James Sickinger is Associate Professor of Ancient History at Florida State University. He is the author of *Public Records and Archives in Classical Athens* (Chapel Hill, 1999) and serves as an editor and contributor to *Brill's New Jacoby*, including an edition, translation, and commentary on the Parian Marble (BNJ 239). He has also published numerous articles and book chapters on Greek law, history, and Athenian ostracism.

Pierre Chiron is Professor emeritus of ancient greek at Paris-East University, honorary member of Institut Universitaire de France, President of International Society of Classical Bibliography (editor of *L'Année Philologique*). He works as a philologist on the history of ancient Rhetoric. He published critical editions of treatises like Demetrius' *On Style* or Anaximenes' (?) *Rhetoric to Alexander*, new translations into French of Aristotle's *Rhetoric*, Lysias' and Demosthenes' discourses. He has recently published inquiries on the greco-latin *progymnasmata*: *Manuel de Rhétorique. Comment faire de l'élève un citoyen*, Les Belles Lettres, 2018; *Les Progymnasmata en pratique, de l'Antiquité à nos jours/Praticing the Progymnasmata, from Ancient Times to Present Days*, Éditions Rue d'Ulm, 2020. A selection of his articles was gathered and edited by Ch. Guérin and F. Woertherunder with the title *Rhétorique, philologie, herméneutique*, Paris, Vrin, 2019.

General Index

Achilles 182
Adeimantus 6, 122, 139, 142–146, 180, 304, 355
Agesilaus 182
anagrapheis 54 n.4, 57, 469–470
Andocides (orator's grandfather) 68 n. 26
Antiphon 8–9, 47, 49, 51–52
Anytus 104, 108, 177
Aegospotami 8 n. 39, 9, 11–12, 27, 30, 81, 115 n. 49, 119–123, 127, 129, 139, 141–147
Alcidamas 33
Alexander the Great 9, 85, 96, 314 n.23, 344, 348, 352, 358–359, 373, 380–382, 384, 388–389, 398–403, 405–408, 431–433, 435 n. 26, 438–442, 447–448, 453 n. 27, 459 n. 38, 482, 485
Allusion(s) 11, 74, 81–85, 101, 180, 236, 414 n. 11, 468, 472, 482, 484
Amazons 373
ambassador 15, 206, 286, 307, 417–418
Amnesty 9, 11, 30, 31 n. 33, 73, 76, 101, 103–104, 108, 135, 160, 379 n. 17
Amphipolis 7, 211, 331 n. 52, 348–349, 416 n. 19, 417, 420 n. 35, 422, 424
Andros 370
Androtion 7, 14, 257–271
Antalcidas, the Peace 96, 151, 165, 198, 208, 285
Antenor 182
Antipater 96, 381–382, 432, 439
Anytus 104, 108, 177 n. 14
Aphobus 32, 242–253
apocheirotonia 228–229, 231
Apophasis 432–434, 438
Archelaus 71
Archedemus 146, 159–160, 162
Archinus 104, 108, 104, 108, 151, 153
Arche 112, 115
Arginousai 6, 8 n.39, 9, 12, 419 n. 34, 156 n. 44, 157, 158, 160–164, 166, 177, 183 n. 35
Argos 83, 85, 91, 111, 180, 467

Argument(s)
Aristogeiton 378–379, 389 n. 60, 433, 435 n.23, 465 n. 2, 378–379, 389 n. 60, 433
Aristodicus 51
Archestratides 135–136, 138
Archidamus (II) 181
Archidamian War 174, 177 n. 15
Archidamus (III) 181
Archippe 227
Alcibiades 2, 5–6, 8–9, 12, 27, 54, 71, 88 n. 22, 91, 122, 135–147, 180–181, 467, 329 n. 38, 406, 467
Alcibiades the Younger 122, 137, 140, 143, 145, 147, 162, 164, 177, 181
Alyzeia 225, 232
Amorges 11, 90–93, 98
Anakrisis 34–35
Anaximenes 9, 19, 174, 481–482, 485 v. 17, 490
Ancestors 13, 88, 156 n. 44, 161 n. 60, 175 n. 11, 189, 190, 194–195, 197, 199, 209, 218 n. 70, 293, 299, 364, 436–437
andragathia 178
Areopagus 191–194, 371–372, 403, 431–434, 437–439, 442
Aristeides 93, 195
Arthmius of Zelea 465 n. 2
Artaxerxes 93–95
Asia Minor 86, 92 n. 33, 95
Aspendus 96
ateleia 275–276, 280, 284–285, 286 n. 37
atimia 104, 226 n. 8, 386 n. 45
Athens 5–6, 8–9, 11–13, 15–19, 23, 25 n. 9, 26 n. 13, 27–28, 30 n. 32, 31, 33, 34 n. 47–48, 54–55, 57 n. 16, 58–61, 63, 65–68, 70–77, 81, 83, 88–90, 92 n. 30, 93–96, 101–104, 105 n. 20, 108–113, 115–116, 120–125, 128 n. 29, 128 n. 31, 135–147, 151–161, 166, 171–172, 174–177, 179, 181, 183–185, 189
Athenian League (Second) 192, 196, 225, 229, 280, 452 n. 24

Athenian Empire
audience(s) 4, 12, 14, 17–19, 25–34, 36–39, 47, 51, 63, 65 n. 8, 65 n. 11, 66, 72, 77, 111, 115–116, 135, 139, 143, 147, 152–153, 166, 185, 190–192, 206, 209, 212–213–214, 218–29, 226, 232 n. 42, 235–238, 260, 272, 275, 279, 287, 293–298, 300–304, 307, 318 n. 40, 324, 331–333, 334 n. 70, 335, 337, 343, 349, 351 n. 45, 354–358, 365, 368–370, 414 n. 11, 415, 417–419, 424–425, 427, 429, 435, 437, 444, 449 n. 5, 456, 458, 465, 468, 473–474, 481, 491
auloi 172
Autochthonous 298
Autolycus 371–372
Autonomy (autonomia) 303, 308, 425, 435, 437

basanos/slave torture 234, 247–248, 251–252, 302
Betrayal 6, 142–143, 145 n. 77, 442
Black Sea 253, 345
Boeotia, Boeotians 11, 54–55, 59, 90, 135–137, 157, 337, 348, 378, 383
Brasidas 177, 182
Bribery 68, 327, 328 n. 35, 354, 432, 472
Bosporus 276 n. 3, 473
Burial(s) 158, 162, 301, 367
Byzantium 83, 85, 192, 195, 276 n. 3, 285 n. 35, 416, 416 n. 18, 418, 421 n. 40, 425, 457, 476

Callias 93–94, 468
Callimachus 173, 178
Callistratus 4, 226, 228, 229 n. 23, 285, 365–66, 367 n. 13, 414 n. 8
Carthage 5, 485
Catana 59, 60–61
cavalry 54, 59–60, 109, 136–137, 145, 185, 383
Cephalus 147 n. 93, 468–469
Ceramicus 28 n. 24, 125, 158
Chalcidice 308, 383
Chaeronea 3, 9, 15–17, 18 n. 24, 34 n. 47, 87, 161 n. 60, 181, 291, 293–294, 297, 302, 316–317, 319, 325, 338, 343–345, 352–359, 363–364, 366–370, 377–378–381, 383–393, 397–398, 406, 427, 435–437, 443–444, 489
Chersonnese 16, 61, 184, 86, 377, 441, 459 n. 39
children 16, 61, 184, 207, 211, 246, 248–249, 251, 301, 357 n. 79, 377, 441, 459 n. 39
Chabrias 9, 14, 202, 262, 275–288
Cholleidai 185
Cimon 102
Circumference 297–298
Cleisthenes 177, 181, 330–331, 333
Cleitophon 104
Cleocritus 178 n. 15
Cleon 330
Cleophon 177, 181, 184, 195, 354
Cleruch(s) 184, 451–453, 456, 458, 459 n. 39, 460
Cnidus 89, 145, 148, 192, 206 n. 7, 208 n. 19, 215, 216 n. 57, 218 n. 70, 219, 229 n. 23, 279 n. 15, 286
Colonus 10, 56, 58, 61
common knowledge 32 n. 39, 180, 225, 236, 365 n. 9
Conon 89, 112, 120, 122, 145–147, 156, 177 n. 14, 181 n. 29, 192, 215, 225, 228, 276, 280, 285–286, 355, 381 n. 21, 451, 465 n. 2
Corinthian War 3, 64, 86–87, 142, 153, 165, 207–208, 212–214, 220–221, 276, 466
Coronea 85, 145, 148
Court(s) 5, 16–17, 34, 36, 38, 47, 87, 107 n. 25, 107 n. 25, 124, 136–140, 143–146, 147 n. 93, 171, 173, 178, 180, 194, 197 n. 37, 198, 210, 217 n. 61, 227, 228 n. 21, 235, 250 n. 30, 265, 333, 344, 349, 352, 363, 366, 368, 371–372, 377, 384–385, 389, 418 n. 26, 420, 447, 472, 486
collective memory 18, 64, 128, 206, 214, 219, 318–319, 365, 447, 449–450, 457 n. 37
conspiracy 71, 123, 146 n. 86, 165, 200, 295 n. 20, 419 n. 34

General Index — 501

Corinthian War 3, 64, 86–87, 142, 153, 165, 207–208, 213, 214, 220–221, 276, 466
Corcyra 94, 196, 225, 226 n. 6, 228, 232, 286
Cos 192, 195
Council 28, 57, 72, 159, 193, 194 n. 27, 268, 368, 400, 402, 433, 434 n. 22, 468
Ctesiphon 325 n.13, 343–344, 350 n. 41, 352 n. 47, 356, 436, 440
Critias 70, 76
credibility 35 n. 50, 81, 258, 271, 332
crowning 344, 356
Cyprothemis 451
Cyprus 14, 71–72, 174 n. 9, 200, 275, 277, 287
Cyrus the King 181 n. 29, 200
Cyrus the Younger 83, 163, 177
Cyzicus 71–72, 196

Dareius (king of Persia) 180 n. 22
Deceleia 5, 172, 177, 180, 186
Deceleian War 174, 177
Delion 177
Delian League 93, 143, 225 n. 2, 456 n. 35
Decree(s) 14, 17, 28 n. 26, 32 n. 40, 163, 210 n. 30, 380, 384, 387 n. 49, 388, 390, 398, 402 n. 19, 403, 413, 448 n. 4, 460, 465 n. 2, 466, 472–477
Demades 9, 18, 27 n. 20, 352 n. 52, 377, 380 n. 18, 382–383, 397–399, 401–410, 433, 438
Demochares 242 n. 2, 244, 247, 249 n. 26, 470, 471 n. 21
democratic party 116, 129, 138, 145
Demophantus 465 n. 2
Demosthenes' father 242 n. 2, 243, 247, 252
Demosthenes' mother 241, 246–250, 253, 300
Demosthenes' sister 241, 242 n. 2, 246, 248–250, 253
Deceive, deception 25, 107, 216, 426, 451 n. 16, 487
Demes(men) 53, 57–58, 60, 185

desertion 136–137, 352 n. 49, 372, 436, 443
Dicaeopolis 185
Dikasts 175–176
Diodorus Siculus 154, 174
Diondas 314 n. 23, 315, 384, 387–92, 398–399, 401–402, 409–410
Dionysius of Halicarnassus 11, 64–65, 81–82, 84, 102–106, 229, 292, 333, 415 n. 16
Dionysius I 181 n. 29, 210 n. 34
Dionysodorus 471
direct speech 333–334, 336, 338
Doxa 26, 34, 163, 484, 486
Dowry 244, 246 n. 18, 248–249, 417
Draco 102, 468
Duris of Samos 460

eisangelia 13, 225, 228–229, 231–235, 237–238, 310, 363, 455 n. 31
Eikos (eikota)/probability 234, 328, 486
Egypt(ians) 14, 83, 174 n. 9, 211, 219, 230, 275, 277, 285, 287
Elatea 337, 352
Eleusis 104–105, 126 n. 24, 140, 185, 209 n. 29, 315
Elis 83, 416 n. 20, 467
Embassy 8 n. 39, 15, 92, 94–96, 210, 307, 310, 312–318, 323–326, 328–331, 338, 346, 348, 350, 354, 392 n. 70, 407, 414 n. 6, 421–422, 431, 467
enargeia 333, 335, 357–358
Enkomion 206
Envoy 16, 91, 343, 346, 349–350, 432, 443
Epicrates 65 n. 16, 147 n. 93, 384–387
Epicerdes 276 n. 3, 475 n. 38
Epicrates 385–387
Epidaurus 370
Epilycus 68 n. 28, 88, 90, 93–95, 98
exegetai 468
Ephialtes 50 n. 4, 51, 194
Epigamy 109
Eratosthenes (member of the Thirty) 61, 106
Erchia 185
Eretria 55, 57, 58, 61, 71, 88

Erythrae 448, 451 n. 17
ēthopoeia 206 n. 6
Euboea 11, 55 n. 10, 58, 81, 84–86, 88, 308–309, 345, 424
Euripides 436
Euryptolemus 159–160, 350 n. 37
Euthycrates 382–384
Euxenippus 440
Euxitheus 9–10, 47–51
Euxitheus' father 49
Exiles Decree 432, 448, 459 n. 38
experience 30, 34–35, 102, 116, 139, 153, 252, 331, 333, 335, 337, 344, 347, 484

Facts 31, 34–35, 37 n. 63, 38 n. 65, 39
Family 7, 10, 13–14, 32, 56, 60, 63, 67–68, 74, 76 n. 74, 205–206, 214–219, 242, 247, 249, 251–253, 371, 413, 451
flattery 18, 165–166, 384, 386, 397, 401–402
Four Hundred 10, 53–61, 64, 70 n. 37, 71–72, 107
Five Thousand 10, 54, 56–61, 71–72, 104
Freedom 101
funeral speeches 3, 8, 153 n. 18, 298, 357, 417 n. 26, 417 n. 26
future 1, 5–6, 13, 28, 67 n. 17, 81, 89, 111, 144, 189, 191, 193–194, 196, 199, 201–202, 244, 253, 296, 425, 473–474, 476, 483

general(s) 6, 84, 120 n. 2, 122, 137, 142 n. 53, 145, 155, 157–165, 199, 202, 214, 229 n. 23, 230, 276, 282–284, 304, 350, 354, 356, 407, 49 n. 34, 425
Gorgopas 14, 275, 277, 287
Grain 71–72, 178, 276 n. 3, 345, 443 n. 54, 473
Graphê paranomôn 159, 378, 380, 382, 387, 390
Gylippus 177, 182
Gylon 242–244, 246 n. 18

Hagnonides 433
Halonnesus 414–415, 419, 422
Haliartus 84, 136, 138, 145

Harmodius and Aristogeiton 2, 207, 215, 465 n. 2
Harpalus, Harpalus affair 9, 252 n. 34, 403, 431–433, 435, 438, 442
Heraclides Ponticus 453
Hellenotamiai 50
Hellespont 6, 8 n. 39, 54, 55 n. 6, 59, 120, 163, 165, 178–179, 182, 280
Herms 2, 72
Hermon 178
Herodes 47–48, 51
Homer 300, 436
hoplites 68 n. 26, 104, 108–109, 110 n. 38, 111, 115, 156, 277
hostages 184
Hierum 473
Hipparchus, son of Charmus 465 n. 2
Homonoia 103, 130 n. 37
Hoplites 68 n. 26, 104, 108–109, 110 n. 38, 111, 115, 156, 277
hortatory intention 475, 476 n. 43
hybris 104, 333
Hyperbolus 181, 195
Hyperides 126, 126 n. 23, 156, 162, 287, 307, 310, 312, 314–315, 318, 330 n. 43, 338 n. 93, 351 n. 45, 354 n. 61, 367 n. 13–14, 368–369, 377–393

Iatrocles 334
imageability 334
imagination 277, 294, 323, 334, 339, 358
India 441
Iphicrates 196–197, 202, 207, 209, 211–212, 214, 219, 226, 228–230, 286, 455 n. 31
Isocrates 3, 8 n. 39, 12–13, 19, 31, 37–38, 93, 122 n. 13, 136–137, 140, 145, 152, 171–186, 189–202, 213, 225 n. 3, 287, 350, 419, 451, 455–458, 482–492

Jason 213, 227, 229
Judgment 82, 116, 455
Jury/jurors 216–217, 225, 232 n. 43, 233–237, 243

Kairos 32–33, 379, 384, 388–391
kyrbeis 469–470

Lacedaimonians 157–158, 160, 172, 174–175, 177
Lamia 392
Lamian war 403, 404 n. 28, 406 n. 33, 433 n. 17, 441 n. 45
law(s) 7, 17, 34, 161, 195, 265, 268, 327, 364, 366, 368, 378, 385, 434, 469, 473 n. 30, 477 n. 48
Lenaia 185
litigation 140, 193, 471
liturgies 10, 32, 53, 56, 60, 178, 210, 218, 252, 275, 473, 486
logographer(y) 36, 135, 448, 491
Laughter 152–153, 338
League of Corinth 96, 302, 439
Leocrates 16, 354–355, 363–372, 437
Leosthenes 287, 432
Leptines, law of 275, 285–287, 473–475
Leucon 473–476
Lies 30 n. 32, 35 n. 50, 115, 141, 311–312, 313 n. 19, 316, 325 n. 13, 331, 456
Lycius 53, 55 n. 6, 59
Lycophron 363
Lysander 6, 8 n. 39, 9, 70, 120, 121 n. 6, 136, 139, 161, 163–164, 177–178, 179 n. 20, 355
Lysicles (general) 378, 437
Lysimachus 198, 373

Macedonia, Macedonians 15–19, 27, 71–72, 84 n. 11, 180, 228, 291, 302, 304, 310–315, 318, 343–345, 348, 353–354, 363–364, 373, 377, 380, 383, 392, 397–398, 401–402, 407, 413–414, 417–418, 420, 422–423, 432, 435–436, 439–449, 481, 490
Marathon, battle of 391–392, 457
Memory 392–393, 431, 435, 444, 447–460
Mantinea 83, 467
Mausolus 284, 451
Meidias 32 n. 39, 249–250, 308
Megara 68, 85, 311, 432, 436 n. 33
Megalopolis 85, 439–440, 467 n. 8
"men of Peiraeus" 105, 116, 125
"men of the city" 116

Menexenus 151–153, 157, 165–166, 209 n. 29
Mesogeion 185
Metics 16, 369, 377, 379, 386–387
Metroon 477 n. 46
Methone 84, 425
Milyas 247, 251, 253
Miltiades 2, 181, 195
Mockery 336–337
Moerocles 472–473, 477
Mounichia 114, 207, 221
Mystification 304
Myth 3, 190 n. 5, 191, 201, 293, 296, 301–302–303, 305, 417, 419
Mytilene 8, 47–49, 83, 155, 157, 160, 174, 213, 221, 280
Mytilenean revolt 9–10, 47, 49–51

narration 16, 24, 26, 29, 32, 34–35, 123, 249, 307, 323, 335, 337
Narrative 125, 140, 146 n. 82, 154, 173, 180, 182, 205–207, 215, 219, 225–226, 230, 232 n. 43, 233–235, 237, 247 n. 19, 272, 296, 329, 333–336, 345, 349 n. 29, 425 n. 55, 431, 438, 453–454, 457, 460
Navy 89, 120, 156, 456 n. 35
Naxos, battle of 275, 278–282, 284 n. 32, 286–288
Negotiations 64, 68–69, 76, 90, 96–97, 447
Nemea 2, 145, 148
Nestor 182
Nicanor 432, 485
Nicias 8 n. 39, 31 n. 36, 88, 237 n. 69
Nicias (Peace of) 88, 94–95, 172, 177, 467
Nicolaus (Syracusan) 174
Nicomachus 469–470
Notion 183 n. 35

Oaths 94, 96, 128, 233 n. 52, 248 n. 22, 283, 467
Olynthus 84–86, 308, 311, 331–333, 383, 425
Oracle 366

Oratory 8–9, 23–29, 31–35, 37–39, 67–68, 77, 156 n. 44, 166, 181 n. 27, 182, 190 n. 11, 206 n. 5, 287, 323, 325, 348–349, 365, 379 n. 14, 381 n. 21, 391, 434–435, 439, 449–450, 456, 457 n. 37, 459, 484, 490–491
Olympia 432, 467
Olympic Games 136, 432
Oropus 55, 59, 83, 85, 285, 287, 424

Paches 174
Pallene, Battle of 64, 425, 74 n. 21, 75 n. 64
Panactum 185
Paralus 219, 400
Pasio 227–228, 233
Pathos 182, 184, 286, 313
Patrios demokratia 102
Patrios politeia 70, 75, 102–103
Pausanias II 103 n. 10, 106 n. 22
Pedaritus 182
Peiraeus 5, 16, 89, 103, 125, 227, 377, 454, 473
Peisistratids 74, 75 n. 64
Pella 16, 310, 323–324, 329, 331, 346, 349–350
Peloponnese 83, 192, 309–311, 347, 439
Peloponnesian War 2, 3 n. 16, 7, 12, 31 n. 35–36, 47, 63, 69, 72–73, 90, 110 n. 38, 119, 120, 128, 135, 137, 140, 142 n. 56, 143–145, 147, 155, 161–163, 166, 171–177, 180, 183–184, 186, 355, 456 n. 35, 458, 466, 471
Pentecontaetia 181
Performance 35 n. 50, 36, 54, 95, 232 n. 42, 275, 283, 293, 333, 336, 358, 470
Pericles 2, 11, 88, 101, 103, 126, 152, 161 n. 60, 177, 180–185, 195, 248, 294, 357, 404, 406, 452, 455–456
Persepolis 441
Persia, Persians 11, 67, 83, 85, 92–95, 98, 112, 128 n. 29, 180, 181 n. 29, 183, 192, 197–198, 200, 277, 299, 344, 391, 436, 441, 451–452, 454, 457
Persian War(s) 3 n. 16, 28, 68, 85–86, 91, 176, 299, 457, 487
Phormisius 9, 11, 101–108, 111, 116

philanthropia 350–351
Philocles (general of Aegospotami) 6, 121 n. 6
Philocles (general of the 4th century B.C.) 431 n. 1, 433, 435 n. 23
Philocrates 9, 15–16, 27, 84, 307–311, 323–324, 326–327, 339, 343–348, 356 n. 74, 413, 416, 421 n. 40, 422, 424, 426, 476, 468 n. 10
Phocion 400, 403, 404 n. 28, 407 n. 39, 284 n. 31, 349 n. 33
Phocis 86, 309, 327–328, 358 n. 85
Phormio 177, 180, 227, 233
Phrynichus 53–56, 60, 91, 471–472
Phyle 74, 185, 485, 486 n. 21
Plataeans 465, 475 n. 41
Plato 3, 124 n. 17, 126 n. 24, 151–166, 483, 486
Plethos 111
Polyeuctus 398, 407, 433, 440 n. 44
Potidaea 84–86, 232, 416–417, 421 n. 39, 425, 450 n. 12, 439
Precedents 16, 363–365, 371, 484
Present 13, 28, 189–193, 199, 201–202
Prodosia 228 n. 22, 436
Proklesis 431–432
Philip II 3, 8 n. 39, 9, 15–17, 34 n. 47, 84 n. 11–12, 85, 96, 181, 227, 233, 291–292, 308–317, 323–324, 327–338, 435–436, 441 n. 48, 443, 467–468
Pydna 416 n. 19, 425, 84
Plague 172
Plataiai 176
Pnyx 185, 316, 319
Proxenia 95, 382
Pylos 177, 181 n. 27
Python of Byzantium 416, 418, 421, 425

reconciliation (of 404/3) 74, 76, 103, 106, 121 n. 8, 128, 175, 449
relatives 159, 162, 207, 302, 304, 307, 356, 357 n. 78, 369, 471
reception 29, 36–37
revision (of speeches) 38, 65 n. 8
Rhodes 83, 84 n. 12–13, 87 n. 19–20, 192, 195, 458
Rhodians 284, 457

Rhamnous 185
Rhetoric 12–13, 15, 33, 39, 65–66, 129, 146 n. 86, 151–152, 165, 183, 189, 198, 200–201, 205, 250 n. 27, 252, 291, 295–299, 302, 305, 318, 330, 422, 428, 435, 442, 482, 484, 490
rhetoric of deflection 291, 293–305, 354
rhetoric of defeat 15, 294–295, 297, 437
Rumour 29, 33

Sacred War, Third 2, 85, 309, 327
Samos 18, 55 n. 6, 71–72, 83, 196, 232, 447–448, 450–460
Salamis 201, 277, 391–392, 457
Satraps 86, 93, 451
Satyrus 262, 264, 333
Scapegoat 343–344, 355, 356 n. 74, 359
Second Athenian Naval Confederacy 83, 233 n. 49, 452, 487
Sicily 5–6, 8 n. 39, 54, 55 n. 6, 60, 90–91, 177, 180, 183, 207, 209, 220
slaves 16, 108, 156, 172, 244, 250–252, 262, 264, 269, 355, 369, 377, 379, 384–385, 389, 416 n. 17
Social War 192, 194–196, 208 n. 20, 209, 258, 260, 271, 280–284, 311, 455 n. 31
Socrates 34, 68, 85, 124 n. 17, 152–166, 357, 483
Solon 7, 102, 192, 197, 469
Soteria 11, 101, 103, 106, 109, 111, 113
Sparta, Spartans 2, 5, 7, 11, 47, 64–67, 69, 71, 85, 80, 90–95, 97–98, 105, 11, 135–137, 143, 155, 157, 177, 180, 198, 208, 215, 285, 311, 313 n. 19, 423, 435, 439–440, 467, 485
Speech-writing 172
Sphacteria 174, 185
Spiritualization 15, 291, 299
Stratocles 318, 433, 441
Symposium 16, 323–324, 331, 333–334
Synegoros 35–36, 136–137, 207, 247
Syracuse 6, 60, 95, 182, 485–486

Teisias 136
Testimony 14, 27 n. 19, 33, 35, 225, 226 n. 8, 233–234, 247, 251–252, 317, 331 n. 50, 335, 349 n. 30, 403, 406, 471, 487
Themistocles 181, 195
Thebes, Thebans 2, 8 n. 39, 9, 14–15, 179, 285, 291, 307–309, 312–313, 315, 317, 319, 327–328, 357–359, 383, 391–392, 403, 406–408, 424, 435–436, 439, 441–442, 449 n. 6, 467, 485–486
Theocrines 472–473
Theodorus (father of Isocrates) 172
Theophemus 470–471
Theramenes 61, 70 n. 38, 71, 76, 87, 104, 106–108, 111, 122–123, 155, 159–161
Thessaly, Thessalians 84–85, 213, 221, 229, 315 n. 29, 414 n. 9
Thasos, Thasians 84, 276 n. 3, 285 n. 35, 476
Theban Alliance 312, 387, 391
Thorubos 235, 237
Thrace 48, 85–86, 138, 207, 211, 226, 283, 285, 439
Thrasylochus 250
Thrasybulus 102–103, 105–106, 108–109, 111, 114, 129, 138, 145, 147–148, 159–160, 177–285, 472
Thrasymachus of Calchedon 103
Thermopylae 84–85, 309, 328
Thirty (the) 9–10, 30, 61, 63–65, 67, 69–77, 83, 101–102, 108, 111–112, 114, 116, 123, 129, 135, 143, 146 n. 86, 160–161, 163, 165, 178 n. 15, 184, 218, 269, 332, 449 n. 9, 471, 485
Thirty Years' Peace 94
Timarchus 310, 348, 356 n. 74
Timotheus 9, 18, 179 n. 20, 192, 196–197, 207, 209, 212–214, 225–238, 28–287, 427, 447–448, 450–460, 487
Timemata parechomenoi
Tissaphernes 91–94, 180
Tradition 2, 7, 10, 25–26, 29, 63, 76, 102, 115, 127, 161, 248 n. 24, 250, 317, 367, 398, 401, 404 n. 28, 406, 409, 418, 448, 457, 460, 483–484, 487
Treason 11, 119–120, 122–123, 139, 142 n. 53, 212 n. 43, 228, 285, 287, 308, 310, 312, 347 n. 22, 363, 366, 367 n. 12–13, 371, 373, 382, 436

Treaties 67, 81, 344, 466–467, 468 n. 10, 474 n. 36
Trierarch(s), trierarchy 58, 178, 207, 209 n. 28, 218, 250, 282 n. 25, 470, 471 n. 21
Troezen 68, 370, 386
Troy 299–300
truth 4, 7, 9, 12, 23–24, 33, 58, 84, 129, 141, 144, 151–152, 155, 157, 165, 175, 252, 258, 300, 312, 316, 318–319, 324, 330, 357, 414 n. 11, 421, 427, 434 n. 21, 437–438, 441, 443, 460, 483–484

Tyrannicides 280
Tyrtaeus 436

walls 11, 69 n. 35, 72–73, 75, 81, 88–89, 90 n. 27, 95, 97, 112, 127, 143, 165, 165 n. 84, 184
warships 174 n. 9, 427
witnesses
women 16, 242, 248, 251–252, 332, 355, 369, 377, 426, 441, 468

Zeus Soter 373

Index of Passages

Aelian
Varia Historia
5.12 — 432 n. 10

Aelius Theon
Progymnasmata
p. 102–105 (Patillon–Bolognesi) — 484

Aeschines
1.53	454, 459
1.80	37 n. 59
1.131	352 n. 50
1.162	420 n. 47
1.164	418 n. 30
1.166	348
1.167–169	348 n. 24
1.169	348
1.171	351 n. 43
1.173–176	331 n. 48
1.173	272 n. 30
1.175	491 n. 32
1.181	352 n. 50
2	35 n. 51
2.2	324 n. 4
2.4	337 n. 87
2.6	310 n. 10
2.12–13	348 n. 28
2.12–19	326 n. 18
2.13	350
2.15	350
2.16–17	348 n. 28
2.21	348 n. 28, 349
2.22	241 n. 1, 352 n. 50
2.30	350
2.30–33	348
2.31	417 n. 23
2.33	348
2.34	338 n. 95
2.34–35	349
2.36–37	350
2.38–39	348 n. 28
2.39	350
2.41–43	348 n. 28
2.47–48	348 n. 28
2.51–52	348 n. 28
2.54	324 n. 4
2.56	326 n. 18
2.61	347 n. 21
2.70	176
2.74–78	31 n. 36
2.76	181 n. 27
2.78	241 n. 1, 252 n. 34
2.79	347, 352 n. 50
2.82	348 n. 28
2.88	352 n. 50
2.92	324 n. 4
2.93	241 n. 1, 252 n. 34
2.98	324 n. 4
2.99	352 n. 50
2.100	176
2.103–107	338 n. 96
2.106	352 n. 50
2.109–113	338 n. 97
2.113–117	349
2.118	349
2.121–123	326 n. 18
2.123	348
2.124–127	330 n. 42
2.126	324 n. 4
2.127	241 n. 1, 252 n. 34
2.139	352 n. 50
2.149	212 n. 43
2.150	237 n. 68
2.151	352 n. 50
2.153	324 n. 4, 331 n. 50
2.153–158	332 n. 59
2.154–155	336 n. 82
2.157	332 n. 54, 336 n. 83–84, 337 n. 86
2.171	252 n. 34
2.172–77	87
2.175	88
2.176	124 n. 17
2.177	352 n. 50
2.178	329 n. 34
2.180	241 n. 1, 252 n. 34
2.183	241 n. 1, 252 n. 34
3	8 n. 39

3.7	176, 352 n. 49	3.151–152	443 n. 52
3.11	436 n. 29	3.152	352 n. 49
3.16	331 n. 48	3.152–158	356
3.32–48	436 n. 29	3.153	346 n. 17, 356
3.48	344	3.154	176, 357
3.49	344 n. 8, 436 n. 29	3.155	352 n. 49
3.49–50	325 n. 11	3.157	357
3.49–167	345	3.159	352 n. 49, 407 n. 41, 443 n. 52, n. 54
3.53	325 n. 13		
3.54	345	3.161	407 n. 41
3.55	352 n. 49	3.163–166	344 n. 4
3.56	313 n. 19	3.165	439 n. 38
3.57	351, 359	3.165–166	439 n. 40
3.58	346 n. 17	3.168	272 n. 30
3.60	346	3.170	352 n. 49
3.61	346	3.171–172	241 n. 1
3.62–64	346	3.175	352 n. 49
3.63	96	3.175–176	443 n. 52, 491 n. 92
3.66	346	3.176	352 n. 49
3.69	346	3.181	352 n. 49, 443 n. 52
3.70	467 n. 9	3.187	352 n. 49, 443 n. 52
3.71	347 n. 21	3.202	331 n. 48
3.71–73	346	3.211	356 n. 77
3.72–74	346	3.220	330 n. 44
3.73–74	346	3.225	356 n. 77
3.73	346	3.227	354 n. 63
3.76	346	3.235	356 n. 77
3.80	347 n. 22	3.237	344 n. 8
3.81–82	347 n. 22	3.239	441 n. 49
3.85	83–84	3.243	212 n. 43
3.93	414 n. 10	3.244	352 n. 49, 443 n. 52
3.99	35 n. 50	3.247–248	351
3.101	344 n. 8	3.252	351, 355, 364 n. 3
3.103	176	3.253	352 n. 49, 443 n. 52
3.106	1 n. 1,	3.259	443 n. 54
3.121	252 n. 34		
3.131	353, 356	**Agora** 19 P26.455–460	323 n. 3
3.132–133	344 n. 4		
3.133	252 n. 34, 440	**Alcidamas**	
3.137–141	352 n. 53	*On those who write*	
3.140–151	436	*written Speeches*	483
3.141	352		
3.145–146	404	**Amphis**	
3.148	352 n. 49, 353 n. 57	*PCG* 23	264 n. 19
3.149	354		
3.150	354		
3.150	181 n. 27		

Anaximenes (?)
Rhetoric to Alexander

1421 b 12	488
1422 a 2	489
1422 a 39–41	489
1422 b 20–24	486
1422 b 30–33	489
1422 b 40–1423 a 8	485 n. 19
1423 a 29–1423 b 32	490
1424 a 8–1424 b 27	490
1425 b 18–35	418
1426 a 11	489
1427 b 12–30	489
1428 b 26–29	491 n. 33
1429 b 15–17	486
1432 a 4	487
1432 b 15–19	488
1433 b 11–14	482 n. 3
1433 b 33	488
1435 a 13–15	487
1436 a 25	483 n. 11
1437 a 39	488
1444 a 16 b 7	491 n. 32
1445 b 32–34	488
32.3	418 n. 27

Andocides

1.4	71 n. 46
1.27	72
1.36	72
1.73	128 n. 28, 184 n. 38
1.74	443 n. 53
1.76	128 n. 28
1.77–79	129 n. 332
1.81	30 n. 32
1.90	449
1.90–91	101 n. 1
1.95–96	465 n. 2
1.95–96	465 n. 2
1.96–98	87 n. 21
1.101–102	72
1.106	74, 128 n. 28
1.109	73 n. 56
1.110–116	468
1.115	468
1.116	468
1.140	128 n. 28
1.142	74
2.13–16	72
2.19–21	72
2.20–21	71 n. 46
2.26	237 n. 68
3	37 n. 61
3.3–9	87
3.6	88, 97
3.9	88
3.10–11	10
3.10–12	466
3.11	176
3.11–12	105
3.12	465 n. 2, 466
3.13	90
3.14	90
3.20	90
3.21	74
3.23	89
3.24–26	97
3.27	90
3.28	90
3.28–32	68, 90
3.29	88, 93
3.29–31	90
3.32	90, 97
3.33	97
3.34	97
3.36	88–89
3.37	1 n. 1
3.39	88, 97, 176
3.41	97

To His Comrades

65 n. 8	

Androtion

BNJ 324	257 n. 1
BNJ 324 F 18	210 n. 34, 221

Antiphon

5.14	1 n. 1
5.20	48
5.67–73	10, 47
5.74–79	47
5.94	1 n. 1
6.2	1 n. 1
6.45	1 n. 1

Archippus
Fr. 48   140 n. 43

Aristophanes
Acharnians
32–33   185
406   185
Birds
1591–95   96
Frogs
1425   138 n. 22
Lysistrata
1009–1012   96
Thesmophoriazousai
837   121 n. 6
Plutus
173   212 n. 41
178 (with scholia)   277 n. 11

Aristotle
Politics
1268a   357 n. 79
1273b35–41   102–103
3.8.3   426 n. 56
5.9.6–7   426 n. 56
Nicomachean Ethics
5.1134b23–4   182
Rhetoric
1355b30–1356b15   421 n. 41
1358b4   205 n. 1
135820   65
1359b23–24   66 n. 13
1364a   285 n. 34
1364a1   285 n. 34
1364a19–23   367 n. 13
1377b 16–1378a6   143 n. 62
1378a 20–23   144 n. 62
1384b   450
1396a6–7   367 n. 13
1396a6   457 n. 37
1396a7   450 n. 12
1401b32–34   352 n. 52
1408a32–36   236 n. 63
1408a 33–36   32 n. 39, 141 n. 47
1414a30b3   26 n. 16
1.3.1   205 n. 1
1.7.13   367 n. 13
2.2.1   181 n. 27
2.22.4–9   339 n. 98
2.23.6   337 n. 88
3.5.2   181 n. 27
3.7   141 n. 47
3.8.1   181 n. 27
Sophistical Refutations
Fr. 611.35 (Rose)   453

[Aristotle]
Athenaion Politeia
19   74 n. 60
24.3   357 n. 79
25.4   51
28   181 n. 27
28.3   147 n. 87
29.3   102
29.4–5   57 n. 15
29.5   54 n. 4, 104
30.1   54 n. 4
31.1   57 n. 17
32.1   54 n. 4, 58 n. 21
33.1   58 n. 24, 71
34.1   181 n. 27
34.3   70, 103
39.1–5   104
39.6   101 n. 1, 106
40.2   104
40.2–3   104
40.3   449
40.2–3   104
43.4   228 n. 20
53.4   370 n. 21
53.7   370 n. 21
61.2   228 n. 20
61.6   84
67.2–4   87
Oeconomicus
2.1350b   451

Arrian
Anabasis
1.7–9   441 n. 47
1.10.3   406 n. 34
2.2.3   400 n. 4–5
2.13.4   439 n. 38
3.6.3   439 n. 38

6.14.1–3	96	3.23	89
16.10	439 n. 38	3.27	89
26.2–3	96	3.28	89
		3.29	89
Athenaeus		3.29–31	89
6.251b	432 n. 10	3.32	89
		3.36	89
Cratinus		3.37	89
PCG 258	404	3.243	232 n. 47
		4.4–6	83
Curtius		4.4–8	425 n. 54
3.1.19	400 n. 4–5	4.9	427 n. 65
10.2.1	431 n. 1	4.9–12	425 n. 54
10.2.6–7	432	4.17	84
6.1.19–21	439 n. 41	4.23	212 n. 41
		4.47	84
[Demades]		5.5	84
On the Twelve Years		5.9–10	83
1.9	377 n. 2	5.10	85
9–10	368 n. 17	5.16	85
48	432 n. 10	5.18	85
BNJ 227 T 21	398 n. 2	5.20	85
BNJ 227 T 24	398 n. 2	6.11	84
BNJ 227 T 49	406 n. 33	6.14	85
BNJ 227 T 120	401 n. 12, 403 n. 21,	6.15	426 n. 60
	404 n. 28	6.17	85
		6.20–25	425 n. 54
Demosthenes		6.23	424
1.5	84, 426 n. 62	6.27–28	427
1.9	84, 425	6.29	85
1.13	84	6.30	424
1.21–22	84	6.35	85
1.22	426 n. 60	6.36	85
2.6	84	8.5	467
2.7	84	8.14	417 n. 21
2.11	84	8.35	417 n. 21
2.13	350	8.36	84
2.14	84	8.38–51	86
2.15	350	8.38–67	257 n. 4
2.17	426 n. 60	8.40	84
2.18–19	426 n. 59	8.40–43	426 n. 62
2.25	1 n. 1	8.52–67	86
2.36–37	350	8.57	176
2.39	350	8.64–67	425 n. 54
3.13	89	8.75	427
3.14	89, 427 n. 65	8.73–75	84
3.20	89	9.11–27	86

9.12	85	16.6	83
9.15	85	16.16	83
9.16	426 n. 60	16.25	83
9.17	85	16.27	467
9.17–18	85	16.28	83
9.18	85	18.20	162 n. 60
9.19	85	18.57	344 n. 8
9.21–25	423 n. 49	18.59	344 n. 8
9.23	85	18.63	466
9.25	86	18.66–68	466
9.26	85	18.72	292
9.32	85	18.85	6
9.36	86	18.129	316 n. 30
9.40	86	18.129–130	241 n. 1
9.41	466 n. 4	18.136	416 n. 18
9.41–44	465 n. 2	18.160–226	436
9.49	426 n. 60	18.168	252 n. 34
9.55–70	86	18.169	8 n. 39
9.57	85	18.169–180	87
9.59–62	85	18.170	338 n. 90
9.68	85	18.174	338 n. 91
9.73–75	86	18.174–179	338 n. 91
10.8	86	18.178	352 n. 54
10.9	86	18.192–194	392 n. 71
10.11–27	257 n. 4	18.192–195	466
10.12	86	18.195	368
10.13–17	426 n. 62	18.199	466
10.19	82	18.206	466
10.27	82	18.208	367 n. 16, 466
10.31–32	86	18.213	314 n. 26
10.31–33	86	18.222	388
10.34	86	18.222–223	387 n. 49
10.47	86	18.223	389 n. 62
10.55–70	257 n. 4	18.225–226	330 n. 43
10.64	86	18.225–227	331 n. 48
10.65	86	18.231	350 n. 40
12.18	416 n. 18	18.244–247	316 n. 32
14.13	82	18.245–246	466
15.3	284	18.248	443 n. 54
15.3–4	83	18.249	355
15.9	232 n. 47	18.257–258	56 n. 11
15.19	83	18.259–260	241 n. 1
15.22	83	18.264	352 n. 48
15.24	83	18.270–275	466
15.27	83	18.282	354 n. 63
15.29	83	18.283	176
16.4	83	18.285	377 n. 2

18.285–288	354 n. 64	19.192–195	333 n. 63
18.298	350 n. 40	19.196	332 n. 54
18.300	392 n. 71	19.196–198	426 n. 61
18.310	1 n. 1	19.197	337 n. 87
18.315	350 n. 40	19.197–198	334 n. 68
19.3	326 n. 16	19.198	335 n. 77
19.4	326 n. 19	19.199	241 n. 1
19.8	323 n. 1	19.220	348 n. 25
19.9	327 n. 25	19.237	212 n. 40
19.9–14	347 n. 23	19.246	331 n. 48
19.9–16	327 n. 22	19.248	327 n. 24
19.15–153	329	19.253–254	331 n. 52
19.19–22	327 n. 26	19.271–272	465 n. 2
19.20	348 n. 25	19.276–277	64 n. 3
19.26	327 n. 26	19.279	329 n. 37
19.27	327 n. 25	19.281	241 n. 1
19.35	327 n. 26	19.287	241 n. 1
19.39	350 n. 40	19.302–307	349 n. 23
19.43	328 n. 31	19.305	347
19.45–46	37 n. 59	19.306–309	332 n. 58
19.49	327 n. 26	19.314	327 n. 24
19.53–66	328 n. 28	19.326	348 n. 25
19.58	328 n. 31	19.331	414 n. 6
19.64–65	358 n. 85	19.337	337 n. 87
19.65	2	20.1	285
19.72	329 n. 38	20.17	268
19.74	327 n. 26	20.29–87	473
19.80–82	324 n. 4	20.30–33	473
19.81	426 n. 60	20.31–32	345 n. 11
19.83–85	328 n. 28	20.34–35	473
19.84	328 n. 29	20.35	474 n. 37
19.87	426 n. 60	20.35–36	473
19.91	122 n. 12	20.36	474 n. 37
19.98–110	328 n. 32	20.36–38	476
19.101	328 n. 33	20.37	473
19.102	350 n. 40	20.41–42	60 n. 33
19.116	310 n. 10	20.41–48	475 n. 38
19.120	329 n. 27	20.41–69	473
19.139	350 n. 40	20.42	176
19.140	350 n. 40	20.52	2
19.154–176	329	20.59	474 n. 37
19.196–198	426 n. 61	20.59–63	476
19.167	327	20.60	474 n. 37
19.175	329 n. 41	20.61–63	474 n. 37
19.178	323 n. 1	20.63	474 n. 37
19.189	335 n. 74	20.64	475 n. 39–40, n. 42
19.191	355 n. 71	20.68	89, 237 n. 68

20.68–74	122 n. 12	22.67	258
20.69	465 n. 2	22.67–68	263
20.70	280	22.68	89, 260
20.72–74	89	22.73	259–260, 265
20.75	265	22.74	265 n. 21
20.75–86	276	22.75	265
20.76	286	22.78	260, 270
20.77	237 n. 68	23.104	272
20.78	278	23.119	196
20.79	287	23.120	196
20.80	278	23.144–211	87
20.81	281–282	23.149	196, 212 n. 43
20.82	281–282, 287	23.171–172	285 n. 34
20.83	281–282	23.171–178	283
20.84	212 n. 41, 232 n. 47	23.129	211 n. 39
20.108	268	23.130–132	212 n. 43
20.127–30	465 n. 2	23.132	211 n. 39
20.155	268	23.144–211	87
21.1	249	23.149	196
21.18	235 n. 55	23.198	212 n. 43
21.62–63	212 n. 43	23.202	232 n. 47
21.71	454	23.210	245
21.77	249	23.212	178
21.78	249, 250	24.1	268
21.79	250	24.2–3	258
21.80	250 n. 30	24.5	268–269
21.110	85	24.6–8	271 n. 26
21.154	86 n. 17	24.8	272 n. 27
21.160–167	58 n. 26	24.9	258
21.164	285 n. 34	24.24	269
22.13	1 n. 1	24.36	271 n. 26
22.14	417	24.38	268
22.15	417	24.51–52	269
22.47–78	257	24.57	269
22.48–49	260	24.59	269
22.51–52	268	24.65	269
22.53	263	24.69	269
22.56	260	24.76	269
22.56–57	264	24.82	270
22.57	267	24.90	269
22.59–69	264	24.91	269
22.60	264	24.101	269
22.61–63	264	24.104	272
22.61–64	258	24.110–159	257
22.63	264	24.111	262 n. 16, 270
22.64	267	24.119–120	270
22.66	266	24.122	270

24.123	269	24.200	269
24.124	258, 269	24.200–201	269
24.125	269–270	24.206	269
24.126	270	25.97	1 n. 1
24.129–130	270	27.2	243, 249 n. 27
24.130	258	27.4	244–245
24.133	324 n. 8	27.5	244–245
24.137	270	27.6	235, 244
24.143	269	27.8	237 n. 68, 245
24.152	269	27.13	244 n. 13
24.154	269, 271 n. 26	27.15	246
24.157	271 n. 26	27.18	244 n. 13
24.159	260	27.19	250
24.160–161	260	27.33	252
24.160–162	261–262	27.37	237 n. 68
24.160–175	261, 263	27.40	247
24.160–186	257, 270	27.45	245
24.162	268	27.61	244 n. 13
24.163–164	268	27.65	249
24.165	263	27.65–66	245
24.167	269	27.69	245
24.168	260, 269	28.1	243
24.169	265	28.2	243
24.169–171	263	28.13	252
24.170–171	262, 266–267	28.15	249 n. 25
24.170–175	264	28.15–16	246
24.171	267	28.17	250
24.172	264	28.19	245 n. 14, 249 n. 25
24.173	266	28.21	249
24.174	266	29.2	251
24.174–175	262	29.11	251
24.175	258 n. 7	29.11–12	251
24.176–177	262	29.12	251
24.176–186	262–263	29.17–21	251
24.177	269	29.25	251
24.178–179	262	29.26	248, 251
24.180–181	262, 269	29.30–33	252
24.181	259–260, 265	29.38	251
24.182	262–263	29.43	249 n. 25
24.183	265	29.45	249 n. 25
24.183–185	262	29.52	251
24.186	262, 270	29.55	251
24.187	258	29.56	248, 251
24.192–193	269	32.4–9	334 n. 69
24.197	272 n. 27	36.22	227 n. 12
24.197–198	269	36.43	227 n. 9
24.199	262 n. 16	36.48	227 n. 10

36.53	238 n. 72	[Demosthenes]	
42.12	385 n. 38	7.2	414
46.13	228 n. 18	7.6	419
47.22	477	7.7	424
48.11	385 n. 38	7.7–8	420
48.54	385 n. 38	7.9	420 n. 37
49.55	217 n. 63	7.9–13	417
52	227 n. 14	7.10	416
52.8	227 n. 10	7.11	1 n. 1, 416
53	227 n. 14	7.11–12	423
54.4	217 n. 63	7.16	426
56.2	385 n. 38	7.18–23	425
57.60	237 n. 68	7.18	421
58.27–28	230 n. 351	7.19	421
58.56	477	7.13–19	417
60.4	298	7.19–23	422
60.9	298	7.20	422
60.10	299	7.22	421
60.11	1 n. 1	7.26	422, 424
60.18	162 n. 60	7.27	424
60.19	304	7.28–32	424
60.19–21	372 n. 71, 392 n. 71	7.31	350 n. 39
60.19–22	162 n. 60	7.32	416
60.20	157 n. 45	7.39	416
60.21	304	12.8	468
60.22	354	26.6–7	2
60.27	300	26.11	368 n. 18
60.29	300	40.25	181 n. 27
60.31	301	40.53–54	236 n. 53
60.32	302	43.31	210 n. 32, 220
60.34	302	44.7	385 n. 38
60.35	302	47.22	470
Letters		47.67–68	468
2.1	432 n. 6	47.71	468
2.2	432 n. 17	49.9–10	445 n. 31
2.14	435 n. 23	49.22	217 n. 63
2.14–16	432 n. 7	49.47	229 n. 23
2.15	432 n. 6	49.55	217 n. 63
2.21	432 n. 7	49.66	229 n. 23
2.26	432 n. 7	58.53–56	473
3.31–32	433	58.56	477
3.37	434 n. 18	59	227 n. 14
3.37–38	432 n. 7	59.2	227 n. 10
3.42	432 n. 6	59.30	237 n. 68
3.43	432 n. 7	59.94–106	465 n. 2
		59.94–107	87

59.105	475 n. 41	1.63	431 n. 4, 434
59.107–114	206 n. 4	1.64	434 n. 23
		1.67	434 n. 23
Didymus		1.68	432 n. 5
On Demosthenes		1.70	431 n. 3
col. 1.30	86	1.71	443
col. 7	64 n. 3	1.75	286
col. 8.8	416 n. 18	1.78	443
col. 11–27	64 n. 3	1.80	443
cols. 4.59–6.62	86	1.81	443
		1.82–83	432 n. 5
Dinarchus		1.83–84	431 n. 4, 434
1	18, 434	1.86	431 n. 4, 432 n. 5, 434
1.1	431 n. 4	1.88	434 n. 23
1.4	432 n. 5	1.89	398, 431 n. 3
1.5	438	1.90	431 n. 3
1.5–11	439	1.94	432
1.6	432, 434 n. 22	1.95	252 n. 34
1.7	398, 403 n. 25	1.101	398, 404 n. 22
1.10	442 n. 49	1.103	432
1.11	398, 403 n. 25, 434 n. 23, 439	1.104	431 n. 4, 433–434, 439
1.12	443	1.105–106	435 n. 23
1.13	434 n. 23	1.108	431 n. 4, 434
1.14	213 n. 46, 233	1.113	433–434, 435 n. 23
1.14–16	225 n. 14, 381 n. 21	2.1–2	435 n. 23
1.15	252 n. 34, 434 n. 23	2.1–3	434 n. 21
1.18	431 n. 4, 442 n. 49	2.6	435 n. 23
1.24	441	2.14	433
1.26	434 n. 23	2.15	398, 435 n. 23
1.29	433, 434 n. 23	2.17–19	434 n. 21
1.31	434 n. 23	2.20	435 n. 23
1.32–72	8 n. 39	2.20–21	434 n. 21
1.34	440	2.21	433
1.34–35	313 n. 19, 435 n. 23	2.22–23	435 n. 23
1.37	418 n. 28	2.24	466 n. 4
1.40	431 n. 4, 434	2.24–25	465 n. 2
1.42	235 n. 56, 466 n. 4	2.26	435 n. 23
1.43	410 n. 47	3.1	431 n. 1
1.45	432	3.2	431 n. 4, 435 n. 23
1.46–47	434 n. 23	3.4	385 n. 38
1.48–63	434 n. 19	3.5	431 n. 4
1.53	434 n. 23	3.6	435 n. 23
1.55	434 n. 19	3.16	431 n. 4
1.58	432	3.17	225 n. 14, 458
1.60	434 n. 23	3.18	435 n. 23
1.61	431 n. 4, 434		

518 — Index of Passages

3.21	431 n. 4	14.110.2–4	83
3.22	435 n. 23	15.23.3	96
		15.28.3	452
Dio of Prusa		15.29.1–4	277 n. 10
15.21	368 n. 18	15.29.3–4	277 n. 12
		15.32	277 n. 5
Diodorus Siculus		15.32.5	277 n. 5
12.4.4	93	15.34.3–35.2	278 n. 14, 279 n. 16
13.24.2	174	15.35.1	284 n. 32
13.33.1	60 n. 33	15.35.2	279 n. 16
13.52.2	71	15.36.5–6	225 n. 4
13.98.2–99.6	157	15.41	219
13.98.3	157	15.46	83
13.99.2	157	15.47.2–3	226 n. 6
13.99.6	157	15.47.3	229 n. 28–29, 455 n. 31
13.100.1–2	160		
13.100.2–3	160	15.68–69	285 n. 34
13.101.1	160	15.76.1	83
13.101.2	161	15.79.3–6	83
13.101.3	164	15.81.6	232 n. 46
13.101.7	164	15.84.4	83
13.102.1	161	15.87.6	83
13.102.5	164	15.90	83
13.103.1	164	15.92.2	285 n. 34
13.105	142 n. 52	16.3.1	349 n. 31
13.105.3	178 n. 16	16.4.3	349 n. 31
13.105–106	139 n. 37	16.6.2	84
13.106.1–6	161	16.7.2	84
13.106.1–7	120 n. 2	16.7.3–4	281
13.107	127 n. 25	16.8.2	349 n. 31
13.107.4	165	16.8.3	416 n. 19
14.2.1	165	16.8.5	84, 349 n. 31, 416 n. 17
14.3	63 n. 1		
14.3.2	165	16.31	84
14.3.2–7	127 n. 25, 165	16.38.1	84
14.3.6	165	16.38.2	328 n. 29
14.3.7	165	16.53.3	327 n. 22
14.4.2	165	16.54.3–4	327 n. 22
14.4.4	165	16.55	348 n. 27
14.6.2	83	16.55.3–4	333 n. 63
14.39.3	451 n. 17	16.55.3	349 n. 31
14.83.4–7	89, 215 n. 17	16.56.2	85
14.83.5–7	192 n. 17	16.60.2	85
14.85.3	89	16.71	417 n. 21
14.86	220	16.72	417 n. 20
14.86.6	208 n. 20	16.74	417 n. 21
14.91–92	84	16.82.2–3	84

16.84	285 n. 34, 352 n. 48	*Isaeus*	
16.85.2–86.6	378 n. 4	1	209 n. 26
16.86.2–3	381 n. 24	*Lysias*	
16.86.4	352 n. 48	7	333 n. 62
16.87	348 n. 27	13	414 n. 4
16.87.1–3	368 n. 17, 377 n. 2		
16.87.3	354 n. 62, 406 n. 33	**Duris of Samos**	
16.88.1	378 n. 6	BNJ 76 F65–67	460 n. 40
16.88.1–2	432 n. 8		
16.89.2–3	96	**Ephippus**	
16.95.3–4	349 n. 31	BNJ 126 F 5	447
17.4.7	407 n. 41		
17.4.8	441 n. 49	**Eubulus**	
17.8.2–14.1	441 n. 47	F 67	450 n. 12
17.13–14	357		
17.15.1	358	**Euripides**	
17.15.3–4	407 n. 43	*Philoctetes*, fr. 797 Nauck[2]	482
17.15.4	407 n. 42		
17.22.5	400 n. 5–6	**Frontinus**	
17.48.1	439 n. 38	2.1.9	381 n. 25
17.62.6–63.4	439 n. 38		
17.62.7	439 n. 40	**Gorgias**	
17.63.1–3	439 n. 41	*Helen*	
17.73.5	439 n. 38	10.2	152
17.73.5–6	439 n. 41	10.4	152
17.108.6	431 n. 1	10.6	152
17.109.1	432 n. 8	10.11	152
17.267	439 n. 40	10.12	152
18.8.1–2	406 n. 33		
18.8.2–7	432 n. 8	**Harpocration**	
18.8.7	453 n. 26, 459 n. 38	A247	174
18.48.1	406 n. 34	Γ21	182
18.86.2–3	381 n. 24	Π42	182
18.183–184	96	s.v. Ἀγνίας	221
		s.v. Αὐτόλυκος	372 n. 26
Diogenes Laertius		s.v. Ἑλληνοταμίαι	64 n. 5
1.55	357 n. 79	s.v. Νεώρια	64 n. 5
10.1	432 n. 10, 454 n. 30	s.v. Ξενικὸν ἐν Κορίνθῳ	212 n. 41
		s.v. Πηγαί	64 n. 5
Dionysius of Halicarnassus			
Ad Ammaeum		**Hegesias of Magnesia**	
1.4	257 n. 2, 275 n. 1	BNJ 142 T 3, FF 7	442 n. 51
4	83–86	BNJ 142 T 3, FF 10–12	442 n. 51
Demosthenes		BNJ 142 T 3, FF 16	442 n. 51
3	103	BNJ 142 T 3, FF 17	442 n. 51
13	414 n. 4	BNJ 142 T 3, FF 20	442 n. 51

Hellenica Oxyrynchia
7.3	174
7.1 (=*FGrHist* 66 F1, c II, 1)	210 n. 34
10.1 (Chambers)	112
19.2	174

Herodotus
5.92	426 n. 57
6.42.2	92 n. 34
7.132	85
8.136	85
8.140–143	85

Hyperides
1.4	367
1.7	402 n. 19
3.19	402 n. 20
3.20	402 n. 20
3.20–30	323 n. 3
3.28–30	310 n. 9
4.1	384
4.4	380
4.5	380
4.6	380
4.7	380 n. 19
4.7–8	384
4.9	384
4.10	381
5.1	310, 385 n. 38, 432 n. 5, 434
5.2	432 n. 5
5.3	432
5.4–9	384
5.5–7	433–434
5.6–7	435 n. 23
5.7	385 n. 38
5.8	432 n. 5
5.9	431 n. 3
5.9–10	431
5.11	385 n. 38
5.13	385 n. 38, 435 n. 23
5.14	385 n. 41
5.14–22	384
5.15	385 n. 41
5.16	385 n. 41
5.17	385 n. 41
5.18	385 n. 38, 432 n. 9
5.21	435 n. 23
5.22	385 n. 41
5.26	385 n. 38
5.26–28	386
5.27	385 n. 38
5.28	386
5.29	386
5.29–30	386
5.30	386
5.31	387
5.31–32	432
5.33	386 n. 47
5.34	432 n. 5
5.38	435 n. 23
6.2	1 n. 1
6.3	287
6.19	156

Fragments
fr. 1	381 n. 26
fr. 6	381
fr. 8	380, 381 n. 22
fr. 11	382
fr. 15a	383
fr. 15b	383
fr. 27	377 n. 3, 379
fr. 27–39	368 n. 18
fr. 27–39a	377 n. 1, 378
fr. 28	379
fr. 29	379
fr. 30	379
fr. 31	378
fr. 32	379
fr. 35	379
fr. 36	378
fr. 38	378
fr. 39	378
fr. 39a	379
fr. 76	382–383
fr. 77	382

Against Diondas
136v 20–25	392
137r 2–8	315 n. 27
137r 13	314 n. 26
137r–136v	388, 391
137v 2–8	392
144v 23–28	389
144v 28–31	384

144v 28–145v 2	388	130	68 n. 126
145r 2–3	389 n. 62	157	68 n. 126
145r–144v 9–22	388	*SEG*	
145v 2–11	390	14:47	259
145v–144r	388	19	89
145v 12–144r 24	391	21.541	184 n. 43
173r 31–175r8	383	37.725	450 n. 12
173v 25–28	314 n. 23	45.1162	450 n. 12
174r 25–32	389 n. 60	51.1001	471 n. 24
174r 30–32	389	145	89
175v 1	389 n. 58	*Syll.*³	
9	355 n. 72	276A	454 n. 30
19	354 n. 66		
28	406 n. 307	**Isaeus**	
		2.6	207, 208 n. 19, 209 n. 5
Idomeneus			
BNJ 338 F 10	324 n. 7	4.7	208 n. 19, 209 n. 5, n. 28
Inscriptions		5.6	206 n. 7, 208 n. 19, 23
IG I³ 6	469 n. 14	5.7	208 n. 23
IG I³ 102	472	5.8	216 n. 60
IG I³ 104	468 n. 11	5.11	207, 208 n. 19
IG I³ 125	475 n. 38	5.37	206 n. 10, 208 n. 19
IG I³ 227	475 n. 38	5.42	206 n. 7, 208 n. 19, 209 n. 28
IG I³ 71	88		
IG I³ 363	456 n. 35	5.46	206 n. 10, 208 n. 19
IG 2² 33	475 n. 38	5.47	215 n. 55
IG 2² 543	472 n. 29	6.1	207, 209 n. 4, n. 28
IG II² 43	452	6.13–14	209 n. 27
IG II² 240	382 n. 32	6.27	206 n. 9, 207, 208 n. 19, 209 n. 5, 28
IG II² 1660	89		
IG 2² 124	283–284	6.47	209 n. 27
IG 2² 543(= *IG* 2³ 1.414)	472 n. 29	6.60	209 n. 28, 455 n. 31
IG 2² 1186	350 n. 36	7.9	207, 208 n. 19
IG 2² 1606	279 n. 18	7.13	237 n. 68
IG 2² 1607	279 n. 18	7.27	209 n. 26
IG 2² 1612.313–316	471 n. 21	8.43	209 n. 27
IG 2² 1627, 421–430	217 n. 66	9.4	208 n. 19
IG 2² 1628, 563–570	217 n. 66	9.14	208 n. 20
IG 2² 1629	217 n. 66	9.14–15	207, 209 n. 5
IG 2² 1039–1047	217 n. 66	10	208 n. 20
OGIS		10.20	208 n. 19–20
265	96	10.22	208 n. 19
Osborne & Rhodes		11.8	206 n. 8
41	469 n. 14	fr. XVI 66 B–S	207 n. 17, 208 n. 19, 209 n. 26, n. 28
48	283		
83	432		

Isocrates		7.66	237 n. 68
3.22	176	7.84	189
3.26	418 n. 28	8.12	237 n. 68
4.21	175	8.16	177 n. 14
4.28	418 n. 28	8.22	176
4.30	419 n. 32	8.37	174
4.35	176	8.41	194
4.98	176	8.46	200
4.119	179	8.61	177 n. 14
4.120	451	8.75	181
4.122	175	8.82	357 n. 79
4.142	177 n. 14	8.84	194
4.154	177 n. 14	8.84–86	184
5.9–11	37 n. 63	8.84–88	183
5.42	418 n. 28	8.86	179
5.47	1 n. 1	8.92	182, 186
5.58–61	181	9.22	199
5.59	181	9.23	200
5.61	177 n. 14	9.25	201
5.62	179	9.25–26	201
5.67	177 n. 14	9.27	200
5.81	172	9.29	200
5.114	350, 455	9.31	201
6.21	176	9.32	201
6.42	419 n. 32	9.43	350 n. 36
6.44	176	9.46	200
6.50	176	9.51	200
6.52	237 n. 68	9.52	177 n. 14
6.52–53	182	9.56–57	177 n. 14
6.63	237 n. 68	9.59	200
6.92	176	9.64	200
6.104	176	9.66–71	200
7.1–2	192	9.67–69	200
7.1–4	192	9.74	200
7.3	192	9.80–82	200
7.4	192	10.2	152
7.6	192	10.4	152
7.12	177 n. 14	10.6	152
7.16–17	102	10.10	152
7.21–23	489	10.11	152
7.24–25	193	11.5	181
7.26–27	102	12.9	173
7.37–38	193	12.57	178 n. 15
7.51	193	12.59	198
7.55	193	12.61	198
7.64	179, 237 n. 68	12.77	176
7.65	177 n. 14	12.99	179

12.105	177 n. 14	16.28	180
12.111	199	16.29	180
12.116	199	16.29–30	180
12.118	199	16.41	177 n. 14
12.132–133	199	17.11–7	251 n. 31
12.143	199	18.3	30 n. 32
12.172–174	37 n. 63	18.5–19	177
14.14	30 n. 32, 176	18.9–10	30 n. 32
14.23	176	18.23	177 n. 14
14.26	182 n. 30	18.31	176
14.27	208 n. 20	18.38	30 n. 32
14.31	179	18.42–44	30 n. 32
14.56	237 n. 68	18.44	128 n. 28
14.111	451	18.47	177
15.5	455 n. 33	18.52–54	30 n. 32
15.11	83	18.58	178
15.12	483	18.59	8 n. 39, 177
15.19–20	483	18.59–61	177, 179
15.93	486	18.60	177
15.94	486	18.61	177
15.101	455	18.65	177
15.101–139	487 n. 26	18.68	128 n. 28
15.111	177 n. 14	21.2	177 n. 14
15.111–112	232 n. 47	21.7	216 n. 61
15.128	177 n. 14, 179 n. 20	*Letters*	
15.132–134	456	8.8	177 n. 14
15.161	186		
15.183–184	483 n. 8	**Justin**	
15.234–35	177 n. 14	*Epitome*	
15.278	488	5.8	127 n. 25
15.307–08	177 n. 14	6.5.2	212 n. 41
15.313	197	8.2.8–12	328 n. 29
15.314	197	8.6.4–8	416 n. 20
15.315	197	9.3.4–11	435 n. 24
15.316–317	197	9.4.4–5	354 n. 62
15.318–319	198	11.2.7	441 n. 49
15.319	176, 184 n. 17	11.3.6–4.8	441 n. 47
16.4	237 n. 68		
16.5–21	180–181	**Libanius**	
16.6	180	*Hypothesis* to Demosthenes	
16.9	180	5.1	310 n. 8
16.10	180	6	416 n. 18
16.15	180	7	423 n. 47
16.18	180	*arg.D.* 23.6	270 n. 25
16.20	180		
16.21	180	**Lycurgus**	
16.22	180	1.1	365 n. 7

1.8	354, 373	1.93	3, 365
1.10	365	1.95–96	365
1.12	365 n. 7	1.97	373
1.14–15	436 n. 33	1.98	364 n. 6
1.16	351 n. 45, 371, 377 n. 1, 379	1.100	436
		1.107	365 n. 7, 436
1.16–19	436 n. 33	1.119	466 n. 4
1.18	373	1.124	466 n. 4
1.21–27	436 n. 3	1.124–126	465 n. 2
1.27	365 n. 7	1.126	466 n. 4
1.36	368	1.129	365 n. 7
1.36–37	377 n. 1	1.133	373
1.36–38	368	1.136	373
1.37	369	1.142	372
1.37–54	87, 369	1.144	367, 371, 386 n. 47
1.39	378 n. 10	1.147	373
1.39–40	370	1.150	373
1.39–42	355	1.168	436
1.39–43	378 n. 9	F 3	372 n. 26
1.40	369		
1.41	368–369, 377 n. 1, 406 n. 37	**Lysias**	
		2.1	1 n. 1
1.42	357 n. 78, 370, 443 n. 54	2.10	176
		2.18	128 n. 29
1.43–44	371	2.18–19	129
1.46–51	364, 367 n. 15, 436 n. 32	2.43	128 n. 29
		2.54	1 n. 1
1.47	372	2.58	30 n. 32, 120, 142 n. 54, 179, 181
1.49	316 n. 34		
1.52–54	371	2.58–59	28 n. 24, 30 n. 32
1.53	386 n. 47	2.59	121 n. 7
1.57	373	2.60	162 n. 65
1.59	373	2.61–64	12
1.59–62	436 n. 32	2.63	128 n. 29
1.61	364 n. 6	2.64	128 n. 29
1.62	364 n. 6	2.65	128 n. 29
1.68	436	2.66	128 n. 29
1.71	373	2.72	237 n. 68
1.75	364 n. 6	12.5–24	111
1.75–76	365 n. 7	12.13	107
1.78	373	12.36	31 n. 34, 121 n. 9, 146 n. 86
1.80	364 n. 6		
1.81	176	12.43	121 n. 9, 179
1.84	364 n. 6	12.43–44	109
1.85	373	12.44	109 n. 33
1.89	373	12.46	162 n. 65
1.90–93	366	12.47	450 n. 9

12.50	32 n. 40, 61 n. 37	18.9	59 n. 31
12.61–64	11	18.19	30 n. 32
12.62–78	87	18.24	176
12.62–79	61 n. 37, 119	18.59	179
12.65	107	19.17	179
12.68	128 n. 28	19.39–40	228 n. 18
12.71–72	109	19.55–59	32 n. 40
12.72	109 n. 33	21.1–5	32 n. 40
12.74	128 n. 28	21.6	329 n. 38
12.79	112 n. 42	21.9	6 n. 32, 30 n. 32, 121 n. 9, 179
12.87–100	107		
12.92	121 n. 9	21.10	142 n. 51
12.95	107	25.7–11	60 n. 35
12.96	107	25.12	176
12.100	484 n. 14	25.25–26	121 n. 9
13.5	179	30.4	469
13.5–48	471	30.17	40 n. 18
13.9–11	96	30.17–20	469
13.33	139 n. 33	30.18	469
13.43	121 n. 9	30.19	469
13.48	121 n. 9	30.20	469–470
13.49–97	471	30.21	470
13.70	471	31.8	121 n. 9
13.72	472	33.7	165
13.92	450	34.1	11
14.3	135	34.2	11
14.7	135	34.3	11
14.13	176	34.4–5	11
14.16	121 n. 9	34.5	11
14.17	141	34.6	11, 128 n. 28
14.21	137–138	34.7–8	11
14.25	139, 146	34.8	11
14.25–26	144	34.9	11
14.26	139	34.11	101
14.27	139	fr. 87 (Carey)	405 n. 31
14.30	143	fr. 170 ll. 155–156 (Carey)	121 n. 8
14.30–38	8 n. 39	fr. 170.184–189 (Carey)	59 n. 31
14.35	139		
14.37	143	**[Lysias]**	
14.38	122, 139, 355 n. 71	6.6–7	32 n. 39
14.38–39	180	6.19–20	366 n. 21
14.39	143	6.27	366 n. 21
14.40	143	6.32	366 n. 21
16.4	121 n. 9, 179	6.46	178 n. 18
16.8	162 n. 65	20.1–2	61
17.3	176, 217 n. 61	20.1–3	61
18.2	8 n. 39	20.1–10	53

20.2	60	4.1	282 n. 25
20.3	54	4.2–3	282
20.4	54, 60	*Iphicrates*	
20.5–6	60	2.1	211 n. 39
20.5–7	54	3.4	211 n. 39
20.5–10	61	*Timotheus*	
20.6	55	1.2–3	232 n. 46
20.7–10	57, 60	2.1.2–3	225 n. 4
20.10	54, 61	4	197
20.11	53	4.2–3	229 n. 27
20.11–12	55, 57, 60		
20.11–36	53 n. 1	**Onesicritus**	
20.12	56	BNJ 134 T 8	373 n. 31
20.13–14	57, 61		
20.13–15	61	**Pausanias**	
20.14	54–55, 59–61	4.28.2	83
20.14–16	57	6.3.16	215 n. 57, 451 n. 17
20.14–22	60	9.1.4–8	83
20.17	54		
20.18	54	**Philochorus**	
20.18–21	61	BNJ 326 F 56a	313 n. 21
20.18–22	59	BNJ 326 F 56b	313 n. 21
20.22	54, 59	BNJ 328 F 56a–b	315 n. 28
20.23	54, 56, 60	BNJ 328 F 40	89
20.23–30	60	BNJ 328F 49–51	84
20.24	8 n. 39	BNJ 328 F 55a	467
20.24–26	61	BNJ 328 F 147	210 n. 34
20.24–27	54, 59	BNJ 328 F 139a	71
20.28	54, 61	BNJ 328 F 139b	72
20.29	54	BNJ 328 F 147	221
20.30–31	61	BNJ 328 F 149a	63 n. 3
20.33	56	BNJ 328 F 149b	63 n. 3, n. 5
20.34–36	61	BNJ 328 F 154	453
20.35	54	BNJ 328 F 157	85–86
		BNJ 328 F 161	467 n. 9

Nepos
Conon

5	451 n. 17	**Philostratus**	
Alcibiades		*Vitae Philosophorum*	
8	142 n. 52	1.510	359 n. 18
36	142 n. 52		
37	142 n. 53	**Photius**	
Chabrias		495b	368 n. 18
1	277 n. 1	Lex. s.v.ὀρθῆς	379 n. 11
2–3.1	277 n. 10		
3.1	277 n. 12		

Index of Passages — **527**

Plato
Gorgias
521a3–b1   166
521d6–9   166
Symposium
221C   182
Phaedrus
248b   121 n. 6
Menexenus
234a1–2   151
234b10   151
234c1–235d7   33 n. 45
235a2–b2   296
235a5–7   298
236a8–c1   152
236c5–7   153
236c8–9   152
236c11–d2   153
242b5–c5   3 n. 16
243b7–d2   155
243d1   156 n. 44
243d   124 n. 17
243e–244b   126 n. 24
244d1–3   3
246a6   153 n. 15
246c2   156 n. 44
248e   357
249d10–e2   165
32b1–c3   161
521a3–b1   166
521d6–9   166

Plutarch
Agesilaus
37   285 n. 34
Alcibiades
12   136 n. 9
25.6   54 n. 2
32.1–3   406 n. 33
36   142 n. 52
36–37   139 n. 38
37.5   127 n. 25
Alexander
3.8   416 n. 17
9   435 n. 24
9.3   381 n. 24
11.6–13   441 n. 47

28.1   448
46   373 n. 31
De glor. Ath.
3 347a   333 n. 61
Demosthenes
5   83, 367 n. 13
9   416 n. 18
9.1   432 n. 9
14.2   441 n. 49
15   238 n. 71
15.4   459 n. 39
15.5–6   324 n. 7
18.2   353 n. 18, 443 n. 52
18.2–3   313 n. 21
20.2   352 n. 49
20.4–5   441 n. 49
21   368 n. 17
22.4   349 n. 33
23.1–3   441 n. 47
23.3   407 n. 41
24.1   403 n. 23, 439 n. 40
24.2   358 n. 87
25.1   431 n. 1
25.3   431 n. 1
25.4–5   432 n. 6
26.1   431 n. 4, 433 n. 17
26.2   432 n. 7, 435 n. 23, 27
27.6–8   406 n. 33
28.1   448
31.4   401 n. 13
Lysander
13–15   127 n. 25
14.8   105
Nicias
29.1   60 n. 33
Pelopidas
18.7   435 n. 24
Pericles
10   51
23.4   88 n. 23
25–26   452
37.1–2   406 n. 33
Phocion
1.1   406 n. 33
1.3   401 n. 13
6.1   284 n. 31
6.2–3   278 n. 14

12–14	85	848e–f	387 n. 49, 406 n. 37
15	85	848f	388
16	353 n. 18, 368 n. 17	848f–849b	368 n. 18
16.4	407 n. 39	849a	368 n. 17, 372 n. 29, 377 n. 3, 378 n. 7, 406 n. 37
16.5	349 n. 33		
21.1	400 n. 6, n. 10		
24	370 n. 21		
25–26	452	*Isocrates*, 9	
26.1–2	96	(Mathieu & Brémond 1929) 487 n. 26	
26.3	406 n. 33		
29.3	434 n. 18	**Polyaenus**	
		Strategemata	
[Plutarch]		3.10.7	84, 225 n. 4
Moralia		3.10.7–10	232 n. 46
188c	400 n. 6, n. 10	3.10.9	452
221a	432 n. 8	3.11.3	277 n. 8
741b	449 n. 9	3.11.9	277 n. 8
796a	193 n. 19	3.11.11	278 n. 14
811c	401 n. 11	4.2.2	381 n. 25, 435 n. 24
818e–f	439 n. 40	4.2.7	435 n. 24
835a	64 n. 3	6.8	451 n. 16
836d	228 n. 22, 229 n. 30		
837b	451 n. 17	**Polybius**	
837c	225 n. 3	2.62.6–7	82
843d–e	372 n. 26		
844a	246 n. 17	**Polyeuctus**	
845c	432 n. 8	Fr. 1.1. (Sauppe)	406 n. 35
845f	443 n. 52	Fr. 1.2 (Sauppe)	401 n. 12, 406 n. 35
846a	431 n. 1		
846b	431	*POxy*	
846c	433 n. 12	11: 1378, col. ii, 19–21	86 n. 17
846c–d	434 n. 18		
847c	459 n. 39	**Quintilian**	
848f–849a	443 n. 54	3	481
848f–849b	368 n. 18	4	481
849a	368 n. 17, 372 n. 29	9	481
851a	368 n. 18, 443 n. 54	**Rutilius**	
Vit. X or.		2.12	379 n. 12
836d	228 n. 22, 229 n. 30		
837a	173	**Scholia in Aeschines**	
839C	185 n. 44	3.57 [125]	351 n. 42
840c	324 n. 7		
843d	378 n. 6	**Scholia to Demosthenes**	
846a	387 n. 49	Schol. 20c Dilts to Dem. 19.3	326 n. 17
847c	400 n. 6	Schol. 25c Dilts to Dem. 19.4	327 n. 21
848a	388	Schol. 399 Dilts to Dem. 19.196	333 n. 60
848e	400 n. 6	Schol. 403 Dilts to Dem. 19.197	336 n. 80

Schol. 408 Dilts to Dem. 19.197	337 n. 87	1.119–25	96
Schol. 411 Dilts to Dem. 19.197	336 n. 80	2.1.32	6, 113, 355
Schol. 415 Dilts to Dem. 19.198	335 n. 74	2.2.11	70
		2.3.11	63 n. 1

Seneca the Elder
Controversy
6.5   211 n. 39

Stephanus of Byzantium
Ethnika s.v. Oreus   85

Suda
phi 354   349 n. 34

Strabo
13.1.39   173
14.1.18   453, 454 n. 30

Theophrastus
Characters
8   313 n. 9
8.4   331 n. 50
25.4   217 n. 63
fr. 696 (Fortenbaugh) 334 n. 70

Theopompus
BNJ 115F 27   348 n. 27
BNJ 115 F 105   284 n. 32
BNJ 115F 164   309 n. 6
BNJ 115F 166   309 n. 7
BNJ 115 F 244   431 n. 1
BNJ 115 F 245   431 n. 1
BNJ 115F 282   348 n. 27
BNJ 115F 284   416 n. 20
BNJ 115 F 328   313 n. 21
BNJ 326F 164   309 n. 6
BNJ 326F 166   309 n. 7

Thucydides
1.1   171
1.1.1   173 n. 8
1.22.2–3   142 n. 56
1.31–44   94
1.67   96
1.73   2
1.114.3   88 n. 23
1.115–17   452

2.3.25	703
2.13.7	371
2.14	58 n. 23
2.14–17	185
2.19.2	185
2.22.2	185
2.34.2	158 n. 53
2.36.3	161 n. 60
2.45.2	248 n. 24
2.46	357
2.65	184
2.65.4	406 n. 33
2.65.7	123 n. 16
2.65.7–11	183
2.65.10–12	76 n. 73, 123 n. 16
2.65.12	164, 183
2.79	210 n. 29
3.1.2	185
3.2–18	47
3.18–50	174
3.25–50	47
3.38.4–7	330 n. 45
3.52–68	182 n. 30
4.16	94
4.23	94
4.41.1	185
4.85.1	175
4.102–108	182 n. 32
4.118.10	96 n. 41
5.6–11	182 n. 32
5.18	467
5.24.2	177 n. 15
5.25.1	177 n. 15
5.25.3	177 n. 15
5.26	171
5.26.3	177 n. 15
5.26.6	177 n. 15
5.28.2	173 n. 8
5.44.3	96
5.47.5	467
5.47.11	467
5.56.1–2	467
5.56.3	467

5.74–79	47	8.68.3	54 n. 3
5.79.1–2	111	8.71.2	59 n. 32
6.1.15	370 n. 21	8.72	128 n. 28
6.6–8	91	8.73.4	55 n. 6
6.16.1–3	88 n. 22	8.74.2	58 n. 25
6.24	237 n. 69	8.76.6	103
6.27.3	71 n. 41	8.86	128 n. 28
6.28.2	2	8.90.1–2	54 n. 3
6.34	95 n. 40	8.92.2	57 n. 12
6.38.2	121 n. 6	8.94–97	59 n. 27
6.53.3	2	8.96	58 n. 23
6.59.4	74 n. 60	8.97.1–2	71
6.91.6–7	143 n. 59	8.98.1	72 n. 50
6.93–7.86	182 n. 33	8.104–6	55 n. 6
6.105	94		
7.18	91	**Xenophon**	
7.18.1	143 n. 59	*Agesilaus*	350 n. 36
7.20	183 n. 34	*Anabasis*	
7.27.5	59 n. 32, 172	1.1–10.19	83
7.28.1	58 n. 23	*Cyropaedia*	
7.75.5	217 n. 63	1.2.1	350 n. 36
7.85.4	60 n. 33	*Hellenica*	
7.87.2–3	60 n. 33	1.1.11–26	71
8.1	6	1.4.17	6
8.1.3	58 n. 23	1.4.18–19	406 n. 33
8.5.4–5	91	1.6.24	156
8.5.45	180 n. 23	1.6.25	158
8.6.3	143 n. 59	1.6.28	157
8.12.1	143 n. 59	1.6.29–31	157
8.19.1–2	91	1.6.29–33	157
8.23.1	55 n. 6	1.6.33	157
8.28.2–4	91	1.6.34	158
8.28–55	182 n. 31	1.6.36	163
8.35.3–4	215 n. 57	1.7	146 n. 84
8.42	219	1.7.2	146 n. 82
8.43.3–4	219	1.7.4	122 n. 12, 159
8.48.4–51.3	54 n. 3	1.7.5	159
8.48.5	55 n. 9	1.7.6	159
8.53	128 n. 28	1.7.8	357
8.53.1	108	1.7.11	159
8.54.3	91	1.7.12	159
8.54.3–4	54 n. 3	1.7.13	159
8.60	55 n. 10	1.7.14	159
8.64.5	55 n. 9	1.7.15	160
8.65.3	104	1.7.18	350 n. 37
8.67.2–3	57 n. 15	1.7.25	160
8.67.3	55 n. 4	1.7.34	160

1.7.35	6, 146 n. 84, 160	4.1.32	95 n. 40
2.1.21	178 n. 15	4.3.10–12	89
2.1.22–29	120 n. 2	4.3.10–14	215 n. 17
2.1.23	178 n. 15	4.3.11–12	192 n. 17
2.1.25–26	142 n. 52, 143 n. 61	4.4	83
2.1.25–32	139 n. 36	4.4.7–18	220
2.1.32	6, 122	4.5.11–18	212 n. 41
2.2.1–23	127 n. 25	4.8.4	216 n. 17
2.2.2	111	4.8.9–10	89
2.2.3–4	182	4.8.12–16	90
2.2.10–11	182	4.8.24	95 n. 40, 219
2.2.11	70	4.8.34	211 n. 39
2.2.16–17	96	5.1.10	277 n. 9
2.2.19	179	5.1.10–12	277 n. 7
2.2.19–20	74	5.1.25	211 n. 39, 219
2.2.20	88	5.1.28–36	90
2.2.22	111	5.1.30–34	96
2.3.2	75 n. 69	5.1.31	83
2.3.10–11	182	5.3.26	96
2.3.11	75 n. 69	5.4.61	278 n. 14
2.3.13	184 n. 37	5.4.63–66	225 n. 4
2.3.13–14	76	6.1.7	229 n. 26
2.3.25	70	6.2.2–11	226 n. 5
2.3.41	74	6.2.12–13	226 n. 6
2.3.48	104 n. 15	6.2.13	229 n. 28, 455 n. 31
2.4.2–5	138 n. 29	7	83
2.4.10–39	125 n. 19	7.1	221
2.4.10–43	138 n. 29	7.1.1	96
2.4.13–17	114	7.1.26	83
2.4.21	178 n. 15	7.1.33–40	96
2.4.28–39	76	7.4.1	83
2.4.39	105	7.4.10	111
2.4.39–42	111	*Hieron*	
2.4.40–42	103	5.1–2	426 n. 57
2.4.43	104	*Memorabilia*	
3.1.4	145 n. 75	3.5.10	156 n. 44
3.5.7–16	112		
3.5.16–25	136 n. 4	**Valerius Maximus**	
3.5.18–19	84	7.2	432 n. 10
3.5.23	137 n. 19		

www.ingramcontent.com/pod-product-compliance
Lightning Source LLC
Chambersburg PA
CBHW031719230426
43669CB00007B/185